Dedicated to:

Gabe and Sam, my buddies for life,

Do not repay evil for evil or abuse for abuse; but, on the contrary, repay with a blessing. It is for this that you were called—that you might inherit a blessing. 1 Peter 3:9

With love,
Paw Paw

ABOUT THE AUTHOR

JONATHAN WHITE is professor of Interdisciplinary Studies in the Frederik Meijer Honors College of Grand Valley State University, Allendale, Michigan. He also served as an instructor in the Bureau of Justice Assistance, State and Local Anti-Terrorism Training program for 15 years. He has lectured in the FBI Academy, in the Department of State Anti-Terrorism Assistance program, in all branches of the U.S. Armed Forces, and in law enforcement agencies throughout the world. The Founding Director of GVSU's School of Criminal Justice and former Dean of Social Science, he holds a PhD in Criminal Justice and Criminology from Michigan State University and a Master of Divinity from Western Theological Seminary.

Terrorism and Homeland Security

Jonathan R. White

Frederik Meijer Honors College
Grand Valley State University

CENGAGE
Learning·

Australia • Brazil • Mexico • Singapore • United Kingdom • United States

Terrorism and Homeland Security,
Ninth Edition,
Jonathan R. White

Product Director: Marta Lee-Perriard

Sr Product Manager: Carolyn Henderson Meier

Content Developer: Christy Frame

Product Assistant: Valerie Kraus

Sr Marketing Manager: Jennifer Levanduski

Art and Cover Direction, Production
Management, and Composition: Lumina
Datamatics, Inc.

Manufacturing Planner: Judy Inouye

Cover Image: Oleg Zabielin/Getty Images

Library of Congress Control Number: 2015951183

For product information and technology assistance, contact us at
Cengage Learning Customer & Sales Support, 1-800-354-9706.

For permission to use material from this text or product,
submit all requests online at **www.cengage.com/permissions.**
Further permissions questions can be e-mailed to
permissionrequest@cengage.com.

Student Edition:

ISBN: 978-1-305-63377-3

Loose-leaf Edition:

ISBN: 978-1-305-66020-5

Cengage Learning
20 Channel Center Street
Boston, MA 02210
USA

Cengage Learning is a leading provider of customized learning solutions
with employees residing in nearly 40 different countries and sales in more
than 125 countries around the world. Find your local representative at
www.cengage.com.

Cengage Learning products are represented in Canada by Nelson
Education, Ltd.

To learn more about Cengage Learning Solutions, visit
www.cengage.com.

Purchase any of our products at your local college store or at our
preferred online store **www.cengagebrain.com.**

Printed at CLDPC, USA, 08-21

BRIEF CONTENTS

CONTENTS

I began work on the first edition of this book 30 years ago and have reworked it several times to describe constant changes in causes, groups, tactics, and issues. Terrorists constantly employ new methods of murder and destruction as the face of terrorism changes. Yet, no matter how terrorism mutates, one aspect remains constant. Technology provides the means for a relatively small group of violent people to terrorize nation-states, including superpowers.

Professors who have used previous editions of this book have asked for changes and updates to this text. In addition, they have offered valuable critiques, suggestions for new material, and corrections of factual errors. Many of them asked me to reduce historical coverage and to increase discussions of trends and future directions. I hope this new addition meets their expectations, although I do utilize historical discussions to place contemporary events and probable future issues in context.

While this is a new edition, the purpose of the book remains the same. It is designed to introduce criminal justice and other social science students to the field of terrorism and homeland security. The book is also meant to provide a pragmatic background for the law enforcement, intelligence, and military communities. It is a basic, practical introduction for people who will or already do face the threat of terrorism. Many theories, polemics, and models are summarized and compared, but readers will find no grand theory. The purpose is to expose readers to a vast array of issues, campaigns, theories, and opinions.

As stated in the previous editions, issues surrounding terrorism are emotionally charged. Therefore, the information in this text is presented from a variety of positions. The purpose is to explain various points of view without taking sides. Students are exposed to differing interpretations of issues that have spawned heated controversies. Hopefully, the text presents enough information to allow students to make informed decisions.

Overview

This text is designed to provide readers with basic information. The purpose is to provide the background for understanding terrorist movements in many parts of the world. Part I focuses on practical criminology. It begins with a chapter on definitional and historical issues. This is followed by a discussion of criminology, processes of radicalization, and various types of terrorism. Chapter 3 is now completely devoted to the financial aspects of terrorism at the request of multiple professors throughout the United States. It also discusses virtual economies. Chapter 4 has new information about the media and terrorism. One of the foremost changes is an examination of research on the new types of media that are influencing terrorist behavior. Chapter 5 has an enhanced discussion of gender roles and the increasing involvement of women in terrorism. It also discusses tactics and force multipliers.

The remainder of the book builds on the information in Part I. Part II focuses on international terrorism motivated by ethnicity and nationalism. I have included presentations on Boko Haram and al Shabaab in Chapter 7 of Part II even though they claim to be part of a larger jihadist movement. I believe they are more motivated by tribal and familial issues than religion, but these discussions would have fit equally well in the chapter about jihadist violence. Part III examines international ideological and religious terrorism. The final section deals with domestic terrorism and homeland security.

New to This Edition

There are several new items in the ninth edition. Here is a summary of the major additions and updates.

In Every Chapter:

More focus on current activities and future projections
Hypothetical examples used to illustrate major points
General chapter summaries and specific summaries of new chapter objectives

Chapter 1:

Updated examples of terrorist activities
Analysis of comparative definitions
Review of impact of definitions on policy
Streamlined historical material highlighting major events

Chapter 2:

Updated criminology with a new emphasis on the value of practical criminology for law enforcement and security forces
Added emphasis on the importance of recognizing terrorist behavior for state and local law enforcement
Discussion of lone wolf attacks
Updated cases related to recent terrorist events and new case studies
Enhanced discussion of radicalization processes
Expanded examination of prison radicalization
Added summary of the debate about the existence of radicalization

Chapter 3:

Refocused exclusively on terrorist financing
Defined terrorist financing and money laundering
Comparison of terrorist financing and money laundering
Review of national and international efforts to control terrorist financing and money laundering
Discussion of underground economies
Examination of private and virtual economies
Expanded examination of the hawala network
Discussion of gathering intelligence on financial terrorism

Chapter 4:

Analysis of social media
Updated research findings on empirical and qualitative studies of media-terrorism
Comparison of "old media" and "new media"
Analysis of media biases when covering gender issues

Chapter 5:

Reorganization of chapter structure
Examination of all subjects, including gender, within a tactical framework
Summary of recent research on gender and terrorism
Examination of stereotypes of femininity in Muslim women
Analysis of the impact of terrorism and counterterrorism on Arab women
Summary of research on gender and suicide bombing

Chapter 6:

Political analysis of separatist terrorism
Role of negotiation in separatist terrorism
Speculation about future potential areas of separatist terrorism

Chapter 7:

Description of nationalistic terrorism
Reduced discussion of anticolonial historical material
Addition of recent research findings
Analysis of endemic violence in Nigeria
Discussion of political situations in Somalia and Nigeria
Addition of in-depth discussion of Boko Haram
Analysis of African Mission in Somalia (AMISOM)
Addition of new material on al Shabaab and its relation to endemic terrorism

Chapter 8:

Summary of the Syrian civil war
Explanation of changes in international jihadist terrorism
Summary of terrorism in Syrian civil war with reference to Muslim versus Muslim
   fighting

Chapter 9:

Coverage of summer 2014 fighting in Gaza
Summary of Hamas encounters with the Islamic State of Iraq and al Sham (ISIS)
Impact of the Syrian civil war on the Hezbollah–Hamas relationship
New analysis of the rise of Fatah and associated splinter groups
Review of the future of Hamas–Palestinian Authority unity pledge
Discussion of the issues from both Israeli and Palestinian views
Updated assessment of al Aqsa Martyrs Brigades

Chapter 10:

Discussion of United Self Defense Forces (AUC) in conjunction with death squad terrorism
Removal of dated material concerning Europe and Nepal
Discussion of Bacrims
Completely revamped section on the National Liberation Army (ELN) and the Revolutionary Armed Forces of Colombia (FARC), including peace negotiations
Updated information on Naxalite violence in India

Chapter 11:

Introduction to twenty-first-century Jihadi Salafism
Addition of modern jihadist ideologues Abu Bakr Naji and Abu Musab al Suri
Review of material on *A Call for Global Islamic Resistance* and *The Management of Savagery*
Summary of al Qaeda core's relationship with al Qaeda in Iraq (AQI)
Analysis of the Islamic State of Iraq and al Sham (ISIS)
Summary of current activities of ISIS
Examination of Al Qaeda core's split with ISIS
Expanded discussion of al Qaeda franchise with new analysis, including al Qaeda in the Arabian Peninsula (AQAP), al Qaeda in the Islamic Maghreb (AQIM), Mokhtar Belmokhtar, Ansar al Sharia–Libya, Ansar al Sharia–Tunisia, Ansar Bayt al Maqdis, and al Nusra
Addition of material on new jihadist groups

Chapter 12:

Summary of political debates about the meaning of domestic terrorism
Inclusion of background on Public Enemy Number 1 (PEN1)
Examination of mass shootings
Analysis of racial terrorism and new work on the Ku Klux Klan
Addition of section on extremism versus terrorism
Summary of updated information about domestic jihadist attacks
Presentation of new empirical data on ecoterrorism

Chapter 13:

Analysis of emerging threats to the U.S. homeland
Reorganization of chapter based on input from reviewers
Questioning of the need of intelligence reform
Review of methods of verifying intelligence assumptions

Chapter 14:

Inclusion of new RAND study on information sharing and homeland security
Future analysis of homeland security needs

Chapter 15:

Expiration of some provisions in the USA PATRIOT Act
Summary of the impact of the USA FREEDOM Act
Response by various stakeholders to the USA FREEDOM Act
Critique of National Security Letters
Examination of the Foreign Intelligence Surveillance Court (FISA)
Examination of bulk data gathering techniques

Chapter 16:

Examination of community policing and homeland security
Evaluation of law enforcement militarization and use of military equipment
Militarization of the "war on drugs" metaphor impact on community partnerships
Review of law enforcement tactical units

Ancillaries

For the Instructor

MindTap for Criminal Justice from Cengage Learning represents a new approach to a highly personalized, online learning platform. A fully online learning solution, MindTap combines all of a student's learning tools—readings, multimedia, activities, and assessments into a singular Learning Path that guides the student through the curriculum. Instructors personalize the experience by customizing the presentation of these learning tools for their students, allowing instructors to seamlessly introduce their own content into the Learning Path via "apps" that integrate into the MindTap platform. Additionally, MindTap provides interoperability with major Learning Management Systems (LMS) via support for industry standards and fosters partnerships with third-party educational application providers to provide a highly collaborative, engaging, and personalized learning experience.

Online Instructor's Manual includes learning objectives, key terms, detailed chapter outlines, chapter summaries, lesson plans, discussion topics, student activities, "What If" scenarios, media tools, and a sample syllabus. The learning objectives are correlated with the discussion topics, student activities, and media tools.

Online Test Bank.   Each chapter's test bank contains questions in multiple-choice, true false, completion, essay, and new critical thinking formats, with a full answer key. The test bank is coded to the learning objectives that appear in the main text and indicates the section in the main text where the answers can be found. Finally, each question in the test bank has been carefully reviewed by experienced criminal justice instructors for quality, accuracy, and content coverage.

Online PowerPoint® Lectures.   Helping you make your lectures more engaging while effectively reaching your visually oriented students, these handy Microsoft Power-Point slides outline the chapters of the main text in a classroom-ready presentation. The PowerPoint slides are updated to reflect the content and organization of the new edition of the text, are tagged by chapter learning objective, and feature some additional examples and real-world cases for application and discussion.

Cengage Learning Testing Powered by Cognero.   This assessment software is a flexible, online system that allows you to import, edit, and manipulate test bank content from the *Terrorism and Homeland Security* test bank or elsewhere, including your own favorite test questions; create multiple test versions in an instant; and deliver tests from your LMS, your classroom, or wherever you want.

For the Student

MindTap for Criminal Justice.   MindTap Criminal Justice from Cengage Learning represents a new approach to a highly personalized, online learning platform. A fully online learning solution, MindTap combines all of your learning tools—readings, multimedia, activities, and assessments into a singular Learning Path that guides you through the course.

Acknowledgments

This book was not produced in a vacuum, and I am grateful to many people. Foremost is Marcia for understanding the many months of new research and writing. Senior Product Manager Carolyn Henderson Meier and Content Developer Christy Frame were wonderful and supportive. The copyeditor Sarah Wales-McGrath was amazing. Kailash Rawat was patient and helpful throughout the copyediting phase of the book. I am also grateful to academic colleagues who reviewed work and made valuable suggestions. They include:

Julie Baldwin, University of Arkansas at Little Rock
Aaron M. Carver Sr., University of Mount Olive
David Admire, Southern Utah University
Keith E. Johnson, Mansfield University
Magdalena A. Denham, Sam Houston State University

I ask that all of you accept my heartfelt gratitude.

PART 1

Terrorism in Historical and Social Contexts

CHAPTER 1

The Shifting Definition of Terrorism

LEARNING OBJECTIVES

After reading this chapter, you should be able to:

▶ Explain the reason *terrorism* is difficult to define.

▶ Summarize the impact of context on definitions of *terrorism*.

▶ Explain the importance of defining terrorism.

▶ Outline contemporary attempts to define terrorism.

▶ Explain where the term *terrorism* originated and how the meaning changed during the history of the nineteenth century.

▶ Explain how socialism, anarchism, and communism were mistakenly associated with terrorism.

▶ Summarize the differing meanings of terrorism in Russia from the People's Will through the rise of Lenin, Trotsky, and Stalin.

▶ Summarize the early history of the Irish Republican Army.

▶ Define the term *selective terrorism* as used by Michael Collins.

Anthony Correia/Shutterstock.com

FBI Headquarters, Washington DC

During World War II, soldiers on several fronts often executed prisoners. It was a routine event on the Eastern Front, and Japanese and Americans killed captives on Guadalcanal. German SS troops executed more than 200 American captives during the Battle of the Bulge. We may call these actions murder today, but few people would use the term *terrorism* to describe them.

In the summer of 2014, the Islamic State of Iraq and al Sham (ISIS) (also known as the Islamic State, the Islamic State of Iraq and Syria, ISIL, and Daesh) released videos showing the beheading of American and British hostages. ISIS also filmed mass executions of Iraqi military prisoners. Most of the world's leaders called these murders, and American political leaders frequently refer to ISIS as a terrorist nation/state.

The difference between these two examples might cause heated and passionate debate because terrorism is difficult to define. Both of these actions involved a form of terror, but the term *terrorism* is applied selectively. In addition, the meaning of *terrorism* changes over time. The term was originally used to describe the actions of the French government. It would be applied to groups fighting against capitalism a few decades later and would be employed to describe both Russian revolutionaries and eventually the Soviet government. In the twentieth and twenty-first centuries, the term became synonymous with nationalistic, revolutionary, radical religious, and nihilist groups.

Defining the term is not an academic exercise. The definition helps to determine policy, behavior, and international opinion. It becomes part of a nation's application of military force and its criminal justice system. Defining terrorism can literally be a matter of life and death. This chapter will focus on the problems of defining terrorism and offer a brief history of its shifting meaning.

Difficulties with Definitions

Terrorism is difficult to define because it is not a physical entity that has dimensions to be measured, weighed, and analyzed. It is a **social construct**; that is, terrorism is defined by different people within shifting social and political realities (Schmid, 1992). The term has spawned heated debate because it is nebulous and pejorative. As a result, there are many definitions of terrorism and no single accepted understanding.

Some scholars have opted for a simple definition stating that terrorism is an act or threatened act of violence against innocent people for political purposes (Laqueur, 1987, 1999). Some nations have criminalized terrorism, defining it as a violation of law (Mullendore and White, 1996). Alex Schmid tries to synthesize various positions in an **academic consensus definition** (see Schmid and Jongman, 2005, pp. 1–38, 70–111). Schmid says most definitions of the term have two characteristics: (1) someone is terrorized and (2) the meaning of the term is derived from the terrorists' targets and victims. Many victims of government violence claim that repression is terrorism, while governments tend to define terrorism as subnational violent political opposition (Bady, 2003). There is no standard meaning of the term *terrorism*.

H. H. A. Cooper (1976, 1977b, 1978, 2001) first approached the problem by stating that there is "a problem in the problem definition." We can agree that terrorism is a problem, but we cannot agree on what terrorism is.

social construct: The way people view reality. Groups construct a framework around a concept, defining various aspects of their lives through the meanings they attribute to the construct.

academic consensus definition: A complex definition based on the work of Alex Schmid. It combines common elements of the definitions used by leading scholars in the field of terrorism.

Definitions Influenced by Social Context

The **social context** surrounding the term *terrorism* influences how it is defined. Consider the following examples and the differing meanings of *terrorism*:

A. In early 2010, a colleague of mine returned from the U.S. State Department's Anti-Terrorism Assistance program in Jordan. He was working with 27 Jordanian police officers—12 Christians, 12 Muslims (all Sunnis), and three agnostics. They never argued about religion, but they were appalled when he outlined the operational methods of Hezbollah. The reason: The Jordanian police officers vehemently stated that Hezbollah was not a terrorist organization. It was a militia fighting the Israeli Defense Forces. Hezbollah is a Shi'ite group, but that made no difference to the Sunni Muslim, Christian, and agnostic police officers. In their minds, Hezbollah was a legitimate militia resisting Israeli aggression.

B. In January 2015, three men claiming to belong to al Qaeda in the Arabian Peninsula (AQAP) and influenced by ISIS attacked the offices of *Charlie Hebdo,* a French satirical magazine based in Paris. They murdered 13 cartoonists who had satirized Islam and then killed two police officers. They would murder four more people before they were killed a few days later. Every government in the

social context: As used in this book, the historical, political, and criminological circumstances at a given point in time. It is the way people in a culture define actions and issues within a society's general outlook on reality. The social context affects the way terrorism is defined.

West and most governments around the world called this terrorism. More than 1 million people and 40 world leaders marched through Paris to show solidarity against terrorism. Yet, one Islamic leader asked why the world made so much ado over the deaths of 17 people when hundreds of Muslims were being killed around the world every day. He said Western deaths were considered to be the result of terrorism, but Muslim deaths passed unnoticed.

C.   The definition becomes even more complicated in war zones. In Afghanistan, North Atlantic Treaty Organization (NATO) forces are fighting two major enemies, a loose association of Central Asian fundamentalist Muslims called the Students, or the Taliban, and another terrorist group known as al Qaeda. News reporters, politicians, and military officers often lump the two organizations into a single group of terrorists, but there are profound differences. Al Qaeda operates as an international terrorist group, while the Taliban forms divergent regional militias and uses **selective terrorism** to support guerrilla operations. More important the theological tradition of the Taliban differs from al Qaeda's infatuation with a violent interpretation of a twentieth-century militant Egyptian theologian. Linking the two organizations under the single umbrella of terrorism results in a profound misunderstanding of the Afghan war (Christia and Semple, 2009).

D.   On November 5, 2009, **Nidal Malik Hasan** went on a shooting spree at Fort Hood, Texas, killing 13 people. There were many reports that Hasan had embraced radical Islam and that he had decided to attack soldiers at Fort Hood as part of a global jihad against the West (Simpson and Gorman, 2009). A former high-ranking intelligence officer immediately called this an act of terrorism, yet many government officials stated that it was the act of a mentally deranged soldier (Sherwell and Spillius, 2009). In this case, even the country that had been victimized by murder seemed unable to decide on a definition of terrorism.

E.   There have been dozens of attacks by domestic right-wing extremists since a bombing in Oklahoma City in 1995. In addition, groups representing a violent interpretation of Christianity, anti-government groups, sovereign citizens, and members of the common-law court movement have killed more than 30 police officers in the past few years. When attacks against law enforcement officers occur, state, local, and federal authorities charge suspects with violations of statutory law. Neither the media nor the public routinely refer to those convicted of such crimes as terrorists, yet their actions are similar to attacks that are called *terrorism overseas*.

selective terrorism: A term used by Michael Collins during the Irish War of Independence (1919–1921). Collins did not launch indiscriminate terror attacks. Rather, he selectively targeted the British military, the police force it sponsored, and the people who supported the United Kingdom.

Nidal Malik Hasan: (b. 1970) an American soldier of Palestinian descent. Hasan was a U.S. Army psychiatrist who became self-radicalized and embraced militant Islam. In November 2009, he went on a shooting spree at Fort Hood, Texas, killing 13 people and wounding almost three dozen others. He was wounded, arrested, and charged with several counts of murder.

The Importance of Defining Terrorism

Aside from the social context, the term *terrorism* is difficult to define because it is pejorative. It is loaded with politically explosive meanings. Therefore, the manner is which terrorism is defined has political consequences. Only nation-states have the freedom to apply the label to their enemies, and the term dehumanizes the people who receive the label. When people are deemed to be terrorists, governments give their security forces expanded powers of investigation, search, and detention. In many cases, they utilize military force to kill opponents without thought of capture or benefit of trial. For example, the United States has employed missile attacks from drones that not only kill terrorists but also destroy innocent civilians in the surrounding area.

Terrorists are treated differently from criminals and other enemies of the state. They are atypical criminals entitled to neither human rights nor civil liberties. This is especially true when terrorists operate from foreign bases. Representatives of the state may take actions outside the law because people supporting the state frequently believe that terrorists are somehow less than human. The state also has the power to look at all of its citizens and people from all parts of the world as potential terrorists. Therefore, governments can expand social control and limit civil liberties in response to terrorism (Cebeci, 2012).

Definitions of terrorism are also important because they impact policies. Haviland Smith (2008), a retired counterterrorist specialist from the Central Intelligence Agency (CIA), believes the United States has been less than effective in countering terrorism because of the way the terms *terrorism* and *insurgency* are conflated. Political leaders have used the terms interchangeably, but terrorism, he says, is generally a law enforcement and intelligence issue, while insurgencies are primarily military matters. In addition, the United States sends the wrong policy message to the world. If you are an insurgent against a repressive government that is friendly toward the United States, you can be called a terrorist. Conversely, if you are fighting against a government with an anti-American policy, you are a freedom fighter. This inconsistency has resulted in many poor policy decisions, according to Smith.

> ✓ **Self-Check**
> > Why is terrorism difficult to define?
> > What does Cooper mean by saying there is a problem with the problem definition?
> > What examples illustrate contextual meanings of *terrorism*?

Attempts to Define Terrorism

Alex Schmid and Albert Jongman (2006, pp. 5–6) surveyed many scholars who specialize in terrorism and looked for commonalities in the definitions they received. Not surprisingly, the use of force or violence appeared in 83.5% of the responses. Political activities were mentioned in 65% of the definitions, while fear appeared in 47%. About one-third of the definitions mentioned differences between victims and targets, planned actions, and tactical methods. Interestingly, only 6% of the respondents pointed to endemic criminal activity in terrorism despite the fact that almost all acts of terrorism involve violations of criminal law.

Definitions and Policy

Ayla Schbley (2003) believes that it necessary to emphasize the criminal nature of terrorism and move the focus beyond debates about politics. If defined from a political perspective, justifying terrorism simply depends on a person's viewpoint. This is wrong, he writes, because violence targeting defenseless symbolic victims can never be justified by any legal authority. Terrorism is a crime. Therefore, he defines terrorism as any violent act upon symbolic civilians and their property.

Boaz Ganor (2002) sees attacks on civilians as the key element differentiating terrorists from legitimate revolutionaries. Ganor says that debates about the meaning of terrorism are centered in theory, but in the practical world, they need to be defined by terms that transcend theoretical issues. A clear definition is crucial for a nation's policy and for international cooperation. If the world community is not clear about the meaning of terrorism, terrorists will continue to operate under the guise of legitimacy.

Ganor also argues that confusion arises because policymakers in the West use incorrect terms and phrases to describe terrorism. The reality of terrorism is glossed over with casual references to "guerrillas," "the underground," and "national liberation." As a result, many Western governments get caught in a semantic trap and fail to develop a cohesive international policy against terrorism. Terrorists use the same labels to justify their activities.

The solution, Ganor believes, is to focus on noncombatant civilians. When civilians are the exclusive objects of attacks, the resulting actions are terrorism. Accordingly, he says that terrorism is the use or threatened use of violence against civilians or civilian targets to attain a political objective. Violence is the essence of terrorism, the aim is always political, and civilians are the targets. These features distinguish terrorism from insurgencies and guerrilla wars.

By utilizing the terminology of conventional and unconventional wars, Ganor believes it is possible to differentiate among multiple forms of violence. For example, "soldiers" target military objectives, even though civilians are frequently killed in subsequent fighting. "War criminals," however, target civilians, their prisoners, and other noncombatants. "Guerrillas" attack military and security forces as well as political leadership. Terrorists are different. They target civilians to send a symbolic message.

If Western governments would recognize the threat to civilians, several things could be accomplished, Ganor believes. Terrorism could be defined, and nations could craft international agreements for antiterrorist cooperation. In addition, legislation could be enacted, offensive action could be authorized, and punishment could be sanctioned. Nations that support terrorist groups could legitimately be identified and diplomatically isolated.

Group Target: A collection of a particular people who are attacked by terrorists simply because they belong to a particular group.

Eric Reitan (2010) approaches the problem differently. He argues that attacks on military and security forces can be acts of terrorism. Traditional definitions, he writes, do not distinguish terrorism from criminal violence or any form of war. Like Ganor, he recognizes the importance of the target, but he expands the victims beyond civilians. Civilians, security forces, and political leaders are a **"Group Target,"** he says. If forces outside the law attack them for political purposes, it is terrorism.

Sound policies, Reitan writes, demand that governments distinguish terrorism from all other forms of violence. The Group Target concept does that. For example, Timothy McVeigh parked a truck loaded with explosive fertilizer by the Murrah federal building on April 19, 1995. One hundred and sixty-eight people were killed, including many toddlers in a daycare center. He did so because he hated the American government and its symbols. Anyone belonging to or associated with the U.S. government was McVeigh's enemy, including any law enforcement or military personnel who happened to be in the building. Reitan believes that the Murrah building symbolized a Group Target to McVeigh.

Reitan concludes that group targeting is the distinguishing feature of terrorism. If an attack is launched against a target simply because it or its members belong to a particular group, the action is terrorism.

An Insurmountable Problem?

Defining terrorism is important and it impacts policy, but H. H. A. Cooper's observation remains: There is a problem with the problem definition. The problem causes some researchers to suggest that the definitional dilemma may be insurmountable. Other researchers, analysts, and practitioners say the definition of terrorism is irrelevant. Some people even conclude that terrorism may be justified at times.

Jacqueline Hodgson and Victor Hodges (2013) write that defining terrorism is crucial because it identifies the people who are terrorists and it defines the specific acts that can be legitimately called terrorism. Yet, it is impossible to provide a precise definition of terrorism. Three factors inhibit efforts to describe terrorism. First, if the definition is too narrow and excludes attacks on state officials, security forces, or military targets, any resulting law or policy will be of little practical value. Conversely, if the definition includes the state and its personnel, the government can use its power to label legitimate freedom fighters as terrorists.

Hodgson and Hodges conclude that when political leaders are given the power to apply the label, they make judgments they are not qualified to make. Labels are applied inappropriately at times as a result, but the public must accept this because governments need antiterrorism policies and antiterrorism laws. Therefore, it is necessary to live with imperfection and to define the indefinable. As a result, enforcement will be discretionary and arbitrary, and at times, policies and actions will be unjust. They say there is no choice except to tolerate some form of injustice within policies, laws, and enforcement because doing so is necessary to take antiterrorist actions.

There is another approach. Nearly 30 years ago, Walter Laqueur (1987, p. 72) offered a simple definition of terrorism, and it is similar to the definition given by the RAND Corporation's longtime counterterrorism expert Brian Jenkins. Terrorism is the use or threatened use of force against innocent victims for political purposes. (You may notice how closely this resembles Boaz Ganor's definition. Ganor replaces *innocent* with *civilian*.) Yet, Laqueur seems not to worry about the definition. He adds a wry comment about the definition in a footnote. No doubt, he says, academics will write volumes about the definition of terrorism in papers and maybe even entire books on the subject. Ironically, none of the publications will help anyone understand the topic.

The *Stanford Encyclopedia of Philosophy* (2011; accessed February 2015) has an interesting entry in its discussion of the definition of terrorism. There may be situations where an action seems to be terrorism but is not. If terrorists can demonstrate that their actions will correct an evil action that is bad enough to justify stopping it with violence and the outcome is good enough to compensate for their actions, the perpetrators may not be committing an act of terrorism. This is true only if there is no other method for achieving the outcome and the targets are limited to military, security, and political actors. No other people or properties may be attacked. (Laqueur might add that these points provide material for an interesting intellectual debate, but they do not add one iota to our understanding of terrorism.)

> ✓ **Self-Check**
>
> \> What are the most common concepts in scholarly definitions of terrorism?
> \> How does Ganor's definition differ from other definitions?
> \> Is the definition of terrorism important for national policy?

Shifts of Meanings in History

Entire nations change their approach to national security, intelligence, and law enforcement based on the way they define terrorism. This can be demonstrated by recent changes in American defense and law enforcement policies in response to terrorism, and this U.S. experience does not represent a new trend. When the term *terrorism* was first introduced in Western history during the late eighteenth century, governments adjusted their policies based on the way they defined the threat. They continued to do so for the next two centuries.

Terrorism did not begin in a vacuum. Many Americans became acutely aware of modern terrorism after the first World Trade Center bombing in 1993 and after the bombing of the federal building in Oklahoma City in 1995. Yet, modern terrorism began decades, even centuries, before these events. Terrorism, at least from the Western perspective, grew from the French Revolution (1789–1799), and the word was originally used to describe the actions of a government, not of a band of revolutionaries. Terrorism developed throughout the nineteenth century, changing forms and ideology. The meaning of terrorism changed in the twentieth and twenty-first centuries as well. As Christopher Hewitt (2003, pp. 23–45) observes, the definition of terrorism and antiterrorist policies changes with political tides. The political atmosphere, in turn, changes with history.

The Origins of Terrorism in Western History

The meaning of terrorism has changed with political tides in Western history. Terrorism began as government repression in France, but the French transformed its meaning by referring to Spanish guerrilla tactics in the Napoleonic Wars. By the middle of the nineteenth century, the word was used to describe the actions of revolutionaries. Nationalists copied revolutionary tactics in the early twentieth century, and they were deemed to be the new terrorists. The meaning of terrorism came full circle when Communists in the Soviet Union used terrorism to subjugate the population. After World War II, terrorism appeared in anticolonial movements, political extremism, and religion. All the differing forms of revolution and violence resulted in changing definitions and multiple policies.

The birth and evolution of the Western democracies also gave rise to a paradox, the relationship between democracy and terrorism. F. Gregory Gause III (2005) points to a variety of studies about this relationship, and he comes to a depressing conclusion: Terrorist attacks occur more frequently in democracies than in countries with any other form of government. Citing U.S. State Department statistics between 2000 and 2003, Gause finds that of nearly 530 attacks, almost 390 occurred in countries practicing full or limited democracy. This democracy factor would come into play in the nineteenth century and continue into the twenty first century (see the following "Another Perspective: Terror and Democracy" feature).

ANOTHER PERSPECTIVE

Terror and Democracy

Many terrorism analysts believe that terrorists need democratic states to function. Totalitarian states, they argue, make it impossible to engage in covert activities. Terrorists need freedom of speech, freedom of thought, and freedom of action. Jenny Hocking (2004) takes the opposite view. In reaction to a terrorist attack in Bali, Indonesia, in 2002, the Australian government followed the path of the United States, Hocking says. Political rights have been trampled in the name of the war on terrorism. A counterterrorist network has invaded civil liberties in Australia, and the Australian Intelligence Security Service has been given permission to pry into the lives of law-abiding citizens. Terrorism is a threat, but overreaction to it also threatens democracies. The internment of terrorist suspects without charge or trial is a greater threat than terrorism.

The French Revolution

The term *terrorism* appeared during the French Revolution (1789–1799). It began with political and economic unrest in 1787, and the government was toppled in 1789. The revolutionary committee that controlled the government executed the king in 1793, beginning a series of mass executions that lasted until the summer of 1794. Edmund Burke, a noted British political philosopher of the eighteenth century, used the word to describe the situation in revolutionary Paris. He referred to the violence as a **Reign of Terror**, and he used the word *terrorism* to describe the actions of the new government.

Members and associates of the Committee of Public Safety were called terrorists by French nobles, their families, and sympathizers. They were responsible for 17,000 legal executions. Some scholars estimate that there were 23,000 additional illegal executions (Tilly, 2004).

Reign of Terror: The name given to the repressive period in France (1794–1795). The revolutionary government accused thousands of French nobles and clergy of plotting to restore the monarchy. Executions began in Paris and spread throughout the countryside. Large mobs attacked and terrorized nobles in rural areas. Summary executions (executions on the spot without a trial) were quite common.

Guerrillas and the Spanish Peninsula

In the Napoleonic Wars, the meaning of terrorism started to undergo a subtle transformation. Napoleon invaded **Spain in 1807**, and his army would face a type of threat that it had not experienced up to that point. Small bands of Spanish partisans began to attack French troops. Frequently armed and supported by the British Army, the partisans attacked the French in unconventional manners. They could not gather and face a French corps on a battlefield, but they could murder off-duty soldiers, attack supply columns, and engage in hit-and-run tactics. The Spanish called the partisans patriots, but the French referred to them as terrorists. Thus, the meaning of terrorism shifted away from governmental repression to the resistance of some people to governments. This transformed definition would be maintained through the nineteenth century (Tamas, 2001).

Spain in 1807: The Peninsular War (1808–1814) began when Spanish and French forces divided Portugal in 1807. Napoleon, whose army entered Spain in 1807, attempted to use his forces to capture the Spanish throne in 1808. British forces under Sir Arthur Wellesley, later Duke of Wellington, joined Spanish forces loyal to the king of Spain and Spanish partisans to fight the French.

Guerrilla warfare did not originate in Spain, but it was particularly savage there. It served as an asymmetrical method of resisting the French Revolutionary Army. It began a decade before the invasion of Spain when armed citizens loyal to the king fought against the French Revolution. It continued in Spain, and David Bell (2007) says that it came to full fruition when the 1812 French invasion of Russia failed. Russian guerrillas decimated the massive French Army during its retreat from Moscow during the winter of 1812–1813. Few armies could resist Napoleon in the field, but groups of disbanded soldiers and armed citizens were another matter. Bell believes that this signaled an ideological transformation in the meaning of war. Whether his thesis is correct, one aspect of his argument is certain: These guerrilla movements helped set the stage for terrorism.

> ✓ Self-Check
> > Do you think there is a relationship between terrorism and democracy?
> > What did the term *terrorism* first signify in France?
> > How did the meaning of terrorism change from the French Revolution through the Napoleonic Wars?

1848 and the Radical Democrats

The meaning of the term *terrorism* changed in Western minds essentially because of the nature of European violence in the 1800s. The French Revolution did not bring democracy; it brought Napoleon. The Napoleonic Wars continued until 1815, and then a new international order emerged. Although democracy continued to grow in the United States and in the United Kingdom, royalists reasserted their power in the rest of Europe. Under the surface, however, democratic ideas continued to grow. These ideas led to further political struggles and demands for freedom.

The democrats of the early 1800s were not united. Most of them believed in middle-class democracy, and they were reluctant to take to the streets if a legislative process was available. They believed that they could create constitutional monarchies and evolve into a system of democracy as the United States had done. The main objective of most European middle-class democrats from approximately 1815 to 1848 was to obtain constitutions to ensure liberty. Several of the German states began writing constitutions, but they were thwarted by monarchal forces and decisively defeated between 1848 and 1849. Austrian and Russian monarchs simply controlled all governmental processes. In the wake of failure, disgruntled democrats began to speak of nonlegislative avenues for change.

Radical democrats demanded immediate and drastic change. They were not only interested in developing constitutions but also wanted to distribute evenly the wealth created by trade and manufacturing. Many **Socialists**, including a group of Socialists called **communists**, argued for centralized control of the economy. **Anarchists**, sometime allies and sometime foes of the Socialists, sought to reduce or eliminate centralized government. The wealthy owners of industry, known as capitalists, were politically powerful, and many people from the middle class prospered when capitalist enterprises expanded. The capitalists opposed all forms of socialism and anarchy. Radical democrats felt that the capitalists were little better than the royalists. The radical democrats wanted all people to be equal, and they argued that democracy should be based not only on freedom but also on economic equality. This meant that the class structure and distribution of wealth had to be reorganized. This frightened the newly emergent capitalist and middle classes in the same way the French Revolution had scared European royalty. The radical democrats called for class revolution.

The revolution came in 1848. The conservative system established by governments after the Napoleonic Wars was antidemocratic. As constitutional movements failed in many countries, people grew restless. Parisians took to the streets in February 1848, and they overthrew the government. Many people in other European capitals followed suit, and by autumn, almost every major European country had experienced unrest or revolution. In some cases, as in Berlin—which was the capital of Prussia at the time—the army came to restore order. In other cases, such as France, a new republic was proclaimed. The middle class saw some gains, but most workers did not.

Governmental control was slowly restored in Europe between 1848 and 1849, but new class awareness and unrest emerged. The 1848 revolutions fostered working-class distaste for the distribution of wealth and power. George Woodcock (2004, p. 81) says that the 1789 French Revolution ushered in a new class structure, but it also resulted in a new economic system—capitalism—and a centralized state. The 1848 revolutionaries fought against the economic system. They lost and went underground.

This action, Michael Burleigh (2007) writes, signaled the beginning of modern terrorism. It started with the nation-state and the French Revolution, and organized governments used terrorism far more effectively than revolutionary groups. Yet, Burleigh says, secretive revolutionary groups formed the nexus of modern terrorism after 1848, a transformation that took place in Western Europe. Claudia Verhoeven (2009), on the other hand, moves the point of origin further east. She argues that modern terrorism began in Russia. Though Russia experienced its first terrorist campaign in the 1870s, several small groups organized individual cells a decade earlier. This, she concludes, represents the origin of modern terrorism. Regardless of geographical location, Burleigh and Verhoeven make the same point: When groups went underground after 1848, terrorism as it is known today came into its infancy.

radical democrats: Those who tried to bring democracy to all classes. They sought a more equitable distribution of wealth throughout all economic classes, believing that concentrated wealth and class inequities prevented societies from becoming truly democratic.

Socialists: Radical democrats who sought wealth equality in capitalist societies. Some Socialists sought governmental guarantees of living standards. Others believed that the state should control industry and divide profits among all members of society. Others believed that people would form cooperative relationships on their own with no need of a government.

communists: Socialists who believed in a strong centralized economy controlled by a strong central government. Their ideas were summarized in *The Communist Manifesto,* written by Karl Marx and Friedrich Engels in 1848.

anarchists: Those in the nineteenth century who advocated the creation of cooperative societies without centralized governments. There were many forms of anarchy. In the popular understanding of the late nineteenth and early twentieth centuries, anarchists were seen as violent Socialist revolutionaries. Today, antiglobalists calling themselves anarchists have little resemblance to their earlier counterparts.

Socialists

Three strains of radical democrats coalesced after the failed revolutions of 1848: communists, socialists, and anarchists (Figure 1.1). Socialists wanted to completely democratize society and assume control of industrial production. They believed that a strong state would ensure that profits from industry were distributed in an egalitarian manner. Communism represented a particular form of socialism, one that advocated a strong centralized government, the elimination of all classes except the working class, and a complete state monopoly over all forms of industrial and agricultural production. Socialists and communists agreed that wealth was not a private entitlement. It belonged to all workers. Although many socialists embraced communism, communists denounced socialists who failed to advocate for strong state controls. Many socialists emphasized democracy over the centralized power of communism (see Levin, 2003). The radical democrats believed political power should be held in common. Their concept of socialism was especially popular among some groups of displaced workers. Unfortunately, the upper and middle classes frequently believed terrorism and socialism were the same thing (A. Roberts, 2002).

One of the chief spokespersons and intellectuals in the socialist camp was the founder of communism, Karl Marx (1818–1883). He finished a Ph.D. in philosophy

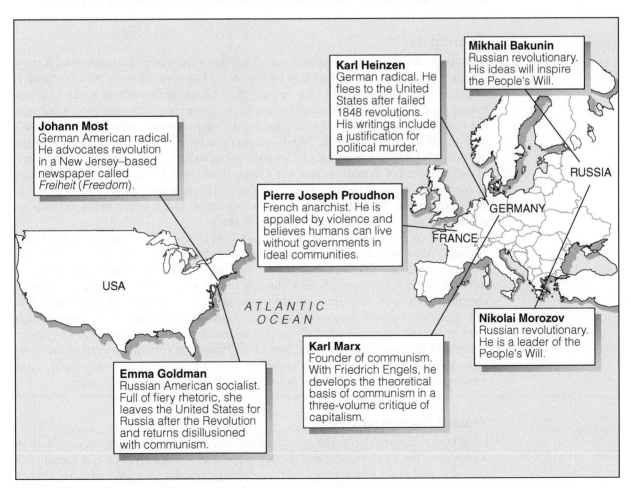

FIGURE **1.1** Anarchists and Socialists

in 1841 and moved to Paris shortly thereafter. He met Friedrich Engels and formed a lifelong friendship. He outlined theories of socialism in several writings, including a three-volume critique of capitalism. Marx believed that social structure is arranged by the material circumstances surrounding human existence. People shape the environment through work and even produce more than they need. Marx referred to this extra production as *surplus*. In medieval societies, nobles controlled the surplus production of peasants, but control shifted to capitalists with the end of the Middle Ages. Marx and Engels claimed that the capitalist economic system exploited the lower classes for the benefit of others. They called for a change in the system.

Despite the many labels applied to him and the derogatory statements of his enemies, Karl Marx was not a terrorist. Marx referred to "revolutionary" change, but he never clarified what he meant by revolution. Further, he did not advocate political bombing or assassination. In fact, on most occasions, he publicly condemned it. He believed socialism was to be a reflection of democracy, not violence. A massive seizure of power by the general population might be justified, but individual acts of murder were not.

The process of democratization was slow, however, and some of the radical democrats began to feel violent revolution was the only possible course of action. A few radical democrats went underground, choosing subversive violence as a means to challenge authority. They became popularly known as terrorists because they hoped to achieve social revolution by terrorizing the capitalist class and its supporters.

Anarchists

Anarchists shared many ideas with socialists about the egalitarian nature of society, but they disagreed on the function of the state. The term *anarchy* was not new. It originated several hundred years earlier, when Greek philosophers spoke of eliminating governments, but the nineteenth-century anarchists were also concerned with the distribution of wealth. This frightened the upper classes, which already associated socialism with terrorism. Pierre Joseph Proudhon (1809–1865) was one of the advocates of modern anarchism. His political activities eventually landed him in a French prison, but Proudhon was not a man of violence. He called for the extension of democracy to all classes, to be accomplished through the elimination of property and government. Property was to be commonly held, and families living in extended communes were to replace centralized government.

Proudhon disagreed with Karl Marx and other socialists about the role of government. Most socialists saw centralized government as a necessary evil. Like the democrats, the socialists believed government had to exist to protect the individual rights of citizens. Communists took the role of the state further, insisting on a strong central government. Proudhon, on the other hand, believed that all government was evil. Proudhon had revolutionary ideals, but he was a man of peace. He believed that anarchy would develop peacefully as people learned about the structure of governments and the capitalist economy. Not all of Proudhon's disciples were of the same peaceful bent. They came to see themselves as revolutionaries, and they would have growing influence on terrorism in the second half of the nineteenth century.

Violent Anarchism

Despite the rhetoric, both the socialists and anarchists engaged in more talk than action after the 1848 revolutions. Both groups debated the efficacy and morality of violence, and most of the people who called for revolution spoke of mass action, not individual violence. Walter Laqueur (1999, p. 12) says that the socialists and anarchists rejected terrorism on practical and theoretical grounds. Practically, terrorism could not promise strategic success, and many of the revolutionary theorists rejected violence in general. Marxists and anarchists favored strikes, demonstrations, and other mass actions.

Richard Jensen (2004) also believes that the initial calls in history for revolution cannot be associated with terrorism. Even though socialists and anarchists disagreed about the path for creating a new society, they avoided violence. Those who advocated violence usually did so only rhetorically; however, this changed in the 1880s as anarchists began assassinating heads of state. The media sensationalized anarchist events, leading people to conclude that anarchism was a vast international conspiracy of terror. By 1880, the press and politicians had collapsed all forms of socialism into the generic term *anarchism*, and anarchists were deemed terrorists in popular opinion.

How did this change occur? Jensen says that several factors merged to create a culture of terrorism among some members of the anarchist movement. He outlines some of the reasons, and other researchers have identified a number of factors (Laqueur and Alexander, 1987; Laqueur, 1999; Epstein, 2001; Woodcock, 2004; Clutterbuck, 2004; Grob-Fitzgibbon, 2004). Taken together, these factors reveal a pattern in the transformation of some anarchists from rhetoric to violence.

Another factor influencing the adoption of violent action was the invention of dynamite. Alfred Nobel blended explosive material with chemicals, cotton, and refined clay to produce an explosive 20 times more powerful than black powder. To be sure, the power of dynamite was often overestimated. One anarchist claimed that 10 pounds of it could sink a battleship. But dynamite gave an individual or small group a psychological edge. For the first time in history, a small group had a technological force multiplier that allowed it to launch a major attack. Rhetoric gave birth to propaganda by the deed, but dynamite fostered the philosophy of the bomb.

Anarchism and Nationalism

If the 1800s witnessed the growth of anarchism, it also saw the growth of nationalism in the West. As anarchists called for an end to government, nationalistic organizations demanded the right to self-government. Many nationalists adopted the tactics of the anarchists to fight the foreign powers occupying their lands. Nationalistic groups throughout Europe turned to the philosophy of the bomb, and nationalist terrorists began to follow the pattern set by the violent anarchists.

Nationalistic groups did not view themselves as terrorists. They believed that anarchists were fighting for ideas. Nationalists believed that they were fighting for their countries. Anarchists were socially isolated, but nationalists could hope for the possibility of greater support. Governments labeled them terrorists, but nationalists saw themselves as unconventional soldiers in a national cause. Nationalists believed that they were fighting patriotic wars. They adopted only the tactics of the anarchists, not their ideology.

The nationalistic Irish Republican Army (IRA) grew from this period. Unlike anarchists, the IRA did not reject the notion of governmental control; rather, the IRA wanted to nationalize it. The IRA believed Ireland was entitled to self-government. Their weakness relative to the government's power caused them to use the terrorist tactics fostered by the anarchists. In the twentieth century, other nationalistic groups in Europe followed the example of the IRA.

Though two distinct positions had emerged, it is not possible to completely separate nineteenth-century anarchism and nationalism. Grant Wardlaw (1982, pp. 18–24) sees a historical continuity from anarchism to nationalistic terrorism. Richard

Rubenstein (1987, pp. 122–125) makes this point by looking at contemporary anarchist and nationalistic groups. Rubenstein says that the stages terrorists must go through to employ violence are similar for both types of terrorism; the moral justification for anarchist and nationalistic terrorism is essentially the same.

Terrorism in the modern sense came from violent anarchists in the late 1800s. The anarchists were based in Western Europe, but they carried their campaign to other parts of the world. The most successful actions took place in Russia before the 1905 and 1917 revolutions. Anarchist groups assassinated several Russian officials, including the czar. Anarchism also spread to the United States. In America, it took the form of labor violence; American anarchists, usually immigrants from Europe, saw themselves as linked to organized labor. The anarchist movement in America did not gain as much strength as in Europe, and American anarchists were generally relegated to industrial areas. Right-wing extremism was not part of the anarchist movement, but by the mid-twentieth century, right-wing groups began to imitate the tactics of violent anarchists.

Self-Check

> Describe the various schools of revolutionary thought in the mid-nineteenth century.
> What impact did dynamite have on modern terrorism?
> Explain the surprising relationship between nationalism and anarchism.

ANOTHER PERSPECTIVE

Noam Chomsky Examines Terrorism and Morality

Noam Chomsky (2002) approaches terrorism with two critical questions: (1) How should terrorism be defined? and (2) What is the proper response to it? He says that the problem of defining terrorism is complex, but there are many straightforward governmental responses. Almost all of these definitions cast terrorism within a moral framework; that is, terrorism becomes a criminal act where innocents are victimized. These circumstances require a government to act; yet, the response frequently evokes a paradox. Governments define terrorist acts as immoral, but they tend to respond by acting outside the bounds of morality. They justify their actions by citing the original immoral act of a terrorist group.

Chomsky finds this approach unacceptable. The same moral framework that allows a society to define an illegal act as terrorism requires that the response to terrorism be conducted within the bounds of morality. Terrorism, Chomsky says, is something "they" do to "us," and it is never about what "we" do to "them." Citing just-war doctrine, Chomsky says the response to terrorism cannot be terrorism. A moral truism states that any illegal activity is immoral no matter how a state wishes to justify its response to an event.

The definition of terrorism provides a moral constant. For example, if an official definition states that terrorism is the use of violence against innocent people to change political behavior, a state is morally obligated to live within the bounds of this definition. It cannot use violence against innocents to force its political will. If terrorism is a crime, the response to it must not be criminal if the response is to be morally legitimate. The contradiction comes, Chomsky concludes, because the United States operates within a moral definition of terrorism only when its own interests are served. As a result, oppression, violence, and illegal actions are rarely defined as terrorism when they are condoned by the United States or its allies.

Terrorism and Revolution in Russia, 1881–1921

The historiography of the Russian Revolution and the fighting that took place afterward have changed drastically since the collapse of the Soviet Union. Histories written during the Cold War tended to be either pro- or anti-communist. As documents and archives became available to Western writers after the collapse of the Soviet Union views of Russia changed, and new histories and biographies emerged. Sheila Fitzpatrick (2001) views the revolution from a perspective that begins with revolt and ends several years after the rise of Communism as **Joseph Stalin** (1878–1953) purged and executed his enemies in the 1930s. Robert Service (1995) concludes a three-volume biography of **Vladimir Lenin** (1870–1924) with a picture of a ruthless man who forged policy by force of will. Service's Lenin is a man who was not interested in power for its own sake and who genuinely wanted to create a better socialist state. Confrontations forced him to compromise in the end. Katerina Clark (1998) presents the tremendous cultural shifts from 1913 to 1931 by focusing on St. Petersburg from late czarist times until Stalin consolidated power. Christopher Read (1996) divides this era into two periods—the collapse of czarist Russia and the building of the new socialist order. Service (2005) brings another perspective, completely rewriting the history of Russia from the fall of the czar to the rise of **Vladimir Putin**.

At the time of the revolution, however, the West viewed the communist state with horror. They equated communism with anarchism and revolution. Class revolution became a reality in Russia, and the West feared that Russia would export revolution through terrorism. Late nineteenth-century Russia differed significantly from the other great powers of Europe. Class distinctions between nobles and peasants were virtually the same as they had been before the French Revolution, and Russian peasants were beset by poverty. Industry had come to some of Russia's cities, but Russia's economic and governmental systems were not adequate to handle the changes. Czar Alexander II (ruled from 1855 to 1881) vowed to make changes in the system, but when he attempted to do so, he found himself in the midst of revolutionary terrorism.

The People's Will

Three groups in Russia after 1850 felt that they could reform and modernize the Russian state, but they disagreed about how to do it. One group, whose views Czar Alexander shared, wanted to modernize Russia from the top down. Another group, the intellectuals, wanted Russia to become a liberal Western democracy. Violent anarchists took another path. They believed that Russian problems could be settled through revolution. Narodnaya Volya (the People's Will) advocated violent socialist revolution. When it launched a campaign of revolutionary terrorism in the 1870s, it faced confrontation with conservative elements such as the church, police, and military. Members of the People's Will came to believe that it was necessary to terrorize these conservative organizations into submission.

The motivations behind the People's Will evolved from Russian revolutionary thought. According to Laqueur (1999, pp. 15–16), the philosophy of anarchist terrorism in Russia was embodied by Mikhail Bakunin and Sergey Nechaev. Their revolutionary thought developed separately before they met each other in the 1860s, when they formed an intellectual union. Both spoke of revolt against the czar, and both endorsed violence as the means. Yet, even in the nation that would experience a violent anarchist campaign and eventually a communist revolution, Bakunin and Nechaev basically stuck to rhetoric.

Although they were ideologically linked to anarchism in western Europe, they were distinct from their Western supporters. Russian anarchists were writing for a

Joseph Stalin: The dictator who succeeded Lenin. Stalin solidified Communist control of Russia through a secret police organization. He purged the government of all suspected opponents in the 1930s, killing thousands of people.

Vladimir Lenin: The Russian revolutionary who led a second revolution in October, bringing the Communists to power. Lenin led the Communists in a civil war and set up a dictatorship to enforce Communist Party rule in Russia.

Vladimir Putin: (b. 1952) a former KGB (Soviet secret police) officer and second president of the Russian Federation from 1999 to 2008. He served as Russia's prime minister after his second presidential term and return to the presidency in 2012.

general population in the hope of sparking a democratic revolution. Laqueur says that their significance lies in their influence on later revolutionaries and the violence and assassinations those later revolutionaries committed. They were not radical revolutionaries in Laqueur's view.

Sheila Fitzpatrick (2001, pp. 19–21) presents a different view. Russian economic progress dominated the last part of the nineteenth and early part of the twentieth centuries. The problem was the attitudes of peasants and industrial workers. According to Marx, agrarian peasants did not have enough motivation to join the proletariat in revolution, but Fitzpatrick says that Russia was different. Revolutionary sympathy was high among the peasantry, giving them a closer relationship with many urban workers. Revolutionary rhetoric and writings had touched the lower classes, but Russian economic prosperity had not. The lower classes were receptive to revolution, although as Christopher Read (1996, p. 294) illustrates, no single theme dominated the revolutionaries until it was imposed by the state under Lenin.

Regardless of the debate, the writings of the Russians were powerful. Nechaev (reprint 1987, pp. 68–71) laid down the principles of revolution in the "Catechism of the Revolutionary." His spirit was reflected in writings of the late twentieth century. Rubenstein (1987) compared the "catechism" to Carlos Marighella's *The Minimanual of the Urban Guerrilla* and found no essential differences. Both Laqueur and Rubenstein believe that Nechaev's influence lives on. Bakunin (1866, pp. 65–68) believed that the Russian government had been established on thievery. In "Revolution, Terrorism, Banditry," he argues that the only way to break the state's hold on power is revolt. Such rhetoric did not endear Nechaev and Bakunin to the czar, but it did make them popular with later revolutionaries. Laqueur (1999) concludes that such revolutionary pronouncements correctly belong with Russian expressionist literature, not terrorist philosophy.

These philosophies guided the People's Will. They murdered the police chief of Moscow and went on a campaign of bombing and killing. In May 1881, they succeeded in striking their ultimate target: They killed Czar Alexander II. Ironically, this brought about their downfall. The People's Will was eliminated, Alexander III (ruled from 1881 to 1894) ended all attempts at reform, and revolutionaries went underground. Nicholas II (ruled from 1894 to 1917), who succeeded Alexander III, was a man who would be toppled by revolutionary forces.

Czar Nicholas and the Revolutions of 1905 and 1917

Nicholas faced his first revolution in 1905, after his army lost a war to Japan. In addition to losing the war, Russia was consumed with economic problems and bureaucratic inefficiency. A group of unemployed workers began demonstrations in St. Petersburg, and some enlisted men in the Russian navy mutinied. Their actions were brutally suppressed by Nicholas's army and police forces, feeding the spirit of revolution that burned below the surface. Russian revolutionaries needed another national disaster to create the atmosphere for revolution. It came in 1914, when Russia entered World War I (1914–1918).

By 1917, the Russian people were tired of their economic woes and their czar. In February, a general strike in St. Petersburg turned into a revolution. Unlike in 1905, the Russian Army joined the workers, and a new Russian government was formed. They envisioned a period of capitalist economic expansion that would save the beleaguered Russian economy. **Workers councils (or soviets)** were established in major Russian cities.

The primary mistake of the February revolutionaries was that they kept Russia in the war, a decision that was unpopular with the Russian people. This had two

workers councils (or soviets): The lowest-level legislative body in the Soviet Union following the October Revolution. *Soviet* is the Russian word for "council."

immediate ramifications. It created unrest at home, and it inspired the Germans to seek a way to remove Russia from World War I. The Germans found their answer in Vladimir Ilyich Lenin who orchestrated a second revolution in October 1917 and removed Russia from the war.

Lenin and Trotsky

The Russian Revolution utilized terrorism in a new manner, and this had an impact on the way people viewed terrorism in the twentieth century. Lenin and one of his lieutenants, **Leon Trotsky** (1879–1940), believed that terrorism should be used as an instrument for overthrowing middle-class, or bourgeois, governments. Once power was achieved, Lenin and Trotsky advocated terrorism as a means of controlling internal enemies and as a method for coping with international strife. Russia was very weak after the revolution. It faced foreign intervention and was torn by civil war. By threatening to export terrorism, Lenin and Trotsky hoped to keep their enemies, primarily Western Europe and the United States, at bay.

With their threat, Lenin and Trotsky instilled the fear of Communist revolution in the minds of many people in the West. To some, terrorism and Communism became synonymous. Though the Russians, and later the Soviets, were not good at carrying insurrection to other lands, Western leaders began to fear that Communist terrorists were on the verge of toppling democratic governments. Despite Lenin and his successor, Joseph Stalin, having the most success with another form of terror—murdering their own people—fear of Communist insurrection lasted well into the twentieth century, and some people still fear it. Even as the Soviet Union tottered into dissolution, Western analysts still saw terrorism through the lens of Western–Soviet confrontation (see Livingstone and Arnold, 1986; Sterling, 1986). Former CIA analyst Michael Scheuer (2006, pp. 20–23) believes that this perspective hinders the ability to comprehend terrorism today.

In fairness to analysts of the Cold War, Lenin's victory and subsequent writings have inspired terrorists from 1917 to the present. Although Communist terrorism was not part of an orchestrated conspiracy, it did influence behavior. Some terrorists scoured the works of Lenin and Trotsky, as well as other Russian revolutionaries, to formulate theories, tactics, and ideologies. Although not a simple conspiracy of evil, this influence was real and remains today.

Leon Trotsky: A Russian revolutionary who led foreign affairs in Stalin's government and later became the commander of the Red Army. He espoused terrorism as a means for spreading White revolution. He was thrown out of the Communist Party for opposing Stalin and was assassinated by Communist agents in Mexico City in 1940.

✓ **Self-Check**

> How did revolutionary thought develop in czarist Russia?
> Describe the two revolutions under Nicholas II.
> How did Lenin and Trotsky influence the direction of revolutionary thought?

Selective Terrorism and the Birth of the Irish Republic

In August 1969, the British Army was ordered to increase its presence in Northern Ireland in an effort to quell a series of riots. Although the army had maintained bases in Northern Ireland for some time, rioting in Londonderry and Belfast was suddenly far beyond the control of local police and the handful of British regular soldiers stationed in the area. On August 18, 1969, British Army reinforcements began arriving,

⏱ Outdated History?

Michael Scheuer (2006, pp. 20–23), former director of the CIA's bin Laden unit, believes that the focus on history is often misplaced. There are two types of terrorist "experts," he contends—retired governmental and military officials and informed commentators. The latter group is made up of academics and journalists. Scheuer believes that these people are far from experts because not only do they fail to understand history, but they are also stuck in a time frame. Media consciousness about terrorism developed and grew in the 1970s. Two issues dominated terrorism at that time: the Cold War and violence around Israel and Palestine. Expertise about terrorism came from studying both the emergence of theory, with its roots in the West, and the anticolonial movements associated with the early part of the Cold War. Terrorism was a historical phenomenon, an outcome of confrontations that grew from the influence of Western history. Ideological groups such as the Baader-Meinhof Gang and the Red Brigades came from political battlefields. Nationalistic groups such as the Puerto Rican Armed Forces of National Liberation (FALN) and the Basque Nation and Liberty (ETA) were motivated by patriotism, but they adopted leftist agendas and the tactics of leftist terrorists.. The anti-Western attitude of Palestinian groups like Hezbollah and the Abu Nidal Organization was tinged with a left-wing philosophy and a style of operation similar to their counterparts in ideological and nationalistic movements. Western expertise was honed over two decades, from 1970 to 1990, Scheuer says, and it has very little to do with terrorism today.

Jihadist terrorism comes from a different tradition. It does not rely on political and theoretical developments in the West, and although jihadists frequently embrace the cause of the Palestinians, they do not seek to establish an independent Palestinian state or replace a destroyed Israel with a new Arab country. They come from a religious tradition dating from the twelfth century in the Western calendar, and they operate in a manner far different from terrorist groups in the late twentieth century. Expertise on the old-style groups is not applicable to the jihadists, Scheuer concludes. So-called terrorism experts are outdated. They are stuck in the past and examine modern terrorism through a perspective "yellowed with age."

Consider these issues in terms of future developments:

- Unlike most criminals, terrorists study the past to develop tactical models. Is there merit in studying the history of terrorism? If so, what is the time frame for beginning such study?
- Does the history of terrorism teach lessons across cultures? Are there certain aspects of terrorism that remain constant across time and location?
- How is the form of twenty-first-century terrorism different from its previous manifestations? How is it similar?

hoping to avoid a long-term conflict. Their hopes were in vain. The meaning of terrorism in Ireland changed with history. Unlike revolutionary France, Europe in 1848, and the differing forms of terrorism in Russia, terrorism in Ireland developed over a number of centuries (Lee, 1983).

The Irish have never ruled their island as a single political entity, and they have experienced some type of foreign domination since a series of Viking incursions in 800 CE (Costigan, 1980; Cahill, 2003). The Vikings were driven out in the eleventh century, only to be replaced by invading Normans in the twelfth century (Simms, 2000). England began to colonize the northern part of Ireland in the late 1500s. This not only brought conflict between the colonizers and the colonized, it created a direct collision between Protestants and Catholics (Bradshaw, 1978; O Corrain, 2000; Curtis, 2000, pp. 16–18, orig. 1936; Herren and Brown, 2002). Finally, after the United Kingdom was formed in 1801, Ireland was literally absorbed by Great Britain (see Cronin, 1984; Foster, 2001, pp. 134–172). This last act created a new type of Irish person, the *Republican*, a citizen who wanted to be free of the British in a *Republic* of Ireland.

The Early Irish Republican Army

By the twentieth century, the struggle in Ireland had become a matter of divisions between Unionists, people who wanted to remain in the United Kingdom of Great Britain and Ireland, and Republicans, people who wanted independence. A host of other conflicts were associated with this confrontation, but the main one was the Unionist–Republican struggle. The Unionists often had the upper hand because they could call on support from the British-sponsored police and military forces. The Republicans had no such advantage, and they searched for an alternative.

Costigan (1980) believes that the Republican military solution originated when the Irish Republican Brotherhood (IRB) formed in the 1850s. Support came from exiles and emigrants around the world. Irish Catholics had emigrated from their homeland to the United States, Australia, Canada, and New Zealand, but they never forgot the people they left behind. Irish immigrants in New York City created the Fenian Brotherhood as a financial relief organization for relatives in the old country. After the U.S. Civil War, some Irish soldiers returning from the U.S. Army decided to take the struggle for emancipation back to Ireland. Having fought to free the slaves, they believed that they should continue the struggle and free Ireland. They sponsored a failed revolt in 1867, and others launched a dynamite campaign in London a decade and a half later. Although the IRB pledged to work peacefully, it gradually evolved into a revolutionary organization.

J. Bowyer Bell (1974) has written the definitive treatise on the origins and development of the Irish Republican Army (IRA). He states that it began with a campaign of violence sponsored by the IRB in the late 1800s. Spurred on by increased nationalistic feeling in the homeland and the hope of home rule, the IRB waged a campaign of bombing and assassination from 1870 until 1916. Its primary targets were Unionists and British forces that supported the Unionist cause. Among their greatest adversaries was the British-backed police force in Ireland, the **Royal Irish Constabulary (RIC)**.

The activities of the IRB frightened Irish citizens who wanted to remain united with Great Britain. For the most part, these people were Protestant and middle class, and they lived in the northern counties. They gravitated toward their trade unions and social organizations, among them the Orange Lodges, to counter growing IRB sympathy and power. They enjoyed the sympathy of the British Army's officer corps. They also controlled the RIC.

The Fenians of the IRB remained undaunted by Unionist sentiment. Although Irish Unionists seemed in control, the IRB had two trump cards. First, IRB leadership was dominated by men who believed each generation had to produce warriors who would fight for independence. Some of these leaders, as well as their followers, were quite willing to be martyred to keep republicanism alive. In addition, the IRB had an organization. It not only served as a threat to British power, it also provided the basis for the resurgence of Irish culture.

Royal Irish Constabulary (RIC): The police force established by the United Kingdom in Ireland. It was modeled after the London Metropolitan Police, but it represented British interests. After the Free State was formed, the RIC became the Royal Ulster Constabulary (RUC). In turn, the RUC gave way to the Police Service of Northern Ireland (PSNI) as part of Irish and British attempts to bring peace to Northern Ireland after 1995.

The Easter Rising

At the turn of the twentieth century, no person embodied Irish culture more than Patrick Pearse (1879–1916). The headmaster of an Irish school, Pearse was an inspirational romantic. He could move crowds to patriotism and inspire resistance to British policies. He was a hero among Irish Americans, and they sent hundreds of thousands of dollars to support his cause. He told young Irish boys and girls about their heritage, he taught them Gaelic, and he inspired them to be militantly proud of being Irish. He was also a member of the **Supreme Council of the IRB**. When the possibility of home rule was defeated in the British parliament, Republican eyes turned to Pearse.

By 1916, the situation in Ireland had changed. The British had promised home rule to Ireland when World War I (1914–1918) came to an end. Whereas most people in Ireland believed the British, Unionists and Republicans secretly armed for a civil war between the north and the south. They believed a fight was inevitable if the British granted home rule, and each side was determined to dominate the government of a newly independent Ireland. Some Republicans were not willing to wait for home rule.

With British attention focused on Germany, leaders of the IRB believed that it was time for a strike against the Unionists and their British supporters. On Easter in 1916, Patrick Pearse and James Connolly (1868–1916) led a revolt in Dublin. Pearse believed that the revolt was doomed from the start, but he also believed that it was necessary to sacrifice his life to keep the Republican spirit alive. Connolly was a more pragmatic socialist who fought because he believed a civil war was inevitable.

The 1916 Easter Rising enjoyed local success because it surprised everyone. Pearse and Connolly took over several key points in Dublin with a few thousand armed followers. From the halls of the General Post Office, Pearse announced that the revolutionaries had formed an Irish republic, and he asked the Irish to follow him. The British, outraged by what they saw as treachery in the midst of a larger war, sent troops to Dublin. The city was engulfed in a week of heavy fighting.

Whereas Pearse and Connolly came to start a popular revolution, the British came to fight a war. In a few days, Dublin was devastated by British artillery. Pearse recognized the futility of the situation and asked for terms. Bell (1974) points out the interesting way Pearse chose to approach the British: He sent a message using a new title for himself, commanding general of the IRA, to the general in charge of the British forces. The IRB had transformed itself into an army: the IRA.

If Connolly and Pearse hoped to be greeted as liberators, they greatly misjudged the mood of Ireland. Had the British played to Irish sympathy, they might have stopped violent republicanism. Their actions, however, virtually empowered **Sinn Fein**. The British handed down several dozen death sentences for the Easter Rising. Hundreds more people received lengthy prison sentences. Pearse became an Irish legend. Standing in front of a firing squad, he gave an impassioned plea for Irish independence. Connolly, who had been badly wounded, was tied to a chair and placed before a firing squad. Public sympathy shifted to the rebels.

Two important people managed to escape the purge. Eamon de Valera (1882–1975) received a prison sentence instead of death because of questions about his nationality. He had been born in New York City and was brought to Ireland at an early age. Michael Collins (1890–1922), who was in a cell where prisoners slated for execution were being segregated from those selected for internment, walked to the other side of the cell and found himself among the internment group. It saved his life. De Valera would emerge as a revolutionary and political leader, and Collins would become the leader of the IRA.

Supreme Council of the IRB: The command center of several Republican terrorist organizations, including the Irish Republican Army, the Official Irish Republican Army, and the Provisional Irish Republican Army. The name was transposed from the Irish Republican Brotherhood.

Sinn Fein: The political party of Irish Republicans. Critics claim it represents terrorists. Republicans say it represents their political interests. Despite the debate, Sinn Fein historically has had close connections with extremism and violence.

ANOTHER PERSPECTIVE

State Repression

Edward Herman (1983) says terrorism should be defined in terms of state repression. During the Cold War, the United States supported several Latin American dictatorships because the dictatorships were anti-communist. These governments, which had some of the worst human rights records in history, routinely jailed, tortured, and executed political opponents. The United States not only ignored the repression, it also funded the activities and trained the repressive military and police forces. When the amount of human suffering from these dictatorships is compared to violence caused by insurgent terrorism, the pain caused by modern terrorism shrinks to insignificance. The "real terror network," Herman argues, is found in repressive government. University of Virginia sociologist Donald Black (2004) summarizes the paradox evident in Herman's earlier work. Counterterrorism, he says, is more violent than terrorism.

The Black and Tan War, 1920–1921

Sinn Fein, the political party of Irish republicanism, continued its activities in spite of the failure of the Easter Rising. When World War I ended, many of the Republicans were released. There were several moderates in Ireland, represented by the Parliamentary Party, and they sought to reopen the issue of home rule. They believed that this was the only nonviolent way to approach the Irish question. Bew (1999) says that the moderates were also willing to cede the northern province, Ulster, to the Protestants who wished to remain united with Great Britain. If the Protestants were forced into a united Ireland, they reasoned, violence would continue.

Bew believes Sinn Fein took advantage of the moderate position and championed the cause of a united Ireland. The ideologues of republicanism expressed themselves in extremist terms. They not only rejected home rule but demanded a completely **Free State** devoid of any British participation in Irish politics. For Sinn Fein, anything but a united Ireland was out of the question. The British government also vacillated. Conservatives, especially the military officer corps, were reluctant to abandon the north either to home rule or to an independent Ireland, whereas others sought to solve the Irish problem with some sort of home rule. Bew argues that Sinn Fein moved into the arena by discrediting the Parliamentary Party. Moderation fell by the wayside as extreme republicanism increased.

Free State: The given to the newly formed Republic of Ireland after Irish independence.

Selective Terror

Michael Collins was appalled by the amateur tactics of the Easter Rising. Revolution, he believed, could be successful, but it would not develop from a popular uprising. It needed to be systematic, organized, and ruthless. After being released from prison as part of a general amnesty, Collins studied the tactics of Russia's People's Will and the writings of earlier anarchists and terrorists. Collins developed a strategy called selective terrorism. Devising a plan that would later influence terrorists as diverse as the proto-Israeli group Irgun Zvai Leumi and Ernesto "Che" Guevara's Communist revolutionaries in Cuba, Collins reasoned that indiscriminate terror was of no value. Random or large-scale attacks would alienate public opinion. Conversely, launching an attack and waiting for the population to spontaneously rise to rebellion was equally futile. To be effective, terrorism had to selectively and ruthlessly target security forces and their symbols of authority.

After months of planning, recruiting, and organizing, Collins launched a new form of the IRA. He began by gathering intelligence, learning the internal workings of British police headquarters, and obtaining a list of intelligence officers. The first attacks were devastating. Using the information from the extensive preparation, Collins's men ambushed off-duty police and intelligence officers and murdered them. They then began attacking police stations. IRA terrorists would emerge from a crowded sidewalk, throw bombs and shoot police officers, then melt back into the crowd before authorities could respond. A master of strategy, Collins continued a campaign of terror against Unionists and the RIC.

The British responded by sending a hastily recruited military force, called the Black and Tans because of their mismatched uniforms, and Ireland became the scene of a dreadful war. Each side accused the other of atrocities, but both parties engaged in murder and mayhem. The conflict became popularly known as the Tan War or the Black and Tan War. It was a fierce struggle between the IRA's selective terrorism and British repression. It ended with independence for the southern provinces and British control of Northern Ireland. Failure to win freedom for the entire republic cost Michael Collins his life. It also served as the main source of terrorism directed at the United Kingdom through most of the twentieth century.

> **Self-Check**
>
> > How did the IRB evolve toward militancy?
> > How did the Easter Rising impact republicanism?
> > What is the meaning of "selective terror," and how did Collins employ it?

Emphasizing the Points

The United States has changed national security and law enforcement policies based partially on the way it defines terrorism. This is a situational definition, however, because the meaning of terrorism has changed through history. The ideas behind modern democracies were contained in the Enlightenment, giving birth to revolutions in the American colonies and in France. Terrorism was a product of the class-based revolution in France, and the term described the actions of the government. It would go through many changes in meaning until it once again was used to describe government repression. Many of the chapters in Part 2 will summarize recent regional histories to show how the definition continues to fluctuate.

SUMMARY OF CHAPTER OBJECTIVES

- Terrorism is difficult to define because it is a social construct and not a physical entity. Furthermore, the term is pejorative because it evokes a variety of politically charged responses. The way terrorism is defined often has life or death consequences.
- The term *terrorism* is defined within social and political contexts, and it means different things in different time periods. The meaning even changes within a historical time frame as contexts change. This is the primary reason that no single definition of terrorism will ever be successful.

- Definitions of terrorism are important because they guide policy, but there are differing frameworks for definitions. Some approaches emphasize the criminal nature of terrorism. Others focus on the types of targets that terrorist select. While many academics offer definitions, they are probably not as important as policy definitions.
- Terrorism originated during the French Revolution. It described the actions of the government. In the nineteenth century, the French applied it to guerrillas in Spain, and it was used to describe the actions of radical democrats in the 1848 revolutions. By the century's end, it was used as a label for anarchists and nationalists.
- Socialism refers to controlling an economy by direct democracy and utilizing economic profits to ensure the well-being of citizens. Anarchism is a philosophical concept that originated in ancient Greece. In the eighteenth century, anarchists generally disavowed the power of national governments. Some anarchists were violent, engaging in bombing and assassination. Communism in its ideal form is socialism with economic production and profits being owned and distributed by workers.
- Modern revolutionary terrorism is closely associated with a series of revolutionary activities that began with the People's Will and continued through the Russian Revolution. After the Communists seized power, they returned to the practice of the French revolutionaries and used terrorism to maintain political power.
- Irish revolutionaries fought for independence for several centuries. The Irish Republican Brotherhood was created in the mid-nineteenth century. They soon adopted the tactics of the 1848 revolutionaries, waging a campaign of terror that culminated in the Black and Tan War.
- After the failure of the Easter Rising, Michael Collins used the term *selective terrorism*. His intention was to target specific government officials and supporters. He sought to terrorize them until they accepted IRA terms.

LOOKING INTO THE FUTURE

If past behavior is the best predictor of future behavior, as psychologists frequently argue, then the definition of terrorism will remain elusive. Aside from confusion surrounding the term and multiple agencies using a variety of meanings, there are important international repercussions due to the lack of an internal agreement on a standard definition of terrorism. This will continue to remain problematic and complicate international relations. The main reasons are that it will allow murderous subnational groups to operate with impunity in some parts of the world, and it will give repressive governments additional legitimacy.

In the first case, assume that Country A suffers an attack on innocent civilians by a subnational group wishing to change Country A's political policies. The citizens of Country A call this an act of terrorism. The group responsible for the attack is based in Country B, but when diplomats from Country A complain, the leaders of Country B respond by saying the group represents a legitimate political organization. While this may result in an incursion into Country B's sovereign territory and may even led to war, there is no international legal standard to delegitimize the subnational group.

The second case is similar. Assume that a repressive dictator controls Country C. The people suffer under the dictator's hands, and there is no hope of peaceful political change. All forms of dissent are severely punished. The only hope of liberation can come from a revolution. As a result, a small group forms and begins to grow. It engages the government's forces and leaves citizens alone. The dictator calls this action terrorism, and the international community lacks a legal standard to contradict this logic.

For the foreseeable future, international diplomats and UN representatives will talk about the problems created by the lack of a standard definition of terrorism. That is probably all they will do. There seems to be little hope of agreeing on a standard definition in the near future.

KEY TERMS

Social construct, p. 3
Academic consensus
   definition, p. 3
Social context, p. 3
Selective terrorism, p. 4
Nidal Malik Hasan, p. 4

Reign of Terror, p. 9
Spain in 1807, p. 9
Radical democrats, p. 10
Socialists, p. 10
Anarchists, p. 10
Communists, p. 10

Joseph Stalin, p. 15
Vladmir Lenin, p. 15
Vladmir Putin, p. 15
Workers' Councils (or
   Soviets), p. 16
Leon Trotsky, p. 17

Royal Irish
   Constabulary, p. 19
Supreme Council
   of the IRB, p. 20
Sinn Fein, p. 20
Free State, p. 21

CHAPTER **2**

Practical Criminology, Radicalization, and Types of Terrorism

Aftermath of a Riot

Stefan Feldmann Demotix/Corbis News/Corbis

LEARNING OBJECTIVES

After reading this chapter, you should be able to:

▶ Explain the value of practical criminology for law enforcement and security forces.

▶ List the differences between terrorists and ordinary criminals.

▶ Explain the importance of radicalization and alienation.

▶ Summarize two recent case studies of radicalization.

▶ Describe opposing views about prison radicalization.

▶ Summarize the controversy regarding the use of the concept of radicalization.

▶ Identify three different types of terrorism.

▶ Define lone wolf terrorism.

▶ Explain the ways small and large groups use terrorism.

▶ Describe the manner in which guerrillas and insurgents use terrorism.

O n Sunday August 5, 2012, Wade Michael Page walked into a Sikh temple in Oak Creek, Wisconsin. He began shooting. Six worshipers were killed inside the temple. Three other Sikhs, including the temple president, were injured trying to stop him. He then followed fleeing people into the parking lot, where he killed two more victims. As police responded, he shot and wounded one of the officers. The police were able to stop him by shooting and killing him. No one knows why he did it.

This was one of many mass-shooting events in the past decades. Each murderer had a unique background and access to firearms. As details emerged, investigators found that Page had a background in violent racist music. He was a neo-Nazi involved in the white supremacy movement, and he played in a variety of bands. While not on tour, he spent a lot of time surfing white supremacy websites.

The Southern Poverty Law Center (2012) reported that Page began his path to violent racism while serving in the U.S.

25

Army in the 1990s. He gravitated toward hate music and eventually identi-fied with the white supremacy movement. He expressed a vitriolic hatred of Muslims after the September 11, 2001, attacks, and perhaps he thought he was attacking a mosque. Wearing colorful turbans over uncut hair as part of their religious tradition, Sikhs are sometimes confused with Muslims. Yet, Page made no threats and left no statement about his motive.

Even though investigators could not find the reason for Page's actions, one aspect was clear. He had traveled down an ideological path that ended with murder. He had acted alone and ended the lives of his victims as a lone at-tacker. Some researchers and analysts have a name for Page's journey to hate and murder. They call it radicalization. They also use a special term to describe such attacks. It is lone wolf terrorism.

The Criminology of Terrorism

There are two branches of criminology in the practical world of criminal justice. When using the word *criminology* in an academic setting, images of psychological and sociological theories appear in the minds of researchers and teachers. This is clas-sic criminology, which traces its origins to **Cesare Beccaria** and uses the most modern theories of individual and group behavior. When the word is mentioned in a law enforcement agency, a different image appears. Practical criminology focuses on the common actions of lawbreakers. Police officers are not as concerned with theories of criminality as they are with the practical aspects of criminal behavior. They want to know what criminals do so that they may deter them from committing a crime or catch them after the crime is committed.

The purpose here is to consider this second branch of criminology, the applied actions in crime prevention and apprehension. This distinction is important because although terrorists commit crimes as they struggle for a cause, they differ from or-dinary street criminals. Terrorists have organizational structures, belief systems, and motivational values that separate them from ordinary criminals. The behavioral dif-ferences are even more pronounced during political insurrections. When guerrillas employ terrorism, they usually do so within the context of a political and military strategy. Law enforcement personnel should recognize the differences between typical criminal behavior and terrorist activity if they want to prevent crime and apprehend criminals. Law enforcement officials are frequently the first governmental agents on the scene of a terrorist incident. If they fail to recognize that the scene may be some-thing more than an ordinary crime, they may well miss the point of the investigation.

For example, should malicious destruction of property always be classified as a simple misdemeanor or felony? If someone unlawfully enters a farm, destroys cages, and frees the animals, is this simply malicious destruction? Many law enforcement officers would answer *yes*; but consider the Animal Liberation Front (ALF). In instruc-tions to members and sympathizers, the ALF advocates the systematic destruction of farms that produce fur for clothing. Their website gives potential recruits tactics for the most effective destruction of mink farms. (See http://www.animalliberationfront .com/index.html.) If a deputy sheriff or state trooper happens on such an attack, it will probably be classified as malicious destruction of property, even though it may well be part of a larger operation.

In terms of terrorism, law enforcement agencies, intelligence organizations, and military forces need to take a practical criminological approach to terrorism. This is

Cesare Beccaria: (1738–1794) One of the found-ers of the discipline of criminology. His work *Of Crimes and Punishments* (1764) is the classic En-lightenment study of the discipline.

One of the issues that has dominated the discipline of criminal justice over the past few decades is the debate about the academic function of the discipline. Some scholars favor a theoretical approach to the field, while others believe that professors with previous professional experience are better suited to address the discipline. This debate takes place not only on college campuses but in the worka-day world of criminal justice as well.

Here are some examples of the differences between practitioners in the field and theoretical social scientists:

Professionals—tend to focus on criminological findings that will result in crime fighting and solutions for community problems.

Professionally oriented social scientists—tend to conduct studies that will help professionals reduce crime.

Theoretically oriented social scientists—tend to focus research on increasing the body of scientific knowledge regardless of application.

In reality, all three approaches are necessary and valued. Each "type" of criminology has a valid purpose.

FIGURE **2.1** Theory vs. Practice

especially true for state and local agencies because individual officers are usually the first people to arrive on the scene of a terrorist incident, and if terrorists are active, they frequently have unexpected encounters with law enforcement prior to and after an incident. Troopers, deputies, patrol officers, and investigators will be more effective if they develop practical criminological skills. Recognizing the characteristics of terrorist behavior improves prevention and investigation.

Differences Between Criminals and Terrorists

Terrorist investigations do not follow the pattern of most criminal investigations because terrorists seldom behave like normative street criminals. D. Douglas Bodrero (2002), the former commissioner for the Department of Public Safety in Utah and a former member of the International Association of Chiefs of Police Committee on Terrorism, offers a comparative analysis between terrorist behavior and that of ordinary criminals. Bodrero argues that typical criminals are opportunistic. This means that criminals tend to be impulsive. Most street criminals do not plan their crimes extensively, and they react to easy opportunities on the spur of the moment. Criminals are usually not committed to a cause. Even career criminals do not believe in crime as an ideology or religion. Crime is just a method for obtaining goods. Because of this lifestyle, criminals tend to be self-centered and undisciplined. Except for a small proportion of career criminals, ordinary street criminals are untrained. Their goal is to obtain cash or goods and get away.

Bodrero and most police officers base crime prevention and apprehension strategies on these assumptions about street criminals for one simple reason: They work. By protecting (or hardening) targets, denying opportunity, and conducting aggressive patrols, many ordinary street crimes like burglary can be suppressed (W. Harris, 1998). In addition, making police an extension of the community can reduce crimes that seem to defy suppression, such as domestic violence (Trojanowicz et al., 1998). By using criminal intelligence files to keep track of known felons, criminal associations, and crime patterns, police suppress criminal activity. Police search for hangouts of local criminals, they know their friends and family, and they maintain sources of information about suspicious activity. These procedures not only serve as the basis of community policing, they are the essence of criminal investigation.

Bodrero (2002) says terrorist behavior differs from standard patterns of criminal behavior because terrorists are highly motivated and loyal to a particular cause. Whereas ordinary criminals are opportunistic, terrorists are focused. They may select targets of opportunity, but the targets have symbolic value. Terrorists use crime to make a symbolic statement about a political cause.

If criminals are uncommitted and self-centered, terrorists find strength in a cause and the ideology or religion behind the cause. They are supported by an organization and sent on a mission. They are team oriented even when they act as individuals. For example, suicide bombers do not act alone; their preparation involves teamwork. Being part of something greater than themselves becomes the basis for action. Even in the case of lone wolves, the ideology is all-consuming. They might act alone, but deep-seated beliefs cause loners to feel that their actions are part of the vanguard of a movement. Terrorism is an organizational process, whether support is real or implied through ideology (Schweitzer, 2000; Khashan, 2003; Kaplan et al., 2005; Azam, 2005).

Ideology and religion are not limited to suicide bombers; they also influence individuals who will become terrorists for a single event. For example, Buford Furrow entered a Jewish daycare center in August 1999 and began shooting people. He was a lone wolf. He had no extensive logistical network or support organization. Yet, Furrow was consumed by an ideology of hate and a religion that demonized Jews. He was not an uncommitted opportunistic criminal acting alone. He was an agent of an ideology on a divine mission. Again, as Bodrero (2002) indicates, this is not the pattern of typical criminals. Bodrero says that criminals are undisciplined, untrained, and oriented toward escape. Terrorists are exactly the opposite. They have prepared for their mission, they are willing to take risks, and they are attack oriented. Lone wolves might be untrained, but they are prepared and attack oriented.

In summary, terrorists and criminals exhibit practical behavioral differences. These include:

1. Criminals are unfocused. Terrorists focus their actions toward a goal.
2. Criminals may live in a criminal underworld, but they are not devoted to crime as a philosophy. Terrorists are dedicated to a cause.
3. Criminals will make deals to avoid punishment. Terrorists rarely cooperate with officials because they do not wish to betray their cause.
4. Criminals usually run when confronted with force. Terrorists tend to attack.
5. Criminals strike when the opportunity to do so is present. Terrorists strike symbols after careful planning.
6. Criminals rarely train for crime. Terrorists prepare for and rehearse their operations.

These differences influence the ways criminal intelligence is gathered and the process of criminal investigations. Terrorism investigations involve long-term observation, informant development, and evidence collection. They usually involve a lengthy process of piecing together elements of a complex criminal conspiracy (see Lee, 2005; Dyson, 2008).

The significance of Bodrero's argument can be measured in the investigative response to terrorism. When investigating a crime, police officers can take advantage of the behavioral characteristics of typical criminals. The most hardened criminals will usually act in their own self-interest, and they will make deals to receive a lesser sentence. When searching for a fleeing felon, law enforcement officers find it productive to question known associates and keep family and friends under surveillance. These tactics do not work in countering terrorism. Law enforcement, military, and security officials need to focus on ideology, group and individual behavior, and sharing information over broad geographical regions to successfully investigate terrorism.

> **Self-Check**
>
> > What is "practical criminology"?
> > Why does law enforcement focus on practical interpretations of criminology?
> > What are the differences between terrorists and criminals?

Radicalization

John Horgan (2009) argues that many psychological approaches have mistakenly focused on the root causes of terrorism. Such studies miss the point. Rather than searching for the "roots of terrorism," Horgan believes researchers should search for the **routes to terrorism**. In other words, Horgan is concerned with the psychological processes that lead people to terrorist groups, the issues that keep them in groups, and support mechanisms for people who want to leave.

routes to terrorism: As used by John Horgan, refers to the psychological and social factors that motivate people to join and remain in terrorist groups.

The process of becoming a terrorist involves three distinct phases. In the first phase, a person must decide to become a terrorist, and this is followed by a decision to remain in a terrorist group. Both of these decisions return to the arguments about justifying violence, but there are points where people decide that they can no longer accept terrorism. Horgan believes this leads to a third process, disengagement—the behavior of people who decide to abandon terrorism. Horgan believes these pathways to terrorism are more important than searching for a definitive profile of terrorist behavior.

If Horgan is correct, his research suggests that a more effective approach to profiling is to identify actions and policies that may help prevent the desire to join or remain in a group. It also suggests a need to understand and support the factors involved in deciding to leave a group. Horgan asks researchers to focus on the process of radicalization rather than methods to prevent it.

Practical Criminology and Radicalism

Radicalization involves the processes that change a person's socially acceptable behavior into terrorism. John Horgan (2009, p. 155) states that it is unrealistic to assume that programs or policies can prevent radicalization. He also notes that most of the people who hold radical views are not violent. **Violent radicalization** is the problem of terrorism, Horgan believes. Movement toward violence is a social and psychological process influenced by peer groups and terrorist causes. Brian Jenkins (2009) believes that since it is a process, people moving toward violent radicalization exhibit observable signs. Family members, peers, and people closely associated with an individual may witness the behavioral changes. If this is true, others may observe them, too.

radicalization: As used in this context, refers to the psychological process of adopting extremist positions.

violent radicalization: Refers to the process of adopting extremist positions and engaging in violence based on a new set of beliefs.

The term *radicalization* is used by law enforcement, intelligence, military, and other agencies. Popular media employ it frequently. Yet, there is not complete agreement about the meaning of the term. Some people even question its existence (Porter and Kebbell, 2011). However, if researchers like John Horgan and Brian Jenkins are talking about radicalization, it has an applied meaning. In terms of practical criminology, radicalization can be seen as a *process* that *causes* violence.

Radicalization is believed to cause terrorism when the motivation for political change combines with the process of developing deep-seated doctrines that lead toward violent action. It occurs on an individual level when a person decides to join a group and on a group level when an organization decides to employ terrorism (Tsintsadze-Maass and Maass, 2014). Peter Neumann (2007), who heads an organization designed to study radicalization in the United Kingdom, says that such an approach allows the examination of the political, economic, and social factors that underpin political violence.

alienation: Happens when an individual or group becomes lost in the dominant social world. A person or group of people is alienated when separated from the dominant values of society at large.

Another concept closely associated with radicalization is **alienation**, a term used in several branches of the social sciences, as well as in other disciplines such as theology. Many sociologists define alienation as a process by which an individual or group becomes separated from the values, norms, and mores of the dominant social world. This leads to self-estrangement. The concept was initially popularized by Karl Marx's work on economic alienation, and many sociologists of the nineteenth and twentieth centuries expanded his approach, focusing on concepts like social isolation, lack of meaning, and normlessness.

Many terrorism analysts began looking at radicalization and alienation in the first part of the twenty-first century; their focus tended to be on individuals attracted to Islamic extremism. Some researchers found that individual decisions were less important than the social-psychological patterns of an entire group. Members of groups became radicalized together. A clique of friends moved collectively toward terrorism, and individual identities were absorbed and redefined when the clique joined a terrorist movement (Borum, 2004; Sageman, 2004, pp. 152–156; Horgan, 2005, pp. 80–105). Further analysis indicated that paths to radicalization developed differently for different causes and different types of groups. Ethnic, nationalistic, political, and religious terrorists were radicalized in a multitude of ways (Post, 2007).

The Process of Radicalization

A number of researchers believe that members of terrorist groups go through decision-making processes while they are being violently radicalized (Sageman, 2004, pp. 152–156; Borum, 2004; Ryan, 2007; Post, 2007; Hoffman, 2009; Rinehart, 2009; Kershaw, 2010; Ganor, 2011). Research in the area has been expanding over the past decade, and there are many emergent findings. One position maintains that radicalization can be understood as a process of socialization: It is the result of learning to engage in radicalized violence (Wilner and Dubouloz, 2011). Case studies provide rich data to determine individual paths (Ganor, 2011; Vidino, 2011). Another area of growing research is the process of de-radicalization. Although more data is needed, some preliminary findings suggest that if a person can go through a process of radicalization, the person can reverse the path and become de-radicalized (Gunaratna and Ali, 2010; Horgan and Braddock, 2010). Empirical evidence is still emerging, however, and our knowledge of radicalization is incomplete (Dalgaard-Nielson, 2010).

Marc Sageman (2004) was one of the first analysts to suggest that radicalization could be modeled and observed. Sageman presents radicalization as a six-step framework. It starts with alienated young men who find other groups of alienated young men. They "discover" religion as a way of giving meaning to their lives. Terrorism enters the equation if the newfound religious orientation turns to violence. Regardless, it remains difficult to join a terrorist group. These young men must meet a broker, an activist who knows actual terrorists, and be accepted by an actual terrorist group.

Sageman's framework applies to groups of males, but radicalization also occurs among women. Some recent research suggests that women are attracted to religious

STEP 1 Alienated young man

STEP 2 Meets other alienated young men and forms bond

INTERIM They become a "Bunch of Guys"

STEP 3 Groups gravitate toward religion

INTERIM They outdo each other in zeal to express love for the group

STEP 4 Religion interpreted in militant terms

INTERIM Most groups stop at this point

STEP 5 Militant group meets terrorist contact

STEP 6 Militants join terrorists as a group decision

FIGURE **2.2** Summarizing Sageman's Model

study groups as a social outlet in traditional cultures in which they are not given the same opportunities as men. The group gives them a means of social expression and acceptance apart from the male-dominated culture. Radicalization depends on the nature of the study group and the beliefs of dominant males in their lives. If these groups and dominant males emphasize militancy, the women in a study group may become radicalized toward religious violence (Ali, 2007; International Crisis Group, 2009). Paradoxically, women who struggle against a male-dominated culture may reject radicalization as an expression against a male-dominated ultraconservative religious culture (King, 2009).

Johnny Ryan (2007) maintains that there are behavioral commonalities as groups move toward violence. Radicalization is the result of "Four Ps": persecution, precedent, piety, and perseverance. He believes that these four concepts present a single interpretive framework that can be used to understand militant rhetoric and violent behavior. Ryan does this by comparing militant Islamic groups with Irish Republican militancy. He argues that both types of groups feel they have been persecuted and that both groups have experienced this over an extended period of time. The history of persecution presented a precedent for resisting the persecutors. Violence became a righteous or almost sacred action of devotion for both Republicans and Islamic militants. Ryan believes both ideologies have continued over time, and each generation is called upon to make new sacrifices.

The message of radicalization is recognizable and based on experience. Ryan says that al Qaeda and its associated networks explain revolutionary theory in an ideological manner similar to the IRA. Both Republican and Islamic militants present historical grievances to prove that revolutionary violence is the only alternative to an unjust system. He believes that radicalization cuts across cultures. It can be understood by the formula of heroes and martyrs, grievances against the superior power, and utopian goals that are articulated in the revolutionary message. It is an observable process and can be used to explain violence.

Other researchers have come to the conclusion that there is no single process of being radicalized, but that radicalization can occur in a variety of ways. John Horgan (2009) finds that radicalization occurs as individuals make decisions within the group. These observable points can be found when an individual decides to join a terrorist group, when the group moves from rhetoric to violence, and when an individual makes the decision to either stay with or leave the group.

Michael King and Donald Taylor (2011) say that radicalization is a process that is not specifically applicable to any national, political, religious, or ideological group.

They examine several models in an attempt to find commonalities in research findings. Beginning with Marc Sageman and Sageman's subsequent work with the New York City Police Department, King and Taylor believe that some form of deprivation or alienation takes place in the initial steps of the model. Steps toward radicalization are a logical response to feelings of alienation.

King and Taylor also believe that three other models dominate the research field in radicalization. The first model focuses on social and economic deprivation and the resentment resulting from it. Deprivation leads to blaming an outside group for the group's situation, and the outside group is demonized. This provides an opportunity for violent radicalization.

The second model is based on long-term learning. As in the previous model, a group feels that it is victimized. In other words, the people in the group feel deprived because they can never hope to live as well as the group that is victimizing them. Some members of the group eventually seek to understand the reason they are deprived. The answers lead to resentment, and the process is exacerbated when the group has religious goals or is seeking a religious explanation for deprivation. In this model, a group's orientation is refocused, and radicalization is learned over a period of time.

A third model maintains that radicalization is the result of psychological interpretations of events. Individuals in deprived economic circumstances gravitate toward one another and generally resent the position of a superior group. They develop options to attack what they see as unfair treatment. Aggression eventually emerges if the group becomes morally outraged and develops a solidified sense of injustice. Once the group takes a terrorist action, the radicalization process is completed.

King and Taylor combine all the models to suggest three areas for further study. The first area is to seek to understand how people react to relative deprivation. A second factor involves understanding how a group interprets its identity. This means that researchers need to locate and describe social processes involved in creating subjective reality. The final area involves personality types. King and Taylor believe it is necessary to understand why people exposed to the same social environment react in different ways—most of them do not engage in terrorism.

Hussein Solomon (2014) examines radical Islam in South Africa. Increasing violence in Africa makes him fear the rise of violence in his own nation. He argues that the sources of radicalism are to be found in militants who misinterpret religion. They are located in mosques, missionary organizations, and religious schools. He believes that charismatic militant religious figures are also potential sources of violent extremism. His work is basically a call to action. There is little evidence to support or rebuke his fear because radicalization in South Africa has not been studied sufficiently. Solomon implores researchers and security personnel to look at experiences from other countries and apply their methodologies and findings to South Africa.

Testing Radicalization with Recent Case Studies

Two recent case studies shed light on the process of radicalization. Etri Tsintsadze-Maass and Richard Maass (2014) examined radicalization in the Weather Underground, a violent domestic extremist group that conducted a number of bomb attacks from 1969 to 1975. Elena Masters and Rhea Siers (2014) look at the topic through the lens of one individual. They examine the radicalization of Omar Hammani, a young American who left Alabama to join a terrorist group in Somalia.

Tsintsadze-Maass and Maass say that most research on radicalization assumes that people adopt a violent extremist ideology through a rational thought process. It is based on the idea that actors analyze their own personal goals, the reasons they can no longer

1. Group pressured from external political, economic, and social forces
2. Group isolated from other interpretations of reality
3. Group members develop and think alike
4. Believe that leader's biases are factual and normal
5. Lack of structured decision-making process

FIGURE **2.3** Conditions Leading to Groupthink

tolerate the current political situation, the need to resort to violence, and the probabilities of success. Groups move to terrorism because they think violent action will correct political injustice. The decision to engage in violence is logical, according to most studies of terrorism. But Tsintsadze-Maass and Maass object to this way of thinking.

The decision to engage in terrorism is irrational, they believe. Logical thinking suggests that actors adopt behaviors because they think doing so will allow them to achieve their goal. There are times when terrorists select violence in a most illogical manner, and they pursue a course of mayhem and destruction when they have no chance of beating or even changing the system. Such behavior is the result of **groupthink**.

Five issues are common to groupthink scenarios. First, an external issue creates stress within the group. Second, the group is isolated from other groups or actors. Third, group members have similar backgrounds and believe systems. Fourth, members believe that bias leadership is normal. Finally, the group lacks a systematic method for making decisions. Tsintsadze-Maass and Maass test their theory or irrational decision making by conducting a historical study of an American terrorist group.

The **Weather Underground** formed in 1969 when a small group of potentially violent people broke away from a larger anti-war and social justice student movement known as the Students for a Democratic Society (SDS). The SDS had more than 100,000 members on college campuses throughout the nation, and their numbers gave them a voice in discussions of economic justice, problems of racism, and foreign policy. Social activism and multiple demonstrations gave the SDS the power to influence political behavior.

Tsintsadze-Maass and Maass argue that the rational choice for anyone wishing to change the direction of American society would have been to strengthen the SDS. Logically, to gain political power, people would have increased membership, expanded peaceful public demonstrations, and used voter activism. If the power of the SDS diminished, its relevance would suffer. Extremist political positions espousing violent rejection of social norms are frequently unattractive to potential followers when the majority of people are satisfied with the social system. Therefore, breaking away into a smaller group to espouse more radical views would be illogical and irrational. Yet, this is exactly what the Weather Underground chose to do.

Leadership in the Weather Underground believed that violence was necessary to overthrow the U.S. government. Its members agreed. They came from similar backgrounds, they thought alike, and they acted alike. They called for a massive militant demonstration and expected large numbers of students to join them. When this failed to happen, leaders of the Weather Underground failed to understand that their message did not appeal to the majority of activists who were working for greater social and economic justice. Instead of recognizing the futility of their position, the small group launched a bombing campaign in the hope of inspiring a revolution. Their goal was illogical and unattainable. Tsintsadze-Maass and Maass argue this situation was the result of groupthink.

groupthink: A mode of problem solving based on consensus. It occurs when members of a group value agreement about the way a problem will be solved rather than solving the problem. Once the members agree on a course of action, they follow it even when there is no chance of success.

Weather Underground: A left-wing domestic terrorist group operated from 1969 to 1975.

The Weather Underground did not engage in critical thinking. No alternative paths were accepted. Members of the group wanted to support one another. They wanted to think alike. They created a common stereotype of the enemy. They believed their actions expressed a moral absolute. Bombs failed to change political behavior; in fact, they actually increased external threats to the group. Yet, group members never questioned either their extremist views or their violent actions. Members of the Weather Underground dismissed public criticism and rejected any form of self-doubt. They continued to engage in violence, even though it was obvious to everyone else that they could not be successful. All these factors led to further bad decisions, but group members accepted the illusionary world they had created. None of this was logical. Tsintsadze-Maass and Maass conclude that groupthink is responsible for irrational terrorism.

Elena Masters and Rhea Siers (2014) study rationalization by looking at a young Alabama man who chose a path of violent religious extremism. Omar Hammami, discussed further in the section on al Shabab in Chapter 7, grew up with a Christian mother and a Muslim father. He converted to Islam from Christianity when he was a teenager, but he fell away from orthodox religion after bitter differences with his father. He became increasingly militant, eventually leaving college and becoming the American face of terrorism in Somalia.

Masters and Siers followed Hammami's path to see if there was some type of systematic manner of radicalization. Hammami went through many differing experiences on a complex journey of self-discovery. His motivations followed several paths with virtually no order. At times, he sought adventure. At other times, he wanted public praise or self-fulfillment. Much of his behavior was teenage rebellion. Personal conflict with his father made him determined to do something his father would never do. His indoctrination was far from systematic, and he moved from one form of religion to another. He finally settled on militancy. Masters and Siers could find no systematic pattern in his behavior.

Hammami simply made decisions the way most people make decisions, except that he chose violence in the end. Despite his choice, he never totally committed to terrorism. He was more interested in his personal views and his interpretation of the world. Although he was the face of Somali terrorism on the Internet and was known by many young Somalis in America for his militant rap videos, he broke with the leaders of his group in 2013. By September of that year, the leaders killed him and ended his eclectic journey into violent radicalization.

Other Cases of Radicalization

Concrete examples provide illustrations of radicalization. Bruce Hoffman (2009) and Boaz Ganor (2011) have used case studies to explain radicalization in Europe. Individual cases in the United States may also be used. **Umar Farouk Abdulmutallab** tried to destroy a Northwest airliner as it entered American airspace after a six-hour flight from Amsterdam on Christmas 2009. He attempted to detonate explosives hidden in his underwear. Passengers noticed Abdulmutallab's suspicious behavior as the plane neared Detroit, and he was subdued after trying to light the explosives. An American intelligence official assessed the incident by concluding that local issues in the Middle East had driven Abdulmutallab to a global act of terrorism (Dickey, 2010).

Abdulmutallab's story illustrates the complexity of radicalization. He would seem to have been a poor candidate to fall under the influence of Arabian militants. Born to a wealthy Nigerian family, he received an elite education and went to the United Kingdom to complete boarding school and college. Yet, he felt alone and isolated. Raised

Umar Farouk Abdulmutallab: (b. 1986) according to a federal indictment, smuggled a chemical bomb and chemical igniter in a syringe onto a Northwest flight from Amsterdam to Detroit on December 25, 2009. He was born into a family that practiced Islam but became radicalized while attending school in the United Kingdom. He was allegedly trained by terrorists in Yemen, who supplied the explosive compound.

with a set of tolerant Islamic values, his experience in London challenged his concept of right and wrong. He was alienated. He eventually found solace on militant websites and gravitated toward radicalism. Falling under the influence of a militant preacher, Abdulmutallab eventually joined a militant group in Yemen and began the attempted suicide mission (Hosenball, Isikoff, and Thomas, 2010; *New York Times*, 2010).

In another instance, **James W. von Brunn** walked into the U.S. Holocaust Memorial Museum in Washington, D.C., on a summer day in 2009. He began shooting, sending frightened tourists scrambling for cover. He was wounded by security guards, but not before he fatally wounded Stephen T. Johns, one of the officers trying to stop him. It was not the first time von Brunn had encountered law enforcement. He had tried to take the Federal Reserve Board hostage in 1981 and was sentenced to prison for the attempt. Von Brunn wanted to wage war on the federal government.

Von Brunn's radical development did not take place in a vacuum. He had a long history of being a loner and a white supremacist. According to news reports, he consumed information from neo-Nazi groups, and he believed that Jews were in league with nonwhite races to destroy white Americans and Europeans. Von Brunn developed antigovernment, racist, and anti-Semitic views over decades, and he maintained a hate-filled website after his release from prison. He attacked the Holocaust Museum as a final act of rage (Stout, 2009; Wilber, 2010).

James von Brunn's life had the makings for success. Born in the Midwest, he was strong, good-looking, and educated. He entered military service in World War II and returned to enter advertising in New York City. He married into an established East Coast family in 1951 and seemed to be on his way to a successful career. Unfortunately, there was another side to von Brunn. He hated Jews with a militant passion. His hatred abated during the war, but it increased after moving to New York City. He began writing about his views, growing increasingly bigoted against both Jews and nonwhites. It eventually cost him his marriage but not his deeper journey into anti-Semitism (Ruane, 2009).

The reasons for von Brunn's radical descent into hatred are not clear, but there were influences in his life that seem to have spawned an individualized journey into bigotry. He belonged to a German–American friendship group in the late 1930s that served as a front for the Nazi Party. After his divorce, according to the *Washington Post*, he traveled a path into deeper paranoia and virulent anti-Semitism. This eventually led to his attempted attack on the Federal Reserve Board in 1981. After being released from prison, he developed even stronger beliefs and began writing and managing a website. Two years before the museum attack, the only son from his first marriage committed suicide. In 2009, he apparently decided he had had enough and that the government and the Jews were going to pay (Ruane, 2009).

Downtown Boston was busy on April 15, 2013. The streets were crowded with runners, and the sidewalks were jammed with spectators. It was the Boston Marathon, and runners were crossing the finish line. Suddenly, cheering was replaced with screams of pain and cries of horror. A bomb had exploded on the sidewalk. A second bomb detonated a few moments later, increasing casualties and confusion. Three people were killed, and 260 were wounded. As the story unfolded, two young immigrants from Kyrgyzstan, **Dzhokhar** and **Tamerlan Tsarnaev**, seemed to be responsible for the attack.

Tamerlan was killed in a shootout with the police a few days later, and Dzhokhar, although wounded, was taken into custody. According to federal prosecutors (*United States of America v. Dzhokhar Tsarnaev* [2013]), Tsarnaev stated that Muslims were all one people, the West was killing them, and Muslims were going to strike back. He was radicalized because the two brothers believed the United States was at war

James W. von Brunn: (1920–2010) an American white supremacist and anti-Semite. He entered the Holocaust Museum on June 10, 2009, and began shooting. He killed a security officer before he was wounded and subdued. He died in federal custody while awaiting trial.

Dzhokhar Tsarnaev: (b. 1993) and **Tamerlan Tsarnaev** (1986–2013): two brothers who were members of an immigrant family in Boston. Dzhokhar was a naturalized American citizen. They believed the West was at war with their religion and decided to strike back by bombing the 2013 Boston Marathon. Law enforcement officers subsequently killed Tamerlan. Dzhokhar was wounded and taken into custody.

with his faith. The Internet reinforced this belief, and the government claimed that Tsarnaev had learned to make the bomb from a radical online magazine.

According to the federal indictment, the brothers built the bombs inside a pressure cooker, which increased the explosive power. Their acts demonstrated the ability of individuals to conduct a terrorist attack on their own.

Commonalities in Radicalization

In the examples of Abdulmatallab, von Brunn, and Hammami, there are several common forms of behavior. First, it is interesting to note that the three men all came from well-to-do, middle-class environments. The *New York Times* reports that most international attacks against the United States in the twenty-first century have come from well-educated terrorists from the middle class (Mackey, 2010). Gerald Post (2007) argues that such regularities are common to the radicalization process. All three men became deeply angered and filled with moral indignation. This was reinforced by identifying with a victimized group and the desire to violently redress grievances. They were alienated from mainstream thought as they expressed anger, and they sought to address their situations by doing something meaningful. Finally, there was some type of event that triggered their decision to take violent action.

Recall that Brian Jenkins (2009) believes there are common behavioral patterns associated with radicalization. These patterns may be observed by family members, friends, and other associates. If Jenkins is correct, this would suggest that there is some merit in identifying the behaviors associated with radicalization and in training security personnel to search for and recognize them. This is not to suggest that the National Counterterrorism Center is incorrect in its proposal that security and law enforcement agencies have a broader mission than counterterrorism and that indicators may be valuable to such agencies.

For example, assume that you are the chief of a midsize American police agency of 120 personnel. Your officers have recently been trained in the six-step model gleaned from Sageman: (1) alienated youth, (2) join other alienated youths, (3) they seek orientation in religion, (4) their religion is militarized, (5) they encounter an actor who knows terrorists, and (6) the actor introduces them to the terrorists and they join. Because there are differing paths to radicalization, there are more models, but we will use this model for illustration.

Assume the training has taken place, and your officers are looking for these behavioral patterns during investigations and routine patrol operations. If this happens, you would soon be receiving field contact information and reports that identify alienated young people and the groups they join throughout your jurisdiction. This would help identify potential problems in schools, communities, and other organizations. It would also help identify potentially harmful directions in which alienated young people could move, such as gangs or other criminal groups. Although the original purpose was to gather information on terrorism, the overall result produces a more comprehensive picture of your community. It is part of a concept known as Total Criminal Intelligence.

With 120 personnel, department budgets, and community safety concerns, you have many problems in your jurisdiction. The probability of terrorism in your jurisdiction may be low, but if it happens, its impact will be critical. In addition, after the event has occurred, the media, citizens, and elected officials will ask you what you did to prevent it. By training officers to recognize the signs of radicalization, you will have taken a proactive step before an incident and have another tool that allows for better deployment of resources because the process gives you a more strategic view of the community (see Saupp, 2010).

Empirical research suggests that even though radicalization resembles other forms of behavior, there are some distinct issues involved. In religious radicalization, people exhibit distinctive forms of behavior, and these may appear in any sequence (Gartenstein-Ross and Grossman, 2009). They adopt rigid, literalist interpretations of religion. They trust only selected radical sources of theological information, and they tolerate no deviance from their interpretation. These patterns can be seen across many religions (White, 2010).

When Islam is involved, there are other behavioral indicators. People being radicalized accept the idea of the "clash of civilizations," and they believe that the West is at war with Islam. They selectively interpret government actions to prove the point. They also aggressively and vehemently attempt to convert other Muslims to their point of view and publicly denounce those who will not follow them. They either break away from mainstream mosques or join an organization that supports their interpretation of religion. Finally, they begin adopting traditional forms of dress (Gartenstein-Ross and Grossman, 2009).

Eli Berman's (2009, pp. 30–35) suggestion about violent groups is also worth noting when security forces are dealing with terrorism. The number of terrorist groups is rather small, while the number of radicalized people is very large. The key to counterterrorism is to focus on radicalized individuals when they try to join the militant group. John Horgan (2009, p. 155) complements this idea with another tactic: It is virtually impossible to control all the factors that may radicalize a person, but there are points when terrorists want to leave the organization. It is important to know how to extricate people. They might always be radicalized, Horgan points out, but if they are not engaged in violence, they are not terrorists.

Individual Journeys

There is evidence to suggest that radicalization is not always a group process, or at least that it involves individual reflection whether a group plays a role or not. Post's (2007) research shows that individual psychological and sociological factors create the framework for interpreting reality. The influence of social structure serves as the major background for interpreting reality for most individuals. Post says that ideology is transferred from generation to generation within this framework, and he believes that traditions of radicalization are passed in this manner.

Earlier research by Martin van Creveld (1991) and Thomas P. M. Barnett (2005) reinforces the pattern presented by Post. Radicalization tends to happen with individual interpretation of larger actions. The probability of individual radicalization increases when a relatively weak group feels that its existence is threatened and that it has been victimized by a superior power. Feelings increase if the superior group dominating the threatened group is believed to be morally depraved. These situations create the social and psychological conditions for a person to become radicalized. All social conventions pass and the radicalized victim comes to believe that terrorism is the only weapon for the weak to use against the strong.

> **✓ Self-Check**
>
> \> What are the three key questions about radicalization, according to Horgan?
>
> \> How does groupthink reinforce radicalization?
>
> \> What common patterns of radicalization appear in case studies?

Two Views of Prison Radicalization

As demonstrated by the previous section, several scholars and practitioners in the field of terrorism believe radicalization is the beginning of a process that may lead to extremist views and political violence. This discussion has overflowed into studies of prison systems. Many people believe that prisons are academies for crime; that is, less experienced inmates learn how to become more effective criminals from older inmates. A similar argument is applied to terrorism. Terrorists must be separated from the general population. Otherwise, they will convert inmates from the general population and transform them into fellow terrorists. In other words, prisons run the risk of becoming schools for terrorism.

Many scholars are leery of such simple generalizations, but they do believe that prisons present opportunities for radicalization. Excellent researchers, such as Mark Hamm (2007 and 2009) have uncovered processes and stages for conversion to, immersion in, and acceptance of violent radical philosophies or religions within prison walls. Such research is more sophisticated than generalizations about terrorist schools. However, other scholars and practitioners find little or no evidence for prison radicalization.

The Process of Radicalization in Prison

Recent reports suggest that groups are being radicalized in prison, and Mark Hamm (2007) has conducted a definitive study of prison radicalization in the United States. The process in prison usually involves a charismatic leader who gathers a number of individuals in an entourage. A leader will often target selected prisoners for a group or will dominate new inmates, intimidating them until they join the group. Hamm maintains that this recruitment is similar to procedures used by street gangs.

Terrorists also use recruiters who are not incarcerated. This is most frequently associated with religion, and the person who recruits and radicalizes potential terrorists may be a visiting chaplain. A chaplain has access to prisoners and may claim freedom of religion while delivering a radical message. Hamm says militant chaplains also distribute radical literature in the form of religious works.

Most of the people who enter prison have to adjust psychologically to the loss of freedom, constant monitoring, and threatened violence from other prisoners. This frequently leaves a new inmate, especially someone in prison for the first time, in a state of crisis. Recruiters for a radical cause often recognize differing types of crises, and they try to bring individuals to the radical cause with strategies that match the psychological state of the person they hope to entice.

Hamm found five common patterns of converting people to violent radical causes. The first contains people in crisis, who will respond to religious overtures for emotional support. A second involves people seeking protection in the prison environment. These people will convert because the radical group offers safety. The third group of potential converts—Hamm calls these people searchers—have had little exposure to religion, and they are fascinated by both the multiplicity of religious expressions inside prison and the feeling of belonging among members of the group. The fourth involves a personality that is common in prison—manipulating people for personal gain. Finally, Hamm classifies chaplains from the outside as free-world recruiters.

Behind almost every conversion, according to Hamm, lies a friendship or kinship link, but sometimes, a new inmate simply meets somebody in the yard and converts to a new faith. Radicalization tends to take place among two factions and three major groups. The first faction involves various Muslim groups who use cut-and-paste

PRISON RADICALIZATION—Mark Hamm's research for the National Institute of Justice concludes that inmates are recruited and radicalized in a number of ways:

Crisis Convert—joins a radical group as a result of a personal crisis

Protection-Seeking Convert—seeks a group out of fear

Searching Converts—have been exposed to religion, but seek deeper meaning while in prison

Manipulating Converts—are controlled by a strong member inside a group

Free-World Converters—result from chaplains outside of the system who spread literature and preach radicalization

Source: Hamm, 2007.

FIGURE 2.4

versions of the Quran, and the second group centers around white supremacy. This results in three major groups: (1) Islamic extremists, (2) Christian extremists who use selected biblical passages to justify their views, and (3) white supremacists who have adopted the Norse pantheon of Odin, Thor, Frida, and the other gods and goddesses (Martin, 2007; Hamm, 2009).

Patterns of prison radicalization in other countries seem to follow patterns similar to those uncovered by Hamm, but the level of the threat they represent varies. In Central Asia, the prison systems are deteriorating, and it is difficult to monitor outside religious leaders who make visits to inmates. Militant Islamic missionaries use this situation as an opportunity to radicalize individuals. Militant converts are growing inside Central Asian prisons, threatening to further disrupt correctional operations. In addition, individuals seek to join other militant groups outside the prison after they are released. Prison radicalization is a growing threat in Central Asia (International Crisis Group 2009).

The United Kingdom, on the other hand, has experienced growing prison radicalization, but it does not present as great a problem as in Central Asia (Gartenstein-Ross, 2009). At this point, researchers know that radicalization takes place inside prisons, but there is not enough evidence to indicate how dangerous the threat is.

Questioning Prison Radicalization

Other research studies point in a different direction. Richard Pickering (2012) says the Prison Service in the United Kingdom has developed a program to prevent radicalization. Officials monitor the behavior of outside chaplains, move to isolate and counter inmates who champion radical ideas, search for the presence of radicalization in prison, and continue searching during the management period for released inmates. Although he maintains that these activities are important, the Prison Service has little evidence that radicalization occurs in British prisons.

A government-sponsored study in the United Kingdom found that many terrorists have been in prison, but there is scant evidence that they were radicalized within the walls. Pickering believes that radicalization has multiple causes, and it is difficult to differentiate the ways people develop violent extremist views. Further, radicalization is a nebulous concept and hard to quantify. The best preventive approach, he concludes, is standard inmate monitoring. A person is shocked upon entering prison. Pickering says radicalization may be possible, but it is more important to ensure that a new inmate does not withdraw into self-isolation.

Louise Porter and Mark Kebbell (2011) examined 21 male inmates convicted of terrorism in Australia and found that they shared several commonalities. Exposure to radical theology was the most common denominator in their decision to engage in violence, and almost all of them expressed religious intolerance. Sixteen of the men adapted radical views from exposure to the Internet. Most of the subjects had close family ties, but they were not connected with their respective communities. Interestingly, they tended to separate themselves from the local Muslim community and their mosques as their extremist views increased. All claimed a desire to seek revenge for a perceived injustice or attack on their faith. The men did not turn to violent theology because they were isolated. They became isolated after they turned to extremism. A final important point: They taught theology to themselves.

Although the 21 subjects shared these characteristics, Porter and Kebbell point out that the remainder of their social behavior was similar to the rest of the population. They tended to be older than terrorists in other countries, but most of the men were married, had children, and were employed. Two of them were professionals with advanced education, and only one was a committed felon before he became radicalized. Some of them claimed to have trained with terrorist groups in other countries, but the researchers doubted these claims. Each of the attacks that led to their arrest and conviction for terrorism had been unsophisticated. The attacks did not bear the marks of basic tactical training. Basically, they looked and acted like most other people, which led Porter and Kebbell to conclude that the men convicted of terrorism were just ordinary individuals. They had little influence in the prison community.

Clarke Jones (2014) reviewed cases from several Asian and Western countries. He say mainstream beliefs are that prisons housing terrorists are schools for recruiting and training new terrorist, and this fact means that terrorists should be separated from the general population to eliminate their influence. These concepts are based on limited research on radicalization.

The discussion of prison radicalization takes place in the media, government circles, and academic settings. These portrayals overemphasize the existence of radicalization. Jones is not suggesting that the process of developing violent extremist views is unimportant, but the ideas are misrepresented. Prison officials equate radicalization with the fear of Islam. Both staff and fellow prisoners treat many Muslim inmates poorly as a result. In addition, since Islam is perceived to be the problem behind radicalization, there is little differentiation between Muslim inmates in general and their radical counterparts. Both sets of people are lumped together. Ironically, Jones concludes, when convicted radicals are placed in the general population, peer pressure causes them to conform to the norm.

Bert Useem and Obie Clayton (2009) take the argument further. Their research found no statistical data to demonstrate massive radicalization in U.S. prisons, and the actual probability that it will occur is far less than popularly believed. Radicalization in prison is one of the most discussed and least understood subjects in modern American corrections. Prisons seem to inhibit radicalization for a number of reasons. Inmates are subjected to rigid, structured order, and there are social boundaries between prisoners who hold extremist views and those who do not. The institution continually emphasizes and reinforces a message of nonradicalization, rewarding inmates who behave accordingly. Most inmates in the United States have completed less formal schooling than the general population, making the abstract ideas in complicated radical ideologies difficult to understand. Useem and Clayton say that although they found no evidence of prison radicalization, it could happen. Vigilance is the key to preventing it, just as with most of the other problems in American prisons.

Rejecting the Term

There is another position that is in opposition to both the acceptance of theories about the process of radicalization in general and prison radicalization. Some scholars question the value of the term *radicalization*. Others vehemently reject it. From the perspective of practical criminology, some practitioners believe that research in radicalization and alienation will produce valuable knowledge. The National Counterterrorism Center (2010c, p. 133), a federal agency created in 2004 to integrate information gathered on international terrorism, officially says that this type of information does not help analysts understand the process of radicalization. Indicators of radicalization reflect experiences and behaviors seen in all people. In addition, people who are radicalized are motivated by local issues, and radicalization is so diverse that its myriad sources are difficult to discern. Therefore, the so-called signs of radicalization are really only signs of human behavior. According to the National Counterterrorism Center, there is little need to study the processes of radicalization.

Neither scholars nor practitioners are quite sure about the meaning of radicalization. It has been operationally defined, and most working definitions approach it as the process of adopting violent extremist views. Yet, as Mark Sedgwick (2010) notes, there is no consensus about the definition of radicalization. Many researchers use the term, but it is used in a variety of different contexts. Security experts see radicalization as a problem for law enforcement, while those concerned with eliminating relative economic deprivation seek to integrate minority groups into the dominant system. On a grander scale, foreign policy experts look at radicalization as a problem created by networks of groups, schools, and national or regional ideologies. All of these contexts are different, and each approach has its own set of assumptions and research agendas. Sedgwick believes that the term *radicalization* simply confuses everybody. He proposes a solution: Abandon the use of the word as an absolute, definitive concept.

Chetan Bhatt (2010) believes radicalization is associated with alienation. He looks at Muslim populations inside the United Kingdom and argues that Western governments seek to integrate and assimilate immigrant populations. This poses a problem because many immigrants choose to maintain their native identity, including political and religious affiliations. This does not represent a path toward political violence; however, it does indicate a rejection of Western norms. It is possible to argue that continued identification with traditional values is a form of purposeful alienation. The new country's values and norms are rejected, while the old country's ways are incorporated in a different society.

Bhatt compares Pakistani militia movements to the activities of Central Asian immigrants in northwest London. The issue does not appear to be alienation. Bhatt argues that the Muslim community is exposed to a wide array of militant thinking, and this thinking may impact the subsequent decisions of young people to support militant groups or to take violent action. Militant ideology is not the main source of the decision to engage in violence; rather, the growth of international organizations that train paramilitary fighters is the source of militancy. The primary culprit is Pakistan's intelligence agency. By supporting militant groups that use terrorist tactics, Pakistan has created new associations between international paramilitary groups and Muslim immigrants in the United Kingdom. Militancy is not a result of alienation; it is a conscious decision to maintain national identity and sacrifice for a greater cause.

Frazer Egerton (2011) states that the common perception of the Salafi–jihadist movement is related to alienation. Yet, writers in this field seldom define what they mean when they use the term *alienation*, and the term is generally undertheorized and over-applied. The discussion of alienation, he asserts, is intuitive but unsubstantiated. One of the common approaches, he argues, is to look at structure. It is commonly assumed that young Muslim males between the ages of 15 and 30 are alienated from social structures and as a result, they are frustrated and are attracted to violent ideologies.

In other versions of structural alienation, young males are seeking meaning, and they move toward religion to find that meaning. As a young man becomes more and more involved in religious activities, he moves toward radical interpretations of the religion and subsequently to violence. A variant of the religious journey involves the relationship between economic deprivation and terrorist violence. This version of structural alienation maintains that poor economic conditions alienate young men from society and lead them to take out their frustration in violence. Another popular version of structural alienation involves ethnic exclusion. Proponents of this theory maintain that when people are excluded from normative society due to their race or ethnicity, they respond with violence.

Egerton concludes that while such theories are attractive and are used to explain terrorist violence, they are overly generalized. For example, very few people respond to alienation with terrorist violence. In addition, most religious behavior, even fervent, intolerant religious beliefs, does not lead to terrorism. Egerton suggests that social scientists avoid referring to alienation. He says that the concept is nuanced and complex and linking it with alienation only makes things more confusing. Radicalization and alienation exist in degrees, and they are manifested in several different ways. To suggest that someone is alienated is to ignore the complexity of human behavior. Researchers will obtain more fruitful results by examining militant ideology and finding the concepts that attract followers.

Some researchers simply reject the term *radicalization*. Arun Kundnani (2012) says the use of the term *radicalization* has become normative in practical and scholarly approaches to terrorism, but it distorts both perspectives. When it is used in the West, radicalization has become synonymous with Islam. It has been used by a host of scholars and self-proclaimed experts who claim that a process of de-radicalization can be created. Others believe they can intervene and prevent radicalization. The result is that the whole Muslim community is potentially susceptible to the process and because of this, Islam is viewed with suspicion.

Kundnani may be correct, but in terms of practical criminology, security personnel are served by looking at the behavioral characteristics of violent extremists. This may provide tools to counter violence. *Radicalization* is a broad term that has little practical value. Violent extremists, however, tend to have their own ways of talking and acting. These actions are unique to particular ideologies. Law enforcement, intelligence, and military units are best served by learning the behavior cues, jargon, and indicators of the particular type of terrorism they face.

Self-Check

> Why do some officials and scholars fear prison radicalization?
> What evidence contradicts the concept of prison radicalization?
> Why do some people reject the idea of radicalization altogether?

Types of Terrorism

Regardless of your interpretation of the radicalization process, terrorism is the result of extremists deciding to use violence. It may appear to be random, unorganized, and senseless. Yet, these common assumptions are incorrect because terrorism has a purpose. It is designed to frighten a targeted audience, coercing its victims to behave in a particular manner. While the greatest form of political violence is due to nation-states engaged in war or political repression, security forces often deal with lesser forms of subnational conflict. Accordingly, law enforcement and related security operations are concerned with three types of terrorism: (1) individuals using terrorist tactics, (2) small groups using terrorism as a strategy, and (3) terrorist tactics used to support guerrilla warfare or insurgencies.

Lone Wolves

William Pierce (MacDonald, 1989), the late white supremacist, wrote a series of magazine short stories that eventually evolved into a novel, *Hunter*. The book is a fictional account of a violent right-wing extremist who decides to launch a terrorist campaign. The protagonist is fearful of sharing his plans with others lest he be betrayed. He decides to form an organization that cannot be penetrated by the police or an informant. This organization, in Pierce's words, is the mind. The main character goes on a killing spree, targeting nonwhites, Jews, couples of mixed race, and white "race traitors." He is a lone wolf.

Lone wolves represent the most basic form of terrorism. It requires only a person who is so aggrieved that he or she will engage in violent action to make a statement. Criminals and people in mental crisis may engage in serial bombings or single mass shootings, but lone wolves differ. Like other terrorists, they engage in purposeful violence to impact a target audience. Their victims are not the audience they are seeking. They are addressing the people who see and/or hear about the attack.

Sometimes, lone wolves assume that their attack will result in their capture or death. They engage in an attack and become terrorists for a single event. Nidal Malik Hasan's attack at Fort Hood, discussed in Chapter 1, falls in this category. In another example, Buford Furrow entered a Jewish daycare center in August 1999 and began shooting people. He had no extensive logistical network or support organization. Yet, Furrow was consumed by an ideology of hate and a religion that demonized Jews. He was not an uncommitted opportunistic criminal acting alone. He was an agent of an ideology on a divine mission.

At other times, lone wolves plan a campaign. In September 2014, Eric Matthew Frein allegedly attacked a rural Pennsylvania State Police post. According to media reports, he shot two troopers from a hidden position in the woods outside of a rural post, killing one officer and wounding another. News reports stated that he was angry about several issues in American society, and he wanted to commit mass murder. Multiple police agencies conducted an extensive search for many days, and Frein was captured before he could complete his plans.

Recently, some terrorist groups have called on individual sympathizers to take action on their own, and sometimes, individuals are motivated to follow the advice. At other times, an individual such as Eric Frein becomes so upset that no external group is necessary. Single issues also motivate individuals. For example, antiabortion activist Eric Rudolph planted multiple bombs and led investigators on a seven-year search due to his anger over a single issue. Some actions are planned, and terrorists train for the event. However, most attacks are amateurish. The variety of lone wolf attacks makes it difficult to categorize activities.

Lone wolves represent a special problem. As Pierce said, it is virtually impossible to infiltrate thought processes. Still, there are certain counteractions that are effective against them. When law enforcement officers have reasonable suspicion that a person is committing or is about to commit a crime, it is reasonable to gather and share intelligence about that individual (Carter, 2009). In addition, a police force that has its personnel deeply engaged in solving community problems and relating closely to people in the community will find that individual citizens will share information that might identify potential lone wolves (White, 2013).

DATE	ATTACK	LOCATION
October 2014	Police officers attacked with hatchet	New York City
October 2014	Suspected jihadist kills soldier then storms Parliament	Ottawa, Canada
September 2014	Workers attacked with knife; woman beheaded; suspected religious motivation	Oklahoma City, Oklahoma
May 2014	Jihadist kills four in Jewish museum	Brussels, Belgium
May 2013	Soldier stabbed and killed by jihadists	London, England
April 2013	Boston Marathon bombing: three killed, 260 wounded	Boston
March 2012	Seven people killed by al Qaeda–inspired man	Toulouse, France
July 2011	77 people killed by right-wing extremist	Oslo and Utoya Island, Norway
March 2011	Two U.S. airmen killed	Frankfort, Germany
February 2010	Antigovernment extremist crashes plane into federal building	Austin, Texas
November 2009	13 killed in Fort Hood shooting	San Antonio, Texas
June 2009	Jihadist kills U.S. Army recruiter	Little Rock, Arkansas

Source: *Time* (http://time.com/3533581/canada-ottawa-shooting-lone-wolf-terrorism/)

FIGURE **2.5** A Sample of Lone Wolf Attacks

Small Groups and Urban Terrorism

The second type of terrorism involves groups operating without the support of an actual or de facto state. Previous research demonstrates that small groups tend to be weak, while larger groups have more staying power and sometimes have the resources to maintain a campaign. For the most part, small groups tend to last less than 18 months (Gurr, 1988a and 1988b; see also Damphousse and Smith, 2004). Small groups can create chaos, but they have little chance of overall victory. Their primary objective is to project an aura of power; that is, terrorism gives the illusion of strength. Small groups use terrorism as a strategy. Due to their relative weakness when compared to security forces, the only thing they do is create terror. Small groups follow an urban model of terrorism.

Frantz Fanon (1925–1961) inspired anti-imperial violence after World War II, and his influence remained with Western ideological groups in the 1960s and 1970s. Born on Martinique in 1925, Fanon studied medicine in France and became a psychiatrist. When Algeria revolted against French rule in 1954, Fanon went to Algiers to work in a mental hospital. His experiences there caused him to side with the rebels. Fanon believed the pressures caused by exploitative imperialism were the primary causes of mental illness in Algeria. He produced two works, *The Wretched of the Earth* (1982) and *A Dying Colonialism* (1965), as a result of his Algerian experiences. He died of cancer in 1961, a year before the Algerian War ended, and he was unable to play a leading role in revolutions; his thoughts, however, were strongly imprinted on Africa, Asia, and Latin America (see University of Singapore, 2007).

In *The Wretched of the Earth*, Fanon indicts colonial powers and calls on all the colonized to practice terrorism. He writes that Western powers have dehumanized non-Western people by destroying their cultures and replacing them with Western values. Even when Westerners are not present, a native middle class embraces Western values and turns its back on the general population. Natives in the middle class abandon native intellectualism and their own culture and replace them with Western traditions. The masses end up suffering a perpetual identity crisis: To succeed, they are forced to deny their heritage. Fanon argues that the natives can follow only one course of action: revolution.

To be sure, Fanon was no Gandhi. His only argument was for violent revolt, including guerrilla warfare and acts of terrorism. He claimed that decolonization was destined to be a violent process because it involved replacing one group of powerful people with another group. No group would willingly surrender power. Therefore, according to Fanon, achieving freedom was inherently violent. Political action and peaceful efforts toward change were useless. Only when oppressed people recognized that violence was their only alternative would they be assured of victory. Fanon saw guerrilla warfare and individual acts of terrorism as tools of revolution. Guerrilla war was the initial method of revolt because third-world revolutionaries could not mount direct, conventional campaigns at the beginning of their struggles. Fanon's concept of guerrilla warfare was based in rural revolution, but urban terrorism would become the major weapon rendering colonial administration impotent.

Terrorism was to be limited to specific acts. Fanon argued that terrorism should not be used against the native population in general. Like Communist Chinese revolutionary leader Mao Zedong, he believed doing so would alienate potential supporters. Instead, he proposed two targets for terrorism: white settlers and the native middle class. The purpose of terrorism was to terrorize Westerners and their lackeys into submission. Individual murders, bombings, and mutilations would force the white settlers to leave the country and frighten the native middle class away from their colonial masters. Brutality would be the example. It would bring on governmental repression, but this would only cause more natives to flock to the terrorist cause.

Fanon's ideas flourished in Latin America, but they came with a twist. Beginning in Brazil, some revolutionaries believed cities would be the focus of Latin American revolution, and they embraced Fanon's idea of urban terrorism. They felt a revolutionary could create the context for an impromptu general uprising through the use of spontaneous violence. Directly reflecting Fanon, these revolutionaries believed terrorism could communicate with the people and infuse them with the spirit of revolt. The foremost proponent of this idea in Latin America was **Carlos Marighella** (1911–1969; see O'Connor, 2007).

Marighella was a Brazilian legislator, a leader of the nationalistic Communist Party, and eventually a fiery revolutionary terrorist. Brazilian police killed him in an ambush in 1969. In two major works, *For the Liberation of Brazil* (1971) and *The Minimanual of the Urban Guerrilla* (1969), Marighella designed practical guides for small group urban terrorism. These books have had more influence on recent revolutionary terrorism than any other set of theories. Marighella wanted to move violence from the countryside to the city, and although his call to terrorism was politically motivated, his model was apolitical. He designed a method for organizing a campaign of terror that, for the past 40 years, has been employed by groups ranging across the political spectrum—from the Japanese Red Army to the Freemen of Montana.

Marighella believed the basis of revolution was violence. Violence need not be structured, and efforts need not be coordinated among groups. Violence created a situation in which revolution could flourish. Any type of violence was acceptable because it contributed a general feeling of panic and frustration among the ruling classes and their protectors. Marighella's most original concept was that all violence could

Carlos Marighella: (1911–1969) A Brazilian Communist legislator and revolutionary theorist. Marighella popularized urban terrorism as a method for ending repression and eliminating U.S. domination of Latin America. He was killed in a police ambush in São Paulo in 1969.

be urban based and controlled by a small group of urban guerrillas. From Brazil, this concept of revolution spread throughout the world.

The hierarchy of Marighella has been replaced by uncoordinated activities in many groups, but Marighella might have been satisfied with this, since his four-stage model did not require coordination. Urban terrorism was to begin with two distinct phases: one designed to bring about actual violence and the other designed to give that violence meaning. The violent portion of the revolution was to be a campaign employing armed revolutionary cells to carry out the most deplorable acts of violence. Targets were to have symbolic significance, and although violence was designed to be frightening, its logic would remain clear with regard to the overall revolution. That is, those who supported the revolution would not need to fear terrorist violence themselves (see Moss, 1972, pp. 70–72; Marighella, 1969; Smith and Damphousse, 2002, pp. 6–13).

The terror campaign was to be accompanied by a psychological offensive to provide peripheral support for terrorists. The psychological offensive would not only join students and workers in low-level challenges to governmental authority, it would also be used to create a network of safe houses, logistical stores, and medical units. In essence, the supporting activities would carry out standard military support functions.

A campaign of revolutionary terrorism in an urban setting could be used to destabilize governmental power. A psychological assault would convince the government and the people that the status quo no longer held. They would come to feel that the terrorists were in control. When this situation developed, Marighella believed, the government would be forced to show its true colors. With its authority challenged and the economic stability of the elite eroded, the government would be forced to declare some form of martial law. This would not be a defeat for terrorism but rather exactly what the terrorists and their supporters wanted. Governmental repression was the goal of terrorism at this stage.

This view might appear to be contradictory at first glance, but there was a method to Marighella's madness. He believed the public supported governmental policies because they did not realize the repressive nature of the state. The terrorist campaign would force the government to reveal itself, thereby alienating the public. With no place else to turn, the public would turn to the terrorists, and the terrorists would be waiting with open arms. As the ranks of the urban guerrillas grew with the rush of public support, Marighella believed, the revolutionaries would gradually abandon their terrorist campaign. Their efforts would focus more and more on the construction of a general urban army, one that could seize key governmental control points on cue. When the urban army had reached sufficient strength, all its forces would be launched in a general strike.

Marighella's theory has only one weakness: It rarely works. Even so, several small terrorist groups have followed it, even unknowingly at times. Marighella writes that the purpose of the urban guerrilla is to shoot. Any form of urban violence is desirable because a violent atmosphere creates the political environment needed for success. Terrorism can be used to create that environment, and terrorism can be employed with minimal organization. Therefore, terrorism is to be the primary strategy of the urban guerrilla.

Marighella (1969) outlines the basic structure needed for an urban terrorist group in the *Minimanual of the Urban Guerrilla*. The main operational group of a terrorist organization should be the firing group. Composed of four to five terrorists each, several firing groups are needed to construct a terrorist organization. They can join as needed to concentrate their power, but their small size ensures both mobility and secrecy. For Marighella, the firing group is the basic weapon of the urban guerrilla.

In a single theory, Marighella provides the justification for violence and the organizational structure a small group needs to begin killing. Unlike Fanon, Marighella endorsed violence for the sake of violence. Terrorists operating in this way use terrorism as a strategy. It is the only type of attack they can launch. Guerrillas are capable of other types of operations. Therefore, terrorism becomes a tactic for guerrillas. Globalization, modern communications, and new weapons technology allow subnational groups to wage another type of campaign, an insurrection. Some military theorists believe this is a third model of terrorism.

Guerrillas and Large Group Terrorism

Sometimes, large groups use terrorism, especially when they have external support or when they enjoy popular appeal from an indigenous population. These groups may have the ability to launch a revolution, lead an insurrection, or launch a guerrilla war. This leads to the final type of terrorism, tactical operations in subnational wars. In this case, terrorism is used as a tactic against specific enemies and their supporters, and guerrillas refuse to employ indiscriminate violence. Targets are selected with care.

Guerrilla war is an age-old phenomenon. Several nationalistic rebellions after World War II were based on guerrilla war, including the long campaign that toppled the Chinese government in 1949. Mao Zedong (1893–1976) inspired both fellow Communist and Nationalistic revolutionaries, but the Cuban Revolution from 1956 to 1959 captured the minds of left-wing ideologues. They came to view guerrilla war as a statement of struggle against capitalist powers, and terrorism had a special role in this revolution (see Wickham-Crowley, 1992, pp. 51–59).

The Cuban Revolution did not create guerrilla warfare, but it popularized it throughout the world. Although only one other guerrilla movement has succeeded in overthrowing an established government—the Nicaraguan Sandinistas in 1979—guerrilla

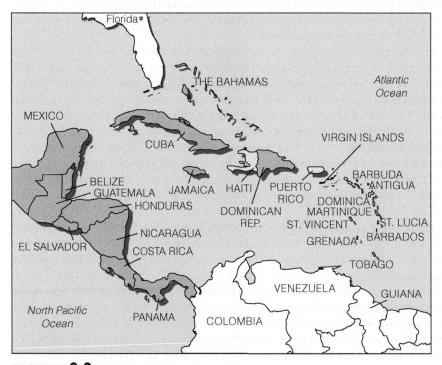

FIGURE **2.6** Central America and the Caribbean

war is the preferred method of fighting among Latin American revolutionaries. Unlike the model for urban terrorism, the guerrilla model began with a successful structure and then moved toward a theory (see March, 2005; O'Connor, 2007).

The process began in the hills of Cuba. The Cuban revolutionary leader Fidel Castro tried to seize power in 1956, but he was soundly defeated. Retreating to the rural regions of Cuba, he surrounded himself with a ragtag group of revolutionaries, including a friend, **Ernesto "Che" Guevara** (1928–1967). Guevara was born in Argentina in 1928. After earning a medical degree at the University of Buenos Aires, he turned his attention from medicine to the plight of the poor. He believed poverty and repression were problems that transcended nationalism, and revolution was the only means of challenging authority. He served the regime of Guatemala in 1954 but fled to Mexico City when Communists were purged from the government. There he met Castro.

Guevara immediately impressed Castro, and the two worked together to oust the Cuban military dictator Fulgencio Batista (1901–1973). After failing to seize power in 1956, Castro began to meet secretly with rural partisans. Castro organized a command-and-support structure, enlisted partisans, and formed regional guerrilla forces. As Castro's strength grew, he moved to more conventional methods of warfare and triumphantly entered Havana in 1959. Throughout the campaign, Guevara had been at Castro's side.

Inflamed with revolutionary passion, Guevara completed a work on guerrilla warfare shortly after Castro took power. Far from theoretical, it can be deemed a how-we-did-it guide. Translated copies of Guevara's *Reminiscences of the Cuban Revolutionary War* appeared in the United States as early as 1961, but the book did not enjoy mass distribution until the end of the decade. It describes both Guevara's evolution toward Marxism and the revolutionary process in Cuba, and it details the structure and strategy of Castro's forces, as well as the guiding philosophy of the **Cuban guerrilla war**. Guevara also outlines the revolutionaries' methods of operation and principles of engagement. With the advantage of hindsight, it makes a stirring description of how victory was achieved.

Guerrilla revolutions based on the Cuban experience are typified by three phases, each designed to progress from and complement the previous one. In phase one, Guevara-style revolution begins with isolated groups. In phase two, the isolated groups merge into guerrilla columns. The final phase brings columns together in a conventional army. The goal of the strategy is to develop a conventional fighting force, or at least a force that renders the conventional opponent impotent. Although Guevara's work focused specifically on the Cuban experience, it had two important effects. In Latin America and to revolutionaries there, in particular, Guevara became an icon. In addition, guerrillas throughout the world studied the guide and copied the tactics used during the revolution (see Burton, 1976, p. 70; J. K. Clark, 1988; Asprey, 2002, pp. 698–710; Taber, 2002, pp. 25–37).

Terrorism plays a limited role in Guevara's guerrilla framework. Although Guevara's focus was on the countryside, he saw the need for small urban terrorist groups to wage a campaign of support. These actions, however, should be extremely selective; their purpose is to keep governmental forces off balance, terrorizing them in their "safe" areas, never letting them relax. The main purpose of terrorism is to strike at the government's logistical network; a secondary purpose is to demoralize the government. Terrorism is a commando-type tactic.

The theory of guerrilla war came after the appearance of Guevara's work, which was popularized by a French socialist named Régis Debray. In *Revolution in the Revolution?* Debray (1967) summarizes his concept of Latin American politics. He writes

Ernesto "Che" Guevara: (1928–1967) Fidel Castro's assistant and guerrilla warfare theorist. Guevara advocated guerrilla revolutions throughout Latin America after success in the Cuban Revolution. He was killed in Bolivia in 1967 while trying to form a guerrilla army.

Cuban guerrilla war: A three-step process as described by "Che" Guevara: (1) revolutionaries join the indigenous population to form guerrilla *foco*, as Guevara called them; (2) small forces form columns and control rural areas; and (3) columns unite for a conventional offensive to overthrow government.

that the region has one dominating issue: poverty. Poverty threads through the entire fabric of Latin American life and entwines divergent cultures and peoples in a common knot of misery. Poverty is responsible for the imbalance in the class structure, as the wealthy cannot be maintained without the poverty of the masses. Debray sees only one recourse: The class structure must be changed and wealth redistributed. Because the wealthy will never give up their power, revolution is the only method of change.

Debray's prime target was the United States. Behind every power in the south stands the United States, according to his thesis. Debray held the United States responsible for maintaining the inequitable class structure, and he shared the common Marxist belief that North American wealth caused Latin American poverty. It seemed quite logical, therefore, to target the United States.

As did Frantz Fanon, Debray continually talked of revolution. He saw little need for terrorism, however, and he minimized the role of urban centers in a revolt. Debray believed revolution was essentially an affair for poor peasants, and it could begin only in a rural setting with regional guerrilla forces. Terrorism had no payoff. At best, it was neutral, and at worst, it alienated the peasants needed for guerrilla support. According to Debray, for a revolution to work, it needed to begin with guerrillas fighting for justice and end with a united conventional force. Terrorism would not accomplish this objective.

Response to Differing Types of Terrorism

Separating the types or forms of terrorism is not an academic exercise. It is practical criminology. Each type of violent extremism calls for a different response. Lone wolves are best countered by routine law enforcement operations, especially when employing community policing. Small groups are also a law enforcement problem, although they require shared intelligence and regional task forces. Multiple law enforcement agencies need to cooperate with each other when confronting small groups. Large groups may be associated with guerrilla wars or insurgencies. The police have a role, but their power should be augmented by military force. Guerrilla wars and insurgencies are primarily a military problem.

✓ Self-Check	> What are the differences among the three types of terrorism?
	> How do small groups employ the urban or Marighella model?
	> How did Debray modify Guevara's work on guerrilla warfare?

Emphasizing the Points

Criminologists seek to explain the reasons people commit crimes. When law enforcement, intelligence, and military personnel confront terrorism, it is helpful to move beyond criminology and confront the problem with practical approaches. Part of that process suggests that security personnel should recognize the behavior of people as they adopt violent extremism. Many researchers refer to the adoption process as radicalization, but the term is used in a variety of ways. Security forces probably cannot stop radicalization or de-radicalize extremists. They may, however, be able to recognize behaviors associated with violent extremism. Finally, three types of terrorists confront governments: lone wolves, small groups, and large groups. Each type demands a specific response.

SUMMARY OF CHAPTER OBJECTIVES

- Theories of terrorism are important, but law enforcement, intelligence, and military forces are also served by developing a practical understanding of the type of terrorism they are facing.
- Criminals tend be to unfocused opportunists with no loyalty to a group. Terrorists are goal oriented, motivated by a cause, loyal to each other, and focused.
- Radicalization is the process of adopting violent extremist views and acting them out with terrorist actions. Many social scientists believe this is caused by alienation.
- A recent case study suggests that radicalized subjects do not make decisions rationally. Another study of a radicalized individual revealed an eclectic pattern of decision points. Other case studies seem to indicate that there are multiple paths to radicalization.
- Many people believe that prisons are schools for radicalization. Some researchers in the United States and Europe believe they have found patterns of radicalization. Other research suggests that there is little radicalization in prisons.
- There is no single definition of the term *radicalization*, and some critics believe it is used to label Muslims in the West. Security forces are best served by learning the common types of behaviors associated with violent extremists within a particular ideology.
- Three types of terrorism involve lone wolves, small groups, and large groups. Lone wolf violence seems to be increasing, and some groups encourage it.
- Lone wolf terrorism involves an individual taking action on his or her own initiative. Lone wolves may be trained or untrained. Many lone wolves launch only one attack, and they are captured or killed at its end.
- Small groups use terrorism to create an aura of false power. They follow an urban model that uses terrorism as a strategy. Large groups can use terrorism selectively and frequently employ it as a tactic.
- Guerrillas and insurgents are trying to win popular support against their enemies. They do not use indiscriminant terrorism; rather, they select their targets with care.

LOOKING INTO THE FUTURE

Debate about and interpretation of the Constitution is an ongoing process in the course of American political and legal life. It will continue as long as the United States is governed by the document.

This is the 1st Amendment to the United States Constitution:

Congress shall make no law respecting an establishment of religion, or prohibiting the free exercise thereof; or abridging the freedom of speech, or of the press; or the right of the people peaceably to assemble, and to petition the government for a redress of grievances.

Think of examples of radicalization and try to define the term within the framework of the 1st Amendment. Examine your definition to see if it violates this amendment. It is legally acceptable to become a radical extremist about any social, political, or economic idea. Your definition of radicalization should conclude with some criminal act if you want to practically apply it to law enforcement.

Your definition and many others will play a role in the future of terrorism. There is a fine line between accepting an unconventional view of reality and attempts to violently impose that view on others. The key aspect is the point where the position leads to violence. This issue is at the base of democracy and it will continue to be.

KEY TERMS

Cesare Beccaria, p. 26
Routes to terrorism, p. 29
Radicalization, p. 29
Violent radicalization, p. 29
Alienation, p. 30

Groupthink, p. 33
Weather Underground, p. 33
Umar Farouk Abdulmutallab, p. 34

James W. von Brunn, p. 35
Dzhokhar Tsarnaev, p. 35
Carlos Marighella, p. 45

Ernesto "Che" Guevara, p. 48
Cuban guerrilla war, p. 48

CHAPTER 3

Terrorist Financing and Money Laundering

LEARNING OBJECTIVES

After reading this chapter, you should be able to:

▶ Define money laundering.

▶ Define terrorist financing.

▶ Compare terrorist financing and money laundering.

▶ Describe national and international efforts to control terrorist financing.

▶ Outline financial intelligence gathering and investigative efforts.

▶ Summarize illegal and legal methods of terrorist funding.

▶ Describe networks and systems in informal economies.

▶ Describe the Hawala system.

▶ Summarize views on the political economy of terrorism.

▶ Summarize the debate about narcoterrorism.

ID1974/Shutterstock.com

The New U.S. $100 Bill

The Islamic State of Iraq and al Sham (ISIS), also known as the Islamic State, the Islamic State of Iraq and the Levant (ISIL), or Daesh, emerged from al Qaeda in Iraq. In June 2014 in the midst of the Syrian civil war and the sectarian violence in Iraq, ISIS laid claim to territory and acted as if it were a nation-state. It was a different type of terrorist group and financed itself in an unusual manner. ISIS was large enough to take and hold geographical areas, including oil fields and economic centers in Iraq and Syria. This ability placed ISIS in the unique position of raising money by special "taxes" on people in conquered territory, taking possession of wealth by force, kidnapping for ransom, and most importantly, selling oil in an underground economy. According to ABC News (2014), ISIS made $3 million a day in the summer of 2014, making it the most well-funded terrorist group in history.

All terrorists need money, and as a group's size and complexity increases, its need for income also grows. Large terrorist groups pay salaries to individual members and meet living expense for their leaders. Some groups even pay pensions to former members. Groups raise money in numerous legal and often illegal ways. They run legitimate businesses, raise money through crime, accept donations, and engage in many other economic activities. This chapter will focus on the methods terrorists use to raise money, their participation in formal and informal financial systems, measures to stop terrorist financing, attempts to investigate groups and individuals, the structure of terrorist economic networks, and a debate about the existence of narcoterrorism.

Financial Flows

When modern terrorism began to emerge after World War II, security forces frequently concentrated on investigative measures, law enforcement, and military force, to counter it. Counterterrorists emphasized tactical control of areas where terrorists operated, and financing was frequently overlooked or ignored. This approach changed by the 1980s as security forces came to realize the crucial role that money played in terrorist operations. In Northern Ireland, for example, law enforcement officials and terrorism analysts realized that the IRA had made a **Capone discovery**; that is, it developed an organized crime network to finance its operations (Adams, 1986). A decade later, American analysts demonstrated that Middle Eastern terrorists were raising funds in the United States through grocery coupon fraud (Kushner and Jacobson, 1998). Other investigators found legal businesses laundering millions of dollars for terrorist organizations (Navias, 2002). Many terrorist organizations used petty crime, money laundering, and the transfer of illegal contraband to finance operations (Hinnen, 2004).

> **Capone discovery:** A term used by James Adams to explain the Irish Republican Army's entry into organized crime.

Awareness of the importance of financing evolved slowly, partly because of the inherent contradiction in the cost of a single terrorist event when compared to the cost of a campaign. Stated simply, a terrorist operation usually does not cost a lot of money, but the overall budget for a campaign is quite high. The *Economist* (2003) reports that terrorism is cost-effective in terms of the causalities and destruction terrorist events cause. Events like the 1995 Oklahoma City bombing or the multiple bombing attacks on trains in Madrid in 2004 cost only a few thousand dollars. A single attack like the 2009 Fort Hood shootings might only cost a few hundred dollars. Yet, as Neil Livingstone and David Halevy (1986) explain, it takes a lot of cash to run a terrorist group for any length of time. For example, 9/11 was inexpensive, but holding al Qaeda together cost several thousand dollars per month (L. Wright, 2006, pp. 168–169). After 9/11, some analysts saw the importance of terrorist financing. They began research projects on fund-raising, money laundering, and the storage and transfer of funds (Jacobson and Levit, 2009).

Money Laundering

It is popularly believed that the term *money laundering* first appeared in the 1920s. Organized crime families earned money through prostitution, distribution of illegal goods, robberies, burglaries, and other illegal activities. While this gave gangsters an abundant income, it also created a problem. They had to account for their assets without linking the source of the money to the crimes they committed. They wanted to move money from the informal underground economy where it could not be used to the formal economic system where they could spend it. They had to make their incomes appear to be legitimate. Organized criminal syndicates opened laundromats, funneled illegal money through them, and reported tremendous incomes. Illegal gains were transferred into legal profits, and both law enforcement agencies and the Mafia called the process money laundering (Durrieu, 2013, p. 13). Both sides knew that these businesses probably could not make such profits, but forged business accounting records showed the money was "clean." It could be used in the legitimate economy.

Roberto Durrieu (2013, p. 19) explains the process. Assume that three criminals make $3 million by smuggling drugs, and they divide it equally. When they do work, the odd jobs they perform pay far less than $1 million per year. They obviously want to enjoy it, but when the money is used in the legitimate economy, it becomes part of formal record keeping systems. Banks report large deposits, real estate transfers create multiple financial documents, and other transactions are taxed. The criminals know that any sudden change in lifestyle might bring attention from law enforcement. They may even know that when Al Capone was finally convicted, he was charged with income tax evasion.

The three criminals need to launder the money; that is, they need to give the illusion that their sudden increased income was derived legally. They must conceal the process by which they gained the money to enjoy the fruits of their illegal labor. Laundering allows them to do this.

placement: Placing illegal monetary profits in the legitimate financial system.

layering: Concealing the source of illegal income in confusing, sometimes multiple financial actions.

integration: Presenting illegally gained money in the formal economic system as if it were the result of a legal activity.

Money is laundered in three steps. **Placement** involves putting criminal proceeds in the legitimate financial system. Placement can take place in a single action, such as showing the monetary gains as profits, or it may be laundered through repeated transactions to conceal its origins. This second process is called **layering**. The final step is **integration**. This involves assimilating illegally obtained money in the formal economy and giving funds the appearance of legitimacy (Tofangsaz, 2015).

It is hard to trace some money because it is hidden in underground networks or in informal transfers. The U.S. Department of the Treasury (2015) explains that organized crime and drug networks use extensive money laundering systems. Criminal groups will launder money several times, converting illegal income to another form of funds and often further laundering it by other means.

Empirical research shows that terrorists do not usually engage in complicated laundering systems. While terrorists use the same networks and channels as organized criminals, they usually layer illegal money in one step, such as converting cash into a money order, buying prepaid charge cards, or wiring cash to a group's financier. Terrorists also launder significantly less cash than organized crime or drug networks. One empirical study involving almost 200 money laundering techniques indicated that the maximum sum of money for organized criminals was $69 million, while the maximum amount for the terrorist cases involved $4.8 million.

black market peso exchange: A method for converting illegal profits in U.S. currency to Colombian pesos in an effort to hide the illegal funds. Terrorists have frequently used the system, although they launder less money than organized crime or drug networks.

One common method for laundering drug money from Colombia is known as the **black market peso exchange**. Terrorists, especially the Revolutionary Armed Forces of Colombia (FARC), have used this network, although not as much as drug dealers. In the peso exchange, drug dealers sell their products in the United States and accumulate large amounts of U.S. currency. Unlike in terrorism investigations, law enforcement officers are well versed in disrupting drug networks simply by following the path of such money. As a result, the dealers need to find a way to hide the cash. They do so by selling the money to brokers in Colombia, who pay the dealers in Colombian pesos. This creates no financial record in the United States. Brokers purchase goods in the United States and smuggle them to importers in Colombia. These goods are marketed and sold in Colombia and in other countries at greatly inflated prices. The importers make

FIGURE **3.1** The Process of Money Laundering

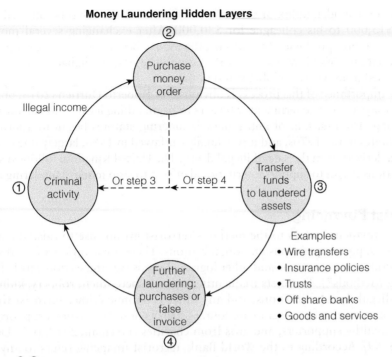

FIGURE **3.2** Money Laundering — Hidden Layers

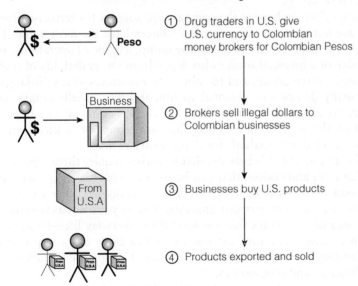

FIGURE **3.3** The Black Market Peso Exchange

a profit, pay the excess pesos to the broker, and the broker, after taking a commission, sends the money to drug dealers in the United States Dealers convert seemingly legitimate pesos into dollars, and all the money looks legitimate (Zill and Bergman, 2014).

A variation of the peso exchange involves selling goods or services at inflated prices. For example, recall the three hypothetical drug dealers who are trying to account for a sudden influx of $1 million each. One of the subjects can "sell" his car worth $15,000 to his colleague for $30,000. After exchanging several more over-priced goods and producing bills of sale, the money begins to take on the appearance of legitimate profits (Tofangsaz, 2015). As with the peso exchange, this method can also be used to move cash globally and informally.

The importance of this process is obvious, but Roberto Durrieu (2013, pp. 19 and 98–119) says it took governments 50 years to begin taking legal action against money laundering. The first talk of anti-money laundering statutes began to appear in the United States in the 1970s, and it was finally outlawed in 1986, largely due to massive incomes derived from the sale of illegal drugs. The United Kingdom followed suit, and both nations began to support international efforts to stop money laundering in 1988.

Terrorist Financing

Terrorist financing refers to the methods terrorist groups use to raise the material needed to support operations and organizations. There are a variety of legal and illegal methods to meet income and other logistical needs (see the section entitled "Illegal Funding Methods"). Terrorists frequently engage in petty theft, robbery, kidnapping, selling illegal drugs, extortions, and any other economic crime. Terrorist financing also involves money from legitimate sources such as donations from a supporting diasporas, wealthy supporters, and gifts from charities (Freeman, 2012, p. 7; Derriueu, 2013, p. 69). According to the World Bank, terrorist financing refers to any money used to support terrorism, including people who support, plan, or engage in an act of terrorist violence (Durrueu, 2013, p. 68). Funds may also be delivered by a combination of legal and illegal sources, and some groups are self-supporting or sponsored by states (Tofangsaz, 2015).

There is no data evaluating the comparative sources for terrorist financing, and researchers are not clear on what types of sources have the most value. The importance of financing depends on the size of the group, its type of operations, and its purpose. The value of a financial source also depends on the availability of resources, the particular needs of the group, and the ability to obtain resources (Tofangsaz, 2015). Terrorists usually do not seek personal wealth, and they usually obtain resources to support terrorist activities (Durrieu, 2013, p. 67). It is difficult to gather systematic information on the acquisition of money because groups or at least terrorist operations must be funded, but methods for doing so are varied.

Hamed Tofangsaz (2015) believes that terrorists require three types of financing. He states that cash and entities that can be used as cash—such as cash cards, credit cards, and checks—are used for weapons, bribes, and myriad other activities. Tangible goods are also an aspect of terrorist financing, but they are not as important as cash. These items include the things that are needed for everyday life—food, accommodations, clothing, travel, and anything else needed to carry out an operation. Finally, terrorist financing also involves intangible income. Groups need sanctuaries, training spaces, intelligence, and propaganda.

Tofangsaz argues that terrorist financing develops in distinct phases. Terrorists need to obtain money, transport and store it, and distribute it to the operational group. Obtaining money involves fund-raising, and as mentioned, this happens in a

FIGURE **3.4** Stages of Terrorist Financing

variety of manners. Fund-raising is followed by security. Terrorists must be able to move and hold their financial resources. The final stage is distribution. Resources must reach individual terror cells.

Sometimes, economic support for terrorism does not involve actual money. Goods and services may be substituted for cash. Victor Dostov and Pavel Shust (2014) suggest that support may also come from a rapidly growing sector of the legitimate economy, customer loyalty programs. Airline miles, hotel and rental car points, and other customer bonuses can be traded for goods and services. These benefits can be used, in turn, to finance terrorism.

Customer loyalty rewards constitute a private economy, and programs have grown rapidly over the past 20 years. Awards of loyalty points from hotels, cash back rewards on credit cards, free rental cars, cash discounts for purchases, and frequent flyer miles have become a form of pseudocash. Reward programs have taken the character of surrogate payments in goods, services, and cash back incentives, making some of them act as private currency. International efforts to thwart terrorist financing do not have the resources to monitor the array of programs, according to Dostov and Shust, but terrorists may use them as income sources.

Loyalty programs do not fall in the realm of financial record keeping. However, Dostov and Shust point out that corporations keep extensive records on loyal customers, records that reveal transaction histories, behaviors, preferences, and exchanges to third parties. Companies also monitor rewards closely to avoid fraud. Most customer reward transfers are electronic, so they automatically create a record. In addition, there are few technical problems in gathering and analyzing data. It is usually as simple as entering a customer's name and reward identification number. Even though governments lack the capacity to investigate suspicious behavior, public–private partnerships could become a valuable tool in preventing or stopping terrorist financing if rewards are being used to support terrorism.

Dostov and Shust use the money laundering model—recall that it is placement, layering, and integration—to analyze customer loyalty programs, and they find potential risks. Terrorists may use points for purchases, rewards may be used across international borders, and customer loyalty awards are housed in an unregulated, decentralized private economy. If frequent flyer miles can be used for cash, cash cards, gifts of free flights, or private currency, they can be used to finance terrorism.

Comparing Money Laundering and Terrorist Financing

As awareness of money laundering grew, law enforcement agencies and intelligence organizations began to realize that terrorist financing might be a separate process using differing methods. At first, many governments and agencies began to employ anti-money laundering techniques to investigations of terrorist financing. In fact, after 9/11, when anti-money laundering programs permeated international counterterrorism efforts, many analysts equated terrorist financing with money laundering. Laws and operations that worked against laundering could be used to stop financing, or so many people believed.

Recently, financial analysts and economists have begun to question the logic of linking the two concepts. Approaching terrorist financing with anti-money laundering tools equates terrorism with organized crime. The two concepts are hardly identical. Organized criminals are in business to make money, and they launder illegal profits to enjoy their benefits. Terrorists fight for a cause, and when they reap profits, they only want to use them in support of that cause. Both organized crime and terrorism are based on money, but it is used differently in each case (Tofangsaz, 2015).

Separating financing from laundering does not mean that terrorists do not launder money. When terrorists gain money illegally, they may need to hide its source. At other times, they may be using donors, charities, or some other entity where they avoid linking the money with its origin. For example, it is illegal to donate money to support terrorist groups in the United States. A donor may donate money to a front organization, and the recipient layers the money to give the appearance that it is being used for a purpose other than supporting terrorism. The donor's crime goes undetected, and terrorists get the funds. In such cases, terrorist groups employ money laundering techniques (Durrieu, 2013, pp. 69–70). Many times, however—maybe most of the time—terrorists have no need to launder money.

Think of it this way. Organized criminals use money laundering to obtain money and spend it. They commit the crime *before* they get the money. When terrorists raise money, either legally or illegally, they usually commit the crime *after* they get the funds. Criminals seek resources to accumulate them, whereas terrorists want to disburse them. The difference between money laundering and terrorist financing is the direction of the flow of cash, goods, and services. This may mean that terrorist financing should be attacked with methods other than anti-money laundering techniques. Researchers and analysts, who see terrorism as a distinct category of crime, tend not to believe that anti-money laundering is an effective weapon in the arsenal of counterterrorism (Tofangsaz, 2013).

Terrorists and organized criminals move and store cash differently. To begin, much terrorist financing takes place in the legitimate economy. They can use banks, credit cards, check exchanges, and other legal economic transactions. When this is the case, there is no need to hide these activities from governments or law enforcement. Organized criminals begin with dirty money and must hide their initial transactions.

Similarities may come into play when using underground networks because terrorists and criminals move along the same routes. When terrorists use informal financial methods to move and store cash, they deal with the same people who move and store cash for criminals. Yet, funds are moving in opposite directions. Terrorists are moving money to commit a crime, while money launderers are moving away from a crime. Money laundering requires a criminal predicate, whereas, terrorism does not (Tofangsaz, 2015).

Roberto Durrieu (2013, p. 70) points out that terrorists may need to make the money dirty. This process involves hiding the legal origin of money used to support terrorism. For example, in the United States, it is illegal to donate money to any designated terrorist group. Assume that a hypothetical donor wants to send money to a group whose cause he avidly supports, and the group wants the money. Yet, neither they nor the donor wants the source of the funds to be identified because the donor could be arrested. The money has to be "dirtied." Layering takes place when the donor gives money to a legitimate organization, say a charity, and that organization gives it to another legitimate organization outside the country such as a nongovernmental organization (NGO). The NGO engages in legitimate activity while supporting the outlawed group. Since the money has been dirtied, it can flow to the terrorists. The donor has been protected.

Toward a Theory of Terrorist Financing

Some analysts believe the primary reason that officials do not understand the financing process is that they lack a theoretical framework. Graham Myres (2012) says that governments equate terrorist financing with money laundering because there is no theory of financing. Terrorism, he says, has been the target of social science studies but not financial research. Terrorists have financial strategies and disburse funds. They acquire resources, fund operations, move money, and launder and dirty it. Myers concludes that analysts should create a theory to explain terrorist financing. It would enhance efforts to understand terrorism.

Michael Freeman (2012, pp. 3–12) of the Naval Post Graduate School is concerned about the lack of a theory to explain terrorist economies. He wants to place terrorist financing in some sort of framework. Without a theory, he argues, analysts cannot adequately explain how groups raise money, how money is budgeted, and how it is invested. Researchers also need to know how these processes change over time.

Freeman argues that researchers need a theory that accounts for the need for money, the amount of money needed, sources of income, and the interaction of these three factors with counterterrorist operations. He then proposes a framework to capture information based on six criteria: (1) the quantity of money needed, (2) the need for legitimacy, (3) the security of assets, (4) the sources of income, (5) the ability to control the flow of resources, and (6) the simplicity of a group's financial system. He says that all these factors will vary based on the importance of the criteria at a given point of time. As a group's needs change, some factors become less important while others become more essential.

Freeman's proposal can be explained by an example. Quantity and source of income would be crucial criteria for a group with few resources. In this situation, counterterrorist research and investigation should be directed toward the acquisition of funding. Another group might have an abundance of resources. This increases the importance of security and flow of funds. Such a theory, Freeman believes, enhances knowledge about operations.

Analysts do know that terrorist financing is critical because terrorists want as much money as possible. Freeman says that money is a force multiplier. Without it, a group is weakened. Groups with income can launch more attacks, maintain an infrastructure, provide goods and services, protect assets, and provide incentives to potential recruits. Good financing allows groups to build training camps, maintain logistical networks, travel, and purchase weapons. Money is important, and analysts need a theoretical framework to explain it.

✓ **Self-Check**

> How is money laundered?
> What are the differences between money laundering and terrorist financing?
> How could a theory of financing increase our understanding of terrorism?

Efforts to Control Terrorist Financing

The financial environment is important to terrorists. Fund-raising is a business activity in the world of private corporations, and it is a business-like operation in terrorist organizations. Unlike corporations, terrorists are not in business to make money, but they need money to stay in business (Tupman, 2009). They also need a financial-friendly environment to flourish. Several countries in Asia, Europe, and North America have taken formal action to make their economies less friendly to terrorists. They have enacted laws to ban terrorist fund-raising and to regulate the banking industry. This makes the business of funding terrorism more difficult. Many nations lack the will or capacity to oversee their economies. These unregulated areas are conducive to crime and terrorism (Petraeus and Amos, 2006, pp. 8–43). Even economically developed regions are vulnerable to private currencies like Bitcoin and underground economic networks (Brantly, 2014).

Regulation and Enforcement

After its long experience with the Irish Republican Army, the United Kingdom was one of the first nations to address terrorist financing. The British developed several tools to fight it. Parliament passed four specific laws against terrorist fund-raising before the start of the twenty-first century. One law simply banned possession of terrorist funds. Another prohibited any effort to assist terrorist groups in fund-raising. A third measure criminalized concealment of funds if money was connected to terrorism. Finally, if law enforcement or intelligence officials can establish reasonable suspicion that funds are connected to a terrorist group or an act of terrorism, the government is empowered to freeze all financial assets of anyone involved and to impound them (Ridley and Alexander, 2012).

Several other countries have followed the United Kingdom's lead, creating financial intelligence units and financial investigative forces. Such units gather information on transactions and provide a means to enforce compliance with economic regulations. Their goal is to reduce money laundering and terrorist financing, and they work very well in the banking industry and other financial exchanges in a formal economy. They regulate the flow of funds, but they have limitations. Their effectiveness depends on a nation's willingness and ability to regulate its financial system (Rashdan, 2012). Regulation works only in a formal, well-developed economy.

Nicholas Ridley and Dean Alexander (2012) examined regulations in the United States. Although in the past, the United States and United Kingdom led efforts against organized crime and money laundering, the United States did not pay too much attention to terrorist financing until the aftermath of 9/11. President George W. Bush issued an executive order that enabled the government to seize funds associated with any group on the State Department's designated terrorist list within days of the attacks. The USA PATRIOT Act further required financial institutions to report suspicious activity, develop anti-money laundering procedures, and to assess customers. President Barrack Obama strengthened regulatory power in 2010 by criminalizing efforts to aid or support terrorist groups, even if actions take place outside of the country. In June 2010, the U.S. Supreme Court ruled that material support of terrorism included not only economic support but also provision of expert advice, training, services, and personnel.

Ridley and Scott (2012) note that several federal agencies created financial enforcement and intelligence units. While the Internal Revenue Service (IRS) had a long-standing Criminal Investigative Division, the FBI created the Terrorism Financing Operations Section (TFOS). The Department of the Treasury created the Office of Terrorism and Financial Intelligence, and after the start of the Iraqi insurgency, it formed a financial investigative unit to gather, analyze, and distribute intelligence on terrorist financial networks in Iraq. The Department of State opened the Counterterrorism Financial Unit, and the Drug Enforcement Administration gathered intelligence on the nexus between terrorism and illegal drugs with the Office of Counternarcotics Enforcement.

Regulation, intelligence gathering, compliance, and enforcement increased, but Ridley and Alexander believe both Europe and the United States made a fundamental mistake. They equated terrorist financing with money laundering. European countries first recognized the mistake when they realized that efforts to stop the financing of al Qaeda were not working. Officials in the United States noticed this, too. It began to include efforts to uncover terrorist financing, expanding the tasks of investigative, and enforcement units.

Ridley and Alexander see this shift as a positive step, but they do not believe it has gone far enough. The United States needs to place more emphasis on terrorist financing. They also think that interagency squabbling over turf hinders intelligence gathering activities, and they are dismayed that organizations continue to horde information rather than share it. They urge greater scrutiny of seemingly innocent transactions and believe that government agencies should cooperate more with the private sector to uncover terrorist financing.

The U.S. efforts to regulate and eliminate terrorist financing extend beyond its borders. In Asia and the Pacific, it encourages developed and developing nations to expand their economies and adopt anti-terrorist financing measures (APEC, 2013). In Europe, it participates in a joint European and American initiative, the Terrorist Finance Tracking Program (TFTP). The TFTP began as a secret American intelligence gathering program, and it eventually emerged as a formal regulatory agency in the European Union (Plachta, 2014). The United States also seeks to implement uniform anti-money laundering and terrorist financing regulations around the globe, in both developed and developing regions (FATF, 2014).

Efforts by the United Nations

Terrorist financing and money laundering usually involve international funding, and they have become part of the global economy. At the urging of the United States and the United Kingdom, the UN General Assembly adopted the International Convention for the **Suppression of the Financing of Terrorism** in December 1999. It was later strengthened by the addition of provisions that criminalized terrorist financing, empowered governments to seize and freeze assets used by terrorists, and required financial institutions to report suspicious behavior (Thony and Png, 2007).

Another important action was the creation of the **Financial Action Task Force on Money Laundering (FATF)** a decade earlier and its subsequent strengthening in the twenty-first century. Its purpose was to bring the international financial community into harmony by strengthening regulations and introducing more uniform practices. FATF originally contained 40 recommendations, and it was strengthened when nine special recommendations that targeted terrorist financing were added between 2001 and 2006. The special recommendations called for more regulation, reporting suspicious activities to law enforcement, and moves against informal economic systems (Troutsoult and Johnson, 2012).

The nine special recommendations asked all member states to implement UN financial instruments. They also reinforced previous efforts to criminalize terrorist financing, asset seizure, and suspicious activity reporting. The fifth recommendation called for international cooperation in investigation and law enforcement efforts against terrorist financing. Later measures asked for stronger anti-money laundering standards, rules for wire transfers, monitoring NGOs, and measures against suspects transporting cash (Thony and Png, 2007; Othman and Ameer, 2014). On the surface, FATF appears to be very strong.

Critics and terrorism analysts note several weaknesses in FATF. The first has little to do with financing and reverts to the problem of defining terrorism. Debates about the meaning of terrorism allow funds to flow to terrorist groups. For example, a government may consider a paramilitary group to be a terrorist organization, but another nation might see the same group as a legitimate revolutionary or liberation movement. The first nation outlaws the group because it practices terrorism, and the second nation supports the group as an ally. International prohibition of terrorist financing is impossible without a standard definition, and as W. A. Tupman (2009) notes, there is still no standard definition of terrorism, and nobody is close to providing one.

There are other shortcomings in FATF. Critics note a widespread absence of laws allowing the seizure of assets used to support terrorism. Much of FATF is aimed

Suppression of the Financing of Terrorism: A 1999 UN resolution designed to thwart terrorist financing. It was strengthened after 9/11 by provisions that criminalized terrorist financing, empowered states to seize terrorist assets, and required financial institutions to support suspicious activities.

Financial Action Task Force on Money Laundering (FATF): A resolution passed by the United Nations in 1990 and strengthened from 2001 to 2006 urging member states to adopt measures to hamper money laundering and terrorist financing. It contained 40 recommendations. Nine special recommendations were added to focus specifically on terrorist financing.

at informal financial systems, but transactions in these markets take place in secret, where government regulations do not apply. Criminals using these markets are likely to keep informal networks secret, and the majority of people who use them have no criminal intention. They simply do not have access to institutions such as banks. Even when the formal system is discussed, many countries have neither the means nor the will to enforce the recommendations (Thony and Png, 2007).

Enforcement efforts aimed at underground networks are ineffective and often counterproductive in developing countries. In fact, informal systems may well be the thriving sector of an undeveloped nation, and its people may view them as normal and acceptable. Informal exchanges usually take place in cash so that there are few records, which makes transactions difficult to trace. Many people see FATF as an attempt to impose regulation of traditional economies, and the recommendations often violate cultural, social, and religious practices. FATF is ill suited for many areas of the world (Trautsolt and Johnson, 2007).

Critics also have concerns about due process. Assets can be seized and frozen based on the suspicion of terrorist activity. This means that a government may take action before prosecuting a suspect. It also implies that a person can lose assets because he or she is associated with a person or organization engaged in suspicious activity. For example, assume that a charity is financing a terrorist group. A large donor might have assets seized simply because he or she is associated with the charity. This could happen without formal charges or criminal prosecution (Plachta, 2014). The United Nations tried to remedy this by allowing individuals to petition the government for a formal hearing if assets are frozen (Thony and Png, 2007).

Despite criticism, supporters claim that FATF works well in economically developed countries. It promotes risk assessment and transparency in the banking sector, maintains communications with nonprofits and NGOs, supports expansion of regulation, and seeks to improve efforts against money laundering and terrorist financing. It actively monitors states that are unaware of or supporting illegal monetary practices and maintains a list of noncooperative nations (FATF, 2015). Rick McDonell, the executive secretary of FATF in 2015, points out that a global anti-money laundering and terrorist financing is a complex, massive undertaking. FATF operates without treaties or enforcement powers, and it relies on peer pressure and diplomacy to achieve compliance. This means it cannot change established economic practices in a brief span of time. Regulation and reform of financial systems will evolve slowly over time, and laws based on FATF recommendations have produced financial intelligence that has led to prosecutions for terrorist financing. McDonell also points out that a top-level minister represents every nation that is involved in FATF (Millman, 2014).

Qualitative data also suggest that efforts like FATF are important. It is difficult to assess the effectiveness of anti-terrorist financing measures because researchers lack the data and means to create an accurate assessment of anti-terrorist financing regulations. Simply studying conviction rates underestimates their effectiveness, and comparing convictions across international borders in varied economies produces misleading data. Current and former intelligence and law enforcement officials, however, see the situation in a different light. Qualitatively, FBI agents believe that dozens of terrorist convictions have resulted, and several terrorist plots have been stopped because banks reported suspicious activity. Law enforcement agencies in Europe feel the same way. Intelligence agents believe that anti-money laundering and terrorist financing activities provide hundreds of leads. While critics are leery of regulatory measures, practitioners believe that regulations developed from FATF recommendations can be used to stop terrorism (Jonsson, 2010).

The international economy is a morass of differing systems separated by currencies, traditions, cultures, mores, and a host of other issues. There are systems within systems, and the intermeshed international economy is susceptible to fraud, criminal behavior, money laundering, and terrorist financing. Any attempt to counter criminal financial operations is destined to be complicated. It may be easy to find the weaknesses with FATF, but it represents an effort—a massive effort—to counter money laundering and terrorist financing. The long-term focus is improvement of monetary systems, increased security, and compliance. Improvement over time will probably be the best measure of FATF's effectiveness.

✓ **Self-Check**
> What efforts has the United States made to combat terrorist financing?
> What is the purpose of FATF?
> What are the strengths and weaknesses of FATF?

Financial Information as an Investigative and Intelligence Tool

When security officials began to believe that money trails would be the best tool to use against terrorism, they equated terrorist organizations with drug gangs and organized crime. Conventional wisdom suggested that terrorist groups could be dismantled simply by "following the money." There were arguments for waging "financial warfare" by freezing assets and tracing the funds used by terrorist groups (Navias, 2002). The U.S. government endorsed this approach, arguing that counterterrorist investigations should focus on sources of financing and mechanisms to transfer money (National Strategy for Combating Terrorism, 2006, p. 7). These financial approaches supposed that attacks on terrorist financing with anti-money laundering tactics would reduce terrorism.

This approach was too simple. It assumed that terrorists would act only in the legal, formal economy. In reality, terrorists participate in underground criminal networks that are relatively immune to financial regulations. So-called formal financial warfare would not be effective because underground economies operate under different rules (Basile, 2004). Experience in Canada suggests that conventional financial investigations against terrorists are ineffective and that traditional measures do not work, at least on the surface (Montpetit, 2008).

As criticism of counterterrorist financial investigations increased in the media and among the public at large, security forces came to realize that the nature of money trails in terrorism was misunderstood. Many people assumed that terrorists operated like drug networks; but that was not the case (Giraldo and Trinkhunas, 2007, p. 293). Whereas, an intensive financial investigation of money laundering networks could result in the successful prosecution of an international drug ring, the same tactic did not work against terrorist groups. This was true even with large international networks. Counterterrorism specialists and investigators came to realize that financial investigations could be used as a tool in a process, but by themselves, investigations of the flow of funds would not stop terrorism.

Drug dealers and organized criminals require massive organizations to collect and launder large amounts of money. Terrorists do not operate like that. Terrorists do not launder money frequently; as noted earlier, it takes relatively little money to launch an individual terrorist operation (Liu, 2012). Traditional financial investigations are not effective against terrorists because of the limited amounts of money required for a terrorist operation, but when financial transactions become one aspect of larger investigative or intelligence operations, they help to provide a comprehensive picture. Terrorists do need money, and they get it by both legal and illegal methods. If financial information is added to evidence gained by other investigative techniques, it can provide a more comprehensive picture of terrorist activities (Levitt and Jacobson, 2008, p. 15).

Terrorist networks operate much like a business franchise, although transactions frequently take place in the underground economy. Money is moved across international borders. Therefore, financial investigations are conducted internationally and require international agreements to stem the flow of money. As result, one aspect of counterterrorism involves tracing money and using the information in concert with other intelligence to produce a comprehensive picture of terrorist operations (Williams, 2007, pp. 77–82; Levitt and Jacobson, 2008, p. 15).

John Cassara (2006) argues that the United States has been less than effective in its efforts to fight terrorism because law enforcement agencies have not used sufficient forensic accounting tools. It is possible to track terrorists' money laundering, cash purchases, banking accounts, and stock and business investments. Cassara also says that tracking money can create better intelligence—criminal intelligence and national security intelligence. Mapping the financial activities of suspected groups and individuals gives intelligence a comprehensive focus. **Forensic accounting** can be used to solve crimes and to gain information.

Forensic accounting: An investigative tool used to track money used in illegal activities. It can be used in any crime involving the exchange, storage, or conversion of fiscal resources.

Illegal Funding Methods

Terrorists raise money by a variety of legal and illegal means. Some of the illegal methods include running criminal enterprises, engaging in the drug trade, conducting illegal business activities under a legal cover, smuggling money, illegally transferring money, and a variety of other methods. Middle Eastern terrorists engage in smuggling and document fraud. Document fraud raises money for terrorist organizations and provides terrorists with false identification. In Central Asia, terrorist organizations trade illegal arms, launder money, and distribute drugs. Latin American terrorism is tied to drug production and public corruption. In the United States, domestic terrorists engage in fraud schemes and robberies to finance political violence (Mili, 2006).

Raising money for illegal operations is nothing new. The Brazilian terrorist-philosopher Carlos Marighella argued that "urban warfare" begins with a campaign of **expropriation**—that is, robbery (1969, 1971; see also Burton, 1976). Terrorists around the world use a variety of criminal methods to raise funds. Violent activities involve kidnapping, extortion, and robbery. Less violent methods include fraud, larceny, smuggling, dealing in contraband, forgery, and counterfeiting (Nance, 2003; Williams, 2007, p. 77). Interpol estimates that counterfeiting and intellectual property theft is responsible for $200 billion annually in illegal profits in the United States alone, and the amount doubles to $400 billion when the international community is included. This involves pirated CDs and DVDs, counterfeit clothing, and stolen computer software (Noble, 2003). Counterfeiting and fraud are common practices among the American extremist right (Pitcavage, 1999a, 1999b, 1999c).

expropriation: A term used by Carlos Marighella for armed robbery.

Domestic extremists are not the only violent fanatics who raise funds in the United States; international terrorists also engage in fraudulent activities in America. From approximately 1981 to 1986, the Abu Nidal Organization engaged in various criminal activities in Tennessee and the St. Louis metropolitan area to generate funds

(E. Harris, 1995). Hezbollah ran cigarettes from North Carolina to Michigan and used some of the profits to fund operations in Lebanon (*United States of America v. Mohamad Youseff Hammoud, et al.*, 2002). There are a variety of schemes across the country that use baby formula. American baby formula is treasured throughout the world because of its nutritional value. Terrorists sometimes steal formula and use illegal distribution networks to raise money (Clayton, 2005). In Cincinnati, law enforcement officers broke a ring of convenience stores that were selling stolen goods to finance terrorist organizations (Coolidge and Prendergast, 2003). Police in Dearborn, Michigan, arrested two men for making false identification papers for Middle Eastern groups (U.S. Immigration and Customs Enforcement, 2005).

The Internet has become a tool for fraud. Terrorists use online activity in identity theft and in gaining access to bank and credit card accounts. They also sell items at Internet auctions. Security fraud is another method of raising funds. For example, a group might buy a large amount of stock in a company that is fairly inactive. They then fill the web with stories of new products, new technology, or some other item that will cause the company's stock to increase. As the stock value increases, terrorists sell the stock at an inflated price even though the company has seen no real increase in value. Before the stock drops back to its normal level, the terrorists make a huge profit. This process is known as pump and dump, and it is frequently used by dishonest stock speculators and other criminals (Hinnen, 2004).

Terrorists use extortion and protection rackets to raise money. Terrorist organizations force legitimate businesses and other people to make payoffs to avoid being attacked. Loretta Napoleoni (2003, pp. 27–28) reports that the Shining Path of Peru taxed farmers for protection. Rebels and death squads in Colombia did the same. Zachary Abuza (2003b) says similar tactics are used in Southeast Asia. In essence, Abuza concludes, terrorists use the same fund-raising techniques that criminals have used for years, in addition to their unique methods of gathering money.

Stolen vehicles also play a role in fund-raising (Sallot, 2006). North American cars, especially SUVs, are attractive to terrorists. When used as car bombs, the large capacity of SUVs provides far more explosive power than smaller vehicles. They can also be used to raise cash. A stolen SUV can be sold in the Middle East or Central Asia for nearly $100,000.

Examples of illegal fund-raising extend to all forms of crime. At the heart of illegal activity is fund-raising, and terrorists have learned that crime can pay. Traditional crimes, especially large embezzlement schemes in the global economy, represent a source of income for small groups as well as large organizations (Labeviere, 2000, pp. 54–55; Napoleoni, 2003, pp. 203–205; D. Kaplan, 2005). After raising funds, terrorists frequently spend them in underground networks to support operations.

Tobacco has become an important source of money for terrorist organizations. By 2012, al Qaeda in the Islamic Maghreb (AQIM) had become the primary source of income for the al Qaeda network (Rogers, 2012). AQIM achieved this prominent position by smuggling cigarettes. David Cid, former director of the Memorial Institute for the Prevention of Terrorism, says that cigarettes are easy to buy and easy to smuggle. They can also be counterfeited. The Afghan Taliban produces millions of fake Marlboros and distributes them through Afghanistan and China. The Irish Republican Army raised an estimated $100 million over a five-year period by smuggling cigarettes. The Kurdish Workers Party raises money by taxing cigarettes as they cross the border. Many of the drug smuggling routes in North America have been used for cigarette smuggling. Drug detection methods do no work against cigarettes, and penalties for illegally possessing cigarettes are much lighter than those for possessing drugs (Wilson, 1999).

Legal Methods of Raising Funds

Terrorists do not limit their financial activities to underworld networks and illegal revenue sources. Many groups engage in legitimate business activities to raise and distribute money (Navias, 2002). Activities include soliciting contributions, operating businesses, running nongovernmental organizations (NGOs), creating charities, using wire transfers, forming or using banks, and using informal money transfer systems. Sometimes, people smuggle large amounts of money across international borders. At other times, foreign workers send money back to organizations in their home countries. One terrorist group legally raises the money through normal employment (National Strategy, 2006; Levitt and Jacobson, 2008; and Montpetit, 2008).

According to several researchers (Emerson, 2002, pp. 183–219; Ehrenfeld, 2003, pp. 21–22; Napoleoni, 2003, pp. 111–179), charities have been involved in funding terrorism. Data from national and international law enforcement sources agree with these findings (Scott-Joynt, 2003; Isikoff and Hosenball, 2004; U.S. Department of State, 2004b). Many people who contribute to charities do not know they are supporting terrorist organizations. Others believe the efforts they are supporting are not terrorist operations; rather, they seem them as legitimate military operations. Zachary Abuza (2003b, p. 93) writes that terrorists often set up a phony charity or skim the proceeds from legitimate organizations. Either way, charitable funds are frequently diverted to terrorist groups.

> ✓ **Self-Check**
> > How do financial tools impact investigative and intelligence functions?
> > What are some of the common illegal methods of funding terrorism?
> > What types of legal activities fund terrorism?

Underground Networks and Systems

David Carter (2009) points to an important characteristic of terrorist organizations. When terrorists move goods, people, weapons, money, or contraband, they must do so through underground networks. It is not possible to build a network overnight; they develop only through long-term trust. This means, Carter concludes, that terrorists use existing criminal networks for logistics, including financing activities, and they are vulnerable to intelligence-gathering activities. Even researchers who disagree about the stability of networks see the importance of the underground economy (Biersteker and Eckert, 2007). Even if illegal economic routes are not stable, money still flows through a network. The examination of underground economic systems shows links among people and groups.

The FBI estimates that the global underground economy produces $500 billion per year. An underground economy requires secret institutions, and terrorists have found various enterprises for hiding money (Maier, 2003). Rachel Ehrenfeld (2003, pp. 10–30) says that terrorists run banks and create phony companies to launder or hide their funds. They also engage in secret transactions and form alliances with organized crime.

Friedrich Schneider (2002) says the underground economy and its ties to crime are so important to terrorists because all the transactions remain hidden. Organized criminal and smuggling networks have long had the means of hiding money through seemingly legal transactions. Terrorists take advantage of these networks. Schneider believes that terrorism has become a big business. Terrorists not only move funds but also smuggle stolen goods and contraband. As mentioned earlier, document fraud and forgery are money-raising activities.

Terrorism is linked to organized crime throughout the world, and in some cases, it is almost impossible to distinguish between terrorist and criminal activity. Tamara Makarenko (2002) says that Russian organized crime groups trade weapons for drugs in Colombia. She also finds that both terrorists and criminals take advantage of political instability in regions like Central Asia and the **Triborder region** in South America (around the common border of Argentina, Brazil, and Paraguay; Figure 3.5). In the Middle East and Southeast Asia, terrorists and criminals kidnap for profit. She believes that terrorist and criminal organizations have grown into global enterprises.

The **globalization** of crime and terrorism has created opportunities for vast profits in the diamond trade. African diamonds, or "conflict diamonds," are obtained illegally and sold through an underground network. According to Global Witness (2003), a British human rights organization, al Qaeda spent 10 years moving into unregulated diamond trading in West Africa. In the early 1990s, it infiltrated legitimate trading centers to establish a base. After success in mainstream trading, al Qaeda slowly and quietly switched from legitimate trading centers to underground criminal networks. Then, taking advantage of weak governments and regulations in Africa, it established its own international trading network. The new system allowed al Qaeda and allied jihadist groups to make tremendous profits while providing a ready-made network to hide and launder money. It should be noted that the 9/11 Commission (2004, p. 171) examined claims about al Qaeda's involvement in the diamond trade and came to a different conclusion. The commission found no evidence that diamonds were used to support al Qaeda. Global Witness disagrees and believes it has presented evidence of al Qaeda's activities.

Triborder region: The area where Brazil, Paraguay, and Argentina join. The major city is Cuidad del Este.

globalization: A common global economic network that ideally unites the world through production and international trade. Proponents believe it will create wealth. Critics believe it creates corporate wealth and increases the distance between the rich and the poor.

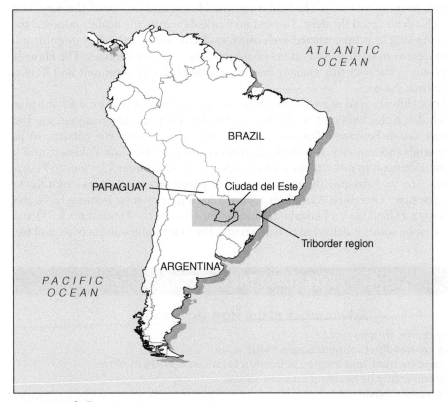

FIGURE **3.5** The Triborder Region

The Triborder region is the area in South America where Paraguay, Brazil, and Argentina have a common border. Quite a bit of criminal activity takes place in the region, and the Paraguayan city Ciudad del Este is particularly known for its lawlessness. The region is also home to more than 20,000 Middle Eastern immigrants. Hamas, Hezbollah, and other terrorist groups have been known to frequent the area.

The Hawala System

Hawala system: A system of exchanging money based on trust relationships between money dealers. A chit, or promissory note, is exchanged between two *Hawaladars*, and it is as valuable as cash or other traded commodities because the trust between the two parties guarantees its value.

Informal financial networks are hidden from public view, and transactions take place in a self-regulated, underground market. Probably the most well-known hidden financial exchange is an ancient trading network called the **Hawala system**. Many international criminals and terrorists funnel money through it. The system originated several hundred years ago in China under the name of Feng Chin, or "flying money." Today, it is primarily used in Pakistan and India, though there are Hawala dealers around the world. It is a legitimate means of transferring money without using money or moving actual funds across international borders, although it may violate currency transfer regulations in some countries. It is a network based on long-term trust relationships and the knowledge that each dealer is impeccably reliable for all debts (see the section later in this chapter titled "Expanding the Concept: Advantages of the Hawala System").

Several hundred years ago, Central Asian merchants were frequently robbed of the gold and silver they carried in caravans to pay for goods. They developed a system of noncash exchange as a result. Rather than carrying money, caravan leaders would visit merchants and pay for goods with a promissory note. When the caravan reached its destination, the leader sold his goods, and the distributors would pay the caravan leader with promissory notes. The leader returned home and presented the note, and the local chit dealer paid the debt. The system worked because the dealers honored the promises. As long as people trusted each other, each chit was worth silver or gold, and merchants, caravan leaders, and others could thus travel without money. The Hawala system is one version of this ancient practice (Jamwal, 2002; Schramm and Taube, 2002; Sharma, 2006).

Today's Hawala system works much as the old system did (Figure 3.6). Imagine that Asadullah Kahn lives and works in Los Angeles. He is an American citizen, but his parents live in Peshawar, Pakistan. Asadullah wishes to assist his parents, so he regularly sends them money. It is difficult, however, to get funds into Pakistan, and it is even more difficult to move them across the North-West Frontier Province to Peshawar. Postal service is frequently unavailable, and parcel services can take months to deliver a package. Therefore, Asadullah goes to a local jewelry store because he knows the owner is a *Hawaladar*, a Hawala dealer. Asadullah gives the *Hawaladar* $500 and tells him that he wants it delivered to his parents. The *Hawaladar* subtracts a small fee,

---

EXPANDING THE CONCEPT

Advantages of the Hawala system:

- Money moves with no record.
- Money crosses international borders with ease.
- It is based on trust, and long-term trusting relationships are in place.
- Money can easily be bartered for contraband.
- No tax records exist.

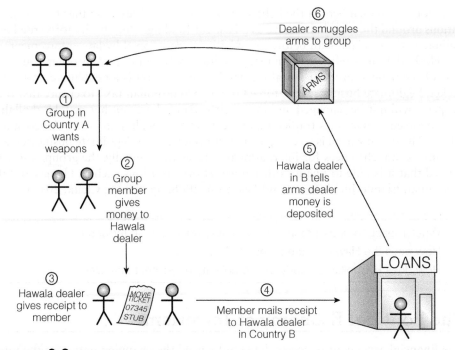

FIGURE 3.6 The Hawala System

usually 1 or 2 percent, and sends word to a *Hawaladar* in Peshawar that Asadullah sends his parents the balance. Asadullah's parents visit the Peshawar *Hawaladar*, and he pays them the promised money. No money actually moved from Los Angeles to Peshawar, but Asadullah's parents received nearly $500. The system works because the *Hawaladars* in Peshawar and Los Angeles implicitly trust each other. They know the debt will be honored (see U.S. Department of the Treasury, 2003).

Change the imaginary scenario a bit, and the impact on terrorism can be demonstrated. In the revised situation, imagine that Asadullah is not a hardworking son seeking to support his parents but an operative for the Lashkar-e-Taiba, a Kashmiri terrorist group. Asif, Asadullah's contact in Peshawar, needs $5000 to buy AK-47s. After raising funds in the United States, Asadullah visits the Hawaladar, hands over $5000, and asks the *Hawaladar* to get the money to Asif. The Peshawar *Hawaladar* gives Asif the money, not knowing its use. Asif buys the weapons and delivers them to contacts in the Lashkar-e-Taiba. There is no record of the transaction and no way to trace the flow of funds. The Hawala system was not established to support terrorism, but it hides transactions in the modern world of international banking (Sharma, 2006).

Hezbollah as an Example

Hezbollah can serve as an example of the complexity of terrorist financing (Levitt and Jacobson, 2008, pp. 65–68). The group is discussed in full later in this text, but for now, please understand that it is a political party, a social welfare organization, and a militant group. It uses all types of sources for funding, and it moves money in underground networks and laundering systems. Most of Hezbollah's funds come from state funding, with Iran acting as the principal sponsor. Hezbollah receives an estimated $200 million per year from Iran. There are numerous Lebanese Shi'ites dispersed throughout the world, and Hezbollah receives quite a bit of money in direct donations from members of the Lebanese diaspora. Charities and other front organizations around the world also serve as a base for funding. One charity forwarded $50 million a year to Hezbollah before its activities were stopped by law enforcement.

Hezbollah also relies on criminal activities in Lebanon and in other countries. One of the main sources of illegal income inside Lebanon is an extensive protection racket. Legitimate businesses are forced to pay a "Hezbollah tax" to ensure that their property will not be damaged and that their personnel are not harmed. Hezbollah is also involved in narcotics trafficking and cigarette smuggling in North America and Africa. The organization is so complex that it even manages legitimate businesses, and it controls branch offices for international wire services. Finally, the group is so well funded that it is able to finance other terrorist organizations such as Hamas and the Palestinian Islamic Jihad (Levitt and Jacobson, 2008, pp. 65–68; Chalk, 2012).

✓ Self-Check	> What impact do underground financial networks have on terrorism?
	> How does the Hawala system operate?
	> How does Hezbollah embody the complexity of terrorist financing?

The Political Economy of Terrorism

The financial aspects of terrorism have influenced the changing nature of the international economy. After the collapse of the former Soviet Union in 1991, the United States became the world's only superpower. Promoting an economic system that emphasized international production, trade, and consumption, American economic policies focused on reducing the trade barriers between nation-states. Some countries have prospered under globalization of the world economy, but others have grown weaker and poorer. Globalization is based on the belief that international trade barriers should be removed so that commerce and industry can develop in an international free market. Terrorism has taken hold in some of the areas left behind in the rush toward globalization, and this has changed the nature of terrorist financing (see Barber, 1996, pp. 48–49).

Loretta Napoleoni (2003) examines this process, formulating a new theory about the financing of terrorism. Agreeing with Adams's early findings and other studies that found links between organized crime networks and terrorism, Napoleoni goes far beyond a summary of the immediate circumstances. In *Modern Jihad,* she argues that terrorism has evolved as an economic entity. The fall of the Soviet Union and subsequent globalization have produced what she calls the **new economy of terrorism**. Napoleoni says that the origins of the new economy of terrorism grew from the Cold War (1945–1991). As Bruce Hoffman (1998, pp. 43–65) says, colonial revolts began at the end of World War II, and Napoleoni (2003, pp. 11–28) sees this as the beginning of a macroeconomic shift. Western nations began to use underground methods to fund their struggles in the colonies, and revolutionaries sought their own sources of money. The origins of the new economy of terrorism can be traced to anticolonial revolts.

new economy of terrorism: A term used by Loretta Napoleoni to describe the evolution of terrorist financing from the beginning strategies of the Cold War to the present. Economic support and antiterrorist policies interact to form the new economy.

To demonstrate the birth of this new economy, Napoleoni turns to France. After World War II, when France was still a colonial power in control of many foreign lands, nationalists revolted against French rule all over the world. In Vietnam, the revolutionary nationalists were called the Vietminh. Although they had international Communist backing, the Vietminh needed money. They muscled their way into opium production, sold the drugs, and used the profits to keep their guerrillas in the field.

Ironically, France tried the same concept. When the war against the Vietminh became politically unpopular, the French government found it difficult to finance military operations. Napoleoni says the French took over opium profits and used them to finance the war. As a result, drug trafficking became one of the primary methods governments used to finance activities during the Cold War.

Napoleoni says that as the Cold War developed, the Soviet Union and the United States fought each other by proxy; that is, they did not fight each other directly. The Soviets used allies to attack countries loyal to the United States, and the United States used its friends to attack Soviet-backed countries. Napoleoni believes that modern terrorist groups evolved from these surrogate conflicts and that they looked for ways to become independent from both superpowers. The desire for autonomy led terrorist groups to join criminals in an underground economy.

Napoleoni cites several examples to support this idea. She says a radical Marxist group in Peru, the Shining Path, turned to the drug trade in northern Peru, regulating drug production to fund their activities. The Revolutionary Armed Forces of Colombia (FARC) went a step further and joined the Colombian drug trade. Militant Palestinians went in another direction, using robbery and extortion to raise funds. The IRA started diverting funds from American charities before turning to organized crime. Napoleoni says these sources of financing fueled most of the terrorist activities of the 1970s and early 1980s.

The ETA (separatist group in Spain) changed the structure of terrorist financing. Instead of seeking links to an underground economy, ETA tried to gain control of the economy. They forced Spanish businesses out of the Basque areas of northern Spain and weakened the entire state. The Basque region became a **failed state**, a place where Spain could no longer exert power. When this happened, ETA established an illegitimate economy in a **shell state**. It paid salaries to terrorists, provided for the families of fallen members, and even ran a pension system for retired terrorists. ETA was successful because the Spanish economy had failed in the Basque region, leaving the area in a hopeless political mess. ETA was strong enough to enforce stability.

The new terrorist economy can be understood from the example of ETA. Napoleoni believes that globalization has created pockets in the world where failed or weak states are left to govern with little economic or political power. Terrorists and criminal groups grow in such places, running their own underground economies and providing some form of political stability because they are strong enough to resist the state. Illegitimate groups form a shell state, an organization that acts as a government in a place where the government is not strong enough to act.

As globalization increased, according to Napoleoni, it not only created economic vacuums where shell states could form but also fueled the growth of a global underground economy. It provided illegal trade routes for drugs, arms smugglers, contraband dealers, and human trafficking. Terrorist groups funded themselves through these activities, and they could not exist without them.

Napoleoni believes that modern terrorism is an international force supported by groups in shell states that continually change both their organizational structures and political goals to maintain income from an international underground economy. They hide their economic views with religious rhetoric or patriotic slogans, but their most important objective is to raise funds. Without funding, a terrorist group cannot exist. The prime goal of a group, then, is to maintain its finances. Napoleoni concludes that powerful groups even become strong enough to invest in legitimate markets, and in some instances, they move so much money that they affect the global economy.

Complementing Napoleoni's work is a model developed by Mario Ferrero (2002), who argues that modern radical Islamic groups use violent activity as a means of

failed state: An area outside a government's control. Failed states operate under differing warlords, criminal groups, or competing governments.

shell state: A political situation where a government nominally controls its own state but where large regions are either anarchic or under the control of others. A government is unable to enforce law or provide for other forms of social order in a shell state.

providing economic stability. Jihadist groups cannot keep outsiders away or fire slackers for being unproductive. Numerous recruits flock to training camps and meetings, including people who are less than totally motivated. The slackers threaten stability by using a group's limited resources. To control this, jihadists increase rhetoric and violence to drive all but the most loyal members away from the group. This leaves enough resources to support the true believers.

Jeanne Giraldo and Harold Trinkunas (2007, pp. 7–11), of the U.S. Naval Postgraduate School, suggest that the political economy of terrorism is related to failed states and areas where governments cannot exert political control over their own territory. This has resulted in autonomous terrorist groups with their own funding sources. The terrorism generated by such groups is not related as much to a new style of terrorism or religious motivation as it is to their ability to generate funds. They control their economic circumstances, and funding creates violence.

Like Napoleoni, Giraldo and Trinkunas believe that the old Marxist groups were constrained by their sponsors. Unlike Napoleoni, they do not see the long emergence of a political economic system through the evolution of Cold War financing. They believe that the key is self-sufficiency. Financial and political autonomy allows terrorists to operate without the constraints of a sponsor. Further, by participating in the global economy, they can function much like a government, controlling the flow of cash, goods, and services.

If these macroeconomic theories of terrorism are correct, they have meaning for the nature of counterterrorism. Many criminologists believe that crime can be reduced when potentially deviant groups have a vested interest in the economic structure of society. Macroeconomic theory suggests that counterterrorism policies should be aimed at providing the world's peoples with economic stability, opportunity, and participation in the mainstream economy (see Barnett, 2005, p. 49). Economic policies to counter terrorism would thus involve supporting states in danger of failure, providing opportunities for people to participate in and benefit from economic systems, and eliminating underground economic networks. When a state fails and a terrorist group creates its own shell state, the group has no incentive to participate in legitimate economic enterprises. As Benjamin Barber (1996, p. 299) says, when economic globalization threatens the ability of ordinary people to meet their needs, they will find other ways to survive. Indeed, this reflects Napoleoni's thesis. Poverty does not cause terrorism, but economic and political failures may result in a shell state where terrorism can be organized and funded.

> **Self-Check**
> > What is a macroeconomic theory?
> > How does it apply to terrorism?
> > What political assumptions must be made to see the logic of a macroeconomic theory?

narcoterrorism: A controversial term that links drugs to terrorism in one of two ways: Either drug profits are used to finance terrorism or drug gangs use terrorism to control production and distribution networks.

Narcoterrorism

A heated issue surrounding the discussion of terrorist financing is the relationship between terrorism and drugs. The term *narcoterrorism* refers to groups using either terrorist tactics to support drug operations or drug-trade profits to finance terrorism. Rachel Ehrenfeld championed the concept of narcoterrorism in her early works, and she expanded on the idea (Ehrenfeld, 2003). According to her research, terrorists are involved in the international production and distribution of drugs; indeed, she believes that the narcotics trade is one of their primary sources of money. The U.S. government tends to accept this position, but it is nonetheless extremely controversial.

The Link Between Drugs and Terrorism

Steven Casteel (2003), an executive with the Drug Enforcement Administration (DEA), told a U.S. Senate committee that terrorism and the drug trade are intertwined. Organized criminals, smugglers, and drug dealers naturally linked up with terrorist groups, he says, because all these organizations move in the same circles. Like Napoleoni, he believes that globalization has intensified this relationship. He says that the relationship between drugs and terrorism has been in place throughout history.

David Adams (2003), reporting for the *St. Petersburg Times*, says that Hezbollah and Hamas use the Latin American drug trade to raise funds. He writes that U.S. military units have tracked their activities in South America, and the military is concerned about the large amount of money involved. According to the U.S. Central Command, hundreds of millions of dollars have been raised in Latin America. The military's prime concerns are the Triborder region, the Venezuelan island of Margarita, and the areas controlled by FARC in Colombia. The DEA agrees with this assessment. An official from the U.S. Department of State puts it succinctly: "Whether it is from Latin America or elsewhere, terrorist groups are financed through drugs. This is demonstrable, not debatable" (J. P. Walter, 2002).

Other governments also believe that terrorism and drugs are linked. The French Ministry of Defense issued a report stating that drugs are the primary currency used to finance international terrorism. The French government points to the Shining Path and FARC to show the influence of cocaine. The ministry claims that radical Islamic groups get most of their money through the drug trade in Central and Southeast Asia. Afghanistan is the primary source of heroin in Europe, and the profits from these drug sales fund all international Islamic terrorist groups (Chouvy, 2004). Officials in India believe that Lashkar-e-Taiba and al Qaeda have smuggled drugs and other contraband through Africa, Central Asia, and Eastern Europe (*Times of India*, 2003). According to many in the Indian government, militant Islamic groups are funded by the drug trade.

Joshua Krasna (1997) takes the argument to another level. He says that if people are willing to expand the definition of national security beyond the framework of military defense, drugs pose a security problem. Defining security as social safety, Krasna says that the drug trade threatens political and economic stability by disrupting society. The drug trade limits the ability of legitimate governments and increases the power of insurgent and terrorist groups. Terrorists, for their part, use drugs not only to exploit the social safety concerns of their enemies but also to fund terrorist activities.

Nothing illustrates Krasna's point better than the unfortunate situation in Mexico. Seven major drug trafficking organizations dominate the political landscape in northern Mexico. Officially labeled drug trafficking organizations by the U.S. government, these drug cartels bring a high level of criminality to the U.S.–Mexican border. Violence spills over into Arizona and Texas, and the cartels have directly influenced urban gang activity in Los Angeles, Chicago, New York, Dallas, and San Francisco. Another alarming trend is the link between one of the groups, Los Zetas, with Hezbollah. This has spawned concern over an emerging link between drug trafficking and terrorism. Los Zetas uses Hezbollah in West Africa to launder drug profits, while Hezbollah uses the payoffs from Los Zetas to finance terrorist operations. There is speculation about an even closer link between Los Zetas and Iran, as some analysts believe that the drug cartel may have been involved in an assassination plot against the Saudi ambassador to the United States in late 2011 (Chalk, 2012).

Narcoterrorism Controversies

Not everyone accepts the link between drugs and terrorism. Some people argue that terrorists may use drugs as a source of income, but they also use several other illegal activities to raise money. Selling drugs is only one method, and the drug problem is not caused by terrorism. Other people believe that the use of the term *narcoterrorism* is an attempt to take political advantage of the fear of terrorism. If drugs and terrorism come to mean the same thing, it will be easier to take actions against drug dealers. Critics believe that combining the drug problem with terrorism confuses two different issues.

The 9/11 Commission (2004, pp. 171–172) dismisses the idea that drugs were linked to al Qaeda's attack on New York and Washington, D.C. There is no evidence, the commission writes, that indicates bin Laden used underground drug networks or narcotics trafficking to support the September 11 attacks. The Taliban used narcotics trafficking to support itself in Afghanistan, but bin Laden used a network of donors based in Saudi Arabia and the Gulf States.

In the same article in which he explains narcoterrorism, Adams (2003) acknowledges the critics. He points to skepticism about the military and DEA assessments of Latin America. Many critics believe these organizations have overstated the problem. Other people point to misunderstandings. Terrorists are not necessarily linked to the drug trade, even when they appear to be involved with drugs. Many Arabs live in the Triborder region, and they support Hamas and Hezbollah. Just because drug traders flourish in this region does not mean that either the Arabs or the terrorist groups are associated with drugs.

David Kaplan (2003) says the financing of militant Islamic groups has very little to do with the drug trade. Based on a five-month study for *U.S. News & World Report*, Kaplan blames Saudi Arabia for funding the spread of an intolerant form of Islam. Violent intolerance, he says, spawned the rise of terrorist groups, and the sect most sympathetic to an intolerant version of Islam comes from Saudi Arabia. Charities are responsible for the bulk of terrorist financing, he believes, and the money funds radical mosques, militant schools, and Islamic centers that support the jihadist movement. Saudi money can be traced to violence in Algeria, Bosnia, Kashmir, the West Bank, Gaza, Indonesia, Somalia, and Chechnya. The spread of militant Islam is not about drugs.

Pierre-Arnaud Chouvy (2004) does not agree with the position of the French military. He argues that the term *narcoterrorism* is too vague to describe either drug traffickers or terrorists, and it does not help address either problem. The problem with drugs involves supply and demand. Western Europe and North America provide ready markets for drug use. Typical Afghan farmers fight to survive. They produce opium, the base for heroin, because it is a cash crop. Western Europe has the demand, Chouvy says, and Afghanistan has the supply. Opium production has nothing to do with terrorism. *Narcoterrorism* is a convenient term for the French government to use, appealing to public emotions and giving the police more power.

Civil libertarians are especially critical of attempts to link terrorism and drugs (TalkLeft, 2003). Agreeing with Chouvy, they see the attempt to link narcotics and terrorism as a ploy by states. If terrorism were to disappear, the drug trade would remain. But if governments link drugs with terrorism, they can reinvent the meaning of crime. Drug dealers will become terrorists, and a frightened public will grant the government expanded powers to combat drugs. In addition, courts more readily grant search warrants and wiretaps against terrorists. Civil libertarians often believe governments want to define drug pushers as narcoterrorist kingpins in an effort to increase their own power.

Michael Scheuer (2006, pp. 42–44) takes the middle ground in the debate over narcoterrorism. In an examination of Osama bin Laden, Scheuer writes that the analyses of al Qaeda's use of heroin to finance jihad range from believable to fantastic accounts. Some reports of the narcotics connection are true, some are simply asserted without evidence, and a great deal of propaganda is obviously false. Nevertheless, the narcotics trade in Afghanistan makes billions of dollars. It would be naïve, Scheuer concludes, to assume that bin Laden has not been able to take advantage of some of those funds.

✓ Self-Check

> Define the two elements of narcoterrorism.
> What arguments support the idea?
> Why do some analysts reject the idea of narcoterrorism?

Emphasizing the Points

Money laundering is the process of converting the proceeds of crime into assets that can be used in the formal economy. Terrorist financing refers to illegal and legal methods of funding terrorism. For many years, analysts equated money laundering and terrorist financing, but today, the two processes are examined differently. Terrorists may also have a need to launder dirty money, such as NGO support of a militant group. Even with the shift in analysis, it is difficult to assess the effectiveness of antilaundering and antiterrorist financing efforts. The most prominent international tools are FATF recommendations, but the effectiveness of FATF measures are subject to debate. The federal government has created financial law enforcement and intelligence units to counter money laundering and terrorists financing, and the United States and Europe have championed a host of anti-terrorist economic measures. Terrorists employ a variety of illegal methods to obtain resources and sometimes move assets in hidden networks. Terrorist financing remains complex because there is no single method or path for obtaining resources. Some analysts have concluded that one of the most lucrative ways of raising money is selling illegal drugs.

SUMMARY OF CHAPTER OBJECTIVES

- *Money laundering* is a term that was first used to describe the actions of organized crime groups. They gathered money in a variety of illegal ways and claimed that their gains were profits generated by laundromats. It is the process of converting proceeds from crime into legitimate money.
- Terrorist financing refers to the methods used to fund terrorist groups or operations. It is extremely complicated because terrorists employ a variety of legal and illegal moneymaking methods.
- After 9/11, governments in the United States and Europe increased anti-money laundering efforts, assuming that this action would reduce terrorist financing. Many analysts slowly recognized subtle differences. Criminals commit crime then launder the proceeds. Terrorists, by contrast, distribute funds to commit crimes.

- The United States and Europe have sponsored international efforts to combat money laundering and terrorist financing, and the UN FATF recommendations are prominent among them. Critics contend that most nations do not comply with FATF recommendations and the regulatory system is ineffective. Supporters counter by arguing that the complex system will take time to construct. They also point to increased arrest and conviction rates based on financial investigations and intelligence.
- Financial investigative and intelligence units permeate federal law enforcement agencies and the intelligence community.
- Terrorists raise funds by a number of legal and illegal methods. Illegal methods include robbery, counterfeiting, fraud, cigarette smuggling, extortion, kidnapping, and a variety of other criminal activities. Terrorists also raise money through legal operations. They divert funds to support terrorist operations. Charities and business operations are the most frequent legal activities.
- Funds are disbursed in an underground economy or through traditional money laundering activities. These include hidden money transfers such as the Hawala. They also smuggle cash, launder money, convert it to consumer products, or keep the money or goods within the organization.
- The Hawala system is based on an old method merchants used to exchange money without risking transport of actual cash. It is based on agents who exchange promissory notes. Today, some terrorists use this system to fund operations.
- The political economy of terrorism involves groups that have the ability to act autonomously in shell states and failed states. Becoming a de facto government power, they control the movement of money, goods, and services.
- There is a debate about the relationship between illegal drugs and terrorism. Proponents believe that terrorists use drugs to finance operations, and they use the term *narcoterrorism* to describe this activity. Opponents argue that governments use the term to increase their own power by defining common criminals as terrorists.

LOOKING INTO THE FUTURE

Rapid changes in global economic networks and exchange mechanisms suggest that traditional economic structures are fading. Private exchange systems like Bicoin and Pay Pal are growing, and most economic transactions are electronic. New and changing economic systems provide opportunities for terrorists. They will also be vulnerable to terrorist attacks, especially when they are first introduced.

Forensic accounting will become crucial for effective national and international law enforcement agencies. U.S. law enforcement agencies will need to develop forensic accounting skills to face the future, but they probably will lag behind the capabilities of terrorists on the state and local levels. University trained accountants have many more lucrative employment opportunities when examining pay scales in state and local police agencies. Yet, there are alternatives. For example, partnerships with federal agencies can provide state and local forces with needed expertise. Teaching officers to recognize suspicious economic activity provides another path for future law enforcement. The U.S. Treasury Department's Suspicious Activity Report represents a step in that direction. No matter how they accomplish it, future law enforcement officers must develop the tools to thwart economic crime to deal with the economics of terrorism.

A second future need in law enforcement involves cyber skills, and these talents will be applicable to many forms of investigation and enforcement far beyond counterterrorism. Police of the future will need to improve computer competency and form partnerships with experts to assist in investigations. The FBI has been increasing efforts in this area for the past decade, and the future will bring a greater demand for cyber skills. The future may also bring greater cooperation among forensic computing experts in law enforcement, the military's Cyber Command, and private industry.

KEY TERMS

Capone discovery, p. 53
Placement, p. 54
Layering, p. 54
Integration, p. 54
Black market peso
    exchange, p. 54

Suppression of the
    Financing of
    Terrorism, p. 61
Financial Action Task
    Force on Money Laun-
    dering (FATF), p. 61

Forensic accounting,
    p. 64
Expropriation, p. 64
Triborder region, p. 67
Globalization, p. 67
Hawala system, p. 68

New economy of
    terrorism, p. 70
Failed state, p. 71
Shell state, p. 71
Narcoterrorism, p. 72

CHAPTER 4

Terrorism and the Media

LEARNING OBJECTIVES

After reading this chapter, you should be able to:

▶ Define the new media environment.

▶ Describe the characteristics of the new media.

▶ Explain how the Internet has impacted terrorism.

▶ Describe the way narrative can be presented in a hybrid frame.

▶ Summarize research trends with respect to terrorism and the media.

▶ Discuss the role of the media in constructing social reality.

▶ Explain the tension between security forces and the media.

▶ Describe how the media can be viewed as a weapon.

▶ Explain how news frames are used to present a story.

▶ Describe the special relationship between terrorism and television.

amer ghazal/Alamy

Social Media, the New Propaganda Tool

James Oliver Rigney Jr. (October 17, 1948–September 16, 2007), whose pen name was Robert Jordan, began publishing a massive fantasy series entitled *The Wheel of Time* in 1990. Sadly, he passed away in 2007, but Brandon Sanderson completed the 14-volume series masterfully. The books tell stories of a world where demons fly, women weave special powers from a mythical city called Tar Valon, young men and women seek their destinies, and good forces battle evil for control of creation. Of course, the series is the product of Rigney's imagination, yet the books contain quite a bit of truth about the human experience. One theme that occurs throughout the series is the way tales are passed by word of mouth. Readers are allowed to experience men and women struggling against evil through the eyes of the main protagonists. After the confrontations, the story spreads through fictional kingdoms, and the stories change. By the time they are told for the fifth, sixth, and seventh times, the stories do not resemble the original narrative. This is the way human beings share stories, and not merely the product of entertaining fiction.

On May 2, 2011, commandos from the U.S. Navy's elite counterterrorist SEAL Team landed in a compound north of Islamabad, Pakistan. Their target was one of the most infamous terrorists of all times, Osama bin Laden. The raid was successful. Shortly after the raid, President Barack Obama called President George Bush to give him the news. A few minutes later, Obama came on the major networks and announced that bin Laden was dead. Then the stories of the stories started to spread. Military experts and former commandos first appeared on cable television to give "authoritative" accounts of the raid. Network news broadcasts and nationally syndicated newspapers expanded stories of the raid the following day, complete with illustrations and graphics. The White House released an official version of the raid. A few days later, a SEAL publicly contested the official version, and television producers began focusing on documentaries to explain what "really" transpired. Within weeks, there were several versions of the story about the death of the world's most wanted terrorist. A year later, a firsthand account would be released in the book *No Easy Day* (Owen and Maurer, 2012). The narratives of bin Laden's death were told and retold with slight variations in the different renderings.

Events become stories in literature and in day-to-day life. Most stories are forgotten, but some of them are repeated. Twice-told stories evolve into sagas, and sagas change to legends. The *Wheel of Time* series demonstrates this process through literary fiction. The many versions of bin Laden's death arose in the world of electronic mass-mediated information. Hybrid narratives spread from two sources, the older slower mass media of print, radio, and television and the newer instantaneous social media and Internet.

The New Media Environment

Terrorists frequently seek to tell stories to publicize a cause. This implies that terrorist groups have a special relationship with the news media, and as terrorism evolved into an ideological phase in the 1960s and 1970s, it became a drama made for television. Terrorism provided the spectacle, and television news networks became the medium. The symbiotic relationship seemed to be made to last, but journalists and reporters realized they were being manipulated. Security force managers also learned that they often were pictured heroically when responding to terrorist violence, so instead of avoiding the media, they sought to portray the positive actions of their personnel. Terrorists still tried to maintain control of the message. They used media reports to magnify fear, but as media editors and producers constructed the stories, terrorists lost control. They searched for a solution, and they found a new weapon in a media revolution in the early twenty-first century.

In the past few years, mass media transformed into virtual communities of chat rooms, e-zines, forums, websites, YouTube postings, Facebook communications, and Twitter's social network. Not only did these forms of communication represent a new media, they gave terrorists the ability to completely control their message. The battlefield migrated from television to instant communication.

Defining the New Media

The mass media of newspapers, radio, and television could be defined as mass communication. The new methods of interaction also involve communication, but they

new media: Any virtual network that allows communication. It includes blogs, multiple Internet postings, and any social network.

allow selective connections among communities. Communication scholars refer to these selectively controlled methods of interaction as the **new media,** and they define the concept broadly. John Amble (2012) says the new media refer to any virtual network where communication takes place. New media include blogs, multiple Internet postings, and any social network. They are innovative, they frequently involve two-way communication, and they are growing at an astonishing rate.

Amble states that terrorists were quick to understand the power of the new media. They began to employ it in the 1990s as the Internet expanded, and they increasingly relied on it after it grew exponentially in the twenty-first century. He points to the rapid expansion of the Internet between 2000 and 2011 as connections spread across the globe.

In this time period, it grew by 2,000 percent in the Middle East and by an astronomical 15,000 percent in Pakistan. As the Internet developed, terrorist narratives started to spread. Government officials and media elites no longer held a monopoly on message selection. Anybody could create a narrative and make it available to a mass audience.

Aside from network expansion, Amble says that other factors influenced the growth and impact of the new media. As technology developed, the price of network devices dropped. Cell phones, computers, and other devices were cheap and plentiful. They were in the hands of billions of consumers. Additionally, improved digital technology increased the quality and quantity of communications. Devices became smaller and more powerful. Finally, increased bandwidth increased the ability of servers to process traffic. A communications revolution created a host of virtual communities.

Syrian civil war: A war that began in March 2011 in an attempt to overthrow President Bashir Assad. It is characterized by multiple groups fighting multiple enemies and has resulted in the deaths of thousands of people caught in the fighting. Opponents are divided along sectarian, ethnic, and political lines. It has attracted fighters from many countries, including nation states in Europe, North America, and Asia.

Jytte Klausen (2015), the primary investigator on a National Institute of Justice (NIJ) grant studying the impact of social media on terrorism, led a team of researchers who were investigating Twitter. Her team collected and analyzed data from 59 Westerners who joined jihadist groups in the **Syrian civil war** from January through March 2014. She says that Twitter, the most popular form of electronic communication for the target group, plays an important role in the strategy of violent radicals. It provides instant communication straight from the front lines with user-controlled narratives.

Twitter is particularly powerful, according to Klausen. It legitimizes messages because it brings the perception of authenticity, and it is socially accepted. For example, reporters in the old media of newspapers, radio, and television frequently cite Twitter as a legitimate source of information. In addition, journalists, analysts, and scholars working in the field of terrorism frequently follow each other on Twitter. It is readily available and highly mobile because it is specifically designed for cell phones. Appearances of authenticity increase as postings (tweets) are augmented with pictures and videos. Once tweeted, postings can be linked to other platforms or forwarded to multiple users. They can also be embedded in websites. Consumers believe they are receiving authentic information as they are vicariously placed in battle zones.

Characteristics of the New Media

There are several distinguishing characteristics that differentiate the new and old media. Television, radio, and print, to a lesser extent, are relatively rapid in the scope of human history, but slower than the new media. The old media is controlled by small groups of elite stakeholders who distribute selective information to targeted audiences. It transmits one version of a story to many people, and while elites may interact with the sources of a narrative, the audience can only consume the information. Consumers cannot collaborate or participate in developing a story.

None of the characteristics of the new media apply to the old. John Amble (2012) points out that several consumers can engage a story in multiple fashions. They may even become contributors, editing and commenting on stories they forward. In other words, Amble says, consumers become part of the stories they post. They control the message, interpret it as they wish, and forward it to selected audiences. If old media communication is characterized as one-way and one-to-many, new media is multipath and many-to-many.

The New Media and the Internet

In addition to the explosion of the new media, the Internet has a growing influence on the direction of terrorism. Metteo Vergani (2014) discovered this in a case study of an Italian convert to Islam who joined an al Qaeda-affiliated group in Syria. Vergani says that online experiences combine with actions, social ties, and the new media to allow potential terrorists to participate in a group. Physical proximity is not required, and virtual reinforcement of radical beliefs helps participants justify their extreme positions. Any participant can have access to propaganda and unfiltered news. Like-minded people can link across great distances, experimenting with new roles and identities. The new media and the Internet provide a platform for reinforcing polarization, violence, and hostility.

Jytte Klausen's (2015) study of Twitter revealed that Syrian jihadists give the illusion that Western recruits freely communicate with their old social networks at home. However, this is far from the truth. In reality, Western recruits surrender all communication devices when they arrive at a training camp, and they are threatened with death if they try to communicate with family and friends. While Twitter feeds give the illusion that messages are freely posted by a variety of fighters, only the most trusted recruits are allowed to post. The group controls the message. Vergani (2014) says the Internet takes over when the tweet stops.

In Vergani's case study, al Qaeda controlled the original symbols and ideology to present a single image, which is just as Klausen found. The ability to communicate was limited and regulated, but once a story was posted, the dynamics of the Internet came into play. As consumers engaged the story, some of them chose to participate in it. Stories were recast on the Internet resulting in multiple narratives far beyond the control of the group who released an original grassroots story. Multiple consumers were free to transform and personalize narratives. There were no limits to the manner in which a story could be retold each time it was remixed. Stories circulated and grew in much the same way that stories are passed through communities and cultures. Vergani says that these findings are applicable to communication within the new media and narratives evolve into hybrid stories more quickly than in the past due to the number of Internet platforms and their instant availability.

The subject of Vergani's case study entered a Syrian al Qaeda-linked group through the standard jihadist narrative; that is, the West has oppressed Muslims by establishing puppet governments, and it is the duty of all real Muslims to fight both the puppets and the West. Muslims are called to either come to or create a war zone, and wage jihad. This represents the tightly controlled message of the terrorist group; however, the original story is told and retold. In Vergani's study, the subject went to Syria to join a devoted brotherhood where jihadists are happily and willingly martyred for a cause. Yet, the narrative was retold on the Internet, and new elements of the story developed. Rebellious symbols were added with stories of adolescent angst. In turn, teenage unrest turned into revolutionary left-wing activity. One version of the tale combined jihadist martyrdom with Latin American Marxists, and contradictions continued to increase. Vergani's subject was pictured with scantily clad young women allegedly praising him for jihad, images al Qaeda would consider pornographic. The religious fanaticism of

Osama bin Laden was combined with the atheism of Che Guevara. Finally, a glorious Arab past was combined with an abstract history of Italian glory. The new grassroots story was a hybrid that differed greatly from the original.

Another combination of new media and Internet power can be seen in the emergence of propaganda e-zines, such as al Qaeda in the Arabian Peninsula's (AQAP) *Inspire*. It is a slick publication that urges consumers to wage war on their own home ground. The first sections of each professional e-zine are designed to motivate readers and provide them with information from the jihad. The next section focuses on "Open Source Jihad." It contains specific instructions for waging terrorism, for example, "Build a Bomb in the Kitchen of Your Mom."

The precise nature of the instructions is problematic for two reasons. First, the information is frequently simple and correct. Although some ideas are far fetched, others are on target. Anyone wanting to engage in violence has the instructions for doing so. Second, the information is more likely to encourage violence. If you say, "Lose weight," you are not likely to motivate an overweight person. If you say, "Here's a one-month meal plan of 1,800 calories a day and a three-day-a-week exercise routine," your words are more likely to result in action. "Open Source Jihad" does not say things such as, "Come to Yemen and wage jihad" or "Form a terrorist cell." However, it does tell potential terrorists how to take a standard pressure cooker, mix certain chemicals, and construct a workable fuse. This type of instruction is more likely to result in action (Lemieux et al., 2014). In fact, it actually did motivate bombers in Boston to attack the 2013 marathon with an exploding pressure cooker (Kahn, 2013).

Other Aspects of the Internet

The Internet impacts news coverage of all events and often exceeds the ability of the established media to report an event. It is also used for communication, propaganda, reporting, recruiting, training, and as a tactical weapon. Either side can directly control information or hack into opponents' websites. Both sides can mine data and gather intelligence. The Internet can be a weapon, and either side may use it effectively. Terrorists have learned to use it on several levels.

Todd Hinnen (2004) says that the Internet is used most frequently as a communication device and that sending unsecure email is the most common way terrorists use it. Unsecure email is easy to penetrate, and evidence from it is frequently used in criminal prosecutions. Hinnen cites charges against a Colombian terrorist group for arms trafficking based on evidence gathered from email. Terrorists, aware of the dangers of unsecure email, use a variety of methods to hide communications. One way, Hinnen writes, is to give an email account's password to several members of a group. A member can then draft a message but never send it. Other members log on, read the draft, and then delete it after all have viewed it. Because the message is never sent, there is no email record. A second method involves setting up a secure website, such as TerroristGroup.com, with its own email server. All members of a terrorist group would receive an address, such as jsmith@terroristgroup.com. If email stays exclusively within the secure site, it is difficult to trace.

Terrorists understand the power of the Internet. They run their own websites, and they sometimes hack into existing sites to broadcast propaganda videos. Yassen Zassoursky (2002) says that these abilities enhance the power of terrorist groups, and he believes that the Internet's communication capabilities give terrorist groups an opportunity to attack the global community. Sonia Liff and Anne Sofie Laegren (2003) reinforce Zassoursky's thesis by pointing to Internet cafés. They say that cybercafés enhance the Internet's striking power because they make communication untraceable.

Steganography is frequently said to be one of the Internet's greatest vulnerabilities in light of criminal and terrorist communication. The process refers to embedding hidden information in a picture, message, or other piece of information. The process is not new. A Roman general once shaved the head of a slave, had a secret message tattooed on the slave's head, and waited for the slave's hair to grow back. When the message was covered, he sent the slave to the recipient with instructions to shave the slave's head (Lau, 2003). Obviously, the Internet presents possibilities for faster communication, and it does not present the risk of permanently displaying the message if the messenger goes bald! A steganographic message can be encrypted, placed in plain text in a hidden file, or sent via a covert channel (Westphal, 2003). There are numerous potential purposes for using steganography in terrorism. It could be used to hide communications, steal information from security forces or an organization within the critical infrastructure, or provide opportunities for an electronic attack (Wingate, 2006).

> **Steganography:** Embedding a hidden encoded message on an Internet site.

There are two positions on the steganographic threat to the United States. Stephan Lau (2003) says one position claims that steganography is used by terrorist groups to communicate and launch cyberattacks. After 9/11, for example, media reports claimed that al Qaeda was hiding information in steganographic images. Some believe that it will be used in denial-of-service attacks or to deface websites. Lau takes a different position, claiming that fear of steganography is the stuff of urban legends. Although steganographic programs are readily available and difficult to detect or counter with security hardware, programs offering statistical analysis of data contained in any Internet transmission readily reveal irregularities and the location of any hidden image. Entrepreneurs are marketing these programs to corporations and governments, but Lau believes the threat is not in the hidden image. He says that there is no evidence to show that terrorists' use of steganography is a threat. The real threat, Lau argues, is the American government's enhanced ability to decipher private communications based on a threat that does not exist.

In the areas of propaganda, reporting, and public relations, the Internet has been a boon for terrorist groups. It allows terrorist groups to present messages and to portray images that will not appear in mainstream media. Paul Wilkinson (2006, pp. 144–157) says that terrorists have always used some medium for communication. In the past, it ranged from tavern gossip to handbills. Thus, it is logical to assume that the Internet serves the same purpose, now literally at the speed of light. Major terrorist groups run websites to present alternative views. For example, before its demise in 2009, the Liberation the of Tamil Eelam (LTTE) ran a news service formerly called the Eelam-Website Violent single-issue groups use websites for propaganda as well (see the section later in this chapter titled "Expanding the Concept: As Sahaab versus al Hurra").

The Internet can also be used for recruitment and training. Abdul Bakier (2006b) finds Salafi jihadists using websites and email to make training manuals available. The Internet has become more important as more females join the **Salafi movement**. One blogger, who identifies herself as the mother of bin Laden, claims that the Internet gives women the opportunity to become *mujahidat* (female holy warriors). Bakier finds some sites are specifically aimed at recruiting or retaining females. Other sites encourage suicide bombings. Discussion groups examine tactics and provide basic weapons orientation, and some militant scholars provide in-depth theological apologias to justify religious violence. One site has an entire first-aid course to deal with battlefield wounds. Bakier says that more and more groups are using recruiting sites.

> **Salafi movement:** Used by orthodox Muslims to follow the Prophet and the elders of the faith. Militants narrow the use of the term and use it to justify violence. The Salafi movement refers to those people who impose Islam with force and violence.

The Internet is also used in target selection, reconnaissance, and, sometimes, as a tool to support an attack. Maps, satellite imagery, and diagrams provide ready-made intelligence sources. Stephen Ulph (2006a) sees terrorists increasingly using Internet searches to find economic targets. He believes this trend is notable because terrorists

EXPANDING THE CONCEPT

As Sahaab Versus al Hurra

Al Qaeda's media campaign has proved difficult for the United States to counteract. Al Qaeda's underground video network, known as As Sahaab, wages an effective propaganda campaign using the Internet. Evan Kohlmann (2005), an NBC terrorism analyst, explains the process. Local camera operators film studio sequences of a propaganda statement or live-action footage of mujahedeen along the Pakistan–Afghanistan border. The footage is edited on a computer, dubbed or subtitled, and handed over to an Internet group called al Fajir, which posts links to the clip in Arab chat forums. (Ironically, most of these forums are hosted in North America.) Television networks pick up the broadcasts. Western networks heavily edit them, but, on networks like al Jazeera, they sometimes appear as full-length broadcasts, according to the Discovery Times Channel (2005). In its own media offensive, the United States launched al Hurra, an Arabic-language 24-hour satellite station, in early 2004. The results have been disappointing. One prominent Arab writer called the $62 million project the American *Pravda*, after the Communist news organization in the former Soviet Union (Cochrane, 2004). The Discovery Times Channel agreed, stating that most Arabic-speaking viewers distrust the news produced by al Hurra. In essence, a few thousand dollars invested in website cams, PCs, and video software have made more of an impact than a multimillion-dollar television enterprise. The United States has yet to capitalize on the Internet for spreading propaganda.

Sources: Kohlmann, 2005; Discovery Times Channel, 2005; Cochrane, 2004.

across the globe can unite and research a particular target in a matter of minutes. He also finds terrorist groups attracted to data mining. One terrorist training manual points out that it is possible to gather information on enemy targets simply by using the Internet. Ulph (2006b) also sees the Internet as a potential weapon. Terrorists want to take hacker warfare to their enemies. Groups post methods to steal passwords and instructions for breaking into secure areas. There are instructions on systems and denial-of-service attacks, as well. As a logistical tool, the Internet can also be used to assemble people for a violent action. Clearly, the Internet has become a weapon in many arsenals.

But there is another side to the story. Security forces also use new media, and they do so effectively. Researchers have access to databases, government reports, and other information. Security forces also monitor websites and chat rooms (Wright, 2008). New laws in a number of countries have given law enforcement and intelligence agencies the authority to monitor Internet content for criminal activity, although such surveillance is controversial in Western democracies (Brown, 2009). Law enforcement networks in the Regional Information Sharing System (RISS) have the ability to share criminal investigative information, and they provide local, state, and federal law enforcement with secure communications. The Internet can thus be used to combat terrorism and other forms of criminal activity. Terrorism researchers and security specialists use Twitter to communicate, gather intelligence, and to follow select terrorists (McCants, c.2014).

✓ **Self-Check**

> What is the new media, and how can it be characterized?
> How do the new media and the Internet interact?
> Is the Internet a potential weapon for terrorism? Why or why not?

Trends in Research

Jeffery Ian Ross (2007) raises several important points about the need to research the relationship between terrorism and the old news media. In essence, many criminologists and analysts discuss it, but there remains much to be learned. Studies tend to repeat one another, revealing little new material. Terrorism requires interdisciplinary research because it involves so many aspects of the human experience, and its relationship with the media has not been fully explored. Ross concludes that the range of publications and research adds very little new knowledge.

Ross believes that there are several areas in need of new research, though we do know something about the relationship between the media and terrorism. First, meanings are socially created, and Ross demonstrates that reporting is part of the social construction of terrorism. Second, terrorists are aware of the power of the media and seek to manipulate their message through it. Third, while the media enhances the power of terrorism, it does not cause it. Finally, terrorists will increasingly use the Internet to communicate as the relationship between the media and terrorism grows stronger in the future.

A Set of Empirical Findings on Twitter

Jytte Klausen's (2015) detailed empirical analysis of Westerners using Twitter in the Syrian civil war is a perfect answer to Ross's call for more research. Her team's findings demonstrate several aspects of the use of new media. The main purpose of terror media is to generate propaganda. Klausen says Syrian jihadists glorify martyrdom. We fighters are supreme, they say, and the enemy is worthless. Dead jihadists are frequently cleaned up before being photographed, and corpses may be posed with smiles as if the subjects died happily. Videos show comrades lovingly burying their dead, while enemy dead are gruesomely depicted. Many photographs and videos show executions to create fear in a psychological war. By mid-June 2014, one particularly violent Syrian-Iraqi group began posting pictures of crucified victims. It also featured pictures of piles of severed heads and videos of victims being buried alive.

Frequency distributions of types of tweets revealed common categories from Syrian jihadists. In written communication, Klausen found that tweets centered around religious indoctrination, battle reports, interpersonal communication, everyday life, and delivering threats to the West. Religion dominated written communication, with four out of five tweets focusing on religious dogma. Klausen's team originally believed they would find postings dominated by practical communication and discussions with friends back home. Instead, they found Twitter feeds presenting unsophisticated dogmatic religious statements.

Pictures and videos revealed a different pattern. The most common visual images emphasized combat and territory gains. Pictures depicting lifestyles were the next most common. They emphasized the glory of jihad. The final frequency-ranked video tweets focused on innocent victims murdered by enemies; portrayals of martyrdom followed, and the least common category included images of retribution (although Klausen did record 93 pictures and videos of retribution). An interesting spin-off revealed a growing gender role in religious violence. The next chapter of this text presents evidence that females tend to play supporting roles in nationalistic and religious-based terrorist movements, but Klausen reveals a growing Western network of women who are playing an important role in jihadist communication. Wives and mothers of European jihadists are linking with their counterparts in Syria and Iraq.

Televised Gender Stereotypes

Television also impacts the way women are viewed in terrorist organizations. Although women have played significant roles in modern terrorism and have frequently assumed positions of leadership, television tends to portray women as minor figures in a male-dominated occupation. Brigitte Nacos (2005) finds that television depicts female terrorists in a manner similar to the way women politicians are portrayed. The result is that women are cast in supportive and nurturing roles devoid of any personality characteristics required for tough political action. Women are treated with typical gender clichés that are, in turn, captured and restated in television reporting. Television generates the same stereotypes for female terrorists and politicians.

Nacos presents several images created by television news frames. She discusses the "physical appearance" frame, which focuses on the way a woman looks in front of the camera. The "family connection" frame is used to create the appearance of a "typical housewife." The "terrorist for the sake of love" depicts a lovelorn female entering a life of terrorism due to her relationship with her male companion. The "women's lib" frame paints a picture of a nontraditional woman seeking to define herself in a more masculine role, as does the "tough as men—tougher than men" news frame. Finally, news frames also depict women as bored, frustrated housewives who are out of touch with reality.

The result of such depictions, Nacos concludes, is that television misrepresents the threat of terrorism by misstating the dangerous role that female terrorists play. Instead of looking at the actual activities of women, television portrays them via gender stereotypes. The traditional method of framing female politicians has weakened in recent years, Nacos says, but the same is not true for the images of women terrorists. As a result, women are able to use their television-generated images to avoid detection. Gender-biased reports weaken our ability to respond to terrorism.

> ✓ **Self-Check**

> > Why is it necessary to gather empirical evidence about the media and terrorism?
> > What do Twitter postings reveal about Westerners fighting in Syria?
> > What biases appear from research on gender and reporting?

The Media and Socially Constructed Reality

Communication and socially constructed images are part of human culture. Traditionally, people told stories around campfires. The invention of writing radically changed communication, but oral traditions remained strong because most people were illiterate. The printing press revolutionized writing, and increased education added to its impact as literacy spread. Harnessing electricity allowed communication across great distances, but the invention of radio and television transformed images into symbols. New media represents another transmogrification. As the late Marshal McLuhan said, the medium is the message. Unless a person experiences terrorism, various media define it.

When a television report covers terrorism, it presents a number of images that represent reality. Newspaper articles frequently print photographs to enhance a report, and reality in a radio report becomes the images multiple listeners are creating with their minds. The same factors apply to new media. Consumers experience an event through the media, not by actual participation. It is important to remember that all of these interpretations do not represent objective reality. They are presented within a social context and interpreted by individuals. Further, whether on television or Twitter, a report is framed and presented within a social context. The meaning of terrorism is socially constructed, and the media provides a large part of the interpretation (Munson, 2008).

News Frames and Presentations

Although communication scholars debate the definition, David Levin (2003) says reporting patterns are packaged in segments called **news frames**. The purpose of a news frame is to assemble words and pictures to create a pattern surrounding an event. The news becomes a symbolic representation of an event in which the audience is allowed to participate from a distance. Television and other media spin the event so that it can be translated into the understanding of popular culture. They use rhetoric and popular images to set the agenda, and the drama becomes the hook to attract an audience.

News frames form the basis for communicating symbols. Karim Karim (2001, pp. 18–19) says the news frame creates a narrative for understanding a deadly drama. Characters are introduced, heroes and villains are defined, and victims of violence become the suffering innocents. The people who produce the frame provide their interpretation to the audience. Because the news frame exists within the dominant political context of the producers, it is not necessary to expend a great amount of energy on propaganda. The audience has been indoctrinated by journalists and mainstream reporters who present governmental officials as protectors and terrorists as villains. The news frame provides the "correct" symbolism for the consumer.

Simon Cottle (2006) believes that news frames help "mediatize" the presentation of terrorism; that is, they shape the way an event is communicated. The news frame is used by all media, but it is especially applicable to television. The news frame, although intentionally used, is one of the least understood aspects of broadcast journalism because its complexity goes unnoticed. Discussions of news frames usually focus on a specific story, or they involve reducing ideas to common elements. Actually, Cottle says, selecting from among the different styles of news frames presents an issue in a particular fashion. The classic approach in television is the **reporting frame**. It is usually short and designed to provide the latest information. Although facts and figures are presented, the story fails to focus on context or background. It is superficial, reducing reality to violent actions and reactions, while the underlying causes of conflict are ignored.

Types of Frames

Other frames complement the reporting frame, according to Cottle. A dominant frame presents a story from a single point of view. An authority figure or institution defines the story in this type of frame. Closely related is the conflict frame, which presents a story frame with two views, each side having experts or witnesses to support a position. A contention frame summarizes a variety of views, and investigative frames champion the role of the press as the protectors of democracy. Cottle identifies other frames designed to serve the community, enhance collective decision making, and enrich social understanding of an event (see the section later in this chapter titled "Expanding the Concept: Communication Frames"). Frames can also campaign for a single interpretation of an event or provide in-depth coverage beyond the shallowness of a reporting frame. Finally, Cottle says, television news presents a mythic frame, which reinforces deeply held values. This frame is frequently used to depict those people who have sacrificed their lives for a cause. The combination of all these communication frames complicates the presentation of the news on terrorism.

news frames: Visual, audible, or written packages used to present the news. Communication scholars do not agree on a single definition, but news frames generally refer to the presentation of the news story. They contain a method for beginning and ending the story, and they convey the importance of characters and actions as the story is told.

reporting frame: The simplest form of a news frame. It is a quick, fact-driven report that summarizes the latest information about a story. It does not need to contain a beginning or an end, and it assumes that the consumer understands the context of the facts.

Communication Frames

Simon Cottle (2006) says that news frames are complex because they are composed of a variety of communication frames. Terrorism is reported within the following types of frames:

- Reporting frames: superficial, short, and laced with facts
- Dominant frames: one authority's view
- Conflict frames: two sides, with experts
- Contention frames: a variety of positions
- Investigative frames: exposure of corrupt or illegal behavior
- Campaigning frames: the broadcaster's opinion
- Reportage frames: in-depth coverage with background
- Community service frames: information for viewers
- Collective interest frames: reinforcement of common values
- Cultural recognition frames: a group's values and norms
- Mythic tales frames: hero stories

Ambiguous Stories and News Frames

News frames give the story a structured meaning, but sometimes a story defies structure. The frame is centered on getting viewers' attention, presenting information, and revealing the results. But what happens when the results are inconclusive? Frank Durham (1998) answers this question by looking at the crash of TWA Flight 800, a passenger airliner that exploded over the Atlantic Ocean shortly after taking off from JFK Airport in New York City in 1996. Durham believes that the news frame works when a report is based on sources with definitive explanations of an event. There were no solid answers in the TWA crash, however, and no authority emerged with a definitive story on the crash. Durham tracked reporting in 668 stories from the *New York Times* for one year following the explosion. Dominant news frames emerged, but all were proved incorrect.

Durham concludes that ambiguity destroys the ability to create a sustainable news frame. Reporters covering TWA 800 expected to find facts that would reveal a logical cause. They looked to terrorism, a missile strike, and finally mechanical error. In the first months following the crash, neither facts nor logical conclusions pointed to an answer. As a result, Durham says, the *New York Times* could not produce a news frame for the story.

Durham's conclusion might have an interesting effect on understanding terrorism. If terrorism is reported in well-defined news frames, both the media and the consumer will assume that there is a political beginning, a violent process, and a logical end. If there is ambiguity about the story, however, the method by which reporters gather the story and present it becomes the story because there is no logical conclusion. Currently, most media outlets report terrorist events within the logic of a well-defined frame (see Althaus, 2002). When violence is ambiguous and continual, the frame loses meaning, and terrorism is reported as an endless cycle of violence. As Leon Uris (1977, p. 815) writes in *Trinity*, a novel about Anglo-Irish conflict in Ulster, there is no future in Ireland, just the cycles of the past. And cycles may not be amenable to news frames.

Neglecting the Domestic Front

Brigitte Nacos, Yaeli Bloch-Elkon, and Robert Shapiro (2008) do not question the media's focus on counterterrorism, but they do suggest that the focus is improperly centered on overseas actions. While international events are important, domestic terrorism is just as crucial. The problem is that the media has virtually ignored domestic security issues.

The public depends on the mass media for information about issues. In turn, public perceptions formed by news stories frequently set the agenda for political policies. There is a strong correlation between the issues that the public thinks are important and the actions taken by political leaders. Communication scholars argue that one of the most important roles of the free press in a democracy is to make sure that critical issues stay in the news. At the same time, heightened competition for audiences creates an atmosphere in newsrooms in which shocking and dramatic information trumps complex stories dealing with nonsensational issues. In other words, attacks against known terrorist leaders in Yemen or Pakistan draw more attention than mundane congressional hearings on port security.

Nacos and her colleagues looked at several hundred news accounts in the first decade of counterterrorist action after 9/11 and found that the American news media did not believe there was a need to focus on domestic security. The media's main focus was on perceived threats overseas. For example, the researchers examined all of the terrorism stories on ABC News, CBS News, and NBC News during a 39-month period. The three networks aired a total of 85 stories related to homeland security. During the same time frame, the networks ran 373 stories dealing with the threat of terrorism. Most of the stories about security were aired after some type of public security breach. The researchers believe their findings indicated television's preference for sensational events.

The threat of terrorism is real, and it demands some type of response. While some scholars are quick to condemn any type of military action or the use of deadly force in response to political violence, Nacos and her colleagues did not question the necessity of acting with force. Their focus was on the national security agenda as portrayed by media reporting. There is a need to examine the threat, they argue, but the need for domestic security is just as important. By not analyzing the complex factors related to securing the American public, the media has deemphasized homeland security. The researchers conclude that this is a dangerous situation.

Terrorism and Television

Benjamin Barber (1996, pp. 76–83) analyzes the problems of news frames and popular images on television in *Jihad vs. McWorld*. The title suggests that he is examining the world of the jihadists, but, in fact, he is looking at global economic inequities and the resulting ideologies that drive people into different systems. Instead of moving people to discuss solutions to problems, Barber believes, the media flourishes on one overriding factor: entertainment. He humorously calls the 24-hour news networks the **infotainment telesector**.

The infotainment telesector is not geared for depth; rather, it is designed to create revenue. "News" becomes banter between a host and a guest, and debates devolve into shouting matches between controversial representatives of various points of view. Issues are rarely systematically discussed. Hosts perpetually interrupt their guests or provide answers to their own questions. Many news talk shows feature debates between pleasing personalities who frequently have no grasp on the complexities of terrorism, yet they fill the airwaves with opinions. There are some excellent cable and network news shows, but there are also a host of news entertainment productions.

These contexts of the infotainment telesector and the desire to beat the other networks have a negative effect on homeland security. Documents are leaked, confidential plans are unveiled, and vulnerabilities are exposed. Terrorism is made more

infotainment telesector: A sarcastic term to describe cable news networks. It refers to news organizations producing stories to entertain their audiences under the guise of presenting objective information.

horrific to create better drama. News film is constantly replayed, giving the illusion that attacks are repeated time and time again. News hosts spend time interviewing reporters from the field who speculate on the facts surrounding an event. This leads to a dilemma for policymakers. Freedom of the press is guaranteed in the First Amendment to the Constitution, but television coverage frequently becomes part of the story it is covering.

Over the years, several studies have pointed to the close relationship between terrorism and television. H. H. A. Cooper (1977a) was one of the first analysts to point to the issues, explaining that terrorist acts were made-for-TV dramas. Abraham Miller (1982) published one of the first books on the subject, pointing out that television brought terrorist events into our homes. More recently, Yassen Zassoursky (2002) says that television and the Internet give terrorists an immediate international audience. Gadt Wolfsfeld (2001) says acts have become so graphic and sensational that they grab media attention. In one of the best standard-setting studies, Alex Schmid and Jany deGraaf (1982) say that the relationship between terrorism and the media is so powerful that Western democracies may need to take drastic action and even implement censorship.

David Levin (2003) says that the purpose of television news coverage is to keep the audience primed with emotion and excitement. News organizations use a standard drama pattern to accomplish this. It is designed to keep the viewer tuned to the station. The attention-getting theme is the essence of the drama.

A drama pattern is constant in any unfolding event. On-the-scene reporters send reports back to the anchor, who calmly sits at the desk gathering information, sometimes asking urgent questions to clarify issues for the audience. The hidden meaning of the report intimates that the station has crucial information on "breaking news," and members of the audience need to know it. The anchor is the authority figure who is able to process information for the viewers. Reporters are the researchers sending the latest information back from the scene. The overriding message of the drama is "stay tuned." It is the pattern of Greek tragedy, and it works for television—whether covering the weather, terrorism, election results, or *Football Night in America* (see the following section titled "Expanding the Concept: TV Drama Patterns").

EXPANDING THE CONCEPT

TV Drama Patterns

What makes a good news drama?

Change: The situation is changing, and the outcome is unknown.

Information: The latest news and breaking news about the situation is on this station.

Stay tuned: You must keep watching; the best is yet to come.

Expertise: Only this station is qualified to explain the situation.

On-the-scene reports: Reporters are there telling you what is happening, even when they do not know.

Control: The anchor controls the information from the studio, giving you a vicarious feeling of control.

Participation: You are allowed to vicariously participate in the event.

Money: The station breaks away to sponsors but promises even more drama after the commercial.

End of the Western Monopoly on the Old News Media

Control of the drama pattern was held by a Western monopoly until recently. New networks such as **al Jazeera** and al Arabia have challenged the West's—especially the American—hold on international news. If there is an effect from 24-hour cable news slanted toward a particular interpretation, new national perspectives influence it (Gilboa, 2005). In addition, localized networks present other perspectives and definitions of terrorism. Judith Harik (2004, pp. 160–161, 189) points out that Hezbollah has learned to do this by projecting a positive image on Lebanese national television. She says Hezbollah took advantage of **al Manar** television, Lebanon's network, as the Israelis withdrew from Lebanon and again during the **al Aqsa Intifada**.

Al Manar television presented a sympathetic view of the al Aqsa uprising, and Hezbollah was quick to take advantage of al Manar's 24-hour coverage. The method of reporting was the key to success. The news was interspersed with inspirational religious messages. Hezbollah was able to get al Manar to focus on Hezbollah's role in the intifada and to run programs on its former glories. In an effort to demoralize the Israelis, al Manar broadcast pictures of Israeli casualties and ended with the question: "Who will be next?"

Power came in the form of visual images. Harik believes al Manar television helped elevate Hezbollah to heroic status. She cites one example whose effect swept through Lebanon: Faced with heavy fighting in a West Bank village, Israeli forces withdrew. The Israeli Defense Forces (IDF), using Israeli mass media, denied they had abandoned the village. But al Manar presented another view. When the Israelis withdrew, Hezbollah fighters entered the village along with Palestinian mujahedeen. Hezbollah raised its flag over the village, and someone took a picture. As the IDF was denying it had retreated, al Manar showed the village with the Hezbollah flag flying high overhead. Hezbollah achieved a media victory.

Television makes the viewing audience participants in a terrorist attack. Viewers have short- and long-term psychological damage after seeing terror attacks on television, and this damage shapes anxiety and attitudes. Anat Shoshoni and Michelle Sloan (2008) measured the reactions of 300 university students in Israel after they had been exposed to terrorist violence on television. Looking at levels of anxiety and anger, they wanted to see if attitudes and perceptions of the enemy and the willingness to accept negative group stereotypes would be affected. Unlike the immediate experiences of anxiety and anger, attitudes are generally formed over a long period of time.

The experiment began with a survey to measure anxiety and attitude. After the survey, students were shown two 7-minute video clips, one of a terrorist attack and the other of nonterrorist violence from the same group, and the researchers conducted a second set of measurements. As they had expected, Shoshoni and Sloan found that anger and anxiety increased, but they also saw that long-term attitudes changed within the same time frame. In other words, the violent vignettes not only increased short-term fear, they were also responsible for fear and anxiety long after the students viewed the videos.

Television seeks drama, and terrorism provides an unfolding dramatic event. Tyler Cowen (2006) argues that terrorism is a spectacle that has a focal point, various actors, and a storyline. Television news coverage works well with such spectacles. Dramatic moving shots can be played over and over, while in-depth analysis gives background to an eager audience. Terrorist leaders need the unfolding drama, too. It allows them to motivate followers and increase their control over an organization.

al Jazeera: An international Arabic television network.

al Manar: Hezbollah's television network.

al Aqsa Intifada: An uprising sparked by Ariel Sharon's visit to the Temple Mount with a group of armed escorts in September 2000. The area is considered sacred to Jews, Christians, and Muslims. Many Palestinians were offended, and a new round of violence ensued.

> **Self-Check**
>
> \> What various frames construct the multiple realities of terrorist events?
>
> \> Why do terrorism and television have a special relationship?
>
> \> How has the growth of non-Western media impacted interpretations of terrorism?

Issues in the Media

The new media environment involves propaganda and persuasion. Nobody would claim that it is objective. The way issues are reported and framed in the old media is another matter. For example, Fox News claims to be "fair and balanced." Critics maintain it is not, but supporters believe that it presents objective reports. National Public Radio (NPR) reporting is debated in the same manner, and conservative critics frequently believe that NPR has a liberal bias. Many critics also claim that MSNBC has become the mouthpiece for political liberals. Such debates are not easily resolved, and the arguments favoring one side or the other are frequently full of opinions rather than hard evidence. Before leaving the discussion of the media, it would be helpful to review some of these issues.

Biases in the Old Media

While some representatives of the old media admit their slanted perspectives, the U.K.'s *Guardian* for instance, many mainstream media claim to be objective when presenting information about terrorism. They know governments and terrorists are trying to manipulate news stories, so they seek an ideal—objectivity. Many reporters believe that it is their job simply to tell the truth. They seek to be fair and balanced, as Fox News claims to be. These assumptions are naïve, according to former CBS employee Bernard Goldberg (2003, pp. 103–114). All news comes with a slant, and reporters are expected to create news frames reflecting their outlet's orientation. For people outside the newsroom, the debate is intense. At one end of the spectrum, critics claim that the media has a liberal bias. Critics fume, claiming that print and electronic media are inherently anti-Western and anti-American (see Bozell, 2005; Anderson, 2005). These critics claim reporters are sympathizing with terrorism at worst or undermining the government at best.

Pundits and other nonscholars attack this position. They claim that the media has been taken over by conservatives. Conservative talk show hosts and guests banter about pseudofacts, which reinforces right-wing ideology. Guests are invited on these programs only to be bombarded with conservative ranting. The critics claim that the news media is dominated by bullies and hatemongers who seek to silence any voice but their own. Reporting on terrorism cannot be objective in such a format, as it is designed to create fear and limit individual freedom (see Anderson, 2005; Willis, 2005).

Is there bias in the coverage of terrorism? Some scholars think so, but it is much more subtle and complicated than the writers of popular diatribes believe. Rather than joining the debate by measuring the amount of conservatism or liberalism in news content, Daniel Sutter (2001) analyzes the economic aspects of news production. He asks, What incentives would generate a bias, and why would a profit-making entity risk losing an audience? One of Sutter's answers comes in the form of an analogy. Suppose the public is composed of 600 television news viewers who are liberal, moderate, or conservative. By statistical distribution, 300 viewers would fall in the middle, or moderate, category. The remaining 300 would divide equally between liberals and conservatives. A news organization, as a profit-making entity, has an incentive to attract the largest possible audience. If the news moved either to the right or left, it would be threatened with the loss of mainstream viewers. Sutter sees no incentive for a liberal or conservative bias. Or does the media have a bias that is neither liberal nor conservative? (See the following feature titled "Another Perspective: Media Ownership.")

ANOTHER PERSPECTIVE

Media Ownership

Edward Herman (1999) focuses on the social construction of reality and political bias when he examines the media, but not from the perspective of most critics. The bias is economic, he says, and it is dominated by multinational corporations. The American media is part of a vast propaganda machine promoting the values and goals of business corporations. He conducts case studies examining advertising, ownership, and content to demonstrate the point. Stories affecting corporate profits are manipulated in a positive way. Dictators are portrayed as moderate or benign when they favor corporate investments and profits, even as the same leaders repress or massacre their own citizens. Newspapers use catchphrases such as "free trade," "third-world elections," and other simplifications to hide the powerful economic forces behind political action. The political bias is neither liberal nor anti-American; it is based in its market orientation.

There is a caveat in his logic, Sutter admits, because some media organization owners are willing to sacrifice profit to stand for a political position. In addition, some journalists insert their own feelings into a story, even when these feelings do not reflect the owner's position. These factors are countered by trends in the profit-driven media. First, if the entire media were to exhibit a bias, one owner would need to have a monopoly on all media outlets. One company can afford to take a position, Sutter says, but the entire industry will not. Second, journalism is a profession. Work is reviewed and approved by editors and also reviewed by colleagues. Individual bias is readily identified, but each journalist or reporter thinks and presents news separately. This process prevents an overall bias in the industry. Third, as news organizations expand, there will be pressures for a bias to develop special audiences among liberals and conservatives. Yet, the media will remain market driven, and the entire industry will not take up the biases of a limited, specialized audience. Finally, news organizations are increasingly led by boards and groups of owners driven by the desire to make money. They do not have the incentive to introduce bias that alienates their mainstream viewers.

David Baron (2004) takes a different approach, suggesting that bias appears on two levels: the individual discretion of the reporter collecting information for a story and the public's desire to watch or read the most captivating story. Small portions of a reporter's individual bias may slip into the story, but the corporation presenting the news will limit it. The business wants the greatest number of viewers, hence revenue, it can attract; therefore, it keeps reporters focused on captivating issues. The organization also wants to tailor the report to the beliefs and values of the audience. Therefore, there is very little incentive for bias. The one exception deals with reporters' salaries. Less objective news appealing to a specialized, politically biased audience can mean lower overall wages for reporters. Baron says that reporters who frame stories within a political bias do not need critical thinking and discernment skills. Therefore, station managers can pay them less and increase profits. There is a risk in this process, however, because bias may lower consumption, resulting in less income and lower profits. News corporations want to avoid risk and will keep major biases out of their stories.

Tim Groseclose and Jeffrey Milyo (2005) come to a different conclusion, stating that the American media has a liberal bias. Using multiple variables, Groseclose and Milyo selected a variety of media outlets, including newspapers, magazines, and television and radio news shows, to study. They limited their study to news items, eliminating editorials, commentaries, book reviews, and other opinion pieces from their study. They then selected think tanks and research organizations those media outlets used to provide information, guidance, and evaluation on governmental programs and policies. Next, they divided Congress into liberal and conservative members and counted the number of times liberals and conservatives cited a think tank. Finally, they compared the number of times each selected news source cited the same think tank and compared this to the congressional numbers. They concluded that the news media cited the think tanks referenced by liberal members of Congress more than they cited the think tanks referenced by conservative members. Groseclose and Milyo concluded that the American news media has a strong liberal bias.

Fouzi Slisli (2000) is not concerned with a liberal or conservative orientation; instead, he focuses on the use of pejorative labels. He believes adjectives introduce bias into the news. Citing sensationalism and failure to conduct in-depth reporting, Slisli says that the American media is full of oversimplifications and stereotypes. The media plays to the lowest level of understanding among its viewers. Large groups of people are lumped together in news reports that have no intention of examining complexities. False categories are created to further simplify issues.

David Levin (2003) examines the reporting of peace processes, intimating that it has the problems of simplification, the inability of the audience to understand complexities, and a network's desire to attract an audience. The news is aimed at particular audiences, and different organizations approach audiences in a variety of ways. Information and education stations approach the news differently than do 24-hour cable news networks that focus on entertainment and emotions. It is difficult to explain sufficiently well the nature of the conflict, the various political positions, internal fighting within governments and terrorist organizations, and other issues surrounding attempts to bring peace to areas such as Sri Lanka, the Basque region of Spain, Israel and Palestine, and Ireland. Many people prefer simplicity and entertainment. Thus, many news programs and some networks search for an unreflective audience, playing to the most susceptible members of the audience. Some producers even attempt to find a supermarket-tabloid audience by searching for the lowest common denominator among them, that is, people who want to be spoon-fed and entertained. These shows exploit emotions, favor sensation over facts, fail to examine issues in depth, and place entertainment value above information.

Information networks approach the same issues with different objectives. They seek to educate their audiences. Their shows are thoroughly researched and focus on the complexity of information. Their purpose is to inform, and they seek an audience that wants to reflect, criticize, and analyze. They introduce the intricacies of competing interpretations of information and accept ambiguity as normal. When trying to bring peace to an area plagued by political violence and terrorism, subtlety and complexity are the norm.

Richard Miniter (2005) shifts the argument to accuracy. He states that the media used to have a conservative bias, but now it has tilted toward liberalism. This is not the problem, however. The issue for the media is that it is spreading incorrect information about terrorism. He identifies 22 misconceptions about terrorism accepted as truth by most newspapers, magazines, and broadcasters. The myths come from a variety of sources, including honest mistakes in reporting, American and foreign government disinformation, and contrived leaks. Although the myths are accepted by much of the media and the public, they obfuscate terrorism because they are untrue (see the section later in this chapter titled "Another Perspective: Miniter's Media Myths"). Miniter is an investigative journalist, and he cites many credible sources. However, other investigative journalists citing other credible sources disagree with some of his findings (for example, see Gordon and Trainor, 2006; Ricks, 2006).

Creating Critical Reflection in the Audience

Whether biased or not, superficial coverage in the old media will not create an informed electorate. There is another type of conservatism beyond popular definitions and classical political science definitions. Some institutions provide social stability and preserve the status quo of social structure (see Manning, 1976, pp. 102–103). The media may be playing this role far beyond exhibiting a liberal or conservative bias. Todd Fraley and Elli Roushanzamir (2006) say that the current conditions of subnational and supranational violence are shifting and distorting all media presentations of violence, including terrorism. They sadly conclude that the mass media is spreading more propaganda than news in a world dominated by media corporations. The flow and amount of information, however, could serve to raise the awareness of news consumers, creating a new **critical media consciousness**. Yet, consumers frequently accept small snippets of events and move on to new ones in a never-ending stream.

Steven Chermak and Alexander Weiss (2006) found this to be the case when they examined community policing. News agencies projected positive images of law enforcement efforts and community responses. The same principle probably applies to security forces responding to a terrorist attack. Media coverage shows security officials on the scene restoring order and helping victims. These are positive images that work against terrorism. In stories on community policing, Chermak and Weiss found that after initial reports on successful community policing, reporters simply moved on to other stories. There were no attempts of critical in depth analysis in their study.

Whether in the new or old media, superficial narratives and constant flows of differing stories do not lend themselves to critical thinking. Fraley and Roushanzamir (2006) believe that news consumers need to develop analytical abilities that look beyond the news frame and examine the issues behind terrorism and other political events. If they do, the researchers believe, political freedom will expand throughout the world. If consumers remain at the current level of understanding, corporations will continue to remain in charge of mass media outlets, and emerging subnational and supranational groups—such as multinational terrorist organizations—will fight for control of emerging media. If the established media only stabilizes the existing social order, this will result in polarization with other forms of media, such as the Internet.

There is also quite a bit of controversy on the relationship between the media and violence with no clear results. Barrie Gunter (2008) conducted an in-depth historical study of the influence the media has on social aggression and violent behavior. Concern about the impact of images of violence began with movies in the 1920s, and it continues today. Gunter says a variety of researchers approach the topic with a multitude of methodologies, but there are problems inherent in the decades of study. Most models assume that media violence is linked to negative behavior. That model may be acceptable to policymakers, Gunter argues, but it is not acceptable to social scientists. And it is not conducive to critical reflection.

Research on media-induced violence is full of differing results due to a variety of factors. First, the causal variables are unknown. For example, if someone is exposed to revolutionary social media or left-wing stories in the old media and that person commits an act of terrorism, was it caused by exposure to the media or some other unknown social factor? Researchers do not know. Second, consumers may prefer media violence as entertainment while never accepting violent behavior in everyday life. Finally, causal relationships are often oversimplified in casual reports.

critical media consciousness: The public's understanding of the media and the way stories are presented. A critically conscious audience would not simply accept a story presented in a news frame. It would look for the motives for telling the story, how the story affected social constructs and actions, and hidden details that could cause the story to be told in another way.

ANOTHER PERSPECTIVE

Miniter's Media Myths

Richard Miniter (2005) says that popular images, conservative and liberal views, and urban legends are popularized through the media. Many of these media-based "truths" cannot stand the test of investigation. A selection of myths follows.

The Myth	The Truth
In an email, Lt. Col. Oliver North allegedly warned Senator Al Gore about Osama bin Laden.	North was testifying to another senator about Abu Nidal, a Middle Eastern terrorist.
Former Soviet Union backpack nuclear devices were stolen by al Qaeda.	The weapons appear to be secure and are more difficult to steal than popularly believed.
Jihadists are most likely to infiltrate from Mexico.	Canadian media has little respect for the abilities of Canadian police and intelligence services, and jihadist sympathizers operate a strong lobby in Canada. Miniter says the evidence indicates that jihadists will come from the north.
Conservative media personalities argue that political correctness keeps us from using racial profiles to target terrorists who travel by air. If we could use racial profiles, we could identify terrorists.	Racial profiling does nothing to single out terrorists within ethnic groups. Comparing air travelers with a comprehensive terrorist knowledge base would work, but civil libertarians, both liberal and conservative, prevent that.
Liberal media personalities claim that the defense contracting company Halliburton made tremendous profits in Iraq.	Halliburton has shown little profit from Iraq, both for investors and for conspiracy theorists.
A popular Internet and Arab-media myth states that Israeli intelligence warned Jews to avoid the World Trade Center on September 11, 2001.	Although the exact number is unknown, hundreds of Jews died in the 9/11 attacks, including five Israelis.

Miniter believes that all media serve as a source of disinformation. The primary reasons are sloppy reporting, editors who fail to check facts, and rumors that are accepted as truth. People gravitate to belief in conspiracies as a result.

Miniter says that the American government can help stop disinformation by making its reports readily available and by releasing the entire transcripts of officials' interviews before items are reported in the news.

longitudinal studies: In social science, studies that involve examinations of the same subjects over long periods of time.

Gunter concludes that studies of the relationship between behavior and media violence need to be **longitudinal studies**. They need to concentrate on multiple variables and realize that the impact of the media does not take place in a vacuum. Despite the large number of studies, current evidence is not conclusive, and it is often couched in political catchphrases. If Gunter is correct, the contagion effect of the media on terrorism should be examined in the same framework. Currently, very little is known.

ANOTHER PERSPECTIVE

Wilkinson's Analysis of the Media

Paul Wilkinson (1997) argues that terrorists must communicate their efforts, and they use the media to do so. He concludes the following about the relationship between the media and terrorists:

- Terrorists and the media have an interdependent relationship.
- Terrorist groups have an underground communication system, but they need the mainstream media to spread their messages.
- Mass media serve as the terrorists' psychological weapon by creating fear and anxiety.
- Terrorists may trap the media into spreading their message.
- The media may inadvertently shift blame for an incident from terrorists to victims or governments.
- Governments benefit when media sources portray the savage cruelty of terrorist groups.

Self-Check

> Why do some people assume the old media has biases?
> What evidence points to political bias when covering terrorism?
> Why should the old media produce a critical media conscious?

Censorship Debates

Debates over censorship arise because many people assume that acts of terrorism are induced by reckless media coverage and that media outlets provide terrorists with information. This again raises Barrie Gunter's point about utilizing inconclusive selective evidence. Censorship tends to reflect the attitudes of the censors.

For example, recall that social scientists do not believe there is conclusive evidence about the behavioral effects of violence in the media. Yet, the leader of one media watch-dog group says that long-term exposure to media violence causes violent behavior and insensitivity toward victims. He says that the surgeon general, the American Medical Association, and the National PTA "know" this to be true (Klite, 2000). Although he advocates internal self-regulation, he argues that the media must be censored. After all, common wisdom "proves" that media violence causes violent behavior. If a legislative body granted censorship power to the watchdog group, presentation of media violence would probably reflect the mores and values of the group's censors. In addition, the group would most likely lobby to extend censorship to the Internet and all forms of the new media. In the worst case scenario, they might even begin to monitor individuals to ensure that nobody viewed any unapproved material. These issues illustrate the controversial nature of censorship and explain the rationale behind heated debates.

Many of the concerns about all forms of media and censorship are based on common unproven assumptions or single examples. Yet, censorship already occurs regularly with no outcry and quite a bit of support. When terrorist organizations open websites or release propaganda videos on the Internet, intelligence agencies block and remove the offending items, frequently distributing copies for the exclusive use of security forces. These actions are generally supported in the West and they are rarely questioned.

Paul Wilkinson (1997) believes that governments face three choices when it comes to maintaining freedom of the press and combating terrorism. A popular position is to assume a laissez-faire attitude. This hands-off approach assumes that market forces will determine the norms. A second choice is censorship, meaning that a governmental agency would have veto power over news reports. A final choice is to let the press regulate itself. Wilkinson says that reporters would not behave in an irresponsible manner if they knew what they could do to avoid aiding terrorists. He notes that governments and security forces seldom provide direction for news organizations (see the preceding feature titled "Another Perspective: Wilkinson's Analysis of the Media").

The arguments about censorship are heated and deal with core issues of democracy. At the center of the debate is the right to free speech and the question of whether free speech necessitates media access to information. The media answers in the affirmative, claiming that the public has a right to know and reporters have the freedom to inform. Critics respond that free speech does not imply unlimited access to information. There is a right to speak; there is no right to know. In another sense, the censorship debate also focuses on truth, or factual information. Because terrorists and governments understand that media images are important in terrorism, they both spend great amounts of energy trying to manipulate the media. Manipulating the media and withholding information are very different from governmental control of the press (see Cram, 2006; Ross, 2007; Weimann and von Knop, 2008).

Looking at actions shortly after the United States started the Bush administration's war on terrorism, Doris Graber (2003) summarizes both sides of the argument. She argues that freedom of the press is crucial during times of national crisis, but that is when the media is most vulnerable. She believes that people who seek increased censorship do so by developing strategic arguments based on sloganeering and knowledge of select audiences. These efforts are attempts to manipulate people into supporting censorship by using verbal tactics to make arguments that it seems illogical to disagree with. Officials in the war on terrorism augmented this process by withholding information and encouraging lower-ranking officials to do the same. Although the Obama administration abandoned the metaphor of war when approaching terrorism, the president continued many of the practices of his predecessor.

Graber says several arguments were used in favor of censorship. The first focused on national security, a powerful excuse when used in times of emergency. According to this position, information must be controlled to ensure the survival of the state. Another position was to claim that the public wanted the information withheld. A former democratic senator voiced his support for controlling information after 9/11, claiming that the American people overwhelmingly supported these governmental efforts. According to this logic, America was fighting a new type of war, and some form of censorship was required. Finally, limited censorship was justified under the banner of patriotism. Ultimately, governmental officials claimed that they were asking for trust, not censorship. They would release information when it was safe to do so.

Freedom of Information (FOI) Act: A law ensuring access to governmental records.

According to Graber, it was mainly journalists who presented the anticensorship view. They cited a variety of governmental mistakes and misdeeds, all hidden under the cover of national security. They condemned governmental officials who fought against the **Freedom of Information (FOI) Act**. They also argued that terrorism was essentially a war of information. Instead of trying to silence sources, the government should focus efforts on getting out the facts. Finally, every governmental clampdown cast officials in a bad light. The anti-censorship camp reserved its harshest criticism for media outlets that decided to self-censor as a service to the government.

Graber concludes that arguments for and against censorship in times of crisis are as old as warfare. They will not be resolved in the current struggle with terrorism. However, she states, the United States is fighting for freedom and democracy, and only an informed public is capable of successfully defending liberty. Editors, she argues, should hold back information to protect citizens and security forces, but those decisions belong to the media, not the government.

Gabriel Weimann (2008) argues that two issues come into play when debating government regulation, use of communication technology by terrorist groups and cyberterrorism. Terrorists use the media, but they have access to their own forms of communication through the Internet and more recently social media. These forms of communication demand the attention of scholars and analysts, but Weimann maintains that most efforts are aimed at cyberterrorism. The emphasis needs to shift to communication, he believes. The major problem with the Internet, Weimann says, is the way it is used every day. Terrorists maintain hundreds of websites and use the Internet for research and communication. Although his article was written before the popularity of social media, tools like Twitter have increased the power of communication. Counterterrorism should be aimed at learning how terrorists use the Internet and devising methods to thwart their effectiveness.

Weimann says governments may be tempted to censor or regulate the media in the name of security, but this is a dangerous course of action. The foundation of Western democracy is based on free speech and communication. Censorship, regulation, and gathering data from communications threaten the basis of democracy. It does not take much imagination, he says, to see the harm that invasive government operations might have. In the end, censorship could do more to damage freedom than the terrorist attacks themselves.

✓ **Self-Check**

> What factors influence the way a story is covered?
> How is news simplified?
> Why are both potential censors and reporters concerned about censorship?

Emphasizing the Points

Modern terrorism has been a media sensation, but this situation is changing. The new media environment gives all actors the power to participate in a narrative. This often produces multiple narratives with contradictory symbols. Although research has been improving, there is a need for more interdisciplinary research on the relationship between the media and terrorism. The media provides the backdrop for the social construction of terrorism, and news frames create images for social interpretation. This means that there is extensive competition to present a point of view and a news frame, which leads to charges of bias from all sides. This is especially true in television because terrorism is a made-for-television drama. Some scholars and analysts have called for limited censorship because the media is so powerful.

SUMMARY OF CHAPTER OBJECTIVES

- The new media environment refers to instantaneous communication through a variety of platforms. It includes social networks, web pages, e-zines, chat rooms, blogs, and similar forms of communication.
- The new media allows for vicarious participation in an event and opportunities for reframing narratives. It also provides tools for two way mass communication.
- An exponential expansion of the Internet has been the basis of the new media environment. Its power is multiplied because devices are available and powerful, and costs have been reduced.

- Hybrid narratives appear as an original story is told and retold. Stories grow and take on new characteristics. Contradictory symbols frequently appear in hybrid narratives.
- Interdisciplinary research on the relationship between terrorism and the media is lacking. New research has revealed the importance of the new media environment. Research also shows that gender roles are shaped by the way terrorism is covered.
- Both the old and new media create images in the minds of consumers, which results in socially constructed reality. Most people participate vicariously in an event based on the common definitions derived from these images.
- News frames refer to the way narratives or video images are presented to consumers. They shape stories about terrorism.
- News frames set the stage for a story, introduce characters, give narratives of actions, and either provide a conclusion or lead consumers to a variety of conclusions.
- There is a special relationship between terrorism and television. Terrorism has a close relationship with television because it provides an unfolding drama. Television news reports are often designed to entertain and excite audiences. Some critics maintain that television reporting focuses more on entertainment than information.
- New non-Western international outlets often provide sympathetic views of terrorism. Western media elites no longer have a monopoly on the old media.
- Some media commentators believe that there is a liberal bias in television news reporting. Others feel that conservative views dominate the airwaves. There are some networks on cable television that cater to particular political audiences, and they adjust their reports to match the opinions of their viewers. The power of media has prompted some security experts to call for censorship when reporting about terrorism.

LOOKING INTO THE FUTURE

The importance of the new media environment will probably expand rapidly in the near future. Newspapers have experienced a growing lack of readership, and this problem is getting larger. Young people increasingly rely on Internet platforms for news. This implies that many counterterrorist battles will take place on the Internet and in social media. As these areas grow, competition will become more complex. Terrorism may increase as isolated individuals see themselves as no longer separate from fellow ideologues. Virtual networks reinforce extremism and allow followers to participate in virtual groups. The faceless nature of many interactions exacerbates radical behavior. This may be a boon for counterterrorism efforts, however. Many web users and participants in social media incorrectly assume anonymity while communicating. Twitter, Facebook, the Internet, and new technologies can continue to be an increasing source of intelligence for security forces.

KEY TERMS

CHAPTER 5

Force Multipliers, Gender Roles, and Tactics

Kurdish Guerrillas

Sebastian Meyer/Corbis News/Corbis

The Center for American Progress (Sofer and Addison, 2012) raised the alarm about an unaddressed problem in counterterrorism. The role of females in terrorist groups is increasing around the globe, but the current U.S. strategy for countering terrorism makes no mention of the problem. In fact, the issue of women in terrorism is not even discussed. This is ironic because the number of female suicide bombers has been increasing in recent years, and terrorist groups are expanding recruitment efforts to attract women.

The Center says the threat is not new. Secular groups have been using females for decades, and the Kurdish Workers' Party (PKK) used women in 76 percent of its attacks in the last two decades of the twentieth century. Religious terrorist groups soon followed suit. The first known female suicide bomber struck in April 1985 when a young Muslim woman drove a truck laden with explosives into an Israeli Army convoy. The Pakistani Taliban and al Qaeda formed female suicide cells after the first female suicide bomber struck in Pakistan in 2010.

It should be noted that the use of women in terrorist attacks does not constitute a tactical change. The same basic tactics

LEARNING OBJECTIVES

After reading this chapter, you should be able to:

▶ Summarize the tactics of modern terrorism.

▶ Define force multipliers.

▶ List and describe four force multipliers.

▶ Outline the tactical importance of female terrorists.

▶ Explain the reasons researchers and the public have ignored women in terrorism.

▶ Define the types of threats posed by technological terrorism.

▶ Explain the effects of biological, chemical, and radiological weapons.

▶ Characterize the possibility and possible outcomes of nuclear terrorism.

▶ Summarize transnational economic targeting in the tourist, energy, and transportation industries.

▶ Summarize theories of suicide bombing.

▶ Explain the reasons researchers and the public have ignored women in terrorism.

▶ Describe the roles women play in nationalistic, ideological, and religious groups.

of bombing, ambush, robbery, assassination, kidnapping, and hostage-taking remain the same. The organizational structures are also relatively constant. The change is due to the expanding roles of females in terrorist organizations, especially in male-dominated conservative movements. This shift is also impacted by stereotypes. Society at large casts women in nurturing roles and is often unwilling to see them performing nontraditional tasks in both legal and criminal organizations. Feminist criminologists have been aware of this problem for decades, but the idea is new to most of the media. As a result, when women strike, the attack receives greater attention, and the media becomes a force multiplier.

Tactics and Force Multipliers

While the term *terrorism* is difficult to define, the process of terrorism is not. Terrorism is simply a way of fighting. In fact, Max Boot (2013) advances the argument that guerrilla warfare and terrorism dominate the history of warfare. Conventional war, he concludes, is not the normative method of fighting. Terrorists fight in the shadows, and security forces must be prepared to operate in that environment.

six tactics of terrorism: As defined by Brian Jenkins: (1) bombing, (2) hijacking, (3) arson, (4) assault, (5) kidnapping, and (6) hostage-taking.

Brian Jenkins (1984, 2004a, 2004b) says that there are **six tactics of terrorism:** bombing, hijacking, arson, assault, kidnapping, and hostage-taking. Recently, the arsenal of terrorism has grown to include threats from weapons of mass destruction (WMD), but the public does not clearly understand these threats. Technology has also modified bombing to include virtual attacks through computer systems (B. Jenkins, 1987; Brackett, 1996, p. 45; J. White, 1986, 2000; Parachini, 2003).

force multipliers: A method of increasing striking power without increasing the number of combat troops in a military unit. Terrorists have four force multipliers: (1) technology to enhance weapons or attacks on technological facilities, (2) transnational support, (3) media coverage, and (4) religious fanaticism.

Jenkins says that the six tactics can be enhanced by **force multipliers**. In military terms, a force multiplier increases striking power without increasing the strength of a unit. Terrorists routinely use force multipliers because they add to their aura. All political terrorists want to give the illusion that they can fight on a higher, more powerful level.

Four force multipliers give terrorists more striking power (see the following feature titled "Another Perspective: Force Multipliers"). Researchers have known for many years that technology can enhance a terrorist group's ability to strike (see Ketcham and McGeorge, 1986, pp. 25–33; Bunker, 1998; Linstone, 2003; Brookbank, 2006; Wright, 2008). Cyberterrorism and potential WMD attacks are examples of technological force multipliers. Daniel Benjamin and Steven Simon (2002, pp. 365–382) demonstrate that media coverage and interpretation of terrorist events often serve as force multipliers. One incident can be converted into a "campaign" as electronic media

---

))) ANOTHER PERSPECTIVE

Force Multipliers

Transnational support increases the ability of terrorist groups to move and hide across a nation.

Technology allows a small group to launch a deadly attack.

Media coverage can make a minor group appear to be politically important.

Religion transcends normative political and social boundaries, increasing violence and decreasing opportunities for negotiation.

The Most Common Tactic of Terrorism

Although terrorist tactics change over time, the most common weapon of terrorism has been and is still the bomb. In 1848, anarchists talked about the "philosophy of the bomb," meaning that the only way to communicate with the social order was to destroy it. In the late 1800s, militants used bombs to attack governments and businesses. The Irish Republican Army (IRA) found the bomb to be their most important weapon after 1969, and by 1985, the organization was deploying extremely sophisticated ones. Groups in the Middle East, Sri Lanka, and eventually throughout the world found that bombs could be delivered by suicide attackers. Hijackers first used bombs to take over planes, and then, on September 11, 2001, terrorists turned civilian airliners into bombs.

---

scramble to break the latest news. A frightening new force multiplier has been the introduction of religious fanaticism in terrorist activities (B. Hoffman 1995; Laqueur, 1999; Juergensmeyer, 1988, 2003; von Hippel, 2002; Stern, 2003b). The introduction of religion has introduced suicide attacks into the arsenals of terrorism.

Although terrorist tactics change over time, the most common weapon of terrorism has been and is still the bomb. In 1848, anarchists talked about the **philosophy of the bomb,** meaning that the only way to communicate with the social order was to destroy it.

Terrorists tend to increase their effectiveness in bombing by applying improved explosive technology to their weapons just as conventional military forces constantly improve the killing power of their munitions. In 2004, *New Scientist* reported that Middle Eastern terrorist groups were working on a two-stage military-style weapon called a mininuke. This type of explosive is designed to spread fuel in the air and then ignite it. Known as a **thermobaric bomb,** it actually explodes the air in the blast area. One analyst speculated that an attack on a Tunisian synagogue in 2002 used this technology (Hambling, 2004).

Although the tactics are simple, they always represent a variation on a theme. Force multipliers enhance destructive power, whereas innovation is used to achieve shock and surprise. Again, this is nothing more than the tactics used by conventional military forces, but in terrorist attacks, they are used outside the rules of a war with front lines and a beginning and an end. This explains why terrorism is different from war, even though terrorists and military forces sometimes use the same tactics. Terrorist tactics, though simple, create terror because they are designed to exclusively attack civilians and symbolic targets. The only purpose of a terrorist attack is to send a message of chaos.

philosophy of the bomb: A phrase used by anarchists around 1848. It means that social order can be changed only through violent upheaval. Bombs were the first technological force multiplier.

thermobaric bomb: A two-stage bomb. The first stage spreads either a fuel cloud or finely ground powder through the air. The explosive material mixes with the oxygen present in the atmosphere. The second stage detonates the explosive material, which explodes in all directions in a series of shock waves. The cloud can penetrate a number of barriers. A person breathing the material explodes from the inside out when the material is ignited.

> ✓ **Self-Check**
> >   Describe the basic tactics of terrorism.
> >   Define and describe force multipliers.
> >   How do force multipliers affect the tactics of terrorism?

Technology

Terrorism is influenced by technology. Some analysts believe that when the technological impact is so great that it turns a tactic or weapon into a strategy, it is possible to look at the resulting activity as a specific type of terrorism (see Pape, 2003, 2005).

Others believe that this technique confuses the issue and that types of terrorism refer only to tools any terrorist group could use (see Dyson, 2004). Striking a balance between these two positions, this section will examine four types of terrorism that are potentially powerful enough to transform the nature of terrorism. As stated earlier, these types may be different only in terms of the weapons used in terrorist attacks, but special types of terrorism have become so individualized they deserve a separate review.

Cyberterrorism

cyberterrorism: Uses computers to attack other networks or to conduct physical attacks on computer-controlled targets. The most frightening scenario involves an attack designed to create catastrophic failure in the economy or infrastructure.

Cyberterrorism refers to the use of computers to attack technological targets or physical attacks on computer networks. The National Conference of State Legislatures (2003) defines cyberterrorism as "the use of information technology by terrorists to promote a political agenda." Barry Collin (2004), who coined the term in the early 1990s, believes it involves disrupting points where the virtual, electronic realm of computer networks and programs intersects with the physical world. Miami attorney Mark Grossman (1999) argues that the threat of cyberterrorism is real, and international legal systems are not prepared to deal with it. Cyberterrorism is computer hacking with a body count, according to Grossman. The Council on Foreign Relations (2004) defines cyberterrorism by the ways terrorists might use computers and information networks. The targets for cyberterrorism include computers, computer networks, and information storage and retrieval systems. Terrorists differ from hackers, the council argues, because their purpose is to launch a systematic attack for political purposes. The most common tactic to date has been the defacement of websites.

Cyberterrorism is an attractive, low-risk strategy. Michael Whine (1999) claims that computer technology is attractive to terrorists for several reasons. Computers allow terrorist groups to remain connected, and they provide a means for covert discussions and anonymity. Computer networks are also much less expensive and work intensive than the secretive infrastructures necessary to maintain terrorist groups. Bowers and Keys (1998) believe cyberterrorism appears to be a threat because of the nature of modern society. To function, Western society increasingly needs information and the flow of information, and cyberterrorists threaten to interrupt or confuse that flow of information. This leads Tiffany Danitz and Warren Strobel (1999) to remind policymakers that violent political activists also use the Internet as a command-and-control mechanism. They say there is no doubt that computers are vulnerable to crime, and terrorists do use and will continue to use them.

Enemies are preparing to launch cyberattacks. A group calling itself the Cyber Caliphate claimed to have hacked the headquarters of the U.S. military's Central Command (Centcom) in January 2015. Although they actually invaded public social media, the attack symbolized their desire to strike the United States (Cooper, 2015). The most significant breach to date, in 2008, also involved Centcom. An infected flash drive was placed in a computer on a U.S. base in the Middle East. It entered both classified and unclassified cyberspace from there, allowing access to operational plans and other secure data. Known as Operation Buckshot Yankee, the incident catalyzed the creation of a new military unit, the U.S. Cyber Command (Lynn, 2010).

The greatest fear is catastrophic or multiple failures from cyberterrorism. Both the public and private sectors are experiencing attacks on websites and computer systems. Some attackers simply wait outside the targeted system, gathering enough data to infiltrate and steal corporate or government secrets. Other attacks are more nefarious. The main fear is that a worm, virus, or some other type of weaponized computer signal will suddenly strike a target. Due to automation and the computerized control of large segments of the infrastructure, a massive failure at one point could cause a series of failures that could lead to the closure of an entire support structure (Matusitz, 2010; Helms, Constanza, and John, 2012).

There are frightening scenarios for catastrophic failure. For example, if a terrorist organization could infiltrate the banking or investment sector of the economy, a program could conceivably start draining accounts. This would create an economic crisis. In another scenario, imagine a major switching station on the power grid of a large metropolis. If the computer program running the station were attacked, the station could be the source of a catastrophic failure. As other portions of the grid picked up the slack from the downed station, they would find circuits overloading and could begin shutting down. It is conceivable that a large segment of the country could be without power for days. Finally, suppose that a malicious program were to enter a nuclear power plant. It is possible that the offending virus could cause a meltdown and explosion. Technological societies are vulnerable to such cyberattacks (see Mallesh and Wright, 2011).

WMD: Biological Agents

Terrorism by WMD presents a potential strategic scenario and even served as the United States' excuse for invading Iraq in 2003. WMD include biological agents, or biological weapons, which have been used for centuries. Modern arsenals contain **bacterial weapons** and **viral weapons**, with microbes cultured and refined, or weaponized, to increase their ability to kill. When people are victims of a bacterial attack, antibiotics may be an effective treatment. Antibiotics are not usually effective against viruses, although some vaccines issued before the use of viral weapons could be effective (see Hinton, 1999; Young and Collier, 2002). Because bacterial agents are susceptible to antibiotics, nations with bacterial weapons programs have created strains of bacterial microbes that are resistant to such drugs. Viral agents are produced in the same manner, and they are usually more powerful than bacterial agents. Biological agents are difficult to control but relatively easy to produce. Terrorists may find them to be effective weapons.

> **bacterial weapons:** Enhanced forms of bacteria that may be countered by antibiotics.
>
> **viral weapons:** Enhanced forms of viruses. The virus is "hardened" so that it can live for long periods and be enhanced for deadlier effects.

There are four types of biological agents: (1) natural poisons, or toxins that occur without human modification; (2) viruses; (3) bacteria; and (4) plagues. The Centers for Disease Control and Prevention (CDC) lists the most threatening agents as smallpox, anthrax, plague, botulism, tularemia, and hemorrhagic fever. Michael Osterholm and John Schwartz (2000, pp. 14–23) summarize the effect of each of these. Smallpox is a deadly, contagious virus. Many people were vaccinated against smallpox in their childhood, but these old vaccinations are no longer effective against the disease. Anthrax is a noncontagious bacterial infection, and plague is transmitted by insects. Botulism is a kind of foodborne illness, and other bacteria can be modified to serve as weapons. Hemorrhagic fevers are caused by viruses. One of the most widely known hemorrhagic fevers is the Ebola virus.

America has experienced two notable biological attacks since 1980. The first modern use of biological terrorism in the United States was engineered in 1984 by followers of a religious group in Oregon. The group spread bacteria in area salad bars in an attempt to sicken voters during a local election. Their intent was to elect their religious followers to local office (Miller, Engelberg, and Broad, 2001). Hundreds of people suffered food poisoning as a result.

The second attack involved anthrax and came in the wake of 9/11. It began in Florida when two workers from a news tabloid were infected by anthrax received through the mail. One of the victims died. In the following days, anthrax appeared again as NBC Nightly News received spores in its mail.

The situation grew worse in October. The office of former senate majority leader Thomas Daschle received its regular mail delivery after lunch on Friday, October 12. Fortunately, staff members were in a class that afternoon, learning how to recognize suspicious packages. When staffers returned to work on Monday, they opened Friday's mail, and someone noticed a white powdery substance in a letter. Alerted by information from Friday's class, the staffer who noticed the substance took immediate action, perhaps saving many lives. The powder contained anthrax spores, and although there were no fatalities, legislative offices were closed in Washington, D.C., for several weeks. Mysteriously, other people died on the East Coast with no explanation of how the anthrax was spreading (Parker, 2002; Schoof and Fields, 2002). By the end of November 2001, the anthrax outbreak had claimed five lives. Cases were reported in Florida; Washington, D.C.; New York; New Jersey; and Connecticut. Two conclusions remain: (1) The public health response was poor and disorganized, and (2) The Department of Justice formally closed the case in 2010.

The United States planned to take massive steps to prevent biological terrorism after these anthrax attacks. Congress created a bipartisan commission to deal with the issue, but the effectiveness of all these efforts has been questionable (Commission on the Prevention of Weapons of Mass Destruction Proliferation and Terrorism, 2010). *Security* (2010) magazine reported that the commission conducted a review of the systems to prevent and respond to WMD attacks and found that preparations were lacking. Most important, in terms of bioterrorism, the commission concluded that the United States had no structure in place to respond to a biological attack. The commission also criticized Congress for failing to properly clarify and oversee the missions of the Department of Homeland Security and for failing to create the education and training systems needed to prepare the next generation of national security experts.

WMD: Chemical and Radiological Weapons

The massive power and heat from atomic bombs place nuclear weapons in a class of their own, but chemical and radiological attacks are basically similar. Radiological poisoning and "dirty" radioactive devices are forms of chemical attack. Chemicals are usually easier to deliver than biological weapons, and they act quickly. Radiological devices act more slowly than most chemicals, but their poison lasts longer and they can be spread like chemicals. Radioactive materials are also more resistant to heat than chemicals, so bombs or other heat-producing devices can be used to scatter them.

There are four types of chemical agents: nerve agents, blood agents, choking agents, and blistering agents (Table 5.1). Nerve agents enter the body through ingestion, respiration, or contact. Blood and choking agents are usually absorbed through

Bioterrorism Report Card	
Capability to Respond to Biological Attacks	F
Control Containment Labs	D+
Review Program to Secure Pathogens	A
Strengthen Disease Surveillance	C
Plan International Biological Weapons Convention	B+
Develop Bioforensic Strategy	A

Source: Commission on the Prevention of Weapons of Mass Destruction Proliferation and Terrorism (2010)

TABLE **5.1**
Chemical and Radiological Agents and Their Effects

Agent	Common Entry	Effect
Nerve	Food, water, air, skin contact	Convulsions, flood of body fluids
Blistering	Skin contact, air	Burns, choking, respiratory failure
Blood/Choking	Breathing, skin contact	Failure of body functions
Radiological	Food, air, water	Burns, long-term skin contact illness

Sources: Organization for the Prohibition of Chemical Weapons, 2000; U.S. Congress, Office of Technology Assessment, 1995.

the respiratory system, and blistering agents burn skin and internal tissue upon contact (Organization for the Prohibition of Chemical Weapons, 2000; for a summary, see Federation of American Scientists, 2010).

Chemicals present an attractive weapon for terrorists because they are easy to control and, unlike biological weapons, the users can avoid the area they attack. Nonetheless, chemical weapons present four problems. First, terrorists must have a delivery mechanism; that is, they need some way to spread the chemical. The second problem is related to the first. Bombing is a popular tactic, but the heat of most explosives incinerates the chemical agents. It takes a lot of chemicals to present a threat. Finally, weather patterns, air, and water can neutralize a chemical threat. Chemical weapons are most effective when used in a confined space, and they are difficult to use effectively in large outdoor areas.

Radiological weapons are closely related to chemical weapons. Exposure to radiation can produce short-term burns and long-term contamination and health problems. Radiological poisoning takes place when a contaminated material comes in contact with any source that conducts radiation. The contacted material, such as food, water, or metal, becomes a contaminated object that could poison humans. Small contaminated pieces of matter can also become a means of spreading radiation through the air.

Some experts believe that terrorists will use radioactive material in a dirty bomb; that is, that a conventional explosive will be used to spread a radioactive agent around a large area. Unlike the incineration that takes place when chemicals are placed in a bomb, radiation is not affected by the heat of an explosion. It is affected only by the type of radiological agent that is used in the device and the dispersal pattern created by the explosion. Most dirty-bomb scenarios are based on the premise that a radiological agent will be used with a conventional explosive.

Countdown to Zero, a film by Lucy Walker, is a documentary about the dangers of nuclear war. She interviews experts and powerful heads of state in the movie, but one of her most frightening interviews, according to the *Times* of London (Goodwin, 2010), came in a jail cell in Tbilisi, Georgia. Her interviewee was a man sentenced to eight years in prison for trying to sell **highly enriched uranium (HEU)** to an undercover officer posing as a member of al Qaeda. In the film, he tells Walker that there is plenty of HEU available and that it is easy to obtain. HEU is so potent that not only could it be used in a dirty bomb, it could also be used to construct a nuclear device. The most frightening aspect of the scenario is that the culprit was a bumbling amateur. If he was able to obtain the material, determined terrorists would certainly be able to do the same.

Other analysts believe that the dirty-bomb scenario is misunderstood. Under most circumstances, P. Andrew Karam (2005) writes, the impact of the radiation from a dirty bomb would not be as disruptive as most people think. Terrorists can spread radioactive material through a bomb, but lethality depends on the type of material used

highly enriched uranium (HEU): Produced by a process that increases the proportion of a radioactive isotope in uranium (U-235), making it suitable for industrial use. The process can also be used to make nuclear weapons. Nuclear weapons are made from either HEU or plutonium.

Sources of Highly Enriched Uranium

Although constructing a nuclear bomb is a sophisticated process, terrorists could build a device with HEU without the assistance of a nuclear state. The United States Research Council has suggested that stocks of HEU be secured. Civilian industries around the globe have created more than 50 tons of HEU. It takes about 80 to 130 pounds to make a crude nuclear bomb. Terrorists could obtain HEU from nuclear reactors used for:

>   Power plants
>   Production of medical isotopes
>   Propulsion engines in ice breakers
>   Power source for space vehicles and satellites
>   Research facilities

Source: Nuclear Threat Initiative, 2009.

---

radiation sickness: Caused by exposure to high doses of radiation over a short period of time. It is characterized by nausea, diarrhea, headaches, and fever. High doses produce dizziness, weakness, and internal bleeding. It is possible to treat patients who have been exposed to doses of radiation, but higher doses are usually fatal. Other than the two nuclear bombs used in World War II, most radiation sickness has been caused by industrial accidents.

in the device. Spreading material through a conventional explosion is not the optimal means for distributing radiation. Most bombs would not cause **radiation sickness** or an upsurge of cancer rates. Karam believes that the primary danger of such a bomb is its psychological effects. The public, in turn, would be prone to panic if they heard about the detonation of a dirty bomb, and public safety officials might refuse to work in the blast area because they would not understand the nature of radioactivity. Many health experts are not trained to recognize symptoms of radiation poisoning, and they might refuse to respond to victims or treat patients.

Karam believes that it is possible to expose thousands of people to intense radiation but that it will probably not be the result of a dirty bomb. He suggests that prevention should focus on preparing for a response rather than trying to detect low amounts of radiation. This involves training public service and medical personnel. Response personnel should understand the low risks of poisoning in the areas affected by a dirty bomb. It is also important, he says, to remind emergency medical personnel and hospital staffs that patients suffering from radioactive poisoning are not contagious.

James David Ballard (2003) looks at the problem of nuclear terrorism another way. Congress has designated a site in Nevada as the repository for all the radioactive waste from America's nuclear power plants, and all this material must be shipped across the country. Ballard wonders what would happen if terrorists seized some of this material. He points out that nuclear waste is a ready-made dirty bomb.

The power plants themselves, as well as other nuclear facilities, present another scenario. Since dirty bombs are less effective than popularly believed, an attack on a nuclear facility with conventional weapons presents a more tempting target. For example, a nuclear power plant could be attacked with a hijacked airplane or a strong explosive device. It could also be overrun in a terrorist attack. A meltdown of its core reactor would lead to the dispersal of concentrated radioactive material over a relatively large area surrounding the plant (Hagby et al., 2009).

✓ **Self-Check**

>   How does technology impact terrorism?
>   Describe the ways cyberterrorists might operate.
>   Describe the effectiveness of differing types of WMD.

Nuclear Terrorism

The most fearful scenario related to WMD involves a nuclear explosion. A stolen atomic weapon conjures the worst images of mass destruction, and it is no secret that several terrorist groups would love to have a nuclear bomb. Nonetheless, it is much easier for terrorists to use a conventional weapon than it is to build a nuclear weapon. Nuclear weapons are also difficult to obtain and detonate. Difficulty has not hampered desire, though. One of Osama bin Laden's former bodyguards told an Arab-language newspaper that al Qaeda wants to build or purchase a nuclear bomb. A top counterterrorism official in the United States confirmed the story (AFP, 2010). Fearing the worst, many governments have installed nuclear detection devices in ports of entry and cities that are attractive targets for terrorists (Daily News and Analysis, 2010).

There are two methods for constructing a nuclear device. The simplest method is to use HEU. Rarely used in military weapons today, it was this type of bomb that was used at Hiroshima, and it can be built without the assistance of a nuclear state. It involves placing two pieces of material in a tube and forcing them to collide to cause a nuclear reaction. The second method involves plutonium, and it is much more complicated. The principle behind a plutonium bomb involves compressing the metal until its density produces a nuclear reaction. Although HEU seems to represent the greatest danger in the hands of terrorists, security experts are not sure whether the worse threat comes from HEU or plutonium. An HEU device is easier to make, but it is far less effective than plutonium. Simen Ellingsen (2008) of the Department of War Studies at King's College London suggests that terrorists prefer the HEU method, even though a homemade HEU device might produce fewer casualties than a conventional attack. He believes that the fear generated by a nuclear explosion would cause public hysteria, thus achieving the goal of terrorism.

The United States was aware of the possibility of a clandestine nuclear attack long before al Qaeda appeared. Micah Zenko (2006) says the American intelligence community has studied the issue for the past six decades not caring whether the attack might come from Russia, China, or some other source. The possibility of an attack is frighteningly real because nuclear weapons and bomb-grade material can be stolen with relative ease. American intelligence agencies believe that it would be rather simple to smuggle a bomb into the United States undetected. Although the United States is woefully unprepared for a nuclear attack from terrorists, it is an ominous possibility made more threatening, Zenko concludes, by fanatics who believe it is their religious duty to obtain a nuclear bomb.

A group of Russian scholars agree with Zenko and expand on his thesis. While Zenko examined the threat to the United States, the Russian researchers believe that nuclear terrorism is a threat to every major country. International terrorists, they argue, want to disrupt their enemies by destroying a large portion of London, Paris, Moscow, or any other international metropolis. However, two factors inhibit their ability to do so: the cost of obtaining a weapon and the technological skills needed to use it. Regardless, the ability of international terrorists to operate globally increases the chances that nuclear weapons will be added to their arsenals (Arbatov, Pikaev, and Dvorkin, 2008).

Scholars from Tel Aviv University suggest that the probability of nuclear terrorism is low (Schachter, Guzansky, and Schweitzer, 2010). The nuclear threat is based on the crime causation model: victim, opportunity to commit a crime, and the desire on the part of the criminal to commit the crime. Al Qaeda—the only nonstate group that has made an effort to obtain a nuclear device—has the desire to make any one of their enemies victims, but it has consistently lacked the opportunity to strike. Further, there is no evidence to suggest that al Qaeda has the ability to obtain a nuclear weapon or to construct one. No state has ever supplied a terrorist group with a nuclear weapon; even if Iran builds a nuclear arsenal, its religious differences with al Qaeda would negate the possibility of sharing one of its weapons with them. Nuclear terrorism, these scholars conclude, is equivalent to "crying wolf." It diverts attention from actual threats, thus increasing the probability of their success.

Michael Levi (2007) steers a middle course in a comprehensive work entitled *On Nuclear Terrorism*. The book gives a balanced, straightforward analysis of the issue and the probability in nontechnical terms. Levi explores the possibility of an attack on the United States, concluding that the country is not ready to deal with it. Careful to avoid writing a "how-to" guide for terrorists, he discusses scenarios for attacks, methods for creating a defensive system, and policy changes needed to prepare for nuclear terrorism. Military experts such as Martin van Creveld (2008) conclude that this is one of the definitive works on nuclear terrorism.

nuclear black market: A nebulous concept referring to illegal or underground methods of obtaining or selling nuclear materials or weapons. For example, the Soviet Union collapsed in 1991, and this prompted many people to fear that a rogue general might secretly sell a weapon to a terrorist group. There is also fear that a country like North Korea might supply one of its nuclear weapons to another nation. These types of transactions would occur outside the public view, therefore, the term *black market* is used to describe them. Some experts do not believe a nuclear black market exists.

Levi (2007, pp. 124–127) reiterates the opinions of others that the easiest method for utilizing a nuclear bomb is to build it. The theoretical homemade bomb would surely strike terror, but it has another major drawback. It is not as lethal as a military weapon. Yet, if terrorists were to obtain a military-grade weapon, it would also come with disadvantages. Nuclear devices have sophisticated security mechanisms that terrorists might not be able to overcome. Nations provide physical security for their arsenals, and they have the technology to detect military weapons. Sheer weight is also an issue. If terrorists were to obtain one of Pakistan's devices, for example, they would find that the warhead is designed to fit on a missile, and it weighs more than a ton. Despite these limitations, Levi says, the possibility of nuclear terrorism is real, and the approach to deal with the problem should be equally realistic.

Levi (2007, pp. 140–142) suggests that the United States should approach nuclear terrorism in two ways. The first involves debunking popular myths about the subject. Policymakers and the public need to understand the basic aspects of nuclear security and must realize that it is never 100 percent effective. Further, irrational fears should be dealt with. For example, building a homemade bomb is complicated. A terrorist cannot go to the Internet, download the instructions, and build it in his or her backyard. Another irrational fear is the **nuclear black market**. It does not exist, Levi says. American officials currently base their possible scenarios on the worst case. Levi believes it is more logical to look at several realistic scenarios and aim preventive measures at high-probability

---

Overcoming Popular Misconceptions about Nuclear Terrorism

Michael Levi (2007, pp. 140–141) says that it is necessary to debunk the myths about nuclear terrorism and to understand the following:

1. Security is never 100 percent effective.
2. The nuclear black market does not exist.
3. Building a nuclear bomb is not a simple process.
4. Nuclear defense should be based on realistic, comprehensive scenarios.
5. We should create total intelligence pictures of terrorist groups beyond nuclear terrorism.
6. Total protection is not possible, but we can tip the scales in our favor.

Levi's Five Goals for Policymakers

1. Support international efforts to stop the proliferation of nuclear weapons.
2. Address nuclear terrorism in conjunction with all other terrorist threats.
3. Mandate nuclear threat analysis based on the most probable dangers.
4. Create a cooperative multiagency defense system.
5. Audit the defense system and reward cooperation.

Source: Levi, 2007, p. 142.

targets. Finally, it is not enough to limit the focus to nuclear terrorism. Levi argues for a comprehensive approach to a particular terrorist group and all its activities. This would provide a better threat analysis than limited attention to nuclear terrorism.

The second response to nuclear terrorism is to revamp defense systems. Protection against any form of terrorism does not involve a single agency working against a single group. Defense involves a multitude of agencies and organizations at all levels of government and liaisons with private organizations. Levi argues that the current bureaucracy does not provide protection because agencies protect their own turf; that is, they do not share information, and administrations are confused and competitive. Oversight of defense systems needs to be clarified and streamlined, and agency managers should be routinely evaluated on their ability to work with other agencies and to share information.

Reforming popular misconceptions and defensive systems will not prevent nuclear terrorism. Levi, quite correctly, concludes that no security network is always effective; America can only tip the scales in its favor. This means that the United States needs to be able to recover from a nuclear explosion, and Levi adds that the country also needs a little luck.

> **Self-Check**
> > What two elements are used to construct nuclear bombs?
> > Explain two positions on the debate about the possibility of nuclear terrorism.
> > What must the country do to prepare for nuclear terrorism?

Economic Targeting and Transnational Attacks

Terrorists may use transnational support or transnational operations as a force multiplier. As the world moves closer to a global economy, terrorists have found that striking transnational economic targets increases the effectiveness of operations. If governments run counterterrorist operations against underground networks and sources, terrorists turn the tables by striking the economic system. Some systems are tied closely to the international economy, and they present tempting targets to terrorists. Three types of transnational attacks can be used to illustrate the issue: tourism, energy, and shipping.

Tourism

On the evening of October 12, 2002, several hundred people were gathered in a resort area of Bali in Indonesia. Many of the people were tourists at a nightclub, and most of the tourists were Australians. Late in the evening, according to an investigator from the Australian Federal Police, who asked to remain anonymous, Indonesians were quietly advised to leave the area around the bar. Shortly before midnight, a firebomb went off inside the bar, trapping the patrons. A second bomb ignited the exterior. Within minutes, more than 200 people had been killed. The perpetrators called themselves Jamaat Islamiyya, and they vowed to strike Indonesia's tourist industry again. They would target hotels and resort areas. Leaders of Jamaat Islamiyya had multiple motives for targeting tourists. They wanted to create fear among foreigners and resented the presence of outsiders in Muslim lands. They also felt that theirs was a method of directly striking the West. One of the leaders claimed that as long as Western troops were in Afghanistan and Iraq, his group would continue killing Westerners in Indonesia. The leaders also felt that they were targeting economic interests (Abuza, 2006b).

There is a relationship between terrorism and tourism, but it is not simple. Terrorism does not seem to have an impact on domestic travel. Terrorism most frequently affects international travelers. If a host country has had widespread media attention focused on a terrorist event, tourism may drop in selected areas (Sonmez and Graefe, 1998). However, the impact of terrorism on tourism is not always clear. Some researchers have found that low-level terrorism gradually reduces tourism over a period of time, while sudden, vicious attacks have an immediate negative impact (Drakos and Kutan, 2003). Other researchers believe that the frequency of violence is more important than the severity of terrorist attacks (Pizam and Fleischer, 2002). Regardless of mixed findings, one aspect is clear. Terrorism against tourists has a negative economic impact; attacks on tourists have economic consequences.

Energy

The economic relationship between energy and terrorism is clearer than the impact on tourism, and terrorists have a vested interest in disrupting oil and gas production. Fossil fuels present tempting targets for two reasons: They represent the power and strength of the industrialized world, and strikes against oil refineries or transfer facilities have an economic impact on the West. Iraq serves as an example. U.S. forces invaded Iraq in the spring of 2003. An insurgency grew during the summer, and it was in full swing by November. The primary economic target of the insurgents was oil production. From June 2003 to February 2006, there were 298 attacks against oil-production facilities. The economic impact from the 26 percent reduction in oil production was devastating. The attacks resulted in $6.25 billion in lost revenue for 2005 (Daly, 2006a).

Al Qaeda noticed the impact of the oil attacks in Iraq. In January 2006, Osama bin Laden broke a 14-month silence to announce that the war against the United States would not be limited to Iraq. Saudi Arabia was a tempting target; bin Laden considered Saudi Arabia as nothing more than an American colony. Oil production at the time represented 40 percent of the country's gross domestic product (Daly, 2006a). Al Qaeda in the Arabian Peninsula, an offshoot of the original al Qaeda, began targeting Saudi oil facilities in 2003 with varied strategies. It sought to destroy production facilities; destroy transfer systems such as pipelines, storage facilities, and shipping; and target individual oil workers, especially foreigners. In an Internet posting, a spokesperson for al Qaeda said the Saudi attacks were designed to destroy the Saudi economy and create an energy crisis in the West. He also mentioned that attacking energy sources brought a good deal of press coverage (Bakier, 2006b). The lessons of Iraq have not been lost on al Qaeda.

The Carnegie Endowment for International Peace (Grare, 2013) reports that Pakistan is experiencing a similar problem in the Balochistan province, which produces 45 percent of the country's natural gas. At issue are the tribal divisions inside Pakistan and the energy produced in Balochistan. The Pashtun tribe controls the central government in Islamabad, and it exploits the natural gas resources in Balochistan to support ethnic Pashtuns. But Balochistan's major fields lie in the Bugti tribal area, and the Bugtis resent and resist Pashtun incursion into their native land. This has led to sharp fighting and a guerrilla war. John Daly (2006b) points out that the situation has become more complicated because of the resurgence of the Taliban along the Afghan–Pakistan border. Some Bugtis, who previously had few ethnic or political links with the Taliban, have allied with the exiled Afghan Taliban as well as al Qaeda members who fled Afghanistan in the wake of the October 2001 American offensive. Daly says that the Taliban believes that the most effective way to destroy the Pakistani government is to attack economic targets. Attacks on gas facilities cripple production and serve as a force multiplier. These areas breed many forms of tribal and ethnic conflicts, including **endemic terrorism**.

Africa presents another set of endemic terrorism. For example, oil has played a crucial role in violence in Nigeria. Oil in the Niger Delta represents a different opportunity for economic attack. It simultaneously funds terrorists and other violent groups while serving as a target for terrorism. In addition, dilapidated storage facilities and pipelines have become an ecological disaster for the impoverished local residents. The result is an environment that encourages subnational violence and that might serve as a base for international terrorism. Jakkie Cilliers (2003) notes that the energy environment in Africa represents an interesting paradox. According to Cilliers, if poverty, endemic terrorism, and criminalized politics are not addressed by the industrial world, areas with situations similar to those in the Niger Delta will evolve in two directions. They will become the base for the emergence of new international terrorist groups and thus provide excellent resources for training and eluding detection. At the same time, the energy resources in the delta will provide a target-rich environment for terrorists.

endemic terrorism: Terrorism that exists inside a political entity. For example, European colonialists created the nation of Rwanda by combining the lands of two tribes that literally hate each other. The two tribes fight to eliminate each other. This is endemic to political violence in Rwanda. The term was coined by J. Bowyer Bell.

Transportation

Transportation systems also present a tempting economic target because attacks on them can produce mass casualties with minimal effort. Another benefit for terrorists trying to strike economic targets is that the costs of protecting transportation are staggering. Transportation is a major concern of homeland security, and it will be discussed in Chapter 13. We restrict our discussion here to examining an economic attack on transportation as a force multiplier. Such attacks are quite effective.

After the September 11 attacks, the federal government immediately budgeted $4.8 billion to protect the aviation industry. In addition, it created a new federal agency, the Transportation Security Administration, with 30,000 employees (Hobijn, 2002). The global shipping industry is also affected by security costs. Indonesia, Malaysia, and Singapore have joined to protest insurance premiums on ships traveling through the Strait of Malacca, a passage way between Indonesia and Malaysia. Rates have soared because insurance companies believe terrorist groups might start cooperating with pirates (Raymond, 2006). Critics of homeland security policies, such as Stephen Flynn (2002, 2004a, 2004b), argue that ports remain unsecured because of the costs associated with increased protection. Although all of these examples represent policy issues, the economic impact is clear. Attacks on aviation, shipping, and transportation facilities increase the cost of security. If terrorists wish to increase the economic impact of an attack, the transportation industry presents a tempting target.

✓ **Self-Check**

> What is economic targeting?

> How do terrorists strike economic targets?

> Why are attacks on energy and transportation targets force multipliers?

Suicide Attacks: Conflicting Opinions

altruistic suicide: The willingness of individuals to sacrifice their lives to benefit their primary reference group, such as a family, military unit, ethnic group, or country. It may involve going on suicide missions in combat, self-sacrifice without killing others, or self-sacrifice that kills others.

Sacrifice in times of conflict is nothing new, and sometimes warriors are sent on missions where they know their lives will be lost. At other times in history, people intentionally have sacrificed their lives for a greater cause. Diego Gambetta (2005) tracks incidents of suicide tactics and attacks since World War II. He believes there are three major types of suicide attacks: (1) suicide in warfare, (2) suicide for a principle without killing others, and (3) suicidal terrorism. Several scholars note that a suicide attack is not a method chosen simply to end one's life. The social and psychological appeal is the idea of sacrificing one's self for the betterment of the community; it is a freely given sacrifice in the form of **altruistic suicide**. Suicide terrorists may be fatalistic, they may be psychologically duped, or they may be wealthy with a bright future. One thing they have in common, however, is that they frequently believe that they are sacrificing their lives for a greater good (Pape, 2003, 2005, pp. 171–195).

Although common logic sometimes dismisses suicide terrorists as psychologically unstable, and early studies suggested that suicide bombers were young, frustrated males, data suggest that neither is true (Howard, 2004). Robert Pape (2003, 2005) presents an extensive empirical analysis of suicide terrorist attacks from 1980 to 2001, and he concludes that the attackers are so diverse it may not be possible to find a single profile.

A Theory of Suicide Terrorism

theory of suicide terrorism: A theory developed by Robert Pape that states that a group of people occupied by a democratic power is likely to engage in suicide attacks when there are differences between the religions of the group and the democratic power and when the occupied religious community supports altruistic suicide.

Instead of searching for related social or psychological factors, Robert Pape (2005) suggests that suicide terrorism can be considered a strategic tool. It is popular because it works, and although suicide attacks began as a form of religious violence, secular groups use the strategy because it is so effective. Suicide terrorism, Pape argues, gives a small group the power to coerce large governments. Suicide terrorists tend to be more lethal than those carrying out other types of attacks, they strike greater fear in the target audience, and each attack hints at future horrific violence. It is a strategy designed to multiply expectations of political victory.

Pape (2005) takes his empirical study of suicide bombing beyond a simple description of how it happens and offers a **theory of suicide terrorism**. He believes three factors must be in place before a suicide terror campaign can take place. First, a nationalistic or ethnic group must be resisting the occupation of a foreign power. Second, the foreign power must have a democratic government whose voters will not routinely allow the indiscriminate slaughter and total repression of the people in the occupied area. Finally, there must be a difference in the religions of the occupying power and the people living under occupation. This is a key point in the theory. Such terrorism does not happen when the occupied and occupier share a single religion; it is caused by differences between the two religions.

Pape (2005, pp. 127–128) says that it is difficult to test this theory because there are so many different factors, but he argues that it might be possible to test it by focusing on evidence from case studies. He does so by looking at the Israeli occupation of the Shi'ite areas of Lebanon, the Sinhalese (Buddhist) control of the Tamil (Hindu) region of Sri Lanka, the fighting between Sunni Kurds and Sunni Turks in eastern Turkey, and Sikhs in India.

The popular conception in Lebanon is that suicide operations are grounded in Islamic extremism; that is, militant Islamic theology causes suicide terrorism. However, Pape's examination of bombings casts doubt on this conclusion. Of the 41 suicide attacks Pape studied, only eight involved the suicide of Islamic militants. Twenty-seven were conducted by Communists who followed no religion, and the remaining three were carried out by Christians. Although Iran supports Hezbollah, the group that first employed modern terrorist suicide attacks, terrorism is homegrown in Lebanon. Bombers come from local communities where self-sacrifice is glorified by religious leaders (Pape, 2005, pp. 128–139).

Sri Lanka presents an interesting scenario because the Hindu Tamil area has been occupied by two powers—native Buddhist Sinhalese and primarily Hindu Indian soldiers. Again, the popular theory of suicide terrorism in Sri Lanka is that the Black Tigers, the suicide organization within the LTTE, brainwash their bombers. The LTTE Black Tigers have conducted more suicide bombings than any other group, and they have assassinated two political leaders—an Indian prime minister and a president of Sri Lanka. Yet, when Hindu Indian soldiers were stationed in Sri Lanka from 1987 to 1990, suicide bombings stopped (Pape, 2005, pp. 139–154).

Pape attributes the cessation of suicide bombings during the Indian occupation to the differences between the Sinhalese Buddhists and the Tamil Hindus. The Tamils believe their existence is threatened by the dominant Sinhalese government, and many of their religious leaders have demonized the Buddhists. Extremist Buddhists respond by dismissing Hinduism. This difference, Pape believes, is the primary cause of suicide terrorism in Sri Lanka. He does, however, note that there are exceptions; in 1991, former prime minister of India was assassinated by the Black Tigers when it appeared that Indian forces might return to Sri Lanka. Pape says that he is not proposing a rule that cannot be broken; rather, he is pointing out a trend.

This logic may also apply to Pape's ideas about democracy. For example, a Christian Russia occupies Chechnya, which is populated by Sunnis with a strong Sufi influence. Russians believe Chechnya is a Russian state, but many Chechens believe they live in independent country. Although Russia has experienced the birth of some forms of democracy, the central Russian government has revoked many of the resulting democratic reforms. Chechens have used suicide operations to oppose Russian occupation, including massive suicide attacks. Again, when considering such a situation, Pape would probably not insist that the occupying power must be a full democracy; rather, he is pointing to a trend, and his evidence suggests that trends exist.

The Kurdistan Workers' Party (PKK) in eastern Turkey conducted 14 suicide attacks from 1996 to 1999, and overall, they were unique. They were the least deadly attacks in the course of modern suicide bombing, killing an average of two people per incident. They started when the popular leader of the PKK called for them, and they stopped at his command. Pape believes that the reason the attacks never became popular is that the Sunni Kurd community identified with the Sunni Turks. Pape (2005, pp. 162–167) found the same trend in the Indian province of Punjab.

Other Research on Suicide Bombing

Studies by many scholars and terrorism analysts confirm Pape's findings. Journalist B. Raman (2003, 2004) says that terrorists favor suicide attacks because they are so intimidating. He points out that suicide bombers can penetrate secure targets with a good chance of success. Audrey Cronin (2003, pp. 9–11) gives several reasons for the popularity of suicide attacks. They generate high casualties as well as publicity for the attacking group. The nature of the attacks strike fear into an enemy, and the attacks are effective against superior forces and weapons. Suicide bombers give terrorist groups maximal control over attacks.

However, other studies bring Pape's finding into question. Domenico Tosini (2009) notes the alarming increase of suicide attacks by terrorist groups and he examines the explanations presented in scholarly studies. Most examinations of suicide bombings are based on the idea of strategic logic; that is, studies assume that both the bomber and the supporting organization are rational actors seeking to accomplish goals. In fact, Tosini finds that almost all the literature focuses on rational choice. He argues that rational choice is not the only explanation for suicide bombing.

Tosini believes the link between suicide and religion has been disproved, given that secular terrorist groups have also employed the tactic. To be sure, religion remains a strong factor for many groups. Not only can it be used to justify attacks; it can also serve as a tool to recruit and retain terrorists. Yet, Tosini believes that rational choice and religion are secondary factors in suicide attacks. The major factor is the social structure and culture of the group engaged in suicide terrorism.

Tosini says that groups take actions inside social structures based on their understanding of reality. This can create group dynamics that lead to suicide terrorism. The dynamic agents involved in a suicide bombing are the armed terrorist group, the group's supporters, and the bombers. These three entities operate in social networks where decisions are made based on interpretations of situations. The decision to engage in suicide bombing is based on the interactions of terrorists, supporters, and attackers within a surrounding social network.

Moving beyond rational choice, Tosini argues that the social climate must readily accept suicide bombings. Supporters of a terrorist group have to embrace the idea and create social rewards for bombers and their relatives. Beyond this, the entire community must accept violence as a normative response to social grievances and believe that suicide bombing is an acceptable expression of violence. Supporting groups need material and symbolic rewards, and attackers must have a deep attachment to idealized representations of their communities. Tosini says that when altruism enters the equation, it produces a culture of martyrdom. This, in turn, combines with two common military approaches to war—dehumanization and depersonalization of enemies.

Tosini's research indicates that suicide bombing is not simply a strategic model based on rational choice. It also calls into question the relationship of religion and democracy to suicide attacks. He argues that suicide terrorism develops when a culture accepts it as an expression of altruistic martyrdom and when terrorist groups within the culture embrace the tactic. A bomber consumed with dreams of becoming a martyr can be launched against innocent people or military targets because enemies have been defined as something less than human. In Tosini's view, suicide bombing takes place through a social process that endorses self-sacrifice as a legitimate expression of normal behavior.

Sara Jackson Wade and Daniel Reiter (2007) examined suicide bombings from 1980 to 2003, and their findings differ from Pape's. Wade and Reiter argue that the form of government is not an important factor. In other words, suicide bombings are not used mainly against democracies. Their data show that differing forms of governments with strong religious minorities experience attacks more frequently than democracies, and they think that Pape missed this point because he used different variables in his research model.

In contrast to Pape, Wade and Reiter believe that Islam is an important factor in suicide bombings, but these are not simply attacks developed to use against the West. They found that Muslim states suffer more suicide attacks than Western states, and more Muslims are targeted in suicide attacks than any other group. A democracy occupying a foreign land with a different religion has little to do with these attacks, they argue. The presence of Islam is more important, and past experience with suicide bombing makes the tactic more acceptable and more likely.

Models for Suicide Bombing

There is a debate about modeling attacks. Rohan Gunaratna (2000) suggests that it may be possible to model some precursors of suicide bombings. After examining suicide attacks between 1983 and 2000, Gunaratna sees three things that all attacks have in common: secrecy, reconnaissance, and rehearsal. He believes that local groups operate in secret to prepare the bomber and the target area. Because locals can blend in with the surroundings, they provide supplies and information. They also conduct the initial scouting or reconnaissance of the target. A support group far away from the target can rehearse the attack in secrecy; the better the rehearsal, the greater the chance of success. The bomber usually conducts the final reconnaissance during the operation, but he or she can detonate the bomb in case of discovery. These factors could serve as the basis for a model.

Another school of thought suggests that models may exist, but there are so many factors that a single set of precursors cannot exist. Audrey Cronin (2003, pp. 6–8) believes that different styles of bombings emerge from different places. The Hamas model, patterned after the actions of Hezbollah, uses a professional group to plan and execute the attack and a support group to prepare the attacker. For many years, researchers believed that this was the only model for suicide bombing (Institute for Counter-Terrorism, 2001).

Cronin finds, however, that different models have emerged over time. The LTTE trained suicide bombers from an early age. The PKK leadership coerced victims to take part in suicide bombings. The September 11 suicide attacks defied the previous models, and bombings in Chechnya represent a different combination of social and psychological factors. There is no single model for suicide bombing.

✓ Self-Check	> Why is suicide used as a weapon?
	> What do empirical studies suggest about suicide terrorism?
	> How might suicide terrorism be stopped?

Tactical Misunderstandings and Gender

Criminologists frequently complain that females are often ignored in the study of crime, unless the study focuses on victimization. Researchers have said the same thing about the study of gender and terrorism (Oliverio and Lauderdale, 2005; Sjoberg, 2009). The main reason for this is a cultural stereotype that brackets women in traditional roles. Many researchers and the general public do not envision women performing the "male" terrorist tasks (Neuberger and Valentini, 1996, pp. 28–36; see also Maleeha, 2012). These attitudes ignore reality. Women have been and remain active in terrorist causes, and their role is increasing. They increase the tactical effectiveness of terrorist groups and the complexity of counterterrorism efforts.

Tactical Roles and Organization

Margaret Gonzalez-Perez (2008) found that the role of women in terrorist groups is more closely related to the political orientation of an organization than to its tactics. She examined 26 terrorist organizations that emerged in the decades after World War II. She separated these groups into those with an international focus and those that embraced domestic issues. (Gonzalez-Perez uses the term **international focus** to refer to terrorist groups operating in multiple countries and the term **domestic issues** to refer to groups within a single country concerned with political or social problems.) Her findings indicate that political and social ideology is closely related to the roles women play in terrorist groups. She says that paternalism, religious traditions, and political orientation are the dominant influences in the process.

Gonzalez-Perez says that women are more attracted to domestic terrorist organizations than to international groups. The reason, she believes, deals with the purposes of the respective groups. Domestic organizations are focused on revolution and social change. Women are attracted to such groups because they have a chance to redefine their roles, and males and females welcome them because they want the same change. Some groups even have a feminist agenda. Women also have opportunities for leadership in revolutionary groups. International terrorists resist outside forces such as capitalism and imperialism. They try to defend a traditional culture that limits the role of women. Yet, women also emerge in traditional organizations when there is a need to recruit personnel and when terrorism becomes a popular means of social expression.

Gathering data from a variety of geographical areas, Gonzalez-Perez offers a strong argument. After examining domestic and international terrorism in the Americas, Africa, the Middle East, Asia, and Europe, her data show that women in domestic groups gravitate toward combat and leadership. The same findings reveal that women in international groups are given more limited roles. International terrorists tend to employ women as supporters, sympathizers, and spies. They seldom receive combat or leadership positions. This pattern remains constant even in social systems that emphasize male dominance. For example, she says that one would think that the machismo influence in Central and South America would blunt female leadership and combat roles, but the opposite is true. Most Central and South American groups have a left-wing revolutionary focus. Women move into active roles because the groups are seeking to restructure their culture and political structure. Every geographical area that she studied produced a common trend: Domestic groups emphasized the role of women even when the group had no stated feminist agenda.

Cindy Ness (2005) offers a similar argument after examining the behavior of women in secular and religious terrorist groups. Using the groups Liberation Tigers of Tamil Ealam (LTTE), Hamas, and Islamic Jihad, Ness argues that modern terrorism began around 1968. Females played an immediate role. Women were relegated to support and service in religious terrorist groups, but they developed combat and leadership positions in secular organizations. Ness argues that this has been fairly constant since the spread of ideological terrorism after 1968. She points to **Ulricke Meinhof** and **Leila Khalid** as examples of female participation in revolutionary terrorism. Both women not only served as combatants, they were also leaders and served as inspiration for supporters. Unfortunately, Ness believes, most terrorism analysts have ignored the role of women in revolutionary groups.

international focus: Gonzalez-Perez uses the term *international focus* to refer to terrorist groups operating in multiple countries.

domestic issues: Gonzalez-Perez uses the term *domestic issues* to refer to groups within a country fighting to change the social or political structure of that nation.

Ulricke Meinhof: (1934–1976) co-created the German Red Army Faction with Andreas Baader in 1970. She was the co-leader of the group. Arrested in 1972, she committed suicide in prison.

Leila Khalid: (b. 1944) was a member of the Popular Front for the Liberation of Palestine. In 1969, she was part of a team that hijacked four aircraft that were destroyed after the passengers and crews disembarked. Arrested in 1970 after another attempted hijacking, she was released as part of a prisoner exchange.

Religious terrorist groups began to emerge in the 1980s while nationalistic and ethnic groups continued to operate. Ness says the roles of women followed a similar path in each of these movements. Conservative male-dominated religious terrorists relegated females to secondary status. Ethnic and nationalistic groups also limited the roles of women. Given the fact that revolutionary groups offered more opportunities for women, one would expect that females would not be as active in religious and nationalistic movements. However, the opposite was true. The reason, Ness explains, is that these movements appealed to a wider audience. Revolutionary groups attracted women, but the groups were small, and so were the number of supporters. Religious and ethnic nationalists recruited from a larger pool of supporters than the earlier left-wing groups. Even though the roles of women were more limited in the traditional groups, there were more women available to work in them. Therefore, Ness explains, more women were involved in traditional movements.

The number of women attracted to religious terrorist organizations also suggests that their roles will expand. Ness believes that because they are so numerous, they will increasingly receive combat assignments. Aside from all of the traditional restrictions of male-dominated religious hierarchies, terrorist groups need personnel. When women are available, they are given combat assignments as the need arises. Ness does not know if this practice will extend to leadership. There is no reason to automatically believe that religious groups will continue to limit the opportunity for female leadership. Women may begin organizing and taking leadership roles, or they may take charge out of necessity when male leaders are captured or killed.

Tactical Considerations

Groups with diverse missions tend to recruit and operate in different ways. Ideology draws certain types of recruits to a movement, and it influences the tactics terrorist groups employ. For example, a revolutionary group trying to overthrow a government and win popular support is not likely to attack with a nuclear weapon. The reason is clear: If political terrorists were to use a nuclear weapon, the public would unite against them, placing the terrorists at a disadvantage. Small groups cannot achieve their objectives against a united mass of people. Religious terrorists, on the other hand, might be tempted to detonate a nuclear device. They have no concern about popular support, and if they lose, they believe a deity will call new followers to carry the struggle forward. Ideology and mission affect operations.

When suicide terrorism reappeared in the 1980s, audiences were appalled. They wondered why a grown man would strap on a bomb and kill himself. Terrorists took advantage of this, and suicide bombings increased. As such attacks became more routine, audiences grew accustomed to seeing suicide bombers. Some terrorist groups, seeking increased psychological impact from suicide attacks, sought new types of bombers. They began using women. Both researchers and the public believed women were manipulated into the act (Deylami, 2013). They refused to accept the idea that women might be devoted to a cause and motivated to sacrifice their lives (Nacos, 2005).

Overlooking Female Terrorists: A Tactical Mistake

If women have been terrorists throughout history, one wonders why their role has been overlooked. Alisa Stack-O'Conner (2007) says female terrorism has been ignored for the same reason that female criminality has been underplayed. Researchers do not tend to think of women as terrorists or criminals, and when they do look at females, researchers usually see them as victims. In addition, law enforcement officers do not tend to arrest females.

Other scholars argue that women have been overlooked because it is generally assumed that terrorism is a violent male occupation. Americans like to think of female terrorists as an aberration, according to Cindy Ness (2005), and American popular culture does not accept the idea that females are terrorists. When females are used as attackers or suicide bombers, Katharina von Knop (2007) believes, they are following a male model instead of assuming roles they would define on their own. Von Knop believes that women have a greater role to play in leadership and maintaining organizations. They do not need to imitate males, von Knop argues. Female warriors differ from their male counterparts. Research from the International Crisis Group (ISG; 2009) in Kyrgyzstan suggests that this is correct. The ISG found that when women move into radical religious groups on their own, they seem to create organizations that provide social organization and sustainability.

Laura Sjoberg (2009) takes the argument further. She is extremely critical of the scholarly literature on women and terrorism. For the most part, her research shows, studies of women in terrorism are generally ignored, and when females are discussed, it is in gendered terms. They are not "terrorists," they are "women involved in terrorism," she says. There are exceptions but most scholars and analysts conclude that women play some type of nebulous role in terrorism. They cannot define the role, and they do not seem to care to do so. Media presentations follow the same tack. Women are neither significant nor worthy of analysis.

Sjoberg vehemently disagrees with such characterizations. Women, she writes, do have a special place in terrorism; women are terrorists in the same way that men are terrorists. There are terrorists who happen to be women, and they have been around for quite some time. There is also no feminist perspective on terrorism; rather, there are feminists who study terrorism in a variety of ways. Sjoberg says that scholars and other researchers are reluctant to study political and criminal violence among women because doing so violates idealized notions of womanhood. Their behavior should be studied from a variety of feminist perspectives, Sjoberg concludes. Such studies would enrich the field.

Sjoberg has a point. Women are playing an increasing role in terrorist operations in all types of organizations. Groups with revolutionary or feminist objectives give them leadership and combat roles. More traditional groups relegate women to support roles, but they are being employed more frequently in tactical operations. Even the most traditional terrorist groups find that there are tactical advantages to using women. In Central Asia, women have even developed their own paths to terrorism, and they sustain them without assistance from groups dominated by men. Finally, while gender-specific roles exist, Sjoberg is correct. There are both men and women who happen to be terrorists. Each gender can be deployed with certain tactical benefits.

Analysts and researchers who assume that female participation in terrorism is an abnormality fail to grasp the nature of terrorism (Nacos, 2005). This leads to tactical and strategic mistakes. For example, popular assumptions suggest that terrorism in Central Asia is an expression of masculinity in a society where females are repressed (Deylami, 2013; Poloni-Staudinger and Orbtals, 2014). Therefore, women in Afghanistan and Pakistan must be rescued. Conversely, when female political leaders in the United States respond to terrorism, voters tend to think they are less effective than males making similar decisions (Holman et al., 2011). The false assumption in such cases is that women cannot effectively respond to terrorism.

Women play important roles in terrorism. Research should focus on the types of functions they perform and methods for countering them. Most counterterrorist tactics focus on methods to prevent young men from joining terrorist groups. The same attention should be focused on young women. Anything else is a tactical miscalculation.

✓ Self-Check

> What roles do women tend to play in differing types of terrorist groups?
> Why do Americans generally ignore female terrorists?
> Why have researchers in general failed to study the roles of women in terrorist groups?

Emphasizing the Points

The tactics of terrorism are straightforward and simple, but they are employed in innovative ways. The study of terrorism is complex as a result of tactical innovation. Force multipliers—technology, transnational support, religion, and the media—enhance the power of terrorist groups. Technological attacks can be made more effective by using WMD, cyberattacks, and/or economic targeting. Suicide bombing has become a particularly terrorizing tactic, but there is no single explanation for either understanding or preventing it. It is important to understand the tactical impact of gender on terrorism, but research on women's roles has been neglected, which leads to strategic and tactical mistakes.

SUMMARY OF CHAPTER OBJECTIVES

- The six basic tactics of terrorism are bombing, arson, hijacking, assault, kidnapping, and taking hostages. Terrorists employ these tactics in a variety of ways.
- Force multipliers increase terrorists' attacking power without increasing personnel.
- Force multipliers include technology, transnational support, media coverage, and religious fanaticism.
- Technology can enhance striking power when it is employed as a weapon or when it becomes the target of an attack. Any form of technology may be used. Cyberterrorism is a growing threat. Computer systems can be infected, or data can be stolen. Terrorists or other enemies might attack computer controlled systems to cause a catastrophic failure in the economic sector or infrastructure.
- Technology also increases the lethality of potential weapons, giving them the potential for mass destruction. Biological agents include bacterial and viral weapons. There are four types of biological agents: (1) natural poisons, or toxins that occur without human modification; (2) viruses; (3) bacteria; and (4) plagues. There are four types of chemical agents: (1) nerve agents, (2) blood agents, (2) choking agents, and (4) blistering agents. Radiological weapons are closely related to chemical weapons, and they could be used by dispersing high doses of radiation in a conventional manner.
- Nuclear terrorism involves the potential employment of a nuclear bomb. There are two methods for constructing a nuclear device. The simplest method is to use HEU in a homemade bomb. The other method would be to gain control of an existing device. Some scholars and analysts believe that this will not happen, and others think that it will. Regardless, the United States is not prepared for

nuclear terrorism. The country needs to develop a cooperative climate among security bureaucracies and create an in-depth multifaceted defense.

- The force of terrorism can be multiplied by the selection of transnational economic targets. Tourism, energy, and transportation present excellent opportunities for increasing the economic impact of an attack.

- Pape's theory of suicide terrorism is based on examining religious differences when a democracy occupies a foreign country or the enclave of an ethnic group. Local religious leaders must create a climate where martyrdom is supported. Other research suggests that religion is not related to suicide bombings. It is difficult to model suicide terrorism because there is no single group or individual profile of suicide attackers. Different groups use different methods, and suicide bombers come from a variety of backgrounds.

- Women have been involved in terrorist groups throughout the history of modern terrorism, but their role has been ignored, just as criminologists frequently overlook female crime. Many researchers and the general public have found it difficult to believe that women could become terrorists.

- Female terrorists impact tactics, and security forces often overlook the threats they pose. Different types of groups tend to use females in different manners. Nationalistic and ethnic groups tend to use them in supporting roles, but women often emerge as warriors and leaders in revolutionary groups. Failure to understand these roles leads to tactical mistakes.

LOOKING INTO THE FUTURE

New technologies promise to increase the lethality of terrorism, although terrorists will use them without changing traditional tactics. The destructive power of standard and improvised weapons will increase, and new techniques for concealing weapons will be developed, which will require improved detection capabilities. Changing methods of how terrorists communicate will lead to an increase in virtual groups, potentially giving local organizations global recruiting capabilities and the ability to strike the industrialized world. Cyberattacks and cybercrime will increase. Local terrorists will mainly engage in low-level attacks, however, because sophisticated tactical operations require extensive logistical support. Suicide bombing will continue and may spread to the West. As research in gender issues and terrorism improves, the tactical capabilities of security forces will be enhanced.

KEY TERMS

Six tactics of terrorism, p. 102

Force multiplier, p. 102

Philosophy of the bomb, p. 103

Thermobaric bomb, p. 103

Cyberterrorism, p. 104

Bacterial weapons, p. 105

Viral weapons, p. 105

Highly enriched uranium (HEU), p. 107

Radiation sickness, p. 108

Nuclear black market, p. 110

Endemic terrorism, p. 113

Altruistic suicide, p. 114

Theory of suicide terrorism, p. 114

International focus, p. 118

Domestic issues, p. 118

Ulricke Meinhof, p. 118

Leila Khalid, p. 118

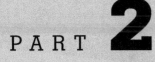

PART 2

International Terrorism: National and Ethnic Movements

CHAPTER 6

Long-Term Separatist Terrorism

LEARNING OBJECTIVES

After reading this chapter, you should be able to:

▶ Explain the nature and characteristics of nationalistic and ethnic separatist terrorism.

▶ Describe the emergence of the modern IRA and terrorism in Northern Ireland.

▶ Outline the basis for negotiating peace in Northern Ireland.

▶ Summarize the nature of Basque culture and its separateness within Spain.

▶ Explain the impact of the Spanish Civil War on the Basque region.

▶ Summarize the birth and evolution of the ETA.

▶ Explain the rise of the GAL.

▶ Outline the Spanish government's approach to Basque separatism.

▶ Describe the rise of the LTTE and the role of the Tamil diaspora.

▶ Summarize the unique aspect of LTTE suicide bombings.

▶ Describe the end of the LTTE and the danger of possible reconstitution.

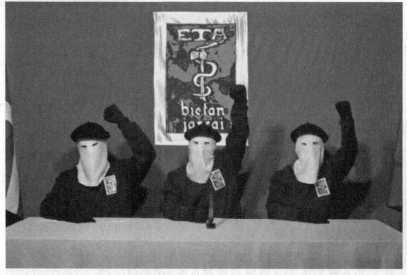

An ETA News Conference

The Basque Nation and Liberty (ETA), an organization that waged a campaign of terrorism against Spain for nearly a half century, released a declaration in October 2011. According to an article in the *New York Times* (Burns, 2011), the ETA stated that it was ending its campaign of violence. It had accepted a cease-fire a few years earlier, and except for a few flare-ups, the fragile peace remained intact. This new declaration went further. It was not a simple agreement to stop fighting. It was a call for a complete cessation of all violence. The long war appeared to be finally over.

The statement was important both for the items it addressed and for the things it did not say. Acknowledging the suffering and the nature of terrorism, the ETA recognized the need to abandon violence. It was not working. In addition, Spanish security forces had become increasingly effective. They had also formed close working relationships with French law enforcement in the Basque region of France, denying an important refuge for the separatists. Finally, the Spanish government had been making political progress in the Basque homeland in Spain. Authorities recognized that separatist issues could not be handled by force alone. As expressed in counterinsurgency doctrine, the government recognized that it had to win a political consensus with the Basque people. The Spanish government was dedicated to this effort, and its actions were paying off.

There were also unspoken issues in the statement. The ETA did not say that it was surrendering, and there was no indication that the group was forever disbanded. The statement also gave no hint that it had dropped its demands for Basque independence or that it would agree to any of Spain's long-term demands. It simply called for direct talks with the Spanish government. The political issues surrounding the decades-long conflict had not been settled.

The first decade of the twenty-first century brought seemingly peaceful political solutions to three violent separatist movements: the renewed troubles in Ireland resulting from civil disturbances in 1969, the ETA's campaign for Basque autonomy, and a long campaign of savage guerrilla warfare and terrorism among two ethnic groups on the island nation of Sri Lanka. All of the conflicts appeared to end. Yet, terrorism involves extremist positions, and extremists are seldom satisfied with compromise. The central question for the next two decades is: Will the political solutions in Ireland, Spain, and Sri Lanka mollify the extremists who call for no compromise? The answer will be determined by the actions of governments as separatists are reintegrated into mainstream politics. Not all of the signs are promising.

Ethnic and Nationalist Separatist Movements

The focus on international terrorism has diverted attention from some of the world's separatist movements; yet, these struggles have shaped modern terrorism. Such wars are asymmetrical, pitting small groups of separatists against larger government forces. This usually leads to the most common tactic in asymmetrical warfare, terrorism (Hanzich, 2003). Since ethnic separatists use the same tactics as ideological terrorists, most analysts and policymakers have approached the two forms of terrorism in the same manner. However, by the end of the twentieth century, some American diplomats began to question this approach, saying that because the structure of ethnic violence had changed, the old models were no longer applicable. The earlier approach obscured the nature of separatist violence (Trundle, 1996; Porath, 2010).

Characteristics of Ethnic and Nationalist Terrorism

Peter Neuman (2007), director of the Center for Defense Studies at King's College London, applauds this shift because it presents an opportunity for understanding and approaching separatists. Unlike religious terrorists, separatists usually have a clear-cut, achievable goal, and they are usually not imbued with the nihilism of ideological groups with pure "absolute" goals. This point presents an opportunity for political pragmatism and negotiation, Neuman argues. Indeed, much of the violence described in this chapter might have been settled much earlier had the governments opposing the separatists moved to the negotiating table. Political accommodation is the most effective method for ending a terrorist campaign, according to a recent study by the RAND Corporation (Jones and Libicki, 2008).

In an earlier RAND study, Daniel Byman (1998) concludes that ethnic terrorism differs from terrorism carried out in the name of ideology, religion, or economic gain. He acknowledges the growing influence of religion on terrorism, but he believes ethnic terrorism is a unique entity, though the line between ethnic and religious violence is blurred. Ethnic terrorists are usually more nationalistic than their religious counterparts. He uses evidence from the Liberation Tigers of Tamil Eelam (LTTE), the Kurdistan Workers' Party (PKK), the Provisional Irish Republican Army (PIRA), and the ETA as evidence for his thesis.

Ethnic terrorists try to forge a national identity. Their primary purpose is to mobilize a community, and they do so by appealing to the nationalistic background of a particular ethnic group. Byman says that terrorist activity is used to make a statement about the group's identity. When the inevitable governmental persecution follows terrorist actions, it draws attention to the group and allows the terrorists to present themselves as victims. This process may increase public awareness of ethnic or nationalistic grievances, and it may lead to new sources of support. Terrorism also polarizes other ethnic groups and forces them to either ally with the terrorists or oppose them.

In the past decade, jihadist networks have come to play a significant role in European terrorism. North African groups operate in Spain and Italy. Middle Eastern networks are active in Germany, Belgium, the Netherlands, France, and the United Kingdom. France also has ties with groups from Algeria (Kohlman, 2004). Yet, a recent analysis of European law enforcement data suggests that separatist violence is the most dangerous threat to Europe. Measured by the sheer number of attacks, separatists present more of a threat to Europe than any other form of terrorism (Renard, 2009). Separatist violence differs from ideological and religious terrorism, and it needs to be examined to unveil its unique qualities.

Violence plays a special role in ethnic terrorism. Whereas political terrorists use violence in a symbolic manner and religious extremists use it to make a theological statement, violence is the *raison d'être* of ethnic terrorism. It keeps an idea alive. Some data even suggest that separatist terrorism is the most violent form of terrorism in the modern world (Masters, 2008). As long as a bomb goes off or a police officer is murdered, the identity and existence of ethnic differences cannot be denied. Violence sustains the conflict, even when political objectives are far out of reach. The fear created by violence serves ethnic interests. Violence also serves to undermine moderates who seek peaceful solutions; yet, peaceful negotiated settlements have proved to be the most effective method for ending ethnic and nationalistic terrorism.

Three Cases of Ethnic and Nationalist Separatism

Nationalistic and ethnic separatist groups studied the tactics of the People's Will and began to copy them in the early part of the twentieth century. Three of these campaigns lasted for many years, and the one in Spain recently ended although tensions remain high. The longest campaign took place in a series of waves in Ireland beginning in 1916 and slowly diminishing in the early twenty-first century. Modern terrorism is associated with the 1916 Easter Rising, the Black and Tan War of 1919 to 1921, and the resurgent Irish Republican Army of 1956 and 1969. Irish nationalists, long angered by the colonial rule of England, incorporated terrorist techniques into their revolt against British rule, and their experiences evolved as weapons technology improved. The Irish Republican Army set the stage for modern separatist terrorism, and terrorism in Ireland is the product of a long, long story.

Another lengthy struggle grew in the Basque region of Spain. During a savage civil war in the 1930s, two ethnic Basque provinces sided against the fascist forces.

When the fascists were successful, the government introduced repressive measures, angering the Basques and causing them to create a government in exile. In the midst of a turbulent series of ideological struggles in the late 1960s, a group of Basque students and workers decided the time was ripe for independence. The Euskadi Ta Askatasuna (ETA) was born, and it is Europe's longest surviving ethnic conflict. It also produced death squads, at times devolving into a dirty war pitting terrorists against self-appointed guardians of the government who operated outside the rule of law.

The island of Sri Lanka has two primary ethnic groups—Sinhalese who dominate the population and minority Tamils. Tensions between the two groups grew after independence in 1948, resulting in sporadic outbursts of violence. Many Tamils left the island, and some of them became economically successful. Their money flowed back to the island as ethnic tensions increased. Fearing repression from the Sinhalese and a deteriorating political situation, a militant group of Tamils, the Liberation Tigers of Tamil Eelam (LTTE), used the money to buy weapons. The Sri Lankan government and the LTTE fought each other savagely from 1983 to 2009, and the LTTE pioneered many methods of terrorist attacks, including the secular use of suicide bombings.

Ethnic terrorism in separatist movements ranges through many parts of the world. Ireland appears to have degenerated into low-level criminal activity by small groups of former terrorists. It also continues to have lingering political hate crimes, including the murder of people of another religious tradition. The LTTE was defeated in 2009, but it may rise again. Despite negotiated peace settlements, the ETA continues to conduct operations. These three examples constitute the longest ethnic–nationalist conflicts since the advent of modern terrorism.

✔	Self-Check	>	What separates ethnic and nationalist terrorism from other forms of terror?
		>	How do separatist movements impact the level of violence?
		>	Why might separatist movements be amenable to negotiated solutions?

Modern Terrorism in Northern Ireland

Eamon de Valera was elected prime minister of the Republic of Ireland in 1927. Although he passed several anti-British measures, he was soon at odds with the IRA. Two important trends emerged. Bell (1997) records the first by pointing to the split in IRA ranks. By the 1930s, some members of the IRA wanted to follow the lead of their political party, Sinn Fein. They felt that the IRA should express itself through peaceful political idealism. They believed that they should begin working for a united socialist Ireland in the spirit of James Connolly.

Another group of IRA members rejected this philosophy. They believed that the purpose of the IRA was to fight for independence. They would never be at peace with the British or the Unionists until Northern Ireland was united with the south. They vowed to carry on the fight. They broke with the de Valera government and formed a breakaway wing of the IRA in the 1930s. The Provisional IRA vowed to keep up the fight, and de Valera turned on them. Robert White (1993, p. 26) says that the IRA was active from 1939 to 1944 in England. They launched an ineffective terrorist campaign in Northern Ireland from 1956 to 1962, when they fell out of favor with Irish Republicans.

J. Bowyer Bell (1997, p. 307) believes that the reason for IRA impotence can be found in the second generation of **Provisionals**. Wanting to follow in the footsteps of their forebears, the Provisionals began to wage a campaign against the

Provisionals: the nickname for members of the Provisional Irish Republican Army. They are also known as Provos. The name applies to several different Republican paramilitary terrorist groups.

Royal Ulster Constabulary (RUC): the police force in Northern Ireland 1922–2001. It was replaced by the Police Service of Northern Ireland (PSNI).

Royal Ulster Constabulary (RUC) in Northern Ireland in the late 1950s. They established support bases in the republic and slipped across the border for terrorist activities. Although the Provisionals initially enjoyed support among Republican enclaves in the north, most Irish people, Unionists and Republicans alike, were appalled by IRA violence. Even the Official IRA—the segment embracing a socialist ideology—criticized the military attacks of the Provisionals. Faced with a lack of public support, the Provisional IRA called off its offensive in the north. By 1962, almost all of its activities had ceased. Some Provisionals joined the civil rights movement; others rejoined former colleagues in the Official wing. Most members, however, remained in a secret infrastructure, hoping events would restore their ranks and prestige.

Just when it seemed that the Provisional IRA was defunct, a Catholic civil rights campaign engulfed Northern Ireland in 1969. The failure of the civil rights movement in Northern Ireland can be directly linked to modern Irish terrorism and the rebirth of the IRA. Alfred McClung Lee (1983, pp. 59–97) notes that the economic situation in Northern Ireland favored the Protestant Unionists. From 1922 to 1969, the government in Northern Ireland systematically reduced the civil rights of Catholics living in the north. During the same period, the economic power of the Unionists increased. When Catholics demanded the same rights as Protestants in 1969, demonstrations grew violent. The British Army was called in to support the RUC.

The IRA and the Modern "Troubles"

According to Lee (1983, pp. 59–97), the political and economic conditions in Northern Ireland provided the rationale for a major civil rights movement among the Catholics. Although the movement had Republican overtones, it was primarily aimed at achieving adequate housing and education among Ulster's Catholic population in an attempt to improve economic growth. The civil rights movement was supported by both Protestants and Catholics, but the actions of the Northern Ireland government began to polarize the issue. Increasingly, the confrontation became recognized as a Unionist–Republican one, and the old battle lines between Protestants and Catholics were redrawn. By 1969, the civil rights movement and the reaction to it had become violent.

The IRA had not been dormant throughout the civil rights movement, but it had failed to play a major role. For the most part, the leaders of the civil rights movement were peaceful Republicans. The IRA could not entice the civil rights leaders to join it in a guerrilla war, and it had virtually destroyed itself in an earlier campaign against the government of Northern Ireland. In 1969, the Provisional IRA was popular in song and legend, but it held little sway in day-to-day Irish politics. Some type of miracle would be needed to rejuvenate the IRA.

Repression on the part of the Northern government was the answer to IRA prayers. The government in Northern Ireland reacted with a heavy hand against the civil rights workers and demonstrators. Max Hastings (1970, pp. 40–56) writes that peaceful attempts to work for equal rights were stymied by Northern Irish militancy. Catholics were not allowed to demonstrate for better housing and education; if they attempted to do so, they were attacked by the RUC and its reserve force, known as B-Specials. At the same time, no attempts were made to stop Protestant demonstrations. The Catholics believed that the RUC and B-Specials were in league with the other anti-Catholic Unionists in the north.

Issues intensified in the summer of 1969. Civil rights demonstrators planned a long, peaceful march from Londonderry to Belfast, but they were gassed and beaten

FIGURE **6.1** Map of Ireland

by the RUC and B-Specials. On August 15, 1969, the Protestants assembled for their traditional Apprentice Boys celebration. Just a few days before, the RUC had enthusiastically attacked Catholic demonstrators, but on August 15, 1969, it welcomed the Protestant Apprentice Boys with open arms. The Catholics were not surprised: Many B-Specials had taken off their reservist uniforms to don orange sashes and march with the Protestants.

Protestant marchers in Londonderry and Belfast armed themselves with gasoline bombs, rocks, and sticks. They not only wished to celebrate the seventeenth-century victory in Derry, but they were also thrilled by the recent dispersal of the civil rights marchers and hoped to reinforce their political status by bombarding Catholic neighborhoods as they marched by. When the Protestants began taunting Catholics, violence broke out. By nightfall, Belfast and Londonderry were in flames. Three days later, Britain sent the British Army in as a peacekeeping force. The British Army became the miracle the IRA so desperately needed.

The Army and Overreaction

According to most analysts and observers, the early policies and tactics of the British Army played an important role in the rebirth of the IRA. In an article on military policy, J. Bowyer Bell (1976, pp. 65–88) criticizes the British Army for its initial response. He says that the British Army came to Ulster with little or no appreciation of the historical circumstances behind the conflict. According to Bell, when the army arrived in 1969, its commanders believed they were in the midst of a colonial war. They evaluated the situation and concluded that there were two "tribes." One tribe flew the Irish tricolor and spoke with deep-seated hatred of the British. The other tribe flew the Union Jack and claimed to be ultrapatriotic subjects of the British Empire. It seemed logical to ally with friends who identified themselves as subjects.

Bell believes that this analysis was a fatal flaw. Far from being a conflict to preserve British influence in a colony, the struggle in Northern Ireland was a fight between two groups of Irish citizens. Neither side was "British," no matter what their slogans and banners claimed. The British Army should have become a peaceful, neutral force, but it mistakenly allied itself with one of the extremist positions in the conflict.

Bell argues that the reaction of Republican Catholics fully demonstrates the mistake that the British Army made. The Unionists greeted the army with open arms, but this was to be expected. Historically, the British Army had rallied to the Unionist cause. Surprisingly, however, the Republicans also welcomed the British Army. They believed that the RUC and B-Specials were the instruments of their repression and that the British Army would not continue those restrictive measures. It was not the British Army of the past. In Republican eyes, it was a peacekeeping force. The Republicans believed that the British Army would protect them from the Unionists and the police.

Such beliefs were short-lived, however. As the British Army made its presence felt in Ulster, Republicans and Catholics were subjected to the increasing oppression of British Army measures. Catholic neighborhoods were surrounded and gassed by military forces searching for subversives, and the soldiers began working as a direct extension of the RUC. Londonderry and Belfast were military targets, and rebels fighting against the government were to be subdued. As confrontations became more deadly, Republican support for the British Army vanished.

Feeling oppressed by all sides, Catholics and Republicans looked for help. They found it, partly, in the form of the IRA. The Officials and Provisionals were still split during the 1969 riots, and the IRA was generally an impotent organization; but the IRA pushed its internal squabbles aside, and the Officials and Provisionals focused on their new common enemy—the British Army. The new IRA policy emphasized the elimination of British soldiers from Irish soil and brushed aside internal political differences (see Hamilton, 1971; R. White, 1989, 1993, pp. 74–88).

The British Army found itself in the middle of a conflict that it had hoped to forestall. Alienated nationalists offered support for the growing ranks of the IRA. Each time the British Army overreacted, as it tended to do when faced with civil disobedience, the Republican cause was strengthened. IRA ranks grew from a few dozen to nearly 2,000, and members adopted an elaborate justification of violence. As IRA ranks grew, Unionists watched with horror. When crackdowns by British Army patrols and incidents of alleged torture by intelligence services increased the ranks of the IRA, Unionist paramilitary organizations grew in response. The British Army also began taking action against Unionist organizations and then truly found itself in the midst of a terrorist conflict (see Moss, 1972, pp. 16–18; Winchester, 1974, pp. 171–180; Munck, 1992; R. White, 1993, pp. 26–28, 64–99, 130–133; Kuusisto, 2001; Alonso, 2001).

In 1972, the British government issued a report on the violence in Northern Ireland. Headed by Leslie Scarman (1972), the investigation concluded that tensions inside the community were so great once they had been unleashed that little could be done to alleviate them. And the policies of the police and the British Army had done much to set those hostile forces in motion. The report concluded that normative democracy could not return until the people in Northern Ireland had faith in all governmental institutions, including the security forces. The report indicated that a legal method was needed to resolve the violence.

Robert White (1989, 1993) explains violence in Northern Ireland as a group process. Socially constructed meanings evolved in three ways: (1) small-group interpretation within the IRA, (2) general interpretation of activities by the Catholic population, and (3) meanings assigned from the interaction between the small and large groups. IRA operatives were recruited according to different patterns, and each recruiting style affected tactics, such as bombings, shootings, or hunger strikes. When the people of Northern Ireland, at least the Catholic minority, felt repressed by the British, this legitimized IRA violence. The IRA could not move without popular support. In addition, popular support came when peaceful actions appeared to produce no results. Finally, as the IRA in the republic and in Ulster grew closer together, they also identified with the Republicans of Ulster. The British were, and remain, outsiders to Republicans.

Unionist Terrorism

Although most Irish terrorism is associated with the IRA and its radical splinter groups, it is not proper to conclude that all Irish terrorism is the result of Republican violence. Unionist organizations also have a long history of terrorism. They represent the Unionist and Loyalist side of terrorism. Historically, it has appeared in three forms: (1) state repression, (2) vengeance, and (3) revolutionary violence for political change. Repression developed because the Unionists held power throughout most of modern Irish history. Vengeance came as Loyalist organizations struck back at Republicans. Finally, some Unionist activity has been directed at the British or other authorities. This happens when extreme Unionists feel that the government is abandoning the Unionist cause (see Elbe, 2000; Wright and Bryett, 2000, pp. 63–66; Bruce, 2001).

Before the 1916 Easter Rising, Unionists feared Irish independence. If home rule were granted, they planned to go to war with the south to gain the independence of the north. They created the **Ulster Volunteer Force** (UVF) as a result. As long as the British remained, however, Unionists had little need of subversive groups. They controlled events in Ireland through the police and military. For example, the Irish Republican Brotherhood (IRB) began importing arms before World War I. Unionists, fearful of Catholic Republican power, decided to arm themselves as well. Although the British government had forbidden importing arms, police officers turned a blind eye as thousands of illegal arms were smuggled one night into the Orange Lodges. The British Army also condoned the smuggling by confining soldiers to their barracks while the arms were distributed.

Ulster Volunteer Force: one of a number of militant Unionist organizations. Such groups wage terrorist campaigns against Catholics and militant Republican organizations.

The Unionist position also enjoyed the backing of the military in other ways. Before World War I, it appeared home rule would be passed by the British Parliament. To influence the vote, British officers began to resign their commissions en masse, forcing a crisis in government. Since the United Kingdom was on the verge of war with Germany, it could hardly fight without the leadership of its officer corps. Home rule was withdrawn, and Ireland remained under British control.

Things changed after the Tan War and the creation of the Republic of Ireland. Although de Valera waged war against his old colleagues, the IRA still brought terrorism to the north. Some Unionist groups formed terrorist enclaves of their own to terrorize the Republicans.

At this point, Unionist terrorism focused on retribution. When Republicans struck, the Unionists hit back. After the IRA was reborn in the 1969 violence, Orange organizations watched in fear. When IRA bombings and assassinations began, the Unionist terrorists targeted Republican leaders, especially outspoken civil rights advocates. Unionist terrorism has never matched Republican terrorism, simply because Unionists were able to use official organizations to repress Catholics in Northern Ireland.

 **Self-Check**

> What impact did the civil rights movement have on political order in Northern Ireland?
> How did the actions of the British Army contribute to the rebirth of the IRA?
> Identify the differences between Unionist terrorism and Republican terrorism.

Anglo-Irish Peace Accord: an agreement signed in 1985 that was the beginning of a long-term attempt to stop terrorist violence in Northern Ireland by devising a system of political autonomy and by protecting the rights of all citizens. Extremist Republicans rejected the accord because it did not unite Northern Ireland and the south. Unionists rejected it because it compromised with moderate Republicans.

Tony Blair: (b. 1953) the Labour Party prime minister of the United Kingdom from 1994 to 2007.

Belfast Agreement: also known as the Good Friday Agreement, an agreement signed in April 1998 that revamped criminal justice services, established shared government in Northern Ireland, called for the early release of prisoners involved in paramilitary organizations, and created the Commission on Human Rights and Equity. Its provisions led to the decommissioning of paramilitary organizations.

Negotiating a Peace Settlement in Ireland

In 1985, the United Kingdom and the Republic of Ireland signed a peace accord regarding the governance of Northern Ireland, but the violence continued. While the **Anglo-Irish Peace Accord** sought to bring an end to terrorism by establishing a joint Irish–British system of government for the troubled area, many Protestant groups felt betrayed, and the Republicans continued to view Britain as a colonial power benefiting from the occupation of Northern Ireland (Dunn and Morgan, 1995). Republican and Unionist narratives had lasted hundreds of years, and their mystical hold on both sets of extremists was hard to break. This discord forced the British government to take a radical step.

Negotiating with Terrorists

Although the United Kingdom and the Republic of Ireland were in direct negotiations and had agreed to share power, Unionist and Republican terrorists continued to fight the settlement and the government. In 1990, the British decided to take another step. Realizing that they had no economic or political interest in controlling Northern Ireland, British intelligence contacted Sinn Fein and began negotiations with the political leadership of the IRA. And then something remarkable happened. The IRA signed a cease-fire, the first in 15 years, in December 1990.

Dean Pruitt (2007) argues this effort turned the peace process in a positive direction. British intelligence units and the IRA kept talking after the ceasefire, and in 1992, Sinn Fein produced a paper calling for peace in Northern Ireland and recognizing that both Unionists and Republicans had to be included in any future agreement. It seemed as if peace would finally develop, but then negotiations began to break down. Terrorists took up their arms again, but a new British prime minister, **Tony Blair**, was determined to end the violence. He formally invited Sinn Fein to the negotiating table. Despite emphatic rhetorical statements to the contrary, counterterrorists and terrorists sat down together. Pruitt says that what had once been a spiral of escalating violence turned into a process of conciliation.

On Good Friday 1998, Britain and Ireland signed the **Belfast Agreement**, which called for independent human rights investigations, compensation for the victims of violence, and decommissioning of paramilitary groups (Northern Ireland Office, 2007). More radical Republicans and Unionists tried to break away. These groups renewed a campaign of violence in 1998, hoping to destroy the Anglo-Irish peace initiatives (Bell, 1998); however, the peace talks gained momentum, and radicals on both sides found that they were losing public support. In addition, people who were jailed for terrorism and violent political activity seemed to be more concerned with reintegrating into their families and communities after their incarceration than with carrying on the struggle (Monaghan, 2004; Hughes and Donnelly, 2004; Carmichael and Knox, 2004). The few remaining violent radicals resorted to criminal activities, and the leadership of the major terrorist groups began suppressing violent activities within their ranks (McGinn, 2006).

The peace process resulted in two important new bureaucratic structures, the **Independent Monitoring Commission (IMC)** and the **Police Service of Northern Ireland (PSNI)**. The IMC investigated claims of both terrorist and governmental abuses, and its actions have resulted in the arrests of Republican and Loyalist terrorists, as well as members of the security forces who acted beyond the law (Henderson, 2006). In 2005, the IRA officially disbanded and handed over its weapons. Its leader disavowed terrorism and urged his followers to cooperate with the police (BBC News, 2005a). The government followed suit by creating the PSNI to replace the RUC.

Independent Monitoring Commission (IMC): a commission created in 2004 to investigate paramilitary actions and alleged governmental abuses during the Irish peace process.

Police Service of Northern Ireland (PSNI): the police force created in November 2001 to replace the Royal Ulster Constabulary.

Rational Political Goals and Negotiated Settlements

Experiences in Ireland exemplify the nature of ethnic and nationalist separatist movements. The long, long story shows the emotional power of narrative, a tale used to justify centuries of revolutionary violence and suppression. It also demonstrates an ironic pattern. When Republican organizations began to engage in violence in the nineteenth century, the British responded with increased violence to put an end to Republican activities. It did not work. When the government sat down to negotiate with terrorists, however, the campaign wound down. Dean Pruitt (2007) contends that this is due to four factors: (1) Military victory was unattainable for either side; (2) allied governments and other organizations lobbied both sides for peace; (3) as negotiations began, both sides grew increasingly optimistic; and (4) the final peace included a broad coalition of diverse groups.

Terrorism in Northern Ireland no longer grabs attention as it did in the past. The major campaigns are over, and the groups have disbanded. Still, the situation remains volatile. Unionist and Republican activists carried out 124 attacks against each other in 2009, and two British soldiers were killed during the same year (Pantucci, 2010). In January 1972, British paratroopers opened fire on Catholic protestors in Londonderry on a day that became known as Bloody Sunday. The British government investigated the incident and absolved the paratroopers, but it later reopened the investigation. The new investigation, one of the most lengthy and costly inquiries in British parliamentary history, condemned the action. David Cameron, the British prime minister, reviewed the report in June 2010. He publicly apologized to the demonstrators for the army's actions, according to the *New York Times* (Burns, 2010). Such an apology would not have been given over the previous two centuries.

> **Self-Check**
>
> > Why did the Anglo-Irish peace accord promise success?
> > What steps did the British take to create successful negotiations?
> > What bureaucratic reforms helped ensure the success of the Belfast Agreement?
> > Why were the negotiations successful?

The Basque Nation and Liberty

In March 2004, a series of bombs exploded in the central train station of Madrid, Spain, killing nearly 200 people. Although the plot was eventually tied to jihadists, the first response from Spain and the international media pointed to the group ETA, or Basque Nation and Liberty. The ETA waged a campaign of violence from 1959 to 2011 that has killed more than 800 people. It has specialized in car bombings and assassinations, and ETA terrorists targeted Spain's number one industry—tourism. The ETA's goal was to establish an autonomous homeland in northern Spain and southern France (Foreign Policy Association, 2004; Council on Foreign Relations, 2002; Goodman, 2003).

Background

The Basque region of France and Spain has been a source of separatist terrorism for more than 50 years. Primarily located in Spain, the Basque region extends over the Pyrenees into France. Basque separatists believed that they should be allowed to either develop a homeland in Spain or maintain a separate culture and language, and this made Basque separatism an important issue in Spanish politics. Many Americans were not aware of the Basque lands because they are unacquainted with the evolutionary nature of European nations. Modern European nation-states appeared only in recent centuries. While many Americans use a word like *British* to describe anyone from the United Kingdom, citizens of the islands frequently describe themselves using such words as *Welsh*, *Cornish*, *Scottish*, *Irish*, or *English*. Modern Spain also developed from separate ethnic groups, and the Basque region of Spain has always had its own language and culture. At times, it was an independent kingdom, and, even though it has not enjoyed full autonomy for almost 1,000 years, Basques hold to their ethnic identity (R. Clark, 1979).

The origins of the Basques, like the Irish, are shrouded in lore and legend, and these stories are ingrained in ethnic narratives supporting separateness. Emerging as a linguistic group between 3,000 and 4,000 years ago, the Basque region challenges popular notions of Spanish nationalistic history. It has been shaped by Spain, but there are more Basques outside Spain than in the country. In fact, more Basques live in Latin America than in Europe. Residents of the region fought the Romans with Hannibal and emerged through the milieu of Iberian history. They have a proud male-dominated history of militarism and independence embedded in the fabric of ethnic identity (Linstroth, 2002). The Basques have been a key factor in Spanish history, but they have had and maintain distinct literary, cultural, and linguistic separateness (Zulaika, 2003). These factors have produced a tradition centered in pride, ethnocentrism, and independence.

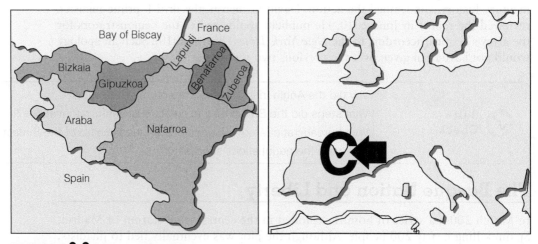

FIGURE **6.2** Map of Spain.

Modern Spain emerged from the unification of several Hispanic kingdoms in 1479 and was solidified at the end of the **War of the Spanish Succession (1702–1714)**. The new monarchy joined the independent kingdoms together in 1716, but it granted the Basque region semiautonomy within the realm. The Basques developed commerce and a middle class, but their autonomy and national identity began to wane in the nineteenth century (Payne, 1971). Although the Basques considered themselves "un-Spanish," Spanish power gradually enfolded the region in the twentieth century. The cultural incursion sharpened ethnic and ideological divisions. The Basque region in France was unaffected by the spread of Spanish culture and contributed to the feeling of ethnic autonomy in Spain.

The Spanish Civil War

Spain's search for national identity and a philosophy of government came to a head in the **Spanish Civil War (1936–1939)**. Republican forces battled fascists, and some Basques sided against the fascists, using the civil war as an excuse to fight for autonomy. As fascist forces grew increasingly powerful, many Basque soldiers lost interest in both politics and the war. They were more concerned with ethnic identity than the governing power of Spain (Seixas, 2005). The same philosophy did not hold true, though, for **Francisco Franco**, the leader of fascist forces. After achieving victory in 1939, Franco forcibly campaigned against Basque national identity. Franco completely incorporated the Basque region into Spain, banning its language and expressions of national culture. Regaining them became the focus of the modern struggle (Moxon-Browne, 1987).

The importance of the civil war is difficult to overemphasize. Franco's repression made the Basque region seem as though it were occupied by a foreign colonial power. Priests were forbidden to make references to the Basque region in religious services, and parents were forced to give their children Spanish first names. The Basque language was banned. Franco applied these rules to the entire Basque region, even though only two of the four provinces opposed his forces in the civil war. After World War II, many Basques believed the Allies would assist their bid for independence or greater autonomy because Franco had supported Hitler; but the United States courted Franco's fascist government in return for American air bases in Spain (Woodworth, 2001, pp. 34–35). This resulted in a resurgence of Basque nationalism during the 1950s and the formation of a government in exile in Paris. The exiled Basques became an idealized expression of nationalism and ethnic identity; while the exiles were virtually powerless, the shadow government attracted a following in the Basque provinces (Muro, 2009). A group of disgruntled middle- and working-class students traveled from Spain to Paris to meet the exiled government in 1959. This would prove to be an incubator for violence.

Twentieth-Century Basque Nationalism

The students were irritated by the rhetoric of the exiles and their willingness to accommodate Spanish authority through lofty speeches and gatherings in Paris. The students wanted action in the Basque homeland. Leaving the exiles, they formed a new group, the ETA, to serve as a stronger expression of national and cultural identity inside Spain. Composed of young, frustrated nationalists who wanted regional autonomy, the ETA advocated neither violence nor terrorism. Its central themes promoted Basque separateness and culture. Like most Basque nationalists, the ETA sought to preserve Basque cultural and linguistic identity. Although the language

War of the Spanish Succession (1702–1714): The first global war exported from Europe, pitting the French and Austrians against each other for familial control of the Spanish throne. Although it involved myriad political factors, it set the stage for the evolution of modern Spain. There are several dates given for the end of the war due to the many peace treaties that ended military operations in Europe and around the world.

Spanish Civil War (1936–1939): a war that pitted pro-communist Republicans against pro-fascist Nationalists. The war ended with a Nationalist victory and a fascist dictatorship under Franco.

Francisco Franco: (1892–1975) leader of the Nationalist forces during the Spanish Civil War and the fascist dictator of Spain from 1939 to 1975.

EXPANDING THE CONCEPT

The Basque Conflict

The Issue. Basque separatists wanted a homeland completely independent of Spain. The nationalists controlled a semiautonomous Basque parliament, but they were divided in their desire for autonomy. A substantial minority of Basques wanted to remain united with Spain.

The Group. Although the Basque region has never been independent, it has its own language and culture. Francisco Franco, the Spanish dictator, tried to crush Basque culture and force the Basques to become Spanish.

The Campaign. The Basque Nation and Liberty (ETA) began a campaign against Spain in 1959. The group was responsible for assassinating Franco's probable successor and many other officials. They agreed to a cease-fire in 1998, but they broke the treaty a year later. The Spanish government gave the Basques regional governing authority, and the Basques used their own language and ran their own schools. The majority of Spaniards believed the ETA to be the most important issue in Spain, and both Basques and Spaniards were tired of ETA violence.

The Situation. The ETA agreed to a second cease-fire, but they resumed violence after the 2006 cease-fire. Spanish and French police forces increased their intelligence operations, resulting in a number of arrests in late 2009 and early 2010. The combat capabilities of the ETA declined. The ETA declared an end to hostilities in October 2011.

Sources: Goodman, 2003; Agence France Presse, 2004; *The Economist*, 2009; Burns, 2011

---

of ethnic minorities is frequently banned or discouraged by the dominant political power, the Basque tongue evolved into an important entity in resisting Spain. The language became the basis of ethnic identity, and many social scientists believe that the early nationalist campaign focused on preserving the Basque language to preserve identity and culture (Spencer and Croucher, 2008). Others think this point is overemphasized (Beck and Markusse, 2008). Irrespective of the debate, the ETA employed the Basque tongue as a nonviolent weapon to separate their homeland from Spain. The words, they believed, should be spoken in the homeland and not in Paris.

The original members of the ETA reflected the composition of the local population, except that most of the members were male. The ETA was primarily a working-class movement, as are many nationalistic terrorist groups, with pockets of students and intellectuals. Its members were raised in Basque enclaves and felt a strong ethnic attachment to their homeland. The overwhelming majority felt that they represented all the members of their community. They began by engaging in public advocacy within the Basque region of Spain, and this tactic eventually gave way to peaceful activism. By 1960, it also created fractures with the ranks. Some members of the ETA wanted to move from activism to confrontation (R. Clark, 1979, 1984).

The ETA Turns to Terrorism

After much internal bickering, some members of the ETA decided that the time had come to actively strike Spain. Their ideas were symbolic, and the ETA's first "attacks" involved spraying walls with nationalistic graffiti. In 1961, members attempted to derail a train carrying fascist civil war veterans to a memorial ceremony, but they failed because they could not figure out how to conduct the operation without injury or death. Franco responded with brutal suppression, and this caused the ETA to examine its methods. The world was engulfed in a variety of revolutionary movements in the 1960s, and the ETA decided to follow the example of the third world. It would take the path of armed revolution. Paddy Woodworth (2001, p. 36) cites this period as the beginning of a "dirty war," a cycle of violence causing violent repression, leading to more violence against the repression, and so on. Terrorism and counterterrorism spiraled upward.

In 1968, the group started a true terrorist campaign. Like many terrorist groups composed of strongly opinionated people, the radicals of the ETA were not prone to compromise and often did not agree with one another. Although the group decided to strike violently, members could not agree on a single strategy. This led to a series of splits in the ETA. A more militant group, the ETA-M, broke away from the ETA in 1974. ETA-M described itself as the military wing of the ETA. Other factions also began to appear.

After embracing violence, one of the most interesting characteristics of the ETA was that its members did not view terrorism as a full-time activity. According to Edward Moxon-Browne's (1987) research, the early recruits maintained some type of employment while serving in the ETA. In addition, most members engaged in terrorism for only about three years. After this, they returned to their full-time occupations. Another interesting aspect is that as ETA violence expanded, women grew more active in the movement. They would eventually move into positions of authority and leadership by the twenty-first century (see Hamilton, 2007).

The development of the early ETA is ironic by some measures. Franco died in 1975, and the Spanish political system began to reform. Spain adopted a new constitution in 1978, and while it did not give the Basque region autonomy, it did restore the Basque language and turned the educational system over to local governments. In spite of these reforms, tensions increased, and the ETA amplified its campaign of violence (Gil-Alana and Barros, 2010). On the other hand, as avenues for regional cultural and political expressions opened, ETA violence slowly began to wane. Unfortunately, this did not happen before the emergence of Spanish death squads.

ETA Tactics and Spanish Death Squads

The ETA evolved, and so did its tactics. As Spanish repression increased in the 1970s, the ETA escalated its attacks. It began a Marighella-style campaign of assassination, robbery, and banditry. It targeted government officials, academic advisors to the government, and members of the police and military. The government responded with martial law, and the ETA responded with more violence. Highly visible shootouts with police forces glamorized the revolutionary image of the ETA among Basque youth. More women joined, at first as supporters, but a few emerged as leaders at the beginning. In 1980, the ETA's most violent year, terrorists killed 92 people. As more and more Spanish officials and police officers were killed, some members of the government became angry enough to take action on their own. If martial law was not strong enough to stop the ETA, they would engage in counterterrorism outside the law. Death squads, such as Warriors of Christ the King and the Basque Spanish Battalion, began to torture and murder suspected terrorists and their supporters (Woodworth, 2001, pp. 39–44).

The death squads evolved into the Anti-Terrorist Liberation Groups (GAL). Composed of Spanish police officers and illegally supported through some governmental agencies, GAL death squads had one common goal: ETA terrorists could strike from the Basque region of France and return beyond the reach of Spanish law. The French government was not willing to cooperate in the suppression of the ETA, so death squads began to slip into France to search for and kill the ETA. The GAL murdered

28 people between 1983 and 1987, sometimes mistakenly killing the wrong people. In 1984, a GAL terrorist entered a French bar frequented by the ETA. Thinking she was executing ETA members or Basque supporters, the GAL terrorist shot a group of gypsies sitting at a table where the Basques usually sat. Both the ETA and the government denounced the death squads, but violence continued (BBC, 1998; Woodworth, 2001, p. 139).

While death squad activity peaked in the mid-1980s, ETA terrorism reached its zenith between 1977 and 1980 and then steadily declined throughout the following decades (*The Economist*, 2009). This was not the result of death squad activity but of Spanish attempts to reframe the conflict and end the suppression of Basque culture. The ETA slowly began losing support in the Basque region. The ETA conducted a sporadic campaign during the 1990s, agreeing to a short cease-fire in 1998. Returning to terrorism in 1999 with a bombing campaign, the ETA decided to attack one of Spain's major industries—tourism. ETA terrorists murdered a total of 30 foreign tourists in 2001 as it continued a bombing campaign against symbols of Spanish power.

Reframing the Conflict

By the late 1980s, the Spanish government had had enough. Unwilling to support GAL, it began investigating law enforcement agencies and related bureaucracies in the Spanish government. It tried to delegitimize the ETA by fostering democracy in the Basque region. Rather than trying to suppress ethnic identity, the government sought to give nationalists a peaceful outlet for their views. One of the biggest changes was the creation of a Basque national police force. This not only served to quash death squad terrorism, it also created the opportunity for self-policing (Greer, 1995). By opening peaceful avenues such as self-policing, both the Spanish and the Basques found it easier to denounce violence. The ETA found it harder to operate.

The Spanish government also made comprehensive social moves in the Basque region by opening political opportunities and allowing cultural expression. The Basques were given total control of the educational system, something Spain was unwilling to do in 1978, and greater political autonomy. Language was accepted as an expression of culture. As the political system opened, the desire for ethnic cultural identity was not strong enough to support violence, especially when the means of suppression were removed. Repressive policies created tension; when they were removed, much of the support for fighting eroded (Wieviorka, 1993).

As Spanish authorities opened opportunities for democracy and national expression, the ETA transformed itself into a social movement. Only hard-core militants were left to preach violence. Faced with decreasing support in Spain, they began seeking sanctuary in France. The French government, however, began taking actions of its own; although the government traditionally had been sympathetic to Basque nationalism, French prosecutors reversed their position (Llora, Mata, and Irvin, 1993).

By the end of the twentieth century, hard-core militants began embracing ideas of class revolution. The ETA and its political wing became more entrenched in working-class ideology. Although the militants never abandoned ethnic separatism, they began to speak of revolution in economic terms. This changed the social structure and gender composition of the ETA, and it further weakened the movement by strengthening Spanish connections to the Basque community. Most Basques were interested in cultural identity, not class revolution. Spain found an effective weapon against the ETA as it opened doors to political participation and cultural expression (Khatami, 1997).

Yet, the violence did not stop. Despite greater opportunities for political and cultural expression, as well as the cooperation of French law enforcement, the ETA continued to operate. Spain took another aggressive step, offering the possibility of a negotiated settlement. When jihadist terrorists struck Madrid on March 11, 2004, it drew attention to the ETA. Although some reporters immediately blamed the ETA for the Madrid train explosions, the ETA was quick to deny it and denounce the bombings. Terrorism analysts in Spain pointed out that indiscriminate murder did not follow the ETA's tactical philosophy. Many people hoped the bombing would lead to a political solution between the Spanish government and the Basque region. The ETA declared a cease-fire in March 2006, and at first it appeared that the ETA and Spain might negotiate a settlement. Some analysts concluded that ethnic terrorism no longer seemed to have a place in a Europe that was seeking greater unification (Rabasa et al., 2006, pp. 115–117). Unfortunately, though violence had waned, sporadic ETA bombings began again in 2007.

The ETA was reluctant to embrace the negotiation strategy of the IRA, even though the Spanish government opened the door, and it would have been an effective method for ending violence (Shepard, 2002; Neuman, 2007). Regardless, the ETA lost much of its original strength by 2010 (*The Economist,* 2010). Following a united French and Spanish law enforcement campaign, most of the major leadership was in custody. Some analysts believed that this would bring an end to the ETA, but others noted that the ETA still had the capacity for murder and violent action (Stewart, 2009). Other analysts believed that proactive political policies were proving more effective than enforcement efforts (Gil-Alana and Barros, 2010). It was probably due to a combination of factors, but the ETA had been weakened.

The story took another turn in the autumn of 2011. The ETA announced that it was abandoning its military campaign, and a communiqué stated that the ETA was offering to end one of the longest ethnic wars in Europe (Burns, 2011). In 2014 ETA militants began turning in their weapons, and the long campaign of violence seemed to be over. However, by the summer of 2015 disgruntled elements of the ETA began planting bombs to disrupt tourism in Spain. Violence has been reduced, but it has not disappeared.

Tamils: an ethnic minority in southern India and Sri Lanka. The Tamils in Sri Lanka are primarily Hindu, and the Sinhalese majority are mostly Buddhist. Ethnicity, however—not religion—defines most of the conflict between the two groups.

> ✓ Self-Check
> > What is the source of ethnic identity for the Basques?
> > How did the Spanish Civil War influence Basque separatism?
> > Why did the ETA inspire Spanish death squads?

The Liberation Tigers of Tamil Eelam

The LTTE (or Tamil Tigers) fought for an independent homeland for nearly 3 million **Tamils** in northern and eastern Sri Lanka. Formed by **Velupillai Pirapaharan** in 1976, the Tamil Tigers used terrorism both as a prelude to guerrilla warfare and as a way to support uniformed guerrillas in the field. The LTTE pioneered the use of secular suicide bombings, beginning in 1987, and it created a special suicide squad known as the Black Tigers. The Black Tigers killed thousands, assassinated prominent political figures, such as former Indian prime minister **Rajiv Gandhi** and Sri Lankan president **Ranasinghe Premadasa,** and murdered moderate Tamils who opposed their cause. The Sri Lankan Army began a series of massive strikes against the LTTE in 2008; by 2009, the LTTE was in full retreat. The government completely displaced the Tamil population, and it actively sought all Tamil Tigers suspected of being guerrillas or terrorists. After killing the leader of the LTTE, the government declared victory in May 2009. The struggle for Sri Lanka produced a long, dirty, and terrible war.

Velupillai Pirapaharan: (1954–2009) founder and leader of the LTTE. Pirapaharan's terrorists conducted more successful suicide bombings than any other terrorist group in the world.

Rajiv Gandhi: (1944–1991) prime minister of India from 1984 until 1989; in 1991 he was assassinated by an LTTE suicide bomber.

Ranasinghe Premadasa: (1924–1993) president of Sri Lanka from 1989 until 1993, when he was killed by an LTTE suicide bomber.

EXPANDING THE CONCEPT

The Sri Lankan Conflict

The Issue. In 1948, the British granted Sri Lanka independence. The island was inhabited by the dominant Sinhalese and the Tamils. Although the constitution granted Tamils representation in the government and civil service, by 1955, they felt that they were being systematically excluded from Sri Lanka's economic life.

The Group. As ethnic tensions increased, some Tamils turned to violence. The Liberation Tigers of Tamil Eelam (LTTE, or Tamil Tigers) were formed in 1976 to fight for the Tamil minority.

The Campaign. The Tigers began a campaign against the Sri Lankan Army, and they targeted India when the Indian prime minister tried to bring peace by deploying security forces. The LTTE is known for kidnapping young children and indoctrinating them in LTTE camps. The Tigers also became masters of assassination and suicide bombings. The LTTE was the first modern secular group to use suicide bombers. Many members lived in a virtual death cult, and the Black Tigers, the suicide wing of the LTTE, were known for carrying cyanide capsules around their necks when they attacked.

The Cease-Fire. The LTTE agreed to a cease-fire in December 2001 and began peace negotiations in 2002. Although occasional outbreaks of violence occurred, many experts believe the LTTE was suffering from a lack of resources.

Renewed Fighting. Hostilities renewed in late 2006. After four years of relative peace, the Sinhalese refused to recognize a Tamil homeland. Both sides began sporadic fighting, and terrorism returned to Sri Lanka.

Conflict Ends. The Sri Lankan military and police forces launched a major offensive against the LTTE in 2008. Segregating the Tamil community, Sri Lankans forced them to either stay in a war zone or go to refugee camps. The next step involved systematically attacking and destroying all LTTE members and their supporters in the geographical region. Sri Lankan forces reduced the LTTE. Pirapaharan committed suicide rather than surrender. Fighting ended in May 2009, bringing one of Asia's longest violent separatist conflicts to an end.

Sources: Council on Foreign Relations, 2004; International Crisis Group, 2006f, 2009b.)

The Origins of Tamil Dissatisfaction

Manoj Joshi (1996) traces the struggle's origins to the autonomy India gained at the end of World War II. As India sought to bring internal peace to Hindus and Muslims, the island of Sri Lanka (formerly known as Ceylon) faced a similar problem. In addition to religious differences, the Tamil minority in Sri Lanka was concerned about maintaining its ethnic identity among the Sinhalese majority. Tamils along the southeastern coast of India supported the Sri Lankan Tamils in this quest. As the Sri Lankan government was formed, some Tamils found themselves in positions of authority. Although they accounted for only 17 percent of Sri Lanka's population, the Tamils were well represented in the bureaucracy. This changed in 1955.

Claiming that Tamils dominated the Sri Lankan government, the Sinhalese majority forced the government to adopt a Sinhalese-only policy. Tamils began to grumble, and some spoke of violence. A Tamil assassin killed the Sinhalese leader in 1959, setting the stage for further violence. Seeking sanctuary in the Tamil region of India, militant Tamils sailed across the short expanse of ocean from Sri Lanka to India to wage a low-level terrorist campaign through 1975. Spurred by their successes, they began larger operations.

The Tamil experience was similar to the situation in Ireland. Buoyed by religious differences and ethnic support, Tamil separatists could begin a guerrilla campaign by waging terrorist war. Their ethnic support base gave them the opportunity to do so. In 1976, Velupillai Pirapaharan, a young Tamil militant, took advantage of the situation and formed the LTTE (The Liberation Tigers of Tamil Eelam; *Eelam* means "homeland"). Pirapaharan faced problems similar to those of other terrorists. He had to raise money, which he did through bank robberies and assassinations, and he needed to eliminate rival terrorists to claim leadership of the movement.

Sri Lanka and the Tamil Tigers

The LTTE eventually emerged as the leading revolutionary group and launched Sri Lanka into a full-blown terrorist campaign. The Tamil Tigers wanted to move beyond terrorism and build a guerrilla force that could eventually evolve into a conventional army. The Sinhalese majority reacted violently in 1983, and Sinhalese protesters flocked to the streets of **Colombo**, Sri Lanka's traditional and economic capital, in a series of anti-Tamil riots. Many Tamils fled to India, and the LTTE returned to terrorism.

Reactions to the riots were a turning point for the LTTE. Unable to foment the revolution from above, the group established contacts with the Popular Front for the Liberation of Palestine. After that time, the Tamil Tigers mounted three on-again, off-again terrorist campaigns. At first, India responded by forming a joint peacekeeping force with Sri Lanka. India's primary purpose was to keep violence from spilling over onto the mainland. India reevaluated its policy after several assassinations and violent encounters, and the government vowed never to send troops to Sri Lanka again.

Colombo: the traditional capital of Sri Lanka and the country's largest city, with a population of 5,648,000. The Sri Lankan government moved the capital to Sri Jayawardenapura Kotte, five miles away, in 1982. Colombo remains the economic center of Sri Lanka.

LTTE Tactics

The LTTE incorporated a variety of tactics after 1984. Their ability to operate was directly correlated to the amount of popular support they enjoyed during any particular period. In 1988 and 1992, they sought to control geographic areas, they moved

---

TIMELINE 6.1 *The Sri Lankan Civil War*

1972	New constitution favors Buddhist Sinhalese.
1976	Pirapaharan forms the LTTE.
1983	Anti-Tamil riots; Tamils hunted and killed.
1987	First LTTE suicide bombing.
1991	Former Indian prime minister Rajiv Gandhi killed by a suicide bomber.
1996	Suicide bomber kills 91 people at Colombo Central Bank.
2002	Government and Tamil Tigers sign a cease-fire.
2004	Cease-fire threatened when a tsunami kills thousands.
2006	Fighting renews.
2008	Military begins large-scale offensive.
2009	Pirapaharan commits suicide. Hostilities come to an end.

Sources: Wall Street Journal Research Staff, November 2005; International Crisis Group, 2006f, 2009b.

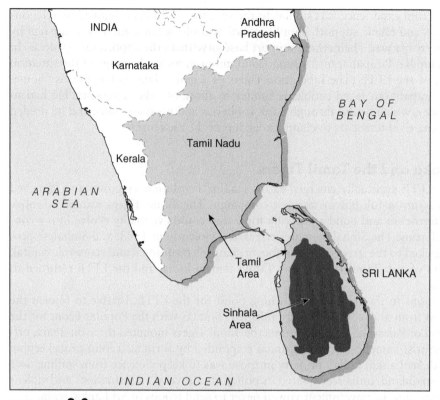

FIGURE **6.3** Existing Map of Sinhalese and Tamil Areas in Sri Lanka; Tamil Areas in India

using standard guerrilla tactics, and they formed uniformed units. They even created an ad hoc navy. In times of weakness, they relied on bank robberies, bombings, and murder. In the weakest times, they employed suicide bombers. They used suicide attacks in 1995 on land and at sea.

Joshi (1996) estimates that before 1983, the LTTE had only 40 followers. The anti-Tamil riots were a catalyst to growth, as links were formed in the Middle East. Terrorist training camps appeared in the Tamil region of India in 1984 and 1985, and the training cadre included foreign terrorists. India responded by signing a joint peace agreement with Sri Lanka and soon found itself under attack from a highly organized terrorist group of between 10,000 and 16,000 people.

When not attacking India, the Tamil Tigers launched operations in Sri Lanka. Although they had once struggled to be recognized as the leaders of the independence movement, the Tigers now ruthlessly wiped out their opponents and terrorized their own ethnic group into providing support. Yet, security forces enjoyed several successes, and by 1987, the Tamil Tigers were in retreat.

According to Joshi (1996), this was a very dangerous period for the group. In fact, it was almost wiped out. Driven into the jungle, the Tamil Tigers practiced terrorism from jungle hideaways. They increased contact with Tamil bases in India, using India for logistical support. Politically adept, the LTTE asked for a cease-fire in 1989, giving India a chance to withdraw from the joint security force. No sooner had the Indian Army left than the LTTE renewed its attack on the Sri Lankans.

In 1990, the LTTE expanded its operations by converting a fishing fleet into a makeshift navy. Suicide boats and other seaborne operations threatened shipping between Sri Lanka and India. By 1991, India was once again targeted by Tamil terrorists, and the Indian navy was forced to respond to the growing threat. Not only did the LTTE fight small-scale sea battles with the Indians, its terrorists also succeeded in assassinating former prime minister Rajiv Gandhi on May 21, 1991. When Indian authorities cracked down on Tamil bases, the Tamil Tigers increased their terrorist attacks against India.

From 1994 to 1995, the Tamil Tigers waged another bombing and assassination campaign, and they did what no other terrorist group has been able to do. Although their bases in India were limited, they had strongholds on Sri Lanka. Supported by these guerrilla strongholds, Tamil Tigers appeared in uniforms in 1994 and fought pitched battles with the Sri Lankan security forces. Suicide bombings increased during the same period. Faced with open revolution, the Sri Lankan government signed a peace agreement in January 1995.

Fighting Renewed

The peace accord broke down, and the Sri Lankan Army went on the offensive. The LTTE suffered several setbacks, but the group made headlines in 1996 with suicide bombings in Colombo. In the spring of 1996, Sri Lankan security forces launched an all-out assault on Tamil strongholds in the northern portion of the island. Some commentators (de Silva, 1996; Berthelsen, 1996) believed this would be the end of the LTTE. They were wrong.

Rohan Gunaratna (1998) argues that the LTTE was in a unique position because it had such a large guerrilla base. The guerrillas were perfectly capable of fighting a protracted war against security forces, and if they were weakened in the field, the LTTE reverted to terrorism. Indeed, this was the LTTE's standard tactic. In the wake of new fighting, the LTTE followed the path of suicide bombing. Although the guerrilla campaign subsided a bit in 1999, suicide bombings increased in 2000, and the LTTE became the secular masters of suicide attacks.

In December 2001, the LTTE agreed to a cease-fire with the government of Sri Lanka. Although the Tigers still threatened violence, their resources were depleted The Council on Foreign Relations (Zissis, 2006) believes that the international community's efforts to thwart terrorism after September 11 were responsible for this situation. Arms shipments were virtually eliminated, and expatriate Tamil communities in Australia, Canada, and the United States were forbidden to gather and ship resources to Sri Lanka. Draining economic resources accomplished what Sri Lankan security forces could not do. The Tamil Tigers lost their striking power.

Facing a weakened LTTE, Sri Lankan security forces developed a new strategy for a final offensive. They created "no-fire zones" and moved into Tamil areas. People in the Tamil areas could stay and fight; stay and hope that they would not be killed or injured; flee, risking injury or death; or move into a no-fire zone. Police and military forces established order in the no-fire zones, interrogating and arresting suspects at will. The Manchester *Guardian* (Chamberlain and Tran, 2009) reported that human rights groups were concerned about conditions in the zones. They resembled unsanitary concentration camps where hundreds of homeless people were interred.

The strategy worked. Every person who remained in the Tamil areas was considered to be an enemy, and the army unleashed a conventional offensive. The LTTE had remained the aggressor through most of the campaign, and it had forced security forces onto the defensive. The role was now reversed, and the Tamil Tigers fought on the military's terms. Unable to use guerrilla or terrorist tactics, the Tamil Tigers fought a defensive battle against conventional assaults. With limited communications and no ability to resupply or use the airport, the LTTE lost ground in every encounter. Many of the commanders began blowing themselves up rather than surrender. Pirapaharan died in this manner. Fighting ended in May, with the remaining Tamil Tigers surrendering (Chamberlain and Tran, 2009).

Government Repression After Victory

The International Crisis Group (2013) reports that government actions in the wake of the LTTE's defeat fostered a wave of Tamil repression. The ICG states that the Sinhalese majority government reverted to policies similar to the ones that caused earlier Tamil unrest. The northern part of the island has always been a Tamil stronghold, and it was the scene of the most ferocious fighting at the end of the war. Rather than repatriating the Tamil population and rebuilding the area, the government kept the area under virtual military occupation. Tamils were not free to move, and many remained in internment camps.

The government also encouraged a "Sinhalesation" of the north. Although the area has been almost exclusively Tamil, it is now dotted with Sinhalese signs along roads and on buildings. New Sinhalese farms were established all along the borders of former Tamil enclaves, and Sinhalese contractors and business firms were favored over those of the Tamils. Massive numbers of troops kept the Tamils at bay. The ICG also reports that Tamils lacked funds and housing. Many were forced to live in poverty. All of this takes place under the watchful eyes of a victorious military force that rules the area with little Tamil input.

Sinhalese military policies had a tremendous impact on the role of Tamil women. Unable to fully function in a repressive economic and political climate, Tamil families were fragile and in disarray. The ICG says that women in the north faced a desperate lack of security. They were constantly victimized, and they had no means of either protecting themselves or redressing their grievances. The Sinhalese security forces that govern their lives expressed no interest in their plight, publicly denying that there was any type of problem. Sexual assault rose, but governmental forces overlooked the problem. The ICG concludes that the Tamils were in political and economic trouble.

An election in early 2015 overturned Sri Lanka's repressive political structure, and it appeared that the country was headed for democratic reform. The Tamils seemed to be on the brink of enjoying the full rights of citizenship, but any reform efforts were slow to develop. The ICG (2015) concludes that reform efforts will work under certain conditions: prosecution of war crimes, just agricultural and economic settlements, and acceptance by both the Sinhalese and Tamils. The current situation, by ICG estimates, is fragile. ICG analysts could have added the large Tamil diaspora to their report. Many Tamils living abroad group have achieved economic successes and obtained business and political power. The diaspora was one of the LTTE's sources of support, and it keeps a watchful eye on events at home. If militants fill there is no hope for ending repression, violence could erupt again.

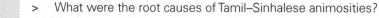

✓ **Self-Check**

> What were the root causes of Tamil–Sinhalese animosities?
> What role did the diaspora play in the formation of the LTTE?
> What guerrilla and terrorist tactics did the LTTE employ?

Emphasizing the Points

Ethnic and separatist movements involve attempts to gain full or partial independence. When such groups employ terrorism, it may be possible for each side to negotiate an end to violence because each position is based on a logical, attainable political solution. Despite the promise of negotiated peace, these movements seem to be more violent than ideological and religious terrorism. Modern terrorism in Ireland grew from dissatisfaction with Catholic emancipation in the north. Basque separatism became violent when the ETA launched a terrorist campaign in support of Basque independence. Both of these cases have resulted in a peace settlement through negotiations, although radical extremists would like to disrupt the agreements. Sri Lankan violence ended with the military elimination of the LTTE. Rather than negotiate with the defeated Tamil minority, the government has continued to routinely suppress them. This may lead to renewed violence and the rebirth of the LTTE or similar organization in the Tamil diaspora.

SUMMARY OF CHAPTER OBJECTIVES

- Many scholars and terrorism analysts believed that the purpose of terrorism had little impact on the tactical and political aspects of violence. Studies over the past 20 years have questioned such conventional wisdom. Newer research suggests that nationalist and ethnic separatist terrorism differs from other forms of terrorist violence. Separatists usually have well-defined goals that can lead to political negotiation, and they are more violent than other types of terrorists. Unlike people who practice indiscriminate terror for an unattainable ideal, the clear objectives of separatist terrorists often seem to offer the possibility of a negotiated political settlement.
- The IRA fought to bring Ulster under Irish control from 1939 to 1944 and from 1956 to 1962, but these attempts were ineffective. The IRA split into factions, and the Irish government worked against it. Fighting renewed in 1969, and the IRA rose from the ashes. Its position solidified when the British Army overreacted to civil disorders. Unionists responded with their own brands of terrorism. Unionist terror came in three forms: (1) repression, (2) vengeance, and (3) revolutionary violence.
- Both the United Kingdom and the Republic of Ireland began to support a serious peace process for Northern Ireland in 1995. Law enforcement policies had weakened the IRA, and the public was tired of violence. Prime Minister Blair also recognized that Sinn Fein was seeking rational political goals. This provided the basis for a long-term political settlement. Extremists in the IRA attempted to derail this process, but they were unsuccessful.
- Modern Spain was formed through the unification of several ethnic areas. The Basque region has existed for at least 3,000 years, and ethnic Basques have never totally embraced Spanish culture. Basques have their own national mythology, literary tradition, culture, and language.
- The Spanish Civil War brought Franco to power, and he violently sought to eradicate Basque culture. This caused a surge of nationalism and resulted in the formation of a Basque shadow government in Paris in the 1950s.
- A group of working-class students formed the ETA in 1959 to express nationalism in the Basque homeland. It began with a campaign of advocacy that transformed into activism. This led to a splintering of the ETA and the formation of a terrorist group. It reached its zenith in 1980, but it remains Europe's oldest violent separatist group.

- Disgruntled Spanish police officers and government officials formed death squads to counter the ETA. These squads eventually merged into the GAL. The Spanish government began taking actions against the GAL in 1987.
- Sri Lanka gained its independence in 1948, giving the Sinhalese majority most of the political power in the country. As Tamils felt discrimination from the Sinhalese, they resorted to violence when peaceful methods failed to address their grievances.
- The LTTE was formed in 1976, and they obtained arms and logistical support from the Tamil diaspora. They developed several effective terrorist and guerrilla tactics and assassinated prominent political leaders. The secular Tamil Tigers mastered the art of suicide bombing, even creating a suicide unit.
- The LTTE was defeated when funds and supplies from the diaspora were cut off. The Sri Lankan government still needs to negotiate an equitable political settlement with the Tamils lest the LTTE be reconstituted in the diaspora.

LOOKING INTO THE FUTURE

This chapter discussed three ethnic–nationalist separatist movements culminating in the IRA, ETA, and LTTE. The ETA continues, and the LTTE has been defeated, although it may have the logistical ability to rekindle. The IRA disbanded with a negotiated settlement, and former Sinn Fein leaders were freed to participate in the political process. Peter Neuman (2007) says nationalistic separatists present a unique opportunity for negotiated settlements because they have recognizable goals.

Separatists are no more rational than other types of terrorists, and their goals are certainly no less absolute. Regardless, Neuman argues that they are easier to bring to the negotiating table than groups like al Qaeda. He also includes Hezbollah, Hamas, and offshoots of the Palestine Liberation Movement as nationalist organizations. Despite their claims to operate under the mantle of religion, they have secular political goals and constituencies to satisfy. They operate like nationalists, and they could become open to political negotiations and settlements.

Neuman understands that negotiations do not develop in a vacuum. The first step is for policymakers to shift their focus of analysis. Instead of focusing on a group's ideology and political objectives, a government should examine a group's attitude about the utility of violence. Many terrorist groups do not begin activities with a violent agenda; they turn to it when they come to see violence as the most efficacious means of achieving their objectives. He points to the IRA as an example. It accepted overtures from British intelligence when its leaders came to realize that total military victory was impossible and marginal objectives could not be achieved with violence. If a group reaches a point where it questions the utility of violence, it might be open to political compromise. Negotiations are always a matter of timing.

Neuman points out that to negotiate, a group must have some type of effective command and control structure. A government must weigh a group's ability to control its members if it seeks a political settlement. If a terrorist group splinters as a result of negotiations, any settlement is jeopardized. When a terrorist group is sponsored by a state, new difficulties arise. Neuman says that a government must assess a group's relationship with its national sponsor and evaluate the need to include the supporting state in discussions.

Neuman's guidelines for negotiating are pragmatic. First, a government cannot be too eager to negotiate, or the offer could backfire. Terrorists might simply use the reprieve to refit and rest. Second, formal negotiations should begin only after a group agrees to a cease-fire. Democracies should clearly indicate that a small group of violent people cannot replace the will of its citizens. Third, negotiations should proceed down two paths—one toward a political settlement and the other toward the welfare of terrorists. It may be necessary to grant amnesty for previous crimes. Although distasteful, it takes momentum away from hard-core terrorists who use punishment as justification for continuing violence. Finally, negotiations must be broad-based. The purpose is to get all parties to participate in a political process, and this can happen only when representatives of the major parties sit at the table.

Terrorists should be given a stake in the democratic process, Neuman concludes, only when they agree to become a part of that process. If negotiations begin, a government must buttress a group's moderates and avoid anything that would strengthen hardliners. For their part, terrorists must abandon violence and participate in politics according to democratic principles. It is the price, says Neuman, terrorists must pay.

Consider these issues in terms of future developments:

- Neuman's arguments are directed toward democracies. How might democracies deal with the types of absolutist goals typified by violent extremism? How can extreme unattainable positions be subject to compromise? What if the electorate or legislature rejects compromises?
- The British government condemned the actions of the paratroopers on Bloody Sunday in January 1972. Some officials called for criminal prosecution. Is it fair to prosecute security forces if terrorists have been given amnesty? Are there crimes so heinous that perpetrators cannot be given amnesty? If so, how might this empower hardliners?
- The LTTE has been defeated, and if reconstituted, it will be developed in the diaspora. Negotiated settlements are effective, but how does the concept apply to Sri Lanka? How might the Sri Lankan government negotiate a permanent settlement? What types of groups should be invited to negotiations?

KEY TERMS

Provisionals, p. 127

Royal Ulster Constabulary, p. 128.

Ulster Volunteer Force, p. 131

Anglo-Irish Peace Accord, p. 132

Tony Blair, p. 132

Belfast Agreement, p. 132

Independent Monitoring Commission (IMC), p. 133

Police Service of Northern Ireland (PSIN), p. 133

War of the Spanish Succession (1702–1714), p. 135

Spanish Civil War (1936–1939), p. 135

Francisco Franco, p. 135

Tamils, p. 139

Velupillai Pirapaharan, p. 139

Rajiv Gandhi, p. 139

Ranasinghe Premadasa, p. 139

Colombo, p. 141

CHAPTER 7

Nationalistic and Endemic Terrorism

LEARNING OBJECTIVES

After reading this chapter, you should be able to:

▶ Define nationalistic terrorism.

▶ Describe revolutionary strategy in Cyprus.

▶ Compare the style of terrorism in Algeria's struggle for independence with terrorism in Cyprus.

▶ Explain the Mau Mau rebellion in Kenya.

▶ Summarize the terrorist issues facing Turkey.

▶ Describe ethnic tensions in China's Xinjiang province.

▶ Explain the rationale behind China's policy toward Uighar separatism.

▶ Briefly summarize Sikh separatism in India.

▶ Define the term *endemic terrorism*.

▶ Describe political conditions in Nigeria and Somalia.

▶ Explain the rise and current status of Boko Haram.

▶ Describe al Shabaab's regional operations and global ambitions.

James Quest/AFP/Getty Images

Aftermath of a Terror Attack, Nairobi, Kenya

Sunday March 11, 2012, began like most other Sundays during the Christian season of Lent at St. Finbarr's Catholic Church in Jos, Nigeria. The priests celebrated the first Mass, and the congregation was dismissed. Congregants for the next Mass were filtering into the church through a gate in the fence that surrounded the church. A small group of Boy Scouts guarded the gate, the only entrance to the church, screening people before they entered. Some security was necessary because northern Nigeria had been the scene of recent religious violence.

Five months earlier, in November 2011, a shadowy group called Boko Haram attacked several targets north of the city of Jos. The group's primary victims were Christians. The Muslim group became increasingly radicalized over the next few years in a country already torn asunder by religious extremism. Both Christian and Muslim militants had attacked one another, but the November attacks were the worst in recent history. When the violence ended, 150 people were dead (Duku, Ogunwale, and Abuja, 2011).

Nigeria is plagued by poverty, political corruption, police brutality, and violent religious fanaticism. As the worshippers at St. Finbarr's filed through the gate on Sunday morning, they were aware that religious services held the potential for violence. They did not resent the group of Boy Scouts who checked each vehicle before it passed through the gate. After all, the Boy Scouts provided an illusion of security.

According to press reports (Agbese, Mahmud, and Muhktur, 2012), the boys refused to let one car pass through the gate. The driver became irritated, and an argument ensued. Heads turned toward the confrontation to search for the cause of the increasingly heated voices. Suddenly, the car exploded in a flash of light. The driver and four of the boys were dead. Another boy lay in the parking lot gasping for life, and three parishioners, including a pregnant woman, were found dead in the debris. A few minutes later, Boko Haram released a statement claiming credit for the attack. Christians went on a rampage. Angry young people stormed away from the church in search of anyone they thought was Muslim. At least 10 people were beaten to death in reprisal attacks. Such is the nature of Africa's endemic terrorism.

Nationalistic Terrorism

Bruce Hoffman (1998, pp. 48–69; 2006, pp. 43–63) of Georgetown University, one of the world's leading experts on terrorism, sees the politics and strategy of anticolonial revolution in the twentieth century as the basis for modern terrorism. It developed as former colonies rejected European dominance of their cultures. Terrorist campaigns were aimed at the security forces, and they also targeted audiences in the imperial homelands. Wise terrorist leaders sought out opportunities to gain sympathy from the international community and anti-imperialist voters in the home country.

A series of anticolonial revolts took place all over the world from the late 1940s to the early 1960s. European powers retreated in the face of guerilla war and terrorism. When revolutionaries of similar language, culture, and traditions fought to create or maintain a common identity, they appealed to a sense of nationalism. In fact, terrorism was justified under a banner of nationalism. Nationalistic terrorism refers to violent terrorism waged on the basis of a shared sense common political unity, cultural traditions, or ethnic freedom. It can be the basis for long-term separatist terrorism—as shown with the Basque region of Spain and struggles in Ireland—and it also appeared in anticolonial struggles after World War II.

Revolts were numerous because Europe had colonized much of the world, but three cases can be used to illustrate differing styles of nationalistic terrorism. Ruled directly by the British, Cyprus became the scene of urban terrorism, and Britain fought rural nationalistic terrorists in Kenya. France fought a brutal multifaceted campaign in Algeria, experiencing multiple forms of terrorism and responding with repressive terror. Though hardly a comprehensive review of anticolonial revolutions, the three cases represent the major patterns that dominated terrorism in the wars of independence. Similar styles of terrorism appear in nationalistic violence today.

Cyprus, 1955–1959

The United Kingdom retreated from its empire throughout the 1950s, sometimes negotiating peaceful withdrawals and, at other times, fighting small uprisings. Having claimed Cyprus (Figure 7.1) as a crown colony after World War I, Britain

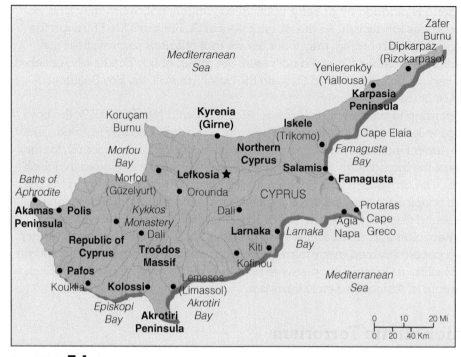

FIGURE **7.1** Cyprus

established its Middle East military headquarters there at the end of World War II, and Cypriots of Greek descent deeply resented British control. They sought unification with Greece, but Turkish Cypriots, formerly governed by the Ottoman Empire, looked to Turkey. Tensions seethed below the surface while the British remained in control (Paul and Spirit, 2008).

Georgios Grivas (1898–1974) had been an officer in the Greek Army. Unconcerned with the Turkish population on Cyprus, he appealed to Greek nationalism. Grivas created an organization to overthrow the British, the Ethniki Organosis Kyprion Agoniston (National Organization of Cypriot Fighters; EOKA). He developed a twofold strategy based on gaining international sympathy and confronting superior British forces in Cypriot cities. (Coyle, 1983, pp. 151–187).

Grivas reasoned that small groups of EOKA terrorists could strike in Cypriot cities, thwarting any potential military offensive against rebel forces. EOKA bombing began with a series of attacks in April 1955. Another series of explosions came two months later, including an attack on a police station. The Cypriots rioted at times during the summer, and the United Kingdom responded with force. A new governor, a former field marshal, imposed harsh penalties, including capital punishment for crimes less than murder. This produced the effect that Grivas had been seeking—press coverage and international sympathy. Terrorists hid in Cypriot cities, and the vast numbers of British troops found few of them (Fairfield, 1959). Responding to international pressure from allies and British citizens who opposed colonial repression, the United Kingdom negotiated a deal with the EOKA in February 1959. As Bruce Hoffman (1998, p. 60) points out, terrorism worked.

The Battle for Algiers, 1954–1962

France began colonizing Algeria in 1830 (Figure 7.2). They brutally used military force to subdue the population in the vast interior of Algeria and flooded the Mediterranean coast with Europeans. By 1881, the north was officially absorbed into France, and after 1889, any European born in the new territory received French citizenship. Some Algerians benefited from the move, but the majority deeply resented the loss of autonomy. They formed patriotic associations seeking to free their homeland, and after France itself had been occupied and liberated, they thought the French would grant independence (Branche, 2008).

By 1953, France, like the United Kingdom, was retreating from its colonial empire, and the French people approved. They relinquished control of colony after colony, but Algeria was another matter. The northern coast was not an imperial holding, most French people reasoned; it was part of France. When Algerian nationalists made overtures for independence, the French government thought that granting their request was out of the question. Algerian revolutionaries formed the National Liberation Front (FLN) and decided to frighten the Europeans out of their country.

David Galula (1963, pp. 9–25) produced one of the best studies of the ensuing conflict. Too impatient to launch a guerrilla campaign from the interior regions of

David Galula: (1919–1967) French captain who fought in Algeria from 1956 to 1958. He returned to Paris to analyze the Algerian campaign, and he produced a critique of the strategy followed in the war. His work inspired the development of counterinsurgency doctrine in the U.S. military.

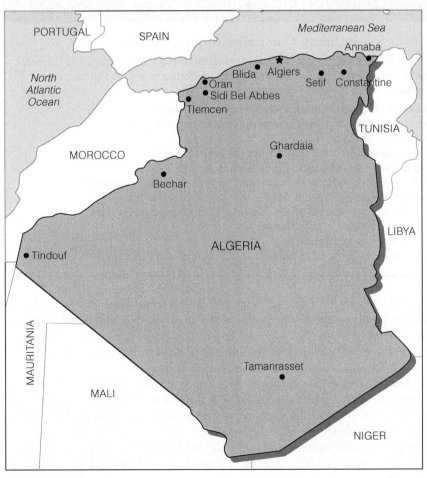

FIGURE **7.2** Algeria

blind terrorism: tactic used by the FLN. It included indiscriminant attacks against French outposts, which involved bombing, sabotage, and random assassination.

Algeria, the FLN decided to strike directly in areas dominated by French colonials and terrorize them with sensational violence. The FLN launched a campaign of **blind terrorism** in 1954. Although its leaders planned to shift to selective terrorism, they never really abandoned indiscriminant violence.

The FLN began its campaign on November 1, 1954, launching 70 clandestine attacks against an unsuspecting enemy. Raphaëlle Branche (2008) says that a most dreadful attack came almost a year later in August 1955, when groups from the FLN slipped into Algerian suburbs and outlying French towns to massacre entire groups of colonial families. Their primary tactic was to slit the throats of their victims, making sure their bodies would be on display the next morning.

Females played an important role in this struggle. FLN leaders noted that French police officers and soldiers were more likely to confront men than women, so they used females to carry weapons and communiqués. As the fighting grew more intense, the role of women increased. Women were able to infiltrate the French areas of Algiers, so the FLN stuffed their handbags with explosives. The women roamed through French urban environments in European dress, depositing their time bombs in highly populated areas. They frequently targeted gathering places known to attract large numbers of French youth (Branche, 2008).

EXPANDING THE CONCEPT

Hoffman Compares Algeria to Iraq

Bruce Hoffman (2006a) describes several interesting parallels between the French experience in Algeria and the initial American response to the Iraq insurgency. These include:

- The absence of a clear doctrine to thwart an insurgency
- Failure to recognize warning signs of an impending insurgency
- Insurgent focus on urban areas
- Failure to separate the population from the insurgents
- The need to avoid alienating the indigenous population
- Promotion of women's rights to counteract support for the insurgency
- The need to emphasize law enforcement over military tactics
- Failure to realize the limited effect of neutralizing insurgent leaders
- The critical importance of intelligence
- The importance of sealing borders
- The critical impact of the humane treatment of captured insurgents

---

Hoffman (1998, pp. 62–65) and Branche (2008) point out that French forces played into the hands of the FLN. As violence increased, they employed tactics of mass arrests, torture, and murder. Algerian opinion quickly turned again France, and by the late 1950s, world opinion was shifting, too. The French made a costly tactical mistake.

Brutal counterterrorist tactics drove Algerian sympathy toward the FLN, and French citizens eventually lost their taste for a dirty war. Galula (1963, p. 5), one of the few observers to grasp the meaning of the French campaign, said the tactics alienated the very people the security forces needed to attract. Counterinsurgency, he concluded, requires public support and sympathy, yet French forces received little support for their murderous behavior. Algeria received independence in 1962. Terrorism triumphed again.

The Mau Mau in Kenya, 1950–1960

Another style of terrorism arose in Kenya in the 1950s. British control of the interior did not take shape until 1908, and the whole of Keya was not fully a colony until after World War I. After the colonial government was established, however, Britain began distributing Kenya's agricultural areas to European farmers, displacing tribes from their ancestral lands. During the 1930s and 1940s one tribe, the Kikuyu, was forced to resettle deep in western Kenya in an area where resources were scarce. Their lands were given to white settlers, and they resented it. By 1950, there was talk of violence in the Kikuyu tribal area. It centered on a group called the Mau Mau (Throup, 1988, pp. 224–233).

The Mau Mau movement represents several factors that bear no resemblance to the anticolonial urban revolts in Cyprus and Algeria. First, it was based in rural areas. Although there was some Mau Mau violence in Kenya's cities, most violence took place in agrarian areas. Second, Mau Mau culture was based on tribal rites and ceremonies where symbols were used to solidify the group. Becoming a Mau Mau warrior involved taking an oath in a mystical tribal ceremony. Third, it brought an overwhelming British military and police response with massive detainment and torture. Fourth, Mau Mau insurgents suffered the brunt of the casualties, losing 10,000 men, while Kenyan loyalists lost 1,700, and European losses could be counted in the dozens. Finally, repression destroyed the Mau Mau, but it brought many of the political reforms that the Mau Mau had been seeking (Kariuki, 1963, pp. 12–24; Percox, 2003: Lonsdale, 2003; D. Anderson, 2005, pp. 224–327). The Mau Mau lost militarily but won the political settlement.

The rebel Kikuyus began assembling in the forests of western Kenya around 1950. Disgruntled Kikuyus began burning fields of European farmers and hamstringing their cattle. The farmers complained to Nairobi, but these small victories emboldened the Kikuyus. The rebel Kikuyus began to engage in magical ceremonies as they prepared for their resistance, and the Mau Mau movement was born. By January 1952, Mau Mau revolutionaries, feeling empowered by their land and magic, began killing Kenyans loyal to the colonial government.

Although highly selective in their targets, Mau Mau warriors began moving back toward the Kikuyu homeland, eventually entering the homesteads where European farmers had displaced them. The Mau Mau grew more daring, targeting farmhouses when they thought they were unoccupied. This dramatically changed in January 1953 when Mau Mau insurgents entered the farmhouse of a politically popular local farmer and police reservist. Hearing a disturbance outside his house early one evening, he took a pistol to investigate. He was ambushed and slashed to death by a group of men swinging **pangas**. Alarmed by his screams, his wife ran outside only to meet the same fate. The men entered the house and broke down the locked bedroom door of the couple's six-year-old son. They slashed him to death in his bed. This event outraged European farmers, and their anger grew when pictures of the young boy's blood-soaked bed were circulated through the white community (D. Anderson, 2005, pp. 92–95). The British responded with force and what they believed to be unbridled moral authority in the face of savagery. The colonial government declared a state of emergency.

panga: a heavy-bladed machete used in agricultural work. It was the weapon favored by people who took the Mau Mau oath.

After the state of emergency went into effect, thousands of British soldiers arrived in Kenya. They were charged with ending the rebellion, and they made military plans to do so. The government recruited and trained a large local force to assist the army. The ensuing campaign was ruthless and violent. In addition, 90,000 suspected rebels were detained in special internment camps. The level of rebel violence dropped as government violence increased.

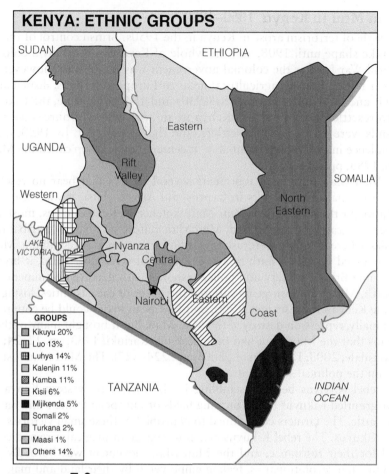

KENYA: ETHNIC GROUPS

GROUPS
- Kikuyu 20%
- Luo 13%
- Luhya 14%
- Kalenjin 11%
- Kamba 11%
- Kisii 6%
- Mijikenda 5%
- Somali 2%
- Turkana 2%
- Maasi 1%
- Others 14%

FIGURE **7.3** Kenya

Unlike urban terrorist campaigns in Cyprus and Algeria, the Mau Mau movement failed in the field. David Anderson (2005, p. 244) explains the outcome by breaking the movement into three phases. From October 1952 through June 1953, Mau Mau units gathered in camps in the lower forests of western Kenya. Morale was high, the mood was optimistic, and they successfully attacked carefully selected targets. Their ranks grew to about 12,000. From July 1953 through April 1954, Mau Mau units were forced to retreat deeper into the forest in the wake of British military offensives. They devolved into forest gangs. The third phase lasted from May 1954 until the summer of 1955. Military and police units laid siege to the forest. Recruitment dropped, and the gangs were isolated from one another. After the summer of 1955, the Mau Mau movement became a paper tiger: It existed only in the minds of the government and European settlers.

Governmental policy was ruthless. Over 90,000 Mau Mau suspects were interned during the state of emergency, and the conditions of custody were appalling. Thousands of suspects were tortured, and a few were executed outside the justice system (Elkins, 2003). These policies backfired. The Mau Mau movement created an atmosphere inside Kenya favoring independence. In addition, the British public grew increasingly disgusted with the colonial government's repressive violence. Kenya would gain its independence, and a former suspected Mau Mau exile would become its president.

✓ **Self-Check**	>	What factors led to revolutionary success in Cyprus and Algeria?
	>	Why did the Mau Mau movement fail to achieve a military victory?
	>	Why did repression ultimately fail in all three cases?

Turkey

Turkey is an enigma in its standing with Europe. The country is 99 percent Muslim and was the home of the last caliphate. Long ago, it was the seat of the Eastern, or Byzantine, Roman Empire, but when its capital Constantinople fell to Mahmet II in 1453, it became the center of Islam. Ironically, Mustafa Kemal, better known as Kemal Atatürk, dissolved the Islamic government in 1923 and established Turkey as a secular republic. Although most of the country is in Asia, Turkey was accepted as a partner in NATO, and it sought close trade ties with Europe and the United States after World War II. It was the first Muslim-majority country to recognize the state of Israel.

Esther Pan (2005b) says that Turkey looks to Europe for both cultural and economic reasons. Many Europeans and Americans encourage it, hoping that Turkey will join the European Union (EU). Other Europeans have been reluctant to accept Turkey, citing demographic, cultural, and religious differences. They fear that if Turkey joins the EU, Europe will be flooded with poorly educated workers, and radical jihadists will strengthen their foothold in Europe. They also worry about Turkey's human rights record.

For its part, Turkey has many people who like the idea of blending religion and government. Other Turks are not enamored of this idea. In May 2007, nearly 500,000 people demonstrated to protest the influence of Islam in Turkey's internal affairs. The Turkish Army has declared that it will not accept a religious government (Associated Press, 2007a). In the midst of this dilemma, Turkey has attempted to modernize its law enforcement agencies and military within the norms of Western democracies. It has opened its doors to Western police agencies, and the Turkish National Police has one of the most highly educated police command staffs in the world. Turkey has also experienced several different types of terrorist campaigns over the past three decades.

Turkey's Struggle with Terrorism

Turkey has suffered 40,000 deaths from terrorism since 1980. In Istanbul, a police commander in Turkey's counterterrorism unit said to the author, "You Americans came to see terrorism as a problem after the World Trade Center. We've suffered thousands of casualties for three decades." Although the largest issue is with the Kurdistan Workers' Party (see the next section), other groups also operate in Turkey. In the mid-1980s, a group known as Turkish Hezbollah appeared in eastern Turkey. It has no connection with the Lebanese Shi'ite group Hezbollah. Formed from a Sunni Kurd–Turk Islamic base, Hezbollah sought to counter the activities of the Kurdistan Workers' Party. Critics claim that it received some forms of clandestine support from the government in the 1990s, but Turkish security forces might disagree. Hezbollah expanded its targets in the 1990s to businesses and other establishments that it deemed to be non-Islamic. Following the path of other terrorist groups, Hezbollah began to kidnap and torture Muslim businesspersons who refused to support its activities. Hezbollah's goal is to establish an Islamic state by force of arms (BBC News, 2000).

Brian Williams and Fezya Altindag (2004) point out that Turkey developed an internal jihadist problem after 1994. They believe that Hezbollah is part of this problem, and they state that that is the blowback, or unwanted effects, from the government's attempt to create Hezbollah as a counterterrorist movement against the Kurdistan Workers' Party. Yet, the real problem started in 1994 when several thousand Turkish young people began to attend militant madrassas, or private religious schools, in Pakistan. They returned to Turkey with an Islamic agenda. Atatürk's secular Turkey was anathema to them.

Williams and Altindag believe that the Pakistani-trained young people eventually became part of a jihadist movement in Turkey, including an al Qaeda splinter group, El Kaide Turka, or al Qaeda in Turkey. By 2001, a group of madrassa-trained young men placed themselves under the leadership of **Habib Akdas**, who had undertaken a task from Osama bin Laden. Bin Laden wanted to punish Turkey for its partnerships with the United States and Israel, and he believed that Akdas was the man to lead the charge. With bin Laden's encouragement, Akdas sought to strike American and Israeli interests in Turkey. Al Qaeda in Turkey would eventually expand its attacks to other Westerners.

Habib Akdas: (birth date unknown) also known as Abu Anas al Turki, the founder of al Qaeda in Turkey. Akdas left Turkey to fight in Iraq after the American invasion. He was killed in a U.S. air strike in 2004.

Habib Akdas and his followers returned to Turkey after the American-led coalition attacked al Qaeda strongholds in Afghanistan in October 2001. Williams and Altindag say that coalition forces found training manuals translated into Turkish, and this prompted the United States to send a warning to Turkey's police and military forces. Akdas bided his time. Not wanting to rush his attacks, he planned for the next two years. Bin Laden wanted Akdas to attack an American air base in Turkey, but Akdas believed it was guarded too well. He searched for softer targets. The U.S. embassy in Ankara and the U.S. consulate in Istanbul also proved to be too well fortified. Akdas decided to turn to British and Israeli targets. He launched suicide attacks against two synagogues in Istanbul on November 15, 2003. He struck the British consulate and a British bank with suicide bombers less than one week later.

The double bombings backfired. Infuriated by the attacks, Turkish citizens demanded that the government take action because the majority of people killed in the al Qaeda bombings had been Muslims. The Turkish National Police unleashed their full power against al Qaeda in Turkey. Williams and Altindag say that dozens of al Qaeda operatives and supporters were arrested, and Akdas removed himself to Iraq to fight the Americans. The militants fanned out across Turkey and began a low-level bombing campaign. Akdas is believed to have been killed in fighting around Fallujah in November 2004 (Global Jihad, 2007). BBC News (2006) reported that Turkish police were able to arrest several important al Qaeda leaders in Turkey in December 2006, including Akdas's replacement.

The Kurdistan Workers' Party and Its Alter Egos

Turkey is currently facing a wave of religious terrorism, but for the past three decades, its major problem came from Kurds, an ethnic group inhabiting parts of southern Turkey, northern Iraq, and northern Iran (see the "*Expanding the Concept: The Kurdish Conflict*" feature later in this chapter). The Kurdistan Workers' Party (PKK) is a Marxist-Leninist terrorist organization composed of Turkish Kurds. It officially changed its name to Kurdistan Freedom and Democracy (KADEK) in 2002 (see the "*Another Perspective: The PKK by Any Other Name*" feature later in this chapter), and it operates in Turkey and Europe, targeting Europeans, Turks, rival Kurds, and supporters of the Turkish government. It represents the same ruthless brand of Maoism as the Peruvian guerrilla organization Shining Path, murdering entire villages whose residents fail to follow its dictates. The PKK/KADEK has developed chameleon-like characteristics, and although it is a revolutionary Marxist group, it has since 1990 employed the language of nationalism. Even more startling, since 1995, it has also used the language of religion.

The PKK was founded in 1974 to fight for an independent Kurdistan (Criss, 1995). Unlike other Kurdish groups, the PKK wanted to establish a Marxist-Leninist state. Although the PKK targeted Turkey, the Kurds claim a highland region spanning southeast Turkey, northeast Iraq, and northwest Iran (see Figure 7.4). Taking advantage of Kurdish nationalism and hoping to launch a guerrilla war, the PKK began operations in 1978.

The plans for revolution, however, proved too grandiose. There was sentiment for fighting the Iraqis, Iranians, and Turks, but not enough support for the Communists. Most Kurds wanted autonomy, not Communism. The PKK was not strong enough to wage a guerrilla war without some type of support, and its political orientation prevented it from allying with other Kurdish groups. The PKK had two choices: It could either wage a propaganda campaign or throw itself into terrorism. Its leadership chose the path of terrorism.

PKK leaders increased their efforts to build a terrorist organization by moving into Lebanon's Bekaa Valley in September 1980. While training there, they met some of the most accomplished terrorists in the world, and after the 1982 Israeli invasion of Lebanon, they quickly found allies in the Syrian camp. For the next two years, the group trained and purged its internal leadership. In the meantime, some PKK members cultivated sympathy among several villages in southern Turkey. By 1984, the PKK was ready for a campaign against Turkey.

Support turned out to be the key factor. Moving from base to base in Turkey, the PKK also received money and weapons from Syria. The relatively weak group of 1978 emerged as a guerrilla force in 1984, and it ruthlessly used terrorism against the Turks and their allies. Civilians bore the brunt of PKK atrocities, and within a few years, the PKK had murdered more than 10,000 people. The majority of these murders came as a result of village massacres (Criss, 1995). Turkey responded by isolating the PKK from their support bases and counterattacking PKK groups. Turkish security forces operated with a heavy hand.

The tactics had a negative effect on the Kurds. Although they were ready to fight for independence, they were not willing to condone massacres and terrorist attacks. The PKK responded in 1990 by redirecting offensive operations. Rather than focusing on the civilian population, the PKK began limiting its attacks to security forces and economic targets. Having expanded into Western Europe a few years earlier, PKK leaders stated that they would strike only "legitimate" Turkish targets. The PKK also modified its Marxist-Leninist rhetoric and began to speak of nationalism.

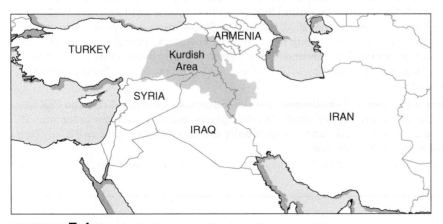

FIGURE **7.4** Kurdish Region: Turkey, Iraq, and Iran

Abdullah Ocalan:
(b. 1948) the leader of the PKK. Ocalan was captured in 1999 and sentenced to death, but his sentence was commuted. He ordered the end of a suicide bombing campaign while in Turkish custody and called for peace between Turkey and the Kurds in 2006.

In a 1995 interview (Korn, 1995), PKK leader **Abdullah Ocalan** reiterated the new PKK position. When asked whether he was a Marxist, Ocalan stated that he believed in "scientific socialism." Ocalan said that this would become a new path because the Muslim population in general, and the Kurds in particular, had suffered at the hands of Marxist-Leninists. He cast his statements in anti-imperialist terms, stating that Kurdistan was only resisting imperialist powers.

In October 1995, Ocalan asked the United States to mediate between the PKK and Turkey, saying that the PKK was willing to settle for a federation instead of complete autonomy. U.S. officials immediately rejected the terrorist's rhetoric, which was nothing new. The PKK had started speaking of federal status in 1990 (Criss, 1995). Irrespective of the form of government, Ocalan wanted semiautonomy. In his October 1995 letter to the United States, Ocalan asked for federal status "like the United States." Earlier that year, he had asked for the same thing, but "like the Russian Federation" (Korn, 1995). The most dramatic announcement came later. By December, the PKK was using the rhetoric of Islam, citing religious texts instead of Marxist-Leninist ideology. Ocalan appealed to Muslim Kurds, in the name of God, to revolt against the so-called secular Turkish government.

EXPANDING THE CONCEPT

The Kurdish Conflict

The Issue. The Kurds are an ethnic group inhabiting northern Iraq, southern Turkey, and northern Iran. When other groups received national sovereignty at the end of World War I, the Kurds remained divided among the three nations. The Treaty of Sèvres (1920) created an independent Kurdistan, but it was never implemented. About 12 million Kurds live in Turkey.

The Group. The Kurdistan Workers' Party (PKK) was formed in 1978 as a Marxist-Leninist group. Its goal was to create an independent socialist Kurdistan.

The Campaign. After training in Syria, the PKK launched a guerrilla campaign in Turkey. By the early 1990s, the PKK turned to urban terrorism, targeting Turks throughout Europe and Turkey. After its leader Abdullah Ocalan was captured in 1999, the PKK pledged to work for a peaceful solution; however, it maintained various militant organizations operating under a variety of names. The PKK maintains links with other revolutionary groups in Turkey and with some international terrorist groups.

The Campaign Renewed. Turkey is being considered for admission to the European Union. The EU, NATO, and the United States list the various entities of the PKK as terrorist organizations. In October 2003, the United States agreed to crack down on the PKK in northern Iraq, but the group remained. Turkey began clandestine incursions into the Kurdish area of Iraq around 2006. (Turkey officially denies this.) Open confrontation began in 2008, and by 2010, PKK units were crossing into Turkey, attacking military outposts.

The Future. After years of challenges, the U.S. Supreme Court ruled that the PKK is a foreign terrorist group. Turkey conducts intelligence, military, and law enforcement operations against the PKK, and it is gradually moving further from Europe, seeking closer ties with the Middle East.

Sources: Council on Foreign Relations, 2004; Dymond, 2004; U.S. Department of State, 2004b; *The Economist* 2008; Liptak, 2010.

ANOTHER PERSPECTIVE

The PKK by Any Other Name

The PKK operates under a variety of names. According to the U.S. Department of State (2004), these include:

- Freedom and Democracy Congress of Kurdistan
- Kurdistan People's Congress (KHK)
- People's Congress of Kurdistan
- Liberation Units of Kurdistan (HRK)
- Kurdish People's Liberation Army (ARGK)
- National Liberation Front of Kurdistan (ERNK)
- Kurdistan Freedom and Democracy Congress (KADEK)
- Kongra-Gel (KGK)

The PKK officially changed its name to KADEK in April 2002 and to Kongra-Gel in 2003.

At first, it might sound surprising to hear the Marxists of the PKK using religious language, but it is politically understandable. The PKK shifted its position to achieve the greatest amount of support. Ocalan had been moving in an anti-Western direction for many years. His terrorists attacked a NATO base in 1986, and they kidnapped 19 Western tourists in 1993. As jihadist rhetoric grew against the West, Ocalan simply copied the language. But there was something more. In June 1996, an Islamic religious government came to power in secular Turkey. Ocalan wanted to prove that he was not an ogre who massacred civilians in their villages; rather, he was simply a good Muslim.

Ocalan's shift to religion gave the PKK new life. Leftist movements in Turkey followed the path of their European counterparts: They went into hibernation. When Ocalan proclaimed a doctrine of Marxist Islam, the PKK managed to survive. A unilateral cease-fire on the part of the PKK in December 1995 placed Turkey in an awkward position. According to Nur Bilge Criss (1995), Ocalan's religious rhetoric played well not only among Kurds but also throughout the Middle East. Writing before the 1996 election, Criss predicted that Turkey would move closer to the Islamic world to counter this threat. He also said that the supreme irony was that Turkey could be drawn away from NATO to an alliance with Iraq or Iran in an effort to counterbalance the Kurds and the Syrians. His predictions turned out to be incorrect.

The PKK represents the pejorative nature of terrorism. When the terrorist label is applied to a group like the PKK, the whole movement is questioned. Kurds have long suffered at the hands of their neighbors. The Iranians have slaughtered them, Saddam Hussein used rockets and poison gas to destroy entire Kurdish villages, and the Turks have repressed them. The PKK is a terrorist organization, but expressing Kurdish nationalism is not a terrorist act. Many thousands of Kurds were victimized by state terrorism long before the PKK unsheathed its sword.

Turkish authorities captured Abdullah Ocalan in Kenya in February 1999, and a security court sentenced him to death in June. Ocalan offered to chart a new course for the PKK a few weeks later. Because Turkey was lobbying to join the EU, it delayed and eventually reversed the death sentence. (Members of the EU may not invoke capital punishment.) It appeared as if there might be a window for peace.

The situation deteriorated after the U.S.-led invasion of Iraq. Kurds in northern Iraq were empowered after they gained freedom from Baghdad's oppression, and the area began to thrive. As their economic power grew, so did the threat to Turkey. PKK operatives and other Kurdish nationalists saw an opportunity to renew their struggle. Although Turkey denied any activity, troops may have crossed the Iraqi border as early as 2006. By 2008, there was no longer a question of secrecy as Turkey launched punitive strikes against the PKK, sometimes by air and at other times with ground troops (*The Economist*, 2008). The PKK responded. During the summer of 2010, it was sufficiently strong to hit isolated army outposts inside Turkey. During the same time period, the Kurds lost a political battle to legitimize the PKK. The U.S. Supreme Court upheld the State Department's designation when it declared that the PKK was a terrorist organization, and the Court ruled that it was a federal crime to support the group (Liptak, 2010).

The rise of ISIS in 2014 may greatly impact the future. The radical version of Islam that fuels ISIS has created strange bedfellows. The vast majority of Kurds are appalled by terrorism, but they want independence. Although they have some autonomy in Iraq due to the weak power of the central government, independence implies that Kurds have strong differences with Turkey, Iraq, and Iran. Yet, the Kurdish militia is fighting ISIS with assistance from its rivals. The Kurds themselves may take stronger action against the PKK. Kurdish fighters cannot stand against ISIS without regional allies.

> ✓ **Self-Check**
>
> > How is Turkey's struggle against terrorism similar to issues in Europe?
> > What types of terrorist groups operate in Turkey?
> > What are the principal goals of the PKK?

China's Problems in Xinjiang

After September 11, China was eager to join America's "war on terror." Beijing claims that international jihadists, trained in Afghanistan and Pakistan, are attempting to overthrow Chinese rule in the Xinjiang (New Frontier) province and establish an Islamic state. In 2003, China asked for international assistance in clamping down on what the government claims to be its own "jihadist terrorists," **Uighar nationalists** who believe Xinjiang is their homeland. Although the Chinese communists link the Uighars to al Qaeda and the 9/11 attacks, the movement predates al Qaeda by 245 years (Lufti, 2004).

Uighar nationalists: China's ethnic Turkmen. Some Uighar nationalists organized to revive an eighteenth-century Islamic state in China's Xinjiang province. Using Kyrgyzstan and Kazakhstan as a base, they operate in China.

The Uighars are ethnic Turkmen, mostly Sufi Muslims, and they have lived in and governed parts of Xinjiang province for 200 years (Figure 7.6.) Many of them are fighting to become independent from China. Chienpeng Chung (2002) says that the ethnic Uighars are mostly Islamic mystics who are inspired by the collapse of the Soviet Union, not by Osama bin Laden. As the former Central Asian Soviet republics gained autonomy after 1991, the Uighars saw it as an opportunity to reassert their independence. Separatists launched a terrorist campaign in the Xinjiang province aimed at throwing the Chinese out. Despite their best efforts, Chung says, the Chinese have not been able to eradicate the rebellion.

China annexed the area in 1759, and the first uprising came in 1865 and lasted 12 years. Chung says that the revolt set the stage for Muslim independence from China, which the Uighars achieved twice, from 1931 to 1934 and then again from 1944 to 1949. They called their land East Turkestan (see Figure 7.5). The Communist Chinese

FIGURE 7.5 The Region the Uighars Wish to Be Autonomous

brutally repressed the Uighars and reasserted control in 1949. The Chinese have settled the area with ethnic Chinese, displacing the Uighars, in an effort to assimilate the area. In 1949, the area was 90 percent Uighar, but it may be less than 50 percent today. Displaced Uighars throughout the world support the separatists. Beijing has asked Washington to list militant Uighar organizations as terrorist groups, and the United States has been sympathetic to Chinese demands. Washington needs Beijing as an ally.

Although one of the militant groups fighting for independence trained in Afghanistan, the majority of militants are not jihadists. To be sure, some separatists are terrorists. Bombings and assassinations have cost almost 200 lives and 600 casualties. Ahmed Lufti (2004) says that it is important to remember that China experienced a terrorist campaign at the time. It is also important to note that the United States does not classify internal Chinese ethnic violence as terrorism, there are religious and ethnic differences that cause strife. Additionally, China is fighting for Xinjiang because it has China's largest oil and gas reserves. The growing Chinese economy needs its resources, but the Uighars feel that it is their country. Groups based in Kyrgyzstan and Kazakhstan leave those countries to raid across the Chinese border, and internal groups run their own campaigns.

Chung says that although this is terrorism, there are two problems with that classification. Most Uighar terrorism is not part of the jihadist movement. Uighars are not fighting an international jihad for a caliphate; they want independence. The greater problem, however, is that many of the separatists are not violent, and they do not endorse terrorism. Chung says that they only want independence. Through the process of labeling, the Chinese have deemed all expressions of Uighar separatism as terrorism based on the jihadist movement. The United States, disinclined to lose China's support against Central Asian terrorism, is reluctant to criticize China when it justifies repression in the name of counterterrorism.

✓	Self-Check	> How did China interpret the "war on terror"?
		> What is the goal of Uighar nationalists?
		> Why do some Uighars want independence?

Sikh Separatism in India

India has a variety of terrorist problems stemming from political, religious, and ethnic strife. The country has a diverse population, including a religious group known as the Sikhs. *Sikh* is a Punjabi word meaning "disciple." Founded over 500 years ago, Sikhism emphasizes an inner journey to seek spiritual enlightenment, followed by external behavior to live in peace with the world. The religion has enshrined 10 great teachers, or gurus, and it embodies elements of Islam and Hinduism (Brar, 2003). After India was partitioned in 1947, some Sikhs sought independence in Punjab, a state where they represented the majority of the population. This gave birth to a small, violent independence movement in 1977.

Golden Temple: the most sacred shrine of Sikhism. Its official name is the Temple of God.

India responded to the revolt by strengthening central authority in Punjab. This move divided the Sikhs into a majority orthodox group that wanted to peacefully resolve the situation and a small radicalized group that wanted to fight India. Issues came to a head in 1984 when Indian military forces entered the Sikhs' most sacred site, the **Golden Temple**, and engaged in a bloody battle with armed militants. Thousands of people were killed (Singh, 2000, pp. 214–215). Small groups of Sikhs formed terror cells that targeted Indian security forces, unsympathetic journalists, and the majority community of Sikhs who called for the restoration of peace (GlobalSecurity.org, n.d.). A few months after the Golden Temple raid, the Sikh bodyguards of the prime minister of India assassinated her.

Sikh extremists planned assassinations all over the world, including the United States. Several cells were active in North America. Extremists compiled a hit list of moderate Sikhs in Canada, and radical members preached violence. One radical pleaded guilty in 2003 to making the bomb that brought down Air India Flight 182 in an explosion that killed 329 people in 1985 (Commission of Inquiry, 2007). By 1988, more than 100 people per month lost their lives due to the Sikh terrorists. Fighting took place as militant Sikhs attacked police and nonmilitant Sikhs, and the police struck back. Violence continued in India through 1994 and then decreased. When one Sikh was asked to explain why the violence had tapered off, he responded that the government killed all the militants (Juergensmeyer, 2003, pp. 86–101).

✓	Self-Check	> Who are the Sikhs?
		> What is the Golden Temple?
		> Describe the course of terrorism, as applied to the Sikhs.

Endemic Ethnic Terror in Sub-Saharan Africa

J. Bowyer Bell (1975, pp. 10–18) used the term *endemic terrorism* to describe the state of terrorist violence in Africa. Endemic terrorism refers to the artificial mixing of rival ethnic groups, tribes, nationalities, or cultures in a nation-state. At times, it is so closely connected with nationalistic terrorism that it is difficult to distinguish between the two. For example, you might argue that China, India, and Turkey have nationalistic challenges. However, you could create a strong case for calling violence in these regions endemic terrorism. The case in East and West Africa differs because nationalism is not applicable, and endemic terror is the cause of much violence.

The borders in much of sub-Saharan Africa and the modern Middle East were drawn in Europe without regard for tribal areas, ethnicity, or religion. This resulted in artificial separations of traditional political associations and cultures. In other instances, rival groups or families were lumped into a single new country despite the fact that they had no common history. Politics in these states often became violent as factions clashed for control of governments. Rulers were notoriously corrupt and/or brutally repressive. Crime flourished, and human rights vanished. Ironhanded rule was one of the few methods that could hold these countries together. Arbitrary arrests, summary executions, and torture allowed the dominant groups to rule over their enemies. Such condition can produce endemic terrorism, which has occurred in the cases of three jihadist groups espousing global rhetoric and engaging in regional violence.

Conditions in Nigeria

Retired Air Force lieutenant colonel Clarence Bouchat (2013) provided an excellent analysis of political and economic conditions—factors that led to endemic terrorism—in contemporary Nigeria for the U.S. Army War College. There is no history of common traditions in Nigeria. It is a state composed of separate religions and cultures constructed from imperial British decisions. Conditions in the conglomerated nation gave rise to two jihadist groups—Boko Haram and its offshoot Ansaru.

The British began creating the modern nation of Nigeria in 1845 when they assumed control of the area's coast. They slowly moved north over the next 100 years, taking charge of diverse regions and incorporating them into a makeshift colony. The people who came under British control were from differing religious, cultural, tribal, and extended family groups. They spoke a multitude of languages and had varied traditions. In 1906, they made the Christian south a colony and began jointly administering it with the Muslim north in 1914. They united both states in a single colony in the 1930s. The main common experience between the two regions was British rule.

When Nigeria gained its independence in 1960, Bouchat points out that it contained 250 ethnic groups and three religious groupings: Muslims, Christians, and those adhering to traditional tribal religions. About 50 percent of the people are Muslims, 40 percent are Christians, and 10 percent practice indigenous religions. Muslims are generally concentrated in the north, and Christians dominate the south. Both religions have leaders who demonize the other side and issue calls for violence in theological terms. Bouchat says these religious rivalries are part of the reason for internal violence, but the root cause of instability is the manipulation of religion for political and economic advantages.

There are internal divisions within the Muslim community. Most Muslims in Nigeria were originally Sufis and remain so today. Strict orthodox Sunni Muslims sent missionaries to the region, and they brought a new tradition of Islam to the northern area, **Salafism**. Salafists combine a strict interpretation of Islam law with a zeal for enforcing their practices. Some Salafists are willing to force their version of religion on others, at times even using violence to spread Islam. They are critical of the more tolerant Sufis.

When Nigeria gained independence in 1960, it was a divided nation and full of internal turmoil. There was no common social structures and several different cultural traditions. Since 1960, Bouchat explains, the country has experienced four different republics, fought a formal civil war, engaged in several internal ethnic and religious

Salafism: tradition of orthodox Muslims who follow the Prophet and the early elders of the faith. Militants are willing to use violence to enforce Islamic law and confront other faith traditions.

conflicts, and generated a terrible record of human rights abuses. The literacy rate in Nigeria is 61 percent, 20 percent of the people live in poverty, and life expectancy is only 47.6 years. It is one of the poorest countries in the world and a hub for cyber-crime, drug smuggling, human trafficking, piracy, violent extremism, and disease.

Ironically, Nigeria has tremendous oil and gas reserves that generate millions of dollars. The problem, according to Bouchat, is that the wealth is controlled by small rival groups of political elites. They struggle with one another to control political power, and the revenue derived from oil income makes them unaccountable to the public. They maintain the status quo with their wealth instead of using it to develop the Nigerian economy. Elites have small groups of supporters and establish social control by politicizing Nigeria's internal diversity. Organized political groups join together in Mafia-like associations and fight each other under the direction of elites.

Geographically, the country is divided into three regions. The north is mostly Muslim with strong Arab, Sunni, and African Sufi influences. Christian and Western influences dominate the other main region, the south. The most violent area of the country is in the most southern part of the north. It is known as the Middle Belt. Bouchat says this is an area of transition. It contains 180 ethnic groups and is subject to multiple cultural and religious influences.

Speculating on the future, Bouchat believes Nigeria could break apart into two or more separate countries, and it may experience renewed civil war. Yet, he argues, breakup is not inevitable. Some important factors bind Nigerians together. Marriage ties unite differing ethnicities and religions. Nigeria has a common education system. National scholars travel the country and share ideas with colleagues across all three regions. There is also some sense of nationalism, and oil and gas income creates

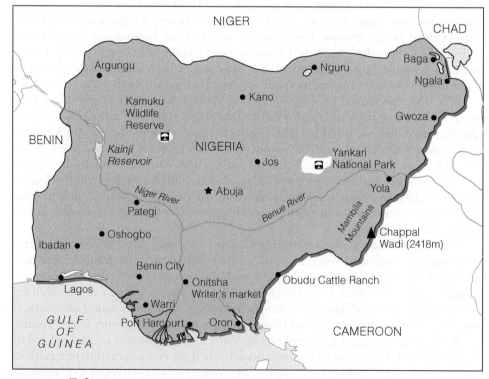

FIGURE 7.6 Nigeria

pressure for unity. If Nigeria develops its economy and moves from poverty, it may solve its social and political problems.

Bouchat may be correct. In March 2015, Nigeria experienced a peaceful transition of government in the midst of a savage terrorist campaign. A Muslim challenger defeated the Christian incumbent in the national presidential election. Although the north voted for the Muslim and the Christian carried the south, they vowed to maintain or transfer power peacefully. They did so, and national unity triumphed over regional and religious difference.

Boko Haram and Ansaru

Boko Haram is one of the most militant Salafi groups in the world, and it is not controlled by any of Nigeria's economic elites. It has kidnapped, raped, burned, bombed, and murdered thousands of people in the past decade (Bouchat, 2013, p. 20). Although it claims to be part of the global jihadist movement and maintains loose connections with other militant groups, its focus is regional. Jacob Zenn (2012), a specialist on Boko Haram conducting research for the Jamestown Foundation, explains that the name Boko Haram originated with local northern Nigerians. The group's actual name translates as "The People Committed to the Propagation of the Prophet's Teaching and Jihad." Locals, though, began referring to it as simply Boko Haram, roughly meaning "Western Education is Forbidden." Members generally subscribe to one or more of three doctrines. They support (1) implementing Islamic law through all of Nigeria, (2) providing rhetorical support for the transnational global jihad, or (3) engaging in criminal activity, especially kidnapping for profit.

Freedom Onoucha (2012), a scholar researching Boko Haram, writes that the ideology behind Boko Haram predates the actual creation of the group by nearly two decades. He traces its birth to 1995 when a number of Nigerian Salafis grew disgruntled with ideas from secular education that seemed to contradict the Quran. It morphed into a formal movement under the leadership of Mohammed Yusuf in 2003. An anti-intellectual who rejected modernity and science, Yusuf urged his young followers to violently reject all things "un-Islamic." They took up his call and embraced his leadership. Followers began to refer to themselves as **Yusufiya**.

Zenn (2012) says Yusufiya violence began to attract attention from security forces in 2003, and it gradually increased over the next six years. The Yusufiya also spawned interest in al Qaeda, primarily through leadership connections with al Qaeda in the Islamic Maghreb (AQIM), a militant group primarily in southern Algeria. Al Qaeda sent money to Yusuf, and he used the funds to send selected followers to AQIM training camps.

According to Zenn's (2012, 2014c) research, Yusuf's role in transforming the group was crucial. His magnetic personality brought young militants under his sway. He converted and wooed potential followers. Although he had contact with AQIM, his focus was on Nigeria. He met and befriended two figures that would join him in leadership, Abubakar Shekau and Mamman Nur. Shekau was charismatic himself and soon became Yusuf's deputy commander. Nur, who had connections with Algerian militants and may have introduced Shekau to Yusuf, emerged as the number three leader. They encouraged militant actions, and violence increased until July 2009, when Nigerian security forces launched an attack on the Yusufiya. They killed 700 militants in a five-day gun battle, including Yusuf. Allegedly, Shekau was wounded and captured.

Zenn (2014a, 2014c) says the actual details of Shekau's detention are sketchy. Either he or someone claiming to be him was released a year after the attack on the Yusufiya. This version of Shekau announced that he had succeeded Yusuf and called

Yusufiya: followers of the Nigerian Mohammed Yusuf. He ordered them to violently reject all ideas not contained in a strict, intolerant interpretation of Islam.

militants to a new organization, popularly dubbed Boko Haram. He expanded the rejuvenated organization's focus, and although actual operations never moved beyond West Africa, he pledged allegiance to a number of jihadist organizations, including AQIM, al Shabab, and ISIS. He also swore personal loyalty to Osama bin Laden and later Ayman al Zawahiri. A BBC News (Chothia, 2015) background report adds that Boko Haram began to kill police officers, political leaders, and critics—including Muslim clerics—soon after Shekau's rise to leadership.

Ambiguity surrounds Abubakar Shekau. Zenn (2013, 2014a) says that no one can be sure who he is. For example, in September 2014, Nigerian and Cameroonian security forces posted a video proving that Shekau had been killed in a firefight. Indeed, the face of the dead man shown in the picture matched the face of an earlier posting by Shekau. The problem, Zenn explains, is that the dead man may be one of many Shekaus. Different Shekaus may have made multiple video recordings. He may have been killed in July 2009 or in subsequent fighting. Security forces may have actually killed him in September 2014. Shekau ideology transformed Boko Haram into a cult-like organization. Its growth and operation will probably continue, Zenn concludes.

Shekau has "died and been resurrected" several times, according to a report from the *Washington Post* (Taylor, 2014). Analysts do not know many details of his life, and they do not know exactly who he is. He voice and cadence seem to change in multiple videos, suggesting that there are many versions of Shekau. His face is always partially covered. Wherever and whomever Shekau is, the person or people playing the role emphasize a common theme that includes violence against Muslims. In an analysis of Boko Haram's leadership and ideology, Jacob Zenn (2014c) concludes that Shekau's endorsement of violence against Muslims divides Baku Haram. In particular, Mamman Nur, his fellow commander and compatriot in the Yusufiya, is opposed to Shekau's style of leadership and murder. Shekau rules Boko Haram with an iron hand, kidnapping young men, forcing them to serve in the ranks, and executing those who try to leave. Repulsive operations such as the kidnapping of 250 schoolgirls in Chibok in 2014 and attacks on villages where hundreds of Muslims are slaughtered cause friction.

Spectacular violence was not always the trademark of Boko Haram. Several sources indicate that the terrorist group's tactics evolved (Onoucha, 2012; Zenn 2014a, 2014b; Chothia, 2015). Boko Haram regrouped from the devastating attacks of July 2009 after the mysterious Shekau emerged in 2010 and claimed the mantle of leadership. Operations began with an attack on a Nigerian prison to free colleagues taken into custody after the July 2009 battle. At first, operations were unsophisticated, and they required little preparation or training. Boko Haram conducted targeted murders and learned as they progressed. From 2010 to 2011, the group mainly killed police officers and political leaders. It stepped up violence in 2012 with bombings of soft targets like markets and churches. From there, the terrorists graduated to mass murders in villages and schools. Killings became indiscriminant, and many Muslims were wounded or murdered. They expanded to political kidnappings in 2013 and then turned to kidnapping for profit. They also began to take and hold territory, declaring a caliphate in 2014. In the same year, Boko Haram increased kidnappings of women and girls for slave labor and sex, and the group also began using males for conscripts.

Zenn (2014c) reports that Mamman Nur and many others were incensed at the killing of fellow Muslims, which sometimes numbered in the hundreds in village massacres. In January 2012, flyers mysteriously appeared in the north announcing the creation of a new group, Ansaru. The flyers stated that Ansaru was a more "humane" form of Boko Haram. It promised to limit attacks and strike only government officials and Christians. Ansaru promised a pan-African approach that would look beyond Nigeria to the rest of the Muslim world. Boko Haram, through Ansaru, moved into neighboring states.

Zenn (2014b) concludes that the international focus of Ansaru and the more regionalized local approach of Boko Haram may keep peace between the groups. Nur will not operate with Shekau, but some of Ansaru's other leaders might. They seem to be willing to let Shekau and Boko Haram lead in Nigeria while Ansaru looks at Chad, Cameroon, and Muslims in other nearby states. The militants may have made a tactical error, however. The mass schoolgirl kidnapping in Chibok in 2014 brought international attention and condemnation. Nigeria's inept military may have been ineffective against Boko Haram, but there are other extremely competent forces in the region. Neighboring countries are concerned with Ansaru's expansion, and the United States and many of its allies support them.

An NBC News (2015b) report discusses what may be a new trend. By April 2015, Boko Haram was losing territory. Combined Cameroonian and Nigerian forces were taking back areas held by the militants, and Boko Haram was retreating. Chad was conducting operations against Ansaru. In May 2015, security forces rescued nearly 700 of the thousands of women kidnapped by Boko Haram terrorists. They told stories of horror. Many had seen their husbands, fathers, and older male children massacred. They suffered as fellow victims died from disease and starvation. They were forced into sex slavery, and many of them were pregnant. They had also been used as slave labor and as human shields against security forces. The world was disgusted with Boko Haram, and so were most of Nigeria's Muslims.

Boko Haram is one of the most violent groups in a violent country. Most Muslims in the north reject their presence, and they have begun to take action. The *New York Times Sunday Edition Magazine* (Okeowo, 2015) reports that Muslim civilians in the north, fed up with inaction from the Nigerian Army, have created several civilian joint task forces. These vigilante groups, sometimes armed with only machetes or sticks, are striking back at Boko Haram. Although the actions of both the vigilantes and security forces can be nearly as ruthless of those of Boko Haram, they demonstrate that the militants are not invincible. Strategically, as Clearance Bouchat (2013, pp. 50–51) speculates, everyone can potentially benefit from Nigeria's oil and gas production. This creates economic pressure to maintain national unity. If income from energy resources is used to develop Nigeria's economy, it could move from poverty into stability. That might well be the death knell for groups like Boko Haram.

Al Shabab's Regional Jihad

On April 2, 2015, a number of Somali militants moved across the campus of Garissa University in northern Kenya at dawn. Although the exact numbers are unknown, Kenyan authorities said they were four young men in the group, and at least two of them had posed as university students. One thing was clear; they were heavily armed. Moving into a dormitory as young people were preparing for the day, they ordered Muslims to evacuate. Then they began killing non-Muslim students. Leaving the dormitory, they moved to a Christian worship service. The killing continued. When security forces eventually arrived to kill the four militants, 147 students were dead. Many more were wounded (BBC, 2015).

The militants came from a terrorist group called Harakat Shabab al Mujahadeen, or simply al Shabab. It began as an insignificant enforcement arm of a sharia court but transformed and grew after an Ethiopian invasion of Somalia. Ideologically, it is part of the international jihadist network, and although it may develop the capacity to actually join it, al Shabab remains a regional group threatening countries in West Africa with low-level terrorism as well as large attacks. Garissa was not its first mass casualty operation. In September 2013, al Shabab struck the fashionable Westgate

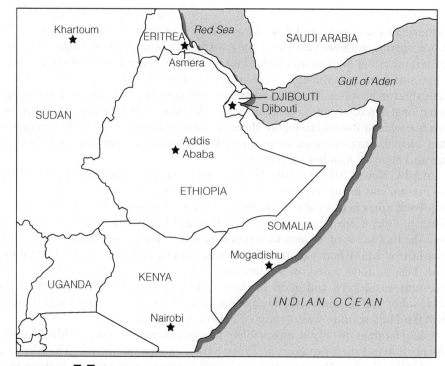

FIGURE 7.7 The Horn of Africa.

Islamic Courts Union (ICU): a confederation of tribes and clans that sought to end violence and bring Islamic law to Somalia. It was opposed by several neighboring countries and internal warlords but brought order to Mogadishu in mid-2006. It retreated after the Ethiopian invasion of Somalia and eventually dissolved.

Transitional Federal Government (TFG): a group established to govern Somalia in 2004 that nominally remained in power until 2012. It was backed by the United Nations, with American support, and the African Union.

Mall in Nairobi, with the terrorists methodically walking through the shopping center killing non-Muslim men, women, and children. It also planted a bomb at a World Cup soccer match in Uganda in 2010, killing 72. Its leaders aspire to global jihad.

Al Shabab is the product of a failed state (See Fig. 7.7.) In 1991, revolutionaries overthrew a long-term military dictator in Somalia but never united to form a government in a country where clans dominate social and political structures. Competing clans created a power vacuum that was eventually filled by a host of local warlords. This gave rise to several humanitarian crises and subsequent international intervention. The United Nations made several unsuccessful attempts to restore order. Somalia degenerated into virtual anarchy, with local warlords controlling sections of the country (Healy and Bradbury, 2010).

According to the Center for Strategic and International Studies (CSIS), various warlords turned Mogadishu into a haven for famine, crime, and human misery (Wise, 2011). Each effort to end the chaos failed. Finally, after more than a dozen attempts, the United Nations created the **Transnational Federal Government (TFG)** in 2004. The TFG was designed to unite rival clans and rid the country of warlords. Formed in Baidoa, a city in southern Somalia, it attempted to forge a union among competing clans. The attempt failed. The TFG could not even move to Mogadishu until 2007, and when it was finally established, the TFG had little influence in the capital and none outside. The TFG eventually gave way to a new Somali government in 2012.

With the capital in turmoil and TFG's failure to bring stability, neighborhoods in Mogadishu started to form their own protective systems. Local authority figures called on neighborhoods to enforce sharia, Islamic law. They introduced Islamic courts and created armed militias to enforce their rulings. People welcomed these steps because they promised to bring an answer to murder and chaos. In 2004 the courts banded together to form the **Islamic Courts Union (ICU).** The courts were strict and punishment was brutal, but they offered an alternative to anarchy from the warlords. As the ICU grew, its militias became stronger, eventually gaining enough power to challenge the warlords. In the summer of 2006, the ICU finally defeated the warlords and drove them from Mogadishu. ICU militias expanded beyond the city, seeking to displace the TFG and bring unity to Somalia. Militias bottled up the TFG in Baidoa and moved into southern Somalia. Unfortunately, as they expanded, they used the rhetoric of jihad, which alarmed non-Muslim West African nations. Christian Ethiopia, concerned because it was the target of much of the rhetoric, invaded Somalia on Christmas Eve 2006. The ICU and its militias melted before the invaders, but one small group stayed to fight. That group was al Shabab.

CSIS reports that al Shabab's leaders vowed to wage a war against the Ethiopians and drive them out (Lyons, 2015). Until this decision, al Shabab was a rather insignificant group numbering no more than 400 men. Having been formed from a defunct Salafi terrorist group, it was particularly fundamentalist. Led by a hard-line sheikh, it eventually came under the command of another hard-liner, Aden Hashi Ayro. In 2007, Ayro launched an attack against the Ethiopians.

Inspired by patriotic resistance, Somalis rallied to al Shabab, and its ranks grew. From 2007 to 2008, it waged a campaign of selective terrorism using improvised explosive devices (IEDs), assassinations, and bombings in southern Somalia. It grew strong enough to support terrorist attacks with periodic hit-and-run guerrilla operations. Public support further increased, and al Shabab grew so large that it evolved into an autonomous movement. As it expanded, its capabilities increased. By 2008, al Shabab could take and hold territory. Increasingly using jihadist rhetoric, it incorporated a tactic that Somalis had never experienced, suicide bombing (Wise, 2011).

Fearing that violence would spread beyond Somalia, many nations in West Africa voiced concern to the **African Union (AU)**. As al Shabab began acting more and more like an international jihadist group, fear increased, and Ethiopia was unable to stop al Shabab's growth. The AU suggested that a multinational African peacekeeping force be deployed in Somalia to usher in stability. The United Nations agreed. The AU created the African Union Mission to Somalia (AMISOM) in January 2007. The bulk of AMISOM troops come from West Africa in the area of Somalia, but it represents most of the nations on the continent. After entering Mogadishu, AMISOM began skirmishing with al Shabab (AMISOM, 2015). Ethiopian forces withdrew from Somalia in January 2009.

AMISOM was more effective than the Ethiopian Army. It was a potent enemy. According to CSIS, al Shabab reached its zenith in 2009, a year after the group's leader Aden Hashi Ayro was killed in an American airstrike (Bryden, 2014). While al Shabab once looked as if it were going to control Somalia, it soon found itself retreating. Several key strongholds started to fall. Another factor in AMISOM's favor was dwindling political support for al Shabab. When al Shabab called for unified resistance to an invasion, it could build a relatively strong guerrilla force to fight Ethiopia. As jihadist rhetoric replaced patriotic calls to duty, al Shabab lost much of its popular appeal. The group's leaders became deeply divided over strategy, tactics, and ideology. With Ayro dead, global jihadists found a new champion, Ahmed Abdi Mohammed Godane. His goal was to place al Shabab in the al Qaeda network. His leadership transformed al Shabab.

According to the BBC, little is known about Godane's early life. He was apparently orphaned and raised by an alcoholic uncle (Chothia, 2014). Keenly intelligent, young Godane escaped from an abusive existence by winning a scholarship to study Islam. He left for school in Sudan and then moved on to Pakistan. He fell under the influence of jihadist thinking and at some point developed a relationship with al Qaeda core. He returned to Somalia as a hardcore jihadist.

Godane had an international focus. According to the, Godane felt the United Nations and AMISOM represented the infidel world, and his first international enemy was right in front of him (Chothia, 2014). Godane's goal was to move al Shabab into the global

African Union (AU): an organization of 54 African states to promote peace, security, and economic development. Combined AU military forces are sometimes deployed in troubled areas of Africa and employed as peace-keepers.

jihad, and AMISOM and UN operations in Somalia provided a gateway. In 2008, he struck his new enemies with a coordinated bombing attack that included an American citizen as a suicide bomber. Godane followed this in 2009 by seeking a formal alliance with al Qaeda core. In 2010, Godane's al Shabab bombed a World Cup soccer game in Uganda to punish that country's participation in AMISOM. Seventy people were killed.

The Kenyan government perceived Godane's international posture and radicalism as a regional threat. Kenya had a large population of Somalis from the diaspora as well as a growing number of refugees from the fighting in Somalia. According to the Jamestown Foundation, al Shabab crossed the porous border between Somalia and Kenya with ease. Kenyan authorities realized that al Shabab could launch operations in Kenya or radicalize local Somalis (McGregor, 2015). CSIS research points out that Kenya has Muslim population of 4.3 million people, many with grievances against the government. Private Saudi donors had also established several religious schools that focused on Salafi doctrine (Bryden, 2014).

Al Shabab had not attacked Kenya for several reasons, according to CSIS (Bryden, 2014). Foreign jihadists traveled to join al Shabab, and Kenya was their pathway, serving as the main arrival point for returning fighters from the Somali diaspora. Kenya was also an important source of medical care for wounded fighters. Additionally, disgruntled Kenyan Muslims were potential recruits for al Shabab. Despite Godane's rhetoric, al Shabab walked lightly in northern Kenya.

The situation changed in 2011. Fearing al Shabab's increasing radicalism, Kenyan troops moved into Somalia for the purpose of creating a buffer zone between al Shabab and Kenya. The Kenyans also believed that many refugees and members of the diaspora would move back to Somalia if a peaceful zone were established. In 2012, the Kenyan government took a further step. It joined AMISOM (McGregor, 2015). Godane wanted revenge.

Godane had a problem, however. The schism he had created between the local Somalis and the internationalists had grown. A great number of al Shabab's leaders wanted no part of an international agenda. Others openly condemned Godane for his leadership style, including American Omar Hammami. Godane, critics claimed, was concentrating power and ignoring locals. They worried because Godane had replaced many Somali commanders with foreigners from al Qaeda core and other international organizations. All of this led to an internal struggle for control of al Shabab, a struggle that soon turned deadly (McGregor, 2015).

Godane responded to his critics with a two-pronged move. First, he began launching small attacks inside Kenya and recruiting Kenyan Somalis. Second, he moved against his rivals. BBC News reports that Godane assumed personal command of his internal security force, dissolved the council that governed al Shabab, and began making command decisions alone (Chothia, 2014). He started ordering the death of his rivals in al Shabab. His second in command and longtime friend was eliminated. Omar Hammami and a number of other leaders were killed. He stepped up assaults against Kenya. In 2013, al Shabab launched the attack on the Westgate Mall. By 2014, his opposition was eliminated, al Shabab operated in Kenya and Somalia, and Godane was completely in charge. Every leader in al Shabab supported Godane, had defected, or was dead. All looked good for Godane until September 1, 2014, when an American missile took his life.

The United States has paid close attention to al Shabab since designating it a foreign terrorist organization in 2008. Fearing its impact on West Africa, the Jamestown Foundation says the United States began a drone campaign against al Shabab, targeting its leadership. Air attacks and commando raids supported drone strikes. Several leaders and key personnel were killed. The United States assisted AMISOM and gained intelligence from al Shabab's defectors. Many of these efforts degraded al Shabab's ability to fight (McGregor, 2015).

One of the main reasons for paying attention to al Shabab has to do with the Somali diaspora in the United States. Over the past few decades, over a million Somalis have been displaced from their homeland, and many of them are in the United States, especially in the Minneapolis area. Many Somali families send money and goods back to their relatives, and stories of the homeland abound in the lives of the second and third generations. Even though many second- and third-generation young people are quite successful in the United States, they feel drawn to the struggle in their ancestral home. Some of them have chosen to join al Shabab, causing law enforcement officials to believe that they will later return to the United States as domestic terrorists (Elliot, 2010).

Stratfor (2015), a private information gathering and analysis company, believes al Shabab has been severely weakened. It has shifted from guerrilla actions to terrorist attacks on soft targets that offer little or no resistance. Spectacular attacks like the Westgate Mall and Garissa University were successful only because there were no security forces in the area, and they represent al Shabab's weakness. Terrorism and murdering civilians are much easier than fighting combat troops.

The future may change, but al Shabab is not the organization it used to be. It has lost most of its territory, including critical ports on the Indian Ocean. Its relatively new enemy, Kenya, now understands that al Shabab is not primarily a foreign problem. It is a domestic problem due to the large Somali diaspora in Kenya, a similarly large number of refugees, and al Shabab's ability to cross the porous border (McGregor, 2015). Leadership and fighting capabilities have been degraded. Global in rhetoric only, al Shabab wages a regional jihad against soft targets.

✓ Self-Check	>	Why does endemic terror thrive in Africa?
	>	How does Boko Haram operate in Nigeria?
	>	What circumstances gave birth to al Shabab, and what factors have weakened it?

Emphasizing the Points

Modern nationalistic terrorism arose after World War II in many European colonies, but it is manifested in a number of ways. Aspiring nationalists used terrorist tactics in former colonies such as Cyprus and Algeria. The Mau Mau rebellion was focused on semireligious tribalism. PKK terrorist in Turkey combined nationalism with ideology. China's Uighars seek regional autonomy based on ethnicity, and India's Sikh's fought for religious separation. Endemic terrorism is a problem in Africa and the Middle East. In sub-Saharan Africa, it has provided impetus for regional jihadists.

SUMMARY OF CHAPTER OBJECTIVES

- The EOKA followed an urban strategy using a small number of terrorists to bring international support for Cypriot independence.
- Unlike the situation in Cyprus, most French people believed northern Algeria to be a part of France, and they saw the separatist movement as an internal rebellion instead of a revolt against a colonial power. As a result, both the FLN and French security forces employed terrorism against each other.
- The Mau Mau uprising was a rural resistance movement by a tribe displaced by colonial agricultural policies.

- Turkey has experienced several forms of terrorism based on religion, ideology, and an ethnic separatist movement. The PKK is Turkey's largest ethnonationalist terrorist threat.
- Ethnic tensions are prominent in China's Xinjiang province because the native Uighar population wants autonomy. The Uighars are ethnic Turkmen.
- China has introduced many ethnic Chinese to the Xinjiang province in an attempt to exert political control. Uighars operating from Central Asia have resisted this policy. After 9/11, China eagerly endorsed the United States' "war on terrorism," claiming that the Uighar nationalists were part of an international jihadist movement.
- Some Sikhs embraced terrorism after a deadly clash with Indian forces. The most damaging attack was on an Indian airliner. They planned an international terror campaign, but it fizzled by the mid-1990s.
- *Endemic terrorism* is a term used by J. Bowyer Bell to describe violence in sub-Saharan Africa. It results from European imperialism and the creation of artificial national boundaries that link unrelated tribal and ethnic groups.
- Nigeria is fractured because it is a conglomerated state created by British imperialists. Oil provides the economic incentive for a diverse population to remain united.
- Boko Haram represents a jihadist movement that began in the northern Muslim region of Nigeria. It seeks a united Muslim caliphate.
- Al Shabab is a jihadist group that arose from the Islamic Courts Union. It has global aspirations but can operate only regionally.

LOOKING INTO THE FUTURE

Nationalism will probably be a factor in several terrorist movements throughout most of the world, including Europe. The postcolonial areas of the globe will remain volatile because many nations have been cobbled together without regard for language, ethnicity, cultures, and religion. The paradox is that such nations are frequently held together by force by a tribal group or particular class of citizens. Groups not holding power will continue to use terrorism as a means of revolution. Nationalistic and endemic terrorism will resist globalism. As populations move from one area of the world to another, they will bring strong loyalties in various conflicts to their adopted homes. They will continue to support some campaigns with sympathy and money, and some people will be motivated to express their views with terrorism in their old homeland, their new one, or some place in between. Nationalistic and endemic terrorism will develop a long reach.

KEY TERMS

David Galula, p 151
blind terrorism, p. 152
pangas, p. 153
Habib Akdas, p. 156
Abdullah Ocalan, p. 158

Uighar nationalists, p. 160
Golden Temple, p. 162
Salafism, p. 163
Yusufiya, p. 165

Islamic Courts Union (ICU), p. 168
Transitional Federal Government (TFG), p. 168

African Union (AU), p. 169

CHAPTER 8

Background to the Middle East

Sir Mark Sykes, British Diplomat

A political revolution began in Tunisia in 2011, and it spread from North Africa through all the Middle East. As repressive governments toppled, many Western political leaders believed that a new surge of democracy would sweep through the area. Experts in Middle Eastern affairs were not quite as confident, and they proved to be correct. At first, regimes fell and people took to the streets demanding free elections. Yet, free elections frequently gave rise to chaos, military rule, and violence. Egypt elected a new government then returned to pseudo-military rule, and many other countries experienced violent internal civil strife. The so-called Arab Spring turned into a bleak Arab Winter.

As demands for democratic reform surfaced in Syria in March 2011, Syrian authorities arrested several young teenage boys for painting pro-democracy graffiti on a wall in Damascus. The boys were tortured while in custody, and one 13-year-old child was murdered. Government authorities sent the boy's mutilated corpse back to his family. People were enraged. Demonstrators flooded the streets, and the Syrian Army responded in its usual fashion by firing into the crowd.

LEARNING OBJECTIVES

After reading this chapter, you should be able to:

▶ Define the Middle East as a historical, geographical, and cultural metaphor.

▶ Briefly sketch the origins of Islam.

▶ Describe the difference between Shi'ites and Sunnis.

▶ Discuss the historical significance of the decline of the Ottoman Empire and the birth of Zionism.

▶ Summarize the impact of World War I on the Middle East.

▶ Describe the formation of Israel and the Arab–Israeli wars.

▶ Explain the emergence of terrorism after the 1967 Six-Day War.

▶ Briefly sketch the history of modern Iran.

The crowds, however, were not deterred. By July, more than 150,000 protestors massed in Damascus. When the government responded with more force, many protestors took up arms. Fighting spread beyond Damascus, and Syria was soon in the middle of a savage multifaceted civil war (Polk, 2013). Over 200,000 people were killed in the first four years of violence.

The Syrian civil war is not a simple conflict pitting one side against another. It involves multiple interest groups representing differing religious sects, ideologies, and tribes. Jihadists fight jihadists, and they also combat other multiple enemies. Violence has spilled into neighboring countries. It has produced strange quasi alliances, with Iran fighting the same enemy as a coalition of American-led Western and Arab nations in one area and opposing them in another. It caused Egyptians to bomb Libya, Saudi military strikes in Yemen, and it threatens to launch a major Sunni–Shi'ite military confrontation pitting Iran and southern Iraq against the Gulf states. The confused nature of the Syrian civil war and many other conflicts are partially the result Europeans who drew new national boundary lines at the end of World War I that separated tribes, religious sects, and families while binding traditional enemies together in artificial national constructs. The new map made the Middle East a tinderbox after 1918. The kindling has produced roaring flames.

Defining the Middle East

Bernard Lewis (1995, pp. 64–67) implies that the Middle East is not a geographical region; rather, it is a concept. It is based on a Western orientation to the world. Historically, the term *Middle East* was used in the West to describe a section of the world that encompasses part of North Africa and southwest Asia directly south of Turkey, including the Arabian Peninsula, Iran, and Afghanistan. Geographically, *Middle East* is a term of convenience with a European bias. If Europe and America are the West, and China and Japan are the Far East, then there is an east "near" Europe, one "far" away, and one in the "middle." Albert Hourani (1997), in a comprehensive history, says the area is dominated by two major concerns: the religion of Islam and the history of the Arab people. Yet, many people who live in the Middle East are not Arabs. Culturally, the Middle East is an area dominated by a religion, Islam, but John Esposito (1999, pp. 214–222) demonstrates that there are many differing cultures within Islam as well as myriad interpretations of the religion.

Bernard Lewis (1995, p. 65) also says that the term *Middle East* is used out of convenience. In a broader sense, people are really speaking about the sociogeographical relationship between Islam and Christianity. Yet, distinctive social meanings attach to the term *Middle East*. It is a region that witnessed the birth of three great monotheistic religions: Judaism, Christianity, and Islam. The Middle East is an area dominated by Islam, but most Muslims live outside the region. The social mores of the Middle East—family and tribal loyalty, male dominance, honor, and resentment of Western imperialism—extend across northern Africa and into Central Asia. The traditional Middle East includes Arabs, but many other people live there.

The Middle East is a historical, social, and geographical concept. It seems to be dominated by questions about Palestine and Israel, but Lewis (2004, pp. 196–204) demonstrates that many other problems beset the region. Lewis (1995, pp. 45–55) also points out that it is the historical tinderbox that ignited several centuries of conflict between Muslims and Christians. The area is the home of Islamic conquests and

Arab empires. It also witnessed the Crusades and Western and Mongol invasions, which were followed by Turkish and then European domination. It gave birth to modern nations in the twentieth century, including Lebanon, Syria, Jordan, Yemen, the independent **Gulf States**, Iraq, Saudi Arabia, Iran, and Israel. It is the home of multiple ethnic groups, and violence in the region has influenced international terrorism. Three issues help illustrate the importance of the region: (1) the birth and spread of Islam, (2) historical confrontations between Christianity and Islam, and (3) the expansion of conflict beyond the traditional geographical realm of the Middle East.

> **Gulf States:** Small Arab kingdoms bordering the Persian Gulf. They include Bahrain, Qatar, the United Arab Emirates, and Oman.

> ✓ **Self-Check**
>
> > Why is the Middle East a geographical concept?
> > What do most people mean when they use the term *Middle East*?
> > How do culture and values shape the Middle East?

A Brief Introduction to Islam

Many aspects of Middle Eastern—and, by extension, international—terrorism are embodied in rhetorical religious sloganeering. If terrorism is to be understood in this context, it is necessary to become familiar with the basic aspects of Islam. For those readers of this book who are unfamiliar with the basics of Islam, this section is necessary; others may wish to skip it. It is not possible to capture the theological richness of any major religion in a short section in a college text, and the following description is a simple overview to provide background information essential to understanding terrorists who misuse religious imagery.

The description here is taken primarily from Western scholars and Islamic sources in English. It is based on the work of Karen Armstrong (2000a, 2000b), Abdullah Saeed and Hassan Saeed (2004), Thomas W. Lippman (1995), Caesar Farah (2000), John Esposito (1999, 2002), Haneef Oliver (2002), Bernard Lewis (1966, 1995, 2004), Heinz Halm (1999), Malise Ruthven (2000), Moojan Momen (1985), Robin Wright (2000), Edward Said and C. Hitchens (1990), Charles Kurzman (2004), Rudolph Peters (1996), and Rueven Firestone (1999).

The Centrality of Mohammed's Revelation

Mohammed was born about 570 by the Western calendar in the Arabian city of Mecca. He was orphaned at an early age and taken in by his uncle, Abu Talib. He was extremely spiritual, by most accounts, and he was exposed to three great monotheistic religions, Judaism, Christianity, and Zoroastrianism. As he grew older, Mohammed became a trader under the tutelage and protection of his uncle. He also became close to his cousin **Ali ibn Talib**, who looked upon Mohammed as an older brother. While on a caravan, he met an older widow, Khadijah. They were married and had a daughter, Fatima. Khadijah was impressed with Mohammed's character and by his spiritual nature. She encouraged him to continue a religious quest, but Mohammed was confused. He had been exposed to several religions, but he did not know which aspect of spirituality was correct. That changed when he was meditating at the age of 40.

Mohammed had a vision of the angel Gabriel (Jabril), who told him that God had chosen Mohammed to be a prophet to the Arabs. (*Allah* is Arabic for "the God." Muslims believe that Jews, Christians, and Zoroastrians worship the same deity.) Mohammed was overwhelmed by the voice of Gabriel, and he begged for silence. Gabriel did not

> **Ali ibn Talib:** (circa 599–661) Also known as Ali ibn Abi Talib, the son of Mohammed's uncle Abu Talib and married to Mohammed's oldest daughter Fatima. Ali was Mohammed's male heir because he had no surviving sons. The followers of Ali are known as Shi'ites. Most Shi'ites believe that Mohammed gave a sermon while perched on a saddle, naming Ali the heir to Islam. Differing types of Shi'ites accept authority from diverse lines of Ali's heirs. Sunni Muslims believe Ali is the fourth and last Rightly Guided caliph. Both Sunnis and Shi'ites believe Ali tried to return Islam to the purity of Mohammed's leadership in Medina.

Abu Bakr: (circa 573–634) Also known as Saddiq, the first caliph selected by the Islamic community (*umma*) after Mohammed's death in 632. Sunnis believe Abu Bakr is the rightful heir to Mohammed's leadership, and they regard him as the first of the *Rishidun*, or Rightly Guided caliphs. He led military expeditions that expanded Muslim influence to the north of Mecca.

Umar: (circa 580–644) Also known as Umar ibn al Khattab, the second Rightly Guided caliph, according to Sunnis. Under his leadership, the Arab empire expanded into Persia, the southern part of the Byzantine Empire, and Egypt. His army conquered Jerusalem in 637.

Uthman: (circa 580–656) Also known as Uthman ibn Affan, the third Rightly Guided caliph, according to Sunnis. He conquered most of the remaining parts of North Africa, Iran, Cyprus, and the Caucasia region. He was assassinated by his own soldiers for alleged nepotism.

Badr: The site of a battle between the Muslims of Medina and the merchants of Mecca in 624. Mohammed was unsure whether he should resist the attacking Meccans but decided God would allow Muslims to defend their community. After victory, Mohammed said that Badr was the Lesser Jihad. Greater Jihad, he said, was seeking internal spiritual purity.

comply. He told Mohammed that Moses had been sent to tell the Jews of the one true God, and Jesus had been sent to the world with the same message. Mohammed, the angelic voice said, had been chosen as the final prophet to complete the message. The first vision stopped after 40 days, and Mohammed came to accept that he had been chosen. Visions would continue periodically until 632, the year of his death.

Mohammed's role as a prophet, as *the* Prophet, is crucial in Islam. He stands in a long line of Jewish prophets—the visionaries later adopted by Christians—and Jesus of Nazareth. Muslims believe that Mohammed was given the direct revelation of God through Gabriel. In Muslim theology, God is vast, all encompassing, and without form. The pronoun *he* is used, but God is gender neutral. The little that can be known about God comes through revelations from the four major prophets—Abraham, Moses, Jesus, and Mohammed—and the law that God has given them. The Hebrew and Christian Bibles contain those revelations, but—according to Islamic theology—humans corrupted the message when writing the stories. One of the greatest mistakes, according to Muslims, was the deification of Jesus. All the prophets are human, and they will be judged by God according to their deeds with an overwhelming, loving mercy that comes from God's benevolence. God has given divine law through the prophets. Mohammed was chosen to correct the errors of the past.

Creating the Muslim Community at Medina

Mohammed won early converts in Mecca, including his cousin Ali, his wife Khadijah, and three influential friends: **Abu Bakr, Umar,** and **Uthman.** Many of the wealthy merchants of Mecca were not impressed. Messages of God's love were acceptable, but Mohammed's emphasis on social egalitarianism called on them to share their wealth. They resented that and asked Abu Talib to remove familial protection from the young Prophet, a request Abu Talib refused. After Abu Talib's death, Mohammed's life was in jeopardy. At the same time, representatives from warring Jewish and polytheistic tribes in Yathrib, later Medina, asked Mohammed to serve as their leader and make peace. Mohammed agreed, provided that they would acknowledge the one God and the legitimacy of Mohammed's calling. They agreed, with the Jews reserving the right to judge Mohammed's calling as a prophet. Legend says that he left for Medina in 622 with 72 families. Most Western historians believe that the families left in waves and that Mohammed escaped to Medina even as Meccans were plotting his death.

Muslims believe Mohammed created the perfect Islamic community at Medina, combining a just government with religion. Mohammed stressed the importance of community over tribal relations and the governance of God's law in every aspect of life. Because there were not enough resources to live in Mecca, Mohammed's followers chose a traditional Bedouin path for survival: raiding passing caravans. In 624, this led to a confrontation with an army from Medina at Badr. It was a small battle, but it was politically important. As a result of their victory at **Badr,** Muslims increasingly came to believe that God was on their side and that their cause would be championed in heaven. Mohammed eventually conquered Mecca, and the new religion spread along trade routes. Suddenly, in 632, Mohammed died, leaving the community of believers to chart the path for the new religion.

The Shi'ite–Sunni Split

The Muslims who followed Mohammed agreed on many aspects of the new faith. God's revelation to Mohammed was critical. The poetic utterances of Gabriel were eventually codified in a single book, the Quran. The things Mohammed had said and done were recorded, and his actions became the basis for interpreting the Quran. All

Muslims came to believe that it was necessary to confess the existence of one God and to acknowledge Mohammed as God's Prophet. They were also expected to pray as a community, to give to the poor, to fast during holy times, and to make a pilgrimage to Mecca if they were able to do so. Problems arose, however, over the question of leadership. According to Arabic tradition, Mohammed's male heir should lead the community, but Mohammed claimed to have revealed a new law that said the importance of the community would take precedence over tribal rules of inheritance. Questions over leadership spawned a debate and eventually a civil war. These questions still affect the practice of Islam today.

The question of leadership focused on the community. One group of people believed the community should select its own leaders, but another group believed that Mohammed had designated Ali, his cousin and son-in-law, as the Muslim leader. The proponents of community selection carried the day, but Ali's followers came to believe that God had given a special inspiration to Mohammed's family. The community selected a political and religious leader, a caliph, but Ali's followers encouraged him to exercise the authority they believed God had bestowed. When Ali's sons, Hasan and Hussein, were born, his followers believed that they also carried special gifts based on their relationship with their grandfather Mohammed.

The Muslim community eventually split over this question. Mohammed's friend Abu Bakr became the first caliph in 632 (see Table 8.1). After Bakr's death in 634, Umar became caliph. The Arabs expanded under his leadership, handing defeats to the Romans, Byzantines, and the Persians. Umar was assassinated in 644 by a Persian captive, and another of Mohammed's friends, Uthman, was selected as caliph. The Arabs continued to expand, and they soon held a vast empire. All was not well, however. As Uthman consolidated wealth, groups of Arab soldiers came to feel that he favored his own family over the community. They broke into his house in 656 and assassinated him. The followers of Ali came forward and proposed that he become caliph. Ali believed that Uthman's family in particular, and Muslims in general, were forgetting the straight path that had been revealed to Mohammed. He led an army against Uthman's family but sought a negotiated peace between the factions. His hopes were in vain, and he was assassinated. The family of Uthman assumed control of the Islamic movement and ruled the first Arab empire.

Sunnis believe that four Rightly Guided Caliphs (Rushadin) served as the true successors to Mohammed. Shi'ites recognize only Ali.

The followers of Ali were not satisfied. They felt that the **Umayyads**, Uthman's family, had abandoned the principles of Islam in favor of worldly goods. This split came to dominate the Muslim community. The Umayyads believed that they represented Islam, even as they fought other Muslims to maintain control of the new Arab empire. Some of the followers of Ali invited **Hussein (Hussein ibn Ali)**, Ali's oldest living son, to meet with them in present-day Iraq. They wanted him to lead a purified

Umayyads: The first Arab and Muslim dynasty. It ruled from Damascus from 661 to 750. The Umayyads were Uthman's family.

Hussein (Hussein ibn Ali): (626–680) Also known as Hussein ibn Ali, Mohammed's grandson and Ali's second son. He was martyred at Karbala in 680. The majority of Shi'ites believe that Hussein is the Third Imam, after Imam Ali and Imam Hasan, Ali's oldest son.

TABLE **8.1**
The Four Rightly Guided Caliphs

Caliph	Period of Caliphate
Abu Bakr	632–634
Umar	634–644
Uthman	644–656
Ali	656–661

Islamic movement, returning to the simple principles of his grandfather, Mohammed. The Umayyad governor was alarmed and sent an army to intercept Hussein. He was killed with a small band of followers at Karbala in 680. His martyrdom cemented the schism between the Umayyad dynasty and the followers of Ali, and Karbala became one of the most important events in Shi'ite history. Its importance is similar to the meaning of the Day of Atonement for Jews and the Easter story for Christians.

Mainstream Muslims following the caliph were conventionally called Sunnis, and the followers of Ali became known as Shi'ites. In actuality, though, several differing types of Shi'ism developed in the formative years of Islam. Zaidi Shi'ites recognize a line of succession differing from Hussein's. Many Zaidi Shi'ites live in Yemen today. Ismalis believe that there were seven Imams who followed Mohammed. They sponsored a cult known as the Assassins in the Middle Ages, but they live quite peacefully on the Indian subcontinent today (see Lewis, 2003a). Today, Ithna Ashari, or Twelver, Shi'ites comprise the majority of Shi'ite Muslims, dominating Iran, southern Iraq, and southern Lebanon.

Initially, there were few theological differences between Sunnis, who comprise an estimated 85 to 90 percent of all Muslims today, and Shi'ites. The main difference focused on the line of succession from Mohammed. Over the years, however, differences did emerge. Ithna Ashari Shi'ites believe that the Twelfth Imam went into hiding in 934. Some of them believe that he divinely transcended life with a promise to return. Another group of Shi'ites believes that he died but was resurrected, and a final group believes that God hid the Twelfth Imam but left part of the imam's spirit on earth. Sunnis claim that all three beliefs are more reminiscent of Christianity than Islam. The split between Sunnis and Shi'ites remains today.

The Golden Age of Arabs

Abbasids: The Caliphate of the second Muslim dynasty. The Abbasids overthrew the Umayyads in 750 and they reigned until invading Mongols defeated them in 1258.

Mohammed's followers spread Islam and Arabic culture through the Middle East in the years after his death. Two dynasties, the Umayyads (661–750) and the **Abbasids** (750–1258), ruled the area in the years following Mohammed. Hourani (1997, pp. 25–37) points out that these caliphs theologically divided the world into the Realm of Islam and the Realm of War. The purpose of Islam was to subject the world to God's will. Indeed, *Islam* means "submission to the will of God," and a *Muslim* is "one who submits."

About 1000, the Turks began to take the domains of the Abbasids. Struggles continued for the next hundred years, until a Mongol advance from East Asia brought the Abbasid dynasty to an end. The Mongols were eventually stopped by an Egyptian Army of slaves, giving rise to a new group of Turks known as the Ottomans. The Ottomans were aggressive, conquering most of the Middle East and large parts of Europe. The Ottomans fought the Iranians on one border and central Europeans on the other border for many years.

European relations with Islamic empires were not characterized by harmony. The West began its first violent encounters by launching the Crusades, which were attempts to conquer the Middle East that lasted from 1095 to about 1250. These affairs were bloody and initiated centuries of hatred and distrust between Muslims and Christians. European struggles with the Ottoman Empire reinforced years of military tension between the two civilizations. Modern tensions in the area can be traced to the decline of Ottoman influence and the collapse of Iranian power in the eighteenth century. When these Islamic powers receded, Western Christian powers were quick to fill the void.

Twelver Shi'ites and the Imamate

Ithna Ashari Shi'ites believe that 12 divinely inspired imams followed Mohammed. Although theological divisions with Sunnis would eventually arise, and the Shi'ites themselves would split into competing sects, the first division within Islam was political. It focused on leadership of the Islamic community.

Ali's followers, known as the Partisans of Ali, believed that he should lead the community. They refused to recognize Abu Bakr, Umar, and Uthman. The Twelvers came to believe that 12 divinely inspired men were sent by God to lead the community. These men were:

> Predicted by the Quran

> God's representatives on Earth

> Infallible

> Existing without sin (like Mohammed and Fatima)

> Inspired by the spirit of God

> Able to recognize their successors

> The best of all men

> Divinely charged to lead with special knowledge of God

The first imams openly opposed the emerging Sunni consensus and met violent deaths. The Sixth Imam ordered that Shi'ites should appear as Sunnis in public, maintaining their religious practices and beliefs only among their fellow believers. This increased Sunni fears that the Shi'ites were subversive.

Martyrdom and voluntary sacrifice became the trademark of the Twelve Imams, and this deeply influenced Shi'ite tradition. A review of the imams and the Shi'ite traditions surrounding their martyrdom reveals the importance of sacrifice.

Imam	Shi'ite Tradition of Death
1. Ali (d. 661)	Assassinated
2. Hasan (d. 669)	Poisoned
3. Hussein (d. 680)	Martyred at Karbala

Karbala is commemorated during the month of Ashura. A traditional Twelver verse says: "Every day is Ashura, every place is Karbala."

4. Ali zain al Abid (d. 714)	Poisoned
5. Mohammed al Baqir (d. 731)	Poisoned or martyred in battle
6. Jafar al Sadiq (d. 765)	Poisoned
7. Musa al Kazim (d. 799)	Imprisoned and poisoned
8. Ali al Rida (d. 818)	Poisoned
9. Mohammed al Jawad (d. 835)	Poisoned
10. Ali al Hadi (d. 868)	Traditions disagree
11. Hasan al Askari (d. 874)	Poisoned
12. Mohammed al Muntazar	Taken into divine hiding and will be revealed as the Mahdi before the Day of Judgment

The Mahdi will restore peace and justice after a final battle with evil. This will herald the return of Jesus, the Imam Hussein, the remaining imams, and all the prophets and saints.

Sources: Momen (1985, pp. 23–45); Ruthven (2000, pp. 174–191, 434)

Bernard Lewis (1995) points to the Age of Discovery as the origin of modern confrontations between the West and Islam. Americans might think of 1492 as the beginning of European discovery, starting with Christopher Columbus, but Lewis points out that this is also the year that the final Islamic stronghold in Spain was destroyed. In addition, although Ottoman Turks conquered Constantinople in 1453 and renamed it Istanbul, 1492 represented a reversal of fortune for expanding Islamic armies. Western Christian military forces gradually gained the upper hand in world affairs through their superior navies and military technology. When the Turks were driven back from the gates of Vienna, nearly 200 years later, it symbolized the ascendancy and domination of the West.

✓ Self-Check

> How is Mohammed's revelation central to both Islam and the Golden Age of Arabs?
> What is the difference between Sunnis and Shi'ites?
> Who were the Abbasids and Umayyads?

Synopsis of Traditional Middle Eastern Issues

To understand terrorism in the Middle East, it is necessary to appreciate certain aspects of the region's recent history. To best understand the Middle East, keep the following in mind:

- The current structure of Middle Eastern geography and political rule is a direct result of nineteenth-century European imperial influence in the region and the outcomes of World War I.
- Many of the Arab countries in the Middle East place more emphasis on the power of the family than on contemporary notions of government. However, Israel rules itself as a parliamentary democracy.
- Most Western government officials and scholars do not believe the modern state of Israel is the biblical Kingdom of David mentioned in the Hebrew and Christian Bibles or the Islamic Quran. They tend to see it as a secular power dominated by people of European descent. Many religious Israelis and their Jewish and Christian supporters disagree with this assessment.
- Arabs in general, and Palestinians in particular, do not hold a monopoly on terrorism.
- Religious differences in the region have developed over centuries, and fanaticism in any religion can spawn violence. Fanatical Jews, Christians, and Muslims in the Middle East practice terrorism in the name of religion.
- Although the Middle East has been volatile since 1948—the year in which Israel was recognized as a nation-state—modern terrorism grew after 1967. It increased after 1973 and became a standard method of military operations in the following two decades.
- In 1993, the Palestine Liberation Organization (PLO) renounced terrorism; however, instead of decreasing tension, the move has created tremendous tension. On the Arab side, some groups have denounced the PLO's actions, whereas others have embraced it. The same reaction has occurred in Israel, where one set of political parties endorses peace plans and another prepares for war. Middle Eastern peace is a very fragile process, and terrorism is a wild card. It can upset delicate negotiations at any time, even after a peace treaty has been signed and implemented (for an example, see Hoffman, 1995).

- All of these issues are complicated by shortages of water and vast differences in social structure. The area contains some of the world's richest and some of the world's poorest people. Most of them are far from water sources.

One can best begin to understand the Middle East by focusing on the world of the late 1800s. During that time period, three critical events took place that helped to shape the modern Middle East.

First, the **Ottoman Empire**, the Turk-based government that ruled much of the Middle East, was falling apart in the nineteenth century. The Ottoman Turks encountered domestic challenges across their empire as various nationalistic, tribal, and familial groups revolted. In addition, they faced foreign threats. The Persian Empire had collapsed earlier, but Great Britain, France, Germany, and Russia intervened in the area with military force. Each European country was willing to promise potential rebels some type of autonomy if they revolted against the Turks. Turkey was reluctantly drawn into World War I, and the victorious Allies partitioned the empire after victory in 1918. A group of military officers took control of Turkey, banned religious government, and in 1924, brought an end to the caliphate (Fromkin, 2001, pp. 406–426).

The second critical event involved a political movement called Zionism. From 1896 to 1906, European Jews, separated from their ancient homeland for nearly 2,000 years, wanted to create their own nation. Some of them favored Palestine, whereas others wanted to move to South America or Africa. In 1906, those who backed Palestine won the argument, and European Jews increasingly moved to the area (Armstrong, 2000a, pp. 146–151). The sultan of the Ottoman Turks allowed them to settle but refused to grant them permission to form their own government. Palestinian Arabs, the people who lived in Palestine, were wary of the Jewish settlers, and tensions rose (Nasr, 1997, pp. 5–8).

Finally, as they fought World War I between 1914 and 1918, European armies occupied the Middle East. European governments continued to make contradictory promises about Arab autonomy as they sought to establish spheres of influence in the region. When the war ended, the victorious nations felt that they had won the area from the Turks. They divided the Middle East, not with any regard for the area's political realities, but to share the spoils of victory. This created long-term political problems. Historian David Fromkin calls this "the peace to end all peace," satirizing the Western depiction of World War I as the "war to end all wars" (Fromkin, 2002, pp. 15–20).

Ottoman Empire: A Turkish empire that lasted for 600 years, until 1924. The empire spanned southeastern Europe, North Africa, and southwest Asia. It reached its zenith in the fourteenth and fifteenth centuries.

Three Sources of Violence in the Middle East

The situation at the end of World War I set the stage for developments over the next century, and it is the basis for terrorism in the traditional Middle East, defined by most Westerners as Israel, Lebanon, Jordan, Egypt, Syria, Iraq, and the Arabian Peninsula. As events unfolded, three factors became prominent in Middle Eastern violence: (1) questions about the political control of Israel and Palestine, (2) questions of who would rule the Arab world, and (3) questions concerning relations between the two main branches of Islam—Sunnis and Shi'ites. Stated another way, these problems are the following:

1. The Palestinian question (control of Palestine)
2. Intra-Arab rivalries and struggles
3. The future of revolutionary Islam

These problems are all separate, but they are also all interrelated. The sources of terrorism in the Middle East are symbiotic. That is, they are independent arenas of

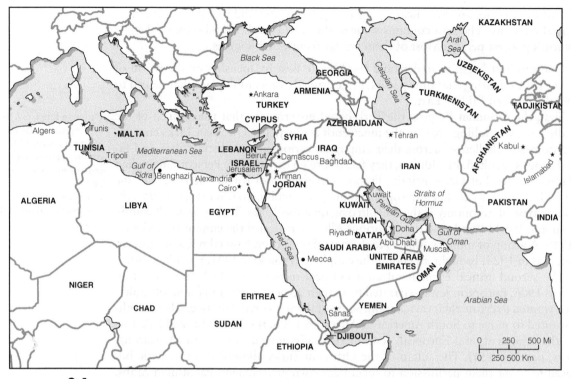

FIGURE **8.1** The Middle East

violence with a dynamic force of their own, but they are also related to and dependent on each other (Figure 8.1).

All forms of Middle Eastern terrorism share certain traits. First, many Arab groups express dissatisfaction over the existence of Israel. They are not necessarily pro-Palestinian, but they find the notion of a European-created, non-Arab state in their lands offensive. Most Middle Eastern terrorist groups are anti-imperialist. The intensity of their passion varies according to the type of group, but terrorism has largely been dominated by anti-Western feelings. Another related factor is the pan-Arabic or pan-Islamic orientation of terrorist groups. Although they fight for local control, most wish to revive a united Arab Islamic realm. Finally, Middle Eastern terrorism is united by kinship bonds. In terrorist groups, as in Middle Eastern politics in general, familial links are often more important than national identification.

When the Israelis practice terrorism, they usually claim their activities are conventional military actions. At times, however, the Israelis have used the same tactics the PLO used in the 1960s and 1970s. It is perhaps more accurate to argue that all Middle Eastern violence, Arabic and non-Arabic, is locked in symbiosis—its various sides are interdependent (see Nasr, 1997; Said and Hitchens, 1990). It can best be understood by looking at political affairs in the Middle East during the build-up to World War I.

The Early Zionist Movement in Palestine

The Zionist movement took place at the same time the Ottoman Empire was breaking up, which created opportunities for several groups that were interested in the region. For Arabs in general, it signaled the possible recreation of the Arab empire as it was shortly after the death of Mohammed. Palestinian Arabs, much more modest in their political views, sought to join with Syria to form a new country. Many Palestinians welcomed the Zionists, thinking that Jews would assist them in the formation of this new country. The Zionists held no such belief: The Jews had no intention of becoming part of Syria. Nasr (1997, pp. 6–7) argues that the Palestinian Arabs represented a cohesive mixture of Muslims and Christians and that they were leery of Jewish settlements. Regardless, Palestinians sold land to the Zionists, who linked their holdings with the ultimate purpose of creating a Jewish state.

Nasr (1997, pp. 9–16) points out that sporadic violence accompanied these new settlements. Tensions became apparent in confrontations between the ethnic groups and conflicts between individuals. Violence was seldom organized, and it did not reflect the forms of terrorism that would engulf the region within two decades. That situation changed during World War I.

In the years preceding the war, Zionism caused confusion in Palestine. Even though most of the Jewish immigrants were European, the Arabs thought of them as Semitic people, and both groups identified with Palestine. Furthermore, the Zionists originally stated they had no desire to displace the Palestinians; they wanted to coexist with them. As Jewish settlers bought land, however, they purchased large parcels next to each other. They established governing councils for their farmland and refused to sell land back to Arabs. They were acting in defiance of the sultan's refusal to allow Jewish self-government (see Hourani, 1997, pp. 323–324).

World War I and Contradictory Promises

Jewish immigration into Palestine played into the political issues of World War I. Because the Turks were allied with the Germans, the British encouraged the Arabs to revolt against the Turks. If the Arabs would fight for the British, the British promised to move the caliphate from Istanbul to Mecca and to name an Arab as caliph. The military commander in Cairo, who promised to restore the caliphate, thought he was promising the Islamic equivalent of a pope and that individual secular Arab states would continue to exist. He did not understand the nature of the caliphate. On October 24, 1915, the British made an unclear promise to the Arabs. In return for a general Arab revolt against the Turks, the British agreed to support the creation of a united, independent Arab state at the close of the war. The British believed this to be sound foreign policy. They believed that the nebulous understanding was not a promise of support to the Arabs. However, the Arabs felt that they had received a promise for the ancient Arab realm of Islam. Although the British had gained an ally at little expense, the circumstances were ripe for resentments (Fromkin, 2001, p. 179).

The British made other promises. Partly in response to the Zionist movement and partly to maintain the goodwill of American Jews, the British promised the Zionists a Jewish homeland in Palestine. The **Balfour Declaration** of November 1917 promised to create the state of Israel. It was backed by Protestant Christians who understood neither the nature of the caliphate nor the importance of Jerusalem, or al Quds to Muslims, in Islam. Supporters of the Balfour Declaration were unaware that their promise directly contradicted the British commander's promise in Cairo, the promise to reestablish an Arab-dominated caliphate. All Arab Muslims would expect the caliphate to include the three most important cities in Sunni Islam: Mecca, Medina, and Jerusalem. The Balfour Declaration threatened to transfer Jerusalem to the new state of Israel (Fromkin, 2001, pp. 274–300).

Balfour Declaration: A policy statement by the British government in November 1917 that promised a homeland for Jews in the geographical area of biblical Israel. Sir Arthur Balfour was the British foreign secretary.

Mark Sykes: (1879–1919) A British diplomat who signed a secret agreement with Francois Georges-Picot in May 1916. The Sykes–Picot Agreement divided the Middle East into spheres of French, British, and Russian influence.

The British also made promises to their allies. Sir **Mark Sykes**, a British foreign service officer, negotiated a treaty with the French to extend spheres of British and French influence in the states of the old Ottoman Empire. On the other side of the region, in ancient Persia (modern Iran), the British approached the Russians with another deal. Iran would be divided into three parts—a northern area controlled by Russia, a southern zone under British rule, and a neutral area in between. When the war ended in 1918, the entire Middle East was controlled by the British, French, and Russians, but it was a powder keg (Fromkin, 2001, pp. 189–196, 291–293).

Explicable in a time when national survival was threatened, these contradictory promises were nothing more than an extension of prewar British imperial policies. They did not alleviate the tensions between the Palestinian Arabs and the newly arrived Palestinian Jews. At the end of the war, the British created a series of Arab countries dominated by strong, traditional family groups. Far from representing a united Arab realm of Islam, the British-led division was challenged internally by rival families and externally by other Arab states. Each family and each of the Arab leaders wished to unite Islam under their own banner. Major states eventually emerged from this scenario: Syria, Iraq, Saudi Arabia, Jordan, and the Gulf States. Some of the new nations dreamed of a pan-Islamic region, but none was willing to let another run it. Other ethnic groups, like the Kurds, wanted autonomy. Christian Assyrians and Jewish settlers in Palestine also wanted independence (Hourani, 1997, pp. 315–332; Fromkin, 2001, pp. 558–561).

The Arabs also could not counter the continuing British influence, and neither a pan-Arabic realm nor a Jewish national state could develop under the watchful eyes of the British. In 1922, Great Britain received permission from the League of Nations to create the **Mandate of Palestine**. The mandate gave Britain control of Palestine and placed the British in the center of Middle Eastern affairs, but it came with a cost. It left neither Arabs nor Jews satisfied. The Arabs believed that they had received a false promise, and the Jews demanded their right to a homeland (Fromkin, 2001, pp. 562–565).

Mandate of Palestine: The British Mandate of Palestine was in effect from 1920 to 1948. Created by the League of Nations, the mandate gave the United Kingdom the right to extend its influence in an area roughly equivalent to modern Jordan, Israel, and the Palestinian Authority.

The Birth of Israel

While the British established the protectorate, in Palestine, feelings of nationalism and anger increased. Both Jews and Arabs resented the British, but neither side was willing to submit to the other if the British were expelled. Sporadic violence against the Jews began in 1921, and the Jews formed a defense force known as the Haganah. They did not see themselves as ordinary settlers, but as fellow colonialists alongside the British. They had come to establish a Zionist state (Burleigh, 2009, p. 90).

Tensions increased throughout the decade, culminating in a riot in 1929 when the Islamic mufti of Jerusalem inspired an attack against Jewish worshippers. More than 60 Jews were killed, and another 60 would be killed in sporadic violence during the remainder of the year. This prompted a debate and a split in the Haganah. Some members wanted to take action against the Arabs and the British, and they saw terrorist violence as the only means to create a Jewish state in Palestine. They called the new group the Irgun Zvai Leumi (Burleigh, 2009, p. 91). Bruce Hoffman (1998, pp. 48–53) states that the Irgun would become the prototype of the anticolonial urban terrorist group. He is not sure whether the EOKA in Cyprus or the FLN in Algeria deliberately based their campaigns on Irgun tactics, but each movement did follow the Irgun model.

An Arab revolt in Palestine began in 1936 and lasted until 1939. It was primarily aimed at the British, but the brewing hatred and distrust between the Arab and Jewish communities also came to the surface. Both Jews and Arabs fought the British, but they fought each other at the same time. Animosity was overshadowed by the events of the early 1940s but resurfaced after the war. Both Jews and Arabs firmly believed that the only possible solution to the problems in Palestine was to expel the British and eliminate the political participation of the other (Nasr, 1997, pp. 17–25).

Michael Burleigh (2009, pp. 95–111) says the British responded to violence with the same ruthless tactics they had applied elsewhere but that the Irgun took matters further. Seeing threats from both the Arabs and the British, the Irgun's leaders—who later became prominent Israeli leaders—plotted a campaign against both sides. At first, the Irgun sought to avoid British casualties. That would change after World War II.

In late 1945 and into 1946, thousands of Jews displaced by the Holocaust flocked to Palestine. Palestinian Arabs, sensing danger from this massive influx of Jews, began to arm themselves. They had little assistance. The British Empire was collapsing, and other Arabs were too concerned with their own political objectives to care about the Palestinians. Officially, the British had banned Jewish immigration, but there was little that could be done about the influx of immigrants. Jews continued to arrive, demanding an independent state (Lewis, 2004, pp. 181–187).

In 1945, the Irgun began a campaign of all-out terrorism. Burleigh (2009) says that the Irgun adopted a twofold strategy: (1) It would attack in the urban centers of Palestine to tie up massive numbers of British soldiers and to terrorize the Arabs into flight or submission and (2) it would wage an international campaign to win sympathy. Many Jews in America and Europe applauded the Irgun's efforts, and its activities grew in ferocity. Individual British soldiers were assassinated, and the Irgun launched a bombing campaign. When three Irgun terrorists were tried and executed for murder, the Irgun kidnapped two British sergeants and hanged them. They bombed prominent places, such as the King David Hotel, killing British and Americans.

If the Irgun's trail of murder and mayhem predated the EOKA and the FLN, it was modeled on a previous campaign of selective terrorism, the Irish Republican Army in the Black and Tan War. In a four-part series on terrorism, the History Channel (2000) pointed to one of the threads running through Jewish terrorism. Leaders of the Irgun studied the tactics of the Irish Republican Army's Michael Collins. They incorporated Collins's methods in the Jewish campaign, and the Irgun's leader took the Irishman's name as his *nom de guerre*. The Irgun knew that it could not hope to defeat the British in a conventional war, but terrorism gave hope for political victory. Within 20 years, Palestinian Arabs would make the same discovery.

In 1947, the situation was beyond British control. Exhausted by World War II, the British sought a UN solution to their quandary in Palestine. The United Nations suggested that one part of Palestine be given to the Arabs and another part be given to the Jews. The Zionists were elated; the Arabs were not. Caught in the middle, the British came to favor the UN solution, and they had reason to support it: The Jews were in revolt.

On May 15, 1948, the United Nations recognized the partition of Palestine and the modern nation-state of Israel. The Arabs attacked the new Jewish state immediately, and the Irgun's terrorism fell by the wayside. Both Arabs and Jews shifted to conventional warfare and would fight that way until 1967.

Arab Power Struggles and Arab–Israeli Wars

Modern Middle Eastern terrorism is the result of continuing conflicts in the twentieth century. This section reviews the formation of some of the most important Arab states in North Africa and southwest Asia. Instead of considering each story separately, the narrative blends Israel's development with the symbiotic nature of the conflict. This approach explains the relationship between intra-Arab rivalries and terrorism.

Although the control of Palestine is always mentioned when dealing with contemporary Middle Eastern violence, since as far back as the post–World War I period, the situation has not been conducive to peace. Britain and France divided the ancient realm of Islam, known as dar al-Islam, and left the area ripe for confusion and bitterness. Aside from the Palestinian issue, other Arabs felt slighted by various peace settlements, and their dissatisfaction continued through the end of World War II. The French and British created states that did not realistically reflect the divisions in the Middle East.

North Africa was completely dominated by Britain and France. Libya was divided into British and French sections, and it did not become independent until 1951. In 1969, Colonel Muammar Gadhafi seized power in a military coup, claiming Libya as an anti-Western socialist state. Egypt achieved its independence before World War II but did not fully break with Britain until Gamal Nasser took power in 1954. Gadhafi sought to follow Nasser's footsteps but broke with Egypt after Nasser's death in 1970 (Halliday, 2005, pp. 167–175).

Syria was under French rule from 1922 to 1946. After several military coups and a failed attempt to form a united republic with Egypt, a group of pan-Arabic socialists, the Baath Party, seized power in 1963. They were purged by an internal Baath revolution in 1966, and Baathist president Hafez Assad came to power in 1970, ruling until his death in 2000. Aside from internal problems (especially problems involving a minority group of Alawites who practiced Muslim, Christian, and pagan rituals), Assad believed that Lebanon and Palestine were rightly part of Greater Syria (Dawisha, 2003, pp. 160–213).

Lebanon has become one of the most violent regions in the area. Ruled by France until 1943, the government of Lebanon managed a delicate balance of people with many different national and religious loyalties. In 1948, when Palestinians displaced by Israel began flocking to the country, the delicate balance was destroyed. Lebanon has suffered internal conflict ever since. Violence has included civil wars in 1958 and 1975–1976, continued fighting up to 1978, an Israeli invasion in 1978, another Israeli invasion in 1982, an Iranian revolutionary intervention following the 1982 Israeli invasion, a fragile peace in 1990, and the growth of a terrorist militia from 1983 to 1996. Several large militias still roam the countryside, despite their agreement to disarm under the terms of the 1990 peace plan. Israel began abandoning Lebanon in the spring and summer of 2000. Militant Lebanese forces moved into the former occupied zones, seeking vengeance on the **South Lebanese Army**, whose members supported Israel (Friedman, 2000, pp. 126–137).

South Lebanese Army: A Christian militia closely allied with and supported by Israel. It operated with Israeli support from 1982 to 2000.

The Persian Gulf region has a different history. In an effort to secure a land route to India, the British established several states from the Mediterranean Sea to the Persian Gulf in the nineteenth and early twentieth centuries. One branch of the Hashemite family received Jordan as a reward for assisting the British; another branch received Iraq. Jordan became a constitutional monarchy ruled by King Hussein from 1952 to 1999 and by his son, King Abdullah, from 1999 to the present. Iraq's path was more turbulent. A 1958 coup eliminated the Iraqi Hashemites from power, and another coup in 1968 brought **Baathist** rule. Saddam Hussein, a Baathist, came to power in 1979 (Dawisha, 2003, pp. 169–171, 276–277).

Baathist: A member of the pan-national Arab Baath Party. Baathists were secular socialists seeking to unite Arabs in a single socialist state.

Saudi Arabia and the Persian Gulf States fared somewhat better because of their immense wealth and independence from Europe. In 1902, the Saud family began expanding its control of Arabia, which included Mecca, the most sacred shrine in Islam, and it unified the kingdom in 1932. The Gulf States remained independent from the

Saud family. The social situation changed in 1938 when oil was discovered on the Arabian Peninsula. As operations intensified, explorers found that the entire region was rich with oil. Poorer states, such as Iraq and Jordan, looked at the Persian Gulf with envy, believing the oil wealth should benefit all of dar al-Islam. Not all has been peaceful in the Persian Gulf or Saudi Arabia.

From 1947 to 1967, the Middle East was dominated by a series of short conventional wars. Arab states failed to achieve unity, often seeming as willing to oppose each other as they were to oppose Israel. Rhetorically, all the Arab states maintained an anti-Israeli stance, but Jordan and Saudi Arabia began to move closer to the West, enthusiastically led by the shah of Iran (B. Rubin, 2003).

In the meantime, Israeli armed forces grew. Composed of highly mobile combined combat units, the Israeli Defense Forces became capable of launching swift, deadly strikes at the Arabs. In 1967, the Israelis demonstrated their superiority over all their Arab neighbors. Although the combined Arab armies were equipped with excellent Soviet arms and outnumbered the Israeli forces, in six days, Israel soundly defeated its opponents and doubled its territory (Armstrong, 2000b, p. 171; Dawisha, 2003, pp. 250–258).

After the 1967 **Six-Day War,** the Palestine Liberation Organization (PLO) began a series of terrorist attacks against Israeli civilian positions. Its military approach mimicked the old terrorist tactics of the Irgun and its violent offshoot, the Stern Gang. These attacks embittered most Israelis and served to define Israeli relations with Arab neighbors. The PLO soon split between moderates and radicals, but terrorism against Israel increased. Israel struck back against the PLO wherever its operatives were located (Nasr, 1997, pp. 40–47).

In the meantime, the Arab states also split into several camps. One group, represented by King Hussein of Jordan, was anxious to find a way to coexist with Israel. A few nations, like Egypt, simply wanted to avenge the embarrassment of the Six-Day War. Egypt would negotiate with Israel, but as an equal, not as a defeated nation. Other Arab views were more militant. Represented by the Baath Party, groups of Arab socialists called for both Arab unity and the destruction of Israel. They formed the Rejectionist Front, a coalition that included several terrorist groups that rejected peace with Israel. Finally, a group of wealthy oil states hoped for stability in the region. They publicly supported the struggle against Israel while privately working for peace. They felt that peace would ensure sound economic relations with their customers in the West.

Despite the myriad positions, the embarrassment of the Six-Day War proved to be the strongest catalyst to action. The Egyptians and the Israelis kept sniping at one another along the Suez Canal. Gamal Nasser, Egypt's president, vowed to drive the Israelis back and asked for Soviet help to do it. Breaking relations with the United States, Nasser moved closer to the Soviet camp. When he died in September 1970, Anwar Sadat, his successor, questioned the policy of moving closer to the Soviets. By 1972, he had thrown the Soviets out, claiming that they were not willing to support another war with Israel. Coordinating activities with Syria, Sadat launched his own war on October 6, 1973 (Esposito, 1999, pp. 72–73, 93–96).

The **Yom Kippur War,** named after the Hebrew festival celebrating God's atonement for all sin and reconciliation with humanity, psychologically reversed the defeat of the Six-Day War for many of Israel's Arab neighbors. Catching the Israelis by surprise in 1973, the Egyptians drove Israeli forces back into the Sinai while the Syrians drove onto the Golan Heights. The Syrians were attempting to launch a tank offensive into central Israel before the Israeli Defense Forces managed to stabilize the front. Israel counterattacked, driving its enemies back, but the Egyptians celebrated their

Six-Day War: A war between Israel and its Arab neighbors fought in June 1967. Israel launched the preemptive war in the face of an Arab military buildup, and it overwhelmed all opposition. At the end of the war, Israel occupied the Sinai Peninsula, the Golan Heights, and the West Bank of the Jordan River. It also occupied the city of Jerusalem, or al Quds to Muslims.

Yom Kippur War: A war between Israel and its Arab neighbors fought in October 1973. Also known as the Ramadan War, hostilities began with a surprise attack on Israel. After initial setbacks, Israel counterattacked and regained its positions.

initial victory. Peace came three weeks later, and the Egyptians felt that their honor had been restored.

Satisfied with this sense of victory, Sadat took a series of bold initiatives. Responding to an overture from the United States, Sadat renewed relations with Washington and stopped the minor skirmishes with Israeli troops by 1975. He visited Jerusalem in 1977 and publicly talked of peace (Esposito, 1999, pp. 96–98).

Former Irgun leader Menachim Begin became prime minister of Israel in September 1977. Begin was committed to maintaining control of the occupied territories, including Jerusalem, that Israel had won in the Six-Day War. Begin's position precluded peace with the Arab states because the Arabs demanded the return of the occupied territories. Despite the obvious differences, Anwar Sadat maintained a dialogue with Washington. Under the mediation of U.S. president Jimmy Carter, Sadat agreed to a separate peace with Israel, provided that Israel would withdraw from the Sinai Peninsula. Begin agreed, and on May 26, 1979, Egypt and Israel signed the **Camp David Peace Accord** under Carter's watchful eye. The decision cost Sadat his life. He was assassinated by Muslim fundamentalists in 1981 for agreeing to peace.

Camp David Peace Accord: A peace treaty between Egypt and Israel brokered by the United States in 1979.

The Return of Terrorism

The Arabs who were rejecting peace with Israel fell into two camps. The radicals rejected any peace with or recognition of Israel. The more moderate group was concerned about the fate of the Palestinians. Egypt's peace with Israel did not account for the Palestinian refugees in Israel or the occupied territories. At the same time, much of the West failed to pay attention to Palestinians' legitimate claims because radical Palestinians were involved in dozens of terrorist attacks.

In the symbiotic world of Middle Eastern terrorism, Palestine was frequently used as a cover for the intra-Arab struggle for power. In 1978, Israel launched a minor invasion of Lebanon, which was followed by a full-scale attack in 1982. During this same period, Middle Eastern governments were consolidating internal power and looking at potential regional rivals. The Iranian government fell to revolutionary Shi'ites, and the American embassy and its occupants were seized by Iran's revolutionary government. As the United States eventually achieved the return of its embassy hostages, Saddam Hussein's Iraq and revolutionary Iran went to war, and thousands died each month on conventional battlefields (Wright, 2000, pp. 15–19). Terrorism continued in other Middle Eastern countries.

In the melee of the 1980s, Middle Eastern terrorism fell into several broad categories, including (1) suicide bombings and other attacks on Israeli and Western positions in Lebanon; (2) various militias fighting other militias in Lebanon; (3) state-sponsored terrorism from Libya, Syria, and Iran; (4) freelance terrorism by high-profile groups; (5) terrorism in support of Arab Palestinians; (6) attacks in Europe against Western targets; and (7) Israeli assassinations of alleged terrorists. Terrorists mounted dozens of operations in support of governments, and several nations used terrorists as commandos. Airplanes were hijacked; airports were attacked; the United States responded with naval action, once accidentally shooting down an Iranian civilian airplane and killing hundreds; and Europe became a low-intensity battleground (Pluchinsky, 1982).

Iran–Iraq War (1980–1988): A war fought after Iraq invaded Iran over a border dispute in 1980. Many experts predicted an Iraqi victory, but the Iranians stopped the Iraqi Army. The war produced an eight-year stalemate and more than a million casualties. The countries signed an armistice in 1988.

Despite the appearance of terrorism, conventional war continued to dominate the Middle East, and Arabs struggled against Arabs. As the **Iran–Iraq War** neared its end, Saddam Hussein turned his attention to Kuwait. Feeling that the British had unfairly separated Kuwait from Iraq before World War I, Saddam Hussein invaded the small country to gain control of its oil production. The result was disastrous for Iraq. Leading a coalition of Western forces and the Persian Gulf States, the United States struck with massive force. Saddam Hussein's army suffered greatly, and terrorism reemerged as a weapon with which to strike an overwhelming military power. As Iraq retreated in the Persian Gulf, terrorists began plotting new methods for striking the United States.

✓ **Self-Check**	> How did misunderstandings between Arabs and Jews develop?
	> Why did terrorism become a part of these misunderstandings?
	> What role did terrorism play in the creation of Israel?

Iran

Americans found it convenient in the 1980s to speak of Iranian terrorism. After all, the Iranians had violated international law in the early stages of their revolution by taking the American embassy in Tehran. They were alleged to have staged several bombings in Lebanon as well as attacks on other American interests in the Middle East. They had planted mines in the Persian Gulf and were responsible for the deaths of U.S. troops. Finally, intelligence sources reported that the Iranians were allied with other terrorist states and supported a shadowy group known as Islamic Jihad—which turned out to be a cover name for an operational group of Hezbollah. The media attributed this rise in terrorism to the rise of Islamic fundamentalism in Iran.

In some ways, this popular conception is correct; but in other ways, it is completely wrong. The 1979 revolution in Iran represented the flames from friction that had started centuries earlier. Far from being a rebirth of fundamentalism, it was more indicative of the religious split within Islam.

Uniquely Persian

Iranians are not Arabs; they are Persians, and they have strong ethno-national ties to the ancient Persian Empire. They have struggled with Arabs for centuries, and these struggles are indicative of Iran's place in Islam. After the martyrdom of Hussein ibn Ali, Mohammed's grandson, at Karbala, Shi'ite Islam moved east. It came to dominate Persia, further separating Persians from many Arab Sunnis. When conquering Arab and Mongol armies rode through Persia over the next centuries, the Persians maintained their historical cultural identity. It came into full flourish when Iran reestablished its own agrarian empire under Shi'ite domination. Iranians resisted the Turks and later European imperialists. Bernard Lewis (2004, pp. 43–45) says that Iran never adopted the habits of nations that conquered them; they remained uniquely Persian.

Negative reaction to European imperialism cannot be overemphasized when considering the politics of modern Iran. There is a healthy Iranian distrust of the West. Karen Armstrong (2000a) shows the religious side of the struggle. During the nineteenth century, Persians developed a hierarchy of Shi'ite Islamic scholars, including local prayer leaders, masters of Islam, ayatollahs, and grand ayatollahs. Armstrong says that the leading scholars formed the **majilis council**, a theological advisory board to the government. In the early twentieth century, the majilis resisted British exploitation by taking political leadership. The scholars' activities helped bring about a constitution in 1906, and they virtually shut the country down in a general strike against British policies a few years later.

majilis council: The Islamic name given to a religious council that advises a government or a leader. Some Islamic countries refer to their legislative body as a majilis.

British Influence and Control

British imperialism came to Iran in the 1800s. After 1850, the British began to view Iran as the northern gateway to India. At the same time, they were also very concerned about German imperialism and possible Russian expansion. For their part, the Russians saw a potential opportunity to gain a warm-water port and expand their empire. They moved into northern Iran and prepared to move south. The British countered by occupying southern Iran. Both countries used the occupation for their own economic and military interests (Nima, 1983, pp. 3–27; see also Esposito, 1999, pp. 41–52).

Oil production had a tremendous impact on the way the British used Iran. The British established the Anglo-Persian Oil Company in 1909 and started taking oil profits out of Iran. Although direct economic imperialism has ended in Iran, Iranians still regard Western oil companies as an extension of the old British arrangement. They believe that the shah stayed in power by allowing Western corporations to exploit Iranian oil.

To some extent, this attitude reflects the history of Iran. The British became very concerned about Iran in the 1920s after the Communist revolution in Russia, believing Iran might be the next country that the Communists would target. No longer in direct control of the south, the British searched for a leader to stem the potential Soviet threat, a leader whose Iranian nationalism would make him an enemy of Russia. They did not believe that such a man would be difficult to find because working-class Iranians hated the Russians as much as they hated the British. The British found their hero in **Reza Shah Pahlavi**. In 1925, with British support, he became shah of Iran (Wright, 2000, pp. 44–46).

Reza Shah Pahlavi:
(1878–1944) Shah of Iran from 1925 to 1941. He was forced from power by a British and Soviet invasion.

Robin Wright (2000) says that Reza Shah was under no illusions about his dependency on British power. For Iran to gain full independence, he needed to develop an economic base that would support the country and consolidate his strength among the ethnic populations in Iran. Dilip Hiro (1987, pp. 22–30) says that Reza Shah chose two methods for doing so. First, he encouraged Western investment, primarily British and American, in the oil and banking industries. Second, he courted various power groups inside Iran, including the Shi'ite fundamentalists. At first, these policies seemed successful, but they created long-term problems.

Reza Shah's long-term failure was a result of his foreign policy. In the 1930s, Reza Shah had befriended Hitler, and he saw German relations as a way to balance British influence. He guessed that Iran would profit from having a powerful British rival as an ally, but his plan backfired. When World War II erupted, the British and Russians believed Reza Shah's friendship with the Nazis could result in German troops in Iran and Iranian oil in Germany. In 1941, the British overran southern Iran, while the Russians reentered the north (Wright, 2000, pp. 45–46).

Prelude to the 1979 Revolution

Mohammed Reza Pahlavi:
(1919–1980) Shah of Iran from 1941 to 1979. The shah led a rigorous program of modernization that turned Iran into a regional power. He left the throne and accepted exile as a result of the 1979 Iranian Revolution.

Reza Shah's reign was over. He fled the country, leaving his son, **Mohammed Reza Pahlavi**, nominally in charge. Mohammed Pahlavi became the modern shah of Iran, but his ascent was traumatic. An Allied puppet in the beginning, the shah had to fight for the same goals that his father had failed to achieve. When he was on the verge of achieving power in the early 1950s, he found himself displaced by democratic and leftist forces. Like his father, the shah fled the country (Kurzman, 2004, pp. 103–124).

In August 1953, Pahlavi returned to the office that had been denied him during Iran's brief fling with democracy. The Iranians had attempted to create a constitutional assembly, but the British believed that they were moving too far to the left and would be swept into a Communist revolution. Playing on their fear of Communism, the British convinced the American CIA that the only hope for stability in Iran was to empower the shah, Mohammed Pahlavi. The CIA conducted propaganda operations, but the new government was so ineffective that it would have fallen without the help of the United States. In the popular Iranian version of the story—the story that most Iranians believe today—the CIA launched a well-orchestrated coup against the government (B. Rubin, 2003). America looked on the shah as a friend, not realizing Iranians viewed America's actions as part of a long tradition of imperialism.

In an extensive account that uses primary sources, Dilip Hiro (1987, pp. 30–100) provides details of the shah's attempt to build his base and of his eventual failure. Once back in power in 1953, the shah formulated a plan to stay in power. Like his father, he believed that only modernization would lead to Iranian autonomy. Yet, he also feared his own people. He created a secret military police force, **SAVAK,** to locate and destroy his enemies. SAVAK was aggressive.

> **SAVAK:** Mohammed Pahlavi's secret police, established after the 1953 downfall of the democratic government.

The shah used a fairly effective strategy with SAVAK. Rather than taking on all his enemies at once, he became selective. He allied with one group to attack another group. SAVAK's enthusiasm for the torture and murder of political opponents complemented the policy. After 1953, the shah found it convenient to ally with the Shi'ite holy men, who welcomed the shah's support and turned a blind eye to SAVAK's activities. Charles Kurzman (2004, p. 126) points out that SAVAK's ruthless tactics, effective at first, would eventually fail.

The Western reforms of Iranian society were popular with the middle class—the members of which profited from modernization. The Shi'ite clergy, however, felt the increasing power of the state as Shi'ite influences and traditions were questioned or banned. From their seminary in the holy city of Qom, the clergy began to organize against the shah, but it was too late. The shah no longer needed the fundamentalists.

According to Hiro (1987), by 1960, the shah's tenuous relationship with the fundamentalist clergy began to waver. This caused the clergy to organize demonstrations among theology students in Qom and marches of the faithful in Tehran. SAVAK infiltrated Shi'ite opposition groups in Tehran, and the army attacked Qom. There were thousands of arrests; demonstrators were ruthlessly beaten or, in some cases, shot in the streets. By 1963, many potential opponents were murdered, and the shah had many others in custody. One of his prisoners was the *hojatalislam* (master of Islam) **Ruhollah Khomeini.** In a gesture of mercy, the shah ordered Khomeini deported to Iraq instead of executing him. That proved to be a mistake.

> **Ruhollah Khomeini:** (1900–1989) The Shi'ite grand ayatollah who was the leading figure in the 1979 Iranian Revolution. Khomeini toppled the shah's government and consolidated power by destroying or silencing his enemies, including other Shi'ite Islamic scholars. Iran was transformed into a theocracy under his influence.

The Revolution

Khomeini's rise to power was a key to the revolution. He was intolerant not only of the shah's American infatuation but of other Shi'ites who refused to accept his narrow interpretation of Islam. The shah and his father had been very successful in limiting the power of the clergy because of the popularity of Western-style reforms. The Shi'ite scholars wisely sidestepped the reforms and attacked the shah where he was most vulnerable, his apparent link to imperialism through America. Khomeini had spoken several times about the shah's love affair with America, and this raised the ire of common Iranians, to whom America seemed no different from their former Russian and British colonial masters (Esposito, 1999, pp. 60–66).

Khomeini's influence increased after he was arrested and deported in 1963. He was promoted to the rank of ayatollah and ran a campaign from Iraq against the shah. Under his leadership, the mosque came to be perceived as the only opposition to the shah and the hated SAVAK. Khomeini headed a network of 180,000 Islamic revolutionaries in addition to 90,000 mullahs (low-ranking prayer leaders); 5,000 hojatalislams (middle-ranking scholars); and 50 ayatollahs (recognized scholars with authoritative writings). The Shi'ite scholars were able to paint the shah in satanic terms, owing to his relations with the United States; they called for a holy revolution and the restoration of Islam. Khomeini led the way from his Iraqi exile (Wright, 2000, pp. 46–48; Kurzman, 2004, pp. 44–45).

Revolutionaries gained momentum after the election of Jimmy Carter as president of the United States in 1976. Carter pressured the shah to end SAVAK's human rights abuses. Fearful of losing American aid, the shah ordered SAVAK to ease off the opposition, thus increasing the ability of revolutionaries to operate inside Iran. There were many different groups. Secular socialists sought to topple the shah and remove Iran from the Cold War. Communists wanted to shift allegiance to the Soviet Union. Many democrats wanted to create an Iranian democracy, and Shi'ite scholars sought to reintroduce religious values within a secular government. Khomeini, who viewed Carter as a manifestation of satanic power, felt no gratitude toward the United States. He wanted to create an Iranian theocracy, with the majilis in charge of spiritual and temporal life. Increasing revolutionary activities from Iraq, Khomeini moved against the shah and other Iranian groups (Rasler, 1996; Figure 8.2).

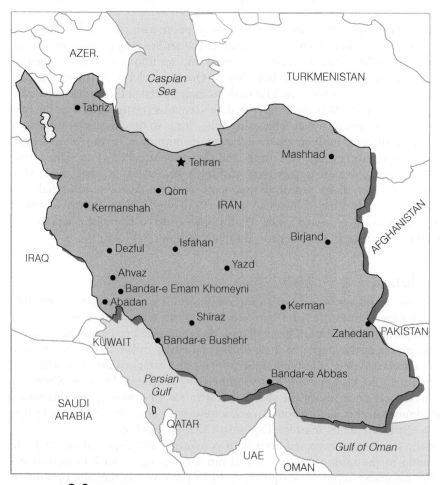

FIGURE **8.2** Iran

The shah pressured Saddam Hussein, then president of Iraq, to remove Khomeini, who was forced to flee Iraq in fear for his life. He received asylum in Paris, where, ironically, he was better able to control the revolution because Paris had a modern telephone system from which he could directly dial Tehran.

By 1977, Khomeini's revolutionary headquarters in Paris maintained an open telephone line to Tehran. Khomeini sent hundreds of revolutionary sermons to a multiple-audiotape machine in Tehran, and his words were duplicated and delivered throughout the Iranian countryside. Khomeini's power increased dramatically (Wright, 2000, pp. 46–49).

Khomeini returned to Tehran in 1978. There was little the shah could do. Although he had unleashed SAVAK and ordered his troops to fire on street demonstrators, the public had risen against him. Several groups were vying for power, but Khomeini seemed to be on top. In February 1979, the shah fled Iran. Khomeini, riding victoriously through the streets of Tehran, was still faced with problems. It was necessary to eliminate all opposition if the Islamic revolution were to succeed. The starting point was to attack all things Western. In his first victory addresses, Khomeini was unrestrained as he called for world revolution. He said it was time to launch a holy war against the West and the traitors to Islam.

The Iranian Revolution of 1979 caused another form of terrorism to spread from the Middle East. Khomeini, filled with hatred for Saddam Hussein after having been driven from Iraq, was at first content to wage a conventional war with his neighbor. However, such direct tactics would not work against a superpower. The United States and the Soviet Union, if they dared to intervene, would be subjected to a lower-level form of warfare. Because the superpowers would win any war fought out in the open, the Ayatollah Khomeini chose to fight in the shadows (Esposito, 1999, pp. 17–20).

In 1982, Israel invaded Lebanon, moving through the Shi'ite areas of the south. Revolutionaries left Iran and traveled through Syria, brokering deals with the Syrians to assist them in resisting the Israelis. The Iranian Revolutionary Guard arrived in the Bekaa Valley and established the nucleus of a new type of revolutionary force, Hezbollah. It subsequently became a multifaceted organization with elements representing terrorism, social services, Lebanese politics, and a military wing of Iranian foreign policy (Esposito, 1999, pp. 154–157).

The Call to Karbala

Khomeini used a mixture of repressive tactics and political strategies to consolidate his power in Iran, and he is best understood within the Shi'ite tradition of Islam. Although many Western observers believe the fanaticism of the revolution was due to a resurgence of fundamentalism, in reality, it gained its intensity from the repressed lower classes of Iran emerging to practice their traditional religion.

As imperialism made its way into nineteenth-century Iran, public plays about Hussein ibn Ali's martyrdom at Karbala gained popularity. The emotional displays of Hussein's death at the hands of the Umayyads and his heroic acceptance of martyrdom became a Shi'ite equivalent of the Christian passion play. Such plays reinforced the distinction of the Shi'ites from all other religions, the uniquely Persian character of Iran, and the nobility of sacrifice for the sake of God (Armstrong, 2000b, pp. 299–319; see Rasler, 1996; Kurzman, 2001).

The Ayatollah Khomeini was guided by the message of Karbala, and he removed Islamic scholars and political leaders who disagreed with his message. He believed that the Iranian Revolution was the first step in purifying the world. Israel needed to be eliminated and returned to Islamic rule. The West was the handmaiden of the Jews, but it also remained the source of imperialism. Its influence was satanic and needed to be destroyed. Holy warriors were called to battle. After Khomeini's death in 1989, several competing schools of thought emerged in Iran. Although opposed by some Islamic scholars and almost all political moderates, a Khomeini-influenced majilis council came to dominate Iranian politics. It was guided by a belief that suggests the martyrdom of Karbala should be experienced every day. Many Islamic scholars rejected this notion, and a number of political analysts believed that most Iranians, although proudly and uniquely Persian, do not wish to usher in a new age of martyrdom (Kurzman, 2001).

> ✓ **Self-Check**
>
> > What social and political factors separate Iran from the Arab-dominated Middle East?
> > How did British imperial policy help shape modern Iran?
> > How did reactions to Western policies influence the 1979 Iranian Revolution?

Emphasizing the Points

Terrorism in the Middle East is the result of historical processes, and the area is a cultural concept, not an actual place. Since extremists couch violence in religious terms, this chapter provides a brief summary of Islam for those who need it. Terrorism is the result of cultural and religious factors interacting with the birth of modern Israel, competition for power within and among Arab states, and the rise of militant religious fervor. Iran presents a set of separate issues, but its problems can also be linked to European imperialism.

SUMMARY OF CHAPTER OBJECTIVES

- The Middle East is a cultural concept. It can refer to a geographical area, but the boundaries are not distinct. The Middle East means different things to different people.
- Islam is one of the world's great monotheistic religions. Believers contend that God is revealed through prophets and that Mohammed was the last and greatest prophet. God's holy law is revealed in the Quran, and Islamic law can be interpreted by the sayings and actions of Mohammed.
- Islam has many different branches. The two main branches—the Shi'ites and the Sunnis—initially split over the leadership of the Muslim community. Today, there are theological and structural differences.
- The collapse of the Ottoman Empire led to the dissolution of the caliphate. British and French forces divided the Middle East into spheres of influence after World War I. Zionist activists had purchased land in Palestine, and they sought to create a Jewish state. European actions led to the creation of modern Israel within the British sphere of influence, and the first modern terrorists were Zionist separatists in Palestine.
- The Arabs and Israelis engaged in a series of conventional wars from 1948 to 1973, and the Israelis demonstrated their military superiority in each one. After the devastating defeat in June 1967, some Palestinians turned to terrorism as a method of confronting Israeli military superiority.

- Modern Iran formed within the context of European imperialism. The British were instrumental in placing Iranian leaders on the throne, and the United States took their place after World War II. Iran disavowed the United States after the 1979 Iranian Revolution.

LOOKING INTO THE FUTURE

Power is shifting in the Middle East. Egypt, Iraq, and Saudi Arabia held sway before the United States toppled Saddam Hussein. There is a new balance today, with Iran exercising influence in Iraq and challenging traditional Arab powers for Persian dominance in the Middle East. Fallout from the Arab Spring, a military coup in Egypt, fighting in Iraq, and the Syrian civil war make predictions about future terrorism perilous. There are too many unknown variables. Arabs may create new nation-states as the Sykes-Picot countries threaten dissolution. Iran's power is ascending, putting it on potential collision courses with Saudi Arabia and other Gulf States. Its nuclear ambitions and developments will shape its relationships with the entire region and the United States. Jihadist violence (discussed in Chapter 11) will also be part of the future. For the present, Israel seems to be satisfied to sit on the sidelines and watch its rivals fight one another; that is, unless Iran continues work on nuclear weapons. Unfortunately, the safest prediction for the future is to suggest that a series of multifaceted conflicts such as the Syrian civil war will continue unless regional powers can restore order. Normalized regional relationships, including dealings with Israel, would help to create a more stable environment. That is not likely to happen soon.

KEY TERMS

Gulf States, p. 175
Ali ibn Talib, p. 175
Abu Bakr, p. 176
Umar, p. 176
Uthman, p. 176
Badr, p. 176
Umayyads, p. 177
Hussein (Hussein ibn Ali), p. 177

Abbasids, p. 178
Ottoman Empire, p. 181
Balfour Declaration, p. 183
Mark Sykes, p. 184
Mandate of Palestine, p. 184

South Lebanese Army, p. 186
Baathist, p. 186
Six-Day War, p. 187
Yom Kippur War, p. 187
Camp David Peace Accord, p. 188
Iran–Iraq War, p. 188
majilis council, p. 189

Reza Shah Pahlavi, p. 190
Mohammed Reza Pahlavi, p. 190
SAVAK, p. 191
Ruhollah Khomeini, p. 191

CHAPTER 9

Terrorism in Israel and Palestine

LEARNING OBJECTIVES

After reading this chapter, you should be able to:

▶ Explain terrorism from Israeli and Arab points of view.

▶ Describe the rise of Fatah and the Palestine Liberation Organization (PLO).

▶ Identify factional groups that emerged from squabbles among the Palestinians.

▶ Describe the origins of the Palestinian Islamic Jihad.

▶ Discuss the origins and growth of Hezbollah after the 1982 Israeli invasion of Lebanon.

▶ Explain the current political and military aspects of Hezbollah.

▶ Outline the impact of the first Intifada and the birth of Hamas.

▶ Describe the current operational capabilities of Hamas.

▶ Summarize the tactics of the al Aqsa Martyrs Brigades.

▶ Describe controversial efforts to control Palestinian behavior.

Joel Carillet/Getty Images

The Wall Separating Israelis and Palestinians

According to Al Arabya News (2014) fighters from Palestinian Islamic Jihad's (PIJ) armed wing, the al Quds Brigade, marched defiantly through Gaza when combat ended after a short undeclared war with Israel in August 2014. Fighting started on July 8, 2014, when Israeli military forces struck Gaza in an effort to stop rocket attacks. Hamas and Islamic Jihad had been launching missiles from Gaza, and the Israelis had had enough. When a shaky cease-fire was established in August, Israel claimed it had killed over 900 militants. Israel usually suffers less in its frequent clashes with Palestinian militants, and the recent war with fighters in Gaza proved to be no different. Although total Palestinian casualties numbered over 2,000 militants and civilians, the Israelis lost 65 soldiers and six civilians. Israel wants the Gaza strip demilitarized. Hamas and its allies do not recognize the legitimacy of Israel and have vowed to eliminate the state. There seems to be little room for compromise.

Fighting broke out again in the spring of 2015. Security forces responded to a terrorist group by making several dozen arrests and demolishing a mosque where the militants gathered. Yet, there was a difference. The security force was from Hamas, and the terrorists belonged to the Supporters of the Islamic State in Jerusalem, a group that pledged loyalty to ISIS. They also arrested several members of Ansar Byat al-Maqdis, Egyptian Salafis who pledged loyalty to ISIS. When ISIS entered the Syrian civil war, many observers felt that Hamas and other Sunni groups would split from an alliance with the Iranian-backed Shi'ite Hezbollah. After ISIS fighters took a Palestinian refugee camp in Syria and beheaded several Hamas supporters, Hamas was driven closer to Hezbollah. In a supreme irony of history, Israel, Hamas, and Islamic Jihad had a common enemy.

Messy Definition

If the word *terrorism* is pejorative around the world, it is even more fraught with emotion when applied to Israel and Palestine. Israelis tend to associate the origin of modern terrorism with the rise of the Palestine Liberation Organization (PLO) and its leader **Yasser Arafat** (1929–2004). The conventional narrative is that Palestinians began using terrorist attacks against Israel when it became evident that Arab conventional forces could not defeat the Israeli Defense Forces (IDF). The PLO was composed of many diverse violent extremists, and it fractured into a variety of Palestinian terrorist groups. Hezbollah became part of the equation after the 1982 Israeli invasion of Lebanon and the IDF's subsequent treatment of Lebanese Shi'ites. The other dominant terrorist group, Hamas, arose in a rebellion in the late 1980s. Several smaller groups, such as the Palestinian Islamic Jihad, operate in alliance with the two dominant groups. All groups murder innocent defenseless people because they are not strong enough to fight Israel's military.

Move to the other side of the argument, and the logic is quite different. Terrorism did not originate with Palestinians; it began with two Zionist organizations in the 1930s—the Irgun Zvai Leumi and the more militant Stern Gang. The future Israelis abandoned terrorism only when they turned to conventional fighting in Israel's War of Independence (1948–1949). From this perspective, Israelis use terrorism as a tool for repression. Proponents of this argument point to Israel's everyday treatment of Palestinians and the massive casualties inflicted by the better armed IDF. Organizations like Hamas and Hezbollah have military wings to resist the IDF, but their main focus is health, social welfare, and education. Israel's continued expansion into Palestinian territories is made possible by the IDF.

As casualties mount, the differences between the two perspectives grow heated. There are calmer voices, but it is difficult to hear rational positions. Hardliners on both sides control the debate. For example, Hamas will not abandon its charter, a document calling for the elimination of the state of Israel. Similarly, expansionists in Israel advocate for removing Palestinians from their homes and replacing them with Israeli settlers. It is difficult to hear the voice of reason in such an environment.

Yasser Arafat: (1929–2004) The name assumed by Mohammed al Husseini. Born in Cairo, he was a founding member of Fatah and the PLO. He merged the PLO and Fatah in 1964 and ran a terrorist campaign against Israel. After renouncing terrorism and recognizing Israel's right to exist, Arafat was president of the Palestinian National Authority from 1993 to 2004.

Fatah and the Six-Day War

On June 5, 1967, Israel launched a preemptive war against Syria and Egypt as they engaged in massive military buildups. The IDF moved against Jordan later in the day after being shelled by the Jordanian Army. The war had a tremendous impact on both sides. For the Arabs, it meant total defeat and humiliation. To Israel, it was an unbounded success. The IDF took Jerusalem, the West Bank of the Jordan River, the Gaza Strip, the Sinai Peninsula, and the Golan Heights. It appeared that conventional arms could not defeat the IDF.

Yasser Arafat thought he had a solution. A few years before the 1967 war, Arafat formed a guerrilla organization, Fatah, in 1959 to wage a campaign against the Israelis. He advocated the use of small-unit tactics and terrorist actions that were patterned after the Irgun Zvai Leumi. Fatah's attacks were annoyances to Israel, but they did not represent a serious threat. Israel was more concerned about the large armies of its Arab neighbors. Frustrated, Arafat merged Fatah into the PLO in 1964 and assumed a leading role. After the Israeli victory in 1967, Arafat was prepared to launch a campaign of terrorism.

Arafat's Fatah moved to center stage after the Six-Day War. The self-made leader of the PLO proposed terrorizing unfortified civilian targets (Wallach and Wallach, 1992). Using a group of Fatah warriors known as **fedayeen**, Arafat began to attack Israel. The initial media coverage of Fatah's attacks caused the PLO's status to rise throughout the Arab world, and Arafat's fortunes rose along with it. All the conventional Arab armies were in disarray. Only the PLO had the courage and will to strike, despite being outnumbered, outgunned, and without a country. They had only the fedayeen (Dawisha, 2003, pp. 256–257).

fedayeen: Warriors who sacrifice themselves. The term was used differently in Arab history; the modern term is used to describe the secular warriors of Fatah.

Arafat conducted Fatah operations from Jordan, despite protests from the government. These hit-and-run strikes drew protests from Israel. They demanded that Jordan put a stop to Fatah's operations. Israel, angered by a lack of action, decided to take matters into its own hands. It attacked a PLO-controlled city in Jordan. The raid did little to stop Fatah, and attacks increased. Fearing an Israeli invasion, the Jordanians expelled the PLO two years later in September 1970.

EXPANDING THE CONCEPT

Important Terms, Dates, Concepts, and People in the Middle East

Arab–Israeli Wars: A generic term for several wars

   1948–1949: Israel's War of Independence

   1956 Suez Crisis: Britain, France, and Israel attack Egypt to keep the Suez Canal open; Israel takes the Gaza Strip

   1967 Six-Day War: Pits Israel against its Arab neighbors; Israel takes Jerusalem, the West Bank, and other areas

   1973 Yom Kippur War: Egypt and Syria strike Israel to regain occupied territories; Egypt is initially successful, but its major army is surrounded in a counterattack (Muslims frequently call it the Ramadan War)

Arafat, Yasser: Leader of the Palestine Liberation Organization (PLO), later the Palestine National Authority (PNA), and later still the Palestine National Council (PNC); widely recognized as the secular leader of the Palestinian movement

Baalbek: Lebanese city in the Bekaa Valley; original headquarters of Hezbollah

Camp David Peace Accords: 1978 peace agreement between Egypt and Israel

Dome of the Rock: The place where Muslims believe Abraham (Ibrahim) had a vision of God

Eretz Israel: The land of Israel under King David; many Jewish fundamentalists feel that God has called them to retake this land and expel the Arabs

Fedayeen: Warriors who sacrifice themselves and others

Gaza Strip: Palestinian strip of land along the Mediterranean

Golan Heights: Region in Syria overlooking Israel

Gush Emunim: Literally, "Bloc of the Faithful"; Jewish group formed in 1974 that believes God literally promised Jews the Kingdom of David

Habash, George: Christian founder of the Popular Front for the Liberation of Palestine

Hawatmeh, Naiaf: One of the founders of the Popular Front for the Liberation of Palestine; later led the Democratic Front for the Liberation of Palestine

Interim Agreement: Follow-up to 1993 Oslo Accords in 1995 to allow elections in Palestinian territory

Intifada: Uprising in Palestinian areas from 1987 to 1993; al Aqsa Intifada was a second uprising from 2000 to 2005

Jabril, Ahmed: Leader of the Popular Front for the Liberation of Palestine; later leader of the Popular Front for the Liberation of Palestine, General Command

Jewish settlements: Legal and illegal settlements in Palestinians lands; in 2004, Israeli prime minister Ariel Sharon proposed withdrawing from the Jewish settlements

Knesset: The Israeli parliament

Labor Party: The liberal Israeli political party

Likud Party: The conservative Israeli political party

Mossad: The Israeli intelligence service

Mujahedeen: Holy warriors

Muslim Brotherhood: An Islamic revivalist organization founded by Hassan al Banna in Cairo in 1928

Occupied territories: Initially, Palestinian territories under the post–World War I British division of Palestine; later occupied by Israel after the 1967 Six-Day War

Palestinian diaspora: The displacement in 1948 of Palestinians living in Israel

Palestine Authority (PA): Formally Palestinian National Authority; a semiautonomous body established after the Oslo Accords

Palestine National Council (PNC): Representative body from the occupied territories, the Gaza Strip, and the Palestinian diaspora

Rejectionist Front: A group of individuals, political parties, and states that reject Israel's right to exist

South Lebanese Army: The security force established by Israel to control south Lebanon after the withdrawal of the Israeli Defense Forces in 1985

Sykes–Picot Agreement: A 1916 agreement between Britain and France for control of the Middle East

Tanzim: Fatah's militia

Temple Mount: The site of the ancient Jewish Temple, a former Christian church, and the al Aqsa mosque

Wailing Wall: The remaining western wall of the ancient Jewish Temple in Jerusalem

West Bank: The West Bank of the Jordan River, formerly controlled by Jordan; seized by Israel in the 1967 war

Wye Accords: 1998 Israeli–Palestinian agreement to abide by previous commitments

Zion: The hill on which Jerusalem stands

Zionist: In contemporary usage, a Jew wishing to reestablish the Jewish homeland; Arabs and many Muslims frequently use the term to refer to all Jews

---

Arafat, Fatah, and the PLO ended up in southern Lebanon. The PLO grew and drew closer to militant Arab states. Ever the chameleon, Arafat became a terrorist celebrity, moving in leftist circles around the world. Fatah's raids continued from Lebanon, but Arafat faced a daunting problem. Fatah was falling apart. Driven by extremist ideologues, small groups began breaking away and operating autonomously. Lacking the ability to control the multitude of new organizations, he formed his own group and took personal command. He named the unit after the month the PLO had been driven from Jordan—Black September.

Arafat longed to strike Israel on an international stage, and he turned to leftist allies. The 1972 Summer Olympics were being held in Germany for the first time since World War II. With information that German terrorists supplied, Black September began planning an international strike. The world would be watching the Munich Olympics, and the Israeli Olympic team would be there. It was a tempting target.

Black September struck the Olympic Village and took most of the Israeli Olympic team hostage, killing those who tried to escape. German police moved in, and the world watched a drawn-out siege. The terrorists negotiated transportation to Libya and moved toward the Munich airport. The German police were not ready to surrender, however, and they launched what would become a tragic rescue operation. Plans immediately went awry. Reacting quickly, terrorists machine-gunned their hostages before the German police could take control. The Israeli hostages and a German police officer were killed. It was a terrorist victory, and European leftists and nationalists saw it as partly their triumph (Shalev, 2006).

The 1982 Invasion of Lebanon

The Israelis tracked down those they suspected of belonging to Black September and killed them. Yet, Arafat grew stronger in southern Lebanon. Lebanon was experiencing endemic multiple internal wars. The country was a mix of differing ethnic groups and religions, and each sect controlled its own militia. Armed band roamed the country fighting multiple enemies. Farther to the north, nationalistic Lebanese Christian and Islamic militias opposed each other as well as the Palestinians and foreign interests. Syria backed its own militia in the hope of increasing its influence in Lebanon, and Iran joined the fighting after the revolution of 1979. Civil war raged in Lebanon, allowing dozens of terrorists to slip across the border and attack Israel (see Nasr, 1997, pp. 125–135; Creed, 2002).

By 1982, the Israelis had had enough. On June 6, a massive three-pronged IDF force invaded Lebanon. The PLO and other militias moved forward to take a stand, but they were no match for the coordinated efforts of IDF tanks, aircraft, and infantry. The Israelis rolled through Lebanon. Soon, they were knocking on the doors of Beirut, and Lebanon's civil war seemed to be over.

Surrounded and bombarded by the Israelis in Beirut, even as the Syrian-backed forces fought the IDF, Arafat knew that the Syrians had no love for him. If the Israelis won, Arafat would be doomed. If the Syrians won, they intended to install their own surrogates in place of the PLO. In August 1982, Arafat left Beirut for Tripoli with 14,000 fedayeen. More than 10,000 guerrillas stayed, but they joined the Syrians.

Self-Check

> Explain the emergence of Fatah from the Six-Day War.
> Why did Black September strike in Germany?
> What impact did the 1982 invasion of Lebanon have on Palestinians?

Factionalism in Palestinian Terrorism

From 1967 to 1982, the PLO was characterized by internal splintering. Arafat found that he could not retain control of the military wing, and several groups split from it. These groups included the Democratic Front for the Liberation of Palestine; the Popular Front for the Liberation of Palestine; and the Popular Front for the Liberation of

Palestine, General Command. Another notable defector, **Sabri al Banna,** created the Abu Nidal Organization, a group that evolved into a global mercenary organization (see Seale, 1992; Gordon, 1999). Kameel Nasr (1997, p. 46) concludes that all of these groups were at their best when they fought each other.

New groups formed after the 1982 invasion of Lebanon. Unable to tolerate Israel's presence in the area, the Syrians rallied all local militias and accepted help from Iran. An Iranian-backed group, Hezbollah, began forming in Lebanon. A popular uprising in 1987, the **Intifada,** gave rise to a new group, Hamas. As Hamas challenged the PLO for power, Arafat disavowed terrorism in 1988 and called for peace. A second Intifada in 2000 created even more groups. The conflict between the Israelis and Palestinians has spawned a multitude of differing organizations.

To place the many divisions in context, the next section lists the dominant groups within the context of the Israeli–Palestinian struggle. You may wish to use this as a quick reference when examining terrorism in Israel and Palestine. Succeeding sections will focus on the current activities of the three dominant groups: Hezbollah, Hamas, and the al Aqsa Martyrs Brigades.

Major Groups

Abu Nidal Organization (Black June): Sabri al Banna (whose code name was Abu Nidal) and Yasser Arafat were once comrades in arms in the struggle for Palestine, but as others broke from Arafat, so too did Abu Nidal's rebel organization, **Black June.** In the end, Abu Nidal and his organization became a mercenary group, not only abandoning Arafat but also completely forsaking the Palestinian cause. The group's international exploits drew more attention than did those of its rival terrorist organizations as Nidal conducted ruthless operations in the 1980s, including:

- The murder of Jordanian ambassadors in Spain, Italy, and India
- Raids on Jewish schools in Antwerp, Istanbul, and Paris
- Attacks on airports in Rome and Vienna
- Assassinations of PLO leaders in Tunis
- The attempted assassination of the Israeli ambassador to the United Kingdom
- An attack on a synagogue in Istanbul

The Abu Nidal Organization evolved into an international group operating in more than 20 countries. It faded from significance by the 1990s, and Abu Nidal was murdered in Iraq in 2002.

Al Aqsa Martyrs Brigades: The al Aqsa Martyrs Brigades are based in West Bank refugee camps. Formed after the beginning of the **al Aqsa Intifada,** the Brigades appear to be Fatah's answer to the jihadists. Some members are motivated by Hezbollah, suggesting to some analysts that the Brigades have Shi'ite elements. Other analysts think that the Brigades are Fatah's attempt to take the Intifada's leadership away from Hamas and the Palestinian Islamic Jihad (PIJ). The Brigades were organized along military lines and became one of the first secular groups in the Middle East to use suicide bombers. Many experts believe that Arafat either directly controlled the Brigades or that they operated with his approval. A command council is responsible for leadership, and terrorist operations are divided into six geographical areas. If Yasser Arafat controlled the Brigades, members directly violated his orders on several occasions. The division commanders control, not the command council, the rank-and-file members.

Black September: Named after the September 1970 Jordanian offensive against Palestinian refugees in western Jordan, Black September was the infamous group that attacked the Israeli athletic team at the 1972 Munich Olympics. Israel spent years

Sabri al Banna: (1937–2002) The real name of Abu Nidal. Al Banna was a founding member of Fatah but split with Arafat in 1974. He founded militias in southern Lebanon, and he attacked Western and Israeli targets in Europe during the 1980s. In the 1990s, he became a mercenary. He was murdered in Iraq in 2002, probably by the Iraqi government.

Intifada: The first spontaneous uprising against Israel, lasting from 1987 to 1993. It began with youths throwing rocks and creating civil disorder. Some of the violence became more organized. Many people sided with religious organizations, abandoning the secular PLO during the Intifada.

Black June: The rebel organization created by Abu Nidal in 1976. He changed the name to the Fatah Revolutionary Council after a rapprochement with Syria in 1981. Most analysts refer to this group simply as the Abu Nidal Organization.

al Aqsa Intifada: An uprising sparked by Ariel Sharon's visit to the Temple Mount with a group of armed escorts in September 2000. The area is considered sacred to Jews, Christians, and Muslims. Muslims were incensed by the militant aspect of Sharon's visit because they felt he was invading their space with an armed group. Unlike the 1987 Intifada, the al Aqsa Intifada was characterized by suicide bombings.

hunting down and killing the members of Black September. The 1972 attack also prompted the Germans to create a new elite counterterrorist group, Federal Border Guard Group 9 (GSG-9), headed by Ulrich Wegener.

Democratic Front for the Liberation of Palestine (DFLP): A Christian, Naiaf Hawatmeh, created the DFLP in 1969 when he broke away from the Popular Front for the Liberation of Palestine. This Marxist–Leninist group seeks a socialist Palestine and was closely associated with the former Soviet Union. In 2000, the group joined Arafat in Washington, D.C., to negotiate with Israeli prime minister Ehud Barak. As a reward, the U.S. Department of State took the DFLP off its list of terrorist groups. The DFLP currently limits its attacks to the IDF.

Fatah: Fatah began as the military wing of the former PLO and was Yasser Arafat's strongest military muscle. Formed in the early stages of the PLO, Fatah was part of an underground organization formed in 1959. It emerged in the open in 1965 after making terrorist attacks against Israel in 1964. Fatah rose to prominence after the 1967 Six-Day War because it became the only means of attacking Israel. Fatah fought the Jordanians for 10 days in September 1970 and regrouped in Lebanon. It joined in the Lebanese civil war (1975–1990) and was eventually expelled to Tunisia. In the first Intifada (1987–1993), Fatah Hawks, political militants in the PLO, organized street demonstrations and disturbances, but emerging religious groups threatened Fatah's leadership among the militant Palestinian groups. Fatah went to the bargaining table in Oslo in 1993 and joined the peace process. It currently holds the majority of seats in the Palestinian government. Although it is now a political party, many analysts associate it with the al Aqsa Martyrs Brigades. The Tanzim Brigade and Force 17 come from the ranks of Fatah, and it has traditionally championed Palestinian nationalism over ideology or religion.

Force 17: Officially known as Presidential Security, Force 17 is an arm of Fatah. It operated as Yasser Arafat's security unit.

Hamas: In December 1987, a few days after the first Intifada began, the Islamic Resistance Movement (Harakat al Muqawama al Islamiyya, or Hamas) was formed. It was composed of the Palestinian wing of the Muslim Brotherhood. The Brothers advocated an international Islamic movement, and most of them did not support violence. Hamas differs from the Brothers' position in that it has localized the Islamic struggle and accepts violence as a norm. Hamas is organized as a large political union, and its primary mission is to oppose the PLO; today, it represents an alternative to the Palestine National Council. Its military wing is called the Izz el Din al Qassam Brigades, named for a martyr in the 1935 Arab revolt against the British in Palestine. In 2004, Israel assassinated Hamas's spiritual leader, Sheik Ahmed Yassin. As soon as Hamas appointed a new leader, the Israelis killed him, too. Hamas is a large organization, but its terrorist wing is rather small. Frequently allied with the PIJ, Hamas competes with other Fatah organizations.

Hezbollah: Hezbollah is the Iranian-backed Party of God, and it operates from southern Lebanon. The local branch of the group forms alliances of convenience with other organizations participated in the al Aqsa Intifada. The international branch is believed to run the most effective terrorist network in the world.

Palestinian Islamic Jihad (PIJ): A small group that emerged from the Muslim Brotherhood in Egypt in 1979 and formed in the Gaza Strip in 1981. Whereas the Brothers spoke of an international Islamic awakening, the PIJ felt that the struggle could be nationalized and had to become violent. The PIJ leaders were enamored with the 1979 Iranian Revolution, and even though they were Sunnis, they sought contact with Iran's revolutionary Shi'ites. The PIJ operates out of the Gaza Strip and forms alliances of convenience with other organizations. It has grown closer to

Hamas since the al Aqsa Intifada. The PIJ seeks to destroy Israel and establish an Islamic state in Palestine.

The group has strong links to the United States. In 2003, the U.S. Department of Justice (2003) took actions against the PIJ in Florida. The Justice Department argued that the group had an organized network of financial supporters around the world, including in the United States, and it brought charges against a professor at the University of South Florida for supporting the PIJ as part of that network. Another government report (U.S. Navy, 2008) cites multiple financial structures as another source of strength. Its presence in a multitude of countries leads to a number of funding sources. These funds have allowed the PIJ to remain in the field and to join Hamas in intermittent rocket attacks against Israel. Many analysts believe that the majority of funding comes from Iran and that the group is still shielded by Syria. They also believe that Hezbollah provides most of the training (Non-State Armed Groups, 2008).

Palestine Liberation Front (PLF): Three different groups call themselves the Palestine Liberation Front: The Abu Abbas faction, based in Iran, follows the old-style leadership used by Arafat; the Abdal Fatah Ghanem faction received support from Libya; and the Talat Yaqub faction sought favor with Syria. The name used by all three groups comes from Ahmed Jabril, a former Syrian Army captain who formed the first PLF in 1961. After the Six-Day War in June 1967, the PLF merged with two small radical groups to form the Popular Front for the Liberation of Palestine, but Jabril broke away and formed the Popular Front for the Liberation of Palestine, General Command. The PFLP-GC split in 1977 after Syria backed Lebanese Christians in the Lebanese civil war (1975–1990), and the anti-Syrians formed a new group, reviving the PLF name.

The PLF had yet another internal war in 1984, and Abu Abbas, a militant leader who rebelled against Syria, returned one faction to Arafat, expelling all Syrian influence. Abdal Fatah Ghanem broke from Abbas and sided with Syria. His group remained active in Lebanon. Talat Yaqub tried to remain neutral. After Abdal Fatah Ghanem died of a heart attack, his faction gravitated toward Libyan support. All three factions of the PLF seek to destroy Israel. The PLF's most notorious action was the hijacking of an Italian luxury liner, the *Achille Lauro*, in 1985. American forces captured the hijackers, but Abu Abbas was released. He went to the Gaza Strip and eventually to Iraq. He was captured during the U.S. invasion of Iraq in 2003 and died in captivity.

Popular Democratic Front for the Liberation of Palestine (PDFLP): The PDFLP is the military wing of the DFLP.

Popular Front for the Liberation of Palestine (PFLP): The PFLP is a Marxist-Leninist Arab nationalist group that emerged after the June 1967 Six-Day War. Egypt initially supported the PFLP but withdrew financing in 1968 when PFLP leaders criticized the Egyptian president. Operating in Lebanon under the command of Wadi Hadad, the PFLP began attacking Israeli airliners in 1968. In 1970, the group staged four hijackings in a six-day period; three of the planes were destroyed in the Jordanian desert in front of international media. Because the PFLP was closely linked to Arafat's Fatah, the Jordanians drove Arafat from their territory in September 1970. In 1975, it allied with Carlos the Jackal, a Latin American terrorist, and the Red Army Faction, a left-wing terrorist group in Germany, to attack an oil ministers' conference in Vienna. Although the PFLP has been successful at times, it has been riddled with factionalism. The first splits came in 1968 and 1969 when Ahmed Jabril and George Habash broke from the PFLP. Wadi Hadad left the organization in 1976 when the Palestine National Council disavowed the use of terrorism outside the vicinity of Israel and the territories it occupied. He formed the Popular Front for the Liberation of Palestine, General Command, but died in 1978. Habash returned to the PFLP in 1976 and directed the campaign against Israel. He eventually reconciled with Fatah and handed leadership over to Abu Ali Mustafa in 2000. Mustafa was assassinated by the Israelis in August 2001. Ahmed Sadat, his successor, retaliated by killing an Israeli official. The PFLP has grown in stature since the al Aqsa Intifada.

Popular Front for the Liberation of Palestine, General Command (PFLP-GC): The PFLP was formed in 1967 when George Habash (1926–2008) agreed to ally his group with Ahmed Jabril's PLF. Habash, a Christian, assumed leadership of the group, but he soon clashed with the Syrian-oriented Jabril. Syria continued to court Jabril, and he broke from Habash in 1968 to form the PFLP-GC. The PFLP-GC advocates armed struggle with Israel; it became one of the most technically sophisticated organizations in the region. It originally operated from southern Lebanon with support from Syria. By the late 1980s, the PFLP-GC was following the lead of the Abu Nidal Organization and renting its services to various governments. Some analysts believe the group was behind various international airline bombings. The PFLP-GC has been eclipsed by suicide bombers since 2000, but Jabril is increasingly emphasizing religion. This places the PFLP-GC closer to jihadist groups, but it still remains one of the most technically sophisticated terrorist organizations in the area. Jabril has always favored military action over sensationalized terrorist events.

Tanzim Brigade: Claiming not to be directly involved in terrorism, the Tanzim Brigade is the militia wing of Fatah.

Self-Check ✓

> What factors led to the breakup of the Palestinian movement?
> How did Hezbollah become involved in the conflict?
> How and when was Hamas formed?

Hezbollah: Local and International

Hezbollah is one of the more enigmatic organizations in the Middle East due to the manner in which it was formed, its historical metamorphosis, and its desire to play a leading role in Lebanon's politics. It grew out of the 1979 Iranian Revolution and maintains close links with Iran. Some analysts argue that it is an instrument of Iranian foreign power, but others insist that Tehran does not and cannot control the organization (Perry, 2010, p. 143). A former U.S. deputy secretary of state referred to Hezbollah as the deadliest terrorist group in the world, and some officials link it to al Qaeda (Byman, 2006; Kaplan, 2003). Others note that Hezbollah suicide attacks peaked in 1985 and 1986, and al Qaeda has denounced the group (Perlinger, 2006). Although it is most frequently associated with violence in Lebanon and Israel, Hezbollah has an international wing believed to be based in Damascus. It also created the organizational style that jihadist groups such as the Egyptian Islamic Group, the Egyptian Islamic Jihad, the Armed Islamic Group in Algeria, and al Qaeda would use.

The Origins of Hezbollah

Hezbollah is a configuration of political actors from the 1979 Iranian Revolution and the Shi'ite community of southern Lebanon. Its roots can be traced to a desire to export revolutionary ideals from Iran and Shi'ite emancipation in Lebanon. The linkage of the two came through Syria's desire to build a relationship with Iran and to control politics in Lebanon. This configuration is complex but logical. The story begins in southern Lebanon after Israel's 1982 invasion.

Shi'ites dominated southern Lebanon. They thought the Israelis would free them from Christian and Sunni domination, but this did not happen. Augustus Norton (2009, p. 33) believes that young Lebanese Shi'ites would eventually have attempted to copy the Iranian Revolution without the Israeli invasion, but the attack made it inevitable.

The Israeli invasion of Lebanon created an unlikely alliance among Iran's **Revolutionary Guards,** secular Syrian Baathists, and southern Lebanese Shi'ites. Iran's foreign policy under the Ayatollah Khomeini's Revolutionary Guards was designed to spread religious revolutionary thought throughout the Muslim world. On the surface, the fervently religious Khomeini had little in common with the secular socialists in Syria, but the Syrians were supporting Shi'ites in southern Lebanon. When Israeli tanks rolled through southern Lebanon, they passed through Shi'ite villages, and the Revolutionary Guards begged the Ayatollah Khomeini for a chance to protect their fellow believers in Lebanon. Alawite Syria and Shi'ite Iran now had a common enemy.

Revolutionary Guards: the militarized quasi police force of the revolutionary government during the Iranian Revolution.

Both nations needed a surrogate to fight the Israelis. If Iran openly intervened in the Lebanese civil war (1975–1990), Israel or the United States might attack Iran. Syria also needed a proxy because its troops were no match for the IDF and, like Iran, it feared the United States. As Shi'ite militias resisted the Israeli invasion, religious leaders thought resistance should be based on faith and not on secular politics. The Revolutionary Guards joined with local Shi'ites to form confederated militia groups. The movement gradually became known as Hezbollah, or the Party of God (Harik, 2004, pp. 39–49).

They were not well organized at first (see Figure 9.1). Hezbollah began as a social movement gravitating around young Shi'ites ready to resist the Israelis. Initially, it was little more than an idea, but small unorganized groups began to fight. Their attacks

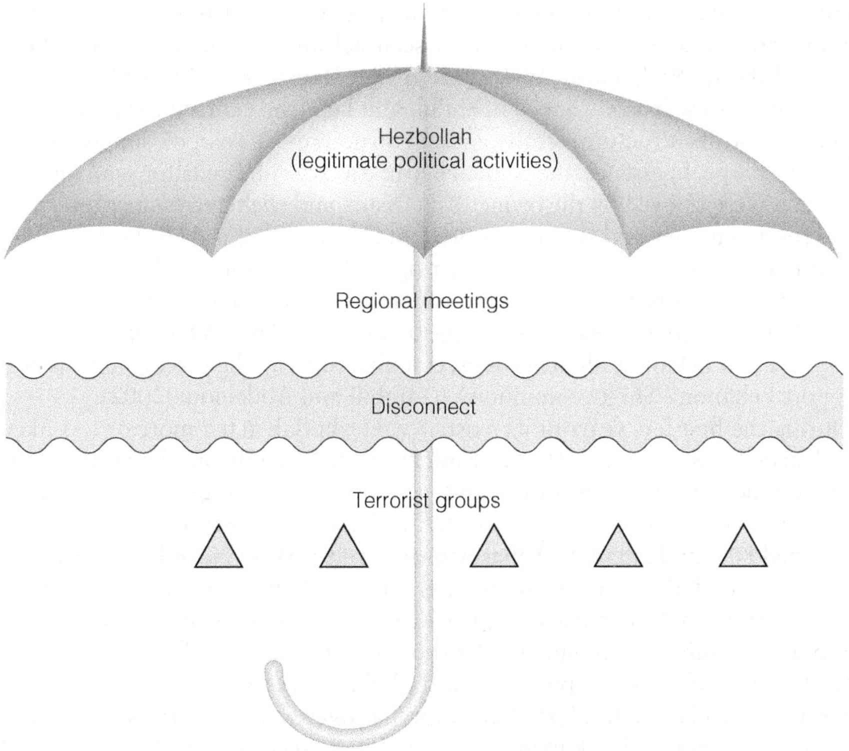

FIGURE **9.1** Hezbollah Umbrella, circa 1985

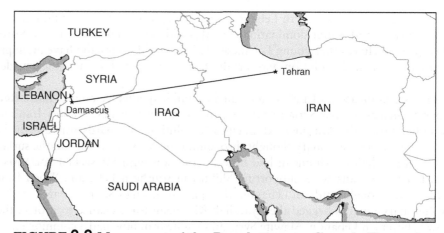

FIGURE **9.2** Movement of the Revolutionary Guards Through Syria to Lebanon, 1982

were characterized by extreme violence and heated rhetoric. It was the beginning of a metamorphosis (Azani, 2009, pp. 2–3, 47–48).

Iranian officials made contact with the Syrians in 1982. Promising reduced oil prices for Syria, the Iranians asked for permission to move 1,000 Revolutionary Guards from Syrian territory across its borders and into the Bekaa Valley in eastern Lebanon. The Revolutionary Guards made connections with the emerging Hezbollah and provided the Lebanese Shi'ite group with money, weapons, and training. Both Syria and Iran wanted to maintain their distance, and the religious leaders of Hezbollah wanted to deny any affiliation with military action. As a result, Hezbollah became a terrorist organization like one no one had ever seen before (see Hiro, 1987, pp. 113–181, 240–243; Taheri, 1987; Kurz, 1994; Wege, 1994; Ranstorp, 1994, 1996).

Hezbollah grew from a council of Shi'ite scholars who claimed to be part of a spiritual movement. Its structure—really, lack of structure—developed simply because no one was in charge. In essence, the council became a large umbrella for semiautonomous groups that were buoyed by the council's charisma and sheltered by its protection. Syrian and Iranian money and supplies poured into the council, and Hezbollah denied any direct connection with the network gathering under its umbrella. Below the umbrella, several Shi'ite cells operated autonomously and received money, weapons, and ideas through hidden channels linked to the spiritual leaders. The leadership also formed alliances with two Lebanese Shi'ite groups, claiming to be a religious movement designed to support Lebanon's Shi'ite community (Gambill and Abdelnour, 2002).

During the first few years of its existence, Hezbollah acted more or less like a terrorist clearinghouse (Reuters, 1996; Azani, 2009, p. 47). Influenced by Iran, Hezbollah met as an independent organization and was always willing to deny its Iranian connections. Hezbollah developed under the leadership of three central figures: **Sheik Mohammed Hassan Fadlallah, Abbas Musawi,** and **Hassan Nasrallah** (Norton, 2009, pp. 33–35). Fadlallah, the target of an attempted U.S.-sponsored assassination, was a charismatic spiritual leader. Musawi provided the loose connections to Iran. Nasrallah was a practical militarist, organizing Hezbollah into a regional force.

In phase one of the development of Hezbollah, from 1982 to 1985 (see Timeline 9.1, "Phases of Hezbollah"), the Hezbollah umbrella covered many terrorist groups, including a shadowy organization known as Islamic Jihad. According to Amir Taheri (1987),

Sheik Mohammed Hassan Fadlallah: (1935–2010) A grand ayatollah and leader of Shi'ites in Lebanon. The spiritual leader of Hezbollah. He was the target of a 1985 U.S.-sponsored assassination plot that killed 75 people.

Abbas Musawi: (1952–1992) A leader of Hezbollah who was killed with his family in an Israeli attack in 1992.

Hassan Nasrallah: (b. 1960) The secretary general of Hezbollah. He took over the leadership of Hezbollah after Musawi's death in 1992. Nasrallah is a lively speaker and charismatic leader.

TIMELINE 9.1	*Phases of Hezbollah*	
1982–1985, Organizing	Different groups carry out attacks under a variety of names.
1985–1990, Kidnapping and bombing	A terrorist organization is created.
1990–2000, Legitimacy	The group organizes social services, a political party, and a military wing.
2000–2004, Coalition	Hezbollah forms temporary alliances with others in the September 2000 Palestinian uprising against Israel (the al Aqsa Intifada).
July 2006	Israel launches an offensive in Lebanon.
August 2006	Israel withdraws, and Hezbollah claims victory.
September 2006	Iran begins to rebuild the Lebanese infrastructure.

Hezbollah leaders met in the city of Baalbek in Lebanon's Bekaa Valley and issued vague "suggestions" to Islamic Jihad. They also provided financial and logistical support for terrorist operations but kept themselves out of the day-to-day affairs of the terrorist group. By keeping their distance, Hezbollah's leaders were able to claim that they had no direct knowledge of Islamic Jihad. More important, though, they were able to keep Iran from being directly linked to Islamic Jihad's terrorist campaign against Israel and the West. The tactic was successful, and other groups formed under the umbrella.

After 1985, Hezbollah began to change. As part of an organization designed to spread the Shi'ite revolution, Hezbollah was not content to act only as an umbrella group to support terrorism (Enteshami, 1995; Reuters, 1996). Its leaders wanted to develop a revolutionary movement similar to the one that gripped Iran in 1978 and 1979. Lebanon was inundated with several militias fighting for control of the government, and Nasrallah saw an opportunity. Following the pattern of the Amal militia, he began changing the structure of Hezbollah. In 1985, he established regional centers, transforming them into operational bases between 1987 and 1989.

After introducing suicide bombers in its initial phase, Hezbollah struck the U.S. Marine Corps and the French Army units based in Beirut on October 23, 1983, forcing the withdrawal of a multinational peacekeeping force. The bombing of the marine barracks resulted in the deaths of 200 marines, and a second suicide bomber killed 50 French soldiers. In its second phase, Hezbollah's leadership launched a kidnapping campaign in Beirut. Westerners, especially Americans, were taken hostage, but Hezbollah, as always, denied any affiliation with the group conducting the operation.

Tactics were extremely effective in the first two phases. Suicide actions and other bombings disrupted Lebanon. The U.S. embassy was targeted for a bomb attack, and Hezbollah managed to kill the top six CIA operatives in the Middle East. Two of Hezbollah's kidnappings were simply designed to murder the victims. Hezbollah kidnapped, tortured, and murdered the CIA station chief in Beirut, as well as a marine colonel working for the United Nations. Judith Harik (2004, p. 37) points out that no evidence directly linked Hezbollah to these actions, and the group denied links to terrorism as they denounced terrorism as a tactic. This strategy made the group extremely effective.

The third phase of Hezbollah's metamorphosis came in 1990. Taking over the organization after the death of Musawi, Nasrallah created a regional militia by 1990. In 1991, many of Lebanon's roving paramilitary groups signed a peace treaty, but Hezbollah retained its weapons and revolutionary philosophy and became the primary paramilitary force in southern Lebanon. It claimed to be a legitimate guerrilla force resisting the Israeli occupation of the area. Hezbollah's militia, however, soon found itself in trouble. Squabbling broke out among various groups, and Hezbollah was forced to fight Syria and Islamic Amal. Diplomatic pressure increased for the release of hostages. Nasrallah took bold steps in response. He sought peace with the Syrians, and with Syrian approval, Western hostages were gradually released. Far from claiming responsibility for the hostages, both Hezbollah and Syria claimed credit for gaining their freedom. Hezbollah's militia began to operate in the open, and it stepped up its campaign against the Israelis in Lebanon. This made the organization popular among Lebanese citizens and gave the group the appearance of a guerrilla unit (see Azani, 2009, pp. 105–135).

Nasrallah had one more trump card. With the blessing of fellow council members, Hezbollah joined the Lebanese political process. Hezbollah's fourth phase brought the organization out of the shadows. Its militia, operating as a guerrilla force, repeatedly struck the Israelis in Lebanon. The success of this action brought political payoffs, and by 1995, Hezbollah had developed strong political bases of support in parts of Beirut, the Bekaa Valley, and its stronghold in southern Lebanon. It created a vast organization of social services, including schools, hospitals, and public works. This final change worked. In 1998, Hezbollah won a number of seats in the Lebanese parliament while maintaining control of the south. When Palestinians rose up against the Israelis in 2000, Hezbollah embraced their cause, and its transformation was complete (see the preceding feature titled "Another Perspective: Nasrallah's Management of Image"). It was a nationalistic group with a military wing, and its stated goals were to eliminate Israel and to establish an Islamic government in Lebanon.

Mark Perry (2010, pp. 141–162) questions conventional approaches to Hezbollah. He argues that the United States bases its view of Hezbollah on stereotypes. Its political leaders do not deny that they manage an armed group, but they claim no responsibility for the kidnappings and bombings of the 1980s. Leaders also admit that they are

ANOTHER PERSPECTIVE

Nasrallah's Management of Image

What is Hezbollah? Judith Harik (2004) says the answer to this question depends on the audience. For the four audiences below, Hassan Nasrallah has four different answers.

1. *Jihadists:* He uses militant language and speaks of holy war.
2. *Nationalists:* He avoids jihad analogies and calls on Sunnis, Shi'ites, Christians, and secularists to fight for Lebanon.

3. *Pan-Arabic:* He points to Israel as a colony of the West and denounces Europe's imperial past.
4. *International:* He cites UN resolutions and claims that Israel violates international law.

Harik concludes that this is not the pattern of an intolerant religious fanatic. Instead, this ability to compromise for various purposes demonstrates Nasrallah's political skills.

allied with Iran, yet Hezbollah is distinctively Lebanese. After Hezbollah forced Israel to retreat from Lebanon in 2006, its popularity soared. Its goal is to become a force in Lebanese politics.

Hezbollah's Operational Capabilities

By the end of the twentieth century, Hezbollah had become one of the strongest non-state groups in the Middle East (Ranstorp, 1994). It became the most technologically sophisticated nonstate actor in the first decade of the twenty-first century (Perry, 2010, p. 162). Its leaders are associated with the Shi'ite seminary in Najaf, Iraq. It is organized in three directorates: a political wing, a social services wing, and a security wing (see Figure 9.3). A separate international group, Hezbollah International, operates outside the domestic structure (J. Goldberg, 2002). Its former leader, master terrorist **Imad Mugniyah**, was killed in Damascus in 2008. A weak Lebanese government allows Hezbollah to maintain strongholds in southern Lebanon, the Bekaa Valley, and central pockets in Beirut. Each directorate is subservient to the Supreme Council, which is currently headed by Hassan Nasrallah.

Most of Hezbollah's activities deal with the politics of Lebanon and the vast social service network it maintains in the south. The security wing is based in Lebanon and is responsible for training guerrillas and terrorists. (Supporters of Hezbollah do not make a distinction between *guerrilla* and *terrorist*.) Guerrillas are assigned to militias that operate along Israel's northern border, especially in the **Shaba farm region**. These paramilitary fighters frequently conduct operations in the open, and they engage in conventional military confrontations with the IDF. Hezbollah can maintain all of these operations because it receives funding from Iran.

Terrorists also operate along the border with and sometimes inside Israel, engaging in murder and kidnapping. Although Israel is their acknowledged enemy, Hezbollah terrorists have also targeted Lebanese Christians and other Arabs unsympathetic to their cause. The primary terrorist tactic is bombing, and Hezbollah has mastered two forms: suicide bombing and radio-controlled bombs for ambushes. Gilles Kepel (2004, p. 34), a specialist in French and Middle Eastern terrorism, believes Hezbollah suicide bombings are directly related to the Shi'ite emphasis on martyrdom.

Hezbollah's international branch appears to have three major functions. (1) In Europe and in the United States, Hezbollah raises money to support operations (*United States of America v. Mohamad Youseff Hammoud et al.*, 2002). (2) Iran uses Hezbollah as an extension of its own power. Hezbollah protects Iranian interests in Lebanon and projects an Iranian-influenced military presence in other parts of the Middle East. Hezbollah also acts as a buffer between Iran and Israel (Byman, 2003). (3) Hezbollah has established a strong presence in South America. It uses this base to raise funds through legitimate and illegitimate methods, conduct propaganda, and launch terrorist operations. Should the United States and Iran ever enter a war, South American members of Hezbollah plan to attack the United States (Gato and Windrem, 2007).

According to Jeffery Goldberg (2002), then writing for the *New Yorker*, Hezbollah International is a shadowy group, and the Supreme Council denies its existence. The international section has cells in several different countries, including the United States, and maintains an extensive international finance ring partially based on smuggling, drugs, and other criminal activity. Imad Mugniyah kept close ties with operatives in the Triborder region and Ciudad del Este (see Chapter 3) and also ran a terrorist training camp off the coast of Venezuela. Mugniyah met with al Qaeda, possibly Osama bin Laden, in the mid-1990s and allegedly taught al Qaeda terrorists methods for attacking buildings.

Imad Mugniyah: (1962–2008) The leader of the international branch of Hezbollah. He has been implicated in many attacks, including the 1983 U.S. Marine and French Army bombings in Beirut. He is also believed to have been behind bombings of the U.S. embassy in Beirut and two bombings of Israeli targets in Argentina. He was assassinated in Damascus in February 2008.

Shaba farm region: A small farming region in southwest Lebanon that was annexed by Israel in 1981. When Israel withdrew from southern Lebanon in 2000, it remained in the Shaba farm region, creating a dispute with Lebanon, Hezbollah, and Syria.

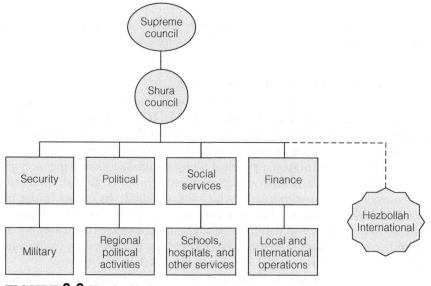

FIGURE **9.3** Hezbollah

Scott Macleod (2008) of *Time* has no doubt that Mugniyah was a deadly terrorist. According to one former CIA agent Macleod interviewed, he was one of the worst the United States has ever faced. The links to Hezbollah are not as clear. Mugniyah certainly had some type of contact with Hezbollah, though the extent of it is unknown. Hezbollah's leaders deny any involvement in Mugniyah's activities. Perhaps he was one of the autonomous operators working independently from the leadership council in Hezbollah's early days. Most analysts do not accept this. They believe that he headed Hezbollah's international wing.

In 2006, Israel launched a month-long attack against Hezbollah in Lebanon and was surprised by the results. Far from operating as a small terrorist organization, Hezbollah fielded thousands of fighters and recruited more. Regardless of its international wing, Hezbollah has transmogrified into a militia capable of fighting one of the strongest military powers in the region. By most estimates, Hezbollah has emerged with strategic and political victory (Cordesman, 2006; Matthews, 2008; and Lindeman, 2010).

Anthony Cordesman (2006) conducted an analysis of the 2006 campaign and says the Israelis entered Lebanon with several specific goals, including:

• Neutralizing Hezbollah's effectiveness before Iran could develop nuclear weapons
• Countering the IDF's image after the 2000 Lebanon and 2005 Gaza withdrawals
• Forcing Lebanon to control Hezbollah
• Rescuing two Israeli soldiers without a prisoner exchange

Writing soon after the war ended, Cordesman cautions that immediate conclusions are often inaccurate. Given that reservation, Israel appeared to achieve only modest objectives, although many Israeli officers thought that the operation had been successful.

The IDF made several mistakes. Matt Mathews (2008), in a review for the U.S. Army, believes that Israel prepared for the war incorrectly. It followed an American doctrine of destroying the enemy's ability to fight with precision weapons and air power, but it did not adequately plan for a ground offensive after the initial strikes. Cordesman (2006) adds that the Israelis had prepared for a strike against terrorists only to find that they had been fighting a more conventional war. They also lost much sympathy due to multiple strikes on civilian targets. In *Infantry* magazine, Yousef Aboul-Enein (2008), of the U.S. Navy, notes that Hezbollah spent years studying the tactics of superior military forces. When the IDF attacked, Hezbollah was able to disperse and hold its ground.

The most important aspect of the 2006 war was the political perception of the results. After years of countering Hezbollah and other groups, the Israelis came to believe that terrorists were weak against a military onslaught. Hezbollah was the aggressor, having fired rockets into Israel in the months prior to the attack, and Israel sought to end this. That did not turn out to happen, as Israel lost sympathy because much of the international community believed that its actions were far out of proportion to the damage it received. In the end, Israel's military forces were not defeated, but the operation was a failure (Harel and Issacharoff, 2008). Hezbollah managed the media's images of the war and set back Israel's strategy to normalize relations with its neighbors (Lamloum, 2009).

After the 2006 war, support for Hezbollah grew to an all-time high. Far from seeking to topple the Lebanese government, supporters maintain that Hezbollah's objective is to become a dominant political force in a coalition of Lebanese political parties (Perry, 2010, pp. 143–145). The Shi'ites inside Lebanon strongly support Hezbollah. They see it as a defensive force but believe its religious base embeds the group in the community. One survey of the 2006 war reported that Lebanon's Shi'ites stood with Hezbollah against Israel. It also found that they would resist the Lebanese government if it tried to disarm Hezbollah's military wing (Haddad, 2006).

The U.S. Department of State (2004b) summarizes: Hezbollah is a deadly international terrorist organization that has developed international links and uses international crime to finance its operations. Its primary sponsor is Iran, and it receives secondary support from Syria—nations that are listed as state sponsors of terrorism. In addition to its murders of Israelis, Hezbollah has killed U.S. citizens and kidnapped and tortured Americans. The State Department previously saw Hezbollah as a group of international murderers, and the view has not changed (U.S. State Department, 2015).

Hezbollah was also involved in the 1985 hijacking of a TWA flight, during which an American was murdered, and two bombings in Argentina in 1992 and 1994. It has been responsible for a campaign of suicide bombings, the murders of Lebanese Christians, international arms smuggling, and a host of international criminal activities, including crimes in the United States.

The future of Hezbollah changed with the Syrian civil war. Bashir Assad, who is fighting to keep power, belongs to the Alawite sect of Islam, and its beliefs are closely related to Shi'a theology. When the war broke out, Hezbollah sent fighters to support Assad. When ISIS formed in 2014, Iraqi Shi'ite militia joined the fray in Iraq with open support from Iran. The United States began operations against ISIS in 2014 and were joined by a coalition of European and Arab nations. Iran rejected the coalition, but Hezbollah, the United States, and Iran oppose the same enemy.

✓ Self-Check

> What circumstances gave rise to Hezbollah, and how did the group change over time?
> What are Hezbollah's current operational abilities?
> What impact has the Syrian civil war had on Hezbollah?

Hamas and the Rise of Sunni Religious Organizations

Arab nationalism: The idea that the Arabs could create a European-style nation based on a common language and culture. The idea faded after the 1967 Six-Day War.

Arab nationalism grew through the early part of the twentieth century and flourished until the June 1967 Six-Day War. Groups spawned from Fatah and independent organizations like the PIJ began their activities by embracing some form of nationalism. Before Abu Nidal degenerated into mercenary activities, he favored Arab socialism as a form of nationalism. In the 1970s and 1980s, Baathist nationalists in Syria and Iraq also believed in socialism. Adeed Dawisha (2003, pp. 253–280) points out that nationalism ultimately failed. It did not unite the Arabs, nor did it raise their standard of living. As nationalism waned, religious fervor took its place. The PIJ began using religious imagery, and other groups were born from religious fervor.

An Overview of Hamas

Ahmed Yassin: (1937–2004) One of the founders and leaders of Hamas. Yassin originally started the Palestinian Wing of the Muslim Brotherhood but merged it into Hamas during the first Intifada. He was killed in an Israeli-targeted assassination.

The story of Hamas is tied to the late Sheik **Ahmed Yassin** (1938-2004). Yassin grew up in Gaza under the influence of the Muslim Brotherhood. He believed that Islam was the only path that could restore Palestine, and he preached reform and social welfare. Many Palestinians in Gaza began to follow Yassin's powerful call. When he told followers to secretly gather weapons in 1984, they obeyed, but it cost him his freedom. The Israelis discovered Yassin's plans and jailed him. He was released in 1986 and decided that in the future, his organization would have a military wing. The Palestinian Muslim Brothers would become the nucleus of Hamas (Institute for Counter-Terrorism, 2004).

Hamas was formed in December 1987 at the beginning of the first Intifada (Isseroff, 2004). Yassin was disappointed with the secular direction of the PLO and wanted to steer the resistance movement along a religious course. Several technically trained university graduates—engineers, teachers, and Islamic scholars—joined the movement. They published the Hamas Charter in 1988, declaring that Palestine was a God-given land, from the Jordan River to the Mediterranean. There could be no compromise with the Israelis, and Israel could not be allowed to exist. Unlike Arafat's PLO, Hamas would fight Israel with religious zeal. Unlike the PIJ, Hamas would be much more than a military organization. It would be a Muslim government, the forerunner of a Palestinian Muslim state (Levit, 2006, pp. 17–18, 30–32).

Izz el Din al Qassam Brigades: The military wing of Hamas, named after the Arab revolutionary leader Sheik Izz el Din al Qassam (1882–1935), who led a revolt against British rule.

Hamas's organization reflects this original charter (Hamas, 1988), maintaining a political wing to oversee internal and foreign relations. Its largest unit, especially in Gaza, is its social wing. According to the third pillar of Islam, *Zakat*, Muslims are to give alms and share with the poor. Hamas runs charities, schools, hospitals, and other social service organizations in Gaza, where unemployment is sometimes as high as 85 percent. These social services have made Hamas popular among the Palestinians. Hamas's military wing, the **Izz el Din al Qassam Brigades**, is named after a martyr from the time of the British occupation of Palestine.

Hamas's relationship with the PLO and the PA has been shaky (Westcott, 2000). The reason can be traced to its religious orientation. Although Yassin and his followers vowed never to use violence against fellow Palestinians, they have always opposed Arafat.

Musa Abu Marzuq: (b. 1951) The "outside" leader of Hamas. He is thought to be in Damascus, Syria. He is believed to have controlled the Holy Land Foundation.

Struggles for Leadership

After the first Intifada, Hamas faced an internal power struggle. Yassin was jailed from 1989 to 1997, and during that time, the American-educated **Musa Abu Marzuq** took over Hamas. His strategy was much more violent than Yassin's had been. He also sought financial backing from Syria and Iran in an attempt to assert greater power in the organization. He assembled a new leadership core and based it in Jordan, leading others to call it the "outside" leadership, in contrast to Yassin' "inside" leadership group, which believed the struggle should remain inside Palestine (Levitt, 2002, pp. 34–37).

Marzuq's leadership also caused a struggle with the Palestinian Authority (PA; Institute for Counter-Terrorism, 2004). In 1996, Marzuq authorized a campaign of suicide bombing inside Israel. The PIJ launched one at the same time, and both campaigns continued into 1997. They were especially savage, targeting civilians and public places. Bombs were designed to kill, cripple, and maim. Some bombs were even laced with rat poison to cause wounds to continue bleeding after treatment. Israel gave Arafat an ultimatum: Crack down on Hamas, or Israel would. The PA arrested a number of Hamas's leaders, and Marzuq's offensive waned.

After Yassin was released from prison in 1997, he gradually reasserted control over Hamas, even though he remained under house arrest. He moved operations back to the Gaza Strip. Violence continued up until 2000 but was slowly decreasing. Leaders of the al Qassam Brigades were incensed at the decrease, claiming that both the inside and outside leadership were placing too much attention on political solutions (see Levitt, 2002, pp. 33–51). In the meantime, Jordanian officials closed Hamas operations in Amman, and the outsiders who could avoid arrest fled to Syria. By 2000, some observers believed a lasting peace might be at hand. They were disappointed (Karman, 2000; Wikas, 2002). The al Aqsa Intifada started in September of that year.

The al Aqsa Intifada

It is hard to overstate the effect of the al Aqsa Intifada on Hamas. Quarreling between the al Qassam leaders and the political wing came to a standstill. Moderates and hardliners drew closer together. As the IDF swarmed into Palestinian areas, Arafat's makeshift government, the PNA, lost much of its power. Hamas, therefore, had the opportunity to assert its muscle. The distinction among the various Palestinian forces began to blur, and Hamas grew stronger by forming alliances with Hezbollah and the PIJ. It then joined the largest suicide bombing campaign the Middle East had ever seen.

In the summer of 2003, PA prime minister **Mahmud Abbas** brokered a limited cease-fire, asking Hamas, the PIJ, and related groups to end their campaigns. However, the peace effort ended in August after a suicide bombing on a bus in Jerusalem. The Israelis responded by renewing a policy of selective assassination; that is, they identified leaders of Hamas and systematically murdered them (see the feature titled "Expanding the Concept: Israeli Selective Assassination" later in this chapter). Hamas passed another milestone in the campaign against Israel: It used a female suicide bomber in a joint operation with a newer group, the al Aqsa Martyrs Brigades (J. Stern, 2003a). Hamas had followed the lead of the Liberation Tigers of Tamil Eelam (LTTE), the Kurdistan Workers' Party, and the Chechen rebels, who also had used female suicide bombers.

Mahmud Abbas: (b. 1935) The president of the Palestinian Authority since 2005, a founding member of Fatah, and an executive in the PLO.

Seeking Election

In March 2004, Yassin was leaving a mosque in Gaza when Israeli helicopters appeared and fired three missiles at him. He met the fate of other Hamas leaders before him and was killed instantly. Hamas announced his replacement, **Abdel Aziz Rantisi,** an old member of the inside faction. However, the Israelis assassinated Rantisi in the same manner, shortly after he took office. A new leader was appointed, but Hamas kept his identity secret (Oliver, 2004; Keinon, 2004).

Abdel Aziz Rantisi: (1947–2004) One of the founders of Hamas along with Ahmed Yassin. He took over Hamas after Israeli gunships assassinated Yassin. He, in turn, was assassinated by the Israelis a month after taking charge.

Khalid Meshal: (b. 1956) One of the "outside" leaders of Hamas, in Damascus, Syria. He became the political leader of Hamas in 2004. After the 2006 election, he continued to lead in exile.

Muqtada al Sadr: (b. 1974) An Iraqi militant and son of a renowned Shi'ite scholar. Al Sadr leads the Shi'ite militia known as the Mahdi Army.

Some analysts believed the new leader was **Khalid Meshal**, an outsider operating from Damascus. At first, this suggested that Hamas would change its focus from Israel to the global jihad because the outside leadership had a larger perspective (Lake, 2004). Analysts looked at two Hamas communiqués issued in August 2004 as U.S. and Iraqi forces battled the Shi'ite militia of **Muqtada al Sadr** in Najaf, Iraq. In the midst of the battle, Hamas's first communiqué condemned the United States for fighting around Najaf, the site of a Shi'ite holy shrine, and it called on all Iraqi people to band together to defeat America. The second statement was different; it called on all Iraqis to support the militia of Muqtada al Sadr. This was stunning, as Sunnis from the Muslim Brotherhood would be unwilling to support a Shi'ite militia in defense of a Shi'a shrine. Evidence indicated that Hamas had undergone some type of internal transformation (Paz, 2004).

Hamas had indeed undergone a transformation, and Khaled Meshal was its new leader, but few were prepared for the impact that this would have on the PA. The transformation began after the 1993 Oslo Accords and the growing disillusionment with Fatah. Despite Arafat's domination of Palestinian politics, Fatah was a corrupt organization. Arafat received millions of dollars from supporters and through international aid, and he doled out funds like a big-city political boss. The majority of the money went to local political leaders instead of to needy Palestinians. Even when the PA seemed to be on the verge of achieving independence, Fatah functioned by its familiar corrupt rules, and it continued to do so after Arafat's death (McGreal, 2006). When elections were slated for 2006, Palestinians were given the opportunity to select a new parliament. They voted Fatah out of power in January, and Hamas won the election.

Hamas Versus Fatah

Hamas controlled the majority of seats in the Palestinian parliament, while Mahmud Abbas retained the presidency. This set the stage for a confrontation between Hamas and Fatah. Tension festered between the rival groups after the election, and Meshal continued to lead Hamas in exile. In Syria, he was free for international travel and fund-raising, something that he could not have accomplished from Gaza, where Israeli restrictions would have limited his movements. This benefited Hamas, ironically, because Meshal's new government needed money. The United States and the European Union refused to recognize Hamas's victory, stating that they would neither support nor discuss settlements with a terrorist organization. They cut off all aid to the PA, which increased bitter feelings between Hamas and Fatah.

Disheartened by the split in Palestinian leadership, Saudi Arabia brokered a power-sharing arrangement between Hamas and Fatah. It was a tenuous agreement, and the United States and the European Union still refused to restore foreign aid to the PA. That brought matters further along. Hamas and Fatah never really considered themselves full partners, and violent skirmishes between the two groups broke out in November 2006. According to news reports, several Arab nations restored peace, but intermittent assaults and counterassaults continued into the summer of 2007. All pretense of power sharing broke down in June when Hamas openly attacked Fatah's strong points in Gaza. Fatah responded by forcibly closing all Hamas offices on the West Bank, but Hamas grew stronger in Gaza. By June 15, Hamas had driven Fatah from Gaza, and Abbas had dissolved the government. He formed a new parliament and cabinet, excluding Hamas. The United States and the European Union restored foreign aid to the West Bank, but Hamas controlled Gaza despite Abbas's actions. Over 200 Palestinians were killed in the fighting (Fisher, 2007).

Rockets and Operation Cast Lead

Meshal wasted no time taking advantage of the new base in Gaza. According to the Council on Foreign Relations (2009), Meshal wanted to attack Israel. In the past, Hamas had relied on suicide bombers—Meshal called them the F-16s of the Palestinians—but control of Gaza gave them a geographical base. They began launching homemade rockets across the border into Israel.

On December 27, 2008, Israel kicked off Operation Cast Lead, a devastating air and artillery assault on Gaza, followed by a ground invasion on January 3, 2009. According to news reports, several nations condemned the Israeli incursion, and the United States urged Israel to show restraint (Patriquin, 2009). Supporters of Israel were infuriated, stating that Israel had a right to defend itself. They asked why there had been no international outcry against Hamas's rocket attacks. Critics emerged, the supporters argued, only when Israel took steps to defend its borders (R. Freedman, 2009). Israel maintained the attack for 22 days, destroying munitions and supplies. It also targeted underground tunnels that Hamas used to bring in military stores. The fighting caused hundreds of casualties.

Controversy over the invasion centered on proportionality. Anthony Cordesman (2009) said that the strategic results might eventually be questionable but that the tactical results were clear. Faced with rocket attacks, Israel responded with overwhelming military force. This temporarily eradicated Hamas's military capability while ensuring that Israeli troops suffered only minimal casualties during the fighting. Such a strategy exacts a high humanitarian toll, Cordesman argues, but it reflects legitimate military action. In addition, it was a tactical success.

George Bisharat and colleagues (Bisharat et al., 2009), writing for an American law journal, argues that the Israeli response was illegal under international law. Two primary factors weigh against Israel. Even though the military response was designed to be overwhelming, the massive response produced hundreds of civilian casualties. In addition, Israel effectively occupied the Gaza Strip. It withdrew from the region in 2005, but it controlled the entry and exit of people and provisions. Such control, Bisharat says, made Israel legally responsible for protecting all the residents of Gaza. The response to Hamas's attacks should have been measured.

Unity?

Despite its turbulent history, Hamas and the Palestinian National Authority reached a compromise in 2014. Both sides agreed to form a unity government. A *Washington Post* report points out some of the sticking points (Booth and Gearan, 2014). Although negotiations between the Palestinian Authority and Israel broke down in 2015, both sides at least discussed the possibility of creating a Palestinian state and a lasting peace. Hamas rejects Israel's right to exist, and if that stand remains unchanged, it might shut the door on future negotiation. The United States lists Hamas as a U.S. State Department Foreign Terrorist Organization (FTO). The implications for its support of the Palestinian Authority are unclear. Israel's political leadership stated flatly that it would not deal with a government that includes terrorists.

The results of unity are unknown as of this writing. Fatah and Hamas fought a brief but vicious civil war in 2007. Other extremist groups operate in the Gaza Strip, and they would like to replace Hamas. An ISIS-related movement started in the same area in 2015, and Sunnis are killing Sunnis. There are many contradictory factors at play. It is possible that both sides may join a unity government, but the major question is: Will it last? That is a perpetual issue in a region filled political irony and changing allies.

Self-Check

> Why did religion merge with the Palestinian movement? How did Hamas obtain power in Gaza?
> Was Operation Cast Lead justified?
> Can there be any hope for peace with Hamas?

Fatah Restructured: The al Aqsa Martyrs Brigades

Suicide bombing became the most important tactic of all the Palestinian terrorist groups at the beginning of the al Aqsa Intifada in September 2000. Hezbollah, Hamas, and the PIJ were in the forefront, giving leadership to local religious groups. Fatah also became involved, but it continued in its secular orientation. Its two main forces were the politically oriented Force 17 and the Tanzim Brigade. Other Fatah splinter groups joined the Intifada, and although they resisted Arafat's control, they also steered clear of religion. This became a problem because local jihadists and religious terrorists dominated the al Aqsa Intifada (Shahar, 2002). If Fatah wanted to play a leading role, it had to move from the secular to the religious realm.

BBC News (2003) reports that Fatah has shown a newfound religious streak that comes from the grassroots of Palestinian society. The al Aqsa Brigades were formed to put Fatah at the center of the new Intifada. The Brigades began as a secular group, but they increasingly used jihadist rhetoric. They were also the first secular Palestinian group to use suicide tactics. Hezbollah, Hamas, and the PIJ do not recognize Israel's right to exist. This is not so with the Brigades. They claim their purpose is limited: Their goal is to stop Israeli incursions and attacks in Palestinian areas, and they intend to punish Israel for each attack. Whether this explanation is accepted or not, one thing is clear: The Brigades became the most potent Palestinian force in the al Aqsa Intifada.

Effective Tactics

The National Counterterrorism Center (2015) states that the tactics of the al Aqsa Martyrs Brigades have evolved over time. They were very active until 2005, but overall activity is difficult to assess for two reasons. First, the groups have splintered and operate autonomously. Some are active, and some are not. Second, the Martyrs Brigades participated in an Israeli amnesty program. Israel's frequent incursions in the West Bank have also deprived the Martyrs Brigades of some key leaders. They may have lost credibility.

In an early analysis the Council on Foreign Relations (2004) says the Martyrs Brigades promised that they would strike Israeli military targets only inside Palestinian territory. This practice was soon abandoned, however, and attacks moved into Israel proper. The Brigades' primary tactics have been drive-by shootings, sniper shootings, ambushes, and kidnap–murders. Yet, as with so many other terrorist groups, their most devastating tactic has been the use of suicide bombers. In a later report, the council reports that the Martyrs Brigades fired rockets into Israel in response to the deaths of two Palestinian teenagers (Danin, 2013).

Yael Shahar (2002) says that when the al Aqsa Martyrs Brigades suicide bombers were unveiled, they were frightening for two main reasons: They were secular, and they sought targets crowded with civilians. They delivered human bombs filled with antipersonnel material that were designed to inflict the maximum number of casualties. Their purpose was to kill and maim as many victims as possible in the most public way possible. Furthermore, as mentioned earlier, they used the first female suicide bomber in the Middle East on January 27, 2002, in conjunction with Hamas. They expanded their targets, and their casualties increased; after initially allowing the PIJ and Hamas to play the leading role in the rebellion, the Brigades moved to the forefront of the rebellion.

Leadership of the Martyrs Brigades

Leadership of the Brigades is a controversial topic. They seem to be directly associated with their parent group, Fatah, but it is unclear how their operations are directed and from where. One school of thought maintains that Arafat led and paid for the Brigades. Israeli intelligence claims that they have proof of Arafat's involvement. Shahar (2002) says that the IDF raided Arafat's headquarters in Ramallah in 2002 and captured PNA documents that show payments to various factions inside the Brigades, payments that were personally approved by Arafat. The Israelis say that Arafat may not have determined targeting and timing but that he paid the expenses and set the agenda.

Other investigations point to another conclusion. The Council on Foreign Relations (2004) believes that Arafat may have run the Brigades but admits that there may be another source of leadership. A BBC News (2003) investigation points to **Marwan Barghouti** (currently in Israeli custody) as the commander. A Palestinian spokesman, Hassan Abdel Rahman, says that the documents Israel seized in 2002 are false and claims that the Israelis planted them (Rothem, 2002). Arafat claimed that he knew nothing about the Brigades.

PBS's *Frontline* (2002) conducted an interview with a Palestinian leader codenamed Jihad Ja'Aire at the height of the first bombing campaign. Ja'Aire claimed that he and all of the other Brigades commanders were under Arafat's control. Arafat provided the direction, Ja'Aire said, and all the members obeyed him. This does not condemn Arafat, Ja'Aire pointed out, because the group operates with a different philosophy. If Israel had accepted the 1967 borders, that is, the borders before Israel added the West Bank and Gaza Strip after the Six-Day War, and stopped incursions into Palestinian areas, Arafat could have called off the attacks.

Whether Arafat had direct control of the Brigades remains a subject of debate, partly because of the way the Brigades are organized. Taking a cue from international jihadist groups, the al Aqsa Martyrs Brigades have little centralized structure. Their administration has been pushed down to the lowest operational level so that each unit might function almost autonomously. Cells exist in several Palestinian communities, and leaders are empowered to take action on their own without approval from a hierarchy. In addition, Israel has targeted the Brigades' leadership for selective assassination; nevertheless, the organization continues.

Beginning a Network

No matter where the leadership authority lies, the managerial relations within the Brigades remain a mystery, even to the Palestinians. In June 2004, some of the leading figures in the Palestinian territories formed the Fatah General Council to investigate the al Aqsa Martyrs Brigades and Arafat's relation to them. This enraged some in the Brigades because they believed that Arafat was manipulating the entire investigation. Claiming that Arafat had abandoned them, disgruntled members of the Brigades surrounded his house and threatened him. If Arafat controlled the Brigades, his hold may not have been very tight (Algazy, 2004).

Marwan Barghouti: (b. 1969) A leader of Fatah and alleged leader of the al Aqsa Martyrs Brigades. A Brigades statement in 2002 claimed that Barghouti was their leader. He rose to prominence during the al Aqsa Intifada, but he is currently being held in an Israeli prison.

The structure of the Brigades is testimony to Michael Scheuer's (2006) comments about the nature of modern terrorism, and it hearkens back to points made by Marc Sageman (2004). Although the leaders of the group are unknown, the Brigades have been effective even without centralized leadership. Their strength comes from the ability of small cells to operate without a strong leader. The Brigades have been effective because they operate within a network (MIPT, n.d.).

✓ **Self-Check**

> What started the al Aqsa Intifada?

> What tactics did terrorists use in the al Aqsa Intifada?

> Do the al Aqsa Martyrs Brigades unite the Palestinians in a common effort? Explain.

))) ANOTHER PERSPECTIVE

David's Kingdom and Israeli Settlements

Many supporters of Israel and a good number of Israeli peace activists do not favor expansion into Palestinian areas. Moshe Amon (2004) writes that although Israel is a secular democracy, it is being influenced by religious extremists. Ultraorthodox rabbis, he maintains, seek to conquer the biblical Kingdom of David. Jewish extremists, with the support of the state, have moved into Palestinian areas to establish permanent settlements. Many militants believe that when David's Kingdom is restored, every person on earth will follow the teachings of the God of Israel. Amon says some of the militants fight Israeli soldiers, and some of their leaders call for the murder of non-Jews. Amon believes this behavior threatens not only Israel's moral character but its very survival.

))) ANOTHER PERSPECTIVE

Controversial Tactics

Israel has engaged in tactics that have enraged the Palestinians and many others. Critics call these tactics Israeli terrorism. Defenders say that Israel has a right to protect itself. The United States almost always supports Israel, frequently using its veto power in the UN Security Council to keep the United Nations from condemning Israeli actions. Controversial tactics include:

• Destroying the homes of suicide bombers' families

• Selectively assassinating Palestinian leaders
• Killing innocents when striking militants
• Excessively using force
• Executing commando raids in neighboring countries
• Invading Lebanon in June 2006
• Invading Gaza in December 2008
• Blockading Gaza
• Violently intercepting ships in May 2010 during the Gaza blockade

EXPANDING THE CONCEPT

Israeli Selective Assassination

Israel targeted Hamas's leaders throughout the al Aqsa Intifada.

Person	Position	Israeli Action
Riyad Abu Zayd	Military commander	Ambush, February 2003
Ibrahim Maqadah	Military commander	Helicopter attack, May 2003
Abdullah Qawasmah	Suicide bomb commander	Ambush, June 2003
Ismail Shanab	Political leader	Bomb strike, August 2003
Sheik Ahmed Yassin	Head of Hamas	Helicopter attack, March 2004
Abdel Aziz Rantisi	Replaced Yassin	Helicopter attack, April 2004
Mahmud al Mabbuh	Political/military leader	Murdered in Dubai hotel, February 2010

Controversial Counterterrorist Policies

Many Israeli police and military units have established excellent reputations in counterterrorist operations. **Mossad**, the Israeli intelligence service, is known for its expertise. Shin Beth, the domestic Israeli security service, is one of the most effective secret police forces in the world. The IDF is an excellent fighting machine. The Israeli police know how to handle bombs, snipers, kidnappings, and everyday crime. The tactical operations of these units are second to none.

Mossad: The Israeli intelligence agency, formed in 1951. It is responsible for gathering foreign intelligence. Shin Beth is responsible for internal security.

Tactical operations, however, differ from policies. Governments decide the broad philosophy and practice of a policy, and tactical operations take place within the guidelines of long-term political goals. Policy involves a strategic view of a problem and the means to settle it. Unlike Israel's excellent tactical record, its counterterrorist policies have stirred international controversy (see *Another Perspective: Controversial Tactics*).

Bulldozing

When Israel first faced suicide bombings, the government implemented a controversial policy called *bulldozing*, whose purpose was to destroy the family homes of suicide bombers. If militant charities and governments were going to compensate families of martyrs, the Israelis reasoned, bulldozing homes would be more painful than the pleasure of economic reward. Soon, the homes of not only families but of suspected leaders in militant groups and others were targeted for bulldozing. In 2004, farms and other areas were bulldozed. The policy expanded to include clearing ground for military reasons and clearing space to build a security fence, that is, a wall separating Israel from Palestinian areas (*Palestine Monitor*, 2004; *The International New York Times*, 2004). Critics maintain that bulldozing is done to further Israel's self-interests.

Invading Lebanon

Judith Harik (2004, pp. 117–124) describes another controversial policy: punishing Lebanon for the sins of Hezbollah. As discussed earlier in the chapter, Israel launched its first invasion of Lebanon to rid the south of the PLO. That ended after an 18-year occupation and the creation of a new enemy, Hezbollah. In 1996, Israel launched a limited offensive in Lebanon to disrupt Hezbollah operations, and dozens of innocent Lebanese were killed in the process.

The Israelis responded with force again in July 2006. Israel was surprised when Hezbollah launched rockets into Israel while Hezbollah ground forces ambushed a military unit inside the borders of Israel. Israel launched an immediate attack, and then announced that it planned to destroy Hezbollah (al Jazeera, 2006). The IDF launched a massive series of strikes for nearly a month. Critics maintained that the operation was overkill. In a war that lasted nearly a month, hundreds of Lebanese civilians were killed, nearly a million Lebanese were displaced, and Lebanon's infrastructure was destroyed (*Daily Mail*, 2007; Chomsky, 2006; Salem, 2006).

The Wall

In an effort to stop Palestinian attacks, the government of Ariel Sharon proposed an idea that dates back to Hadrian of the Roman Empire. The Israelis began constructing a massive wall. On the surface, this might seem to be an uncontroversial issue, but the path of the wall grabbed the attention of the world. The concrete and barbed-wire barrier snaked through Palestinian areas, often putting water and other resources in the hands of the Israelis. It also separated people from services, jobs, and their families. Much of the international community condemned the wall (I. Black, 2003).

Selective Assassination

The most controversial aspect of Israel's counterterrorist policy is selective assassination. Israel has maintained a consistent policy against terrorism. When it is struck, it hits back hard. Israeli commandos and the IDF units have allegedly killed opposition leaders in the past, including Abu Jihad of the PLO and Fathi Shekaki of the PIJ, but the policy expanded during the al Aqsa Intifada when Israel began the wholesale assassination of Hamas leadership.

Reuven Paz (2004) questions the effectiveness of this policy, suggesting that it might internationalize the conflict. Left-wing political leaders in Israel deplore the policy, calling such assassinations "gangster murders" (Kafala, 2001). Human rights groups have condemned the policy and challenged it in Israeli courts (BBC News, 2002). Nations all over the world have condemned Israel for these targeted assassinations as well.

Daniel Byman (2006) defends the controversial policy, arguing that Israel's selective assassinations are publicly transparent. Each proposed attack must go through several stages, excluding legal review. The public is aware of the moral dilemma and various tradeoffs. Byman admits that the policy remains controversial, and says it would be stronger if the judiciary were involved in the process. It is important to note that Israeli deaths from terrorism have dropped since it began employing its controversial policy.

Charles Krauthammer (2004) reflects the feelings of those who support these controversial policies. Israel is under attack, he writes. Though the United Nations, for instance, condemned the security fence, Krauthammer maintains that its construction reduced suicide attacks. Many Israelis feel that harsh policies must be implemented to deter terrorism (Kafala, 2001). Furthermore, the United States has repeatedly taken the position that Israel cannot be condemned for harsh measures until the international community also denounces Palestinian terrorism.

Although supporters claim that Israel should be allowed to take the steps necessary for self-defense, the policies remain controversial. The important question to try to answer is, do harsh policies reduce terrorism or increase the cycle of violence? Thus far, the question remains unanswered, and violence continues from both sides of the fence.

✓ **Self-Check**	> Why might Israeli policies toward Lebanon be described as a failure?
	> Is collective punishment for terrorist violence effective?
	> Do retribution and intensive security measures stop terrorism? Explain.

Emphasizing the Points

The modern conflict between Israel and Palestine is based in terrorism. Fatah imitated the Irgun by using terrorist tactics, but the movement was not united. Palestinian militancy is characterized by factionalism. Terrorism moved to the international arena in the 1980s, but it has remained localized for the past three decades. The current major operational groups are Hezbollah, Hamas, and the al Aqsa Martyrs Brigades. Israeli policies are controversial. Critics claim the Israelis overreact. Defenders maintain that strong tactics are necessary to counter terror.

SUMMARY OF CHAPTER OBJECTIVES

- The pejorative meaning of the term *terrorism* is explosive in Israeli–Palestinian relations. Israel and its allies, especially the United States, have branded the militant groups opposing its statehood as terrorists. Palestinians and their supporters point to the disproportionate amount of force used by Israel in response to violence and refer to that as terrorism. The debate is distorted by extreme positions on both sides.
- Fatah began as a militant organization a decade after Israel's statehood. It absorbed and later dominated the PLO. Its leader, Yasser Arafat, tried to lead the entire resistance movement but was frustrated by numerous factions breaking away to form new terrorist groups.
- Many groups emerged from Fatah and the PLO, and the PLO even formed new groups it could control. The Fatah splinter groups included Abu Nidal Organization (Black June), al Aqsa Martyrs Brigades, Black September, DFLP, Force 17, PLF, PDFLP, PFLP, PFLP-GC, and Tanzim Brigades.
- The PIJ emerged from Egypt in the 1970s. It evolved into a religious organization with the philosophy that while religious law would be implemented after victory, the more immediate objective was the destruction of Israel. Several groups use *Islamic Jihad* in their names.
- Hezbollah is a Shi'ite group formed during the Lebanese civil war with Iranian backing. It evolved over time and currently has multiple functions, including a military wing. Israel, the United States, and many other Western countries call it a terrorist group. Many Muslim counties see it as a legitimate military force.
- Hezbollah has gone through distinct phases, moving from small terrorist operations in Lebanon to political and social action. It also created a defense force and successfully fought Israel in a 2006 war.
- Hamas emerged from the first Intifada. It embraced the principles of religious law and expressed disgust for the secular policies and corruption of the PLO.

It formed a large organization and mastered the art of suicide attacks. It opposes any peace with Israel, and its charter calls for the destruction of Israel.

- Hamas won control of the Palestinian government in 2006. Although the United States has refused to negotiate with Hamas, many people believe that Hamas will target neither the United States nor other Western countries.
- The al Aqsa Martyrs Brigades formed from Fatah, embracing religion and suicide attacks. There are many questions about its leadership. Currently, they operate within a network of independent cells having no central command structure.
- Israel has responded to terrorism with controversial policies. These include bulldozing, invasions of Lebanon, constructing a wall to separate Palestinians from Israelis, and targeted assassinations.

LOOKING INTO THE FUTURE

The future of Israel–Palestinian relations will be defined by Israel's willingness to recognize Palestinian statehood, its decision to either continue or suspend expanded settlements in Palestinian lands, and the ability of each side to control its political extremists. Israel will continue to attempt to strengthen ties with Jordan, Egypt, and Turkey. Doing so will not only give it important alliances, it will increase trade and diplomatic relations. Palestinian poverty and Israel's violations of human rights will continue to create political unrest. Access to water is crucial, and Israel currently controls it. Both sides must eventually reach a position of *realpolitik* to attain peace. Israel and the United States will not deal with Hamas because it is a terrorist group. Hamas rules in Gaza and has pledged to form a joint government with the Palestinian National Authority. The reality is that Hamas has morphed into a political organization with the power to govern, and governing involves realistic compromise. If Hamas wants peace, it must drop its demand for the eradication of Israel and work with the international community to meet the needs of the Palestinian people. Israel and the United States must recognize that Hamas has power and seek to engage its leadership, if they want to reduce tensions and improve social conditions.

There are two wild cards. The first is the Syrian civil war. The rise of ISIS has changed the dynamics of Israeli–Palestinian relations as well as the future of the entire region. The reality is that ISIS presents a threat to several international revivals. The main question for the future is: Will the enemy of my enemy become my friend? To date, the answer has been *no*. The second wild card is Israel's population bomb. Unless Israel forcefully displaces its Arab population, it will soon outnumber the Jewish population. Currently, many Arabs are treated as second-class citizens. Whether Arabs will be included or excluded as full citizens remains to be seen.

KEY TERMS

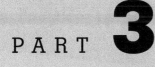

International Terrorism: Ideological and Religious Movements

Revolutionary and Counterrevolutionary Terrorism

LEARNING OBJECTIVES

After reading this chapter, you should be able to:

▶ Define revolutionary and counterrevolutionary terrorism.

▶ Outline the history, philosophy, and influence of the Tupamaros.

▶ Summarize the emergence and current status of FARC and the ELN.

▶ Describe the function and purpose of the MeK.

▶ Describe the rise, fall, and resurgence of the Shining Path.

▶ Outline the issues surrounding Naxalite terrorism.

▶ Explain the operations and tactics of the New People's Army.

▶ Explain the rise of death squads as a reaction to revolutionary terrorism.

LUIS ACOSTA/Getty Images

Civilians Train to Respond to Terrorism

Colombia has been one of the most violent areas of the world since the mid-twentieth century. It experienced a ferocious civil war simply known as The Violence from 1948 to 1958. Analysts estimated that The Violence killed between 200,000 and 300,000 people. Since 1964, the country has been plagued by a revolutionary guerrilla war involving violent political clashes, drug violence, left-wing revolutionary terrorism, and terrorism from right-wing paramilitaries and death squads. Recent fighting has caused the deaths of over 220,000 people, and millions more have been driven from their homes. One of the revolutionary groups, the Revolutionary Armed Forces of Colombia (known by the Spanish acronym FARC), upped the ante by planting hundreds of land mines. Many innocent people have been killed.

Savage fighting pitted Colombian security forces against FARC and other revolutionary groups. Colombia militarized its police and armed peasants in rural areas where FARC operated. This resulted in a "dirty war." FARC massacred villagers, especially Colombia's indigenous people who were thought to be loyal to the government. Security forces and civilian paramilitary units paid back in kind by murdering suspected revolutionaries. Murderous hatred reigned in Colombia.

Although there appeared to be no end to the fighting, an amazing thing happened in 2012. FARC agreed to enter negotiations with the government of Colombia in peace talks sponsored by Cuba and Norway. Fighting continued and discussions were lengthy, but after two years, talking seemed to be having an effect. Even as troops and guerrillas clashed in April 2015, FARC began mine clearing operations with the Colombian army in May. *Deutsche Welle* (2015) reported that this was a virtual miracle. The soldiers and guerrillas were not simply clearing mines in particular sections of the countryside; they were operating side-by-side in mixed units. Terrorism comes to an end when people who will compromise silence violent extremists who will not. If revolutions can be negotiated, peace may come to Colombia.

Revolutionary Terrorism

Modern revolutionary terrorism reached its zenith in the 1960s and 1970s. It was a global movement expressing dissatisfaction in the wake of anticolonialism. Western policy and the U.S. international economic system fell under intense scrutiny, and tensions caused by the Vietnam War fanned the flames of heated political behavior. Small ideological groups appeared in Central and South America, and revolutionary groups emerged in Europe. Guerrilla movements spawned ideological spin-offs. The East–West confrontation came into play as the former Soviet Union supported its own revolutionary groups while Maoist rebellions gave a new twist to old Leninist ideologies. Japan experienced unique forms of violence that combined ideology and religious elements.

Revolutionary and Counterrevolutionary Terrorism Defined

A common misconception is that the American Revolution was based on terrorism. If this were true, rebels would have indiscriminately murdered British citizens and clandestinely destroyed symbolic targets. General George Washington would not have fought to destroy the British army; he would have waged a campaign of symbolic murder in the hope that the horror of it all would change British political behavior. Instead, although many Americans operated as guerrillas, the majority of the rebels joined a conventional army and fought within the accepted norms of conventional warfare. Revolutions cannot be equated with terrorism, although terrorism is sometimes used during the course of revolutions.

When examining ideological terrorism, it is possible to broadly categorize a revolutionary style. Martha Crenshaw (1972), a pioneer in the field, summarized the aspects of revolutionary terrorism early in her career. She says that revolutionary terrorism can be defined as an insurgent strategy in the context of internal warfare or revolution. It is an attempt to seize power from a legitimate state for the purpose of creating political and social change. It involves the systematic use of terrorism to achieve this goal. Violence is neither isolated nor a series of random acts, and it is far from guerrilla warfare or conventional warfare. Revolutionary terrorism differs from other forms of violence because it occurs outside the normal realm of violent political action. It involves acts of violence that are particularly abominable, and it usually occurs within a civilian population. The violence is symbolic, and it is designed to have a devastating psychological impact on established power.

Revolutionary terrorism refers to movements designed to overthrow and replace a political system. After World War II, it involved mainly left-wing and Marxist movements; right-wing groups later copied these models. Some revolutionary groups are sponsored by nation-states.

Revolutionary terrorism involves violent activity for the purpose of changing the political structure of government or the social orientation of a country or region. Maoist terrorism is a form of revolutionary terrorism. Its goal is to establish a Communist society similar to that of revolutionary China. Counterterrorism involves the legitimate legal activities of security forces, but some unofficial groups operate outside the law. When these groups engage in violence, it can be described as counterrevolutionary terrorism.

Modeling Revolutionary Terrorism: Uruguay's Tupamaros

In the early 1960s, a group of revolutionaries called the Tupamaros surfaced in Uruguay (Figure 10.2). Unlike their predecessors in the Cuban Revolution, the Tupamaros spurned the countryside, favoring an urban environment. City sidewalks and asphalt became their battleground. A decade later, their tactics would inspire

FIGURE **10.1** Map of Central and South America

FIGURE 10.2 Map of Uruguay

revolutionaries around the world, and terrorist groups would imitate the methods of the Uruguayan revolutionaries. The Tupamaros epitomized urban terrorism.

In the years immediately after World War II, Uruguay appeared to be a model Latin American government. Democratic principles and freedoms were the accepted basis of Uruguay's political structures. Democratic rule was complemented by a sound economy and an exemplary educational system. Although it could not be described as a land of wealth, by the early 1950s, Uruguay could be called a land of promise. All factors seemed to point to peace and prosperity.

Unfortunately, Uruguay's promise started to fade in 1954. The export economy that had proved so prosperous for the country began to crumble. Falling prices for exported goods brought inflation and unemployment, and economic dissatisfaction grew. By 1959, many sugar workers and members of the middle class faced a bleak future. Uruguay had undergone a devastating economic reversal, and workers were restless. Many of them traveled to Montevideo, Uruguay's capital, to voice their disappointment.

Their logic seemed sound. Uruguay's population center is Montevideo, a metropolis of 1.25 million people. Demographically, the capital offered the promise of recognition. Unfortunately for the demonstrating workers, they did not achieve the type of recognition that they were seeking. Far from viewing the marchers as a legitimate labor movement, the government considered them potential revolutionaries.

Raúl Sendic: (1926–1989) A Uruguayan revolutionary leader. Sendic founded the National Liberation Movement (MLN), popularly known as the Tupamaros. Following governmental repression in 1973, he fled the country. Sendic died in Paris in 1989.

The sugar workers clashed with police, and several union members were arrested. One of those taken to jail was a young law student named **Raúl Sendic** (1926–1989). Disillusioned with law school and his prospects for the future, Sendic had joined the sugar workers. Sendic remained in jail until 1963. When he emerged, he had a plan for a revolution.

Sendic had not seen the brighter side of Uruguayan life in prison. The stark realities of Uruguay's now shaky political system were evident, as torture and mistreatment of prisoners were common. If the population could not be kept content by a sound economy, it had to be subdued by fear. Democracy and freedoms faded as Uruguay's economic woes increased. Sendic described the repression he saw in *Waiting for the Guerrilla*, in which he called for revolt in Montevideo.

After Sendic was released from jail, several young radicals gravitated toward him. María Gilio (1972) paints a sympathetic picture of Sendic's early followers. According to Gilio, these young people were primarily interested in reforming the government and creating economic opportunities. Although they had once believed they could attain these goals through democratic action, the ongoing repression in Uruguay ruled out any response except violence. Gilio believed that the group of people who surrounded Sendic were humanist idealists who wanted to bring Uruguay under direct control of the people.

Others did not hold this opinion of Sendic and his compatriots. Arturo Porzecanski (1973) provides a more objective view of the group's next move. Sendic's group felt excluded from participation in the political system, and Sendic believed that violence was the only appropriate tool to change the political order. In 1963, Sendic and his followers raided the Swiss Hunting Club outside Montevideo. The raid was the first step in arming the group, and the first step toward a revolution.

Urban Guerrillas

According to Porzecanski, the group was not willing to move outside Montevideo to begin a guerrilla war for several reasons. First, the group was not large enough to begin a guerrilla campaign because it represented radical middle-class students. Mainstream workers and labor activists had moved away from the militants' position before the march on Montevideo. Second, the countryside of Uruguay did not readily lend itself to a guerrilla war because unrest grew from the urban center of Uruguay. Third, the peasants were unwilling to provide popular support for guerrilla forces. Finally, Montevideo was the nerve center of Uruguay. All of these factors caused the small group to believe that it could better fight within the city.

National Liberation Movement: The Tupamaros' official name.

In 1963, the group adopted its official name, the **National Liberation Movement** (known by the Spanish acronym MLN). As they began to develop a revolutionary ideology and a structure for violent revolt, the group searched for a name that would identify them with the people, one with more popular appeal than MLN. According to Christopher Dobson and Ronald Payne (1982, p. 206), the MLN adapted the name of the heroic Inca chieftain Tupac Amaru, who had been killed in a revolt against the Spaniards 200 years earlier. Porzecanski notes this story but also suggests the group may have taken its name from a South American bird. In any case, Sendic's followers called themselves the Tupamaros.

By 1965, their ranks had grown to 50 followers, and they were building a network of sympathizers in the city. Instead of following the prescribed method of Latin American revolution based on a rural guerrilla operation, the Tupamaros organized to do battle inside the city, following the recent guidelines of Carlos Marighella. Terrorism would become the prime strategy for assaulting the enemy. The Tupamaros, unlike Castro in Cuba, were not interested in building a conventional military force to strike at the government.

Ross Butler (1976, pp. 53–59) describes the growth of the terrorist group by tracking their tactics. He says that they engaged in inconsequential activities in the early stages of their development. From 1964 to 1968, they concentrated on gathering arms and financial backing. After 1968, however, their tactics changed, and according to Butler, the government found it necessary to take them seriously.

In 1968, the Tupamaros launched a massive campaign of decentralized terrorism. They were able to challenge governmental authority because their movement was growing. A series of bank robberies had financed their operations, and now, armed with the power to strike, the Tupamaros sought to paralyze the government in Montevideo. They believed, as had Carlos Marighella in Brazil, that the government would increasingly turn to repression as a means of defense and that the people would be forced to join the revolution.

The government was quick to respond but found there was very little it could do. The Tupamaros struck when and where they wanted and generally made the government's security forces look foolish. They kidnapped high-ranking officials from the Uruguayan government, and the police could do little to find the victims.

Counterrevolutionary Terrorism

Kidnapping became so successful that the Tupamaros took to kidnapping foreign diplomats. They seemed able to choose their victims and strike their targets at will. Frustrated, the police turned to an old Latin American tactic: They began torturing suspected Tupamaros.

Torturing prisoners served several purposes. First, it provided a ready source of information. In fact, the Tupamaros were destroyed primarily through massive arrests, based on information gleaned from interrogations. Second, torture was believed to serve as a deterrent to other would-be revolutionaries. Although this torture was always unofficial, most potential governmental opponents knew what lay in store for them if they were caught.

The methods of torture were brutal. Gilio (1972, pp. 141–172) describes in detail the police and military torture of suspected Tupamaros. Even when prisoners finally provided information, they continued to be tortured routinely until they were either killed or released. Torture became a standard police tactic. A. J. Langguth (1978) devotes most of his work to the torture that became commonplace in Uruguay and Brazil. The torturers viewed themselves as professionals who were simply carrying out a job for the government. Rapes, beatings, and murders by torturers were common, and the police refined the art of torture to keep victims in pain as long as possible. According to Langguth, some suspects were tortured over a period of months or even years.

Early Successes

In the midst of revolution and torture, the Tupamaros accused the United States of supporting the brutal Uruguayan government. Their internal revolt thus adopted the rhetoric of an anti-imperialist revolution, which increased their popular support. The Tupamaros established several combat and support columns in Montevideo, and by 1970, they began to reach the zenith of their power. Porzecanski (1973) says that they almost achieved a duality of power; that is, the Tupamaros were so strong that they seemed to share power equally with the government.

Their success was short-lived, however. Although they waged an effective campaign of terrorism, they were never able to capture the hearts of the working class. Most of Montevideo's workers viewed the Tupamaros as privileged students with no real interest in the working class. In addition, the level of their violence was truly appalling.

During terrorist operations, numerous people were routinely murdered. The eventual murder of a kidnapped American police official disgusted the workers, even though they had no great love for the United States. Tupamaro tactics alienated their potential supporters. In the end, violence spelled doom for the Tupamaros. By bringing chaos to the capital, they succeeded in unleashing the full wrath of the government. In addition, the Tupamaros had overestimated their strength. In 1971, they joined a left-wing coalition of parties and ran for office. According to Ronald MacDonald (1972, pp. 24–45), this was a fatal mistake. The Tupamaros had alienated potential electoral support through their terrorist campaign, and the left-wing coalition was soundly defeated in national elections.

The electoral defeat was not the only bad news for the Tupamaros. The election brought a right-wing government to power, and the new military government openly advocated and approved of repression. A brutal counterterrorist campaign followed. Far from being alienated by this, the workers of Montevideo applauded the new government's actions, even when it declared martial law in 1972. Armed with expanded powers, the government began to round up all leftists in 1972. For all practical purposes, the Tupamaros were finished. Their violence helped bring about a revolution, but not the type that they had intended.

Tupamaro Organization

The Tupamaros have passed into history, but their organization and operations serve as a model for revolutionary terrorism. It is worth taking the time to examine the MLN because many modern groups form and take actions in similar manners. The Tupamaros were one of the most highly organized yet least structured terrorist groups in modern history. Because they were virtually self-sufficient, Tupamaro growth, operations, and organization were amazing. If they failed to achieve success in the long run, their organizational structure at least kept them in the field as long as possible.

The Tupamaros were nominally guided by a national convention, which had authority in all matters of policy and operations. In reality, the national convention seldom met more than once per year and was disbanded in the 1970s. Christopher Hewitt (1984, p. 8) notes that the national convention did not meet at all after September 1970. John Wolf (1981, p. 31) believes that an executive committee controlled all activities in Montevideo. Arturo Porzecanski (1973), probably the most noted authority on the Tupamaros, makes several references to this same executive committee. For all practical purposes, it seems to have controlled the Tupamaros (see MIPT, n.d.).

The executive committee was responsible for two major functions. It ran the columns that supervised the terrorist operations, and it also administered the special Committee for Revolutionary Justice. The power of the executive committee derived from internal enforcement. The job of the committee was to terrorize the terrorists into obedience. If an operative refused to obey an order or tried to leave the organization, a delegation from the committee would usually deal with the matter. It was not uncommon to murder the family of the offending party, along with the errant member. The Tupamaros believed in strong internal discipline.

In day-to-day operations, however, the executive committee exercised very little authority. Robert Moss (1972, p. 222) states that the Tupamaros lacked a unified command structure for routine functions. The reason can be found in the nature of the organization. Because secrecy dominated every facet of its operations, it could not afford open communications. Therefore, each subunit evolved into a highly autonomous operation. There was little the executive committee could do about this situation, and the command structure became highly decentralized. The Tupamaros existed as a confederacy.

Operational power in the Tupamaros was vested in the lower-echelon units. Columns were organized for both combatant (operational) and staff (logistical) functions. Wolf (1981, p. 35) writes that most of the full-time terrorists belonged to cells in the combatant columns. They lived a precarious day-to-day existence and were constantly in conflict with the authorities. According to Wolf, they were supported by larger noncombatant columns that served to keep the terrorists in the field.

The importance of the noncombatant columns cannot be overemphasized—the strength of the Tupamaros came from the logistical columns. Without the elaborate support network of sympathizers and part-time helpers, the Tupamaros could not have remained in the field. Other groups that have copied their organizational model have not had the ability to launch a campaign because they lacked the same level of support.

Wolf's analysis of the support network includes peripheral support that was not directly linked to the Tupamaro organization. With Porzecanski, Wolf classifies supporters into two categories. One group operated in the open and provided intelligence and background information to the noncombatant sections. The other type of supporters worked on getting supplies to the operational sections. These sympathizers provided arms, ammunition, and legal aid. Both groups tried to generate popular support for the Tupamaros. When the government attacked the terrorists in 1972, its primary target was the support network. Police officials reasoned that if they destroyed the logistical network, they would destroy the Tupamaros.

In looking at the organizational chart of the Tupamaros (Figure 10.3), it is easy to envisage the entire operation. The executive committee was in charge, but it ran a highly decentralized operation. Its main power came from the internal rule enforcement provided by the Committee for Revolutionary Justice. Columns were the major

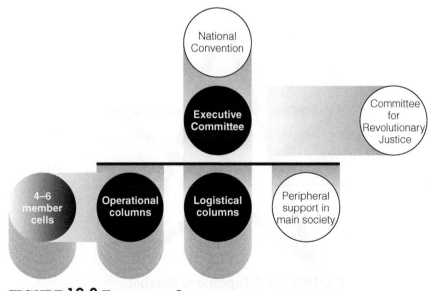

FIGURE **10.3** Tupamaro Organization

units, but they tended to be tactical formations. The real operational power came from the cells, which united for column-style operations on rare occasions. The combat striking power of the Tupamaros came from the four- to six-person groups in the cells. This organization epitomized Marighella's concept of the firing unit. Peter Waldmann (1986, p. 259) sums up the Tupamaros best by stating that they became the masters of urban terrorism. He believes that in terms of striking power, organization, and ability to control a city, no group has ever surpassed the Tupamaros. They epitomized the terrorist role. (See Figure 10.4 for the Tupamaro symbol.)

Influencing Modern Terrorism

As the champions of revolutionary terrorism, the Tupamaros were copied around the world, especially by groups in the United States and Western Europe. Many American left-wing groups from 1967 to 1990 modeled themselves after the Tupamaros. In Western Europe, Tupamaro structure and tactics were mimicked by such groups as the Red Army Faction and Direct Action. The **Red Brigades** split their activities among different cities, but they essentially copied the model of the Tupamaros.

Red Brigades: An Italian Marxist terrorist group that had its most effective operations from 1975 to 1990. It amended the centralized Tupamaro model by creating semiautonomous cells.

William Dyson (2008) argues that although some terrorist structures change and suicide bombing has become more common, terrorists' strategic and tactical practices remain constant. Several groups still follow the model of the Tupamaros. The fact that the Tupamaros created an urban movement is important in terms of the group's impact on violence in Latin America, but it also has a bearing on the way terrorist methods have developed in Europe and in the United States. Historically, Latin American terrorism was a product of rural peasant revolt. The Tupamaros offered an alternative to this tradition by making the city a battleground. They demonstrated to Western groups the impact that a few violent true believers could have on the rational routines of urban life. The urban setting provided the Tupamaros with endless opportunities.

Tupamaro tactics and organization have also been copied by right-wing groups. In the United States, right-wing extremist organizations have advocated the use of Tupamaro-style tactics. Many revolutionary manuals and proposed terrorist organizations are based on Tupamaro experiences.

FIGURE **10.4** Tupamaro Symbol

In the right-wing novel *The Turner Diaries* (MacDonald, 1985), Earl Turner joins a terrorist group similar to the Tupamaros in Washington, D.C. The author describes the mythical right-wing revolution in terms of Carlos Marighella and the Tupamaros. The right does not give credit to the left, but it does follow its example.

✔ **Self-Check**

> What are revolutionary and counterrevolutionary terrorism?
> How did the Tupamaros envision urban revolution?
> In what ways did Tupamaro tactics impact terrorism, in general?

Examples of Modern Revolutionary Terrorism

Revolutionary terrorism began in 1789 with the French Revolution, and it continued from 1879 to 1917 in Russia. After toppling rulers, however, both newly formed revolutionary governments were forced to use terror to suppress the population. Some contemporary terrorists would face the same challenge if they came to power. To avoid rule by terror, revolutionary groups must win the support of the majority of people in country where they operate. Therefore, when revolutionary forces are strong enough, they tend to use selective terrorism in support of guerrilla operations. The Irish Republican Army did this in Ireland's war for independence, and several revolutionary movements have employed similar techniques. The Cuban Revolution serves as an example. Mao Zedong also used selective terrorism in a long sometimes-guerilla, sometimes-conventional war against the Nationalist government and the Japanese in China, and the Vietcong copied many of his ideas in Vietnam. Yet, many groups remain too weak to operate as guerrillas (see Boot, 2013).

Three current movements engaged in revolutionary terrorism are FARC, the National Liberation Army (like FARC, it is known by its Spanish acronym, ELN), and the Iranian Peoples' Holy Warriors (Mujahedeen-e-Kahlq or MeK). At times, FARC and the ELN have been strong enough to sustain a guerrilla army and conduct a campaign of selective terrorism. The MeK has a more difficult situation because it is in Iraq surrounded by Shi'ite militias.

It should be noted the United Self-Defense Forces (known by its Spanish acronym, AUC) was also an active terrorist group operating in Colombia, and it may sometimes have governmental support. Disbanded in 2005, the AUC was an umbrella organization for several counterrevolutionary paramilitary groups, and at times, it practiced selective terrorism by conducting extrajuridical executions. Death squads are considered separately at the end of this chapter.

FARC

Originally liberated by Simón Bolívar in 1812, Colombia became part of a large nation known as Grand Colombia. By 1830, regional interests in Colombia and Panama began to surface, and Panama gained independence during a U.S.-sponsored revolution in 1903. While Panama developed relative stability, Colombia's history was marked by internal violence and political instability. During the last half-century, the country has been in the midst of a dirty war in which terrorists and governmental forces fight a shadow war that is interconnected with drug production (see Figure 10.5).

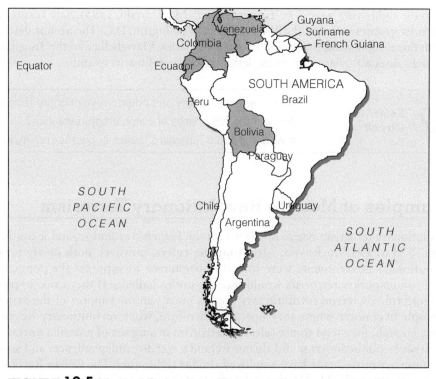

FIGURE 10.5 Map of Colombia, Ecuador, Venezuela, and Bolivia

FARC went through different stages as it gradually formed a guerrilla army. As The Violence came to an end, many opponents of the new government armed themselves and moved to Colombia's remote mountain region. One group attempted to create a self-governing commune centered in a hamlet deep in a rural mountainous area. Its plans were disrupted in May 1964 when government forces attacked the settlement. Members retreated and formed alliances with other displaced guerrillas. FARC was formed as other guerrillas drifted into their ranks, and the new group called itself the Revolution Armed Forces of Colombia (CISC, 2012b).

FARC reached critical mass in the 1970s and grew strong enough to become a true revolutionary guerrilla army. It expanded operations. By 1982, membership had grown to 3,000 people, and it continued to increase. Operating primarily in rural areas, FARC's goals were to topple the government in Bogotá and establish a socialist government (Meacham, Farah, and Lamb, 2014, pp. 9–10; CISC, 2012b).

FARC raised funds by "taxing" marijuana growers, extorting money from local businesses, and kidnapping. Most of its money came from the drug trade. Demand for cocaine in the United States resulted in increased coca production in Colombia's remote mountains. A weak federal government could not effectively control much of the rural countryside, and coca fields increased. As fields got bigger, incomes increased, which resulted in the emergence of several powerful drug dealers. FARC leadership decided to get into the business. Forcing local peasants to move from producing crops into farming coca, FARC bought the harvest and had it refined it into cocaine. Even though the peasants were being exploited by FARC, many of them were not dissatisfied. Coca farming doubled their income of (Meacham et al., 2014, p. 8).

Bilal Saab and Alexandra Taylor (2009) examined the importance of drugs in FARC financing. In 2005, FARC's income was estimated as high as 300 million

U.S. dollars. FARC raised almost half of its money through extortion, kidnapping ransoms, business thefts, and cattle rustling. But most of the income came from illegal drugs. While major criminal organizations in Colombia made their money by producing, redefining, distributing, and trafficking drugs, FARC approached profiteering via another path. Limiting its operations to Colombia, FARC relied on criminals to produce, refine, and traffic the product. FARC made its money by protecting coca farms, cocaine refineries, and domestic distribution routes. Examining data from 1999 as an example, Saab and Taylor found FARC charged $15.70 to protect a kilo of coca paste. If a dealer wanted to transport fully refined cocaine from FARC-controlled territory, the price for protection was $52.60. FARC also provided protection for airstrips that traffickers used. It charged $2,631 per kilo of cocaine on flights within Colombia and $5,263 per kilo to protect drugs if they were temporarily housed at an airstrip.

As FARC became more powerful, it developed multiple enemies. Concerned with illegal drugs, the United States stepped up its assistance to the Colombian government. Some peasants resisted FARC, and the government began arming them to create paramilitary defense forces. Drug producers had a twofold grievance against FARC. First, they did not want the competition. Second, FARC's local units frequently kidnapped drug lords' family members. Criminal organizations had heavily armed private armies that did not fight under limited rules of engagement. FARC responded with violence of its own, and Colombia sank into the abyss of a murderous, multifaceted dirty war (Meacham et al., pp. 9–10).

FARC became a fairly potent force. Making temporary peace pacts with many of the drug lords, they openly targeted the Colombian government. Soldiers, politicians, and law enforcement personnel were killed by the dozens. When the army took action in rural areas, casualties increased. Like revolutionaries from earlier times, FARC expanded territory and ruled by terror. It increased its ability to produce explosives, and it planted land mines to protect the areas under its control. It also developed powerful gas cylinder bombs to use in Colombia's cities. They were particularly ruthless with indigenous people, often massacring entire villages (CISC, 2012b).

Alvaro Uribe won the 2002 presidential election and promised to launch a robust offensive against FARC. He began launching effective military operations against multiple groups that were fighting in Colombia's mountainous jungles and crowded cities. Supported by the United States, he promised that he would bring FARC and other revolutionary forces to the negotiating table and dismantle paramilitary death squads. He was quick to seize on the U.S. reaction to 9/11, claiming that Colombia's contribution to the "war on terror" would be the elimination of revolutionaries and drug dealers. Law enforcement and military operations gradually reversed the tide. FARC slowly eroded (Bustamante and Chaskel, 2008).

By 2008, Uribe's aggressive counterterrorism policy paid off. Some of FARC's key leaders had been killed, including the founder and leader of the group, and its structures were being degraded by effective military action. In 2009, FARC struck back, but Colombian security forces reversed the initial gains. FARC retreated deeply into its territory (National Counterterrorism Center, 2010b).

FARC also developed two ideological problems. First, drug money created wealth. While FARC championed equality and socialism, it evolved into a group motivated by greed. It was embedded in the drug trade, and for many of its members, acquiring money became more important than social equality. Second, while FARC fought for socialism and justice, it used terror to rule the territory it controlled. People began to resent FARC hypocrisy. As profits replaced social reform, members began to desert. Power began to wane. After a hotly contested national election in 2010, Colombia's

Alvaro Uribe: (b. 1952) President of Colombia from 2002 to 2010. He was known for his tough stance against FARC and other revolutionary movements.

**Juan Manuel Santos
(b. 1951):** Became
president of Colombia
in August 2010. He
narrowly won a second
term in 2014, edging out
a conservative candidate
who opposed talks with
FARC.

new leader, President **Juan Manuel Santos,** wanted peace. He offered to negotiate with
FARC. Weakened by Uribe's offensive, in 2012, FARC negotiators sat down with government officials in Oslo (Kamminga, 2013).

There are several obstacles to peace. First, the government and FARC have negotiated cease-fires in the past only to have them fail. Second, conservatives are opposed
to negotiating with FARC, and Santos has promised that any settlement will have to
stand the test of a national referendum. If conservatives ally with the many agricultural
victims of FARC, voters may not approve a settlement. Third, FARC's involvement in
drug trafficking creates substantial incomes for coca farmers and refiners. Members
of FARC have allegedly approached an al Qaeda affiliate in Algeria and Hezbollah
in Lebanon asking for their assistance in drug smuggling. There is a real question
about FARC's commitment to ending the drug trade. Fourth, FARC is a decentralized
organization. Its leaders can negotiate a peace settlement, but local commanders may
ignore it. Finally, FARC represents only one of the groups fighting in Colombia. The
dirty war may continue even if FARC's members lay down their weapons (Jeffers and
Milton, 2014).

The ELN

Liberation theology is a doctrine that originated in poverty. It combines the ideas of
Marx with Christian teachings, specifically focusing on social justice and the poor. It
became popular in Latin America in the 1960s and 1970s, inspiring many Catholics,
Protestants, and social activists. In 1964, a small group of Catholic priests joined an
idealistic group of college students to form a new organization that would fight for
social justice in Colombia. Believing that poverty could not be eliminated through
peaceful means, they decided to effect change by force of arms. They called themselves the National Liberation Army, or ELN (CISC, 2012a).

Father Camilo Torres, one of the early leaders of the newly formed group, encouraged his fellow clergy to join the fight. Some of them listened, with some priests coming from as far away as Spain. The little group had few resources and very little cash.
The priests argued that they could not make money through the drug trade. That,
they said, would be immoral. They could raise money by another crime, however. The
ELN turned to kidnapping, thus accepting a logical contradiction that would appeal
only to an extremist. As they raised funds and armed themselves, they marched into
a revolution. Father Torres was killed in his first battle in 1966 (In SightCrime, n.d.,
circa 2011; and Gumey, 2014).

Through its more than 50 years of existence, the ELN has matured and changed,
moving through four ideological phases. The first phase was marked by liberation
theology. The idealists fought for a socialist democracy to free Colombia's peasants
from poverty. After almost being destroyed in 1973, the ELN rebounded and started
to grow. The regenerated guerrillas shifted their focus as they embraced Cuban-style
socialism. By 1999, the ELN reverted to championing socialist democracy, but members completely abandoned any pretense of religion. Suffering from President Uribe's
military and law enforcement offensive, the group entered its current phase sometime
around 2008 and 2009. Individual units began forming alliances with newly emerging
criminal gangs, and by 2012, the ELN was heavily involved in the drug trade. One
thing has remained constant through the decades, however. The ELN is composed of
proficient kidnappers (CISC, 2012a; Meacham et al., 2014).

Stanford University's Center for International Security and Cooperation (2012a)
reports that membership in the ELN has fluctuated over the years. The small group
of idealistic original members grew to more than 200 people in the early 1970s, only

to be struck and nearly eliminated by Colombian security forces in 1973. By some estimates, it was reduced to 35 members. Recuperating in the years that followed the disastrous defeat, the ELN reached an all-time high in the 1990s, when it fielded about 4,000 guerrillas. After the group abandoned religion in 1999, its ranks began to shrink. The ELN lost even more personnel from 2000 to 2002 due to clashes with paramilitary units, a violent rivalry with FARC, and encounters with security forces. When Uribe came to office and stepped up counterterrorist operations, the ELN shrunk to a new low and saw an estimated 1,500 to 2,000 guerrillas by 2009. The Center for Strategic and International Studies made a similar estimate of strength in 2014 (Meacham, 2014).

While FARC has been estimated to have as many as 35,000 guerrillas, the ELN has never been as popular. One of the more violent and ideologically committed groups, its activities generated popular opposition. The ELN felt pressured at the beginning of the twenty-first century. The group sought a truce with the government in 2002 and again in 2005 but broke off discussions on both occasions. An increasingly violent fight with FARC marked the ELN's continued deterioration through 2009. Weakened ELN members finally sought a truce with FARC in 2009, only to have one local commander break it in mid-2010 by declaring "total war" against FARC. Since that time, relative peace between the two groups has been dominated by geography. FARC tends to operate in rural areas, and the ELN concentrates on Colombia's cities. The groups do not fight when they are separated.

The ELN's command structure has been characterized by power struggles and purges. Currently, the senior commander is Nicolas Rodriguez Batista, who is known by his *nom de guerre* Gabino. He joined the ELN in 1964 at the age of 14. Although Rodriguez is nominally in charge of a central command, he shares power with other central commanders in five different departments that cover the military, political affairs, international relations, finance, and communication. These commanders also share power with regional officers who command large geographical swaths called war fronts. They come together periodically to form a congress but then return to their separate areas. This leads to many independent actions and local alliances among the semiautonomous war fronts. The structure also complicates any efforts to negotiate a peace. It is difficult to lead by committee and even more challenging to negotiate peace settlements when no one has the authority to make a truce (In SightCrime, n.d., circa 2011; CISC 2012a; Voelkel, 2015).

A BBC (2013b) background report on the ELN says that when FARC approached the government to discuss potential peace negotiations in November 2012, some of the ELN leaders expressed an interest. President Santos rebuffed their inquiries, demanding that they first take some type of concrete action. The ELN responded by releasing a kidnapped Canadian oil executive nine months later without requiring a ransom. Yet, as government negotiations with FARC moved from Oslo to Cuba, the ELN was still not involved. Bolivia and Ecuador volunteered to host peace talks.

Opinions about the future of the ELN are divided. Critics argue that elements of the ELN are morphing into *Bandas Criminales* or **BACRIM** drug gangs that have come to replace drug cartels. Various war fronts formed separate alliances with several gangs in 2014 and 2015. Other war fronts fight local BACRIMs for control of the drug trade. An article in the *Miami Herald* does not see the situation so pessimistically (Wyss, 2015). It states that the ELN may eventually agree to peace talks, but such a move must come from a consensus among its commanders. The International Crisis Group shares this opinion (Voelkel, 2015). It states that the ELN is afraid of becoming completely defenseless in a violent environment and concludes that the ELN's path to peace will involve a long, slow walk. It takes time to get a committee to make a decision.

BACRIM: Emerging Colombian drug gangs. A number of violent gangs started to appear after the paramilitary groups were demobilized in 2005. Their ranks include former paramilitary and drug cartel members.

It could indeed be a slow walk to peace, but President Santos may be on the way. In the late spring of 2015, Reuters reported that Colombian officials had met with representatives of the ELN in Ecuador (Murphy, 2015) for preliminary discussions related to peace talks. Santos also opened talks with some of Colombia's BACRIMs. Perhaps there is hope for ending terrorism in Colombia.

The MeK

The U.S. Department of State placed Mujahedin-e-Kahlq (MeK) on its initial list of Foreign Terrorist Organizations (FTO) in October 1997. The MeK was founded in 1965 and thus preceded the Iranian Revolution by 14 years. Its purpose was over-throwing the Iranian government. It has been designated as a foreign terrorist organization by the United States, primarily due to the assassinations of six Americans in Tehran during the 1970s and its anti-American activities during the 1979 Iranian Revolution. Saddam Hussein used its services during the Iran–Iraq War (1980–1988), and it is currently estimated to have about 3,800 members. During the U.S. invasion of Iraq, the group was officially designated as a hostile force, but the MeK negotiated a cease-fire with American forces in April 2003 (Masters, 2014).

The Council on Foreign Relations (Fletcher, 2008) states that the MeK was responsible for attacking a number of Western targets in the 1970s and for support-ing the 1979 **American embassy takeover** in Tehran. It is the largest and most militant group opposed to the Islamic Republic of Iran. The group espouses a mixture of Marxism and Islam, and its original purpose was to overthrow the government of the shah and to replace it with a socialist government. It supported the 1979 revolution, but its philosophy of socialism and women's liberation contrasted sharply with the conservative views of Iran's mullahs.

American embassy takeover: During the Iranian hostage crisis, revolutionary students stormed the U.S. embassy in Tehran with the support of the Iranian government. They held 54 American hostages from November 1979 to January 1981.

Mujahedin-e-Kahlq presents a conundrum for the United States. Officially listed as a terrorist group since 1997, the MeK settled in a camp about 40 miles north of Baghdad in 2003. As soon as the invading U.S. military forces negotiated a peace settlement with the MeK, they found that they could not fit the group's members into a neat package. American military planners had not prepared for MeK prisoners. At first, American forces sought to treat the group's members as prisoners of war, but according to the Geneva Convention, each member was entitled to a separate hearing to determine his or her status. In addition, a significant portion of the membership had been duped into joining during the Iran–Iraq war. Secretary of Defense Donald Rumsfeld changed the members' status in 2004 without a legal review, stating that all members were civilian "protected persons." According to a RAND study (Goulka, Hansell, and Larson, 2009), this decision was the result of improper planning. It also placed the United States in the hypocritical position of having a relationship with a designated terrorist group.

The *Times* of London points out that the relationship became even more uncom-fortable after this point. In 2007, President George W. Bush received a budget of $400 million from Congress to support groups that violently opposed Iran's Islamic regime. One of the groups on the list was the MeK (Philp and Evans, 2009). According to *Vanity Fair* (Unger, 2007), prominent advisors to the Bush administration advocated that the United States form a link with the MeK. It was the best hope for destabilizing Iran, the advisors argued.

According to the Council on Foreign Relations (Masters, 2014), the MeK con-ducted a number of attacks between the 1970s and 2001. These include hit-and-run military attacks against Iran, assassinations of Iranian officials, attacks on Iranian nationals in foreign countries, and large bombings. The group's leader is Maryam

Rajavi, and she hopes to be president of Iran after the current regime is deposed. One of the group's most important goals was to be removed from the U.S. State Department's terrorist list.

An in-depth Canadian press report (Petrou, 2009) suggests that MeK is attempting to demonstrate that it has amended its terrorist past. The MeK held a large rally in Paris in the summer of 2008, and it paid the expenses of several Western politicians who attended the event. The group has been removed from the British and European Union lists of terrorist organizations, and it has shared information with various intelligence agencies. The group is not popular in Iran because of its alliance with Saddam Hussein and the Iran–Iraq War. Though the group has been fairly inactive since 2001, numerous critics have pointed to its abuses of human rights. Others suggest that the MeK is little more than a personality cult built around Maryam Rajavi.

The United States removed the MeK from the list of designated FTOs in 2012, a move that infuriated some government officials yet was praised by others (Pecquet, 2015a). The group has allies in the U.S. Congress and some high-profile U.S. officials (Francis, 2015). When the last U.S. forces left Iraq in 2011, Iraqis allegedly attacked the MeK camp. Sporadic attacks have continued, including a missile attack from Shi'ite forces fighting ISIS in 2015 (BBC, 2013a; Pecquet, 2015b). According to the Council on Foreign Relations, the United Nations recognizes MeK exiles in Iraq as protected people waiting to be transferred to a third country (Masters, 2014). Although the United States no longer recognizes the MeK as a terrorist group, some former government officials vehemently reject the new status. When a congressional representative invited Rajavi to testify at a government hearing, a former state department official and a former United States ambassador left the hearing in anger (Pecquet, 2015a). Many people believe the MeK has not changed its ways.

✓ Self-Check

> How were FARC, the ELN, and the MeK formed?

> What roles do illegal drugs play in Colombian terrorism?

> Why does the West have an ambivalent relationship with the MeK?

Maoist Revolutionary Terrorism

While the Tupamaros exerted tremendous influence on the development of urban terrorism, rural revolutionary guerillas generally incorporated selective terrorism in the traditions of Michael Collins and Che Guevara. Guerrillas in Malaysia, Vietnam, and South Africa used terrorism as a tactic to support a larger strategy. The guerrilla movement failed in Malaysia, but it was at least partially successful in Vietnam and South Africa. Other guerrillas saw few chances for success, and some of these experiences gave way to campaigns of rural terror. Some were influenced by Marxism and others by a more extreme form of Maoism.

Maoist terrorism is a form of revolutionary terrorism, and it can be understood within the same framework Martha Crenshaw originally used to define the term. In practice, Maoist groups tend to be more violent than other revolutionary groups. Critical scholars debate the differences among various Marxist schools of thought, but, in terms of terrorism, Maoist groups exhibit three striking differences from most other revolutionary terrorists. First, they practice ruthless domination in the areas they control, and they rule by terrorism. Second, Maoist groups have a reputation for maintaining internal discipline. They purge and control their own members.

Finally, and most important, Maoist groups follow the revolutionary philosophy of Chinese Communist leader Mao Zedong. Maoist groups are based in rural peasant movements.

Peru's Shining Path

A Maoist group, the Shining Path (*Sendero Luminoso*), launched a campaign in rural Peru that began in 1980 and lasted for the following two decades (Fraser, 2007; see also Taylor, 2006). The Tupac Amaru Revolutionary Movement (MRTA) joined the Shining Path in 1984, although it was much less violent. Peru's revolutionary past was grounded in anticolonialism as the indigenous people sought to free themselves from European rule. **Tupac Amaru** (d. 1572) led a revolt against Spain from 1571 to 1572. Although the country did not gain its independence until 1824, he came to symbolize Peruvian independence. As military coups took control of the government throughout the nineteenth and twentieth centuries, his name was used to invoke a democratic spirit. After a civilian-elected president took power in Lima in 1980, Tupac Amaru came to symbolize another type of revolution. The Shining Path would wage a Maoist campaign of terrorism for the next 20 years using his name.

Scholars have debated the political orientation of the Shining Path almost from its inception. Led by a philosophy professor, **Abimael Guzmán**, the group was deeply influenced by China and its **Cultural Revolution.** Guzmán believed that the leftist politics of Peru's Communist Party were too tame, and he embraced the radical violence espoused by Maoist revolutionaries (Gorritti, 2006). In addition, the Maoist approach matched Peru's economic structure. Most of its economic and political strength came from the countryside. Guzmán moved to build a rural power base, and most scholars view the organization as a violent Maoist movement (Gregory, 2009).

Other scholars do not accept the view that the Shining Path was based on Maoism. Paul Navarro (2010) believes that the entire Peruvian left was influenced by Mao but that the influence was rhetorical. Most Peruvian leftists were mainstream Marxists. While they called for violent revolution, the starting point was thought to be decades away. Peru's communists were not inherently violent. Ronald Osborn (2007) argues that the Shining Path was a hyper-Marxist/Maoist group that was unique among all groups in Latin America because of its proclivity for violence. He says that the Shining Path became the first insurgent force on the left to surpass the military in waging a systematic campaign of violence against civilians.

Guzmán led the Shining Path in a twofold strategy. First, the guerrillas operated in rural areas, trying to create regional military forces. Second, Guzmán attempted to combine Mao Zedong's ruthless revolutionary zeal with the guerrilla philosophy of Che Guevara. The result was a ruthless campaign of violence designed to force peasants into a new egalitarian society. Most guerrillas minimize terrorism because it alienates potential supporters. Guzmán's philosophy was different. Anyone who refused to support the Shining Path was considered an enemy. Not only did Guzmán's followers use terrorism to target individuals, they also engaged in indiscriminate violence against anyone who did not support their call. Some victims suffered from car bombings and drive-by shootings; in other areas, guerrillas wiped out entire villages. The Shining Path's lethal methods demanded the death of all people who resisted or even gave the impression that they did not support the revolution (Theidon, 2006).

The government responded with its own campaign of counterterrorism. Security forces attacked the Shining Path with reckless abandon. Throughout the 1980s, they struck suspected areas of guerrilla support, and they grew more ruthless after the

---

Tupac Amaru: (d.1572) An Inca chieftain who led a revolt against Spain in the sixteenth century. His story has inspired many liberation and democratic movements in South America.

Abimael Guzmán: (b. 1934) A philosophy professor who led the Shining Path from 1980 until his arrest in 1992. Guzmán is serving a life sentence in Peru.

Cultural Revolution: A violent movement in China from 1966 to 1976. Its main purpose was to rid China of its middle class and growing capitalist interests. The Cultural Revolution ended with the death of Mao Zedong.

election of **Alberto Fujimori** in 1990 (Fraser, 2007). Fujimori created a system of secret courts and political repression. He dissolved Congress and ran Peru as a virtual police state. The rural peasants were caught in the middle. Soldiers and guerrillas followed a scorched earth policy, embracing the moral necessity of eradicating all enemies while peasants suffered from the actions of both sides. The struggle degenerated into a series of massacres and individual murders (Theidon, 2006).

Security forces seemed to gain the upper hand in September 1992 when police surveillance teams took Guzmán into custody. Fujimori began a campaign of economic reform despite his draconian measures against Peruvian democracy. The Shining Path, however, responded with a new campaign of terrorism, and the MRTA gained headlines with sensational operations. The government responded with even more repression and police death squads. The fighting ended in 2000 with all guerrillas abandoning terrorism and with the fall of Fujimori. The new Peruvian government created a truth and reconciliation commission, which released a final report in 2003 after a two-year investigation. Two decades of violence had resulted in the deaths of nearly 70,000 people. The Shining Path was responsible for about 54 percent of the total death count (Theidon, 2006).

Despite its practice of murdering anyone suspected of not supporting the revolution, the Shining Path was committed to social egalitarianism, at least rhetorically. The structure of the organization reveals two interesting social patterns. The role of families was prominent in day-to-day operations, and the Shining Path was committed to feminism. It actively recruited and engaged the services of revolutionary females, and Guzman's second-in-command was a woman from 1980 until she was killed in 1988 (Heilman, 2010).

The fighting supposedly came to an end in 2000; however, the *New York Times* (2009) reports that the Shining Path reemerged around 2007, reinventing itself as a drug trafficking organization. According to the newspaper, the Shining Path moved into Peru's cocaine-producing areas and abandoned Maoist practices for the lucrative profits of the drug trade. In 2008, the Shining Path was responsible for more than two dozen murders, making it the deadliest year since the fall of Fujimori.

Lack of leadership remains a problem. According to the Jamestown Foundation (2012), the Shining Path has partially taken over the drug trade in southern Peru. Reports of drug activities have increased, and some evidence suggests that it has formed an alliance with drug gangs in Colombia (Gange, 2015). The probable course for the Shining Path will most likely involve increased criminal activity for profit. The Maoist ideologues appear to be severely weakened.

Alberto Fujimori: (b. 1938) President of Peru from 1990 to 2000. He fled to Japan in 2000 but was extradited to Peru in 2007. He was convicted of human rights violations and sentenced to prison.

Naxalites of India

India has a variety of terrorist problems arising from political, religious, and ethnic strife. It is also in the throes of a Maoist rebellion. To understand the Maoist problem, it is necessary to remember that Indian society was governed by a rigid caste system for centuries. Even though the system has been formally abandoned, many lower-class peasants still suffer from its effects. India's agrarian system is based on large wealthy landholders and unlanded peasants, formerly of the lower caste, who are alienated from the current economic structure. Great economic disparities have led to the growth of left-wing movements that demand a more equal distribution of resources. One of these movements has turned violent (Zissis, 2007) (Figure 10.6).

The Naxalites emerged in a 1967 uprising in West Bengal. Peasants demanding the right to land ownership and better wages staged mass demonstrations with the support of the Communist Party. Police confronted the demonstrators with deadly

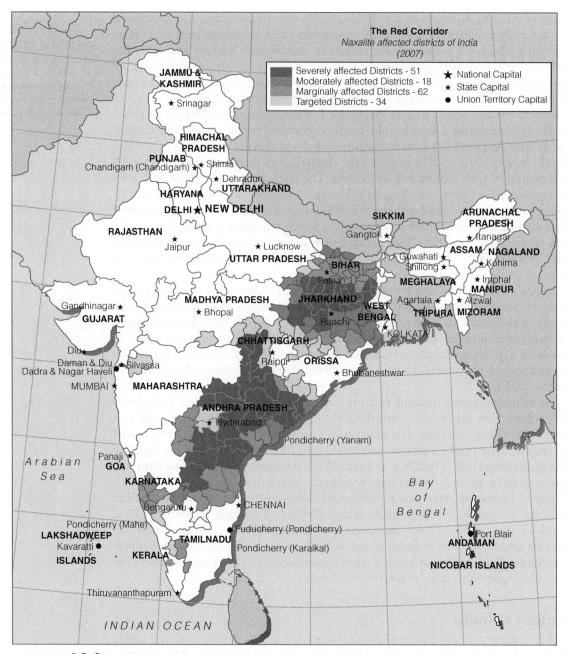

The Red Corridor
Naxalite affected districts of India
(2007)

Severely affected Districts - 51
Moderately affected Districts - 18
Marginally affected Districts - 62
Targeted Districts - 34

★ National Capital
★ State Capital
● Union Territory Capital

FIGURE **10.6** India

force, and protests turned into rebellion. The confrontation occurred in the Indian village of Naxalbari, and the unorganized groups of rebels that gathered in the countryside were known collectively as Naxalites. When tensions between the Soviet Union and China led to a breakup of the Sino–Soviet alliance, the Naxalites chose a Maoist path. Their rebellion was short-lived after Indian security forces targeted the group, and it virtually disappeared by 1975 (Banerjee, 2009).

Some members of the Indian government began to lobby for real reform as a result of the unrest. They saw social injustice at the base of the agrarian rebellion.

Although they attempted to pass reform legislation, they were thwarted by several aspects of India's bureaucratic and political systems. The social separation between landlords and tenants was deeply ingrained in Indian society. The civil service agencies assigned to agricultural areas were inefficient, and there was little cooperation among different units of government. Complete land records did not exist. Many peasants were illiterate, with no economic future other than working as tenant laborers for absentee landlords. When the government finally passed modest reform legislation, it did not allocate enough money to implement the program. In the end, India decided to handle any agricultural unrest as a police problem (Tharu, 2007).

The Naxalites began to emerge again in the 1990s in a variety of smaller movements. Anthropologist George Kunnath (2006) spent a year living with and observing a former member of the Naxalites. He believes that this grassroots movement gained strength because the landlord system had created a virtual feudal state. The Naxalites saw the landlords as unproductive external proprietors who exploited cheap labor. The Naxalites' goal evolved into a movement with three promises: land to the tiller, higher wages for agricultural work, and ending the de facto caste system.

As the group began to solidify, it formed a **Red Corridor** stretching from the northern Nepalese border to south-central India. This became a strong geographical base of power. When two movements—the People's Guerrilla Army of the People's War Group and the People's Liberation Army of the Maoist Center of India—joined the Naxalites 2004, they became a threat to regional stability. By 2005, the Naxalites were challenging India's police with attacks on police stations and jungle ambushes, which produced law enforcement casualties in the hundreds (Turbiville, 2005; Ganguly, 2009).

Red Corridor: The area of Naxalite violence in India. The corridor runs from Nepal through southern India, and from India's east coast to the central regions.

The Jamestown Foundation (2010) reports that the Indian government believes that the Naxalite rebellion has become its number one internal security problem. In the summer of 2010, the prime minister was considering calling on the military to deal with the problem. Other research suggests that the violence has grown because of an ineffective response (Oetken, 2009). Regional police forces have suffered hundreds of casualties, and some observers think the police authorize death squads in response. One of the more controversial moves has been the establishment of a special police force composed of local peasants. With no training and little regard for human rights, the special police frequently operate outside the law. The Naxalites have responded in kind, and more than half the states in India are involved in the dirty war (Guha, 2007; Banerjee, 2009).

There is an interesting aspect to gender roles in the Naxalite movement. When it first began in 1967, females began protest movements that sometimes resulted in violence. Eventually, many joined the militants in the jungles. Many women regarded their activities as a "magic moment," that is, as a time that defined their lives. Although they did not achieve emancipation, they created a new self-identity, apart from their role as peasants, and a women's movement began to emerge (Sinha Roy, 2009). Paradoxically, they also found that they were defined by their participation in the Naxalite movement. Imprisonment, shared dangers, and a spirit of brotherhood created life-long bonds among many groups of men (Donner, 2009).

Shameul Tharu (2007) argues that the rebellion cannot be stopped by either police or military power. It is simplistic, he says, to classify the Naxalite rebellion as a criminal problem. The Indian government needs to address several structural issues, including land reform, political reform, and ending bureaucratic corruption. Sumanta Banerjee (2009) adds that government reform would rectify the peasants' alienation from the land. On the other hand, Naxalite violence and human rights violations against peasants have alienated their potential supporters.

The Aspen Foundation (Van Dongen, 2012) believes that the rebellion is far from over for three reasons. First, India is one of the most underpoliced countries of the world. It does not have enough personnel to confront the Naxalites effectively. Second, reversing their previous public posture, the Naxalites have begun providing social services to the poor inside the Red Corridor. These are effective **no-go areas**, and the Indian government cannot respond in kind. Even if the Indian government could, they have demonstrated no interest in doing so. Finally, the most important reason the rebellion continues is that the fundamental issues that caused the unrest have not been addressed.

Violence surged in 2013 and spilled into 2014. While security forces have retaken much of the forest area controlled by Naxalite militants, military force and increased law enforcement will not end the rebellion. Writing for the *Harvard International Review*, Daniel Epstein (2014) believes that the Naxalites and others have been politically and economically marginalized along with a substantial portion of India's indigenous tribes. The economy in western urban areas is robust, but extreme poverty engulfs the eastern portion of India, especially in rural areas. Epstein concludes that while India must bring security to the Red Corridor, it must also bring west India's prosperity to the east. In addition, all India's people should be vested with the full rights of citizenship. This does not simply involve the Maoist rebels. Unless India makes strides toward economic and political justice, Epstein believes the country may fall apart.

The New People's Army

While many Americans conceive of the Philippine Islands as a monolithic modern state, the reality is different. The Philippines has differing cultures, radical gaps in income, different religious traditions, and divisive politics. In addition to foreign occupation by three different countries in the nineteenth and twentieth centuries, Philippine politics has been characterized as a struggle for democracy in the midst of local revolts. In 1986, a grand **people power revolution** toppled a long-term repressive leader and promised to bring real democracy. The promise failed. Many local revolts continue, including a campaign by the military wing of the Philippine Communist Party, the New People's Army (NPA).

The NPA is the longest-running Communist insurgency in the world. It is a rural movement that began in 1969 as a response to a Philippine dictatorship. It had as many as 25,000 members in the 1980s, though its membership dwindled after the return of democracy in 1986. By the mid-1990s, NPA ranks had slimmed to a cadre of less than 10,000. Today, its estimated strength is less than 7,000 (Montlake, 2007). The group eventually adopted a Maoist revolutionary philosophy, targeting security forces, politicians, judges, and U.S. military personnel assigned to the Philippines. It also gained a reputation for self-purges, killing many of its own members.

The NPA is unique due to its ideological orientation (Coronel, 2007). Most of its power base is in rural Luzon, but it has made inroads in Manila and Mindanao. It sustains operations by levying a "revolutionary tax," which is money extorted from local residents and merchants. The NPA's income averaged about $30 million per year in 2007, and it currently maintains a steady stream of income and logistical material (Montlake, 2007; CISC, 2015). There are many female members who operate as full-fledged guerrillas in the jungle, though the NPA is hardly a bastion of feminism. While girls are recruited at a young age, all aspects of their lives are controlled. Called Amazonas for the mythic race of Greek female warriors, they are not allowed to engage in any activity, including romantic liaisons, without permission from the male leaders (Marshall, 2008).

no-go areas: Geographical areas that the duly empowered government cannot control (this is an informal term). Security forces cannot routinely patrol these places.

people power revolution: A mass Philippine protest movement that toppled Ferdinand Marcos in 1986. Marcos ruled as a dictator after being elected president in 1965 and declaring martial law in 1972. When Gloria Macapagal-Arroyo assumed the presidency in January 2001, a position that she held until 2010, her government proclaimed a second people power revolution.

The rural NPA campaign also symbolizes the paradox of counterterrorism; that is, when faced with terrorism, governments frequently resort to terrorism. In 2006, the Philippine government announced an all-out offensive against Communism, including the NPA. One of the goals was to reduce NPA membership, and the military took this as a signal to move against all leftists (Coronel, 2007). Professors Patricio Abinales and Donna Amoroso (2006) say that the offensive started with extrajudicial murders. Hundreds of people were killed outside the law. When U.S. military personnel began to offer assistance, the public often welcomed the presence of the American troops. They felt that death squad activities would be curtailed when Americans were present. The professors also note that more soldiers than insurgents were killed in the first year of the crackdown.

Many Philippine counterterrorist activities have taken place outside the law since 2000. Over 1,700 people have been murdered in extrajudicial executions, and the United Nations has placed the Philippine government on an international watch list for human rights violations (CISC, 2015). Underground death squads began eliminating suspected enemies in Mafia-style executions in 2001, and murders increased with the campaign against terrorism in 2006 (Abinales, 2008). The Philippine government used the war on terrorism as an excuse to move against church workers, union organizers, lawyers, and human rights workers. The Armed Forces of the Philippines (AFP) have dehumanized the NPA, virtually creating a blood feud that can be ended only through complete annihilation (Montlake, 2007).

The Philippines has been plagued by terrorism since the mid-1970s. Two of the issues that keep the NPA in the field are the structure of political power and the distribution of wealth. The Philippines has democratic roots dating back to 1898, when the United States seized the islands from Spain. Americans quickly established democratic institutions, and they were unique. Instead of giving power to all Filipinos, the new democracy favored prosperous, landed elites. When the United States granted the Philippines independence in 1946, the elites continued to run the government. This resulted in a political structure in which most of the people are excluded from active participation (Hutchcroft, 2008).

Poverty does not cause terrorism, but social inequities can draw people to revolutionary causes. Patricio Abinales (2008) says that the political system is somewhat stable because power is not centralized in Manila. It is maintained through relations with local power structures, and the majority of the people are apathetic about the elitist government. Poverty is another issue, and there is no apathy there. Large gaps in the distribution of wealth provide a pool for revolutionaries. These potential actors are not drawn to terrorism. They are motivated by economic disparity (Coronel, 2007).

> ✓ **Self-Check**
> > What is Maoist terrorism?
> > How is it manifested in the Philippines? In Nepal? In India?
> > What social factors caused Maoists to gain popularity in these three countries?

Death Squads and Counterrevolutionaries

Although a body of theoretical literature addresses revolutionary terrorism, very little has been written on death squads. By some estimates, the subject has been understudied. Death squads have one common base—they protect the established order. Their purpose is to stop social change, and they terrorize those who threaten their position.

Forms of extrajudicial death squads have existed throughout history, and they have resurfaced with modern terrorism. They were prominent in Latin America when revolutionary movements swept through Central and South America.

During the heyday of FARC and the ELN in Colombia, paramilitary units sprang up to fight the guerrillas. At first, the Colombian people, government, and military welcomed these groups. The army even conducted joint exercises with them, and many former members of law enforcement and the military joined their ranks. Officials expressed concern when it became obvious that many of the paramilitary units had strong connections to drug cartels. The army officially severed ties with the paramilitaries in 1989, but some elements of the armed forces continued to cooperate with them. In the early 1990s, several groups began to band together and operated under new names. In 1997, three brothers brought several larger assemblies together to form the United Self-Defense Forces of Colombia (known by the Spanish acronym AUC).

The AUC was effective. According to the BBC (2013b) it hunted and killed leftist guerrillas. This is the type of action that separates death squads from units acting within the rule of law. If AUC leaders suspected persons of belonging to or supporting FARC, they killed them. Deaths were frequently gruesome. Victims were tortured, mutilated, and killed. Many times, the AUC beheaded its captives. They not only killed suspected terrorists, they also began to target their critics, and this soon spread to targeting anybody with left of center political views. Media personalities, politicians, union leaders, and anyone who displeased the AUC became a potential victim. Although the majority of their funding came from drug trafficking, they raised substantial funds from businesses and oil companies who paid for protection from the guerrillas. They also extorted money, kidnapped, and committed other crimes for profit. Their military offensives were marked by rape, robbery, and massacres. The United States placed the AUC on the designated FTO list in 2001.

The Council on Foreign Relations (2008) says the AUC began to demobilize in 2003 when it numbered well over 30,000 men. The government provided legal incentives to men who turned in their weapons; it granted reduced sentences to those convicted of crimes and promised not to extradite persons wanted by the United States. Several drug lords moved to join the AUC to take advantage of the program, but when the government recognized the ploy, many traffickers were extradited to the United States. A scandal in 2007 uncovered AUC relationships with at least 50 high-ranking political officials, and it cast doubt on President Uribe's connections with the organization.

Many death squads are smaller and subtler than the AUC. Death squads come into being when people who hold economic and political power believe that their position is being threatened and authorities are unable to mitigate the threat. The purpose of a death squad is to eliminate opposition when a government is either unable or unwilling to do so. The tactics of death squads vary. They range from semiofficial raids on government opponents to torture and secret murder. In a common scenario, uniformed members of a death squad will "arrest" a victim. The victim is carried away, and there are no records. The arresting officers frighten lucky victims and torture and murder unlucky ones. In other cases, people simply disappear.

Death squads have been associated primarily with right-wing activities, but they are used across the political spectrum. For example, after the 1979 Sandinista revolution in Nicaragua, unofficial groups began to crack down on the press and on potential opposition parties. People who opposed the Communist regime began to disappear. More recently, death squads appeared in Iraq after the fall of Saddam Hussein. Many parties in Iraq used death squads to intimidate their opponents.

Julie Mazzei (2009, pp. 1–24) posits a theory about the emergence of death squads in a work on counterrevolution in Latin America. Mazzei states that paramilitary groups develop based on the perceptions of power elites in the face of economic and political threats. She believes, first and foremost, that death squads must be understood as a method for resisting structural shifts. They are opposed to reform. Prior to mass electronic information networks, this task was delegated to military and law enforcement forces, but modern international pressure, which results from global communications, frequently prevents power elites from using institutional power structures in this manner. Therefore, power elites have begun creating their own extrainstitutional forces to achieve their desired goals.

Perception is the key to Mazzei's theory. Paramilitary death squads come into play only when power elites feel that social changes are undermining their societies and that nothing can be done to stop the process. This does not refer to political movements that displace parties within a legitimate and socially accepted system; it applies to movements that shift the basic structure of a social organization. In Mazzei's study, the hardliners in every country that has seen the creation of death squads viewed reform efforts as an illegitimate method for redistributing wealth and power, and each government in question was either unwilling or unable to stop reform. Mazzei says that both the power elites and members of the paramilitary units justify their actions because they feel that their methods are the only legitimate defense of the social and political order.

Mazzei argues that conditions that give rise to death squads develop when several factors coalesce to form a favorable environment. First, political elites must be entrenched in a society and have a vested interest in maintaining societal structures, and these elites have a history of employing armed force to protect their positions. This combines with a second factor—a reform movement that threatens to break up elite power structures and redistribute wealth and power. Third, the government must be either unwilling or unable to stop the reform movement. Finally, hardliners among the political elites break away from their mainstream counterparts based on the belief that moderate political elites are too soft and unable to stop the reform movement. The only action that will maintain social order, the hardliners believe, is physically eliminating opponents and destroying the mentality of seeking reform.

Augmenting Mazzei's theory is a case study by Brenda Breuil and Ralph Rozema (2009). They looked at the operation of death squads in Davao City, Philippines, and in Medellín, Colombia, and found that perception of social change is indeed the key factor behind death squad activity. Breuil and Rozema explain death squads by social imagination. Their study suggests that entire groups of people in a geographical location within the same socioeconomic structure create and sustain an imaginary perception of the world. These perceptions are shared and accepted within the group, but they are not shared among other groups.

Social acceptance is a critical part of an imagined world. It involves an "in group" and a group that does not belong. The in group behaves the "right" way and lives life "as it should be lived." When an outside group threatens this perception, it also becomes part of a social imagination. The in group comes to believe that members of the outside group are less than human and that they are so deviant that their existence is illegitimate. A group that creates a death squad believes that its place in society is natural and legitimate. Any group threatening that place is illegitimate and is usurping the rightful order. The threatening group is thus dehumanized and deemed unworthy of existence. This justifies the death squad.

✓ Self-Check	> What do most death squads have in common?
	> What factors are present when death squads are created?
	> How is social imagination used to justify death squads?

Emphasizing the Points

Revolutionary terrorists call for radical change in either the structure of government or the underlying political philosophy of governance. Their current origins can be traced to twentieth-century movements in Latin America, especially the urban orientation of Uruguay's Tupamaros. Groups such as FARC and the ELN were originally inspired by the Tupamaros, but they drifted into drug trafficking to survive. Other terrorists, including the MeK of Iran, fight for political dominance. Maoist revolutionaries mirror the revolutionary theories of the Communist takeover in China. Peru's Shining Path was a pioneer Maoist group, and it inspired Communists in Nepal, India, and the Philippines. Counterrevolutionary terrorism is frequently based on the formation of illegal military and police units that torture and kill suspected terrorists and their supporters. They are known as death squads.

SUMMARY OF CHAPTER OBJECTIVES

- Revolutionary terrorism involves violent activity for the purpose of changing the political structure of government or the social orientation of a country or region. Counterterrorism involves the legitimate legal activities of security forces, but some unofficial groups operate outside the law. When these groups engage in violence, it can be described as counterrevolutionary terrorism.
- The Tupamaros established an urban organization. The active cadre conducted terrorism (robbery, kidnapping, and attacking symbolic targets) while waiting on sympathizers to create a revolutionary climate. Many modern terrorist groups have been influenced by the Tupamaros because the group had a major impact on the early development of revolutionary terrorism.
- FARC and the ELN emerged as revolutionary groups in Colombia. They formed alliances with drug cartels, and their influence spread beyond Colombia.
- The MeK fought against the revolutionary government of Iran. Its operations and finances were influenced, and at times controlled, by Iraq. The group has been removed from the U.S. Department of State's FTO list.
- The Shining Path's 20-year terrorist campaign was launched in Peru in 1980. It was a Marxist/Maoist movement that prompted a harsh governmental response. Peru's population was caught in the middle as the Shining Path systematically waged a campaign of terrorism against them. It reemerged around 2007, but its major goal was control of the drug trade. The Shining Path broke into two major factions centered on drug trafficking, and it has branched out into Argentina and Colombia.
- The Naxalite rebellion began in 1967 in West Bengal. It started as several Communist movements agitating for agrarian reform and peasant rights. The first rebellion was repressed with military and police power. In the second phase, Naxalites began to spread and organize in central India, creating a Red Corridor. The third phase began in 2004 when two major groups united and launched an open rebellion.
- The New Peoples' Army is the armed with of the Communist Party in the Philippines. They are the Philippines' most active terrorist group and use guerrilla warfare and selective terrorism.

- Death squads developed as a reaction to revolutionary terrorism. The premise behind extrajudicial arrest, torture, and murder is that normative law cannot cope with terrorist violence. People supporting death squads believe that their existence is threatened; therefore, it is necessary to operate outside the law and terrorize the terrorists.

LOOKING INTO THE FUTURE

Revolutionary terrorism will continue into the twenty-first century, and selective terrorism will be routinely included as an element of guerrilla campaigns. While many eyes are focused on the Middle East, South Asia is a crucial area for the world's social and economic future. Prime Minister Narendra Modi swept into power in 2014 with an ambitious reform agenda that failed to materialize quickly. He still has an historic opportunity to impact the region. India has the potential to become one of the world's great economic powers, but the government must overcome serious weaknesses. The most overriding problem is poverty. This is closely followed by enormous differences in the distribution of wealth, deep social and cultural divisions, and political corruption. These factors make India susceptible to revolutionary terrorism.

The Naxalite rebellion is indicative of a possible future for India. Other tribal, religious, or cultural groups may revolt for their own reasons. If this happens, revolutionary terrorism will spread in India, and the country may become unstable. If Modi or his successors are able to end corruption, give all Indians social and economic opportunities, and end the discrepancy in the distribution of wealth, there will be little incentive to revolt. That is important for every person on earth because instability in a nuclear power is a dangerous affair, especially when hostile and potentially hostile neighbors lay on India's borders.

KEY TERMS

Raúl Sendic, p. 228
National Liberation
   Movement, p. 228
Red Brigades, p. 232
Alvaro Uribe, p. 235

Juan Manuel Santos,
   p. 236
BACRIM, p. 237
American embassy
   takeover, p. 238

Tupac Amaru, p. 240
Abimael Guzmán, p. 240
Cultural Revolution,
   p. 240
Alberto Fujimori, p. 241

Red Corridor, p. 243
No-go areas, p. 244
People power revolution,
   p. 244

CHAPTER 11

Jihadist Networks

LEARNING OBJECTIVES

After reading this chapter, you should be able to:

▶ Summarize the main theological points of Jihadi Salafism.

▶ Summarize the contribution of scholars and strategists to Jihadi Salafism.

▶ Summarize the major points in *A Call to Global Islamic Resistance* and *The Management of Savagery*.

▶ Outline the development of al Qaeda from its creation to the present.

▶ Describe the al Qaeda franchise system.

▶ Geographically locate and identify major groups in the al Qaeda franchise.

▶ Describe the rise and metamorphosis of al Qaeda in Iraq.

▶ Outline the development and current status of ISIS.

▶ Explain the al Qaeda–ISIS split.

▶ Identify some of the major Jihadi Salafist crisis points around the globe.

Abu Bakr al Baghdadi, Leader of ISIS

Jessica Stern and J. M. Berger (2015, pp. 45–47) tell of the Islamic State of Iraq and al Sham—al Sham refers to Syria—(ISIS) blitzkrieg into the Sunni area of Iraq in the spring and early summer of 2014. More than 80 allied Sunni tribes, tribes that fought jihadists during the Iraqi insurgency, aided them. Ibrahim Ali al Badri al Sammarrai, whose *nom de guerre* is Abu Bakr al Baghdadi, was their religious leader. Although they faced an Iraqi army that had been trained and equipped by the United States, the army melted before the onslaught. The United States had spent $25 billion to train and equip the Iraqi army, and much of the equipment fell into ISIS hands. The important city of Mosul fell to the advancing jihadists in early June.

Many facets of ISIS were changing the face of terrorism. For example, it drew nonterrorist allies and recruits to its ranks. It also received hundreds of foreign fighters, including many people from Europe and the United States. ISIS broadcast terrorism on social media. While extremely brutal—they beheaded, shot, burned, and crucified prisoners—ISIS

(image credit, vertical text along photo: Anadolu Agency/Getty Images*)*

also portrayed itself as a benevolent organization. It held captured territory and established local governments, bureaucracies, schools, food distribution networks, and hospitals. Professional military officers formerly in Saddam Hussein's army led military forces. ISIS also became one of the richest terrorist groups in history. Stern and Berger estimate that it generated between $1 and $3 million per day.

In addition to all of its innovative successes, ISIS stunned the Islamic world on June 29, 2014. Spokesperson Abu Mohammed al Adnani said that ISIS was restoring the caliphate, and the group would now simply be called the Islamic State. The caliphate is the historical community of all Muslims that in principle transcends divisions of race, tribes, and nation states. Abu Bakr al Baghdadi, Adnani added, was declared to be the new caliph and named Caliph Ibrahim. All nation states, oaths, and alliances in the Muslim world were null and void, Adnani said. Muslims everywhere were ordered to swear loyalty to the new caliph. Jihad would be waged against the entire nonbelieving world and "heretical" Muslims until the enemies of Islam were defeated in a final great battle. Although a variation on an eschatological theme, ISIS had become the new face of terrorism in the twenty-first century.

Jihadi Salafism

After 9/11, many terrorism scholars and analysts, including this author, said that al Qaeda and its theology of hate did not represent any of the traditions in Islam. Pointing to mainstream interpretations of contemporary Sunni and Shi'a scholars who were also criticizing al Qaeda, they argued that all Islam was a religion of peace. While this is generally true and reflects the opinion of most Muslims today, it is not entirely accurate. Cole Bunzel (2015, pp. 7–11) says that al Qaeda, ISIS, and a number of other militant groups follow a puritanical strain of Islam known as Jihadi Salafism (also referred to as Salafi Jihadism, Salafism, Salafists, or Salafis), a medieval interpretation of Islam that developed when Arabs were being threated by Europeans and East Asians.

Jihadi Salafism represents a minority and frequently internally condemned interpretation of Islam, but it is a distinct theological strain of Sunni Islam supported by a global network of scholars, websites, media outlets, and social networks. Bunzel says it is deeply rooted in a theology of militancy. The **Muslim Brotherhood** champions one school. It formed in Egypt to oppose European imperial rule, to purify religion through education and social service, and to seek the restoration of the caliphate at some distant point in history. A more violent school, represented by ISIS and al Qaeda, seeks to purify Islam and rid Muslim lands of Western influence. ISIS embraces a more extreme intolerant version of Salafism seeking to purge the religion of what it believes are un-Islamic practices, eradicating Shi'ites, and waging offensive wars. Salafis see themselves as the only "true" Muslims, and they have assumed the authority to denounce fellow Muslims "heretics" if they disagree with Jihadi Salafi theology. William McCants (2014a) adds that Jihadi Salafism includes an apocalyptic interpretation of Islam that believes Salafis are called to usher in the final days of creation.

Muslim Brotherhood: An organization founded by Hassan al Banna in 1928 to recapture the spirit and religious purity of the period of Mohammed and the four Rightly Guided caliphs. The Brotherhood seeks to create a single Muslim nation through education and religious reform. A militant wing founded by Sayyid Qutb sought the same objective through violence. Hamas, a group that defines itself as the Palestinian branch of the Muslim Brotherhood, has rejected the multinational approach in favor of creating a Muslim Palestine.

Bunzel (2015) says the Jihadi Salafi members of ISIS stress several concepts. ISIS jihadists are to:

1. Associate only with "true" Muslims
2. Break ties with anyone who questions narrow Salafi interpretations of Islam
3. Base governments on a Salafi interpretation of Islamic law
4. Eliminate any resistance to narrow theology; such resistance is apostasy
5. Kill Shi'ites because they are apostates
6. Root out "traitors" to Islam like Hamas and the Muslim Brotherhood because they compromise with non-Muslims
7. Wage offensive jihad against idolatry wherever it is found ("idolatry" includes all non-Salafi cultures)

Most Muslims scoff at these beliefs and see their faith as a religion of peace. While jihad may be waged in defense of their community, many Muslims see it as an internal struggle against sin. Jihadi Salafism is a strain of Islam, but it is not indicative of contemporary mainstream theology (see Esposito and Voll, 2001; Haneef, 2002; Saeed and Saeed, 2004).

Self-Check

> What is Jihadi Salafism?
> Why would apocalyptic ideas be attractive to Jihadi Salafists?
> What are the core beliefs of the ISIS interpretation of Islam?

Militant Scholars and Strategists

As religions develop, various interpretations arise, and this is especially true in times of crisis. Karen Armstrong (2000b) writes that reformers emerged in Islam during a crisis in the thirteenth century. Taqi al Din ibn Taymiyya introduced new ideas about purity and militancy after Arab setbacks by the Mongols and the Crusaders. **Mohammed ibn Abdul Wahhab** "rediscovered" ibn Taymiyya when he was preaching puritanical reform in Arabia 500 years later. **Sayyid Qutb**, who lacked theological training, militarized the ideas of ibn Taymiyya and Wahhab from Egypt in the twentieth century. Although apologists defend these men as peaceful thinkers seeking to purify the faith, critics maintain that their theological writings gave rise to militancy. In the Salafi movement, the ideas of Taymiyya and Wahhab are championed by Islamic scholars such as **Abu Mohammed al Maqdisi** and **Abu Basir al Tartusi**, although both men reject ISIS.

Although Wahhab has replaced Qutb as ISIS's inspiration, another strain of scholarship is couched in religious language. Works frequently quote religious sources, but their focus is political and military strategy. Two militant strategists of this ilk have exerted a tremendous influence on Jihadi Salafism. Abu Musab al Suri's *A Call to Global Islamic Resistance* is a do-it-yourself manual for global terrorism. Abu Bakr Naji's *The Management of Savagery* is a guide for recreating the caliphate while terrorizing enemies without and within.

Taqi al Din ibn Taymiyya

Western Crusaders began waging war against the Muslims in the eleventh century, and Mongol invaders struck the Arab lands a hundred years later. Hundreds of thousands of Muslims were killed in each invasion. **Taqi al Din ibn Taymiyyah** (circa

Mohammed ibn Abdul Wahhab: (1703–1792) Also known as Abdul Wahhab. A religious reformer who wanted to purge Islam of anything beyond the traditions accepted by Mohammed and the four Rightly Guided caliphs. He conducted campaigns against Sufis, Shi'ites, and Muslims who made pilgrimages or who invoked the names of saints.

Sayyid Qutb: (1906–1966) An Egyptian educator who called for the overthrow of non-Islamic governments and the imposition of purified Islamic law based on the principles of previous puritanical reformers. Qutb formed a militant wing of the Muslim Brotherhood.

1269–1328), an Islamic scholar, was appalled by the slaughter and sought to find an answer in his faith. He believed that Muslims had fallen away from the truth and needed to internally purify themselves. He called for jihad, defining it as the destruction of internal heretics and external invaders.

Ibn Taymiyyah believed that the Crusaders and the Mongols defeated Islamic armies because of Muslim sin. Emphasizing *tawhid*, the oneness of God, ibn Taymiyyah attacked anything not endorsed by Mohammed and the first four caliphs. He forbade prayers at gravesites, belief in saints, and other practices that had worked their way into Islam. He was especially harsh on the mystical Sufis, who believed that deep prayer revealed the will of God beyond the prophecy of Mohammed and the Quran. He called for a purifying jihad to be waged against all people who threatened the faith. Jihad could be waged against nonpuritanical Muslims and nonbelievers (Hourani, 1997, pp. 179–181; Esposito, 2002, pp. 45–46; see also Gerges, 2006, p. 209).

Mohammed ibn Abdul Wahhab

John Esposito (1999, pp. 6–10) says that reform movements are common throughout the history of Islam. Two recent movements became important to the jihadists. In the late eighteenth century, a purification movement started by Mohammed ibn Abdul Wahhab (1703–1792) took root in Arabia. Influenced by ibn Taymiyya, Wahhab preached a puritanical strain of Islam that sought to rid the religion of practices added after the first few decades following Mohammed's death. This doctrine deeply influenced the Saud family as they fought to gain control of Arabia, and it dominates the theology of Saudi Arabia and the Gulf States today. Militant application of Wahhab's puritanical principles spread to India and other parts of Asia.

Strict Muslims who follow the practices of Wahhab argue that they are not militants, but Salafis are. Puritans who agree with Wahhab's theology claim they are trying to rid the religion of superstition and return it to the state envisioned by Mohammed and his first followers (Haneef, 2002, pp. 10–11; see also DeLong, 2004). Critics maintain that intolerant puritanism is responsible for Jahadi Salafism. Throughout history, Wahhab's militant followers have forced their puritanical views on those who disagree with them (Farah, 2000, p. 230).

Sayyid Qutb

Sayyid Qutb (1906–1966) was an Egyptian teacher and journalist employed by the Ministry of Education. He traveled to the United States in 1948 and stayed until 1950 to earn a master's degree. Qutb's experience soured his opinion of Western civilization. He returned to Egypt and became an active member of the Muslim Brotherhood. Qutb was arrested in 1954 after the Brotherhood tried to overthrow the Egyptian government, but he was released in 1964 because of health problems. He published his most famous work, *Milestones*, in 1965. The book outlines the theology and ideology of jihadist revolution, and its militant tone led to Qutb's second arrest and subsequent hanging by the Egyptian government in 1966 (see Bozek, 2009). Qutb's books and articles popularized many militant ideas, but scholars influenced by Wahhab today have replaced him. The most dangerous influences on current Jihadi Salafis are from strategists and political theorists who subscribe to militant puritanism.

Abu Mohammed al Maqdisi: (b. 1959) A Palestinian scholar now living in Jordan. Maqdisi is one of the most influential Jihadi Salafist scholars in the world today. Jailed and investigated many times, Maqdisi has influenced many jihadists.

Abu Basir al Tartusi: (b. 1953) A Syrian jihadist scholar who fled Syria and began preaching and writing from East London in the 1980s. He has denounced many acts of terrorism, but supports Jihadi Salafist ideology. Tartusi has been spotted with an armed group in Syria and supports Europeans who fight the Syrian government.

Taqi al Din ibn Taymiyyah: (circa 1269–1328) Also known as ibn Taymiyya; a Muslim religious reformer in the time of the Crusades and a massive Mongol invasion.

Abu Musab al Suri

In the 1980s and 1990s, American right-wing extremist Louis Beam championed a concept called leaderless resistance. Marc Sageman (2008a) applied the term to the Jihadi Salafist movement. It is not a new concept. Whether resistance or jihad, it simply refers to small isolated cells or a person acting alone attacking a perceived enemy. It is autonomous, noncommunicative terrorism. In *A Call to Global Islamic Resistance,* Abu Musab al Suri popularized the concept in Jihadi Salafist circles.

According to a *Wall Street Journal* article (Samuels, 2012), CNN once referred to al Suri as the "most dangerous terrorist you've never heard of." Inspired by modern Jihadi Salafist scholars, al Suri became disgusted with the elite hierarchy and unsuccessful strategy of Osama bin Laden. Al Qaeda could not work because Western military forces and intelligence agencies were too strong for a small group to defeat. Al Suri called for jihad on the individual level. Simply attack a target, he said, any target anywhere in the world. This strategy will eventually result in victory. According to the SITE (2011) examination of al Suri's 1,600-page manual, Ayman al Zawahiri said it provided a "rich river" for holy warriors.

N. W. Zackie (2013), in a scholarly examination of *A Call to Global Islamic Resistance,* finds that two concepts dominate al Suri's military thinking—individual action and location. Individuals and small groups must remain isolated and secretive. Geographically, jihadists should operate in areas of the world that can sustain terrorism and guerrilla war. The work begins with a long polemical history of the Islamic world. The next section starts by analyzing the reasons the West was not crippled after 9/11 and ends with a strategy for victory. Essentially, this strategy is leaderless resistance. It covers tactics and suggests areas of the world where jihadists can be successful. Although the first part seems to be designed as a religious text, Zackie concludes that it is more of a manifesto. The second part shows that al Suri is a strategic thinker.

Zackie argues that the work can be seen as a military manual, but it does more than this. It can be used to uncover the Salafi worldview. Zackie says the first section is designed to expose and convert people to militancy, get them to accept it, and then inspire them to take action. It is an exhaustive political, social, and legal treatise explaining the current plight of the Islamic world. The argument is logical within the militant puritanical strain of Islam, and it reflects common themes in religious terrorism. The oppressed have been victimized by the powerful, here is the evidence to prove it, this is the critical tipping point in cosmic history, it is time to strike, and the supreme deity is relying on the reader to take action.

The second part contains a plan of action. Al Suri (2005) equates the struggle against the United States and its allies with "light gang warfare." It involves urban terrorism and covert attacks, especially solo actions from wholly separate resistance cells. Jihad should take place on many fronts in all parts of the world. He states that large populated areas where movement is difficult to trace are ideal for resistance, and rugged mountainous areas provide places for concealment. Soft targets create terror, and killing anybody is justified because all non-Muslims and "heretics" are the enemy. Al Suri acknowledges that this may sound like part of the long tradition of revolutionary writings, but he concludes that Jihadi Salafists will adopt revolutionary literature and utilize its tactics.

Abu Bakr Naji

It is one thing to discuss revolution and quite another to justify rule by terror. It is also hard to take any religion and use it to justify mass executions, torture, mutilation, enslavement, rape, and rampant destruction. In fact, al Maqdisi and al Tartusi, two of the most prominent Jihadi Salafist scholars, have condemned such repressive actions. One writer disagrees. He not only justifies rule by terror, he champions it, arguing that ruthlessness is necessary to create the caliphate. Abu Bakr Naji's (2006) *Management of Savagery* explains the unbridled violence of groups like ISIS.

A translation by noted authority William McCants (Naji, 2006) and sponsored by Harvard University's Olin Institute for Strategic Studies is available online. Beginning with a critique of Sykes–Picot, Naji explains why it is necessary to create an Islamic state. Dystopian yet realistic, he calls for organizing well-managed, functioning governing institutions. He also calls for war, merciless war, against all enemies—both internal and external. In terms of governing, he argues that the state must brutally conduct savage public torture and butchery against all who resist. The purpose is to frighten the enemy. It is the age-old message of terrorism. Murder victims to communicate with a larger audience. The Nazis did it secretly. Naji urges the future Islamic state to show brutal repression to the world and brag about it.

Jessica Stern and J. M. Berger (2015) conclude that ISIS employs Naji's logic to rationalize inhuman actions. This logic explains the rational contradiction of portraying ISIS as simultaneously savage and benevolent. It is possible to call the faithful to the caliphate where they all their needs will be met with images of happy children attending school, receiving food and shelter, and playing soccer by using severed heads instead of a ball. The twofold message is designed for different audiences. To enemies, it says fear us because we are coming for you. To the umma, the Islamic community, it says once the "heretics" and unbelievers are eliminated, we will live in a perfect society as God wills. Such contradictory logic provides believers with the religious justification for violence.

When Do Jihadi Salafists Become Devout?

It would seem that only religious fanatics could follow the Jihadi Salafist path. After all, it is reasonable to believe that only a radical extremist could accept the logic of al Suri and Naji. A recent empirical study may suggest otherwise. Religiosity may increase after someone joins a political cause that is inspired by faith. Research from the Combatting Terrorism Center (CTC) at West Point (Mironova, Mrie, and Whit, 2014) looks at the point in time when religion begins to be important to militants. The CTC researchers conducted a survey of two differing populations in the Syrian civil war, the relatively secular Free Syrian Army (FSA) and a sample of fighters in Islamist groups. Their purpose was to determine the primary motivation for joining a group or changing from one organization to another.

The researchers found that issues such as friendship, financial benefits, organizational effectiveness, and simply liking people in the group provided the most motivation for joining. Religion was not cited as frequently, but it did increase after a person entered a faith-based group. Seventy-four percent of the Islamist respondents said they became more religious after joining their group. Of those who were members of the FSA, 37 percent provided an affirmative response to the same question. Ninety-six percent of the Islamists said that religion was crucial to them compared to 42 percent of the FSA respondents. When asked whether religion should be an important element in a new Syrian government, 90 percent of Islamists and 60 percent of the FSA sample said yes.

This study may place the work of Islamic scholars and strategists in a new light. Perhaps group members develop fanatical religious beliefs as they participate in the group. Marc Sageman (2004) makes this argument in an early study of al Qaeda. Jihadi Salafist terrorist groups employ religion to justify their actions, and it is a factor in jihadist terrorism. It may become more important as members participate in the group. Membership in a group may explain fanatical religious extremism. Members increase their zeal to express love of and loyalty to their comrades.

Self-Check

> What is the basis for Jihadi Salafism?
> How can Jihadi Salafism be used to justify violence?
> What themes do al Suri and Naji emphasize?

Al Qaeda from Inception to 9/11

Al Qaeda's origins can be traced to the Cold War. From 1945 until 1991, the United States and former Soviet Union fought one another with surrogates to avoid a direct superpower nuclear confrontation. Islamic radicals hated Communists for their atheism, and this drew the attention of Western intelligence agencies. The United States, the United Kingdom, and France began using radicals against the Soviets, and modern jihadist power grew with Western support (Cooley 2002, pp. 64–104).

Inter-Service Intelligence (ISI): The Pakistani domestic and foreign intelligence service, created by the British in 1948. Supporters claim that it centralizes Pakistan's intelligence. Critics maintain that it operates like an independent state and supports terrorist groups.

Western efforts with radicals surged in 1979 when the Soviet Union invaded Afghanistan to bolster a failing Communist regime. The United States called on Cold War allies throughout the Islamic world to support Afghan mujahedeen who resisted the Soviets. Working with Pakistani **Inter-Service Intelligence (ISI)**, Saudi Arabia, and Islamic charities, the United States funneled weapons and material to the mujahedeen. Several Muslim governments also used the war as an excuse to get rid of their own radicals. They sent local militants to join one of the many mujahedeen groups and ridded themselves of sources of domestic unrest. The Afghans had a place for a wide variety of misfits. The mujahedeen were not politically united, but they had two things in common. Most were deeply religious, and they fought the Soviets with fanatical zeal.

The Soviets left Afghanistan in 1989, and to the mujahedeen, this symbolized a great victory for God over Satan. The United States and several Western powers turned their attention elsewhere, but many of the Jihadi Salafists mujahedeen thought it was time to carry the war to their other enemies, "heretical" Muslim governments, the West, and Israel. As foreign jihadis returned home, they carried the seeds of a new international terrorist network (see, for example, Benjamin and Simon, 2002, pp. 98–102; Cooley, 2002, pp. 64–75; Gunaratna, 2002, p. 18; Kepel, 2002, pp. 136–150; Shay, 2002, pp. 108-109; Ruthven, 2000, p. 365).

Osama bin Laden, Ayman al Zawahiri, and al Qaeda

Although the United States focused attention on the collapsing Soviet Union in 1991, fighting continued in Afghanistan. Shaul Shay (2002, pp. 76–81) writes that the mujahedeen groups continued to struggle for control of the country. Al Qaeda was one of many paramilitary organizations to join the fray, and the United States failed to recognize the problem on two levels. Cooley (2002, p. 122) and Napoleoni (2003, pp. 189–191) say that American oil companies sought alliances with some Afghan groups in hopes of building an oil pipeline from Central Asia to the Indian Ocean. The proposed pipeline would run through Afghanistan. American oil companies paid more attention to potential profits than to the political problems brewing in Afghanistan. On another level, the United States simply ignored issues. As the Afghan groups continued to grow and strengthen, Americans celebrated the end of the Cold War. Only a few people in the United States knew the name Osama bin Laden, and fewer still had heard about a group called al Qaeda.

The report of the **9/11 Commission** (2004, pp. 53–54) notes that bin Laden's reputation began to grow as the mujahedeen searched for a continuing jihad. When international terrorist violence increased in Africa and Asia during the 1990s, bin Laden emerged as a symbol of Islamic discontent. Oil-rich Muslim countries were faced with a growing population of young men who had technical educations but no broad understanding of the humanities, social sciences, or the larger world. They also faced unemployment due to the uneven distribution of wealth in their countries. Bin Laden emerged as a spokesman for the discontented, and his own movement began to take form.

Osama bin Laden was the son of Mohammed bin Laden, a wealthy construction executive who worked closely with the Saudi royal family. The elder bin Laden divorced Osama's mother, but he continued to provide for the family. Because of his father's connections, bin Laden was raised in the Saudi royal court, and his tutor, Mohammed Qutb, was the brother of the Egyptian radical Sayyid Qutb. Bin Laden was influenced by Sayyid Qutb's thoughts. Inspired by the mujahedeen of Afghanistan, bin Laden dropped out of college to join the Soviet–Afghan War. At first, he lent his support to the mujahedeen, but he later formed his own guerrilla unit (L. Wright, 2006, pp. 60–83).

While in Afghanistan, bin Laden fell under the influence of **Abdullah Azzam** (1941–1989), a doctor of Islamic law. Azzam was a Palestinian scholar who was also influenced by Qutb's writings. He came to believe that a purified form of Islam was the answer to questions of poverty and the loss of political power. According to Azzam, the realm of Islam had been dominated by foreign powers for too long. It was time for all Muslims to rise up and strike Satan. He saw the Soviet–Afghan War as just the beginning of a holy war against all things foreign to Islam. At first, bin Laden found the theology of Azzam to his liking and the answer to his prayers for a path to holy war (L. Wright, 2006, pp. 99–106). The two men created al Qaeda to serve as a future headquarters for jihad (9/11 Commission, 2004, p. 58).

Training in Pakistan and Afghanistan under Azzam's spiritual mentoring, bin Laden financed mujahedeen operations and taught the guerrillas how to build field fortifications. By 1986, he had left the training field for the battlefield. Enraged with the Soviets over their wholesale slaughter of Afghan villagers and their use of poison gas, bin Laden joined the front ranks of the mujahedeen. At the end of the war, a bomb killed Azzam, and bin Laden returned home full of zeal for jihad.

The Jihadi Salafist movement took a different course in Egypt. Dr. Ayman al Zawahiri was born into a prominent Egyptian family in 1951. An intelligent, high-achieving student, he fell under the influence of violent religious philosophy in high school after being exposed to militant interpretations of Islam. His passion and intolerance grew in college as he studied at Cairo's al Azhar University. One of his mentors was **Sayyid Imam al Sharif**, also known as Dr. Fadl. Sharif would eventually be jailed for his views, but he converted back to Islam and denounced violent radicalism (see Brachman, 2009). During their time together at al Azhar's medical school, however, Sharif validated Zawahiri's growing radical theology.

Zawahiri was arrested in 1967 and charged with being a member of the Muslim Brotherhood. After his release from jail, he continued his studies to become a physician. Still active in underground politics, he opposed the government of Anwar Sadat. When Sadat signed a peace treaty with Israel, Zawahiri threw himself into the resistance. Egyptian police arrested dissidents from all over Egypt after Sadat's assassination in 1981. Zawahiri was arrested and charged with weapons violations, although he was not officially charged in the assassination. Zawahiri was sentenced to three years in prison; after serving his term, he left for Afghanistan to join the mujahedeen.

9/11 Commission: The bipartisan National Commission on Terrorist Attacks upon the United States, created after September 11, 2001, to investigate the attacks.

Abdullah Azzam: (1941–1989) The Palestinian leader of Hizb ul Tahrir and the spiritual mentor of bin Laden.

Sayyid Imam al Sharif: (b. 1951) Also known as Dr. Fadl, one of Egypt's leading militants in the 1970s. While jailed, he embraced Islam and renounced the violence of al Qaeda–style militancy. He is viewed as a traitor by violent jihadists. He has provided much of the information we have about religious militancy, and he continues to publish works denouncing it. While maintaining his anti-Western and antigovernment views, he sees jihad as a necessary part of Islam. Al Qaeda's version, he claims, violates the morality of Islamic law.

Lawrence Wright (2002) says that bin Laden and Zawahiri were bound to meet each other. Both men were highly educated, members of an elite class, and extremely pious. Bin Laden was a charismatic idealist who needed someone to frame his positions with pragmatism. Zawahiri became that person. He not only had practical abilities, he was also surrounded by an entourage of doctors, engineers, and soldiers. Bin Laden had the charisma, Zawahiri had the brains. According to a U.S. federal agent who spent many months in Pakistan and Afghanistan apprehending and interrogating jihadists (private discussion with author, 2005), Azzam called together five mujahedeen leaders in 1989, including bin Laden and Ayman al Zawahiri, a leader of the Egyptian Islamic Jihad (described later in this chapter), in an attempt to unite the jihadist movement. Bin Laden and Zawahiri left, disillusioned and angry with Azzam, and Zawahiri began sketching out a grand model for al Qaeda.

Using bin Laden's notoriety and charisma among the Afghan mujahedeen, Zawahiri transformed the organization. Zawahiri knew from experience that an umbrella-style organization was difficult to penetrate. He persuaded bin Laden that this was the type of organization to take control of Afghanistan and spread the new Islamic empire. Using Zawahiri's ideas, Osama bin Laden began to recruit the mujahedeen registered in his computer database for al Qaeda, while Zawahiri organized training camps and cells.

Bin Laden's first target was the Saudi government and its "heretical" royal family. As bin Laden's mujahedeen fighters, or "Afghans," as he called them, either went home to their native lands to wage jihad or stayed in Afghanistan to train and fight, bin Laden returned to Saudi Arabia and enjoyed warm relations with the ISI. But the Saudi government, which does not tolerate diverse opinions or dissent, was not happy to see him return. When bin Laden brought several of his Afghans into his Arabian construction business, the Saudis watched carefully. While they looked on, bin Laden became independently wealthy, and his agents began making real estate purchases in Sudan (see L. Wright, 2006, pp. 140–156).

The situation changed in 1990 when Iraq invaded Kuwait. The United States joined Saudi Arabia in a large international coalition opposing the invasion, and bin Laden was infuriated. As thousands of non-Muslim troops arrived in Saudi Arabia, radical Muslims were appalled to find Muslims fighting Muslims under U.S. leadership. The U.S.-led coalition called this military buildup **Desert Shield**, and after an air campaign pummeled Iraq in late January 1991 Desert Shield became **Desert Storm** when the U.S.-led coalition launched a ground offensive in February. They stayed afterward at the invitation of the Saudi government. For bin Laden, this was apostasy.

Ayman al Zawahiri returned to Egypt and became the driving force behind another terrorist group, the Egyptian Islamic Jihad (EIJ). A prototype for al Qaeda, EIJ was loosely bound, with autonomous cells taking action on their own. Zawahiri threw himself into an effort to topple the government, using Egyptians trained in Afghan camps. EIJ terrorists tried to assassinate Egypt's interior minister, and they bombed the Egyptian embassy in Islamabad, Pakistan. The government cracked down, and Zawahiri fled to Afghanistan with several members of EIJ in 1996 (Gunaratna, 2002, p. 45; Keats, 2002).

Bin Laden's protests against Desert Storm brought a Saudi crackdown on his operations, and he was forced to flee the country in 1992 (PBS *Frontline,* 2002). He brought 500 Afghan veterans to Sudan and tried to build a network of businesses and other enterprises. He also began to support terrorist activity. In 1993, his Afghans tried to murder Prince Abdullah (now King Abdullah) of Jordan. U.S. intelligence sources believe that he was behind the attempted assassination of Egyptian president Hosni Mubarak in 1995. According to *Frontline,* bin Laden called for a guerrilla

Desert Shield: The name of the defensive phase of the international coalition created by President George H. W. Bush after Iraq invaded Kuwait on August, 2, 1990. Its aim was to stop further Iraqi attacks and to liberate Kuwait. It lasted until coalition forces could begin an offensive against Iraq in January 1991.

Desert Storm: The military code name for the January–February offensive in the 1991 Gulf War.

campaign against Americans in Saudi Arabia. Several governments put pressure on Sudan to expel bin Laden. He fled to Afghanistan 1996 and rejoined fellow exile Ayman al Zawahiri.

Declaring War on Americans, Jews, and Crusaders

Afghanistan was attractive to both bin Laden and al Zawahiri because the **Taliban**, led by **Mullah Omar**, took power in Kabul and instituted strict intolerant fundamentalist law. Bin Laden moved to Kandahar and established the organizational infrastructure of al Qaeda with his "Afghans," dissidents from multiple Muslim countries. Joined by Zawahiri and other fleeing Egyptians, he consolidated power and absorbed the new jihadists in his ranks. Then bin Laden made a most unusual declaration. Seated in front of a camera in 1996 with Zawahiri and al Qaeda's security director, Mohammed Atef, bin Laden declared war on the United States. In 1998, after absorbing EIJ and other radical groups, bin Laden and Zawahiri formed the **World Islamic Front Against Jews and Crusaders**, and they ordered Muslims to kill Americans and their allies everywhere they found them (Lewis, 2003a).

In August 1998, bin Laden's terrorists bombed the U.S. embassies in Nairobi, Kenya, and Dar es Salaam, Tanzania. The Nairobi bomb killed 213 people and injured 4,500; the Dar es Salaam explosion killed 12 people and wounded 85. These attacks signaled a new phase in al Qaeda terrorism. The Nairobi and Dar es Salaam bombs demonstrated how al Qaeda had matured. For the first time, the group could operate a cell planted in a country hundreds of miles away from al Qaeda training camps. It used sophisticated bombs and demonstrated complex planning. Then came the attack on the USS *Cole* in 2000, a failed millennial New Year's Day attack on Los Angeles International Airport, and then the attacks of September 11, 2001 (see L. Wright, 2006 for one of the best description of these actions, including 9/11). Despite al Qaeda's reputation as an international organization, bin Laden and Zawahiri failed to emerge as the masterminds of a worldwide terror organization. They served mainly as symbols. The 9/11 plot can be traced to another operative, Khalid Sheik Mohammed, who planned the attack and put the people in place to carry it out.

Taliban: The Islamist group that governed Afghanistan from 1996 to 2001.

Mullah Omar: (b. 1959) the leader of the Taliban. After the collapse of the Taliban government in 2001, Omar went into hiding.

World Islamic Front Against Jews and Crusaders: an organization created in 1998 by Osama bin Laden and Ayman al Zawahiri. It represents a variety of jihadist groups that presented a united front against Jews and the West. It was commonly called al Qaeda. The group is currently scattered throughout the Muslim world. Al Qaeda in Afghanistan and Pakistan can be called Al Qaeda core or al Qaeda central.

> **Self-Check**
> > How did the Soviet–Afghan War give rise to al Qaeda?
> > How did bin Laden and Zawahiri create a new organization in Afghanistan?
> > What resulted from the declaration of war and the alliance against Jews and crusaders?

Al Qaeda: Degraded, Transformed, and Franchised

After the U.S.-led offensive in Afghanistan in October 2001, bin Laden and Zawahiri saw their control diminish even further. They were able to indirectly influence bombings in Madrid on March 11, 2004, and an operational commander had direct contact with bombers on the London subway on July 7, 2005. They almost produced mass casualties in the summer of 2006 with a number of simultaneous airline suicide attacks, but good intelligence and police work stopped the attacks in the planning stage. However, their ability to control activity waned, and the nature of Jihadi Salafism changed as bin Laden and Zawahiri lost operational power. Former CIA executive Paul Pillar (2004) saw that al Qaeda's core control structure was disrupted after the 2001 offensive in Afghanistan, which resulted in the creation of a loose international network of affiliated al Qaeda movements. It has suffered more since Pillar's assessment.

Al Qaeda has become a franchise—that is, a brand name. Zawahiri provides core leadership and operates in the tribal areas of Pakistan. He has power because of an alliance with other groups in the area. Alliances include Lashkar-e-Taiba and the Pakistani version of the Taliban. Al Qaeda core's most important ally is a large family that looks more like the mafia than a terror network. The **Haqqani network** runs its own militias, shadow governments, protection rackets, legitimate businesses, and terrorist groups. Dating back to the Soviet–Afghan War, leaders of the Haqqani clan are the major players in Pakistan's tribal region. They can plan and administer highly complex terrorist attacks from a great distance. Yet, Zawahiri and al Qaeda core have been significantly degraded due to U.S. drone attacks in Pakistan and other counterterrorism efforts. Peter Berger (2009) points to the following significant al Qaeda operatives killed by drones:

Haqqani network: A family in the tribal area of Pakistan that has relations with several militant groups and the ISI. The Haqqani family is involved in organized crime, legitimate businesses, the ISI, and terrorism groups. It is the major power broker in the tribal region.

- Abu Laith al Libi: led al Qaeda behind bin Laden and Zawahiri
- Abu Sulyman al Jazairi: member of Algerian jihad
- Abu Khabab al Masri: weapons of mass destruction expert
- Abdul Rehman: Taliban commander, South Waziristan
- Abu Haris: al Qaeda chief in Pakistan
- Khalid Habib: senior al Qaeda leader
- Abu Zubair al Masri: senior al Qaeda leader
- Abdullah Azzam al Saudi: senior al Qaeda leader
- Abu Jihad al Masri: al Qaeda propaganda chief
- Tahir Yulashev: commander, Islamic Movement of Uzbekistan
- Baitullah Mehsud: leader, Pakistani Taliban

Of course, the most public attack on al Qaeda core came on May 1, 2011, when President Barak Obama announced that U.S. Navy SEALs had attacked Osama bin Laden's compound in Pakistan. The nemesis from 9/11 was dead. Al Queda's propaganda arm suffered a blow in January 2015 when an American strike killed Adam Gadahn, al Qaeda core's American spokesperson. Yet, the threat from al Qaeda remains. Seth Jones (2014) of the RAND Corporation explains the reason.

Jones found empirical evidence to explain the degradation of al Qaeda core and its transformation and rebirth as a loose network of jihadist groups. As Paul Pillar (2004) observed, al Qaeda was weakened after the first American attacks in October 2001. The multinational organization began to crumble. Jones says new organizations appeared around the word, some of which accepted the core's leadership and some of which were inspired by it; ironically, other jihadi groups rejected the core altogether. In the following decade, bin Laden was killed, al Qaeda was totally fractured, and the West was forced to face an expanded network that presented a variety of new challenges.

At the end of 2014, Jihadi Salafist groups posed a serious and growing threat to U.S. interests overseas, and they inspired terrorism throughout the world. Jones (2014, pp. 28–33) finds that the number of Jihadi Salafist groups is increasing, and so are their activities. The number of Jihadi Salafist groups rose 58 percent from 2010 to 2013, from 31 to 49. The largest growth in the number of groups was in North Africa and the Middle East. Membership in these groups more than doubled during the same time period. The largest jump in membership was due to rebels from Syria.

The Arab Spring opened several new areas conducive to Jihadi Salafist groups, according to Jones. Libya became a haven for such groups, and Egypt experienced an increase, although many Egyptian security operations have been effective against them. New groups in Libya and Egypt inspired jihadists in surrounding countries, both those swearing loyalty to al Qaeda core and those remaining autonomous or maintaining other allegiances. Syria was a magnet for Jihadi Salafists. ISIS, now separated from al Qaeda core, was the most active group in 2013, accounting for 43 percent of all attacks. It was followed by al Shabab (discussed as a regional group in Chapter 7) at 25 percent, Jabhat al Nusra (al Qaeda in Syria) at 21 percent, and al Qaeda in the Arabian Peninsula (AQAP) at 10 percent. Most attacks have been local, but Jihadi Salafists still threaten the United States and Europe as they plan transnational attacks. Returning citizens fighting with the groups also pose a threat, and Jihadi Salafists inspire homegrown terrorist attacks.

Although the leadership has been degraded, the threat continues due to the franchised approach to terrorism. Bin Laden was an important symbol, and his compound proved to be a treasure trove of intelligence. Yet, threats live on through the franchises.

Major Franchises Swearing Fealty to al Qaeda Core

Diverse al Qaeda movements have appeared in different parts of the world, and their effectiveness is growing (see Fig. 11.1). Some groups have demonstrated an ability to develop and support terrorist attacks beyond their immediate geographical location. Such groups are emerging as threats to regional stability; others threaten Western security. The RAND Corporation counted dozens of active Jihadi Salafist groups in 2013, with several al Qaeda affiliates (Jones, 2014). Some of the major groups are discussed in this section. They are ordered in terms of the author's opinion of the threat they present to Western interests. The most dangerous groups appear first. (For Ansaru, Boko Haram, and al Shabab, please see Chapter 7. ISIS and Jabhat al Nursa are discussed in the following section. With the exception of Ansaru, these groups would also appear—based on threat assessment—shortly after the discussion of AQAP.)

Franchise in Yemen: AQAP One of the Jihadi Salafist groups that has attempted massive attacks in the United States (see Figure 11.2) and supported the 2015 *Charlie Hebdo* murders in Paris grew from the tangled political situation in Yemen. It

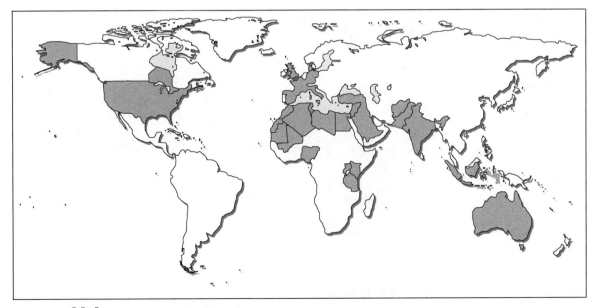

FIGURE **11.1** Global Jihadi Attacks

expanded during violent Yemeni political upheaval in 2014–2015. Its leaders swore loyalty to Osama bin Laden and promised to support Ayman al Zawahiri after bin Laden was killed. The group is known as al Qaeda in the Arabian Peninsula (AQAP).

In June 2015, AQAP spokesperson Khaled al Batarfi announced the death of **Nasir al Wuhayshi,** the group's leader and cofounder. The United States had targeted and killed him with a drone strike. A former aide to bin Laden, Wuhayshi trained in Afghanistan before returning to Yemen. He was arrested by Yemeni authorizes shortly after 9/11. Daniel Byman (2015) says his elimination was not simply another notch on the American gun belt. Wuhayshi transformed a failing terrorist organization in Saudi Arabia into one of the most active international terrorist groups in the world. According to Byman, Wuhayshi was an effective leader and heir to Zawahiri. Under his leadership, AQAP was able to threaten the region, Europe, and the U.S. homeland.

AQAP emerged from the complicated political system in Yemen. A smorgasbord of competing tribes and interest groups remained after a new government was organized in 1990. The government was overthrown shortly after the 2011 Arab Spring, and a new government fled from a tribal rebellion in 2014. As the rebel tribe advanced, AQAP was able to gather strength from some of the tribes that were resisting the takeover.

Wuhayshi and **Qasim al Raymi** formed al Qaeda in Yemen (AQY) after escaping from prison with two dozen other jihadists in 2006. When members of a defeated Saudi group retreated to Yemen in 2009, Wuhayshi welcomed them into the ranks of Yemeni jihadists and formed a new group, AQAP. According to the *Long War Journal* (Jocelyn, 2015), Wuhayshi became the group's leader, and Raymi served as military commander.

AQAP attracted competent jihadists, including bomb-maker **Ibrahim al Asiri** and American Jihadi Salafi cleric **Anwar al Awlaki.** Asiri became a master of his trade and created chemical bombs with the ability to pass through metal detectors. The son of a career Saudi military officer, he joined AQAP with his brother shortly after it formed in 2009. He convinced his brother to become a suicide bomber and attempted to kill a high-ranking Saudi counterterrorism official the same year. The quality of his work served as a force multiplier, and he taught bomb-making skills to others (BBC, 2014).

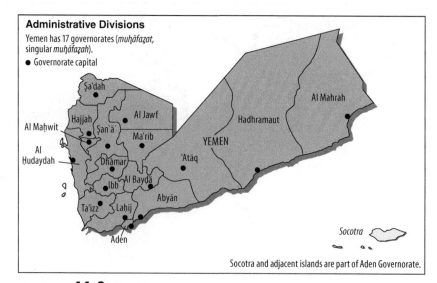

FIGURE **11.2:** Yemen

Awlaki preached at a mosque near Washington, D.C. He joined President George W. Bush in an interfaith prayer service shortly after 9/11 and posted sermons on the Internet calling for peaceful relations between Christianity and Islam. He gradually became convinced the West was waging a war on Islam, however, and he abandoned the United States to join AQAP. He inspired **Nidal Malik Hasan** to go on a shooting spree at Fort Hood in 2009 and may have been involved in a plot to bomb an American airliner over Detroit. An American drone–launched missile killed him in 2011. He still inspires Salafi terrorists throughout the world (Bergen, 2015).

Daniel Byman (2015) says AQAP projects a grave international threat. Members have inspired Salafi terrorism in the United States, Europe, and the Islamic world. AQAP was behind an attempt to destroy a Northwest flight from Amsterdam on Christmas Day 2009. A year later, AQAP terrorists packed chemical explosives in printers placed aboard cargo planes bound for the United States. It was behind another failed plot to bring down a plane with an underwear bomb in 2012. Its glossy *Inspire* Internet magazine motivated two Americans to place homemade bombs at the finish line during the 2013 Boston Marathon. The magazine also gave them the instructions for building the bombs. It sponsored a Parisian attack on the *Charlie Hebdo* offices in January 2015 when three AQAP terrorists called out the names of cartoonists and methodically shot them for lampooning Islam. One of the terrorists subsequently swore allegiance to ISIS shortly before being killed by French police.

The United States has actively waged a drone campaign against AQAP's leadership, increasing attacks in 2014 as the terrorist group gained strength. Awlaki was killed in 2011. A number of other leading figures were killed in late 2014 through 2015. These included a deputy commander, the suspect who planned the *Charlie Hebdo* murders, and Wuhayshi.

Franchise in Iraq and Syria: ISIS (Please see the next section.)

Franchise in Algeria: AQIM Algeria's jihadist civil war in the 1990s spawned the Salafi Group for Preaching and Combat (GSPC) in 1998, and the GSPC gave rise to a new group, al Qaeda in the Islamic Maghreb (AQIM), in 2006. The Congressional Research Service (CRS) says that the GPSC split from the Algerian Islamic Group (GIA) to oppose the GIA's indiscriminate targeting of civilians (Rollins, 2010). In 2006, the GSPC announced its unity with al Qaeda and changed its name to the AQIM. It was able to raise funds from cells in Europe, but its primary income was derived from criminal activities. It made money by kidnapping, trafficking drugs and contraband, and human trafficking (Figure 11.3).

The National Counterterrorism Center (NCTC, 2015) says that the group began changing its targets in late 2006 and early 2007. Using roadside bombs, it began to attack the energy industry. It stepped up its activity in Algiers, the capital of Algeria, and it launched an attack against the Israeli embassy in neighboring Mauritania. The group also introduced suicide bombing, and by the end of 2007 more than 30 people in Algiers had lost their lives to AQIM attacks. This prompted a crackdown by the Algerian government, and AQIM was forced from the capital.

AQIM took advantage of political chaos in northern Mali and consolidated its power there. The group fractured after this. Some cells remained loyal to AQIM but operated independently. Other dissidents joined breakaway organizations such as the Movement for Unity and Jihad in West Africa (MUJWA). **Mokhtar Belmokhtar** formed a new independent group with MUJWA named al Murabituom and attacked a natural gas production facility in southern Algeria in January 2013. More than 80 people were killed.

Nidal Malik Hasan: (b. 1970) A former American soldier of Palestinian descent. Hasan was an army psychiatrist who apparently became self-radicalized and embraced militant Islam. He went on a shooting spree at Fort Hood, Texas, on November 5, 2009, killing 13 people and wounding almost three dozen others. He was wounded, arrested, and charged with several counts of murder.

Mokhtar Belmokhtar: (b. 1972) An Algerian jihadist and organized crime figure. Belmokhtar fought in the Soviet–Afghan War and the Algerian civil war. He joined the Salafi Call for Preaching and Combat and later AQIM. He later broke with AQIM. His is also known for criminal activity.

Various AQIM units and breakaway groups frequently engage in more organized crime than terrorism. They have conducted numerous kidnappings to raise funds and are involved in smuggling. Belmokhtar is especially known for smuggling cigarettes, and one of his many nicknames is Mr. Marlborough. Despite formally severing ties with AQIM, Belmokhtar remains loyal to al Qaeda core (Roggio, 2013; Humud et al., 2014). The future is not clear. French military forces attacked invading jihadists in Mali in January 2013 and drove them back. The French began a withdrawal in the summer of 2015. In the meantime, AQIM and/or its breakaways may have developed extensive ties with Boko Haram. Some analysts believe that elements of AQIM want to shift their loyalty to ISIS. In September 2014, Reuters reported that a breakaway group called Caliphate Soldiers in Algeria swore loyalty to Abu Bakr al Baghdadi, breaking AQIM still further (Chikhi, 2014).

Franchise in Syria and Iraq: al Nusra (Please see the following section.)

Franchise in Somalia: al Shabab (Please see Chapter 7.)

Franchise in Niger: Boko Haram (Please see Chapter 7.)

Franchise in Libya: Ansar al Sharia, Libya Formed in 2012, Ansar al Sharia is composed of Sunni jihadists who seek to create an Islamic state in Libya, according to the Congressional Research Service (Humud et al., 2014). The group has been responsible for attacks on civilians and a number of assassinations. Ansar al Sharia operates primarily in eastern Libya and around Benghazi. One of its most noted attacks against the West was a September 11, 2012, assault on the U.S. Special Mission and Annex in Benghazi. It killed two security officers and the U.S. ambassador to Libya. Ansar al Sharia has loose ties with al Qaeda core through contacts in AQIM (Humud et al., 2014).

Franchise in Tunisia: Ansar al Sharia, Tunisia Founded in 2011 by former mujahedeen from Afghanistan, the Tunisian Ansar al Sharia serves as a conduit for Tunisian fighters bound for Syria. It also seems to be seeking to establish an Islamic state in

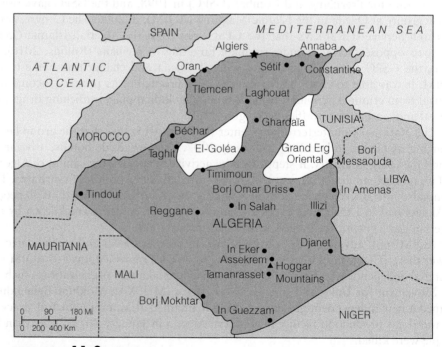

FIGURE **11.3:** Algeria

Tunisia. According to the Congressional Research Service (Humud et al., 2014), all its attacks have been confined to Tunisia. Its primary threat to the West has been attacks on tourists.

Franchise in Egypt: ABM Ansar Bayt al Maqdis formed in 2011 after the Arab Spring. Its primary operational area is the Sinai Peninsula, but it has attempted assassinations elsewhere. Ayman al Zawahiri publically praised the group for its operations, but it has no known contact with al Qaeda core. It embeds al Qaeda videos in its propaganda. ABM may have conducted attacks against Israel, and it promised action against Western powers that engaged ISIS in late 2014.

✓ Self-Check

> How has al Qaeda core been degraded?
> How united is the al Qaeda franchise network?
> What are the various threats posed by the franchise?

Conflict in the Franchise: Jabhat al Nusra and ISIS

The emergence of ISIS took some people in the West completely by surprise. It should not have done so. The roots of ISIS stretched back 10 years. Ahmad Fidal al Khlayleh, known by his *nom de guerre* **Abu Musab al Zarqawi**, was a street thug who was well known to police in Jordan when he left his homeland to fight in Afghanistan in the late 1980s. Covered with tattoos and a heavy drinker, he was not the personification of Islam. After developing a deep hatred of Israel and the United States, he returned to Jordan in 1993 and soon found himself in trouble and in prison (Brisard, 2005, pp. 10–41). Cole Bunzel (2015) says that while he was in prison, Zarqawi formed a close friendship with Abu Mohammed al Maqdisi, who converted him to Jihadi Salafism. He was a new man when he was released from prison in 1999.

Zarqawi left Jordan for Pakistan in 1999 and gravitated to Afghanistan a second time to support the Taliban, probably with the support of Pakistan's Inter-Service Intelligence agency. According to Jessica Stern and J. M. Berger (2015, pp. 16–17), he met bin Laden after entering Afghanistan, and things did not go well. The two terrorists found they had little in common. Bin Laden was cultured and educated, while Zarqawi was an uneducated ruffian. Despite their mutual distaste for one another, bin Laden gave Zarqawi permission to set up a semiautonomous training camp, and he began training jihadists. When the United States invaded Iraq in 2003, he moved to Iraq and established al Qaeda in Iraq (AQI). It would become the basis for the Islamic State of Iraq (ISI), ISIS, and an al Qaeda franchise in Syria called Jabhat al Nusra.

In theory, AQI was extension of al Qaeda; in practice, it was not. Zarqawi was an independent operator. It is unusual to think of the term *moderate* when the word *terrorism* is used, but Zarqawi's approach to violence was even more shocking than other Jihadi Salafists. Jennifer Cafarella (2015) illustrates the different approaches on an imaginary spectrum. Both al Qaeda core and AQI can be placed on the same continuum, but AQI sits on one side and al Qaeda is on the other. They sought the same outcomes from 2003 to 2006, yet they employed violence in different ways.

Al Qaeda killed its enemies indiscriminately, but it grew more "selective" after two American embassy bombings in 1998 accidently killed over 200 Muslims. Only a dozen Americans were killed in the two blasts. Al Qaeda learned that it had to win the support of local populations if it were to achieve its goals. It was the old lesson from Michael Collins in the Black and Tan War. General terrorism did not work, but selective terrorism increased chances for success.

Abu Musab al Zarqawi: (1966–2006) a Jordanian criminal who converted to Jihadi Salafism after trip to Afghanistan in 1989. His radicalism increased after serving a sentence in a Jordanian prison from 1993 to 1999. He returned to Afghanistan in 1999 and moved to Iraq after the U.S. invasion in 2003. He founded al Qaeda in Iraq, a group that became known for extreme violence. He was killed in an American bombing attack in 2006.

AQI took a different approach. Zarqawi's terrorists killed all enemies (and a few friends) irrespective of consequences. For example, bin Laden and Zawahiri wanted to convert Shi'ites and turn them into "true" Muslims. Shi'ites were an abomination to Zarqawi. He wanted to kill as many of them as possible, and he did. AQI bombed Shi'ite markets, celebrations, neighborhoods, mosques, shrines, and religious pilgrimages. Zarqawi's goal was slaughter. From late 2003 to 2006, AQI killed Americans, Iraqi security forces, Iraqi civilians, Shi'ites, and even some Sunnis. The campaign was so violent that when General David Petraeus launched a counterinsurgency in 2007, the United States and its allies fought with the help of former Sunni tribal enemies who flocked to stop insurgents like AQI. In return, the U.S. forces and Iraqi government promised the Sunni tribes security, economic support, and full participation in the Iraqi political system—a promise that the Iraqi government would break in 2012, which spawned the growth and rapid expansion of ISIS.

U.S. intelligence units hunted Zarqawi for nearly three years. Well known for public executions, Zarqawi kidnapped Americans and sawed off their heads with a large knife in a series of Internet videos. His message reflected Abu Bakr Naji's ideal in *The Management of Savagery*: Terrify your enemies with absolute ruthlessness. Zarqawi believed he fought for God in a battle to usher in the end of time.

Zarqawi's participation in jihad came to an end on June 7, 2006. Military and intelligence personnel tracking Zarqawi kept some of his closest associates under surveillance. They spotted one of them going into a house just north of Baghdad and called on the U.S. Air Force. Within minutes, two precision-guided bombs flew into the house, and Zarqawi was eliminated.

The Islamic State of Iraq

U.S. officials released a photograph of Zarqawi's corpse, a mistake when dealing with a culture that glorifies martyrdom. Ironically, Ayman al Zawahiri, who had once written a letter chastising Zarqawi for excessive violence, gave a glowing eulogy for the fallen leader of AQI. He urged AQI to form an Islamic state with support from al Qaeda and to build a popular political entity based on strict Islamic law. AQI followed Zawahiri's advice, creating the Islamic State of Iraq (ISI, not to be confused with the Pakistani Inter-Service Intelligence agency). Its new leader was **Abu Omar al Baghdadi**.

ISI made little headway. While numerous civilians were killed every day, many Sunnis were fed up. They joined General Petraeus's counterinsurgency and drove ISI deep underground. Its membership dwindled, and its ability to operate was severely hampered. When Abu Omar al Baghdadi was killed in 2010, ISI was on the ropes. Its governing council elected another leader who had been radicalized in prison, Ibrahim Awaad Ibrahim Ali al Badri al Samarrai whose *nom de guerre* was **Abu Bakr al Baghdadi**. He was said to be directly descended from the Prophet Mohammed (Stern and Berger, 2015, p. 33).

Abu Bakr al Baghdadi took over at a time when the insurgency seemed to be over or at least winding down, but the Iraqi prime minister made a fatal political miscalculation. The prime minister adopted policies favorable to Iraq's Shi'ite majority and ordered the arrest of some prominent Sunni government officials. He also ordered the United States to leave in 2012, and President Obama complied. The prime minster stopped supporting only Sunnis, including the tribes that participated in the counterinsurgency. He looked away when private Shi'ite militias moved into Sunni areas, frequently massacring the Sunnis. Tribal leaders and other Sunnis looked for a solution. They found it in ISI and later ISIS. Iraqis forced the prime minister from power in 2014, but ISIS had a foothold among the Sunnis.

Abu Omar al Baghdadi: (d. 2010) The first leader of the Islamic State of Iraq who took command after Abu Musab al Zarqawi was killed in 2006. Little is known about his background, and U.S. military forces once believed he was a factious character. He was killed in an American strike in 2010.

Abu Bakr al Baghdadi: (b. circa 1971) An Iraqi Sunni who joined the resistance against the U.S. invasion of Iraq in 2003. He may have been a violent radical before the invasion. Regardless, after being held in prison by U.S. forces, he became a hardened radical. He emerged as a leader of AQI, but unlike Zarqawi, he was articulate and charismatic. He assumed control of the ISI in 2010, entered the Syrian civil war, and changed ISI to ISIS. Abu Mohammed al Adnani declared him caliph of the Islamic State in June 2014.

ISI Reborn

Jessica Stern and J. M. Berger (2015, pp. 38–39) say that when Abu Bakr al Baghdadi became leader of ISI in May 2010, it was in shambles. Baghdadi began rebuilding the organization, bringing trusted allies into leadership positions, packing the ranks with competent former Iraqi military commanders, and recruiting bureaucrats who knew how to create and manage governmental services. This reflected the philosophy presented in Abu Musab al Suri's *A Call to Global Islamic Resistance*. Baghdadi transformed ISI into a Che Guevara–styled guerrilla army. Baghdadi also intended to manage savagery. His minions would use force to terrify external enemies and eliminate all "heretics" in conquered territory.

Writing for the Combatting Terrorism Center at West Point, Michael Knights (2014) says that ISIS did not suddenly appear on the scene in the summer of 2014. Abu Bakr al Baghdadi began a patient and systematic campaign of organizational development when he assumed control of ISI in May 2010. ISI terrorists infiltrated Sunni communities in northwestern Iraq to identify local pro-government leaders. They systematically conducted a campaign of targeted assassinations from late 2010 until 2013.

ISI took other actions. In 2012, it trained highly mobile light infantry units of fighters with experience in Syria, Chechnya, and/or the Balkans. On July 29, 2013, Abu Bakr al Baghdadi's commanders began a new campaign called Soldier's Harvest with these seasoned combatants. The purpose of the operation was to murder individual and small groups of Iraqi soldiers. ISI terrorists assassinated soldiers on the streets, attacked checkpoints, destroyed soldiers' homes, and killed security force officers over the course of the next 12 months. In the process, they essentially isolated the city of Mosul from the highway and communication systems that connected it to Baghdad.

Knights (2014) says Baghdadi also built a highly structured command and control system based on veteran military officers. He created a centralized cell that would determine overall strategy and delegated authority to local commanders. Launching another operation called Breaking the Walls—a car bombing campaign from summer 2013 to summer 2014—Baghdadi's command cell selected targets in 20 Iraqi cities, giving local commanders the power to determine when and how the attacks would be launched. Knights concludes that ISIS's lightening success in June 2014 was the result of multiple actions that weakened Iraqi security forces prior to the offensive.

Jabhat al Nusra

Abu Bakr al Baghdadi also took advantage of the Syrian civil war. As opposition to the Syrian government grew in 2011, many autonomous groups formed to fight the Syrian army. Jenifer Cafarella (2014), a researcher with the Institute for the Study of War, says that Abu Bakr al Baghdadi sent **Abu Mohammed al Jawlani** to Syria with instructions to create an ISI front in Syria. Jawlani kept a low public profile when he entered Syria, and he soft-pedaled rigid Islamic law as he systematically recruited fighters to a new organization. He announced the presence of a new al Qaeda franchise, Jabhat al Nusra, in January 2012 on social media. For the next six months, Jawlani made Zarqawi's mistake of isolating the population by using overt intensive violence. Unlike Zarqawi, he learned this was counterproductive. He abandoned the practice and sought popular support.

Cafarella says Jawlani started to present al Nusra as a nationalist organization expressing loyalty to both jihadist and secular rebels. He publicly downplayed al Qaeda sympathies and did not swear a public oath of loyalty to any jihadist leader. His fighters developed deep ties to many other rebel units and frequently performed specialized

Abu Mohammed al Jawlani: (b. ?) Leader of Jabhat al Nusra. Little is known about Jawlani's background. He is Syrian and left his homeland to fight against U.S. forces in Iraq. He was captured by these forces. After being released from prison, he met Abu Bakr al Baghdadi, joined ISI, and rose through the ranks. Baghdadi sent him to Syria in 2011, where he formed al Nusra. When Baghdadi tried to absorb al Nusra in 2014, Jawlani broke with ISIS and swore allegiance to Zawahiri.

attacks for them. Privately he hoped to recruit terrorists from al Qaeda core to establish a separate operational base for international terrorism in al Nusra's territory. He believed al Qaeda could use this foothold as a platform for attacks on Europe and North America. United States intelligence officers dubbed the terrorists who joined this unit as the "Khorasan Group."

Cafarella (2014) argues that Jawlani implemented many ideas contained in Suri's *A Call to Global Islamic Resistance*. Like Abu Bakr al Baghdadi, he was strategic and methodical. He began a systematic campaign as al Nusra built strength. The first steps were aimed at killing government leaders, military commanders, and off-duty or lightly protected soldiers. The next set of attacks focused on intelligence and security units while Jawlani increased recruitment and training. He created a small army of trained fighters, and al Nusra became the best organization in the rebel ranks. Al Nusra had equipment and funding, and it was effective. Jawlani took and held relatively large sections of Syria, and recruits flocked to the group's ranks, including foreigners, secular fighters, and other rebels.

Stern and Berger (2015, pp. 41–42) agree with Cafarella's belief that al Nusra became the most effective rebel group in the Syrian civil war. Secular and moderate organizations struggled for supplies and weapons, but al Nusra was funded by generous donations. It soon had the upper hand in Syria. In the summer of 2012, Jawlani's al Nusra sought alliances, made compromises, and provided social services in the areas under his control. Back at al Qaeda core, Zawahiri was pleased and assumed that he controlled both of franchises ISI and al Nusra.

ISIS

In April 2013, ISI entered the Syrian civil war. According to Stern and Berger (2015, pp. 42–44), Abu Bakr al Baghdadi merged al Nusra and ISI into a new group, the Islamic State of Iraq and al Sham. Neither Jawlani nor Zawahiri were pleased. No longer soft-pedaling his al Qaeda core connections, Jawlani publicly swore allegiance to Zawahiri. Cafarella (2015) adds that one al Nusra commander said that they did not want to do it, but Baghdadi forced their hand. Stern and Berger say that Zawahiri sent a private letter to Baghdadi nullifying his announcement, and Baghdadi announced that he was ignoring it. ISIS would fight in Iraq and Syria. Baghdadi unleashed his storm of killing in Syria, and he was soon fighting Syrian military forces, secular rebels, Hamas, Hezbollah, jihadist groups, and al Nusra.

ISIS and the Caliphate

Cole Bunzel (2014) says that ISIS was not an isolated entity separate from Islam. While most Muslims, including a large number of Jihadi Salafists, denounced it, ISIS had its own scholars and its own traditions stretching back to ibn Taymiyya. It controlled some of the best and most sophisticated media outlets among the Jihadist Salafi movement, and it did something that al Qaeda core failed to do. It held and governed territory. Stern and Berger (2015, pp. 44–47) point out that it backed up its swagger with its 2014 military campaign, taking about one third of Iraq and Syria. It managed oil production, ran its own banking system, operated schools and health care facilities, and established a government. In June 2014, the second most important city in Iraq, Mosul, fell to ISIS fighters. On June 29, 2014, the group's spokesperson proclaimed that ISIS had restored the caliphate and that Abu Bakr al Baghdadi was the new caliph. From this point on, the spokesperson said, ISIS would simply be known as the Islamic State. Mainstream Muslims gave it the derogatory Arabic name

Daesh, but Jihadi Salafism had a home. Die-hard Salafists, young zealous converts, kids searching for adventure, and hundreds of Western men and women traveled to ISIS territory to join the caliphate. In their minds, the historic Islamic community had been restored.

Conflict within the Jihad

Bunzel (2015) says ISIS's actions created a firestorm of debate in the Jihadi Salafist world. Several Islamic scholars around the world argued that ISIS had the right to create the caliphate. Critics, including some of the most eminent Jihadi Salafist scholars, thought that this was rubbish. They likened ISIS to the first Islamic heretics and claimed that its theology and practices deviated from the straight path of Islam. Al Qaeda supporters said that Baghdadi lacked the power to create a caliphate. ISIS supporters responded by citing Baghdadi's alleged genealogical link to the Prophet.

Stern and Berger (2015, pp. 178–191) say that the declaration led to fighting between al Qaeda core and ISIS. Zawahiri declared that Afghanistan was the seat of the caliphate and that the Taliban leader Mullah Omar was the caliph. Stern and Berger say that as of early 2015, ISIS seemed to be losing the ideological war. No major group had sworn allegiance to Abu Bakr al Baghdadi. By the same token, new groups have sprung up and accepted Baghdadi as caliph. In addition, there was quite a bit of sympathy for ISIS in long-established groups such as AQIM, Boko Haram, and al Shabab. Some leaders in Boko Haram even pledged loyalty to both groups, and groups such as AQIM formed a splinter group that abandoned al Qaeda for ISIS. AQAP was firmly in the al Qaeda core camp under Wuhayshi. Stern and Berger conclude that when al Zawahiri is dead, all bets will be off. As of this writing, the battle for loyalty is still being waged.

Foreign Fighters

Stern and Berger (2015, pp. 77–99) examine another aspect of ISIS—its ability to attract foreigners, many of whom are from the West. They also cite jihadist expert Thomas Hegghamer's claims that Westerners are overrepresented in ISIS media and that their zeal is understandable because they are more motivated than average Syrian rebels. Stern and Berger write that just as there is no clear estimate on the size of ISIS combat strength (estimates range from 20,000 to 35,000 fighters), there is no accurate assessment of the numbers of foreign fighters in ISIS. Yet, men and women from around the world have demonstrated a willingness to join the caliphate.

As John Horgan (2005) correctly noted a few years ago, there is no single method of radicalization. Stern and Berger say this is true concerning paths to jihad. Some experts, including Horgan, say that recruits come seeking meaning for their lives. Others seek adventure, absolution of a sinful past, martyrdom, or a religious calling. Since ISIS is willing to take anyone because the "state" needs all types of talent, men, women, professionals, and others have joined.

In an article from the *New York Times Magazine,* journalist Mary Anne Weaver (2015) interviewed researchers at the International Center for the Study of Radicalization at King's College London. These researchers believe foreign recruits are drawn to ISIS and the Syrian civil war for a number of reasons. Scholarly research has shown that recruitment on social media is important, and economic and educational levels have little to do with the decision to join ISIS. Researchers in one study found that many British recruits were from well-established middle-class homes and had university educations. While there is no common pattern, one former radical noted that

Jihadi Salafism appeals to young people. Surprisingly, very few returning jihadists want to practice their trade when they return. Stern and Berger (2015, pp. 90–91) add that many foreigners quickly become disillusioned and find no way to escape. Young women, for example, frequently find that they are "married" to fighters upon arrival, and they quickly end up pregnant and in abusive relationships.

ISIS has another recruiting theme that is shared with all the al Qaeda franchises. The message is: If you cannot travel to the jihad, practice it at home. That problem is discussed in Chapter 12.

✓ Self-Check	> How did Zarqawi lay the foundation for ISIS?
	> Why did conflict and rivalry evolve among Jihadi Salafists?
	> How has ISIS's formation of a caliphate influenced terrorism?

A Survey of Other Groups

This chapter has focused on Central and southwestern Asia, but the Salafi movement is a global phenomenon. A quick survey of select international groups reveals an array of jihadist movements. Recall that Boko Haram and al Shabab were presented as regional groups in Chapter 7. They are also part of Jihadi Salafism and could have easily been included in this chapter. This section of the chapter will highlight some other prominent groups.

Lashkar-e-Taiba

Jammu and Kashmir: A mountainous region in northern India claimed by both India and Pakistan. It has been the site of heavy fighting during three wars between India and Pakistan in 1947–1948, 1971, and 1999. Kashmir is artificially divided by a line of control (LOC), with Pakistani forces to the north and India's to the south. India and Pakistan made strides toward peace after 2003, but many observers believe that the ISI supports jihadist operations in the area.

The Lashkar-e-Taiba (LeT) was created in 1993 under the watchful eye of Pakistani Inter-Service Intelligence (ISI, not to be confused with the Islamic State of Iraq) to strike at Indian targets in **Jammu and Kashmir**. Its philosophy and operational base have expanded. Peter Chalk (2010) says that many of the homegrown terrorist threats in Europe, North America, and Australia have LeT connections. The group seems to be emerging as a new global jihadist organization working in conjunction with al Qaeda. It is best known for its attacks in India, including a deadly series of attacks in Mumbai in November 2008, and it rejects all forms of Islam except its own interpretation.

According to Chalk, Pakistan officially banned the LeT in 2002, so it operates under a series of different names. The LeT traditionally defined its operations around the Jammu and Kashmir conflict. Its major terrorist operations include:

- 2009: swarm attack on the Sri Lankan cricket team in Lahore
- 2008: multiple attacks in Mumbai
- 2006: attack in Varanasi
- 2005: series of bombs in Delhi
- 2002: massacre in Kaluchak
- 2001: attack on the Indian national parliament
- 2000: attack on the Red Fort in Delhi
- 1993: Mumbai bombings that resulted in 300 deaths

The LeT has also launched numerous attacks in Jammu and Kashmir. Chalk believes that the LeT began to expand operations in Asia and the West in 2003. In 2010 he believed that the LeT might be operating with al Qaeda, and the two groups certainly a common ideology. In addition, the LeT was involved with the 2005 subway bombings in London. Later research suggests that Chalk's conclusion was correct (Rath, 2015). The LeT and al Qaeda seem to be linked through the Haqqani network. It has been especially effective because of its relationship to the ISI. This relationship protects the LeT from crackdowns when the Pakistani government moves against terrorist groups, and it allows LeT planners to have access to intelligence data. The ISI still denies any connection but works informally with the LeT.

Ryan Clarke (2010) believes that the LeT is well entrenched and in a position to launch further attacks. He argues that the LeT was a part of Pakistan's original regional strategy and an arm of the ISI. The growth of militancy in the tribal regions, however, has spawned growth in the LeT. It has moved far beyond the ISI's ability to control the organization. Clarke fears that the LeT will not only continue to execute Mumbai-style attacks but will continue to evolve as part of the international jihadist network.

The Pakistani Taliban

Although the Taliban is most closely associated with Afghanistan, its core emerged from Pakistan after the Soviet–Afghan War. The Taliban seized control of Kandahar in 1994 and controlled 95 percent of the country by 1997. After the American offensive in Afghanistan in October 2001, many members of the Taliban retreated into the Federal Administered Tribal Area (FATA) of Pakistan. They used this area for two

FIGURE **11.4:** Pakistan

primary purposes: (1) as a base for launching anti-NATO attacks into Afghanistan and (2) to form a new Pakistani movement, the Tehrik-e-Taliban or Pakistani Taliban (Afsar, Samples, and Wood, 2008).

There are several bases of political power in Pakistan, and the Pakistani Taliban has grown in importance in the FATA. Tariq Ali (2008, p. 24) believes that the movement does not represent the greatest power base but that it has emerged because of the war in Afghanistan and the complex political situation in Pakistan. Tribal sympathies remain with the Taliban in Afghanistan, and ISI activities have kept the Taliban strong. This has caused the militant religious movement to expand in Pakistani society, something the ISI did not necessarily want to happen. The militants moved into a moral vacuum in Pakistani society, giving them a greater power base.

Red Mosque: *Lal masjid,* located in Islamabad, with a madrassa and a school for women. It taught militant theology. The government ordered the mosque closed in 2007. This resulted in a shootout and a standoff. Government forces stormed the mosque on July 2007, killing more than 100 students. One of the leaders, Abdul Rashid Ghazi, was killed. His brother Maulana Abdul Aziz, the mosque's other leader, was captured while trying to escape in women's clothing.

The United States urged the government to move against the Pakistani Taliban, Pakistan's DAWN (2015) news service reports. It has taken actions in the past. For example, in July 2007 the **Red Mosque** in Islamabad contained a madrassa full of militant students. They not only fanned the fires of rebellion, they also openly called for the prime minister's assassination. As a result, Pakistan's leader ordered troops to close the Red Mosque. The operation ended with more 100 dead militants (Shaikh, 2008).

The deputy leader of the Red Mosque, Abdul Rashid Ghazi, was also killed, and a group of students vowed to take revenge in his name. This spawned the Ghazi Brigades and a series of suicide attacks in several areas of Pakistan, beginning in 2009. The Ghazi Brigades are more closely allied with the Pakistani Taliban than any of Pakistan's other terrorist groups. As a result, they do not enjoy the protection of the intelligence community. They have been targeted by the ISI, the army, and Pakistan's law enforcement agencies (Roul, 2010).

Although the ISI was heavily involved in the formation and maintenance of jihadist groups, such as the LeT and the Taliban, its efforts began to misfire after the Red Mosque incident. The Pakistani Taliban openly challenged the government, and more radical groups emerged. One such group, the Asian Tigers, is actively fighting the Pakistani government and anyone who would ally with it, including fellow jihadists. In April 2010, the Asian Tigers captured and executed an ISI officer, and they publically displayed his body with a note claiming that he worked for the CIA. By summer, the ISI had joined the army in South Waziristan to attack the Asian Tigers. The ISI's goal was to rid the Pakistani Taliban of its rogue organizations (Jamal, 2010).

Bruce Riedel (2008) notes that as the Pakistani Taliban expanded, the U.S. influence waned. No democratic government in Pakistan can support American interests because the United States is anchored only in the military elite. The struggle to limit jihadist networks in Pakistan, the critical battleground according to Riedel, has shifted from American military and intelligence efforts to diplomacy. Riedel argues that American aid can be directed toward the Pakistani military but that it should be conditional. The army needs to remove itself from politics as a precondition to continued aid, and its main focus should shift from confronting India to maintaining internal and regional stability. More important than military aid, though, is the need to assist average Pakistanis and to build an infrastructure. Military aid will not solve the problem of terrorism.

Riedel also states that diplomacy should be based on regional politics. The United States should focus on repairing relations between the two regional nuclear powers—Pakistan and India. Other diplomatic efforts should be aimed at stabilizing relations with Afghanistan. Part of this focus should be the border region between Afghanistan and Pakistan to increase Pakistani security and decrease fears of Indian influence in Afghanistan. This region runs through tribal areas and divides ethnic groups. A realistic agreement about tribal rights within the border region would help smooth hostilities. Finally, in addition to finding common ground between India and Pakistan, it is necessary to move the relationship forward enough to solve the problem of Jammu and Kashmir.

Religious militancy is the result of several issues that make the region a ticking time bomb. If the underlying problems are ignored, Riedel concludes, terrorism will continue, and sooner or later, India and Pakistan will be on the brink of nuclear war. If Pakistan will not agree to address these issues in a constructive manner, groups like the Tehrik-e-Taliban will continue to emerge. Riedel believes that this will consume the region in a wave of terrorism. The potential expansion of terrorism, he concludes, is far more important than al Qaeda.

Thailand

Thailand is experiencing a rebellion in its southern provinces (see Figure 11.5). Although the country is dominated by Buddhism, Islam is the primary religion of the three southernmost states—states that border Islamic Malaysia. Zachary Abuza (2006b) says that Muslims failed in a revolt about 40 years ago because they were ideologically divided. The present-day revolt is smaller but more united. Abuza identifies the main groups involved in the fighting.

The Pattani United Liberation Organization (PULO) was formed in India in 1968 to create a Muslim state through armed struggle. Its leadership is aging, but it maintains a propaganda campaign via the Internet. It held a reunification meeting in Damascus in 2005, hoping to support the insurgency in the south. PULO controls no insurgents, but some of its leaders have made public threats. It claims to be secular, but Abuza says that it has Salafi undertones. New PULO, which was formed in 1995, is much more effective. Its leaders trained in Syria and Libya and have considerable bomb-making skills.

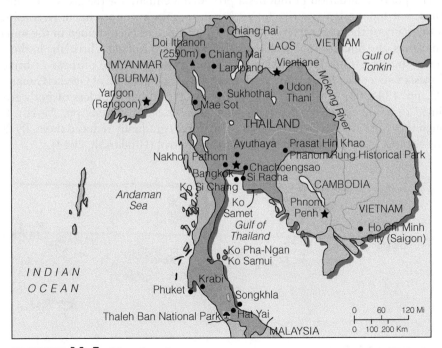

FIGURE **11.5:** Thailand

The Barisan Revolusi Nasional, Coordinate (BRN-C) is leading the insurgency and carries a jihadist agenda. One of three BRN groups involved in the insurgency, BRN-C is active in southern Thailand's mosques. Running a network of madrassas, the BRN-C has become the training ground for militants and fundamentalists. BRN-Cs membership is estimated at 1,000, and it controls 18 schools and a number of teachers. Thai security forces estimate that 70 percent of southern villages have at least one cell.

Complementing the BRN-C is the Gerakan Mujahedeen Islami Pattani (GMIP), with 40 active cells. Afghan veterans reassembled the group in 1995, but it deteriorated into a criminal gang. Abuza says that it began to embrace the insurgency by 2003 and that GMIP has contacts with Jamaat Islamiyya in Indonesia and the Moro Islamic Liberation Front (MILF) in the Philippines. The GMIP staged raids on police and army outposts in 2002.

Ian Storey (2007) notes that the southern insurgency is becoming an international affair. Militant groups in Malaysia have embraced the Muslim rebellion in Thailand, though the Malaysian government does not. Radicals in the Philippines and Indonesia see the revolt as part of the international jihad.

Jihadi Salafism in Indonesia

Jihad also grew in Southeast Asia. Zachary Abuza (2003b, pp. 121–187), in an analysis of terrorism in that region, says that jihadist groups began forming in Indonesia in the early 1990s. The International Crisis Group (2004, 2005a) says that these movements had their origins after World War II when Indonesia gained its independence from the Netherlands. Islamic associations became part of the political process, but they were suppressed by the government and the army in the name of nationalism. Abuza notes that new leadership gained power in 1998, and Islamic groups blossomed, asserting their independence. In 1999, fighting broke out between Christians and Muslims in the eastern islands, and militant Islamic groups grew (Figure 11.6).

The political situation in Indonesia provided a climate for the growth of jihadist groups, but Indonesian security forces began to gain an upper hand. According to Abuza, many of the members of jihadist movements had been trained in the mujahedeen camps of Afghanistan. Lashkar Jihad was formed to fight Christians in the east. A more sinister group, Jamaat Islamiyya, was formed with the purpose of bringing Indonesia under strict Islamic law. Both groups had contact with al Qaeda (Gunaratna, 2002, pp. 174–203; Abuza, 2003b, pp. 138–142), although leaders of both groups claimed to be independent of Osama bin Laden (J. Stern, 2003b, pp. 75–76). Even though they appeared to be growing, security forces gradually reduced them. By 2012 many regions seemed to be under government control (Gindarsah, 2014).

FIGURE **11.6:** Indonesia

In 2014 the *Washington Post* reported a setback in Indonesians' struggle against jihadis (Tharoor, 2014). The threat did not emanate from al Qaeda influenced groups or more established groups like Lashkar Jihad and Jamaat Islamiyya. The *Post* said these organizations were essentially in retreat. The new threat came from ISIS. It was winning support through a string of Salafi websites and the distribution of propaganda. As ISIS has influenced militancy in Africa and the Middle East, it effects were being seen in the country with the largest Muslim population in the world.

Jihadi Salafism in the Philippines

The Philippines has also experienced jihadist violence. Historically, the relationship between the Christian islands in the north and a few Muslim islands in the south has been marked by strife (Figure 11.7). The U.S. Army fought Muslim rebels after the Spanish–American War (1898), and the Philippine government faced both Muslim and Communist rebellions in the 1950s. Religious and ideological rebellions were repeated themes in the Philippines during the twentieth century.

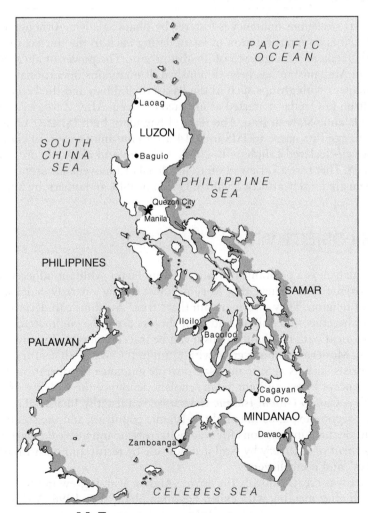

FIGURE **11.7:** Philippine Islands

Abuza (2003b, pp. 89–120) outlines the formation of three recent terrorist groups in the Philippines. The Moro National Liberation Front (MNLF) is a continuation of the old religious struggle. Having proposed negotiations with the Philippine government, the MNLF seeks an independent Islamic state. Breaking away from the MNLF is the more radical Moro Islamic Liberation Front (MILF). It has ties with jihadist movements and seeks to create an Islamic state under strict interpretations of Islamic law. A third group, Abu Sayyuf, claims to be part of the jihadist movement, but it is most closely associated with criminal activity and seems more interested in money than religion.

✓ Self-Check

> What other terrorist groups operate in Pakistan aside from al Qaeda core and terrorists associated with the Haqqani network?
> Where and why has Thailand experienced religious terrorism?
> How did religious extremism evolve in Indonesia and the Philippines?

Emphasizing the Points

Much of today's religious militancy is fostered by Jihadi Salafism. Although most Muslims reject it, it is an interpretation of Islam dating back to the thirteenth century. It spawned al Qaeda and the growth of jihadist groups. The power of al Qaeda core in Pakistan and Afghanistan has been diminished. It maintains operational capabilities through alliances with groups such as the Pakistani Taliban and the Haqqani family. ISIS grew from al Qaeda; it started as al Qaeda in Iraq. After Zarqawi's death, AQI became the Islamic State in Iraq. Abu Bakr al Baghdadi built ISI after taking over in 2010. ISI changed its name to ISIS in 2014 after entering the Syrian civil war. ISIS became the self-declared caliphate in 2014. Al Nusra and al Qaeda are currently at odds with ISIS. There are a variety of other Jihadi Salafist movements around the world. Some of them are loosely affiliated with al Qaeda or ISIS, and others are autonomous.

SUMMARY OF CHAPTER OBJECTIVES

- Jihadi Salafism is a puritanical strain of Sunni Islam. Militant adherents of its most extreme form believe that Muslims must follow a narrow Salafist interpretation of religion. They also maintain that "true" Muslims can declare "false" Muslims heretics, and Shi'ites and nonbelievers are to be eliminated.
- The historical path of Jihadi Salafism can be traced from ibn Taymiyya through Wahhab. Modern militancy grew with Qutb in the twentieth century, and modern theorists such as al Suri and Naji provide guidance for operationalizing jihadist concepts. Less militant Salafi scholars denounce the violence of militants.
- Al Suri's *A Call to Global Islamic Resistance* is a lengthy Jihadi Salafist treatise. The first section explains the plight of Islamic countries, and the second section contains detailed instructions for waging terrorism and guerrilla warfare. *The Management of Savagery* by Naji justifies rule by terror and mass murder of "heretics" and nonbelievers.
- Al Qaeda was created during the Soviet–Afghan War. It grew in the 1990s and expanded after merging with exiled Egyptian jihadists in 1996. A U.S. military

offensive in Afghanistan in October 2001 drove the core organization underground. Many of its leaders and allies have been killed over the course of a long
American drone campaign that has been supplemented by special operations.

- The al Qaeda franchise system grew haphazardly during the first decade of the
core's growing weakness. Regional al Qaeda organizations started with the
core's managerial and financial assistance. Some groups emerged independently
and later swore allegiance to the core. Today, the franchise is a loose alliance of
several groups. AQAP currently presents the greatest international threat.

- AQIM operates in Algeria and surrounding areas, AQAP is in Yemen, al
Nusra is in Syria, Ansar al Sharia has a branch in Libya and Tunisia, Mokhtar
Belmokhtar is in Algeria, and Abu Sayyuf is in the Philippines. Boko Haram
(Nigeria) and al Shabab (Somalia) are discussed in Chapter 7 within the context
of sub-Saharan Africa. There are dozens of other small regional groups.

- AQI was created as an al Qaeda franchise in Iraq after the 2003 American invasion. Its extreme violence and killing sprees soon caused a rift with al Qaeda
core. AQI evolved into the Islamic State of Iraq after Zarqawi's death in 2006.

- ISIS evolved from the Islamic State of Iraq and declared its independence from
al Qaeda core. In 2014, it launched successful offensives in Syria and the Sunni
area of Iraq, and it controlled significant territory in both countries. Its spokesperson declared that ISIS was the new caliphate in June 2014. He also named a
caliph. ISIS has called on Muslims throughout the world to come to the caliphate. Those who cannot are asked to launch terrorist attacks where they live. The
United States began a limited air war against ISIS in September 2014.

- ISIS joined the Syrian civil war in and announced that it was absorbing al
Nusra. Al Nusra rejected the attempt and called on al Qaeda core to mediate.
Attempts to compromise failed, and the core split from ISIS.

- Other Jihadi Salafist groups operate in areas of the world that have large Muslim populations. Some of the major crisis points are Pakistan, Jammu and Kashmir, southern Thailand, Indonesia, and the southern Philippines.

LOOKING INTO THE FUTURE

As long as Jihadi Salafism is able to motivate people to take actions in their native
countries, low-level terrorism will continue to be an international phenomenon.
Attacks have occurred in Asia, Australia, North America, South America, and Europe.
These attacks will continue to range from larger operations such as the *Charlie
Hebdo* attack in Paris to individual assaults like a hatchet attack on police officers in
New York City. Technology will be a key factor. If jihadists are able to obtain chemi-
cal, biological, radioactive, or nuclear weapons, they may use them.

Another future development involves the path of ISIS. The West can support actions against ISIS, but no Western nation or coalition can degrade and eliminate it.
Jihadi Salafism is a problem for Islamic nations. If Muslims band together, ISIS and
the entire jihadist world could be hampered. Although many Americans think that
Muslims do not speak out against terrorism, clerics and lay people denounce jihadists virtually every day all over the world. Scholars publish tracts about the heresy of
Jihadi Salafism, and many governments in Islamic nations take action against it. Keep
in mind that it took the West centuries to quell religious violence after the Reformation. Only Christians could decide to stop fighting. The analogy holds true for Islam.

A darker trend could develop. If ISIS and al Qaeda compromise and form a lasting alliance, they might create a state in which jihadists could base themselves to launch operations throughout the world. Something similar could happen in Afghanistan after international security forces depart. Pakistan is also problematic. If its government were to be dominated by Salafists and the army chose not to intervene, it could present a major international threat. Jihadi Salafism, nuclear weapons, and apocalyptic theology paint a frightening scenario.

KEY TERMS

Muslim Brotherhood, p. 251

Mohammed ibn Abdul Wahhab, p. 252

Sayyid Qutb, p. 252

Abu Mohammed al Maqdisi, p. 252

Abu Basir al Tartusi, p. 252

Taqi al Din ibn Taymiyyah, p. 252

Inter-Service Intelligence (ISI), p. 256

9/11 Commission, p. 257

Abdullah Azzam, p. 257

Sayyid Imam al Sharif, p. 257

Desert Shield, p. 258

Desert Storm, p. 258

Taliban, p. 259

Mullah Omar, p. 259

World Islamic Front Against Jews and Crusaders, p. 259

Haqqani network, p. 260

Anwar al Awlaki, p. 262

Nasir al Wuhayshi, p. 262

Qasim al Raymi, p. 262

Ibrahim al Asiri, p. 262

Nidal Malik Hasan, p. 263

Mokhtar Belmokhtar, p. 263

Abu Musab al Zarqawi, p. 265

Abu Omar al Baghdadi, p. 266

Abu Bakr al Baghdadi, p. 266

Abu Mohammed al Jawlani, p. 267

Jammu and Kashmir, p. 270

Red Mosque, p. 272

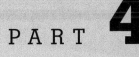
PART **4**

Domestic Terrorism and Homeland Security

CHAPTER 12

Domestic Terrorism

LEARNING OBJECTIVES

After reading this chapter, you should be able to:

▶ Summarize the debate over the meaning of domestic terrorism.

▶ Explain the legal differences between extremism and domestic terrorism.

▶ Categorize the forms of domestic terrorism.

▶ Describe the relationship between racial violence and terrorism.

▶ Outline the evolution and activities of the Ku Klux Klan.

▶ Describe current status of right-wing domestic terrorism.

▶ Explain fluctuations in left-wing criminal extremism.

▶ Define single-issue terrorism.

▶ List single issues that motivate domestic terrorism.

▶ Define the nebulous connection between domestic and international terrorism.

▶ Describe threats from home-grown radicalization.

Ullstein bild/Getty Images

American Terrorists, the KKK

In June 2015, a young man sat with a group of Christians conducting a Bible study at a church in Charleston, South Carolina. He had not come to study anything sacred; his purpose was destruction. After talking to people for about an hour, he drew a pistol and began firing. When he finished, nine people were dead. The rationale behind his crime was simple. He was white, and his victims were black. He hoped to trigger a racial war.

Quite the opposite happened, and multiple races joined together to mourn the loss. Yet, standard debates appeared. Many people claimed it was time to remove the Confederate flag from public buildings and lands. Advocates for various forms of gun control asked for actions to prevent mass shootings. The gun lobby made familiar arguments defending gun ownership. Only a few people joined another debate. As law enforcement officers, prosecutors, and the public discussed the event, they spoke of mass murder. People seldom used the word *terrorism* to describe the crime.

Americans are confused about terrorism inside the United States. When al Qaeda strikes a target within America's borders, most people readily identify it as an act of terrorism. When sovereign citizens shot and killed two police officers outside West Memphis, Arkansas, people generally classify the act as murder. Yet, there is a long history of many types of domestic terrorism in the United States. It goes unnoticed much of the time because the acts are categorized as crime. Crime is normal; terrorism is exotic, and most states have no statute outlawing it.

The Meaning of Domestic Terrorism

A few years ago, I was preparing to give a briefing on domestic terrorism in the federal building in San Francisco. An FBI special agent and I were casually chatting about the briefing before it began, and he asked about the topic. When I said it covered radicalization and domestic terrorism, he shook his head no. You can't do that, he said. Under the current presidential administration, he continued to explain, I would no longer be permitted to use the terms *domestic terrorism* and *radicalization*. The new phrase was *violent criminal extremism*. The instructions were from Washington.

I would have thought this strange, but I understand that the pejorative meaning of the term *terrorism* is politically charged. The topic is approached within an ideological framework. The previous administration had encouraged the use of the phrase *war on terror*. The administration in power at the time of my example dropped that phrase within days of assuming power, and moonlighting contractors like me were ordered not to make references to war in briefings or written material.

Crime is normative in the United States. If individuals or groups of people intimidate or use violence to change behavior, it is classified as criminal behavior. If suspects are from Los Banditos or Hell's Angels, it is called motorcycle gang violence. Groups of violent young people are also involved in gang activities. Drug traffickers engage in drug violence, and criminal conspiracy involves organized crime. Even when people are killed under the banner of racial superiority, it is called racial violence. In reality, many of these activities are so closely related to terrorism that it is difficult to distinguish between the two.

Growing Clarity

The United States has a long history of political violence, but until recently, few scholars characterized it as "terrorism." Three exceptions were H. H. A. Cooper (1976), J. Bowyer Bell (Bell and Gurr, 1979), and Ted Robert Gurr (1988a), all of whom initiated work in this arena before it was popular to speak of domestic terrorism. Cooper and colleagues produced a presidential report on the political context of domestic terrorism. Bell and Gurr looked at the long history of domestic political violence in the United States, and Gurr later developed a typology of domestic terrorism. It included *vigilante terrorism* from the extremist right, *insurgent terrorism* of various revolutionaries, and *transnational terrorism* from foreigners fighting on American soil.

Christopher Hewitt's (2002) analysis of domestic terrorism helps illustrate why American law enforcement has grown increasingly aware of the problem. Terrorism has occurred in recent American history, but it has been approached as typical criminal behavior. Community policing helps solve the problem, Hewitt says, because it is the most effective method of preventing terrorism. In other words, the nature of policing provides a de facto definition.

Law enforcement agencies have made great strides in understanding domestic terrorism over the past decade. This is partially due to the nature of politically motivated crime and violence. As Donald Black (2004) states, the three main ingredients of modern terrorism are (1) an angry group of people or sometimes even a single enraged individual (2) with the ability to travel and (3) with access to technology that can cause massive casualties. All three ingredients are available to people who wish to take criminal action based on various political positions. Stated simply, state, local, and tribal law enforcement agencies have had quite a bit of experience with such criminal activity, and they are getting better at handling it.

In the past three decades, law enforcement agencies have participated in antiterrorist training, especially after the massive Oklahoma City bombing in 1995. Many law enforcement executives came to see that terrorism was no longer an exotic problem that happened only overseas; rather, it was a real criminal problem in the United States. Large urban agencies established units to deal with terrorism, and they frequently operated in conjunction with the federal government. The reaction to Oklahoma City expanded such units, though Chicago; New York; Washington, D.C.; Miami; and Los Angeles had experienced various forms of terrorism for years. Oklahoma City was different—if it could happen there, it could happen anywhere. American law enforcement began to respond. Of course, the process was accelerated in the wake of 9/11.

Understanding is important because terrorism investigation and prevention differs from many other types of patrol and investigative work. Terrorism requires extensive criminal intelligence and deep networks of information. If community policing has a positive impact on neighborhoods, it is essential in antiterrorist operations. Law enforcement cannot operate in many subcultures unless members of those subcultures experience police officers solving problems and meeting community needs. Finally, many investigative methods resemble organized crime and conspiracy investigations. They take time to develop, require patience, and rely on criminal intelligence.

Extremism Versus Terrorism

Another issue surrounds domestic terrorism. The Constitution allows people to hold extremist beliefs, no matter how radical they may be. It also allows people to voice those beliefs most of the time, as long as they are not taking engaging in crime or supporting a terrorist group. Terrorism involves criminal activity, which is why American law enforcement is concerned with the subject. People are free to be extremists, but they are not allowed to engage in criminal activity.

Still, the line between constitutional rights and behavior is sometimes very thin. Freedom of speech serves as an example. The Supreme Court has said that people connected with a terrorist organization are not exercising their right to free speech if they write or speak in support of the group. This is a crime. Subsequent court opinion stated that a person not connected with the terrorist group has a right to speak in favor of its activities even when such activity assists the group (Pochon, 2012).

Categorizing Domestic Terrorism

There is a great deal of tension between theoretical criminologists and practical analysts who look for immediate solutions to a specific problem. Classical, or theoretical, criminologists look for explanations of social phenomena, and they search for theories to explain crime or behavior in general. This crucial work produces theories that guide policies. From a tactical (or practical) perspective, however, immediate responses to crime are not based on general explanations. It is more important to understand the nature of the immediate problem and the possible practical solutions. The same is true for terrorism: An approach appropriate for theoretical criminology does not always lead to a response that solves an immediate problem. U.S. police officers routinely handle terrorism, even though they call it by a variety of names. It would be helpful if law enforcement officers had a practical framework that explained their counterterrorist role (see Figure 12.1).

Tactically, police and security forces should keep two issues in mind. First, beat police officers are usually the first responders to incidents of domestic terrorism. Second, the investigation techniques used in large sensational terrorist incidents are the same techniques a local agency would use to investigate a stink bomb placed in the high school football team's locker room. From a practical perspective, counterterrorism depends on the fundamentals. Good investigative skills such as collecting and preserving evidence and good interviewing techniques are important; it is also important for law enforcement officers to understand the context of the crimes they are investigating. Nevertheless, terrorism investigations differ from those related to routine crime scenes because terrorists behave differently. This calls for increased intelligence, long-term surveillance, and informant development. Therefore, it is important for officers to recognize terrorism when they encounter it.

The FBI categorizes criminal activities on the basis of origin. This categorization is based on gathering and sharing information, but information sharing still remains difficult in police work. According to publicly released information (FBI, 2004), the FBI's classification system has two basic categories: domestic terrorism (DT) and international terrorism (IT). DT involves violent political extremism, single-issue terrorism, and lone wolf activities. IT is related to threats that originate outside the United States. In 2002, the FBI's Joint Terrorism Task Force (JTTF) arrested six suspects near Buffalo, New York, for supporting jihadists. The JTTF called this DT because the activities originated in the United States. The attacks of September 11 are called IT because they originated outside U.S. borders (see FBI, n.d.).

Brent Smith (1994; Smith and Roberts, 2005) places terrorist groups into three broad categories: (1) right-wing extremists, (2) left-wing and single-issue terrorists, and (3) international terrorists. This approach can be used to develop a general typology to refer to when approaching domestic terrorism, keeping in mind the FBI's separation between IT and DT. Some overlap cannot be avoided, but Smith's typology can be expanded to focus on the types of criminal activity that fall under the rubric of DT.

Categorization is helpful because different tactics are used to approach different types of terrorism. Procedures that are effective in one type of investigation may not work as well in others. Knowledge bases, especially knowledge of subcultures, are crucial in many counterterrorism operations. For example, officials working against violent antigovernment groups in southern Missouri probably have little need to understand Sikh religious and cultural traditions. On the other hand, the officers who were involved in responding to the 2012 mass shooting at the Sikh temple in Oak Creek, Wisconsin, would have found such an understanding helpful.

The chapter suggests categories, but virtually any typology will do as long as it recognizes effective tactics for differing types of domestic terrorism. Officers do not respond to riots the same way they respond to barricaded gunmen. Each situation requires appropriate tactics. Approaches to domestic terrorism are similar. The categories suggested in this chapter are racism, antigovernment extremism and other right-wing violence, single issues, and homegrown Jihadist Salafism. The choice of these categories was strongly influenced by the work of Brent Smith and Kelley Damphouse.

> A Typology of Criminal Extremism
> - Antigovernment Crimes (both right and left)
> - Race- and Ethnicity-Motivated Crimes
> - Homegrown Radicalization
> - Single-Issue Crimes

FIGURE **12.1** Criminal Extremism

> **✓ Self-Check**
>
> \> Why does the term *domestic terrorism* create confusion?
>
> \> What is the difference between extremism and terrorism?
>
> \> How does Brent Smith categorize domestic terrorism?

Racism and Terrorism

The tragedy recounted at the beginning of this chapter was one more horrible instance of a long line of racial violence in the United States. Racism has been at the heart of domestic terrorism for more than a century. Groups like al Qaeda and ISIS present a threat, but white supremacist groups and the extremist right have been far more active. For example, Joshua Freilich, Steven Chermak, and David Caspi (2009) present case studies of four white supremacist movements that cite a survey of 37 state police agencies. They found that the overwhelming majority of state troopers were more concerned with right-wing extremists and other racists than jihadists. The troopers had had many encounters with right-wingers and few with al Qaeda–style cells. In addition, from 1990 to 2008, right-wing extremists accounted for 4,300 crimes in the United States, including 275 homicides. Racism and white supremacy have fueled American terrorism.

Violent White Supremacy Movements

skinheads: Young individuals or groups that embrace racial hatred and white supremacy.

The Order: A violent right-wing racist group of the 1980s that killed Jewish radio talk show host Alan Berg and committed other crimes. William Pierce's *The Turner Diaries* inspired the group's formation.

Fourteen Words: Racist words coined by David Lane, a member of The Order: "We must secure the existence of our people and a future for white children."

In a National Public Radio (2015) interview, Peter Bergen stated that within the United States, right-wing white supremacists and antigovernment groups have killed more people than jihadists have. Freilich, Chermak, and Caspi (2009) add to the discussion with the information that white supremacist groups routinely embrace the ideology of neo-Nazis and white separatists. Almost all groups of this ilk are vehemently anti-Semitic. Racist groups have developed a youth subculture based on hate rock. One such group, Public Enemy Number 1 (PEN1), is healthy and growing.

PEN1 grew from the punk rock scene in southern California in the 1980s. It became the largest **skinhead** group in the nation. Freilich and colleagues said that it had 400 members in 2009 and that it was growing. Many law enforcement officials estimate greater numbers today (Morlin, 2015). As PEN1 members were arrested and sentenced to prison for a variety of crimes, they formed an alliance with the Aryan Brotherhood, the nation's largest racist prison gang.

Freilich and colleagues found commonalities among long-lasting movements such as PEN1. Successful groups tend to have a strong core of centralized leadership. They raise money through crime and other activities, and they take advantage of political opportunities. These groups exhibit a sense of social stability, and they are cohesive. White supremacist groups almost always voice **The Order** member David Lane's **Fourteen Words:** "We must secure the existence of our people and a future for white children." Lane died in prison in 2007.

Many white supremacists are either motivated by religion or use it to manipulate followers. The major religious or pseudo-religious movements are Christian Identity, Nordic Christianity, the Creativity Movement, and some forms of **Free-Wheeling Fundamentalism**. Michael Barkun (1997a) says that a new religion, Christian Identity, grew from the extremist perspective. Starting with a concept called **Anglo-Israelism**, or British Israelism, American right-wing extremists saw white Americans as the representatives of the lost tribes of Israel.

Christian Identity is a strange blend of Jewish and Christian biblical passages and is based on the premise that whites are created in the image of a white male deity (J. White, 1997, 2001). It is a religion based on racial supremacy, and its theology is based on a story of conflict and hate. According to this theology, Jews have gained control of the United States by conspiring to create the Federal Reserve System. The struggle between non-Jewish whites and Jews will continue until whites ultimately achieve victory with God's help. At that point, the purpose of creation will be fulfilled. Such theological perversions are necessary when a religion of love is converted into a doctrine of hate.

Barkun (1997a) points out that Christian Identity helped provide the rationale for violence among extremists. Before the Christian Identity movement, American extremism was characterized by ethnocentrism and localized violence. Christian Identity gave a new twist to the extremist movement: It was used to demonize Jews. Christian Identity provided a theological base for stating that white people originated with God, and Jews came from the devil. Such eschatological presumptions are deadly (see Stanton, 1991, p. 36).

Christianity has undergone some strange transformations within the violent circles of right-wing extremism, sometimes known as the hate movement (J. White, 1997, 2001). For example, some extremists have adopted Norse mythology. Following Erich Ludendorff, a member of the German High Command in World War I, extremists began preaching **Nordic Christianity** (also called **neopaganism**) in northern Germany in the early 1920s. This belief system migrated to the United States and took root in Michigan, Wisconsin, Montana, and Idaho in the 1990s. Using ancient Norse rites, adherents claimed to worship the triune Christian deity, but they added Odin (Wotan) and Thor. Odin, the supreme Norse god, called Nordic warriors to racial purification from Valhalla, the Viking heaven. Thor, the god of thunder, sounded the call with a hammer that shook the heavens.

In another religious derivation, **Creativity** rejects Judaism and Christianity altogether (see *Creativity Movement*, n.d.). Formerly called the World Church of the Creator, the movement changed its name to the Creativity Movement after being challenged by a Christian church with a similar name. Founded by **Ben Klassen** in 1973, Creatorists claim that the creator left humanity on its own, and each race must fend for itself. Embracing urban skinheads, Creatorists call for a racial holy war (RAHOWA). They produce racially oriented comic books designed to appeal to alienated white youth. They also publish *The White Man's Bible*, which emphasizes racial purity. Creatorists argue that the concept of an intervening loving God is nothing more than an idle lie. The deistic creator has left white people on their own, and they are expected to fight for their survival. Essentially, Creativity is a deistic religion with more violent tendencies than Christian Identity.

The majority of right-wing extremists retreated to more conservative churches and relied on individual interpretations of scripture to justify antigovernment actions. This group can loosely be described as freewheeling fundamentalists. Unlike those involved with hate religions, freewheeling fundamentalists do not believe that the American government is part of a conspiracy involving the ultimate forces of evil. They do believe, however, that the federal government and local governments are their enemies and that God will assist them as they confront any form of governmental power. Although some freewheeling fundamentalists embrace racism, most followers are neither racist nor violent (see O'Conner, 2004).

Free-Wheeling Fundamentalism: A term to describe white supremacists or Christian patriots who either selectively use Bible passages or personal scriptural interpretations to justify the patriot agenda.

Anglo-Israelism: The belief that the lost tribes of Israel settled in Western Europe. God's ancient promises to the Hebrews became promises to the United Kingdom, according to this belief. Anglo-Israelism predated Christian Identity and is the basis for most Christian Identity beliefs.

Christian Identity: An American extremist religion that proclaims white supremacy. Adherents believe that white Protestants of Western European origin are the true descendants of the ancient Israelites. Believers contend that Jews were spawned by Satan and that nonwhites evolved from animals. According to this belief, white men, women, children are the only people created in the image of God.

Nordic Christianity (neopaganism): A religion that incorporates the ancient Norse gods in a hierarchy under the Christian triune deity, although many adherents simply abandon Christianity. Some law enforcement agencies refer to the movement as Odinism, but the ancient Norse religion is not part of violent right-wing extremist movements. Some analysts refer to the movement as neopaganism.

Creativity: The deistic religion of the Creativity movement. It claims that white people must struggle to defeat Jews and nonwhite races.

Ben Klassen: (1918–1993) The founder of the Creativity Movement.

American's Most Successful Terrorist Group

Max Boot's (2013, pp. 218–225) outstanding work on irregular warfare, *Invisible Armies*, includes a chapter on the Ku Klux Klan. Boots notes that the Klan is one of America's most successful terrorist groups. Emerging in the aftermath of the Civil War, it effectively resisted and ended Reconstruction. It strongly influenced political behavior and still holds sway in some areas of the country today.

Former Confederate general Nathan Bedford Forrest and former Confederate soldiers created the KKK in Pulaski, Tennessee in 1865 (Berlet and Lyons, 2000, pp. 58–62). Forrest had intended to create an antifederal organization that would preserve Southern culture and traditions. When the newly formed KKK began terrorizing freed slaves, Forrest became disillusioned with the movement and tried to disband the organization. It was too late, however, and the KKK began a campaign of hate. By the early twentieth century, the organization had nearly died, but it was revived in the extremist atmosphere after World War I (1914–1918).

Knight Riders: The first terrorists of the Ku Klux Klan. Donning hoods and riding at night, they sought to keep newly freed slaves from participating in government and society.

The KKK has operated in three distinct phases over its history (Berlet and Lyons, 2000, pp. 58, 85–103, 265–286). Shortly after the Civil War, hooded **Knight Riders**, as they were called, terrorized African Americans to frighten them into political and social submission. This aspect of the Klan faded by the end of the century. The second phase of the Klan came in the 1920s as it sought political legitimacy following World War I. During this period, the KKK became popular, political, and respectable. It collapsed, however, in the wake of a criminal scandal. The modern KKK grew after World War II (1939–1945), evolving into its present-day state as a fragmented and decentralized group that is dominated by hate-filled rhetoric.

The Southern Poverty Law Center (2015b) estimates that today the Klan has between 5,000 and 8,000 members. The organization is fragmented, and its members embrace a variety of extremist ideologies. Some local groups try to mask racism with the rhetoric of white civil rights. Dozens of differing groups employ the name Klan, and many times they fight with one another.

Much of the Klan's power is based on its ability to inspire racist ideology. Many spinoff groups began forming in the late twentieth century, and they still exist. These include neo-Nazis, skinheads, white nationalist groups, anti-Semitic organizations, anti-LBGT groups, and some paramilitary organizations. Racist groups, such as PEN1, are centered on hate rock. Other movements, like the White Aryan Resistance, call for lone wolf attacks, and white supremacy gangs like the Aryan Brotherhood flourish in prisons. The KKK is fragmented and full of rhetoric, yet its power comes from its rhetoric as well as underlying racism in the United States.

✓ **Self-Check**

> How is racism related to domestic terrorism?
> What religious influences affect racially inspired violence?
> What is the primary threat from the Ku Klux Klan?

Violent Right-Wing Extremism

Racism is not at the heart of all right-wing terrorism, and other races have violent or potentially violent organizations. For example, some black separatists have a history of criminal behavior. Much violent extremism is based on fear or hatred of government, especially the federal government. While some groups combine racism with antigovernment ideologies, other groups and individuals simply do not recognize governmental power. Conspiracy theories abound in antigovernment circles. Some people believe the U.S. government is in league with a secret organization of Jews and bankers. Others claim the United Nations is attempting to take over the United States and that American military forces are allied with UN troops. These groups sometimes embrace racism, but often they do not.

Antigovernment Extremism

On the morning of April 19, 1995, special news reports on television and radio indicated that some type of explosion had occurred in Oklahoma City in or near the federal building. These reports were quickly amended, and reports of the size and extent of damage increased moment by moment. By noon, it was apparent that the United States had suffered a devastating terrorist attack. As scenes of the injured and dead, including children, and smoldering wreckage dominated the nation's television screens, attention turned toward the Middle East. Conventional wisdom placed blame for the incident on a yet to be identified militant Islamic sect. Many Arab Americans were harassed, and some were openly attacked. The country was shocked when a young white man with a crew cut was arrested for the bombing. It was hard to believe that the United States had produced terrorists in its own heartland.

Sovereign Citizens

The **sovereign citizen** movement is not new, and it is not limited to any racial group or political orientation. The movement has traditionally been linked to white supremacists. It was also related to the militia movement of the 1980s, though issues have changed since then. African American groups such as the **Moorish Nation** can be classified as part of the sovereign citizen movement, as can some Hispanic groups. One Native American group has claimed autonomy from the United States. The Great Recession of 2008 caused a number of people to begin declaring themselves sovereign citizens. Crimes like mortgage fraud and other swindles began to grow. Violent encounters with law enforcement officers also increased (BJA/SLATT, 2010).

Although there they have no centralized structure or organization, sovereign citizens tend to hold some common beliefs. First, they believe that they can declare themselves free of American citizenship as well as U.S. laws and taxes. This transformation can develop in a variety of ways. For example, some people believe that using an odd signature declares that they are free citizens. Others write letters to government officials declaring that they are no longer citizens of the United States. One popular belief is that the United States did not have citizens after the American Revolution, but constitutional amendments added after the Civil War tricked free citizens into accepting American citizenship. If you are aware of that fact, they say, you can simply opt out of the government. Still another group believes there is a missing Fourteenth Amendment to the Constitution that allows them to declare themselves free of citizenship.

The Anti-Defamation League (2010) says that sovereign citizens also tend to believe that there are two governments in the United States. One is legitimate and devoid of regulation except for English common law. The illegitimate government includes all established federal and state governments. Like most right-wing groups, sovereign citizens believe taxes, traffic fines, and other government actions result from a conspiracy of evil.

Sovereign citizens have had violent confrontations with police officers and other government officials, but their most common activity is **paper terrorism**. They file false liens, tying up the property of people who have irritated them. They also write bogus

---

Sovereign Citizens: People who believe that they are not subject to the laws and regulations of the United States. They self-declare that they are individually free of driver's licenses, car registrations, and tax laws. They frequently hold their own legal proceedings and issue orders that have no binding legal authority.

Moorish Nation: An African American group that does not recognize the validity of the U.S. government.

paper terrorism: Uses false documents to clog legal, financial, or bureaucratic processes.

checks or sight drafts against nonexistent accounts. Some sovereigns, like the two who murdered West Memphis police officers, defraud people by conducting seminars to tell participants how they can fill out special forms and renounce their American citizenship. They charge hefty attendance fees. Others carry so-called constitutional driver's licenses and vehicle registrations (ADL, 2010; BJA, 2010).

This is not to suggest that sovereign citizens are a docile group. According to the Southern Poverty Law Center (2015), more than 30 police officers have been killed in confrontations with sovereign citizens. In addition, they have staged well-publicized armed standoffs with law enforcement officers. They have also made violent threats against government officials.

Sovereign citizens represent one other aspect of antigovernment criminal extremism. They tend to merge into other forms of extremism. For example, some sovereigns belong to racist organizations. Others follow a particular religion. Some may be survivalists, while others live in urban environments. There are sovereign citizen compounds where armed militias patrol in fear of government invasion, and there are seemingly normal citizens who hold jobs and refuse to pay their taxes. There is no single sovereign citizen ideology.

Contemporary Right-Wing Behavior, Beliefs, and Tactics

Modern right-wing extremism came to fruition around 1984 and has remained active since that time. According to this author's research (J. White, 1997, 2000, 2002), several issues hold the movement together. First, the right wing tends to follow one of the forms of extremist religion. The name of God is universally invoked, even by leaders who disavow theism (a belief in God). Second, the movement is dominated by a belief in international conspiracy and other conspiracy theories. Followers feel that sinister forces are conspiring to take away their economic status and swindle them out of the American dream. The primary conspiratorial force was Communism, but after the fall of the Soviet Union, it became the United Nations. The extremist right believes that a conspiracy of Jewish bankers is working with the United Nations to create a **New World Order** in which Jews will control the international monetary system. Finally, right-wing extremists continue to embrace patriotism and guns. They want to arm themselves for a holy war (see Barkun, 1997b; Berlet and Lyons, 2000, pp. 345–352).

New World Order: A phrase used by President George H. W. Bush to describe the world after the fall of the Soviet Union. Conspiracy theorists use the phrase to describe what they believe to be Jewish attempts to gain control of the international monetary system and, subsequently, to take over the U.S. government.

In his popular historical work *Dreadnought: Britain, Germany and the Coming of the Great War*, Robert K. Massie (1991) points to the hysteria in Great Britain and Germany during the naval race before World War I. Both the British and the Germans demonized one another, and their national rivalries often gave way to irrational fears. In one of the more notable British reactions, the fear of German naval power gave rise to a particular genre of popular literature. These stories had a similar theme. Secret German agents would land in the United Kingdom and destroy the British Empire through some type of subversive plot. Whether they were poisoning the water supply, destroying the schools, or infiltrating the economic system, the fictional Germans never attacked directly. They were mysterious, secretive, and everywhere. The actions of right-wing extremists fit Massie's description of the hysterical fears in Britain. Extremists believe that alien forces are conspiring to destroy the United States.

Groups grew in the 1980s and 1990s but waned after the 1995 Oklahoma City bombing. Violent members of the right-wing movement melted away from large organizations and began to congregate in small groups. Following the pattern of international terrorist groups, they organized chains or hubs, that is, small groups that operate autonomously. The days of large meetings seemed to fade as well. One Montana criminal intelligence commander told this author he believes that the current leaders of the movement do not know how to arrange large rallies. As a result, he said, the movement in the Pacific Northwest, for instance, looks more like a conglomeration of terrorist cells. By 2010, new groups were emerging under a variety of antigovernment banners.

Increasing numbers of smaller groups led to more individual violence. Additionally, these groups began to form links with single-issue groups, including anarchists and left-wingers. The trend is currently unclear. The groups may be fading as the left wing did in the 1980s, or they may be repositioning themselves. Militias tended to turn to patriotism and more normative behavior after September 11. Other groups did not.

The wild card is the vacuum in leadership. Richard Butler, the leader of the defunct Aryan Nations, died in September 2004. No one had been able to unite the extremist right the way Butler did. Leaders jockeyed for power, but no single leader with Butler's charisma and organizational skills has moved to the forefront. Fragmented paramilitary organizations, however, have grown autonomously.

By 2010, individuals and small violent groups began taking action without a centralized structure. In several areas, two or three people began to operate without contacting other groups or meeting at large convocations. They planned bombings and chemical attacks. In addition, they spoke of a spontaneous revolution. These unrelated groups felt that any act of violence would help create the mayhem necessary to topple the government. The organizational style was new, but the ideology that drove the groups had been transplanted from the hills of West Virginia. It was contained in the philosophy of William Pierce.

The Turner Diaries and Hunter: Blueprints for Revolution

William Pierce was a white supremacist with headquarters in rural West Virginia. He led an organization called the **National Alliance** and purchased Resistance Records, a recording label for skinhead hate music. Pierce held a doctoral degree and worked as a college professor. Until his death in 2003, he drew the attention of watchdog groups, scholars, and law enforcement officers. Pierce wrote two novels that summarized his thought and provided a blueprint for revolution.

Pierce's most noted novel, *The Turner Diaries*, was written under the pseudonym Andrew MacDonald (1985); it is a fictionalized account of an international white revolution. The work begins as a scholarly flashback from "New Baltimore" in the "year 100," and it purports to introduce the diary that the protagonist, Earl Turner, kept during the "Great Revolution," a mythical race war set in the 1990s.

For the most part, *The Turner Diaries* is a diatribe against minorities and Jews. It is well written and easy to read. The danger of the work is that from a technical standpoint, it is a how-to manual for low-level terrorism. Using a narrative—or storytelling—format, Pierce describes the proper methods for making bombs, constructing mortars, attacking targets, and launching other acts of terrorism. Most readers of *The Turner Diaries* will come away with an elementary idea of how to become a terrorist.

The second potential danger of *The Turner Diaries* is more subtle. The book could serve as a psychological inspiration for violence; that is, it could inspire copycat crimes. The frequent diatribes in the book and the philosophy behind it justify murder and mayhem. Pierce presents the destruction of nonwhite races, minorities, and Jews as the only logical solution to social problems. Although Pierce himself was not religious, he used a general cosmic theology, presented in a "holy" work called The Book, to place Earl Turner on the side of an unknown deity.

National Alliance: The white supremacist organization founded by the late William Pierce in Hillsboro, West Virginia. The group has faded, but its influence on small groups and lone wolves remains.

Robert Matthews: (1953–1984) The leader of The Order who was killed in a shoot-out with the FBI.

Brüder Schweigen: German for "silent brothers." The name is used by two violent right-wing extremist groups, Brüder Schweigen and Brüder Schweigen Strike Force II. The late Robert Miles, leader of the Mountain Church of Jesus in Michigan, penned an article about the struggle for white supremacy, "When All of the Brothers Struggle." Miles' article inspired leaders in the two groups to use the name Brüder Schweigen.

Some extremists who have read *The Turner Diaries* have taken action. **Robert Matthews**, for example, founded a terrorist group called the **Brüder Schweigen** (the Silent Brotherhood), or The Order, based on Turner's fictional terrorist group. When arrested, the Oklahoma City bomber Timothy McVeigh was carrying a worn copy of *The Turner Diaries*.

Written in 1989, *Hunter* is another novel by Pierce under his pseudonym, Andrew MacDonald. Although not as popular as *The Turner Diaries*, Pierce's later work tells the story of a lone wolf named Hunter who decides to launch a one-person revolution. He stalks the streets to kill African Americans, interracial couples, and Jews. The book is dedicated to a real-life killer, and like *The Turner Diaries*, it could inspire copycat crimes. In 1999, two right-wing extremists went on killing sprees in Chicago and Los Angeles in a style reminiscent of the violence in *Hunter*.

Extremist literature is full of hate, instructions, and suggestions. Pierce introduced nothing new in the literature of intolerance. However, he popularized terrorism in two well-written novels. Unfortunately, they also served as a blueprint for violence.

Resurgent Violent Right-Wing Extremism

The election of President Barack Obama impacted right-wing and antigovernment extremism, although the government has been reluctant to release evidence of increased activity (see Marshal, 2009). According to a report that was initially restricted but is now available on the Internet, the Department of Homeland Security (DHS; 2009) warned that while no specific right-wing terrorist threat had emerged, several issues drew potential recruits to violent extremist organizations. The report notes that extremists capitalized on the 2008 national election and fears of gun control. The economic downturn and new political climate also made violent extremist groups more attractive. The report says that right-wing extremists exploited these issues in the 1990s and that they were in a position to do so again in 2008. Frustration over illegal immigration and threats from emerging foreign powers increased their potential appeal. The report also says that right-wing extremists would be anxious to recruit military veterans returning from Iraq and Afghanistan.

The report met a storm of controversy, and the Department of Homeland Security recalled it. However, in the summer of 2009, a neo-Nazi entered the Holocaust Museum in Washington, D.C., and began to shoot visitors there. He killed a security guard before he was subdued. In 2010, nine members of a paramilitary group were taken into custody in Michigan for allegedly plotting attacks. In another 2010 incident, a person angered by the Internal Revenue Service (IRS) committed suicide by flying an airplane into a government facility in Austin, Texas. He left a 36-paragraph suicide note that expressed his rage at the federal government. Later the same the year, antigovernment extremists killed two Arkansas law enforcement officers. Between 1995 and 2015, nearly three dozen police officers were killed by antigovernment extremists. The 2009 report warned of this type of violence.

The issue remains controversial. The FBI released a threat assessment of violent DT in 2014. It reiterated many of the points raised in the 2009 DHS warning, but there were and are voices of descent. Professor Philip Jenkins (2009) agrees that actual right-wing threats should be investigated, but he believes that the government will overreact. Congressional representative Peter King from New York, who is chair of the House Subcommittee on Counterterrorism and Intelligence, takes the argument a step further. When a survey of American police agencies revealed that law enforcement officials were more concerned with right-wing extremism than jihadists, King dismissed the idea on ABC television. Jihadists, King said, constitute the greatest threat (Main, 2015).

✓ **Self-Check**	> What role do conspiracy theories play in right-wing extremist ideology? > How do William Pierce's writings influence domestic terrorism? > What types of threats arise from right-wing criminal extremism?

Shifting from Left-Wing Violence to Single Issues

Left-wing terrorist groups dominated terrorism in the United States from about 1967 to 1985. Fueled by dissatisfaction with the Vietnam War, violent radicals broke away from student protest movements. Soon, various groups emerged as they separated from student social protest movements to join ranks with nationalist terrorists. Their favorite tactic was bombing, but unlike right-wing groups, they tried to avoid causing casualties. Various groups made headlines, but their influence faded over time. By the late 1980s, several leftist groups had formed coalitions such as the Armed Resistance Unit, but they were forced to do so out of weakness rather than strength (Wolf, 1981, pp. 40–43).

Single issues dominate left-wing terrorism today, but not all single issues involve left-wing extremism. While the left dominates violence in the name of animal rights, ecological damage, and genetic engineering, antiabortion violence is usually a product of the right. Regardless, the broad spectrum of issues that dominated left-wing terrorism in the last part of the twentieth century has remained dormant in the early decades of the twenty-first.

The Demise of the Left

Several factors contributed to the demise of left-wing terrorism in the United States. One major problem was that intellectual elites controlled the movement (Serafino, 2002). During the time of student activism, leftist elites developed followings and sympathy across a broad spectrum of collegiate and highly educated people. Kevin J. Riley and Bruce Hoffman (1995) note that this gave the left a broad constituency. Nevertheless, the movement lost its base when student activism began to disappear from American academic life. As the mood of the country shifted toward more conservative patterns of behavior, left-wing terrorists enjoyed little sympathetic ideological support.

Riley and Hoffman surveyed several U.S. law enforcement agencies in the mid-1990s to determine their concern with DT. Police departments were worried about terrorism, but left-wing groups were not at the top of their agenda. Only 25 percent of the urban agencies surveyed reported any left-wing activity; rather, they reported much more activity from other types of groups. Riley and Hoffman say that the left-wing groups engaged in symbolic violence. Some identified with Marxist–Leninist ideology, whereas others worked against specific political issues, such as U.S. military involvement in Central and South America. The collapse of the Soviet Union did not bolster the popularity of left-wing causes. In 1995, police perceived right-wing and Puerto Rican groups to be the greatest threats. The greatest concentration of left-wing groups was on the West Coast, but they posed a comparatively minor threat.

Loretta Napoleoni (2003, xix–xxiii) finds that guilt was a factor as left-wing terror faded in Europe. People who may have been sympathetic to the ideology of left-wing terrorists could not tolerate their violent activities as terrorism increased. This may have been a factor in American terrorism as well. Furthermore, left-wing violence waned with the fall of the Soviet Union, and police tactics improved with time, putting many terrorist groups on the defensive (Peacetalk, 2003).

The decline of American left-wing terrorism may reflect a similar trend in Europe. Xavier Raufer (1993) says that German leftists failed when the government stole their agenda. Reagan-era conservatives certainly did not adopt the left-wing agenda, but they did capture the country's heart. American mainstream interests turned from the extremist left. Donatella della Porta (1995) points to a parallel process in Italy. The Red Brigades were able to attract a broad and sympathetic audience, but the government authorities came to understand this and turned the tables, winning the support of the public. Unfortunately, as their power base waned, the Red Brigades increased violence in an effort to gain new recruits. American groups were too weak to do this, though they did grab headlines.

The Rise of Single Issues

Left-wing domestic terrorism did not disappear, however; it was transformed. Leftist movements became more specific, focusing not only on certain political behaviors but on particular causes. When the left faded, single-issue groups emerged to take their place. These new groups grew and began a campaign of individual harassment and property destruction.

Ecoterrorism, Animal Rights, and Genetic Engineering

According to the FBI (Jarboe, 2002), supporters of terrorism related to ecology and animal rights joined opponents of genetic engineering in the United Kingdom in 1992. The new group called itself the Earth Liberation Front (ELF). Composed of radicals from Earth First!, the Animal Liberation Front (ALF), and other disaffected environmentalists, the group migrated from Europe to the United States. Its tactics include sabotage, tree spiking, property damage, intimidation, and arson, and they resulted in tens of millions of dollars of damage. One ELF member recently called for violent action, though both ELF and ALF deny this. Both movements post their activities on websites and e-zines such as *Bite Back* (2015).

The formation of ELF was prefigured when radical ecologists began to sabotage roadworking and construction machinery in the late 1970s. As was the case with the right wing, a novel inspired the ecoterrorists. *The Monkey Wrench Gang*, a 1975 novel by Edward Abbey, told the story of a group of ecologists who were fed up with industrial development in the West. "Monkey wrenching" referred to small acts of sabotage against companies undertaking projects in undeveloped areas. Abbey, however, was an environmental activist rather than a hate-filled ideologue like William Pierce. His novel is a fictional account that inspired others. In *The Monkey Wrench Gang*, the heroes drive through western U.S. states sabotaging bulldozers, burning billboards, and damaging the property of people they deem to be destroying the environment. (This is the same type of low-level terrorism German leftists used in the mid-1990s.) Such monkey wrenching has become a key tactic of ecoterrorists.

Bryan Denson and James Long (1999) conducted a detailed study of ecological violence for the Portland *Oregonian*. They found a shadowy conglomeration of violent ecologists who were unwilling to watch developers move into undeveloped areas. ELF had no hierarchy and was not tied to any particular location. The group used a terrorist tactic long associated with the past, however: ELF targeted its victims with arson.

Denson and Long found that damage from ecoterrorism reached into the millions of dollars. They conducted a 10-month review that considered only crimes that caused more than $50,000 worth of damage. Cases that could not be linked to environmental groups were eliminated. They found 100 cases, with very few success-ful law enforcement investigations. ELF mastered firebombs and would not strike tar-gets when people were present. The goal was to destroy property, though the group's firebombs grew increasingly sophisticated, and they placed bomb-making instructions on the Internet.

According to Denson and Long, most violence associated with ecoterrorism has taken place in the American West. From 1995 to 1999, damages totaled $28.8 million. Crimes included raids on farms, destruction of animal research laboratories at the University of California at Davis and Michigan State University, threats to individu-als, sabotage of industrial equipment, and arson. ELF activities have increased each year since 1999 and have expanded throughout the country (Schabner, 2004). At least some members want to take their actions in a new direction. In September 2002, an ELF communiqué stated that it would "no longer hesitate to pick up the gun" (Center for Consumer Freedom, 2004). That did not happen. After the arrest and conviction of prominent members of ELF, the group began to disappear. Official speculated that a few people had been causing most of the damage (Kirchner, 2015). Ecoterrorism continues under other banners.

A study of global activity looked at both animal rights and environmental ac-tions and questioned the validity of the term *ecoterrorism*. Siv Hirsch-Hoeflen and Cas Mudde (2014) say that very few academics and analysts spend time studying the subject. Combining all groups under the broad term *Radical Environmentalists and Animal Rights (REAR)*, they offer an assessment of the movement.

REAR activists are diverse and international, and they approach their causes in a variety of ways. The majority of people involved in the movement neither engage in violence nor commit crimes. The total number of activists is unknown, but they have operated in 25 countries. Despite this diversity, REAR individuals and groups share some common qualities. They all have uncompromising attitudes and are convinced that their perceptions are absolutely correct. They are not highly organized; rather, they exist in loosely bound grassroots organizations. Finally, whether they act peace-fully and legally or in violation of the law, they believe in direct action.

Looking at criminal activity in the United States from 1970 to 2007, Hirsch-Hoeflen and Mudde found several violations related to criminal activity. REAR ac-tivists committed three assassinations, 30 unarmed assaults, 44 armed assaults, 55 bombings, and 933 attacks on property. Animal rights activists committed the vast majority of attacks but no assassinations. Comparing these statistics to international data from 2003 to 2010, the researchers counted 58 cybercrimes, 80 bombings, 247 arsons, 690 raids to free animals, 808 confrontations at a victim's home, and 3,695 acts of vandalism. The most frequent crimes occurred outside the United States. The United Kingdom experienced 997 violations, Sweden 769, Italy 458, the United States 446, and Germany 379. Most ecoterrorism takes place in the West.

Hirsch-Hoefler and Mudde ask if these activities can rightly be called terrorism. The primary test, they say, is whether the criminal actions are intended to create fear to change behavior. The majority of REAR adherents engage in legal activities. Clearly, assassinations seem to belong in the category, but animal rights activists do not engage in such killings. They are less clear about arsons, assaults, and bombings. Hirsch-Hoefler and Cas conclude that slightly less than 10% of REAR activities can be classified as terrorism. Just as antiabortion activists are painted with the terrorism label because of the actions of a minority of violent people, they say, REAR activists should be viewed in criminal terms. The small number of people who use crime to intimidate a wider audience can correctly be called ecoterrorists.

Antiabortion Violence

For the past three decades, violence against abortion clinics and personnel has risen. Violent antiabortionists began with bombing and arson attacks more than 20 years ago, and they have expanded their tactics since then. Doctors and nurses have been assaulted when entering clinics. A gunman murdered Dr. David Gunn as he entered a clinic in Pensacola, Florida, in 1993. A year later, the Reverend Paul Hill killed a doctor and his bodyguard as they entered the same clinic (Risen and Thomas, 1998). Hill was convicted of murder and executed in 2003. Dr. Barnett Slepian was killed at home in Amherst, New York, in 1998 when a sniper shot him through his kitchen window. Another violent perpetrator, **Eric Rudolph**, evaded federal authorities for years after bombings at the 1996 Olympics in Atlanta, a gay nightclub, and an abortion clinic in Birmingham, Alabama.

Eric Rudolph: (b. 1966) A right-wing extremist known for bombing the Atlanta Olympics, a gay nightclub, and an abortion clinic. Rudolph hid from authorities and became a survivalist hero. He was arrested in 2003 and received five life sentences in 2005.

Abortion is a heated topic that pits pro-life and pro-choice advocates against one another. Most pro-life advocates abhor and denounce antiabortion violence because it is a contradiction of what they represent. Violent antiabortion advocates, however, justify their actions in the same manner as other political extremists. They feel they have the right to define morality in absolute terms. According to Risen and Thomas (1998), both murderers in Pensacola felt a specific holy duty to kill the doctors they confronted. Paul Hill, for example, shot his victims five times, laid his gun down, and walked away. Michael Griffin, Gunn's murderer, felt that God gave him instructions to give Gunn one final warning before he was killed. When Gunn ignored him, Griffin waited for five hours and then shot him three times in the back as he left the clinic. To these extremists, accepting the status quo is more evil than using violence to change behavior. This is the standard justification for terrorism (see the feature later in this chapter titled "Alternative Perspective: Tactics Used in Violent Antiabortion Attacks").

Violence is not the only illegal action perpetuated by those who break the law. The Army of God's manual (n.d.) includes information about "99 Ways to Stop an Abortionist." It discusses low-level tactics such as gluing locks, shutting off water, and slashing tires. These are the tactics of radical ecologists in Germany (Horchem, 1986), but the manual does not credit a source of inspiration for the suggested tactics. The manual also describes methods for confronting workers and women seeking an abortion.

David Nice (1988) attempts to build a theory of violence by examining trends in abortion clinic bombings. Though done in 1988, Nice's research remains applicable today. He found that abortion clinic bombings were positively correlated with every theory of violence except the theory of economic deprivation. There was no relation

ANOTHER PERSPECTIVE

Tactics Used in Violent Antiabortion Attacks

- Suspected anthrax sent through the mail
- Malicious destruction of property
- Threatening letters and phone calls to workers
- False bomb threats
- Individual harassment
- Bombing and arson
- Bombing with secondary devices (designed to kill the people who respond to the first bombing)
- Assaults
- Intentional murder on the premises
- Assassination-style murders

between abortion clinic bombings and economic conditions. Nice concludes that antiabortion violence appears in areas of rapid population growth where the abortion rate is high.

When informal social norms fail to control public behavior, some people want to replace norms with law. If the norm involves an important moral aspect of behavior and laws do not replace former norms, some people feel called to violence. They say that their opposition to a grossly immoral act, such as abortion, justifies their actions. This thought process represents the logic of terrorism. As social controls decrease and the desire to substitute political controls increases, bombings come to be seen as a form of political action. Nice notes that the literature reveals several explanations for violent political behavior. One theory suggests that social controls break down under stress and urbanization. Another theory says that violence increases when people are not satisfied with political outcomes. Violence can also be reinforced by social and cultural values. Finally, violence can stem from a group's strengths or weaknesses, its lack of faith in the political system, or its frustration with economic conditions.

Some of Nice's findings seem applicable to antiabortion violence that has occurred since his study. According to Risen and Thomas (1998), murderers who kill doctors who perform abortions felt that the killings were necessary to make a political statement. Killing was a means of communication. Paul Hill was so excited by Gunn's murder that he successfully publicized it by appearing on *The Phil Donahue Show* and confronting Gunn's son. Activists were also prominent in the geographic area where the shootings took place. All these factors created an atmosphere in which the killers sought to make a stronger statement than merely persuading women entering the clinic not to have an abortion.

Other issues have changed since Nice's study. Deana Rohlinger (2002) argues that current media coverage of abortion issues differs from that of the 1980s and early 1990s. She states that organizations favoring a woman's right to an abortion understood two critical aspects of media coverage in the previous decades. They knew how certain news organizations framed the debate and how they would cover a story. They also understood the power of news coverage and were able to attract media coverage for their point of view. Organizations against abortion did not know how to attract media coverage or how to utilize it as a propaganda tool. If Rohlinger is correct, it would be wise to follow Brent Smith's path of empirical analysis. Nice's theory of bombing and frustration could be tested against the ability of the antiabortion movement to affect outcomes by media publicity.

Carol Mason (2004) argues that frustration may be building on the pro-choice side. She believes that the antiabortion movement has not only effectively conveyed a message but glorified apocalyptic violence. Antiabortion terrorists become heroes in the antiabortion movement, even though their actions are publicly denounced. She uses the case of Eric Rudolph to illustrate her point. Wanted for a string of violent antiabortion acts, Rudolph was finally captured after years of being a fugitive. Rudolph was allowed to play the role of right-wing folk hero, Mason says, after he was taken into custody. She believes that such glorification could lead to a backlash.

Laws protecting access to abortion have not resulted in a backlash. Studies by and Joshua Freilich and William Pridemore (2007) found that laws protecting access to abortion had little effect. They neither reduced attacks nor caused a backlash from groups opposing abortions. They found that extremists who attack clinics and providers are more concerned with their cause than with obeying the law.

Freilich and Pridemore also found that about 40 percent of the clinics in the United States had experienced some form of attack, vandalism, or harassment. Incidents ranged from murder to vandalism against property. The study of self-reported victimization revealed that extremists practiced several methods of attack. Employees reported that they had been harassed, subjected to picketing at home, stalked, threatened; received nuisance telephone calls; and had their property damaged. They also had personal data and their pictures distributed on "wanted" posters and displayed on the Internet.

After the murder of a physician in the vestibule of a Lutheran church in Wichita, Kansas, Amanda Robb's article in a popular magazine (2010) raised questions about lone wolves. The doctor, who ran a late-term abortion clinic in Wichita, was murdered just before a Sunday worship service. Robb argues that the murderer was not a lone wolf but the product of a right-wing mindset that promotes antigovernment violence. Critics of positions like this feel that the government and liberals in the media are trying to create an atmosphere of political repression. They argue that the government wants to use individual acts to move against people with conservative political beliefs (*New American*, 2009).

Examining evidence about the effectiveness of terrorism, James Lutz and Brenda Lutz (2008) found that antiabortion terrorism falls into a unique category. There are a variety of political and tactical debates because the movement is based in religion, but it does not represent a single theological perspective. The vast majority of people in the movement protest with peaceful tactics, causing the violent actors to form their own subcategory. From this perspective, antiabortion violence is effective. It is contagious among the subset, and it is effective. Murders and other violent attacks are designed to frighten health care workers and to change their behavior, and these tactics work. They deter doctors and nurses from performing abortions, and potentially violent people are inspired to take action. Lutz and Lutz conclude that there can be no doubt that violent antiabortion terrorism has made abortions more difficult to obtain in the United States, even though the majority of antiabortion activists denounce violence.

There is no easy solution to the abortion debate, as proponents of each side believe that they are morally correct. Those who are pro-choice feel that they are defending constitutional rights, and those who are pro-life often believe that they are following God's will. The abortion debate represents a political issue in which the positions have been defined by extreme political positions, and this frustrates other people who believe a moral solution lies between the two extremes. The atmosphere surrounding the abortion debate is similar to extremist positions surrounding terrorist conflicts in other parts of the world.

Self-Check

> What single issues have replaced left-wing ideological terrorism?
> Is the use of the term *ecoterrorism* justified?
> Is antiabortion violence terrorism?

Homegrown Jihadists

While Christian and quasi-Christian religious extremists on the right have engaged in violence, the United States has also experienced homegrown Islamic criminal violence. These homegrown extremists are Americans or American residents who adopt the jihadist philosophy. Many law enforcement officials fear that a new style of jihadist group is appearing, a hybrid of foreign and homegrown terrorists. Such groups have been involved in over 60 foiled attacks, ranging from a plan to go on a shooting spree at Fort Dix, New Jersey, in 2007 to an attempt to detonate a car bomb in New York City's Times Square in 2010. ISIS inspired seven domestic plots and two attacks between the October 2014 and June 2015 (Inserra, 2015).

Homegrown terrorists are produced in a number of ways (Holden and White, 2010). The United States has experienced two styles of homegrown attacks or attempted attacks. The first involves individuals who become radicalized by personal experiences. These personal experiences can vary from listening to radical sermons to being encouraged to commit suicide bombings by family members. The second might involve a similar path to radicalization, but it also involves some type of foreign connection. For example, Nidal Hasan went on a shooting spree in Fort Hood, Texas, killing several U.S. service personnel and wounding others. He appears to have been influenced by radical preaching and literature on the Internet. Faisal Shazad attempted to detonate a bomb in Times Square. He apparently received training in Pakistan. There is a fear that returning jihadists will launch domestic attacks, but data suggest this does not happen as frequently as predicted.

Some homegrown terrorists choose not to strike in the United States. For example, **John Walker Lindh** and **Adam Gadahn** left the United States to join the jihad overseas. Such actions always leave the possibility of returning home. If that happens, a new third type of threat could come in a hybrid form: a returning homegrown jihadist experienced and trained in terrorism. Authorities fear that American citizens may join experienced international sleeper cells hiding in America (see Thachik, Bowman, and Richardson, 2008).

The country has had some experience with hybrid terrorists. One instance includes black Muslims who were recruited away from the faith in which they were raised or converted to a traditional form of Islam. Afterward, they experience further conversion into militancy. Still another model involves normative American Muslims radicalized in their mosques. Finally, some Muslims are radicalized while in foreign countries and then return to the United States. Mark Hamm (2007, 2009) says that prison recruiting creates a problem because it is much easier to radicalize people in jail. For example, a group of convicted armed robbers in Southern California formed a jihadist cell in this manner.

John Walker Lindh: (b. 1981) An American captured while fighting for the Taliban in 2001 and sentenced to 20 years in prison.

Adam Gadahn: (1958–2015) The American spokesperson for al Qaeda. His *nom de guerre* was Azzam al Ameriki. He was killed by a drone strike in January 2015.

((●)) ANOTHER PERSPECTIVE

Hamas in the United States

- In the summer of 2004, the Department of Justice charged several people with terrorist activities, including money laundering, threatening violence, possessing weapons, and a series of other related crimes. The indictment charged the suspects with being members of Hamas.
- In October 2003, law enforcement officers found small Cincinnati grocery stores raising millions of dollars for Hamas through price fraud.
- In September 2003, agents seized two men in the Virgin Islands after they left the mainland to launder money for Hamas.
- In Dearborn, Michigan, law enforcement officials charged two men with bank fraud. The alleged purpose was to raise money for Hamas.

Source: United States of America v. Mousa Mohammed Abu Marzook et al., 2003

The Charlotte Hezbollah Cell

A deputy sheriff moonlighting as a security guard in Charlotte, North Carolina, noticed a group of people buying cigarettes at a discount tobacco store. He noticed them because they were buying hundreds of cigarette cartons and loading them into vans. The deputy assumed it was a cigarette smuggling operation and called the Bureau of Alcohol, Tobacco, and Firearms (ATF). Buying cigarettes in one state and then selling them in another can be criminally profitable because of varying state tobacco laws and tax systems. When the ATF agents started investigating, they were surprised at what they found. The FBI, CIA, and many other agencies were also interested in the case.

Hezbollah was operating in Charlotte.

In this case, the suspects purchased cigarettes in North Carolina and ran them to Michigan. North Carolina had a tax of $0.05 per pack on the cigarettes ($0.50 per carton). Michigan, however, taxed cigarettes at $0.75 per pack and $7.50 per carton. North Carolina did not require a tax stamp, but Michigan did. Smugglers transported the cigarettes from North Carolina to Michigan, stamped them with Michigan tax stamps, and then sold them at regular prices without paying the taxes.

The U.S. attorney for western North Carolina, Robert Conrad, assumed the suspects were smuggling North Carolina cigarettes to Michigan and profiting by not paying tax. This turned out to be the base of the investigation, as the smugglers kept some of the money, but other illegal profits took a strange path. Conrad followed some of the money to Vancouver, Canada; other profits went overseas. Conrad's office traced the money to Lebanon. Far from a simple cigarette scheme, the smuggling operation turned out to be an operation to support Hezbollah. The Charlotte Hezbollah cell, as it came to be known, was broken because investigators and prosecutors looked beyond the surface.

Source: United States v. Mohamad Youseff Hammoud et al., 2002

In 2006, after British authorities uncovered a homegrown jihadist plot, FBI director Robert Mueller stated that the United States had to be vigilant against similar plots. International jihadists are a threat, Mueller said, but like the United Kingdom, the United States could be threatened by its own citizens. One of the incubators for homegrown jihadists is the American prison system. America's prisons are already awash with many variations of Islam, and Wahhabi missionaries covertly preach religious militancy in the prisons. Aware of this danger, some institutions have established special units to gather information about religious militancy and to intercept violent missionaries (Moore, 2006).

Although prisons and jails are recruiting grounds, homegrown jihadists appear in different areas. In June 2006, JTTF officers in Miami and Atlanta arrested a group of jihadists who were not involved in any network but who, authorities claimed, were plotting to blow up the Sears Tower in Chicago. The group did not even follow Islam. Its leader made up a religion combining Islam and other beliefs. According to media reports, the suspects were amateurs who had no real understanding of explosives, Islam, or the jihadist movement. Mueller said that such groups might become the greatest domestic threat. They are self-recruited, self-motivated, and self-trained. Their only direct contact with the jihadists is via the Internet (Josson, 2006). The jihadists who pulled off the March 11, 2004, Madrid attacks were amateurs, too.

Homegrown terrorism is not an American problem alone, nor is it limited to radical Islam. It is a "bottom-up event," in which a person hears a radical message and decides to pursue the radical goal. Lorenzo Vidino (2009) argues that this is hardly new, citing several cases to illustrate the point. For example, in 1977, a group of 10 homegrown religious radicals stormed three sites in Washington, D.C., taking more than 150 hostages. This is just one of many homegrown instances in the second half of the twentieth century. While it may differ in scope from modern suicide bombing, Vidino concludes that it represents an extension of a problem. Homegrown terrorism is not something new.

Homegrown jihadist terrorism began drawing attention after 9/11. In May 2007, a group in New Jersey planned to enter Fort Dix and murder American soldiers. They were indicted after police were informed of their videotaped training exercises (Hauser and O'Connor, 2007). A month later, the New York City Police Department and the New York JTTF completed an 18-month investigation of an attack planned for JFK Airport (MSNBC, 2007). In 2009, FBI agents arrested an Afghan-born permanent legal resident of the United States and two friends for planning suicide attacks in New York City. They were tied to groups in Pakistan and had possible links to al Qaeda, according to the *New York Times* (Rashbaum, 2010). The plot was followed by an attempted bombing in Times Square by a Pakistani-trained homegrown terrorist in 2010, according to ABC News (Katersky, 2010).

Brian Jenkins (2010) found that 46 publicly recorded attacks or attempted attacks came from homegrown jihadist terrorists between September 11, 2001, and December 2009. Far from having been recruited by a nefarious network of hidden operatives, most of the people involved in the cases were self-radicalized, seeking to join the jihad on their own. Jenkins believes that the attacks were thwarted because American law enforcement changed its focus from apprehension after the fact to prevention. This is effective when criminal intelligence is gathered and analyzed on a local level, he argues. He also warns about overreacting. Although a single event can produce massive casualties, the United States experienced more domestic terrorism in the 1970s than it did in the first decade of the twenty-first century. Intelligence gathering is necessary, Jenkins concludes, but it must take place within the norms of democracy.

> ✓ **Self-Check**
>
> > How are homegrown terrorists involved in the jihadist movement?
> > How are homegrown terrorists supported?
> > What are the characteristics of homegrown terrorists?

Emphasizing the Points

There is some confusion over the amount of domestic terrorism because most terrorists are arrested and charged with violations of statutory crimes. There is also a fear that political dissent may be criminalized. A practical approach for law enforcement and criminal intelligence agencies is to categorize the type of terrorist activity motivating attacks or attempted attacks and apply the unique prevention and investigation techniques that work best in each instance. Racism is a part of terrorism in the United States. Although it is fragmented today, the Ku Klux Klan and its offshoots have a long history of domestic terrorism. Racists and antigovernment extremists today dominate domestic terrorism, and the left has been subsumed in single-issue terrorism with the exception of antiabortion violence. Law enforcement and other officials are preparing for homegrown jihadists. While jihadists have called for it, home grown Jihadi Salafism has not materialized.

SUMMARY OF CHAPTER OBJECTIVES

- There is confusion over the meaning of domestic terrorism and political disagreement over its meaning. Law enforcement officers and criminal intelligence agencies do best by avoiding the debate and focusing on successful tactics that work against the individual or group acting in violation of the law.
- Extremism differs from terrorism, and it is not a crime. Very few criminals are terrorists, but all terrorists act outside the law.
- There are several typologies for classifying domestic terrorism. Placing a type of terrorism in a category based on tactics, operations, and likely targets is an effective counterterrorist tool. The categories used in this chapter are racism, antigovernment extremism, single issues, and homegrown Jihadist Salafism.
- Racism has been an important factor in America terrorism. It dates back to the Civil War and is still prominent in many areas today.
- The Ku Klux Klan is one of America's most successful terrorist groups. During its three-phased history, the KKK used violence and intimidation to change the political behavior of African Americans and opponents of racism. Although fragmented today, the KKK's legacy lives on in a number of racist groups.
- The current status of right-wing terrorism today is dominated by violent antigovernment extremism. Sovereign citizens claim that the U.S. government has no power of them. Americans police agencies think right-wing terrorism is more important than the jihadist threat. Right-wing extremists have killed a number of police officers over the past two decades.
- Left-wing ideology was the force behind domestic terrorism in the 1960s and 1970s, but it faded in the late part of the twentieth century. Crime motivated by left-wing issues tends to take place within single-issue groups inside the radical ecology and animal rights movements.
- Single-issue terrorism involves extremist crimes committed to support a particular cause.
- The single issues discussed in this chapter are ecoterrorism, animal rights crime, and antiabortion violence.
- The homegrown jihadist movement involves religious radicals taking criminal action in the name of Salafist Islam. There is no standard pattern of radicalization, and it may range from unorganized individual attacks to highly complex operations supported by an international infrastructure. Research shows that this is not an Islamic problem and that most American Muslims do not support criminal violence.

LOOKING INTO THE FUTURE

In October 2014, four New York City Police Department patrol officers were on duty in a subway station when they stopped to let a freelance photographer take their picture, according to an NBC television affiliate (Dientst et al., 2015). Suddenly, a man with a hatchet lunged at them. Officer Kenneth Healey was severely wounded and fell to the floor. His partner, Officer Joseph Meeker, was wounded in the arm. When the attacker approached the two remaining officers, they drew their weapons and killed him. The man was a recent convert to Islam and had been influenced by Jihadist Salafism.

This type of terrorism may well become the norm in the next decades. Similar attacks have occurred in France, the United Kingdom, and elsewhere. It is the type of terrorism envisioned in the late right-wing extremist William Pierce's serial novel *Hunter*. America is currently a deeply divided society. Issues such as racism, LGBT rights, the role of government, taxes, federal court decisions, religion, gun ownership, abortion, and general politics have completely separated Americans. Fueled by openly partisan newscasts and talk radio, divisions are vitriolic and seem to be increasing.

This atmosphere creates a social climate conducive to extremism and intolerance. It has happened at a time when many political leaders criticize the value of a college education and social polarization is celebrated. A lone individual who is potentially violent and influenced by only one extreme point of view may sink deeper and deeper into radicalism. This in turn could lead to violence. If this social trend continues, lone wolf terrorism may well become a factor in domestic terrorism.

KEY TERMS

Skinhead, p. 284
The Order, p. 284
Fourteen Words, p. 284
Anglo-Israelism, p. 285
Christian Identity, p. 285
Nordic Christianity (neo-paganism), p. 285

Creativity, p. 285
Ben Klassen, p. 285
Free-wheeling funda-mentalism, p. 285
Knight Riders, p. 286
Sovereign Citizens, p. 287

Moorish Nation, p. 287
Paper terrorism, p. 287
New World Order, p. 288
National Alliance, p. 289
Robert Matthews, p. 290
Brüder Schweigen, p. 290

Eric Rudolph, p. 294
John Walker Lindh, p. 297
Adam Gadahn, p. 297

CHAPTER 13

An Introduction to Homeland Security

A Border Patrol Agent on the Job

The U.S. homeland experienced major cyberattacks in 2015. January began with a breach of the Sony Corporation's computer system. It was allegedly masterminded by North Korea because the country's leader was angry about the way he was portrayed in a satirical movie. This attack was followed by a massive data breach in the federal government. As officials investigated the intrusion, they found that it was much worse than expected. Hackers uncovered personal details, including names, addresses, and social security numbers from more than 20 million current and former federal employees and contractors. When United Airlines experienced a massive cyberfailure in July, and the New York Stock Exchange closed for four hours on the same day due to computer problems, officials immediately suspected hackers.

Cyberattacks are potentially crippling. According to NBC News (2015), Lloyds of London and Cambridge University conducted an assessment of a catastrophic cyberattack on the U.S. power grid. In the less-than-probable disruption of 100 networks, estimated losses ranged from $70 billion to $1 trillion.

The FBI director said in July 2015 that his agency lacked the capability to protect the country from sophisticated cyberattacks.

The U.S. economy and social structure is totally integrated with technology, and all systems are vulnerable. A vast network of public and private organizations that controls the infrastructure further complicates security. Even on the local level, all layers of government, local autonomous governing boards, multiple educational institutions, small businesses, large companies, and multinational corporations may control various parts of the infrastructure. Homeland security is charged with protecting all the people served by those systems and the physical infrastructure. If the FBI director is correct, these systems and infrastructure are extremely vulnerable.

Many Meanings of Homeland Security

Homeland security means different things to different people and organizations. The federal government usually refers to the **Department of Homeland Security** (DHS) when approaching the topic. State and local governments apply the term to law enforcement agencies and criminal intelligence organizations. Governors look to the National Guard and state troopers. Health officials consider epidemics and casualties, and emergency responders may think of fires or natural disasters. While counterterrorism analysts tend to approach the topic by focusing on prevention, responders see homeland security as rescue, recovery, and restoration operations.

Scott Robinson and Nicola Mallik (2015) find that homeland security has multiple and unclear connotations. They argue that universities create academic homeland security programs but have no regimented approach for addressing the topic. Although criminal justice suffers the same problem, it is much more pronounced in homeland security. Robinson and Mallik conclude that the current semieclectic approach to the topic is healthy because aspects of homeland security require combining groups of individuals with differing skill sets.

Approaches to homeland security are not merely multidisciplinary. They are orientated toward differing goals, and they require an array of vocational and professional preparation. For example, this book is focused on *analyzing and preventing* terrorism, and this can legitimately be called homeland security. The book makes virtually no mention of bomb disposal techniques, scene management, or first aid. These would be topics for individuals *responding* to terrorism, but that is also homeland security. Essentially, many organizations define homeland security based on their missions.

Department of Homeland Security: (DHS) A federal agency created in 2003 by Congress from the Office of Homeland Security after the attacks of September 11, 2001.

Defining and Evaluating a Mission

Issues surrounding homeland security were confused after 9/11 because the country was dealing with a new concept, a new meaning of conflict, and a change in the procedures used to defend the United States. In the past, military forces protected the homeland, projecting power beyond U.S. borders, but the world changed with the end of the Cold War in 1991. President George W. Bush formed the Department of Homeland Security in 2003 to direct and coordinate efforts to secure the mainland.

Some research indicates that DHS's mission has been successful. State and local agencies have a clearer sense of mission and their role in preventing terrorism because of actions in the DHS. For example, one study indicates that the United States is much more systematic than Canada because the Canadians have not consolidated homeland security (Walby and Lippert, 2015). This is especially true in large metropolitan areas

(Giblin, Burruss, and Shafer, 2014). DHS proudly points to its attempts to coordinate criminal information gathering and intelligence analysis (DHS, 2014). Analysts at the Center for Strategic and International Studies say that much more effort must be focused on cybersecurity and information sharing, but they applaud DHS's efforts in homeland security (Nelson and Wise, 2013).

Critics maintain that DHS's mission is confused and the patchwork of agencies protecting the country is ineffective. Stephen Flynn (2002, 2004a, 2004b) points to weaknesses in port security. Robert Poole (2006) told Congress that aviation security remains inadequate even after the disasters of 9/11. The greatest criticism is aimed at the borders. Although illegal immigration is a hot topic of political debate, the southern border is not secure by any measure. Many counterterrorism experts believe that it will become one of the main infiltration routes for jihadists. The northern border, which does not receive the same amount of attention, is also difficult to secure (Clarke, 2007).

Security Missions

It might be more appropriate to move beyond the confusion about homeland security to look at the missions of various organizations and their common understanding of the concept. Essentially, *mission* and *understanding of homeland security* mean the same thing, but there are many different understandings of homeland security because agencies have differing missions. For example, the Department of Energy (DOE) is responsible for protecting nuclear materials, power grids, and gas lines. DOE's understanding of homeland security is related to its mission. Customs and Border Protection in the DHS, on the other hand, uses its agents to secure U.S. borders and points of entry, with customs agents collecting revenue. It has a law enforcement mission and defines homeland security within this context. The elements of security expand or contract depending on an organization's mission.

There is confusion, to be sure, but it centers on policy, not mission. The policy guiding homeland security in the United States has not been fully developed, and agency leaders are not quite sure how all the missions of the various agencies fit together. Groups inside and outside government are adjusting to new roles. The intelligence community was criticized after the attacks, and the 9/11 Commission and its supporters were successful in implementing reform in the intelligence community. Critics, however, are not impressed with the commission's version of reform. They maintain that the 9/11 Commission was established to investigate the attacks but that it had neither the expertise nor the capability to reform intelligence gathering (Posner, 2004). This leaves the roles of the various intelligence groups in transition. The law enforcement and military communities are trying to find policies to define their roles. The functions of domestic and international laws have not been fully established. Various levels of government and private industry are trying to figure out where they interact. All of these undertakings take time.

Homeland security also involves civil defense, that is, citizens engaged in homeland security. Civil defense did not develop overnight; rather, it emerged slowly from civilian functions during World War II. After 1960, civil defense structures were intended to help government protect citizens in such areas as emergency communications, through private and public broadcasting, direct assistance during emergencies, and designation of evacuation routes and fallout shelters. During the Cold War, various organizations involved in **civil defense** gradually learned specific missions. The idea of "civil defense" will take on a new meaning in the coming years because the

civil defense: Citizens engaged in homeland security.

nature of conflict has changed. Homeland security is much more than the sum of the agencies charged with protecting the United States. A major portion of security is a civic responsibility.

> ✓ **Self-Check**
>
> > Why is there confusion about the meaning of homeland security?
> > How effective is the Department of Homeland Security?
> > How is homeland security related to civil defense?

Agencies Charged with Preventing and Interdicting Terrorism

Congress approved the creation of DHS by uniting 22 agencies in 2002, but many other governmental organizations also focus on homeland security. These organizations exist at all levels of government: federal, state, and local. Two types of private-sector organizations participate in homeland security: businesses providing critical infrastructure and businesses centered on security technology and services. The health care system and energy sector are also part of the infrastructure of homeland security.

The Department of Homeland Security

The DHS was created from the Office of Homeland Security in 2003 as a direct result of the 9/11 attacks. It has several different missions. One group of internal organizations responds to natural and human disasters, and this function is complemented by a group of agencies charged with health and policy. Closely related to this are organizations charged with monitoring science and technology, including the detection of nuclear activities. Other parts of the department are tasked with managing both DHS's internal affairs and some functions external to it. DHS also coordinates its responses with thousands of state and local organizations. There are several internal agencies that have security functions directly related to terrorism prevention.

Formerly, the U.S. Coast Guard was under the Department of Transportation (except in times of war, when it is subsumed by the U.S. Navy). It was the first agency to be assigned to the DHS. The coast guard has many duties, including the protection of coastal and inland waterways, environmental protection, the interdiction of contraband, and maritime law enforcement. For counterterrorism, its primary mission is to intercept terrorists and weapons on the high seas. Coast guard personnel also serve wherever U.S. military personnel are deployed under the command of the armed forces.

Other departments inside DHS have counterterrorist responsibilities. Many DHS agencies are involved in intelligence: Its Office of Intelligence and Analysis coordinates intelligence with other agencies. The Transportation Security Administration is responsible for airport security. The Customs and Border Protection includes customs agents and the Border Patrol. Their work is augmented by an investigative agency, Immigration and Customs Enforcement (ICE), which is DHS's largest investigative arm. The Secret Service also serves under DHS. In addition to providing presidential security, the Secret Service retains its former role in countering financial crime. It is also involved in investigating identity theft, banking practices, and cyberattacks (Figure 13.1).

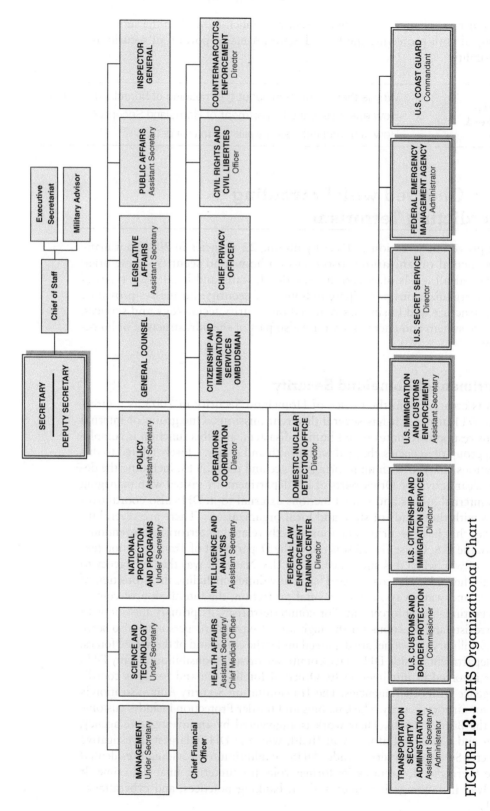

FIGURE **13.1** DHS Organizational Chart

Many DHS employees are employed in law enforcement tasks and have arrest powers. In the new Homeland Security structure, these special agents and federal police officers are trained at the **Federal Law Enforcement Training Center** (FLETC) in Glencoe, Georgia. FLETC instructors also teach basic and advanced classes on terrorism. Before 2003, FLETC was responsible for training all federal law enforcement officers except special agents from the FBI and Drug Enforcement Administration (DEA). These agencies have their own training academies at the Marine Corps base in Quantico, Virginia.

Federal Law Enforcement Training Center: (FLETC) A law enforcement training academy for federal agencies. Operating in Glencoe, Georgia, FLETC trains agents and police officers for agencies that do not operate their own academy.

The Department of Justice

The Department of Justice (DOJ) maintains several functions in the realm of counterterrorism. The most noted agency is the FBI (n.d.). Before 9/11, the FBI was designated as the lead agency for *investigating* cases of terrorism in the United States. After 9/11, Director Robert Mueller maintained that *preventing* terrorism would be the bureau's chief mission. The FBI enhanced its Counterterrorism Division and increased the number of intelligence analysts assigned to it under Mueller's direction. As discussed at other points in this text, the FBI also coordinates state and local law enforcement efforts in its Joint Terrorism Task Forces (JTTFs). The bureau also maintains Field Intelligence offices in its local agencies (see the section titled "Building Intelligence Systems" later in this chapter).

The DOJ is involved in other areas as well (U.S. DOJ, 2006). U.S. attorneys investigate and prosecute terrorism cases and coordinate intelligence sharing (see the section titled "Building Intelligence Systems" later in this chapter). The U.S. Marshals Service (2005) provides protection to federal officials under any type of threat in addition to the securing the courts and apprehending escaped offenders. Marshals are also responsible officials from terrorist attacks. The Bureau of Alcohol, Tobacco, and Firearms (ATF) has for years played a leading role in counterterrorism. Bombs are one of the most frequently used weapons in terrorism, and the ATF has some of the best explosives experts in the world. It is also charged with federal firearms enforcement. Although the FBI is the lead agency in domestic terrorism, ATF's role in explosives and firearms enforcement is crucial. Many FBI investigations would be less productive without ATF help (ATF, 2015). The Bureau of Justice Assistance (BJA) has trained more than 100,000 state and local officers since 9/11 in the BJA State and Local Anti-Terrorism Training (SLATT) program (BJA/SLATT, 2010). SLATT trainers have also been used by various federal law enforcement agencies and the armed forces.

The Department of Defense

Obviously, in times of war, the military organizations in DOD play the leading role. DOD has also assumed counterterrorist functions. It does this in two ways. First, DOD operates the U.S. Northern Command to ensure homeland security. Because the Constitution forbids military forces from enforcing civil law except in times of declared martial law, the Northern Command limits its activities to military functions. It participates in information gathering and sharing, but it is excluded from civil affairs. In times of emergency, however, military forces can provide much-needed assistance to local units of government. This is the second function of DOD. When civilian authorities request and the president approves it, military forces may be used to support civilians in counterterrorism efforts (DOD, 2015). This power can be used in times of national emergency or to assist in disasters or civil disorders.

The Intelligence Community

The federal intelligence community underwent massive changes after 9/11, the invasion of Iraq, and the failure to find weapons of mass destruction (WMD). The Office of the Director of National Intelligence (ODNI) began operations in April 2005. The purpose of the ODNI is to unite America's national security intelligence under one umbrella. The idea dates back to 1955, when several intelligence experts suggested that the deputy director of the Central Intelligence Agency (CIA) should run day-to-day intelligence operations for the agency and that the director should assume the responsibility of coordinating all national intelligence efforts. The 9/11 Commission report suggested sweeping intelligence reforms, including the creation of a single intelligence director. The ODNI resulted from those recommendations (ODNI, 2015).

The ODNI is a new concept in intelligence gathering. It coordinates information from national security and military intelligence. These agencies include the CIA, the National Security Agency, the Defense Intelligence Agency, the National Geospatial-Intelligence Agency, and the National Reconnaissance Office. It also includes intelligence operations from the Department of State. Based on the recommendations of the 9/11 Commission, the ODNI has incorporated federal law enforcement intelligence under its umbrella as well. Law enforcement agencies that report to the director of national intelligence include the FBI's National Security Branch, the DOE's Office of Intelligence and Counterintelligence, the DHS's Office of Intelligence and Analysis, the Department of the Treasury's Office of Intelligence and Analysis, and the Drug Enforcement Administration's Office of National Security Intelligence (Figure 13.2).

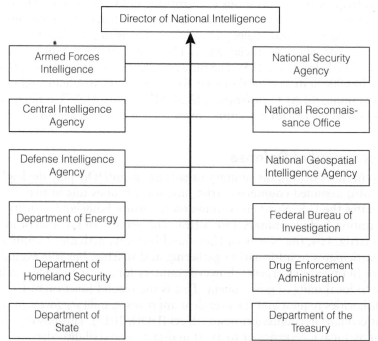

FIGURE **13.2** Office of the Director of National Intelligence

State and local Law Enforcement

The federal government also envisions three intelligence roles for local governments. David Carter (2009) explains the first two. State and local law enforcement agencies need to collect tactical intelligence for the prevention of terrorism and other crimes. They must also use intelligence for planning and the deployment of resources. Chief Gary Vest (2007) explains the third role. Information sharing is at the heart of local intelligence systems. Vest says that agencies are sharing information at an unprecedented scale but that they need to enhance the process by creating systems governed by policies. Vest believes that agencies need to form associations with governing boards that have the power to enforce rules and regulations. These will regulate intelligence within the law, prevent leaks, and provide routine methods for sharing the information.

Carter (2009, pp. 2–6) says that the role of intelligence and information sharing among state and local law enforcement agencies enhances counterterrorism efforts. Large federal systems operate on a global basis, and officers in local communities know their jurisdictions better than anyone else. Community partnerships enhance the amount and quality of information that they can accumulate. The federal government does not have the resources or the community contacts to develop these links. The National Criminal Intelligence Sharing Plan comes to the same conclusion. The ability of state and local agencies to share information is at the heart of preventing terrorist strikes within the borders of the United States (Daniels, 2003). When it comes to terrorism, state and local agencies are crucial to homeland security.

✔ **Self-Check**

> What federal departments and agencies are charged with homeland security?
> Why does the intelligence community interface with law enforcement?
> What roles do state and local law enforcement agencies have in homeland security?

Building Intelligence Systems

Redirecting military and police forces is an essential part of developing a system to protect the nation. The most important aspect of security, however, is the information that guides security forces. If policies and strategy are important to the overall effort, information is crucial for day-to-day operations. For example, Thomas Barnett's (2004) idea of creating an inclusive geopolitical economic policy in which everybody wins is a long-term strategy for reducing international violence. Somewhere between the current state of affairs and the outcome of such a policy is the everyday world of homeland security. This world is driven by intelligence, and security forces can be no more effective than their ability to gain information and process it in a meaningful way.

The Intelligence Process

Information gathering is comparable to academic research. Before beginning, a researcher needs basic knowledge of a field and an understanding of subdisciplines. Much of this background information has no direct bearing on the actual question a researcher is trying to answer, but without background preparation, the researcher cannot even address the question. Command of basic information allows the researcher to move toward applying results. Applied information, with the specificity the researcher seeks, requires both in-depth knowledge about a specific topic and the latest information from the discipline. In the sciences and social sciences, this process leads a researcher from general concepts to applied ideas, from abstract principles to glimpses of reality.

For example, if a terrorist threat is coming from a particular country, intelligence analysts need to have a basic understanding of terrorism, crime, and political power before they are able to begin an examination of the problem. They need to have skills in several social sciences, an understanding of communication and language, and the ability to estimate the influence of nationalist and religious influences on behavior. Such basic knowledge comes from a multidisciplinary liberal education. It may not have a direct bearing on the problem, but basic information provides the skills needed to gather and analyze information about the actual terrorist threat. This is applied information.

Although academic in nature, this process is directly applicable to gathering intelligence. Police intelligence systems can be modeled after academic research. Basic intelligence involves general information about a subject and its subdisciplines. Applied intelligence involves gathering basic information about a target and real-time information about its current activities.

The practical application of this process comes through organizing structures aimed at collecting, analyzing, and forwarding information. Someone in every American law enforcement agency should be assigned to collect and forward terrorist intelligence. In small agencies, this may mean assigning a person who represents several police and sheriff's departments; in moderate-size agencies, the function could be performed in the detective bureau or the planning unit. Large metropolitan and state police agencies need full-time intelligence units. At the state and regional levels, efforts must be made to assemble, categorize, and analyze information and place it within national and international contexts.

This results in a four-step process:

- *Basic information:* Analysts begin work after obtaining an in-depth, multidisciplinary education.
- *Applied information:* Analysts gather information about a specific problem.
- *Real-time information:* Analysts receive actual information as it is forwarded from the field.
- *Analyzed information:* Analysts produce intelligence based on analyzed information.

Ideally, steps two through four are repeated with each new piece of information.

National Security and Criminal Intelligence

As mentioned earlier, in network-to-network conflict, bureaucracies should not change their role. For example, if the CIA were to operate as if it was gathering evidence for a criminal prosecution, it would not be able to function. The same applies to all levels of law enforcement. Police agencies cannot gather information illegally. If they do, they defeat the society they are trying to protect. Each organization in a network has its own function, and the key to success in a network is sharing information.

This leads to the need for two different types of intelligence. **National security intelligence** is gathered to defend the nation. It is not used in criminal prosecutions, and it is not subject to legal scrutiny. **Criminal intelligence** is gathered by law enforcement and prosecuting attorneys. It cannot be gathered, analyzed, or stored without

national security intelligence: A system of agencies and networks that gather information about threats to the country. Any threat or potential threat is examined under the auspices of national defense intelligence. Unlike criminal intelligence, people and agencies gathering defense information do not need to suspect any criminal activity. The FBI is empowered to gather defense intelligence.

criminal intelligence: Information gathered on the reasonable suspicion that a criminal activity is occurring or about to occur. It is collected by law enforcement agencies in the course of their preventive and investigative functions. It is shared on information networks such as the Regional Information Sharing System (RISS). Unlike national defense intelligence, criminal intelligence applies only under criminal law. Agencies must suspect some violation of criminal law before they can collect intelligence.

a reason to believe that a crime is about to take place or has taken place (J. White, 2004b, pp. 73–74).

Richard Best (2001) argues that national security differs from law enforcement. In police work, officers react to information provided voluntarily. Police actions are governed by the rules of evidence, and the ultimate purpose is to protect the rights of citizens, including those who have been arrested. National security intelligence, on the other hand, is used to anticipate threats. It uses aggressive methods to collect information, including, at times, operations in violation of the law. National security intelligence is ultimately designed to protect targets, not individuals' rights.

Best quotes Stansfield Turner, a former director of the CIA, to summarize the differences between law enforcement and national security. "Give the FBI a task," Turner once said, "and it will try to complete the mission within the constraints of the law. Give the CIA the same mission, and it tries to complete the task without concern for legality." Law enforcement's prime concern is public service. The American police will lose public trust if law enforcement relies on covert illegal operations.

Using Best's insight, law enforcement should plan and develop two channels for information. One channel should be aimed at law enforcement intelligence, that is, the types of information police agencies collect. As Best (2001, 2014) describes it, this information is based on criminal activity and the protection of individual rights. It is governed by the rules of evidence. In other words, it must be legally admissible in court. Yet, police agencies will inevitably come upon threats to national security involving information that will not be used in a criminal prosecution. At this point, state and local police agencies should be prepared to pass such information along to defense sources. These two paths for information, one for criminal investigation and one for national security, can serve as the basis for dealing with intelligence collected by state and local police agencies. For example, an officer may stop an individual for suspected criminal behavior. After questioning the person, the officer no longer suspects that a crime is being committed, but the person seems to be associated with a known terrorist organization. The officer gathers information about the person and forwards it to a local fusion center. Neither the officer nor the police agency can keep this information because it does not involve a crime. The fusion center, however, has a group of analysts responsible for national security. They will analyze the officer's information, transforming it into national security intelligence. It will not be used in a criminal prosecution, and it will not be stored by a law enforcement agency or used in a criminal prosecution (see Hammond, 2010).

A Checkered Past

Law enforcement and intelligence agencies present their systems in a positive light, but critics point to two types of failures. First, intelligence processes have been ineffective. The FBI and CIA have been roundly criticized for failing to gather adequate information before the September 11 attacks and ineffectively analyzing the information they did have (Dillon, 2001; Nordland, Yousafzi, and Dehghanpisheh, 2002). The Bush administration and police agencies expressed disapproval of the FBI's information sharing policies (Fields, 2002).

Second, the government has abused its authority in the past. Civil liberties groups fear growing power in agencies associated with homeland security, and others express concern over expanding executive authority (Herman, 2001; CNN, 2006; Keefer, 2006; EFF, 2011).

Rules for collecting criminal and national security intelligence are necessary to prevent such abuses in the future. For example, in the 1950s, the CIA tested drugs on

COINTELPRO: An infamous FBI counterintelligence program started in 1956. Agents involved in COINTELPRO violated constitutional limitations on domestic intelligence gathering, and the program came under congressional criticism in the early 1970s. The FBI's abuse of power eventually resulted in restrictions on the organization.

Americans without their consent or knowledge; the FBI's counterintelligence program **COINTELPRO** exceeded the authority of law enforcement in the name of national security. The government, responding to such abuses, began to limit the power of intelligence operations, unintentionally hampering their effectiveness. Law enforcement and national defense intelligence experienced difficult times during the administration of President Jimmy Carter (1976–1980). Carter was not seeking to dismantle intelligence operations; rather, he wanted to protect Americans from their government. The president tried to correct the abuses of power and end the scandal of using covert operations against American citizens.

Carter's reaction was understandable, but critics believe that he went too far, and no other administration has been able to reconstitute effective intelligence organizations. A *Time* magazine article (Calabresi and Ratnesar, 2002) states the issue succinctly: America needs to learn to spy again. National security intelligence is crucial, but law enforcement has a role, the *Time* authors argue. They also censure bureaucratic structures for failing to share information, and they condemn the system for relying too heavily on machine and and other electronic information. We need information from people, the *Time* authors state emphatically. Another weak point is the inability to analyze information. Intelligence is fragmented and ineffective. Their opinion has been reflected in other studies (Best, 2001; D. Wise, 2002; Hammond, 2010; Fingar, 2011) (see the feature titled "Another Perspective: Types of Intelligence" later in this chapter).

Unlike national defense or security intelligence gathering, police agencies are required to demonstrate a reasonable suspicion of criminal activity before they may collect information. As long as agencies reasonably suspect that the law is being broken or has been broken, law enforcement departments may gather and store criminal intelligence. The USA PATRIOT Act, first passed in October 2001 and renewed in July, 2015, increases the ability of law enforcement and intelligence agencies to share information,

ANOTHER PERSPECTIVE

Types of Intelligence

There are different types of intelligence-gathering systems. The differences are crucial when dealing with civil rights (see Chapter 16), but each intelligence system has its own practical methods for assembling information.

Criminal intelligence is gathered by law enforcement agencies investigating illegal activity. State, local, and federal police agencies are not allowed to gather, store, or maintain record systems on general activities. Their information must be based on a reasonable suspicion that some sort of criminal activity is taking place or has taken place. Certain FBI operations may gather noncriminal intelligence if agents are assigned to national security. They do not use this evidence in criminal prosecutions.

National defense or security intelligence is gathered by several organizations in the DOD, National Security Agency, DOE, DHS, FBI, and CIA. Defense or security intelligence is usually based on one or more of the following sources:

1. HUMINT: Human intelligence from spies, informers, defectors, and other people
2. IMINT: Imagery intelligence from satellites and aircraft
3. SIGINT: Signal intelligence from communications
4. MASINT: Measures and signatures intelligence from sensing devices, such as detecting a weapons system based on the amount of heat it is producing

Defense or security intelligence can be gathered whether the targets are involved in a crime or not.

ANOTHER PERSPECTIVE

David Carter's Recommendations for Law Enforcement Intelligence

David Carter suggests refocusing law enforcement efforts. Police activity, he argues, should be led by intelligence. To accomplish this, police agencies should take an "R-cubed" approach: reassess, refocus, and reallocate.

1. Reassess the following:
   a. Calls for service
   b. Specialized units
   c. Need for new specializations
   d. Community resources
   e. Potential threats
   f. Current intelligence
   g. Political mandates from the community

2. Refocus in these ways:
   a. Establish new priorities based on reassessment
   b. Weigh priorities in terms of criticality
   c. Actually implement changes
3. Reallocate—commit the resources needed to implement changes

Law enforcement intelligence differs from intelligence gathered for national security. Law enforcement agencies must base their activities on a reasonable suspicion that some criminal activity is taking place or has taken place.

Source: Carter, 2009.

---

but David Carter (2009), one of the foremost academic experts on law enforcement intelligence in the country, solemnly warns that the abuses of the past must not be repeated if police agencies want to develop effective intelligence systems (see also Dreyfuss, 2002). If police agencies improve their intelligence-gathering operations, they will do so under more stringent rules than those required for national security (see the feature titled "Another Perspective: David Carter's Recommendations for Law Enforcement Intelligence" above).

Domestic Intelligence Networks

Shortly after 9/11, the IACP joined with the DOJ to create the **National Criminal Intelligence Sharing Plan** (NCISP). The plan established norms for collecting, analyzing, and storing criminal intelligence within legal guidelines. It also suggested how information could be shared among agencies. Its primary function was to set minimum standards for criminal intelligence so that every American police agency knew the legal guidelines for using criminal information. It also sought to create standards for using technology and giving police officers access to information. The standards guide intelligence-gathering activities, and a national coordinating group seeks to maintain them (BJA, 2005; Brooks, 2011).

David Carter (2009, pp. 123–143) points to a number of criminal intelligence networks in operation after 9/11. The **Regional Information Sharing System** (RISS) was created in 1973. RISS has six centers—each serving a selected group of states—that share criminal information with investigators working to combat a variety of criminal activities, including terrorism. RISS expanded operations in April 2003 by creating the Anti-Terrorism Information Exchange (ATIX). Complementing these systems is the FBI's Law Enforcement Online (LEO), which provides FBI intelligence to state and local agencies. The Law Enforcement Intelligence Unit (LEIU) was created by a variety of police agencies in 1956. Today, it serves as a venue to share secure information on organized crime and terrorism.

National Criminal Intelligence Sharing Plan: (NCISP) A plan to share criminal intelligence among the nation's law enforcement agencies. It suggests minimum standards for establishing and managing intelligence operations within police agencies.

Regional Information Sharing System: (RISS) A law enforcement network that allows law enforcement agencies to share information about criminal investigations.

ANOTHER PERSPECTIVE

Homeland Security Information Network

The Homeland Security Information Network (HSIN) is a computer-based counterterrorism communications system connecting all 50 states; five territories; Washington, D.C.; and 50 major urban areas.

The HSIN allows all states and major urban areas to collect and disseminate information among federal, state, and local agencies involved in combating terrorism. It also:

- Helps provide situational awareness.
- Facilitates information sharing and collaboration with homeland security partners across federal, state, and local levels.

Source: DHS, 2015a.

- Provides advanced analytic capabilities.
- Enables real-time sharing of threat information.

This communications capability delivers to states and major urban areas real-time interactive connectivity with the National Operations Center. This collaborative communications environment was developed by state and local authorities.

Carter notes that the DHS has also created an intelligence system. The Homeland Security Information Network (HSIN) is set up to connect all jurisdictions with real-time communication. It includes state homeland security officials, the National Guard, emergency operations centers, and local emergency service providers. HSIN provides encrypted communications on a secure network. Designed to combine the criminal information of RISS with critical infrastructure protection, HSIN is designed to unite all the different organizations involved in homeland security (see the previous feature titled "Another Perspective: Homeland Security Information Network"). Critics maintain that the system is underused and that it duplicates the functions of proven systems like RISS (Jordan, 2005).

Despite the systems and networks that were developed to share information, many agencies still were not part of the information-sharing process. **Fusion centers** came about to correct this. Endorsed by the NCISP, fusion centers were designed to place all intelligence in a single center, combining multiple agencies in a single unit to analyze all types of threats. As a result, a typical fusion center may have analysts and agents from several federal law enforcement and intelligence agencies, military personnel, and local police officers and criminal analysts. It merges information—earning the name *fusion*—into a single process of data analysis. Criminal information is channeled to investigations, and national security intelligence is passed on to the appropriate agency. Once passed on, national security intelligence is not available for criminal analysis or storage in law enforcement files (DHS, 2015b).

fusion centers: Operations set up to fuse information from multiple sources, analyze the data, turn it into usable intelligence, and distribute intelligence to agencies needing the information.

Fusion Centers

Regional Intelligence Center: (RIC) Originally established to gather drug trafficking intelligence, RICs helped provide the basis for fusion centers.

An intelligence fusion center represents a new concept, but it has actually been developing over the past 35 years. Law enforcement agencies were aware of the need to collect and analyze criminal intelligence long before the attacks of 9/11. David Carter (2008) says that fusion centers evolved from **Regional Intelligence Centers** (RIC) created to counteract drug trafficking in the 1980s. There was no single model for these units, and the structure and organization of RICs differed from state to state. The RICs eventually evolved into **High-Intensity Drug Trafficking Area** intelligence centers—HIDTA-RIC.

Carter says the Bureau of Alcohol, Tobacco, and Firearms (ATF) began to centralize its efforts to gather intelligence for reducing gun violence over the next decade, creating **Regional Crime Gun Centers** (RCGC). Realizing the effective operations of the HIDTA-RICs, ATF began coordinating activities with them, and in some jurisdictions, both gun and drug intelligence operated from the same buildings. These specialized intelligence units aimed at specific crimes would become the basis of the fusion centers.

Although the centers were operating by the beginning of the twenty-first century, Carter reports that they had some drawbacks. First, their focus tended to be on local crimes and issues. There were few efforts to share information on a larger, more systematic scale. Second, no funding was available to expand the operation of the centers. These factors combined to produce a third weakness: There was no incentive to expand or increase operations due to the focus on the immediate region. Finally, the centers focused only on specific crimes. The directors of the intelligence centers made no effort to look at exotic crimes like terrorism, and they had no effective method of identifying and passing on national security intelligence. Indeed, the attitudes of the Department of Justice and the attorney general would have prevented such activity.

Despite these weaknesses, cooperation between the HIDTA-RIC and the ATF centers gave law enforcement a new advantage. Information from multiple jurisdictions was being gathered, analyzed, and "fused" into a single intelligence picture of criminal activity. This was the embryo that would grow into a larger intelligence system. David Carter says the intelligence process changed drastically after 9/11 but that the foundation for fusion centers was present well before the event. When the newly created Department of Homeland Security looked for a model to enhance domestic intelligence, it found one in the partnership between HIDTA-RICs and ATF. DHS began funding the centers, and they eventually evolved into fusion centers.

Although each fusion center remains unique and is geared to meet regional needs, the centers follow a common process. Bart Johnson (2007a, 2011) describes the model for fusing intelligence. The purpose of fusion centers is to place experts and analysts from a variety of fields and organizations in a single collaborative work environment. The analysts bring diverse skill sets to provide the resources and expertise necessary to evaluate and disperse intelligence. Raw information comes to fusion centers from law enforcement, other government agencies, and the private sector. The raw information is analyzed to reveal patterns of suspicious activity, the behavior habits of known or suspected terrorists, the vulnerability of targets, and the probability of an attack. This information, known as an **intelligence product**, is returned to the field on a need-to-know basis. When they were initially created, the primary focus was terrorism, but the mission would expand. Although these models differed, the fusion centers together created the basis for state, local, tribal, and federal intelligence partnerships (see DHS, 2015b).

Fusion Center Intelligence

The initial focus on terrorism was understandable given the 9/11 attacks. Yet, fusion centers created a vehicle for several types of operations that could be synchronized. The centers provided a link with private corporations, which was critical because most of the infrastructure is under private ownership. National security intelligence agencies and military forces sent their representatives, and their areas of operations

High-Intensity Drug Trafficking Area: (HIDTA) Specialized RICs in regions experiencing a high level of drug trafficking and drug-related crimes. They evolved from RICs and were the direct predecessor to fusion centers. Some HIDTAs simply expanded to become full fusion centers.

Regional Crime Gun Center: (RCGC) ATF Intelligence center similar to RIC but focused on the illegal use of firearms.

intelligence product: The output of information analysis. Information is analyzed and turned into intelligence. This product is distributed to users.

were separated from the criminal intelligence gathered by law enforcement. They were placed in a secure, top secret setting inside the fusion centers. When a criminal analyst came upon noncriminal intelligence that had a potential impact on national security, it could be passed through proper legal channels within the center (Kanable, 2011).

total criminal intelligence: (TCI) An "all crimes" approach to the intelligence process. The same type of intelligence that thwarts terrorism works against other crimes and community problems.

Fusion centers continued to evolve with an "all crime" or **total criminal intelligence** (TCI) mentality. Carter (2008) shows that fusion centers took the TCI concept one step further by analyzing information about "all threats," and from there analysis went to "all hazards." The primary mission remains analyzing intelligence to identify terrorist threats, but there is a great redundancy in information. In other words, information that can be used to prevent terrorism is also useful in identifying criminal and public health problems. Carter says the same type of information can also be used to target law enforcement activities for community-based crime control and problem solving. Finally, fusion centers created an opportunity to improve the delivery of emergency and nonemergency services.

Practitioners argue that the new efforts have proven to be successful (Johnson, 2007, 2011). For example, a California town experienced a series of armed robberies at gas stations in 2005. At first, this appeared to be a series of local crimes. Officers investigating the robberies gathered standard criminal information to help identify suspects, and in the routine course of the investigations, they forwarded information to a fusion center. Analysts at the fusion center made a startling discovery. The robberies were not being staged for financial gain. The group behind the robberies was trying to collect money to support a campaign of domestic terrorism. The robberies were solved, and several planned acts of terrorism were thwarted.

Such incidental evidence indicates that fusion centers have increased the effectiveness of law enforcement and have enhanced domestic security. There is a need for more systematic research and evaluation to determine the overall effectiveness of the fusion centers. Currently, 72 centers collect and analyze information, coordinating that information with DHS. Still, there are squabbles from time to time about information sharing, and there are struggles among the various bureaucracies for control of information. The ideal goal is to distribute information to agencies that have a right to know and need to know. Sometimes, the ideal is not attained. The rhetoric is based in information sharing and cooperative analysis. Rigorous research is required to determine if this is actually happening.

U.S. Attorneys and JTTFs

The DOJ has created two intelligence systems, one in federal prosecutors' offices and the other in law enforcement. According to DOJ (2015), "The United States Attorneys serve as the nation's principal litigators under the direction of the Attorney General. There are 93 United States Attorneys stationed throughout the United States, Puerto Rico, the Virgin Islands, Guam, and the Northern Mariana Islands. United States Attorneys are appointed by, and serve at the discretion of, the President of the United States, with the advice and consent of the United States Senate. One United States Attorney is assigned to each of the 94 judicial districts, with the exception of Guam and the Northern Mariana Islands where a single United States Attorney serves in both districts. Each United States Attorney is the chief federal law enforcement officer of the United States within his or her particular jurisdiction."

Each U.S. attorney's office has an anti-terrorist assistance coordinator (ATAC). The purpose of the ATAC is to coordinate the collection of criminal intelligence and to share intelligence among federal, state, and local law enforcement agencies. ATACs hold security clearances, so they can view secret national security intelligence. Although they do not use this information in criminal prosecutions, they are authorized to pass the information to agencies charged with national security.

The various JTTFs operate in a similar manner. Each JTTF is made up of officers from all levels of American law enforcement and from a variety of different types of agencies. This gives each JTTF a wide range of authority because officers from different police agencies have different types of law enforcement authority and power. Every JTTF agent also receives a national security intelligence clearance. Like the ATAC, JTTF agents may not use national security intelligence in criminal prosecutions, but they are allowed to collect and use it for national defense. They may also work with various intelligence agencies. In addition, each regional FBI office has a field intelligence coordinator who works with ATACs and JTTFs (Cumming and Masse, 2004; FBI, 2015).

> **Self-Check**
> > How does raw information become intelligence?
> > What is the difference between national security and criminal intelligence?
> > How can existing systems be used to create or to expand future intelligence networks?

Issues in Homeland Security

There are many organizational and bureaucratic problems inherent in organizations. These issues are discussed in Chapter 14. Other aspects of homeland security are directly related to homeland security. These issues include understanding the role of law enforcement, the value of symbolic targets, threat analysis, planning, and how to create a culture of information sharing.

Law Enforcement's Special Role

If military forces are to transform themselves in the fashion suggested by Thomas Barnett (2004), law enforcement must seek and find new roles. More than half of the DHS agencies have police power, and state and local governments look to law enforcement to prevent attacks and respond to the unthinkable. Interestingly, federal, state, and local officers have taken the lead in identifying and disrupting terrorism in the United States. Whether terrorists are homegrown or imported from foreign lands, police agencies are responsible for breaking some of America's most formidable terrorist cells. Law enforcement has a key function in homeland security (see Carter, 2009).

American law enforcement has a long tradition of reactive patrol, that is, responding to crimes and calls for assistance. With the advent of radio-dispatched motorized patrol, response time became the measure of police effectiveness. It was assumed that the sooner the police arrived at the scene of a crime, the more likely they would be to make an arrest. Like fire departments responding to smoke, police effectiveness was determined by the ability to respond quickly to crime.

The problem of terrorism brings the need for preemptive, offensive policing to a new level. If law enforcement simply responds, it will have little impact on the prevention of terrorism. Defensive reactions alone will not stop terrorism, and no government can afford to fortify all the potential targets in a jurisdiction. Even if all targets could be defended, the goal of asymmetrical warfare is not to destroy targets; rather it is to show that security forces are not in charge. Terrorists are free to strike the least-defended symbolic target. Defensive thinking, like reactive patrol, cannot win a fight in the shadows.

If state and local agencies shift to offensive thinking and action, two results will inevitably develop. First, police contact with potential terrorists will increase, but as Sherry Colb (2001) points out, the vast majority of any ethnic or social group is made up of people who abhor terrorism. This increases the possibility of negative stereotyping and abuses of power. Second, proactive measures demand increased intelligence gathering, and much of the information will have no relation to criminal activity. If not properly monitored, such intelligence may be misused.

Another issue appears in the private sector. Kayyem and Howitt (2002) find that offensive action begins in the local community. The weakness in local systems occurs, however, because state and local police departments frequently do not think beyond their jurisdictions, and they do not routinely take advantage of potential partnerships inside their bailiwicks. Kayyem and Howitt believe that partnerships are the key to community planning. One of the greatest potential allies is private security organizations. Unfortunately, many law enforcement agencies frown on private security and fail to create joint ventures with the private sector.

On the positive side of the debate, counterterrorism is not a mystical operation. It requires many of the skills already employed in preventive patrol, criminal investigation, and surveillance. With a few tweaks, police intelligence operations and drug enforcement units can add counterterrorism to their agendas, and patrol and investigative units can be trained to look for terrorist activities in the course of their normal duties. If properly managed, these activities need not present a threat to civil liberties.

The Role of Symbols and Structures

symbolic targets: Terrorist targets that may have limited military or security value but represent the power of the state under attack. Terrorists seek symbolic targets to strike fear into society and to give a sense of power to the terrorist group. The power of the symbol also multiplies the effect of the attack.

Asymmetrical war is waged against **symbolic targets**, and homeland security is designed to secure symbols. Just because a target has symbolic significance does not mean it lacks physical reality. The bombing of the Murrah Federal Building in Oklahoma City in 1995, for example, had symbolic value, and the casualties were horrific. Attacks against symbols disrupt support structures and can have a high human toll. Defensive measures are put in place to protect the physical safety of people and property as well as the symbolic meaning of a target (see Juergensmeyer, 2003, pp. 155–163; Critical Incident Analysis Group, 2001, pp. 9–16).

Symbols need not only be considered in the abstract. Blowing up a national treasure would entail the loss of a national symbol, but killing thousands of innocent people becomes a symbol in itself. Grenville Byford (2002) points out that a symbolic attack may simply be designed to inflict massive casualties—killing people has a symbolic value, and thus killing civilians achieves a political purpose for terrorists. Strategies for protection should be grounded in an understanding of the problem. Ian Lesser (1999, pp. 85–144) outlines three forms of terrorism: symbolic, pragmatic, and systematic. Symbolic terrorism is a dramatic attack to show vulnerability; pragmatic terrorism involves a practical attempt to destroy political power; and systematic terrorism is waged over a period of time to change social conditions. Lesser also points to several examples in which symbolic factors enter into the attacks. In other words, terrorists use symbolic attacks, or attacks on symbols, to achieve pragmatic or systematic results.

The University of Virginia's Critical Incident Analysis Group (CIAG) brought law enforcement officials, business leaders, governmental administrators, and academics together to discuss America's vulnerability to symbolic attack (CIAG, 2001). Symbols

ANOTHER PERSPECTIVE

Community Threat Analysis

Examine the following considerations for defensive planning, or community threat analysis. What other items might be added?

- Find networks in and among communities. Look at transportation, power grids and fuel storage, water supplies, industrial logistics and storage, and the flow of people.
- Think the way a terrorist does. Which targets are vulnerable? Which targets would cause the most disruption? Which buildings are vulnerable? Where is private security ineffective?
- Obtain architectural plans for all major buildings. Protect air intakes, power supplies, and possible points for evacuation.
- Have detailed emergency information for each school.

- Practice tactical operations in each school building after hours.
- Prioritize. Assign a criticality rating to each target, assessing its importance, and rank targets according to comparative ratings.
- Coordinate with health services.
- Discuss triage and quarantine methods. Plan for biological, chemical, and radiological contamination.
- Look at emergency plans for other communities.
- Prepare added security for special events.
- Designate an emergency command post and roles for personnel from other agencies. Practice commanding mock attacks.
- Study past emergencies and determine what law enforcement learned from its shortcomings.

Source: Management Analytics and others, 1995

---

can have literal and abstract meanings, such as a capitol that serves literally and abstractly as the seat of governmental power. The key to security is to offer protection without destroying abstract meanings. For example, the words of one CIAG participant summed up the problem: "We want to protect the Capitol building," he said, "without making Washington, D.C., look like an armed camp."

All societies create symbols, and American democracy is no different. In a time of asymmetrical war, American symbols demand protection. The key to security, the CIAG concludes, is to enhance protection while maintaining openness. The irony is that every added security measure increases the feeling of insecurity. The CIAG report cites metal detectors at county courthouses as an example. Simply going through the detector before entering a building gives a person the feeling that things might fall apart. The key is to make symbolic targets as secure as possible while giving the illusion that very few security precautions have been taken.

Planning for Homeland Security

Everyone knows that planning should take place before a problem emerges. Effective police planning incorporates a description of a goal and methods for achieving it (Hudzik and Cordner, 1983). Planning should be based on the assets available to an agency and a projection of resources needed to meet the goal. A good plan will show how different entities interrelate and may reveal unexpected consequences. Planning brings resources together in a complex environment to manage multiple consequences (see the feature titled "Another Perspective: Community Threat Analysis" above).

The complexities of terrorism can seem overwhelming, so planning is essential. It enhances the gathering, organizing, and analyzing of information (Bodrero, 2002).

Police agencies have long been aware of the need to make reactive plans. Emergency planning, for example, is a tool for dealing with weather disasters and industrial accidents. After riots in Dade County, Florida, in 1980, local agencies developed field force deployment plans similar to mutual aid pacts among firefighters. The tragedies of Oklahoma City and September 11 brought several plans to fruition. Successful efforts in planning can be transferred into offensive strategies.

The IACP (2001) believes planning can be guided by looking for threats within local communities. Police agencies should constantly monitor communities to determine whether a terrorist threat is imminent. Indicators such as an increase in violent rhetoric, the appearance of extremist groups, and an increase in certain types of crimes may demonstrate that a terrorist threat is on the horizon. Planning is based on the status of potential violence, and law enforcement can develop certain responses based on the threat. Prepared responses, the IACP contends, are proactive (see the feature titled "Another Perspective: Information for Planning").

Creating a Culture of Information Sharing

The National Strategy for Homeland Security (Office of Homeland Security, 2002, p. 56; U.S. Department of Homeland Security, 2004b, pp. 3–34) calls for increasing information sharing among law enforcement agencies by building a cooperative environment that enables sharing of essential information. It will be a "system of systems that can provide the right information to the right people at all times." This is an excellent idea in principle.

D. Douglas Bodrero (2002) believes that many of these systems are already in place. The six-part RISS information network, whose policies are controlled by its members, is ideal for sharing intelligence. It has secure intranet, bulletin board, and conference capabilities. The High-Intensity Drug Trafficking Areas (HIDTAs) system and the El Paso Intelligence Center (EPIC) are also sources for information sharing. The International Association of Law Enforcement Intelligence Analysts (IALEIA) routinely shares information with member agencies. These established systems are now complemented by HSIN and a host of fusion centers (U.S. DOJ, Office of Justice Programs, 2006). Critics say that these networks are underused. In the past, Robert Taylor (1987) found two primary weaknesses in U.S. systems: (1) Intelligence is not properly analyzed, and (2) agencies do not coordinate information. Today, critics say the same thing. They feel that information sharing is recommended on the highest levels, but it does not take place (ONDCP, 2015.).

Despite criticism, information sharing is growing into a law enforcement norm. The NCISP has been accepted at all levels of police administration. The systems created after 9/11, older systems such as RISS, fusion centers, and individual agency operations point to a new idea in law enforcement, **intelligence-led policing**. This concept is a continuation of community policing, in which police officers anticipate and solve community problems with citizens before an increase in crime and social disorder occurs. Community policing is based on information gathered from police–citizen partnerships, and intelligence-led policing systematically combines such information with other intelligence data from multiple sources. The purpose of intelligence-led policing is to redeploy resources in areas where they are most needed based on the analysis of criminal information (Duekmedjian, 2006).

David Carter (2009, pp. 39–54) sees intelligence-led policing as the logical outcome of the intelligence process. As police agencies adopted community policing strategies, officers developed skills in problem solving, building community

intelligence-led policing: A type of law enforcement effort in which resources are deployed based on information gathered and analyzed from criminal intelligence.

(((**ANOTHER PERSPECTIVE**

Information for Planning

- List available resources.
- Project potential attacks.
- Identify critical infrastructures.

Factors influencing plans, including:

- Emergency command structures
- Coordination among agencies

- Mass casualties
- Victim and family support
- Preservation of evidence
- Crime scene management
- Media relations
- Costs
- Training and preincident exercises

Source: International Association of Chiefs of Police, 2001.

---

partnerships, and gathering and analyzing the information needed to deal with crime and social problems in a local community. Citing the NCISP, Carter says that these skills have created a reliable and continuous flow of information between the community and the police. It is a gateway to the prevention of terrorism. Intelligence-led policing is an extension of this process. It not only prevents terrorism, it also becomes total criminal intelligence, and it serves to prevent and address all problems in a community.

Intelligence-led policing is part of a process to guide the deployment of law enforcement resources. Carter says that information from citizens defines the parameters of community problems. Law enforcement agencies need to provide information so that citizens can distinguish between normal and suspicious behavior. The law enforcement agencies are to organize community meetings and work with the community to gather information. In addition, they must communicate with the community, working with citizens and advising them of police policy for problems. In this model, the police are to serve as an extension of community needs while advising citizens on the issues that the police see as social problems. All data are scientifically analyzed to guide the distribution of law enforcement resources.

Intelligence-led policing, especially within the framework of counterterrorism, is not without its critics. Critics are afraid that information sharing will lead to massive databases on people who are not subject to criminal investigations. They also fear privacy violations as citizens share information, and they are afraid that anyone who casually encounters a known terrorist suspect will be labeled a terrorist supporter. Critics also say that intelligence-led policing may work in conjunction with national security intelligence gathering, and there will be no oversight of the collection, analysis, and storage of information. They also fear misguided profiling. For example, when a Muslim family moves into a non-Muslim neighborhood, citizens who see the practice of Islam as a suspicious behavior could discriminate against the family (Abramson and Godoy, 2006).

✓ **Self-Check**

> How do diverse, independent law enforcement agencies assist with homeland security?

> Why is planning an important process in protecting both infrastructure and symbols?

> Explain intelligence-led policing and total criminal intelligence.

Intelligence Reform

The *Washington Post* (Priest and Arkin, 2010) ran a series of articles critiquing the intelligence community in the summer of 2010. The project involved a dozen journalists doing research over a two-year period. The *Post* found that the intelligence community had grown so large that no one could account for its costs. In fact, the number of people involved in intelligence and the number of agencies doing the same work were also unknown. It found that over 3,000 public and private organizations operated counterterrorism-related programs at 10,000 locations across the United States. The number of top secret security clearances, for about 854,000 people, was astounding. Over 50,000 intelligence reports were published each year, and no one agency had the authority to manage the overall operation. A panel of experts (*Washington Post*, 2010a, 2010b) concluded that the massive endeavor was unmanaged and ineffective, and it operated with no clear lines of authority. Its worst characteristic was that the intelligence community did not produce credible information about potential threats.

Moving in the Right Direction?

Nancy Tucker (2008), a former executive in the intelligence community and now a professor at Georgetown University, suggests that the failure of intelligence analysis is evidenced by two factors: the surprise attacks of September 11 and the analysis of the WMD program in Iraq. Congress created the ODNI to address such flaws. The ODNI was intended to be a vehicle for continuous reform, an organization to prevent bureaucratic goal displacement and organizational stagnation; however, its massive restructuring met all types of resistance. First, many people believed that the efficiency and methods of the intelligence community needed to be improved. Restructuring created another level of bureaucracy, but it did not address the need for accuracy and efficiency. Second, the new organization confused traditional lines of authority. Specifically, the director of the CIA was to be the one person who could synthesize information and present an apolitical, objective assessment of data to the executive branch of government.

Tucker, however, believes that the reorganization of intelligence under the ODNI has signaled the beginning of improvement. The ODNI is able to balance all the intelligence agencies' needs for information. In the past, the CIA director performed this function but was always forced to guard the interests of the CIA. The ODNI is able to avoid this bureaucratic pitfall, producing a better balance in analyzed information. The ODNI has also been able to attack the problem of **group think** by placing analysts in critical thinking training during the first stages of their careers.

Even with the initial success, she says, the new structure has just barely started the reforms needed to improve the intelligence community. Tucker argues that because Congress created the ODNI, it is therefore responsible for cleaning its own house. The number of committees and budgetary authority lines from Congress is astronomical. Congress needs to streamline its process, and it needs to be assertive. It is difficult to balance the tasks of intelligence gathering within a democracy, especially when the intelligence community is looking at individuals rather than competing nation-states. Congress needs to assert its authority and rigorously review and restrict intelligence activities. In addition, a single national intelligence university should be created to train all analysts from every agency. Specific agency training, Tucker says, narrows the scope of analysis and creates a culture that reinforces loyalty to a particular agency. Another needed reform is to base intelligence gathering and analysis techniques on

group think: Refers to a bureaucratic process in which members of a group work together to solve a problem; however, innovation and deviant ideas are discouraged as the group tries to seek consensus about a conclusion. Powerful members of the group may quash alternative voices. Intelligence groups tend to resist making any risky conclusions lest they jeopardize their individual careers. Peer pressure creates an atmosphere in which every individual comes to the same conclusion.

success. Procedures should be based on methods that work. Tucker believes that all analysis should be based on evidence that the outcome is successful. Finally, the intelligence community needs to reach out to nontraditional venues. There are many institutions that have tremendous analytical capabilities, but the intelligence community ignores them. For example, international retail outlets gather tremendous amounts of information, but they are ignored by government.

Tucker concludes that the system of classifying information, the process of making information secret, can be unreasonable. This happens in two primary ways. First, political actors may classify information to defend their political position. For example, a president can classify information that would be harmful to his party's political position, even though the information has nothing to do with national security. Second, bureaucracies hold classified information for power. Overabundant secrecy and manipulation of "need-to-know" information creates power structures among law enforcement and intelligence agencies. Although not cited by Tucker, almost any law enforcement officer who has worked closely with the FBI knows how an agency can hoard information. Information, Tucker says, should be developed and shared to produce outcomes. Classification should be designed to protect sources, not information. Almost all the information is in the public realm anyway.

Redirecting the Focus of Reform

Uri Bar-Joseph and Rose McDermott (2008) suggest that the problem in intelligence is not the structure of the system; the problem can be found with individual analysts. Official intelligence investigations into shortcomings tend to focus on structures and organization, so they miss this point. Certain types of personalities, Bar-Joseph and McDermott argue, are more prone to fall prey to making erroneous judgments. Some people have traits that influence their ability to objectively analyze information. Personality assessment tests are able to screen people for these tendencies, and intelligence agencies should spend more time examining and selecting analysts.

Bar-Joseph and McDermott base their argument on psychological assessment techniques that have been developed over the past 50 years. To help to ensure that internal prejudices do not filter the information under review, it is important to identify biases that an analyst brings to the job. Psychological assessments can determine which people would discount information not contained in their personal experiences and which people would interpret ambiguous circumstances only within the framework of previous understandings. Both of these traits create an internal circle; that is, new information is interpreted within existing understandings of reality, discounting any new possibility. When this happens, analysts develop conclusions that they expected to find in the first place. This type of reasoning is susceptible to group think, where groups of similar individuals join together to reinforce their own erroneous conclusions. This leads to a three-part pattern: (1) There is new information about a surprise activity before a terrorist attack develops, (2) analysts ignore new information and focus on their previous experiences with terrorism, and (3) the real-life outcome is a surprise. This is reinforced by a bureaucratic tendency to avoid taking risks. When respected peer group members suggest that information be interpreted in a particular manner, it is difficult to go against the current.

Bar-Joseph and McDermott say that there was tremendous pressure to reform the intelligence community after 9/11, and these calls for reform fell into two broad categories. One approach called for comprehensive reform of the intelligence system. This resulted in the formation of the ODNI and a reshuffling of the agencies of the intelligence community. This approach was also responsible for the reasoning behind the creation of the DHS. The second part of the debate focused on reforming the specific components of the system. This type of reform suggested that analysts develop their material as a product for a consumer. Under this model, the intelligence community is like a business producing goods that consumers want to purchase. Unfortunately, the consumer model sometimes creates a product for a consumer looking for evidence to support a particular position. This distorts objective intelligence. For example, in the Bush administration, some political actors wanted to find WMD in Iraq. Analysts, designing information for the consumer, pointed to where the weapons might be, even though the WMD threat never existed.

The key to reform, Bar-Joseph and McDermott conclude, is to shift the unit of analysis away from organizational structures and consumer-driven intelligence products. The entire system needs independent minds that will look at new ways of interpreting data and that will challenge established methods of interpretation. The authors argue that psychological assessment during the analyst selection process will help agencies find the types of people who think in this manner. This change will produce a new method of selecting, training, and promoting analysts. It will also provide, they believe, better information and fewer surprises.

Target-Based Analysis

John Gentry (2008) suggests that the current spate of reform is part of an American tradition. The literature of American intelligence is replete with examples of failures to predict significant events and reform efforts to overcome deficiencies. Gentry believes that most current efforts will fail because they are misdirected. The bureaucracies in the intelligence community have a tremendous stake in preserving the status quo, and employees in each organization believe that they will be blamed for misinterpreting information. This produces a culture that avoids risk taking and reinforces group think.

Reform, if and when it develops, is laboriously slow. Gentry concludes that the intelligence process will work better if local domestic issues and vulnerabilities are lessened. Target-based analysis focuses on two questions: What targets are vulnerable? What capabilities exist to address threats? As David Carter (2009) concludes, intelligence works best when information is based on potential threats and there is a sharing of the information among differing levels of government.

The Need for Reform Questioned

After a major gaff in foreign policy, especially when it involves loss of life, politicians and others are quick to blame the intelligence process. They denounce analysts for failing to predict events, they criticize agencies for bureaucratic policies, and they demand change and reform. Congress holds hearings as it tries to find the guilty party responsible for the intelligence failure. There are people, however, who believe that the intelligence community is not in need of reform, and the political decision makers who act improperly on false assumptions bear the responsibility for many "intelligence failures."

Thomas Fingar (2011), a retired high-ranking intelligence officer from the Department of State, argues that the intelligence community actually does reasonably good work. Its goal is to reduce uncertainty. Analysts provide decision makers with information. Although they are to be blamed when information is not clearly presented or is intentionally skewed, the simple fact is that there is quite a bit of information they do not know. Furthermore, in criminal intelligence, analysts must have reasonable evidence that the actions they wish to analyze are associated with criminal activity. Information is almost always incomplete in criminal and national security intelligence.

Fingar illustrates this situation with a directive from former secretary of state Colin Powell (served 2001–2005), who told his analysts to tell him what they knew, what they thought they knew, and what they did not know. Fingar also points out that analysts did not make policy decisions during Powell's service in the State Department. Secretary Powell and other managers did. If they made mistakes, the analysts can be blamed only if they did not provide the full range of information with an assessment of its quality and veracity.

You can see an example in your college career. Have you ever known a professor who misstated a fact or presented a probable course of action based on faulty information? Most professors engage in activities similar to intelligence analysts, with two major exceptions. Academics are usually not working in a life-or-death environment, and they frequently have weeks, months, or even years to analyze a problem. Intelligence analysts work in time frames involving, weeks, days, and sometimes even minutes. Often, lives depend on their ability to analyze information. Your professors make mistakes. Intelligence analysts do, too.

Analysts are charged with tracking criminals, drug traffickers, and terrorists throughout the world, and they are expected to provide timely information to protect American lives and property. They try to present as complete a picture as possible, realizing that there will always be gaps in the information. When there is a mistake, it is often in the decision, not in the process and analysis that provided the intelligence.

✓ **Self-Check**	>	What prompted calls for intelligence reform?
	>	Do reform efforts look promising?
	>	Why might there be no need for reform?

Emphasizing the Points

Homeland security involves a variety of activities at all levels of government, law enforcement agencies, the military, intelligence agencies, and the private sector. Preventing terrorism is the result of gathering and analyzing information. This is accomplished under two sets of laws, one guiding criminal intelligence and the other focused on national security. While this is extremely complicated, the NCISP has provided guidelines and standards for managing the intelligence process. This takes place in regional fusion centers. Homeland security is ever-changing, and the intelligence process must be continually reviewed and changed to meet new threats.

SUMMARY OF CHAPTER OBJECTIVES

- Homeland security has a variety of meanings to different government agencies, private organizations, and interest groups. The best way to define it is to look at the mission of each particular agency dealing with homeland security.
- After 9/11, several federal agencies were tasked with homeland security. The Departments of Homeland Security, Justice, and Defense have major roles in preventing terrorism. The intelligence community contributes to counterterrorism efforts, and there is a major role for state and local law enforcement to play.

- The intelligence process is very similar to basic and applied academic research. It involves the legal recognition, collection, analysis, and distribution of information. *Intelligence* is "analyzed information."
- Criminal intelligence requires a criminal predicate, and it may be used in criminal prosecutions. It can be revealed at a criminal trial. National security intelligence cannot be used in criminal investigations or criminal trials. It is not subject to discovery.
- The International Association of Chiefs (IACP) of police created a committee to develop national standards for criminal intelligence. This resulted in the National Criminal Intelligence Sharing Plan (NCISP). The Department of Justice created the Global Justice Information Sharing Coordinating Council (Global) to address the problems inherent in sharing information among multiple levels of law enforcement.
- Fusion centers developed from Regional Intelligence Centers. The Department of Homeland Security expanded their operations after the 9/11 attacks. Fusion centers take criminal intelligence from multiple sources and blend, or "fuse," it together to create a real-time picture of criminal activity. They can also forward national security intelligence without using it in criminal prosecutions.
- Law enforcement has a leading role in homeland security because of its presence in communities and its ability to gather information. There are several excellent federal networks, for example, RISS and HSIN. HIDTAs and EPIC assist in distributing antiterrorism intelligence, even though they were designed for drug interdiction. Fusion centers are involved with providing state and local intelligence.
- There are several important issues for homeland security. Law enforcement has a special role in terms of recognizing possible terrorist activity and coordinating preventive measures from multiple community partnerships. Planning is a crucial part of the process. While the infrastructure is critical, symbolic targets also have a special significance. Finally, all partners responsible for homeland security must create a culture of information sharing.
- While intelligence has received quite a bit of attention since 9/11, reformers argue that there are areas where it can be improved. The goal of creating a safe homeland should guide intelligence efforts. Analysts must be trained to recognize broad patterns. Finally, intelligence must be based on threats to known or suspected targets.
- Reform may not be needed. Intelligence will always be incomplete because it is not possible to gather all the information about a target. So-called failures may be the result of poor decision making, not poor intelligence analysis.

LOOKING INTO THE FUTURE

The analysis of criminal and national security intelligence is moving into the cyberworld and social media networks. This has been happening for a number of years, and the trend will probably continue as technology increases. Use of the Dark Web or Deep Web, Internet traffic hidden from most users, will most likely follow this pattern. The growing use of electronic intelligence will not mean that undercover operations and informant development will become passé. Quite the opposite will be true. As cyberanalysis becomes more sophisticated, traditional methods of intelligence gathering will grow in importance to verify the veracity of information. Electronic intelligence will improve human intelligence gathering.

If homeland security efforts are to be successful, the United States must increase efforts in a number of areas. DHS and allied agencies will continue to develop cyber-counterterrorist and cyberwarfare techniques. Both terrorist groups and more conventional competitors such as nation-states are working hard in these areas. In addition, successful American security will depend on hardening the infrastructure and maintaining enough strength and system redundancy to absorb an attack. Finally, agencies charged with homeland security will face criminals and other subnational actors using changing technology as a force multiplier. It will be important for law enforcement, intelligence, and security agencies to stay abreast of technological changes and to develop countermeasures.

The nature of state and local intelligence gathering may change. The New York City Police Department has deployed about 100 officers to foreign countries because information from federal sources has been lacking. Local agencies and regional associations may begin to establish international intelligence networks unless federal cooperation increases.

KEY TERMS

Department of Homeland Security, p. 303
Civil defense, p. 304
Federal Law Enforcement Training Center, p. 307
National security intelligence, p. 310

Criminal intelligence, p. 310
COINTELPRO, p. 312
National Criminal Intelligence Sharing Plan, p. 313
Regional Information Sharing System, p. 313

Fusion centers, p. 314
Regional Intelligence Center, p. 314
High-Intensity Drug Trafficking Area, p. 315
Regional Crime Gun Centers, p. 315
Intelligence product, p. 315

Total criminal intelligence, p. 316
Symbolic targets, p. 318
Intelligence-led policing, p. 320
Group think, p. 322

CHAPTER 14

Organizing Homeland Security

LEARNING OBJECTIVES

After reading this chapter, you should be able to:

▶ Explain the importance of information sharing.

▶ Outline the reasons for bureaucratic complexity in homeland security.

▶ Describe the impact of bureaucracy on information sharing.

▶ Identify the organizations that enhance information sharing in law enforcement.

▶ Explain the impact of the number of individual law enforcement agencies in the United States.

▶ Summarize the organizational problems facing agencies charged with homeland security.

▶ Describe possible solutions to bureaucratic problems.

▶ Explain how the JTTF might serve as a model for the law enforcement mission.

▶ Outline federal homeland security operations.

▶ Identify the National Criminal Intelligence Sharing Program.

▶ Summarize issues associated with border protection.

▶ Explain the need for partnerships to protect the nation's infrastructure.

▶ Define the need for emergency response.

Eduardo Munoz Alvarez/Getty Images

The First Line of Homeland Security

A white police officer shot and killed a teenaged unarmed African American man in Ferguson, Missouri, on August 9, 2014. The shooting led to widespread community protests and confrontations with police. Agencies throughout St. Louis County and some officers from regional agencies arrived to assist the Ferguson Police Department. Although the governor would eventually place Ferguson under the command of the Missouri Highway Patrol, the initial response from local law enforcement did not have the appearance of a police operation.

Ferguson looked like a war zone throughout the night and the next day as the whole world watched events unfold on television. Law enforcement officers arrived wearing camouflaged fatigues and military helmets. They rode in surplus armored vehicles provided by the Department of Defense, and they pointed high-powered rifles at demonstrators. As the local officers moved into the crowd, they fired tear gas from multiple-barreled grenade launchers mounted on the sides of mine-resistant combat vehicles. Many viewers were used to seeing such images from Iraq and Afghanistan. They were not expecting to see such scenes in an American city.

Subsequent reviews by local, state, and federal officials revealed a number of problems with police policies, racial attitudes, law enforcement militarization, use of force, and a host of other issues. Most of these problems are directly related to counterterrorism because state and local law enforcement officers frequently report information that is used in terrorism prevention efforts.

Information to solve noncriminal problems and prevent crime can be obtained only when citizens believe that law enforcement officers represent their community. When people know and trust officers, they form close relationships, relationships that result in the flow of information from the community. This is the lifeblood of effective law enforcement. Heavily armed personnel pointing military-style weapons at demonstrators rarely form meaningful relationships with the people they serve and protect. Counterterrorism begins with community policing.

Bureaucratic Complexity

As stated in Chapter 13, the intelligence process begins with information gathering, and information transforms into intelligence when it is analyzed. This process requires one more step. The structure of multiple layers of law enforcement bureaucracy often inhibits information sharing. This is a problem because unless intelligence is shared, it is useless.

The Impact of Bureaucracy

The RAND Corporation brought several officials from local and state law enforcement together with federal representatives from the defense, law enforcement, and intelligence communities in January 2014 (Jenkins, Liepman, and Willis, 2014). They discussed the role of law enforcement in information gathering and intelligence sharing. They concluded that law enforcement has much to offer to the intelligence community and vice versa. They also felt that many fusion centers fall short of their mission because of differing policies and operations. Although information sharing is essential to counterterrorism efforts, they said that several organizational layers inhibit the flow of information. Organizations created to solve problems frequently stay internally focused and do not share information with other organizations.

If you have studied public administration, you have most likely encountered the classic works on bureaucracy. **Max Weber** (1864–1920), one of the founding masters of sociology, coined the term *bureaucracy* to describe professional, rational organizations. For Weber, every aspect of organizational structure is to be aimed at rationally achieving a goal. In other words, people organize for a purpose, and their organization should accomplish that purpose.

The Numbers Problem

There are thousands of local police departments in the United States, 50 state police agencies, and several federal agencies with law enforcement power. Each organization has its own rules, regulations, policies, and standard practices. In other words, law enforcement in the United States is composed of over 12,000 small to large bureaucracies. This situation is not conducive to information sharing.

Max Weber: (1864–1920) One of the major figures of modern sociological methods, he studied the organization of human endeavors. Weber believed that social organizations could be organized for rational purposes designed to accomplish objectives.

bureaucracy: Governmental, private-sector, and non-profit organizations. It assumes that people organize in a hierarchy to create an organization that will solve problems.

There are ways to overcome the impact of bureaucratic fragmentation. The federal government has bureaucracies such as the DHS, the National Criminal Justice Reference Service, and the Community Oriented Policing Services (COPS) Office. Their purpose is to circulate information. The Bureau of Justice Assistance exists to support state and local police agencies. Law enforcement executives have several associations—such the Major County Sheriffs Association, the Major City Chiefs Association, the International Association of Chiefs of Police, and the National Sheriffs Association—and several state and local groups that provide a conduit for information sharing. Independent organizations such as the Police Foundation, the Police Executive Research Forum, and the National Tactical Officers Association also assist. The Regional Information sharing System (RISS) network is based on information sharing.

Yet, bureaucratic features interfere with information sharing. Critics level harsh attacks against public bureaucracies, claiming that they simply do not accomplish the purposes for which they were established (Liptak, 2002; for classic studies, see Downs, 1967; Warwick, 1975). There are many complaints, including that bureaucracies work toward stagnation. Innovation, creativity, and individuality are discouraged. Career bureaucrats are rewarded with organizational power. Therefore, they look for activities that provide organizational power instead of solutions to problems. Public bureaucracies do not face competition. Within a bureaucracy, it is better to make a safe decision than the correct decision. Bureaucratic organizations protect themselves when threatened by outside problems. Bureaucrats postpone decisions under the guise of gathering information. Policies and procedures are more important than outcomes in bureaucracies. Centralized bureaucracy increases paperwork. Finally, as bureaucracies grow, simple problems result in complex solutions.

Many people counter critics by pointing to the nature of complex organizations. Even efficient private corporations have internal contradictions. Effective organizations must reform and innovate. This applies to government bureaucracies and private corporations. Self-criticism and continual reform are necessary to create efficiency.

Reforming Bureaucracy

1978 Civil Service Reform Act: A federal law designed to prevent political interference with the decisions and actions of governmental organizations.

Government Management Reform Act of 1994: A federal law designed to prevent political interference in the management of federal governmental organizations and to increase the efficiency of management.

Some advocates believe federal reform has begun. A 1995 attempt to reduce paperwork in the federal government is one example. An earlier effort came in the **1978 Civil Service Reform Act**, which gave special executives managerial authority and placed them in performance-based positions. The most recent overhaul of the federal bureaucracy came with the **Government Management Reform Act of 1994**.

Nevertheless, managing homeland security will still require attention to the issues raised in this chapter. Large organizations are difficult to manage, and problems increase rapidly when organizational effectiveness requires cooperation on several levels. Homeland security calls for new alliances among federal agencies and cooperative relations among local, state, and federal levels of government. All of the issues interact with law enforcement agencies.

If the Department of Homeland Security (DHS) can create effective partnerships with intelligence and law enforcement agencies at the federal level, it could focus attention on these issues. However, in addition to thwarting attacks, homeland security has a duty much larger than merely gathering and analyzing information—responding to events. That is a subject beyond the scope of this book. Response involves massive coordination among agencies. Fortunately, all levels of government have extensive experience in this realm. The difficulty is *preventing* terrorism. Prevention requires bureaucratic change, and powerful bureaucrats and bureaucratic procedures do not change easily.

✓	Self-Check	>	What factors add to the complexity of law enforcement bureaucracy?
		>	How does the sheer number of law enforcement agencies complicate bureaucracy?
		>	Why would constant reform improve efficiency?

Bureaucratic Problems

Unlike the ideal rational organizations described by Weber, public service organizations have weaknesses that emerge in the everyday social construction of reality. Personalities are important, varying levels of competency limit or expand effectiveness, and organizations tend to act in their own interests. If all the organizations involved in homeland security are to agree to pool their efforts, several bureaucratic hurdles need to be cleared (see Swanson, Territo, and Taylor, 2001, pp. 643–644; Best, 2001; Bodrero, 2002; Mitchell and Hulse, 2002).

Federal Rivalries

The standard administrative logic is that federal bureaucracies do work together. In reality, this is not always true. Sometimes, federal agencies act more like rivals than partners. The 9/11 Commission criticized agencies for not working together. Anyone who has worked in or with the federal government can relate stories of interagency rivalries. Former FBI director Louis Freeh (2005, p. 192) says that talking about CIA–FBI rivalries might sell books, but it is not true. Former CIA director George Tenet (2007, p. 193) admits that the CIA and FBI had a history of contentious relations, but he and Directors Freeh and Robert Mueller worked hard to overcome them.

For example, as American troops were preparing to enter Iraq in 2003, there was a tremendous dispute between the CIA and the military about the validity of intelligence coming out of Iraq (Gordon and Trainor, 2006, pp. 198–199). Another example is that despite claims to the contrary, individual CIA agents probably refused to share information with the Joint Terrorism Task Force (JTTF) in New York City before 9/11 (L. Wright, 2006, p. 353). Perhaps the best example can be found in the FBI's decision to locate its counterterrorism efforts in its Washington field office. Former FBI executive Richard Marquise (2006, p. 26) says that Washington was the best place to locate counterterrorist headquarters because it positioned the FBI for its inevitable turf battles with the CIA and Department of State. Bureaucracies engage in competition, even when they are working toward the same goal.

Unfortunately, federal agencies distrust one another at times, and their failure to cooperate in some circumstances influences local police relationships. Many federal law enforcement agencies openly resent the FBI, and this attitude is frequently reciprocated. In addition, the creation of new bureaucracies, such as the Transportation Security Administration, exacerbates rivalries. Some rivalry is natural because people tend to look at problems from the perspective of the agency where they are employed. In the real world of bureaucracy, organizations on every level frequently act out of self-interest rather than out of concern for the overall mission (Valburn, 2002).

FBI Versus Locals

In October 2001, FBI director Robert Mueller attended the IACP meeting in Toronto, Ontario. According to police chiefs who attended the meeting, it was not a pleasant experience for him. State and local law enforcement executives criticized him for failing to share information. Mueller vowed that the FBI would never allow this failure to happen again. American law enforcement would witness a new FBI. Despite the intentions of the most forceful bureaucratic leaders, however, orders are not always carried out as planned. There have been success stories of information sharing, but there have also been tales of woe. Many American police executives are not convinced that the FBI is in full partnership with them in efforts to stop terrorism (L. Levitt, 2002).

The purpose here is not to condemn the FBI; rather, it is to acknowledge a bureaucratic issue. Many state and local police executives believe that the FBI will act only in its own interests, and this attitude extends down through the ranks of law enforcement agencies. Many police officers believe the FBI assists local agencies so that they can claim credit for any resulting success, and the FBI has a reputation for gathering information without sharing it. In turn, many FBI agents believe their performance is far superior to that of other federal, state, and local officers. Similar attitudes can be seen in rivalries among state and local agencies, such as the way many state troopers and sheriffs' deputies interact. If police in America are to become part of homeland defense, the relationship between the FBI and state and local law enforcement must improve (Riordan and Zegart, 2002; Emery, 2009; Markon, 2011).

Local Control and Revenue Sources

Some people feel that cooperation between state and local law enforcement will result in the de facto concentration of police power. This attitude was prevalent at the turn of the twentieth century when state police agencies were forming. Many local governments believed that state police forces had too much power, and many states limited the local agencies to patrolling state highways. Civil libertarians believe that consolidated police power will erode civil rights. Local governmental officials worry that their agendas will be lost in federalization. The bureaucratic arguments extend beyond these interest groups (Hitt and Cloud, 2002).

There is also frustration among local governments with the monetary costs of their homeland security responsibilities. Some local governments want homeland security money to be distributed evenly. Larger jurisdictions, like New York City, argue that money should be distributed according to the likelihood of attacks. Even then, New York City officials complain, federal money does not cover the cost of security (Mintz, 2005). Other people worry that homeland security grants are given to local units of government for strange uses. For example, the state of Kentucky received $36,000 in federal money to keep terrorists from infiltrating bingo halls (Hudson, 2006).

Legal Bureaucracy

Another factor inhibiting police cooperation is the legal bureaucracy of criminal justice. For example, many criminal justice scholars believe that the justice system is actually not a system at all but a multifaceted bureaucracy with intersecting layers—or not. Drawing on earlier research, they refer to the justice system quite humorously as the "wedding cake model." Rather than a smooth flow among police, courts, and corrections, they see a cake in which a large bottom layer represents misdemeanors, a smaller middle layer represents serious crimes, and the smallest tier at the top represents a few celebrated cases. Each layer has differing procedures for dealing with different types of crimes, and police departments, court systems, and correctional agencies work apart from one another even within the same layer (see Walker, 1985; Cole and Smith, 2004, p. 8).

Each entity in the criminal justice system is independent, although it interacts with the other parts. There is no overall leader; instead, law enforcement, courts, and correctional agencies refuse to accept single management. From a constitutional perspective, the courts are hardly designed to fit into a criminal justice system. While police and correctional institutions represent the executive branch of government, the courts autonomously belong to the judicial branch (del Carmen, 1991, pp. 275–277). Efforts to increase the efficiency of homeland defense will not change these relationships.

> **Self-Check** ✓
>
> > Describe rivalries among law enforcement agencies.
> > What might be done to overcome those rivalries?
> > Why does inflexibility hamper an organization's ability to operate?

Bureaucratic Solutions

Successful organizations, whether car manufacturers or universities, overcome problems. Bureaucracies contain inherent problems, but they, too, can work for solutions. Law enforcement, homeland security, and intelligence agencies produce a unique product, but all formal organizations have the same internal and external troubles. Law enforcement bureaucracies will interact to solve problems. The lead panel at the first National Fusion Center Conference focused on this issue (Johnson, 2007a). Panel participants from local agencies, the National Guard, the FBI, the DHS, and the intelligence community addressed the problem directly. To combat terrorism, every bureaucratic obstacle that hinders the flow of information and action must be directly addressed (Figure 14.1).

Coordination of the activities of many different types of agencies is essential. Panel members stated that agencies have to develop new methods of coordinating and communicating ideas. This involves coordination committees and communication among

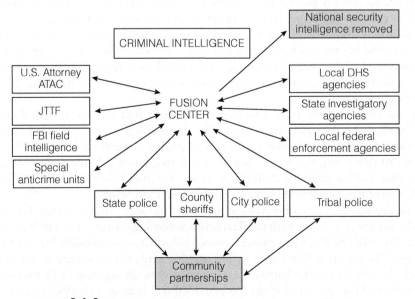

FIGURE **14.1** The Bureaucracy of Information Sharing

> ###))) ANOTHER PERSPECTIVE
>
> ### *Infrastructure Problems in the DOE*
>
> The late *60 Minutes* reporter Ed Bradley (2004) examined the Department of Energy (DOE) and its nuclear facilities. They have many problems, including the following concerns:
>
> - Stolen keys to secure facilities were not replaced for three years.
>
> - Guards were sleeping on duty.
> - Facilities were penetrated during mock terrorist attacks.
>
> Bradley's report concluded that America's nuclear facilities are protected on paper but that the DOE had not implemented real security measures.

actionable intelligence: Information that law enforcement agencies, military units, or other security forces can use to prevent an attack or operation.

leaders. Every person involved in the intelligence effort needs to understand his or her role in the process. As law enforcement officers collect and forward information, analysts at local fusion centers turn the information into **actionable intelligence**. This intelligence is forwarded to the NCTC, where it is analyzed with information from all other sources in the network. This newly created actionable intelligence is returned to the fusion centers as an **intelligence product**. It can be delivered to patrol officers, deputies, agents, and troopers.

intelligence product: Any outcome or output of analyzed information that can be used by law enforcement agencies, military units, or security forces to take an immediate action.

Bureaucracies have problems, but they also offer a process. When law enforcement agencies and the other organizations that aim to prevent terrorism stay focused on the goal, the process can produce results. It is possible to gather and analyze information, assess threats, and mobilize resources to prevent an attack.

Preparing for Successful Law Enforcement Processes

Imagine the following scene: On a snowy afternoon, a road patrol deputy stops a car on a Nebraska highway. Everything looks routine, and the driver, a foreign national, is exceedingly polite. The deputy notices that the car is registered in South Carolina and that the driver has an operator's permit issued in Colorado. The deputy asks questions about the driver's country of origin, his South Carolina or Colorado residence, and his reason for driving through Nebraska. The answers are smooth—too smooth. Had they been rehearsed? When the deputy rephrases the questions, the driver repeats the same answers without variation and seems to be confused by the deputy's questions.

In the course of the interview, the deputy finds that the car is rented and that the driver's name is spelled one way on his license and another way on the rental agreement. Further questioning reveals the driver's immigration papers with a third spelling. At this point, the deputy begins to ask more in-depth questions. The deputy knows that spelling names in multiple ways and creating false identification are methods that have been mastered by many international terrorists.

Terrorism Screening Center: (TSC) A multiagency operation in West Virginia that evaluates information gathered from a variety of governmental sources.

The deputy returns to her vehicle and calls the local fusion center. The analyst puts the deputy in contact with the **Terrorism Screening Center** (TSC) in West Virginia. The TSC tells the deputy to gather as much information as possible but not to make an arrest. The deputy follows instructions and forwards the information. She does not know it, but the driver she has stopped is a suspect in an ongoing JTTF investigation in Florida, and the information she has provided will become valuable in preventing a terrorist attack and arresting the perpetrators *before* the event can take place.

The foregoing example is only imaginary, but in 2002 a Midwestern police officer stopped a vehicle for speeding on an interstate highway. The car contained two men and a number of other items, objects the officer failed to see. The patrol officer failed to notice weapons and explosives in the car, including two loaded automatic weapons behind the driver and a semiautomatic pistol by the driver's hand. He also missed racist literature advocating violence and other extremist propaganda lying open in the car. He failed to see a clue when he first approached the car that would have given warning—a Ku Klux Klan symbol on the back window. Failing to do a proper warrant check, he did not know that one of the men was a fugitive. He gave the driver a speeding ticket, never knowing that his life had been in danger or that one of the men in the car was a member of a terrorist group that was planning a massive attack in Texas. The exact details of the stop are known because the other man in the suspect's car was an undercover police officer working the case (Keathley, 2002).

Law enforcement efforts are improving, and police officers are reporting information. It is also being shared on a number of levels. William Dyson (2011) looked at data from terrorism cases from 2008 to 2011. He found that American law enforcement officers had a tremendous success rate in both investigating terrorism cases and stopping terrorist and extremist attacks. The reason this has happened is twofold. First, law enforcement personnel, through training and awareness, were recognizing possible indicators and warning signs of terrorism. Second, police officers reported this information, and it was being shared by fusion centers and other intelligence agencies. Despite a cumbersome system and all the other problems of bureaucracies, counterterrorism investigations have improved.

New Approaches to the Law Enforcement Mission

The JTTF system might well serve as an outstanding example of law enforcement cooperation. Critics like Cole and Dempsey (2002) believe that gathering security information in the course of criminal investigations is both legal and effective. The RAND Corporation maintains that the JTTF is the most effective tool against domestic terrorism (Jenkins, Liepman, and Willis, 2014). The JTTF offers a sensible alternative by creating a system that separates criminal and national security intelligence. These units also combine local, state, and various federal police officers, as well as corrections officials and prosecutors, in regional units designed to combat terrorism. Local and state officers are given federal authority, and the presence of such officers gives federal agents the ability to act in local jurisdictions. JTTFs have been effective in many cases (Watson, 2002).

An alternative for state and local agencies is to combine training in terrorism awareness with specialized training for selected officers. Rather than bringing an entire department into intelligence-gathering operations, select units could engage in counterterrorist activities. Intelligence specialists like David Carter (2009) see the value in this. Rather than bringing police officers into the intelligence process as full partners, they could be trained to look for indicators of terrorism in the course of normal operations and to pass the information along. Trained police officers may expand their efforts by creating public and private partnerships through community policing efforts.

On the surface, JTTFs seem tailored to the needs of state and local law enforcement, but in some cases, they meet opposition. Local governments have refused to allow their police forces to assist in counterterrorist activities, and some jurisdictions refuse to share criminal intelligence with federal law enforcement. Civil libertarians sometimes see the formation of a JTTF as too great of a consolidation of governmental power. In addition, although academics and governmental officials are fond of using the phrase *criminal justice system*, the courts are not part of the system because they do not belong to the executive branch. State and federal courts may well limit the role of local agencies in homeland security, especially in intelligence-gathering activities.

On the other hand, police are in a perfect position to engage in intelligence-gathering activities and expand their role in national defense. Other Western democracies, such as France and Germany, have done this quite successfully. The Canadians and the British accomplished the same thing but kept more of a public service model than the French or the Germans. The JTTF model may be a start, but law enforcement efforts need to go further. Partnerships with all types of formal and informal organizations and cooperation among all levels of law enforcement in an environment that rewards information sharing are the ultimate answer to preventing terrorism.

The final aspect of preventing terrorism involves applying crime prevention and detection skills. Patrol officers and investigators encounter many more common criminals in their daily routines than terrorists, but the same techniques work against both sets of criminals. For example, former FBI agents Joe Navarro and John Shafer point out that law enforcement officers need to be able to recognize and intervene when they observe suspicious behavior. They need to be able to tell when people are lying, through verbal or written cues, and they need the interviewing skills to move beyond reasonable suspicion of criminal activity to probable cause. In short, they need skills to uncover deceptive behavior. Doing so involves routine police work, and this type of law enforcement not only disrupts criminal activity, it can prevent terrorism when officers recognize suspicious circumstances (Shafer and Navarro, 2004; Navarro, 2005; Navarro and Karlins, 2008; Shafer, 2010). In the end, many aspects of counterterrorism involve basic police work.

✔ **Self-Check**

> How could fusion centers solve problems inherent to information sharing?
> What law enforcement skills are involved in homeland security?
> What is the JTTF, and why is it effective?

Bureaucracies Against Terrorism

There are two views concerning the expanded homeland security bureaucracy. Supporters of one position maintain that consolidating power is efficient. They argue that a large bureaucracy with a clear mission will empower the security forces to perform their mission. The decision to create the DHS was based on this idea (Office of Homeland Security, 2002). Proponents of the second position suggest that decentralizing power personalizes services and helps develop links to communities. They believe localized, informal offices are more adept at recognizing and handling problems. Support for this position can be found among those who seek to trim the homeland defense concept and those who favor limiting the involvement of state and local governments in a larger organization. Although both ideas appear to be new in the wake of September 11, they are actually part of a longtime, ongoing debate.

Intelligence and Bureaucracy

The role of law enforcement and intelligence in homeland security is not exempt from the issues surrounding bureaucracy. Whether federal, state, or local, bureaucratic police work is a political process occurring in the context of official, routine procedures. Intelligence agencies, whether involved with the military or not, face the same problems. Both intelligence-gathering and law enforcement organizations operate within the American political system. They reflect governmental power, and their actions have political ramifications. Internally, conflicts arise from personal rivalries, territorial fights, and power struggles. They are as much a part of these services as they are of any organization (Gaines and Cordner, 1999, pp. 179–180; see also Walker, 1992).

Homeland security involves the use of intelligence and law enforcement. The Bush administration argued that counterterrorism is mainly a military problem. In the United States, however, the lead agency for counterterrorism is the FBI (Best, 2001). The FBI has several charges in this realm. First, under Director Robert Mueller, its charge was to prevent terrorism. Second, it is to coordinate intelligence-gathering and intelligence-sharing activities with the Border Patrol, Secret Service, and CIA. Third, it is to operate as a partner of state and local law enforcement. Finally, because the FBI is in the Department of Justice (DOJ), it is to coordinate its activities with the DHS and the Department of Defense (DOD). Under the intelligence reform law of 2004, all intelligence coordination must take place in the **National Counterterrorism Center** (NCTC) (U.S. Congress, 2004).

This face of homeland security involves a new role for the CIA. When it was originally established at the end of World War II, the CIA was supposed to be the agency that would coordinate all U.S. intelligence data, but the head of the agency, as director of central intelligence, never received the political authority to consolidate the information-gathering power. In addition, the CIA was to operate apart from U.S. criminal law and was not officially allowed to collect data on Americans inside the United States (Best, 2001). Today, the situation is somewhat modified. Chastised by public outcry and by the 9/11 Commission, and with formal orders from the president, the CIA is to cooperate fully with the FBI on counterterrorism intelligence (Office of Homeland Security, 2002; Baginski, 2004). The FBI and CIA are to work jointly on intelligence gathering and sharing inside and outside America's borders.

The DHS was created from the Office of Homeland Security in 2003 and was charged with counterterrorism. The DHS includes law enforcement agencies, such as the Secret Service, the Border Patrol, the new Immigration and Customs Enforcement (ICE),

National Counterterrorism Center: (NCTC) An organization designed to filter information from the intelligence process, synthesize counterterrorist information, and share it with appropriate organizations.

ANOTHER PERSPECTIVE

The DHS and Intelligence

The Department of Homeland Security has a large intelligence section, but its effectiveness is open to question. Several factors plague DHS intelligence:

- It is relatively powerless in the intelligence community.
- The DHS does not maintain terrorist watch lists.

- The CIA has the leading role at the National Counterterrorism Center (NCTC), formerly the Terrorist Threat Integration Center.
- The CIA and FBI compile the president's daily intelligence briefing.
- DHS intelligence has been slow to develop its mission.

Source: Rood, 2004

and the U.S. Customs Service. It has its own military force, the U.S. Coast Guard, which has limited law enforcement power. The DHS is responsible for port security and transportation systems. It manages security in airports through the massive Transportation Security Administration (TSA). It has its own intelligence section (see the preceding feature titled "Another Perspective: The DHS and Intelligence"), and it covers every special event in the United States, from political conventions to football games. It is clearly the largest organization involved in homeland security (DHS, 2004b).

The DOD has a limited but critical role in homeland security. Currently, the main military role in counterterrorism is to project American power overseas. The DOD's military forces take the fight to terrorists in other lands, rather than letting terrorists become a problem within America's borders (Barnett, 2004, pp. 299–303). It also augments civilian defense and provides special operations capabilities. In some cases, military intelligence can also be used in counternarcotics operations. Military forces can be used to protect the borders when so ordered by the president.

This is an impressive array of American power. In theory, led by the FBI and the CIA, multiple agencies will work together to gain information, analyze it, and share the results with every bureaucracy concerned with homeland security. *Cooperation* and *sharing* are the two buzzwords of the day. This is a charge not only to federal bureaucracies but to the FBI and CIA, which are to create a cooperative, sharing atmosphere with thousands of state and local law enforcement agencies. But cooperation does not stop there. The DHS calls on the entire system of homeland security bureaucracies to form relations with local communities and private industry. On paper, this is a massive force designed to stop terrorism and protect the United States of America.

The federal bureaucracy is massive, which presents a problem for agency cooperation. Yet, the bigger challenge is in coordinating the thousands of state and local law enforcement agencies in the United States. They form a network of potential sources of information, and their ability to function and cooperate is crucial to the homeland security mission. If terrorism can be envisioned as a network of terrorists and supporters fighting against a network of security-related agencies and the people they represent, then state and local police agencies are a vital element of America's counterterrorist network (J. White, 2007).

Administrators at the DHS, DOJ, FBI, and Office of the Director of National Intelligence have recognized the importance of state and local law enforcement agencies and the value they bring to homeland security. One of the priorities of the federal government is creating a system where information can flow among the various levels of government, from and through America's police agencies. This is the major bureaucratic challenge facing law enforcement (Johnson, 2007).

State and Local Law Enforcement Bureaucracies

As discussed in Chapter 13, American policing is localized. With more than 800,000 state and local law enforcement officers in the United States, agencies must cooperate to transform organizations. Any plan for changing so many bureaucracies must allow each agency to have the flexibility to change according to local demands. There are issues to overcome and partnerships with external agencies to be created, but it is not an impossible task. America's law enforcement agencies have overcome these problems to build systems in the past, and they can do the same thing in homeland security (see Bodrero, 2002).

The first issue to focus on is building a consensus among police agencies on the task to be accomplished. **Task orientation** will focus the actions of individual

task orientation: As used in this text, the ability to stay focused on the primary mission of an organization.

departments as they meet the homeland security needs within their communities. The task is to provide security. This is accomplished by **threat analysis**, information gathering, and information sharing. Individual tasks will vary. As Richard Marquise (2006, pp. 27–29) says, law enforcement tasks differ between Oklahoma City and New York City, but the mission remains the same. For law enforcement, the primary job is to prevent terrorism. Agencies need emergency service plans and comprehensive preparedness to respond to disasters, but their mission is to prevent attacks. When police officers become first responders, counterterrorism has failed.

Task orientation keeps law enforcement focused on the problem of preventing terrorism. By focusing on the goal, law enforcement agencies avoid three common bureaucratic problems: **goal displacement, mission creep**, and **process orientation**. Goal displacement happens when managers begin focusing on issues other than the purpose of the organization. For example, a good manager takes care of employee needs so that employees can accomplish their tasks. Goal displacement occurs if a manager emphasizes employee needs over a unit's purpose. Mission creep refers to adding too many secondary tasks for a group of workers assigned to an important task. Process orientation involves emphasizing the method of accomplishing a task over the completion of a job. All three problems divert a unit or organization from its goal. Unfortunately, these diversions are common at all levels of bureaucracy.

If multiple agencies are to focus on the task of preventing terrorism, then executives must buy into the concept. Chiefs, sheriffs, and directors set the administrative tone for their agencies. When groups of executives are oriented toward prevention, middle managers—captains and lieutenants—implement policies; sergeants, as first-line supervisors, ensure that the work takes place. Preventing terrorism becomes one of many emergency functions that state and local law enforcement agencies handle. Homeland security transforms into routine police work (J. White, 2007).

Smith and Roberts (2005) demonstrate that terrorists engage in criminal activities before a planned attack. This gives local agencies an opportunity to prevent attacks. To accomplish this, officers need to become aware of the types of activities that take place before an attack. These are known as **preincident indicators**. The indicators for terrorism are known, but they are too sensitive to list in a college textbook. It is enough to be aware that they exist, that officers can learn to recognize them, and that terrorists can be stopped when law enforcement either makes arrests or gathers relevant information.

If terrorism prevention is to be successful on the local level, agencies must participate in systems. Once again, American police agencies have a history of doing this. The Law Enforcement Information Network (LEIN) links agencies to a host of bureaucracies to provide valuable information on everything from vehicle registrations to warrants. The National Crime Information Center (NCIC) maintains information on a nationwide basis. The systems discussed in the intelligence section of the preceding chapter, such as the RISS, the El Paso Intelligence Center (EPIC), and the numerous High-Intensity Drug Trafficking Areas (HIDTAs), attest to the willingness of state and local agencies to cooperate in regional and national networks.

Bureaucratic changes present challenges, but they also provide opportunities. Two recent national innovations demonstrate this, and both processes are crucial to homeland security. As discussed in Chapter 13, community policing changed the face of American law enforcement (Chermak and Weiss, 2006; Duekmedjian, 2006). It began as an idea and spread with support from the federal government, research from university criminal justice departments, creation of community associations and partnerships and regional organizations, and participation of law enforcement executives who oriented themselves to the task of increasing police effectiveness. Homeland

threat analysis: The process of examining a community to determine the areas that might be subject to attack and the criticality of those areas to the functions of the community.

goal displacement: Occurs when process is favored over accomplishments. The process should be reasonable and efficient. Too much focus on the process, however, interferes with completion of job tasks.

mission creep: Occurs when too many secondary tasks are added to a unit. Too many jobs divert a unit from its primary mission.

process orientation: Occurs when more attention is paid to the manner of achieving organizational goals than achieving them. Process is important when it focuses on ethical and legal requirements. Process orientation goes beyond legal and moral norms, and it becomes dysfunctional when an organization's goal is conceived as maintaining procedures.

preincident indicators: The criminal and social actions of individuals and groups before a terrorist attack.

security presents the same opportunity, and community police networks are ideal for the functions it requires.

The second recent innovation is the National Criminal Intelligence Sharing Plan (NCISP). The concept of information gathering, analysis, and sharing began with the Global Advisory Committee to the U.S. attorney general. It moved to a **working group** of executives from all levels of law enforcement. As the working group developed ideas for carrying the concept out, groups like the International Association of Chiefs of Police (IACP) reviewed and amended the recommendations. Like community policing, it was a national team effort of many different law enforcement agencies. When the NCISP was unveiled and endorsed by the IACP, a multitude of police agencies, law enforcement associations, intelligence organizations, and associated bureaucracies endorsed and adopted it.

The many different organizations that comprise state and local law enforcement agencies face a daunting task in transforming bureaucracy, but preventing terrorism requires this transformation. The cooperative efforts of community policing and the NCISP indicate that local law enforcement bureaucracies can meet a challenge and even participate with multiple federal agencies. Such transformation can happen again as agencies develop homeland security missions. In fact, homeland security is an extension of what state and local agencies are already doing (see Carter, 2009).

working group: A term used in the federal government for a group of subject matter experts who gather to suggest solutions to common problems.

Self-Check

> What is the role of the National Counterterrorism Center?
> What factors inhibit effective local efforts to prevent terrorism?
> How might the NCISP impact counterterrorism?

Border Protection

Aside from the myriad functions related to law enforcement and intelligence, the federal government has another major goal: to protect America's borders. The responsibility falls on the DHS and a group of agencies contained within it. The main agencies responsible for border protection include Customs and Border Protection, ICE, and the coast guard. The Transportation Security Administration (TSA) has supporting responsibilities at international airports inside the United States, and agents from the agencies protecting the border are trained at the Federal Law Enforcement Training Center (FLETC). Many of the agencies coordinate their efforts with local units of government, and many DHS personnel are armed and carry arrest power.

American borders are vulnerable in several areas. Long stretches of unprotected areas along the northern and southern borders are open to infiltration, and more than 300 seaports must be secured. The DHS has agencies responsible for securing entry into the United States at airports, and it is responsible for protecting air travel once the entry points are protected. Border agents are responsible for staffing entry points along the northern and southern borders. This activity is augmented by efforts by the coast guard as it patrols the ocean shores and Great Lakes. Finally, another DHS agency has the task of accounting for noncitizens within U.S. borders (DHS, 2005).

Policy Disputes

The scope of activities is daunting, even for an agency as large as the DHS, and the variety of functions multiplies the problems. In some cases, such as keeping track of noncitizens, the DHS cooperates with the FBI and CIA. The DHS has increased the number of people who patrol the borders, and it has tried to shift agents to the least secure areas. The DHS also uses technology such as biometric measuring—identification systems based on body characteristics such as fingerprints, facial patterns, or DNA—to maintain records on aliens (DHS, 2005).

These functions have not come without problems. Critics say that DHS activities, broad as they may be, are not altogether effective (Flynn, 2004a, 2004b). A union representing DHS employees surveyed 500 border patrol agents and 500 immigration inspectors from the Border Protection and Customs divisions. The union president stated that old bureaucratic procedures leave borders unprotected, and members of the union agreed. Only 16 percent were satisfied with DHS efforts. The majority of respondents complained of low morale. DHS administrators countered that only rank-and-file personnel completed the survey (Z. Alonso, 2004).

Some DHS policies have not been popular with other countries. For example, the DHS implemented a policy of fingerprinting and photographing visitors from some other countries; some of America's closest allies were exempted from the process. This policy met with a storm of criticism from nation after nation. Brazil even retaliated, requiring photographs and fingerprints of U.S. visitors to its land. The DHS has also tried more advanced methods of biometric measuring, hoping to create a database of body types. Some have complained that the process was ahead of its time (CNN, 2004a).

Local governments have been asked to assist with border protection, but some of them have balked at the idea. Many local governments feel that they need the trust and cooperation of foreigners living in their areas. If aliens distrust the actions of local governments, governmental functions could be hampered. The education system would be disrupted, aliens would not seek health care, and law enforcement officials would neither get information nor be able to serve people in the jurisdiction (National Immigration Forum, 2004).

The 9/11 Commission Report (2004, pp. 400–407) addressed the issue of border security and suggested sweeping reforms. The commission said that more than 500 million people cross U.S. borders each year, and 330 million of them are foreigners. Bureaucratic reform is essential if these crossings are to be monitored because the system before September 11 was unable to provide security or monitor foreigners coming into the United States. A single agency with a single format, the commission recommended, should screen crossings. In addition, an investigative agency should be established to monitor all aliens in the United States. The commission also recommended gathering intelligence on the way terrorists travel and combining intelligence and law enforcement activities to hamper their mobility. The commission suggested using a standardized method for obtaining identification and passports with biometric measures. In essence, the commission recommended standardizing the bureaucratic response for monitoring the entry of foreigners into the United States.

A more recent empirical examination suggests that all the recommendations from various agencies and the massive reorganization fostered by the creation of the DHS has had less of an impact than originally intended (May, Sapotichne, and Workman, 2009). The primary reason is that it is difficult to change large bureaucracies. Peter May and his fellow researchers demonstrated that workers in smaller bureaus under the grand bureaucracy maintain their routines and systems. Even a massive change in structure does not prevent workers from fighting for turf. Even the powerful disruption of the 9/11 attacks did not alter many of the subsystems. This has many implications for relations among levels of government. If the DHS is unable to change federal bureaucratic relations, it is doubtful that it will have a major impact on state, federal, and tribal systems in areas such as information sharing, immigration, and implementation of a national identity system.

The Immigration Debate

One controversial issue surrounding border protection involves immigration. Many elected officials argue that the United States cannot be secure unless its borders are secure. A few people want to eliminate immigration, but more want to stop only illegal immigration and install tighter controls on immigration from countries that may harbor hostility toward the United States. Other people believe that the immigration debate is overemphasized. They say that the United States is a country based on immigration and that immigrants do not represent a terrorist threat.

Conservative political candidate and pundit Patrick Buchanan (2002, pp. 97–109, 235) summarizes one view. By allowing the unregulated flow of immigrants from the southern border, Buchanan argues, the United States opens the door to terrorist infiltration. The situation is made worse by allowing immigrants from hostile Muslim countries to enter the United States. They can operate as independent terrorists or as agents for a rogue regime. Buchanan takes the argument a step further. By allowing an unregulated influx of Hispanics from the south, the United States risks not only terrorism but the destruction of American culture. Some critics dismiss Buchanan as a right-wing ideologue, but scholars such as Samuel Huntington (2004) make the same argument.

Most of the people concerned with border security make the distinction between legal and illegal immigration, and their primary concern reflects a desire for the rule of law. Kerry Diminyatz (2003) puts forward this idea in a research paper written while training at the U.S. Army War College. The southern border is not secure, and DHS plans for securing the border have not been adequate. This is a security threat not only in terms of terrorism but from a variety of other criminal activities. Diminyatz argues that it is possible to secure the border but that it will take major reforms. The major issues involve economic, social, and political inequities as well as corruption on both sides of the border.

Diminyatz says that the failure to protect the southern border presents four major national security threats: (1) terrorism and weapons of mass destruction (WMD), (2) drug trafficking, (3) human smuggling, and (4) infectious disease. The most significant threat of unregulated immigration comes in the form of terrorism and organized crime. Although this has been a problem for decades, no presidential administration has effectively approached the dilemma. Diminyatz argues that all agencies charged with border security need to be brought into a single organization. The multiple bureaucracies responsible for border security are inefficient, and the structure fails to focus all efforts. To correct the situation, U.S. military forces should be deployed along the border until civilian law enforcement can be consolidated and physical and technological barriers can be established to prevent illegal border crossings.

The federal government seeks to form partnerships with local communities so that state and local law enforcement officers can act as an extension of agencies charged with border security (Seghetti, Vina, and Ester, 2005). However, these law enforcement officials might not welcome the idea of joining a federal partnership to secure the borders. Sometimes local law enforcement agencies refuse to cooperate because they want to maintain informational relationships with the illegal community (National Immigration Forum, 2004). They need information from both legal and illegal immigrants to protect the community and investigate crime. Successful policing requires information, and crimes cannot be investigated without it.

Other methods of enhancing border security have nothing to do with a reorganization of bureaucracy. Congress has considered a number of methods (Garcia, Lee, and Tatelman, 2005). One tool could be the introduction of national identification cards. Another is a law regulating asylum for those from countries openly hostile to the United States. Some members of Congress have suggested creating special laws or legal reviews for legal immigrants who pose a security threat. Others have advocated holding illegal aliens and not deporting them. These positions represent controversies within the controversy. The problem of border security might be best addressed by enhancing an agency's legal authority to deal with the issue. Civil libertarians are wary of such approaches, believing they will result in the abuse of governmental power.

Janice Kephart (2005), a former legal counsel to the 9/11 Commission, believes that the holes in border security come from lax enforcement of existing law. She says that a study of the activities of 94 foreign-born terrorists who operated in the United States from 1990 to 2004 shows the inadequacy of enforcement. Two-thirds of the terrorists engaged in criminal activities before or in conjunction with their terrorist attacks. Note that this reinforces findings from Brent Smith and Paxton Roberts (2005). Terrorists enter the United States with temporary visas and then fail to follow the provisions of entry. They make false statements on applications and lie on other official documents while in the country. They make sham marriages or utilize other loopholes to stay in the country. Kephart believes that border protection starts with rigorous law enforcement and background checks.

Sebastian Mallaby (2007), writing in an opinion column for the *Washington Post*, vehemently argues that the focus on illegal immigration is not relevant to homeland security. Undocumented workers commit fewer crimes than natives, and there is no indication that they convert to jihadist ideology. Immigrants come to the United States because they want to live here, Mallaby says. Homeland security has little to do with immigration reform. Mallaby says that security efforts should focus on two types of targets—those most likely to be hit and those that will cause the greatest loss of life. Immigration is not a factor.

The debate about immigration reveals the problems inherent in law enforcement bureaucracy. To begin with, the nature of the problem is under dispute. Some arguments claim that illegal immigration is not a problem, whereas the opposite side maintains that legal, let alone illegal, immigration is destroying civilization. There is confusion about the relationship between local law enforcement and federal agencies. This is complicated by the number of federal agencies that have a role in border security and immigration. Finally, there are concerns with the efficiency of immigration laws.

Some people argue that they are not being enforced, some want tougher laws, and still others believe border security is not an issue in preventing terrorism. It is difficult to formulate policy in the face of so many contradictory positions.

The immigration debate has grown more heated as the country continues to be divided over ideological positions. The *New York Times* (Archibald, 2010) summarized the issues through an examination of a controversial Arizona law that empowered state and local officers to investigate the status of suspected illegal immigrants. Although the law had public support throughout the country, critics maintained that it would lead to police profiling of Hispanics. The law spawned a heated national debate, lawsuits, demonstrations, and the deployment of National Guard troops on the border with Mexico. If nothing else, the Arizona controversy indicated the problem of addressing a single issue through multiple layers of bureaucracy and competing interest groups.

Border Security: Critique and Reform

There are problems with border security, to be sure. Stephen Flynn (2009) believes that the goals of homeland security are crucial and that America's bureaucracies and leadership are squandering the opportunity to really defend the United States. Flynn says that America has made two crucial mistakes. First, homeland security has been separated from national security. Second, the infrastructure is vulnerable to attacks. Despite all the rhetoric and departmental rearrangements for homeland security, the reality is that the United States has not organized its resources for defense.

Flynn vehemently argues that homeland security should be part of a national strategy to defend the United States. America needs to be able to strike a blow as well as to take one. Although both political parties speak of the war on terrorism, terrorism is not something that can be destroyed only by fighting in other areas of the world. There is no central front, Flynn argues, and America cannot always project its power to fight elsewhere. The United States has marshaled its resources to fight overseas while neglecting to protect its home front.

To illustrate the point, Flynn points to the use of WMD. According to the CIA, the most likely route for smuggling WMD into the United States is by sea. It is difficult to inspect all of the cargo containers arriving at seaports; therefore, the oceans represent an opportunity for terrorists. Flynn points out that the George W. Bush administration did very little to protect the nation's 361 seaports. There was a lot of rhetoric but insufficient action. He finds it hard to believe that in 2004 the United States spent more money every three days to fight the war in Iraq than it did in three years to protect seaports.

The nation's critical infrastructure remains open to attack, Flynn says. In the 2005 national budget, the DOD was allotted \$7.6 billion to enhance the fortification of its bases. In the same budget, the infrastructure for the *entire* nation received only \$2.6 billion. Dirty bombs and chemical threats can be developed from hazardous materials; nevertheless funds for secure disposal of such materials have been drastically reduced. Police and firefighter numbers have been cut, even though they are crucial for security.

Flynn also sees a problem in strategic thinking at the DHS and other agencies. For example, the scientific and medical communities are essential elements of homeland security. Nearly 50 percent of the scientific and medical personnel employed by the federal government retired before 2010. Currently, they are not being replaced quickly enough. The colleges and universities that would produce their replacements are underfunded. In addition, the federal government has virtually ignored private industry, claiming that it is responsible for protecting its own infrastructure. However, Flynn finds that private industry is not doing this.

Even meeting the need for enhanced border security will not protect America against terrorist attack. Security is a dynamic process that combines intelligence, military, and law enforcement power. It requires international coordination and cooperation to counter attacks that are planned overseas. Flynn says that America needs an integrated system for defense.

Flynn believes that jihadists are fully aware of the vulnerabilities in our infrastructure. They will not simply let the United States bring the fight to them; they intend to strike, and the safest and most effective way to hit America is to strike its infrastructure. Jihadists understand the economic effects of their actions. For example, Flynn says that if terrorists managed to shut down the closed-container operations of America's shipping industry for just three weeks, the whole world could be thrown into an economic recession.

Flynn urges policymakers to reinvent homeland security. Defense at home is as important as the ability to wage military action overseas. DHS and other federal bureaucracies should think of security from a broad perspective. There are many benefits to doing so. Flynn argues that developing an integrated system against terrorism would reduce the drug trade, contraband smuggling, and theft. These are residual benefits for a strategic program, he believes.

Despite the system's shortcomings, Flynn believes bureaucracies can overcome the problems. We will never have enough security to prevent every attack, he says, but we should follow the path of the aviation industry. Private and public aviation officials have worked together to lower the possibility of airplane accidents and reduce the devastation when they do occur. Although the air industry experiences horrific disasters at times, people continue to fly. Flynn believes that this is because of the faith people have in the air transportation system. They know that failures, although inevitable, are an aberration. They continue to use the system because they believe in its overall safety. Flynn says that homeland security should have the same goal. In a system of civil defense, people have a civic responsibility to maintain the system. When bureaucracies recover from failure after an attack, people will believe life is getting back to normal, and they will continue to function. This is the goal of bureaucracy, Flynn says. Americans must be able to absorb a major attack and continue to function. That, Flynn argues, should be the model for homeland security agencies.

If police departments follow Flynn's suggestions, they will see security as a "work in progress." Flynn says that if policies become a process, attention will focus on how work is accomplished rather than on the results. Law enforcement agencies should look for weaknesses in the system, probe them, and make changes based on the results. Every agency also needs to forge and sustain a variety of nontraditional partnerships with the community, different levels of government, private industry, and the nonprofit sector. Flynn says that our federal system lends itself to these partnerships because many decision-making functions are reserved for state governments.

Even though Flynn is critical of America's bureaucratic weaknesses, he is optimistic about the future. He believes that bureaucratic leaders, including police executives and managers, will grow to see the problems of terrorism from a more realistic perspective. This will cause them to improve homeland security *before an attack*. Although not every attack can be prevented, most terrorism can be deterred through cooperative partnerships. Prevention demands new skills for law enforcement officers, a culture of information sharing, and new bureaucratic relationships; however, interdiction of terrorism is an attainable goal.

✓ Self-Check

> How do political disputes affect border security?

> Why are state and local agencies hesitant to enforce border security?

> What reforms might enhance border security?

Infrastructure Protection

Another area concerning the DHS is infrastructure protection. Information, energy, communication, transportation, and economic systems are vulnerable to terrorist attacks. Their vulnerability requires all levels of government to develop new capabilities to provide protection. The DHS (Office of Homeland Security, 2002, pp. xi–xii) states that law enforcement agencies will need to develop cooperative links with public and private bureaucracies, including private security organizations, educational institutions, and health care systems. Fortunately, state and local police agencies are not starting in a vacuum. The IACP (IACP, 2001) issued guidelines to provide for cooperation among all levels of government and private industry as well as to identify threats to the infrastructure to defend against them.

Private Versus Governmental Partnerships

Just because some units of government and private industry realize that the infrastructure needs to be protected does not mean that bureaucracies will jump into action. Critics think that too little is being done. Jeanne Cummings (2002) points to two primary weaknesses. As much as a year after September 11, the federal government had failed to provide homeland security funding to state and local governments. State emergency planners complain that they received little federal direction and no federal money. Cummings says that the problem is even worse in the private security industry. After a survey of security at America's largest shopping mall, in Minnesota, Cummings concluded that federal law enforcement does little to assist private security. Keeping Americans safe, Cummings says, depends on state and local efforts outside Washington.

The situation improved over the years. The Department of Justice began to provide monetary aid to state and local governments to assist with homeland security. This was augmented by equipment donations from the Department of Defense and Department of Treasury funds from the forfeiture of assets seized from drug dealers. DHS implemented a massive grant program to assist state and local governments. Cummings was correct about delays in assistance, but the situation improved (DHS, 2015). In fact, today some critics claim that state and local law enforcement agencies have received too much superfluous funding and surplus federal equipment (ACLU, 2014; White, 2015).

Infrastructure protection is another issue. Shortly after 9/11 Richard Clarke (2002) testified before the Senate Subcommittee on the Judiciary. He outlined many of the threats facing the nation's infrastructure, painting a grim picture. Most computer systems are vulnerable to viruses, Clarke believes, because computer users will not pay for proper protection. The government has made efforts to partially address this problem, but more protection is needed. Clarke says that the nation's power system and the technological organizations that support it are vulnerable to disruptions. The Internet and other computer networks that support these systems are also vulnerable to attack. Pointing to the railroad industry as an example, Clarke shows how many low-tech organizations have imported high-tech support systems. If you shut down electrical grids and computers, Clarke maintains, you'll shut down transportation and communication.

The situation slowly improved in some areas, but it remained vulnerable in others, especially in cybersecurity. In 2009 DHS issued a plan for protecting the nation's critical infrastructure (DHS, 2009). It outlined methods for funding and developing partnerships. DHS also created a department charged with infrastructure protection. Cybersecurity has been another matter. Although DHS maintains a cyber response team, a study by the General Electric Corporation (2012) revealed several cyber vulnerabilities. Multiple systems lacked consistent security policies. Improvements to known weaknesses are distributed too slowly and some computer users fail to install them. General Electric found a lack of overall security control. An in depth report both CBS's *60 Minutes* (2015) opined that the U.S. government is prepared for cyber defense, but up to 95 percent of the private sector is at risk.

On the other hand many private corporations have the ability to gather and control information, and doing so is crucial to their ability to function when they compete for business with other companies. Corporations like Walmart, General Motors, and Apple have excellent information-gathering and security systems, and they often share information with governments for the public good. It is quite another matter to hand corporations analyzed criminal and national security intelligence. The problem is that private industry uses information for competition and profit. When government agencies share information, they do so in the public domain for the public good. Government partnerships with private corporations have the potential to give large companies a competitive edge.

The Need for Private Partnerships

All levels of law enforcement are faced with the need for technical specialists and access to privately owned portions of the infrastructure. Protection of the infrastructure does not result automatically with the acquisition of technical expertise equivalent to that of industrial specialists; it comes when specialists in crime fighting and protection establish critical links with the public and private organizations that are working to maintain America's infrastructure. Connections should be developed in two crucial areas. First, the police should be linked to the security forces already associated with infrastructure functions. The American Society of Industrial Security (Azano, 2003) has made great strides in this area, but more needs to be accomplished. Second, state and local law enforcement agencies must establish formal and informal networks with the organizations in their jurisdictions, and these networks should expand to a cooperative federal system.

Government Partnerships

One of the most important aspects of DHS operations is communicating with local communities, law enforcement agencies, and private industries as they relate to intelligence-gathering activities and infrastructure protection. The DHS (2004) says that

---

 ANOTHER PERSPECTIVE

Recommendations for Cybersecurity

The Institute for Security Technology Studies at Dartmouth College recommends following the best practices of security in the computer industry:

- Update software.
- Enforce rigid password security.

- Disable unnecessary services.
- Scan for viruses and use virus protection.
- Utilize intrusion detection systems.
- Maintain firewalls.

Source: Vatis, 2001, p. 19

local efforts are essential to successful security plans. The IACP (2001) believes that local law enforcement agencies will become the hinge on which all local efforts pivot. It will be the job of local law enforcement, the IACP says, to coordinate activities from a host of agencies throughout local jurisdictions all through the United States.

The Federal Mission

As envisioned by federal bureaucracy, homeland security entails coordinating efforts of several local organizations, including private industry, public service, health care systems, and law enforcement. Emergency response planning falls into two broad categories: prevention and reaction (Cilluffo, Cardash, and Lederman, 2001). State and local agencies assume expanded roles in this concept because they are the obvious choice for prevention, and they will be among the first to respond to a domestic attack. If local agencies assume such a role, law enforcement officers will be forced to rethink the ways they do business.

As discussed in Chapter 13, national security intelligence is a function of the federal government. As local agencies become involved in homeland security, they will need to think beyond criminal intelligence. Two new functions become apparent. They must become involved in assessing terrorist threats in their jurisdictions. They must also learn to recognize possible information that may add to national defense intelligence and develop routines to forward such information. This creates a legal problem because law enforcement agencies need to have a reasonable suspicion that criminal activity is taking place or has taken place before they can collect information (see O'Conner, 2004; Carter, 2009).

Expanding Local Roles

If they are to be engaged in homeland security, state and local police agencies will need to expand the role of traditional law enforcement. On the most rudimentary level, officers could be assigned to security tasks and trained to look for information beyond the violation of criminal law. On a more sophisticated level, police intelligence units could be established to gather and pass on intelligence information. The most effective initial practice would be to train patrol officers, investigators, and narcotics officers to look for indicators of terrorism during their daily activities. This would be an effective method of enhancing intelligence, but critics fear governmental infringement on civil liberties (see Chapter 15; Cole and Dempsey, 2002, pp. 186–187).

Assuming that local law enforcement agencies will collect information only within the context of criminal investigations, bureaucratic problems remain. The process of gathering defense intelligence is not readily apparent in American policing. Most law enforcement officers did not enter police ranks thinking that they were joining an army or aspiring to be part of the DHS. Their motivation generally focuses on elimination of crime, not national defense. In addition, local police policies and employment incentives reinforce their original notions. Officers are encouraged to maintain a local view, and police managers reinforce pragmatic actions while discouraging abstract thinking. Police work is extremely political, and law enforcement officers think locally. To paraphrase the late Speaker of the House Tip O'Neill, all law enforcement politics is local. The goal is not to alienate constituencies, but to develop strong community ties to help keep information flowing. Information about suspects, crimes, and criminal activity translates into power and successful individual performance in police agencies, and it solves crimes (Manning, 1976, p. 35).

Thinking Internationally

State and local officers are not rewarded for thinking in terms of international issues or national security. Chiefs of police and sheriffs do not usually praise abstract reasoning. In an early critique of collegiate criminal justice programs, Lawrence Sherman (1978) claims that higher education has done little to help this situation. Criminal justice programs do not produce abstract, critical thinkers for law enforcement; instead, Sherman believes, they impart skills. According to a survey by *Police: The Law Enforcement Magazine*, graduates steeped in academic preparation are not as welcome in law enforcement agencies as recruits with military experience (July 2002). Discipline and the willingness to obey orders are more important than individual thinking and creativity.

Modern terrorism is an abstract, nebulous concept that fluctuates according to historical and political circumstances. To combat terrorism, security forces require groups of people with abstract reasoning skills, knowledge of international politics and history, and specialized expertise in particular regions (Betts, 2002). If the police are to participate as full partners in this process, they need outside specialists with skills not typically available in law enforcement organizations. The ethos behind policing, however, rejects this logic. American law enforcement relishes pragmatic information with immediate applicability in practical situations.

Localized attitudes inspire contempt from intelligence agencies. Unlike analysts in defense intelligence, state and local police officers frequently exhibit no concern for in-depth background information, that is, the kind of information needed to understand intelligence. As a result, intelligence bureaucracies frequently question the competence of police. Intelligence analysts know that information is not usually valuable until it is categorized and placed within social and political contexts. If police agencies are unable to engage in this type of examination, intelligence organizations hesitate to form partnerships with them. These factors present enormous problems as the DHS tries to create a network of information.

> ✓ **Self-Check**
>
> > Why is the infrastructure under both public and private control?
> > Why must government agencies form homeland security partnerships with each other?
> > Why is it necessary to think about international problems at all levels of law enforcement?

ANOTHER PERSPECTIVE

New Approaches to Mission

If state and local law enforcement officers were to begin looking for signs of terrorism, they would need to frame basic questions about potential adversaries. For example, in addition to criminal briefings before patrol or investigative tours, officers would need to think of questions such as the following:

- What is the modus operandi of our enemy?
- How does the enemy's organization function?

- What types of tactics will the enemy use?
- What types of weapons will the enemy use?
- How can information be gathered while still protecting the source?
- What activities in the community might indicate that terrorists may be operating in a jurisdiction?
- How can information be shared securely with other agencies?

Responding to Disasters

No security system can completely stop terrorism, and law enforcement agencies will be called upon to respond when an attack occurs. The process for response and recovery involves planning. Fire departments, regional disaster teams, the health community, and other agencies have **emergency response plans**. Law enforcement agencies have roles under these plans. Their primary responsibilities are to respond and restore order, assist emergency and rescue operations, and support health and human services. They are also charged with investigative and prosecutorial actions. With the exception of the last two functions, the procedures used are similar to those used when responding to natural disasters, civil disorders, or massive infrastructure failures. All of these functions involve reaction.

emergency response plans: Preparations by any agency to deal with natural, accidental, or human made disasters. They involve controlling the incident through an organized response-and-command system and assigning various organizations to supervise the restoration of social order.

Response functions are critical and they save lives, but emergency response planning differs from preventing terrorism. When law enforcement agencies respond to disasters, it does not matter whether the cause was an industrial accident, an act of nature, or a terrorist attack. Multiple agencies, including police departments, respond to emergencies. Plans and actions designed to stop terrorism involve different skills. Gathering information, analyzing it, and sharing findings are part of an intelligence process. Law enforcement's primary role is to prevent terrorism and crime, and its secondary purpose is to react to it to save lives. Reaction to a crisis, although one of the critical missions of police and homeland security agencies, is an emergency function. It has little to do with the cause of the disaster. For example, when a traffic officer responds to a car crash, that is reaction. Preventing automobile accidents is a different function. The same principle applies to preventing terrorism.

✓ Self-Check

> How does prevention differ from emergency response planning?
> Why do law enforcement roles differ in prevention and response?
> Has law enforcement failed when it engages in a responsive role?

Emphasizing the Points

Information sharing is at the heart of homeland security, but bureaucratic complexity creates problems with information sharing. The vast maze of law enforcement agencies form a complex set of bureaucracies that mix with other government and private organizations to form a homeland security network. Ideally, it should operate as a rational bureaucracy. Reenvisioning the law enforcement mission might solve many bureaucratic problems, and the JTTF model would be a method for accomplishing this. Homeland security is further complicated by the national debate about immigration, the large expanse of borders, the number of ports of entry, and the sheer size of the infrastructure. Homeland security will work only with a variety of innovative partnerships.

SUMMARY OF CHAPTER OBJECTIVES

- Information sharing is the lifeblood of homeland security.
- The sheer size of the federal, state, and local law enforcement bureaucracies complicates homeland security. It creates the need for outside agencies designed for communication and information sharing.
- Bureaucracies tend to stifle the flow of information. Organizations must be innovative and constantly be willing to question practices and to change them to effectively share information.
- Estimates of the number of police agencies in the United States are in the thousands. There are 50 state police organizations and more than three dozen federal agencies with law enforcement power. No single policy or practice can synthesize law enforcement in the United States.
- Aside from the number of diverse organizations involved in security, standard bureaucratic problems impact homeland security. These include goal displacement, mission creep, and process orientation.
- Methods for overcoming bureaucratic problems involve increasing information sharing through fusion centers, reenvisioning the law enforcement mission, and employing the JTTF model.
- The JTTF combines all levels and all types of law enforcement organizations in a single unit. Individual task forces can operate all over the country, and they are not limited by jurisdictional boundaries.
- The primary federal agencies involved in homeland security are the DHS, DOJ, and DOD. The NTC maintains links with these agencies and ODNI. The FBI and CIA have a joint operational unit in the NTC.
- The National Criminal Intelligence Sharing Program is a model for information sharing. The IACP has recommended that all law enforcement agencies adopt the plan.
- The problems associated with border protection are the size of the borders, disputes about policy, and debate over immigration.
- The infrastructure is controlled by a mishmash of public and private entities. Law enforcement must work in partnership with these groups to effectively protect the infrastructure.
- Even the most effective homeland security operations will experience failures. Intelligence and information sharing is the goal of terrorism prevention, but police agencies must also prepare to deal with disasters.

LOOKING INTO THE FUTURE

The Brookings Institution prepared a report entitled *A Vision for Homeland Security in the Year 2025* (West, 2012). Although it is not an alarmist document, it does not paint a pleasant scenario. According to the report, the United States will face a complex variety of new threats that may include chemical, biological, radioactive, and nuclear (CBRN) threats, drone attacks, cyberterrorism, and weapons that cannot be envisioned at this time. This situation is exacerbated because stakeholders do not agree on the nature of future threats or their relative importance. Security will depend on multilevel partnerships of differing organizations because one agency cannot deal with all possible threats. Security missions will change rapidly in this environment, and systems will operate in ways their designers never intended. The unpredictability of threats and relations within diverse partnerships create a dangerous environment.

The Brookings Institution makes the following recommendations for the future:

- Train federal and state elected officials in decision making during technological attacks.
- Institutionalize future thinking when dealing with terrorism.
- Organize joint action through infrastructure partnerships.
- Create real-time data analysis and decision-making tools.

If the Brookings report is correct, we need to think about how we will defend the country tomorrow and not how we operate today.

KEY TERMS

Max Weber, p. 329
Bureaucracy, p. 329
1978 Civil Service
    Reform Act, p. 330
Government Manage-
    ment Reform Act
    1994, p. 330

Actionable intelligence,
    p. 334
Intelligence product, p. 334
Terrorism Screening
    Center, p. 334
National Counterterror-
    ism Center, p. 337

Task orientation, p. 338
Threat analysis, p. 339
Goal displacement, p. 339
Mission creep, p. 339
Process orientation, p. 339
Preincident indicators,
    p. 339

Working group, p. 340
Emergency response
    plans, p. 350

CHAPTER 15

Homeland Security and Constitutional Issues

The United States Supreme Court

LEARNING OBJECTIVES

After reading this chapter, you should be able to:

▶ Explain the dangers of restricting freedom in the name of security.

▶ Differentiate between civil liberties and human rights.

▶ List the controversial powers granted to the government by the USA PATRIOT Act.

▶ Summarize the limitations placed on law enforcement in the USA FREEDOM Act.

▶ List constitutional issues that affect homeland security.

▶ Summarize how the Bill of Rights impacts law enforcement.

▶ Cite the issues surrounding executive power to combat terrorism.

▶ Explain due process in the Fourteenth Amendment.

▶ Describe courts' responses to attempts to counter terrorism with increased governmental executive branch power.

▶ Summarize emerging criminal justice scholarship focusing on governmental power.

C ivil libertarians strongly lobbied members of Congress during the spring of 2015. Certain provisions of the USA PATRIOT Act were about to expire, and organizations dedicated to maintaining civil liberties wanted them to disappear. They were especially concerned about provisions that allowed the government to collect massive amounts of intercepted phone calls and data detailing finances, medical records, purchases, and a host of other stored data. One senator agreed with civil liberties advocates and made a procedural ploy in the Senate that caused the sections to expire. Law enforcement officials, the intelligence community, and supporters of the PATRIOT Act were angered. A number of senators voted to allow surveillance.

This series of events represents a political struggle that has been going on since the 9/11 attacks. A frightened Congress passed the PATRIOT Act just 45 days after the terrorist assault.

It greatly expanded governmental powers in the name of national security. Civil libertarians were appalled, believing it to be an overreaction. They feared law enforcement and intelligence agencies would overstep constitutional limitations. President George W. Bush's administration argued that the provisions were tools necessary for effective counterterrorism. President Obama later agreed to continue the policies.

There is a fine balance between freedom and security. When governmental powers are expanded, freedom can be restricted. When regulations limit the government's ability to collect information, security can be threatened. Law enforcement agencies have dealt with this issue for quite some time, and there are decades of statutory and case law outlining procedures for arresting suspects, collecting evidence, and depriving guilty people of their freedom. Expanding security brings concerns for the protection of civil liberties.. Homeland security is bound to encounter the Constitution.

Security and Civil Liberties

USA PATRIOT Act: A law passed in October 2001 that expanded law enforcement's power to investigate and deter terrorism. Opponents claim that it adversely affects civil liberties; proponents claim that it introduces reasonable measures to protect the country against terrorists. The act was amended and renewed in 2006, and the ability to collect and analyze domestic intelligence remained part of the law. Provisions to allow roving wiretaps, increased power to seize evidence, and increased wiretaps were approved in 2011.

September 11 changed the way America views terrorism. The wars in Afghanistan and Iraq claimed the lives of thousands, and massive counterterrorist measures were taken at home. The **USA PATRIOT Act** of 2001, which made significant changes in the structure of federal law enforcement, was passed within weeks of the September attacks. The act was renewed in 2006, after both the Senate and the House introduced several provisions curbing governmental authority. In 2004, the 9/11 Commission issued a report calling for a complete overhaul of the U.S. intelligence system; in response, congress passed the Intelligence Reform and Terrorism Prevention Act in December 2004. The National Criminal Intelligence Sharing Plan (NCISP) set standards for a new system of domestic intelligence gathering and analysis. All of these activities generated tremendous controversy, and the debates took place as America waged foreign wars against an enemy that projected no central front. As America's internal debates continued, terrorist events around the world became deadlier.

The Bush administration faced a barrage of criticism for many of its policies in the wake of 9/11. People expressed concerns over eavesdropping on telephone calls, the collection of domestic intelligence, the treatment of terrorist suspects, and the rendition of suspected terrorists to countries that openly used torture. One of the most contentious issues dealt with the detention of suspected terrorists. The CIA maintained detention facilities in various foreign countries, military forces ran detention centers in Iraq and Afghanistan, and hundreds of people were detained without warrant. The detention facility at Guantánamo Bay, Cuba, became a lightning rod for domestic and international criticism of Bush policies.

military tribunals: Military courts that try combatants outside the civilian court system. Trials take place in front of a board of military officers operating under military law.

While running for president, Barack Obama promised to put a stop to these practices, but his administration continued many of them. Attorney General Eric Holder tried to move a set of trials from **military tribunals** in Guantánamo Bay to New York City, only to back away from efforts to do so. The same thing happened when President Obama sought to close the Cuban detention center. Ironically, the president, who campaigned on promises to move away from Bush's security policies, allowed military tribunals to begin trying cases in 2012. In all fairness to both Presidents Bush and Obama, it is much easier to talk about complexity than it is to manage complex situations.

Security and Civil Liberties Trade-Offs

There are always trade-offs related to security. This applies to social structures and to physical aspects of security. It is possible to use force to create a social structure in which people can have limited fear of crime and illegal violence. The underside is that people in such a society must often fear the powers of the civil government. Crime can be reduced through aggressive apprehension and punishment of criminals, but when the government goes beyond legal norms, people no longer fear only the criminals—they also fear the government that is supposed to protect their rights (Giroux, 2002).

This is both an ancient and a modern principle. When the Athenians were threatened with invasion, they were often willing to suspend the rules of democracy in favor of protection. They shifted from the structure of open democracy to grant more authoritarian power to leaders in times of crisis, and the power would last until the threat abated (Finley, 1983, pp. 24–25). The Romans would follow a similar course in their republic, creating a dictatorship in times of war (Mackay, 2004, pp. 27–28). During the American Civil War, Abraham Lincoln imprisoned opponents without informing them of charges, suspending the writ of habeas corpus (Goodwin, 2005, pp. 354–355). In times of emergencies, some societies have been willing to sacrifice personal liberty in the name of security.

The question of the suspension of liberty lies at the root of arguments concerning homeland security. Proponents at one end of the spectrum argue that the open nature of democratic societies leaves the social structure open to attack. They argue that some limitation on civil liberties is necessary to preserve the greater good. On the other end of the spectrum, people argue that limiting civil liberties is far more dangerous than the more limited threats posed by terrorism. Like Donald Black (2004), they argue that when governments suppress freedom in the name of counterterrorism, their actions are more violent than the terrorists they are trying to stop. There are many differing positions between these two extremes, and the debate complicates any approach to homeland security (Wise and Nadar, 2002).

Because the dispute is unresolvable, a metaphor might be helpful. More than a century ago, tremendous debates raged in the navies of Japan, Europe, and the United States about the construction of battleships. The problem focused on three critical aspects of battleships: speed, armor, and firepower. Any time engineers increased one of the three, they had to decrease the other two. For example, one set of nations decided to develop fast battle cruisers before World War I. This meant that they had to reduce the number and caliber of big guns on the ships as well as the armor plating. Guns and armor added weight and slowed the cruisers. The battleship debate was a zero-sum game.

The debate about homeland security involves similar factors. Decreasing civil liberties limits individual freedom and increases governmental power. It may increase protection from terrorism, but it also increases citizen vulnerability to the abuse of governmental power. Just as it was impossible to build a battleship that had the heaviest guns, the thickest armored protection, and the fastest speed in any navy, so it is impossible to construct a counterterrorist system that ensures complete protection, allows for maximum civil liberties, and protects unrestricted freedom of movement. Issues need to be balanced, and the debate centers on the areas that should be emphasized.

When homeland security is being discussed, the topic of individual rights usually becomes part of the discussion. To engage in a struggle against terrorism, Americans must examine themselves and honestly select a course of action that they will accept. It cannot be imposed by legislative action, military force, or police power. It cannot be defined by self-appointed civil rights guardians. Attorneys and courts are fond of claiming this area for their exclusive jurisdiction, but the issue extends far beyond judicial logic. If Americans want to secure the homeland, they need to engage in a thorough self-examination and decide what they are willing to sacrifice and how they will maintain the most cherished aspects of social freedom (Cole and Dempsey, 2002, pp. 11–12).

civil liberties: Individual rights granted to citizens under the U.S. Constitution.

Bill of Rights: The first 10 amendments to the U.S. Constitution.

Human Rights and Civil Liberties

Civil liberties refers to the individual freedoms people have under a system of law. The Constitution is the law of the land in the United States. It establishes procedures for government and provides for civil liberties. The first 10 amendments, which are known as the **Bill of Rights**, further limit the power of government. Americans enjoy

---

EXPANDING THE CONCEPT

The UN Universal Declaration of Human Rights

In 1948, the United Nations adopted the Universal Declaration of Human Rights. The provisions include the following:

- All human beings are born free and equal in dignity and rights. They are endowed with reason and conscience and should act toward one another in a spirit of brotherhood.
- Everyone is entitled to all the rights and freedoms in the Declaration; and no distinction shall be made on the basis of the racial, religious, political, jurisdictional or international status of the country or territory to which a person belongs.
- Everyone has the right to life, liberty, and security of person.
- No one shall be held in slavery or servitude; slavery and the slave trade shall be prohibited in all their forms.
- No one shall be subjected to torture or to cruel, inhuman, or degrading treatment or punishment.
- Everyone has the right to recognition everywhere as a person before the law.
- All are equal before the law and are entitled without any discrimination to equal protection of the law.
- Everyone has the right to a legal remedy if human rights are violated.
- No one shall be subjected to arbitrary arrest, detention, or exile.
- Everyone is entitled in full equality to a fair and public trial.
- Every defendant has the right to be presumed innocent until proved guilty according to law in a public trial.
- No one shall be subjected to arbitrary interference with his privacy, family, home, or correspondence. Everyone has the right to the protection of the law against such interference or attacks.
- Everyone has the right to freedom of movement, and the right to leave any country, including his own, and to return to his country.
- Everyone has the right to seek political asylum from persecution.
- No one shall be arbitrarily deprived of his nationality nor denied the right to change his nationality.
- Men and women of full age have the right to marry and to found a family. Marriage shall be entered into only with the free will and consent of the spouses.
- Everyone has the right to own property and no one shall be arbitrarily deprived of his property.
- Everyone has the right to freedom of thought, conscience, and religion.
- Everyone has the right to freedom of opinion and expression.
- Everyone has the right to freedom of peaceful assembly and association.
- Everyone has the right to take part in the government of his country, directly or through freely chosen representatives. The will of the people shall be the basis of the authority of government.

Source: United Nations, http://www.un.org/Overview/rights.html

particular freedoms under the Constitution, and the government cannot take these freedoms away. This is civil liberty.

Most people believe that all humans are entitled to basic rights. They should not be enslaved, exploited, or subjected to arbitrary abuse such as genocide or unwarranted punishment. These are known as human rights, and they have been articulated by many governments as well as the United Nations (1948). **Human rights** focus on the legal right to exist in a society in which people are free from arbitrary coercion. People have the right to be free, choose their religion, and have a fair trial (see the section later in this chapter titled "Expanding the Concept: The UN Universal Declaration of Human Rights").

human rights: The basic entitlements and protections that should be given to every person.

Human rights intersect with terrorism and homeland security in two controversial areas. First, terrorist attacks on innocent civilians violate the human right of people to exist apart from political violence against innocent people. Second, governments must respect the human rights of their opponents. Ideally, governments are not allowed to act outside the bounds of human decency and law when countering terrorists. Both positions create political and legal firestorms. Terrorists justify murders by stating that civilians are never innocent because they act within the governmental system (Pew Foundation, 2005). Governments frequently justify inhumane actions against terrorists by stating that they have sacrificed the right to humane treatment because they use terrorism (Porteous, 2006).

Debates about terrorism, governmental authority, and homeland security almost always touch on these issues. Those who favor strong security at any cost tend to overlook human rights abuses and deemphasize civil liberties. Those who favor civil liberties tend to deemphasize security while emphasizing human rights. Many different positions between these extremes argue that the rule of law serves to mediate between these positions.

✓ Self-Check

> How do security and liberty interact with one another?
> Is it possible to increase security and preserve civil rights?
> What is the difference between civil rights and human rights?

Domestic Intelligence Law

Federal counterterrorist laws were toughened after the 1995 Oklahoma City bombing. President William Clinton supported legislation to increase the government's power to limit civil liberties in the face of terrorism. Many civil libertarians criticized Clinton and Congress for these actions. President George W. Bush supported similar legislation in 2001 and again in 2005. After heated debate, the president and Congress reached a compromise in 2006; the provisions of the new law stayed intact. President Obama continued the same policies after taking office in 2009, and he supported continuing the law's provisions in May 2011. Congress had to renew the law again in 2015 if its provisions were to remain intact. Every time surveillance laws have been presented or adopted, they have been at the center of passionate debates.

The USA PATRIOT Acts of 2001, 2005, 2006, 2011, and 2015

In the weeks following 9/11, the Bush administration sponsored legislation that contained increased responsibilities for criminal justice and other agencies. The USA PATRIOT Act of 2001, officially called Uniting and Strengthening America by

Providing Appropriate Tools to Gather and Obstruct Terrorism (USA PATRIOT) Act, had 10 sections, or titles, outlining new powers for governmental operations (for a summary, see Doyle, 2002; U.S. Department of Justice, 2013). Title I was designed to enhance domestic security. It created funding for counterterrorist activities, expanded technical support for the FBI, increased electronic intelligence-gathering research, and defined presidential authority in response to terrorism. This section of the law also prohibited discrimination against Arabs and Muslims.

Some of the most controversial aspects of the PATRIOT Act appeared in Title II, which aimed to improve the government's ability to gather electronic evidence. In other words, it gave police officials expanded authority to monitor communications. It also allowed intelligence and federal law enforcement agencies to share noncriminal information with each other. In addition, it forced private corporations to share records and data with federal law enforcement agencies during investigations and allowed the FBI to seize material when it believed national security was jeopardized. Title II also contained a sunset clause that would automatically end the provisions of the PATRIOT Act unless it was renewed.

Titles III and V also increased law enforcement power. These sections of the PATRIOT Act allowed government investigators to seize financial records. They also provided for expanded powers to investigate money laundering and required additional transaction reports from financial institutions. Educational institutions were required to release records on foreign students.

Two other powerful investigative tools in the PATRIOT Act were special courts for classified warrants and FBI demands for information. The Foreign Intelligence Surveillance Act of 1978 (FISA) established special courts to gather evidence against suspected spies. The PATRIOT Act expanded the power of **FISA courts** to secretly review evidence and empower searches in terrorism investigations. The PATRIOT Act also created an FBI-generated **National Security Letter** (NSL). The FBI could now demand information from many public and private institutions simply by asking for it in an NSL.

Supporters of the PATRIOT Act believed that it increased federal law enforcement's ability to respond to terrorism and that it created an intelligence conduit to improve communication among state, local, and federal police agencies (U.S. Department of Justice, 2013). Supporters believed counterterrorism was strengthened by combining law enforcement and national defense intelligence. Opponents of the law argued that it went too far in threatening civil liberties and expanding police powers. Critics were concerned about sharing noncriminal intelligence during criminal investigations. One of the more pressing concerns centered on FISA courts and National Security Letters (ACLU, 2015b).

FISA courts: Review federal requests for electronic evidence gathering and search warrants without public review.

National Security Letter: A mandatory request from the FBI for public and private records. The recipient is not allowed to discuss the contents of an NSL outside FBI interviews.

Debate and the 2006 Law

The 2001 PATRIOT Act was scheduled for renewal in 2005. Although the House of Representatives voted to renew the law in December, some members of the Senate believed that the 2001 law had been passed too quickly. They argued that many of the provisions expanded governmental authority too far. In addition, they were leery about making some of the intelligence-gathering practices permanent. Although many Republicans wanted to pass the extension of the PATRIOT Act before the 2006 elections, Democratic leaders in the Senate urged caution. Some in the president's own party had reservations about some of the PATRIOT Act's provisions (Holland, 2005).

How the PATRIOT Act had been used in prior years led to these reservations. The Bush administration contended that law enforcement agencies had employed the provisions carefully, using them only to stop terrorist attacks. In testimony before

Congress, officials from the Justice Department assured the nation that no agency had overstepped its bounds. Critics did not agree. They accused the government of having selectively released information and of having hidden unfavorable reports. They also said that agencies were classifying public documents in an effort to hide governmental activities. They were especially critical of "sneak and peek" provisions that allowed the government to search for information without informing the person who was being investigated (Regan, 2004).

Several lawmakers, both Republican and Democratic, were concerned about provisions for gathering secret information and the original PATRIOT Act stipulations denying legal representation in terrorism investigations. In the spring of 2006, the White House and Congress reached a compromise on some of the controversial articles of the PATRIOT Act, and new provisions were approved. Under the renewed act, when the government sought information, the request could be challenged in court. When information was requested in a terrorist investigation, suspects and others involved were allowed talk about it. Suspects were also allowed to seek counsel from an attorney.

Some of the less controversial articles were also renewed in 2006. The government had the right to intercept communications. Criminal intelligence could be given to agencies charged with national security, and the national security community could openly communicate with the law enforcement community. The renewed law also extended the time suspects could be kept under surveillance and allowed the government to seize electronic or other evidence with a warrant. The 2006 law required Internet and email providers to hand over records. Finally, the renewed law expanded the power of federal law enforcement agencies to collect national security intelligence (Associated Press, 2006).

Extending Provisions in 2011

Much of the power of the PATRIOT Act was preserved in 2011 when the Department of Justice argued for the continuation of three key provisions. First, the attorney general asked for permission to continue **roving wiretaps**. These are used when a surveillance target is using disposable phones or intermittent Internet connections. Law enforcement officials may quickly monitor all new communications without returning to a court to obtain a new search warrant.

The second provision dealt with evidence. The PATRIOT Act gave law enforcement officials expanded powers to gather evidence in national security cases. When making an arrest or serving a search warrant, officers could collect all items that might be related to the cases. For example, if a person were taken into custody in a terrorism case, investigators might want to seize all of the electronic equipment in the suspect's home. The 2011 changes allowed them to do so.

The final aspect of the law preserved by the Obama administration in 2011 dealt with eavesdropping. The government gained the right to conduct wiretaps of noncitizens suspected of acts that threaten national security (*The New York Times*, 2012). Leading Democrats in the Senate complained about the president's support for these three provisions, claiming that there were no efforts to ensure that civil liberties would be protected. The attorney general disagreed (D. Taylor, 2011).

roving wiretaps: A method of quickly intercepting disposable phone or Internet traffic. A roving wiretap allows law enforcement officers to monitor subjects when they change communication devices.

Controversy Continued

As the PATRIOT Act was set to expire in May 2015 the debates continued. The overriding concern focused on agencies collecting information on Americans who were not criminal suspects. Bulk data collection from telephone records, financial institutions, and the Internet worried some lawmakers and many civil libertarians. Roaming wire-taps and individual surveillance also caused consternation. In addition, many critics believed the National Security Agency (NSA)and other government organizations simply overlooked civil liberties protections written into the PATRIOT Act (Hammond, 2013).

According to a *New York Times* report, the NSA, an organization dealing with communications intelligence, received secret orders to begin collecting data from millions of phone calls and Internet communications in October 2001 (Savage, 2015). The NSA began gathering bulk data and running it through computer programs to catch key words and phrases that might be associated with terrorism. Suspicious data were reviewed in detail. As word of these efforts began to be leaked to the public, the Bush administration received permission from the FISA court in 2006 to continue the program. In 2013, an NSA contractor fled the country and leaked information about the program, and at that point, the collection process was declassified.

The *New York Times* report states that several groups brought lawsuits to stop the program, but the Obama administration supported and continued it. Many terrorism analysts and the intelligence community believed that bulk data reviews produced useful intelligence and investigative leads. Civil libertarians were outraged. The American Civil Liberties Union (ACLU) was able to successfully challenge the practice in federal court, but the Obama administration asked the FISA court to rule on the matter. The FISA court overruled the federal court, and lawsuits continued.

Debate in 2015

Congressional debate about the renewal of the PATRIOT Act began again in 2015. Lobbyists were active. The ACLU (2015), one of the leading critics of the act, helped lead the attack against it. It stated that several government activities were unconstitutional, including:

1. Intelligence surveillance orders of unknown targets
2. Secret surveillance of noncitizens unassociated with terrorism
3. Mass surveillance of emails, phone calls, and Internet traffic
4. The sharing of private information with the CIA
5. Activists being labeled as terrorists
6. Seizure of property without a hearing

Writing an against the PATRIOT Act for the Electronic Frontier Foundation, Nadia Kayyali (2015) said that the government has adequate national security tools and that three key provisions—roving wiretaps, lone wolf surveillance, and bulk data collections—should be eliminated. Any vote favoring these provisions without a complete overall of the NSA would be unacceptable. NSA "spying," she continued, is unconstitutional. Revocation of the law should not be a partisan issue. Both parties and congressional bodies should join to eliminate it.

Researchers at the Heritage Foundation argued that terrorism has evolved as a major threat to national security (Carafano et al., 2015). Believing that Congress had reached an impasse, the Heritage Foundation favored modifying the law without weakening it. One method would involve folding FISA court rulings into the civil rights provisions contained in the PATRIOT Act. A second alternative would involve creating an impartial third party to hold data until the NSA could obtain a FISA warrant based on reasonable suspicion. A third method would be simply to allow the NSA to go directly to a FSA court with evidence and obtain a search warrant. Carafano and his colleagues pointed out that mega-data from electronic monitoring helped thwart 54 terrorist plots in 20 countries, including 13 planned attacks in the United States. Far from being abandoned, the act should be expanded and controlled by rule of law.

Despite claims by civil rights organizations, Americans seemed to favor retaining the NSA's powers. National Public Radio reported that the majority of Americans wanted the law renewed (Kurtzleben, 2015). The social scientists it interviewed found that support depended on age demographics. Younger people who had few childhood memories of 9/11 seemed to be more concerned with privacy than security. They wanted the NSA's activity to be curtailed. However, older people with vivid recollections of 9/11 were more likely to want to keep all the provisions of the PATRIOT Act.

The Senate began debating the issue in late spring of 2015. The ACLU and its allies lobbied for the elimination of provisions for roving wiretaps, surveillance of suspected lone wolves, and bulk data collections. The Heritage Foundation and fellow conservatives argued for the retention of these powers. The Republican Party split. Senator Rand Paul (R, KY) wanted to scrap the law, while Senators John McCain (R, AZ) and Lindsay Graham (R, SC) argued to keep every provision. Rand caused a procedural delay, and the provisions expired in June 2015.

The USA FREEDOM Act of 2015

The day after provisions in the USA PATRIOT Act expired, both the House and Senate began working on a new law, the Uniting and Strengthening America by Fulfilling Rights and Ensuring Effective Discipline over Monitoring Act of 2015, or the **USA FREEDOM Act of 2015** (for a comprehensive summary, see Council on Foreign Relations, 2015). Supporters believe that it represents major reforms that will ensure the protection of civil liberties. Critics renewed their past arguments, and the constitutional debate continues.

The USA FREEDOM Act bars the bulk collection of Americans' telephone records and Internet data, but implementation has been delayed to allow the intelligence community time to develop new plans. It also limits the government's ability to collect data. Instead of allowing vast dragnets of all information, the FREEDOM Act requires agencies to ask for specific data. If law enforcement agents can demonstrate reasonable suspicion, they can collect limited electronic information on individuals believed to be associated with terrorism. The law restores governmental authority to conduct roving wiretaps and to engage in surveillance of suspected lone wolf terrorists.

FISA is also affected by the USA FREEDOM Act. Federal law enforcement agencies will face greater scrutiny from the FISA court. The new law gives organizations and private companies more authority to publically report FISA requests. Finally, the new law declassifies many FISA interpretations of the law and requires the FISA court to publish unclassified reports on the interpretations they cannot declassify.

USA FREEDOM Act of 2015: Law replacing many of the powers of the PATRIOT Act with greater scrutiny from the FISA court. It also bars the collection of mega-data from dragnet sweeps but allows the collection of specific data based on reasonable suspicion.

> > Why did Congress pass the USA PATRIOT Act so quickly after 9/11?
>
> ✓ Self-Check
>
> > What debates arose from efforts to renew the law?
>
> > How are the FREEDOM and PATRIOT Acts related?

Terrorism and the Constitution

The most controversial facet of counterterrorism laws deals with intelligence gathering and sharing. Many diverse groups across the spectrum of American politics, from constitutional conservatives to civil libertarian activists, worry that the law will encroach on civil freedoms. The American government was founded on the idea of civil liberties. This means that citizens are free from having their government infringe unreasonably on the freedoms guaranteed in the Constitution and the Bill of

Rights. Stated simply, increasing the ability of the government to collect information increases executive-branch power. Therefore, opponents of increased governmental power focus their criticism on the government's intelligence activities, or information gathering. Supporters of increased intelligence activities say that a nation cannot fight terrorism without gathering intelligence (for general comments on intelligence in U.S. law enforcement, see Carter, 2009).

Separation of Powers

When criminal justice and national security agencies gather information about organizations and people, they do so as an extension of the executive branch of government. Any effort to expand executive power will affect the other branches of government. The U.S. Constitution separates the powers of the three branches of government: executive, legislative, and judicial. This is known as the **separation of powers**. Elected bodies of lawmakers (the legislative branch) pass laws, courts (the judicial branch) rule on them, and law enforcement and correctional agencies (executive branch) enforce them. This separation of powers acts as a check and balance to the amount of power wielded by each branch of government (Perl, 1998; Best, 2001; Cole and Dempsey, 2002, pp. 15–16; Carter, 2009, pp. 8–17).

separation of powers: The distribution of power among the executive, legislative, and judicial branches of government. When powers are separated, there is a balance among the powers. No one branch can control the government.

Terrorism and the Bill of Rights

A quick overview of constitutional issues illustrates points where homeland security policies and the Constitution intersect. The main body of the Constitution separates powers and prescribes duties for each branch of government. Powers not explicitly

---

Constitutional Amendments That Are Important to Law Enforcement

First Amendment: Congress shall make no law respecting an establishment of religion, or prohibiting the free exercise thereof; or abridging the freedom of speech, or of the press; or the right of the people peaceably to assemble, and to petition the government for a redress of grievances.

Fourth Amendment: The right of the people to be secure in their persons, houses, papers, and effects, against unreasonable searches and seizures, shall not be violated, and no Warrants shall issue, but upon probable cause, supported by Oath or affirmation, and particularly describing the place to be searched, and the persons or things to be seized.

Fifth Amendment: No person shall be held to answer for a capital, or otherwise infamous crime, unless on a presentment or indictment of a Grand Jury, except in cases arising in the land or naval forces, or in the Militia, when in actual service in time of War or public danger; nor shall any person be subject for the same offence to be twice put in jeopardy of life or limb; nor shall be compelled in any criminal case to be a witness against himself, nor be deprived of life, liberty, or property, without due process of law; nor shall private property be taken for public use, without just compensation.

Sixth Amendment: In all criminal prosecutions, the accused shall enjoy the right to a speedy and public trial, by an impartial jury of the State and district wherein the crime shall have been committed, which district shall have been previously ascertained by law, and to be informed of the nature and cause of the accusation; to be confronted with the witnesses against him; to have compulsory process for obtaining witnesses in his favor, and to have the Assistance of Counsel for his defence.

given to the federal government go to the states. The Bill of Rights also comes into play by protecting free speech and the right to assemble (**First Amendment**), preventing the government from performing illegal search and seizure (**Fourth Amendment**), and preventing self-incrimination (**Fifth Amendment**). The **Sixth Amendment** helps protect these rights by ensuring that suspects have access to an attorney. Interpretations of the Constitution and its amendments have protected American liberties for more than two centuries.

The Constitution guides the United States in war and peace, and it allows certain actions in times of emergency—actions that would be prohibited if there were no emergency. This makes terrorism a constitutionally murky subject, a cloudy area that obscures the boundary separating war and peace, because many people disagree about the nature of terrorism. Many legal scholars argue that terrorism is not a continuing emergency (Cole and Dempsey, 2002, pp. 189–201). For example, America's enemies used terrorists trained in military-style camps to attack civilian targets on September 11. Logically, national security agencies, such as military forces and the CIA, try to prevent attacks, whether they are engaged in a war or not. Criminal justice agencies do not take actions for war—they protect individual rights; local, state, and federal courts are not charged with national defense (see del Carmen, 1991, pp. 73–176). Controversy arises when criminal justice systems and the defense establishment begin to blend their activities.

Fear of Law Enforcement Power

David Cole and James Dempsey (2002) sent out a warning after the 1996 counterterrorist law took effect in the wake of the 1995 Oklahoma City bombing. Stated simply, they feared that federal law enforcement's power was growing too strong in a wave of national hysteria. Their thesis is that counterterrorist legislation empowers law enforcement agencies to enforce political law. By contrast, terrorists must violate criminal laws to practice terrorism. Therefore, Cole and Dempsey argue, it is best to keep the police out of politics and focused on criminal violations. For example, police agencies should not be allowed to interfere with citizens engaged in political associations, even when they are unpopular. (Cole and Dempsey would probably say *especially* when they are unpopular.) Law enforcement has the right to intervene in a citizen's affairs when officers reasonably suspect that a crime has been committed or if a person may be involved in criminal activity. If terrorists are prosecuted under criminal law, the Constitution will be preserved.

Cole and Dempsey point to four cases that illustrate their fears. First, in the late 1960s and early 1970s, the FBI trampled the rights of suspects and citizens through COINTELPRO, its counterintelligence program. Second, from 1981 to 1990, the FBI overreacted against U.S. citizens who expressed sympathy for revolutionaries in El Salvador. The FBI even designated friends of activists to be "guilty by association." Third, in the 1990s, Muslims and Palestinians were targeted by investigations, even though there were no reasonable suspicions that they were involved in a crime. Finally, during the 1990s, political investigations of radical environmentalists and others expanded.

Citing a group of law professors that petitioned Congress to limit political investigations, Cole and Dempsey argue that law enforcement should gather intelligence only when there is reason to suspect criminal activity. They worry that counterterrorist legislation frequently gives the police power to regulate political activity. The real danger is not using reasonable efforts to fight terrorism, they say. There are certain instances when the intelligence community should share information with the criminal

First Amendment: Guarantees the rights to speech, assembly, religion, press, and petitioning the government.

Fourth Amendment: Particularly applicable to law enforcement and homeland security, it limits government search and seizure, including the elements of arrest.

Fifth Amendment: Protects against arbitrary arrest, being tried more than once for the same crime, and self-incrimination. It also guarantees due process.

Sixth Amendment: Guarantees the right to an attorney and a speedy public trial by jury in the jurisdiction where the alleged crime occurred. The amendment also requires that a suspect be informed of any changes justice community. For example, when Osama bin Laden was charged in bombing U.S. embassies in Dar es Salaam and Nairobi, it would have been appropriate for the FBI and CIA to share information. Cole and Dempsey worry that Congress has given these agencies and others too much power to share intelligence without judicial review.

Their argument illustrates the passions involved in counterterrorism efforts. The Cole–Dempsey thesis is endorsed by a host of jurists, civil rights organizations, legal scholars, and die-hard conservatives who support many of the Bush administration's other efforts. There is even support for their position inside law enforcement, especially within the FBI.

Increased Executive Powers

The issues around executive power form the crux of the debate about civil rights and security, and they are no different from the examples cited earlier from ancient Greece and Rome and the American Civil War. Some societies give presidents, prime ministers, and other leaders increased power when a nation is threatened. Because leaders sometimes abuse those powers, civil libertarians are almost always suspicious of additional authority. It is the primary issue involved in discussions about the Constitution, the role of executive authority, and the subsequent actions of law enforcement agencies.

Several constitutional scholars have examined the issue of increasing executive powers to combat terrorism. Lewis Katz (2001) believed in limited government before September 11, but he rethought his position in the wake of the attacks. He finds an analogy in drug enforcement. America launched its "war on drugs" and soon discovered that it could not thwart drug traffickers under constitutional rules of evidence. As a result, police power has been growing since 1971, Katz argues, and citizen protection under the Fourth Amendment has been decreasing.

reasonableness: Assessment of the actions an average person would take when confronted with certain circumstances. This is a Fourth Amendment doctrine.

Leery of government, Katz says that the real test of the Fourth Amendment is **reasonableness**. In normal times, police officers can be held to a higher standard of behavior than in times of emergency. September 11 constituted an emergency. It was not unreasonable to interview Middle Eastern immigrants, Katz concludes, nor was it unreasonable to increase electronic surveillance powers. Although a longtime opponent of a national identification system, Katz now says that such a system would not be unconstitutional, provided citizens were not ordered to produce identification without reasonable suspicion. Actions taken to prevent another September 11, he argues, do not violate the Fourth Amendment when they are reasonable.

Katz does believe that some governmental actions are unreasonable. Eavesdropping on attorney–client conversations, for example, violates the Sixth Amendment, which protects a suspect's right to counsel. Military tribunals deny the presumption of innocence. He argues that we cannot sacrifice the very liberties that we are fighting to preserve. Katz's argument indicates that the balance of powers is a dynamic system, vacillating according to circumstances. In other words, there is no blanket policy of reasonableness, and care must be taken to balance security with civil liberties.

Fourteenth Amendment: Stipulates that a person cannot be deprived of freedom or property by the government unless the government follows all the procedures demanded for legal prosecution.

Sherry Colb (2001) of the Rutgers University School of Law also applies a doctrine of reasonableness. Examining the issue of racial profiling (targeting specific groups of people on the basis of race, ethnicity, religion, or other social factors), Colb concedes that police in America are facing a new enemy. Racial profiling has not helped the police control drugs, she argues, and it violates the due process clause of the **Fourteenth Amendment**. Yet, the scope of September 11 calls into question previous assumptions about profiling. As police agencies assemble profiles of terrorists, one of the characteristics may be ethnicity.

Colb believes that any profiling system, including one with ethnicity as a factor, will yield many more investigative inquiries than apprehensions. The reason is that there are only a small number of terrorists in any group, regardless of their profile, that is, the population of people matching the profile is greater than the population of terrorists in the profile group. By the same token, a number of terrorists may fall within a particular ethnic group, and the urgency of a situation such as September 11 may require action. If a terrorist profile is developed and includes race as one of the characteristics, Colb suggests that some opponents of ethnic profiling may find that they endorse it in the case of counterterrorism efforts.

New guidelines, executive orders, and military tribunals have created strange twists in the criminal justice system. Reporter Katherine Seelye (2002) examined the summer of 2002, when two foreign-born terrorist suspects were arrested on the basis of probable cause and were sent to trial. At the same time, two U.S. citizens, Yaser Esam Hamdi and Jose Padilla, were held by military force without representation. Hamdi was fighting for al Qaeda when he was captured in Afghanistan in November 2001; Padilla was arrested on May 8, 2002, for his alleged involvement in a plot to detonate a dirty bomb in the United States. Hamdi and Padilla, both of whom would have been criminally charged before September 11, were detained much like prisoners of war, whereas two alleged terrorists arrested on U.S. soil were afforded the rights of criminal suspects. Hamdi was released in September 2004.

Ruth Wedgwood (2002), a former federal prosecutor who turned to teaching law, offers an explanation of the irony of Americans being detained militarily and foreigners being held under civilian arrest. She says that al Qaeda attacked civilian targets, gaining an advantage in the U.S. criminal justice system. Al Qaeda, Wedgwood says, has learned that it is best to recruit U.S. citizens for operations because citizens are not subject to arbitrary arrest. Pointing to Jose Padilla, Wedgwood states that his arrest represents a conundrum between reconciling public safety and the law. The issues surface in the difference between intelligence operations and law enforcement administration. In short, she says, going to trial means exposing intelligence sources for the sake of a criminal conviction.

Wedgwood presents the logic of the two situations. Common sense dictates that the detention of terrorists does not follow the pattern of criminal arrests. Terrorists are detained because no writ, no law, and no court order will stop them from attacking. They must be physically restrained, Wedgwood says. The purpose of detention, she argues, is not to engage in excessive punishment but to keep terrorists from returning to society. She admits that the situation presents a public dilemma for a nation under the rule of law.

Wedgwood argues that indefinite detention by executive order is not the most suitable alternative. Terrorists could be given a military hearing to determine whether they continue to represent a threat. A panel of judges might rule on the danger of releasing suspected terrorists from custody. The Constitution is not a suicide pact, she says, citing a famous court decision. Common sense demands a reasonable solution to the apparent dichotomy between freedom and security.

E. V. Konotorovich (2002) is not as concerned about executive orders as Wedgwood is. The stakes are so high, he argues, that the United States must make all reasonable efforts to stop the next attack. Torture is out of the question in this country, but drugs are a viable alternative. Officials are allowed to do body-cavity searches for contraband being smuggled into prisons, Konotorovich argues, and the September 11 attacks make abhorrence of such searches pale in the face of massive terrorism. Drugs should not be used for prosecution, he says, but they can be used to gain information. The threat is real, and legal arguments against obtaining information are an illusion. Americans captured by al Qaeda have been quickly executed. Konotorovich believes that Americans must take decisive actions against such terrorists.

Executive Power and the Courts

The courts frequently limit presidential power through interpretations of the law. For example, one of the first issues related to executive power and 9/11 involved the detention of enemy combatants at Guantánamo Bay, Cuba. The government contended that it could try the defendants in special military tribunals, apart from normal criminal prosecutions and military law. Judges were not swayed by this argument.

Both civilian and military courts, using similar language, handed down decisions blocking the government's efforts to establish special military courts that violate the civil rights established in the American legal system (Bravin, 2007). In the Hamdi case, discussed earlier in this chapter, courts noted that all defendants were entitled to contest the basis of their arrests and this right applied to the suspect. To ensure that an arrest is justified by probable cause, the government cannot hold a person without a hearing.

There are several other cases in which courts have limited executive power. The U.S. Supreme Court ruled that the detainees at Guantánamo could contest the charges against them. In 2006, the courts ordered the government to transfer Jose Padilla, the American originally accused of conspiring to use a dirty bomb, from the military to the civilian criminal court system, where he was convicted of criminal conspiracy in 2007. Later in 2006, the Supreme Court declared that the military tribunal system established for enemy combatants was illegal. In 2007, a military court in Guantánamo dismissed cases against two defendants at Guantánamo Bay on the basis of the earlier Supreme Court decision (Bravin, 2007).

President Obama issued an executive order closing the Guantánamo facility shortly after taking office in 2009. During the summer, former attorney general Eric Holder announced plans to charge some of the leading suspects in the 9/11 plot under federal criminal law. He moved to have the case brought to New York City. Administration officials searched the country for a new detention facility in an effort to move the detainees out of Guantánamo. Both actions met a firestorm of controversy, and the

---

EXPANDING THE CONCEPT

Court Reversals

Despite attempts to increase executive authority related to counterterrorism efforts, several court decisions have reversed White House policies. These include the following:

June 2004: Two decisions that allow enemy combatants the right to contest their arrests

April 2006: A decision that prevents U.S. citizens arrested in the United States from being tried outside the criminal court system

June 2006: The military tribunal system established at Guantánamo is declared illegal because it did not have congressional approval

June 2007: A military tribunal dismisses charges against two enemy combatants based on the June 2006 Supreme Court decision

Source: Bravin, 2007

government backed away from holding the criminal trials in New York City. Speaking on National Public Radio in October 2009 (NPR, 2009), Holder said the January 2010 deadline for closing Guantánamo would be tough to meet but that it would be done. He also promised that the decision on criminal trials would be made within a month. The government achieved neither objective.

Court decisions and executive power remain an unsettled issue. The United States has not been involved in this type of conflict before. Most analysts think that terrorism should be handled within the bounds of criminal law, but both the Bush and Obama administrations have failed to provide a clear path for a course of action. This has resulted in legal contradictions that have limited or threatened individual rights. American courts tend to intervene when this happens. If the executive branch of government will not make policy, the judicial branch will begin to do so.

> ✓ **Self-Check**
>
> > How is the Constitution related to counterterrorism?
> > Why do people in democracies resist concentrating power in law enforcement?
> > What effect do courts have on the power of the executive branch to confront terrorism?

Civil Liberties and Police Work

A *New York Times* investigation revealed that the FBI had been collecting a large amount of data for the NSA, including email and Internet searches from 9/11 to 2008 (Savage, 2015). A court order demanded that the FBI declassify records concerning the program (Clopper and Daughtry, 2015). Documents confirmed the findings of a 2007 FBI internal audit that had indicted agents were collecting and storing massive amounts of information (Solomon, 2007). New evidence also showed that the government was collecting bulk data from domestic and international telephone calls.

As part of the executive branch of government, the FBI stands at the forefront of counterterrorism. Information collected by state and local law enforcement agencies also represents an executive function. Whether civil liberties are protected or abused most frequently depends on the way police departments handle their responsibilities. This applies to federal agencies such as the FBI; the Bureau of Alcohol, Tobacco, and Firearms (ATF); and the Secret Service, but it is also applicable to state and local police departments.

Controversies in Law Enforcement

Effective counterterrorist policy is based on intelligence. The 9/11 Commission Report (2004, pp. 339–348) criticizes federal agencies for failing to recognize and share intelligence. The PATRIOT Act, which was enacted before the commission's findings were released, was designed to facilitate intelligence gathering and to ensure intelligence sharing. Although these efforts remain controversial on the federal level, sharing is logical because the federal government is constitutionally responsible for national defense. The government can make the argument that *any* federal agency can assist in this process. The problem comes when the federal government requests assistance from state and local governments. When the federal government asks state agencies to collect and forward national defense intelligence, many people take notice.

Any attempt to use state and local law enforcement in intelligence-gathering operations will have constitutional implications. The police may be used in homeland security, but there are strong and logical arguments against this and equally powerful arguments supporting it. Regardless, even when the executive branch proposes a course of action, police operations will be influenced by court decisions. Local law enforcement's role in homeland defense cannot be developed in a constitutional vacuum.

The criminal justice system collects *criminal* intelligence, not information regarding national security. It collects information when it has reasonable suspicion to believe people are involved in crimes. Although some people may argue about the type of criminal intelligence the police gather, no one questions their right to gather information about criminal activity (see Commission on Accreditation for Law Enforcement Agencies, 1990; Walker, 1992; Radelet and Carter, 2000; Carter, 2009, pp. 8–17).

The dilemma emerges because terrorism moves the police into a new intelligence realm. Criminals engage in crime for economic gain or psychological gratification. Terrorists are political actors using crime to strike their enemies. This causes terrorists to encounter the police, but not from the standpoint of traditional criminals. To gather counterterrorist intelligence, the police are forced to collect political information. If state and local law enforcement agencies are included in national defense, they will collect information having no relation to criminal investigations. No matter which position you might support, this is a dilemma for American democracy. Law enforcement agencies are not designed to collect political information (Schmitt, 2002).

Although lacking a defined role, the police in the United States have traditionally been associated with crime control. Within local communities, they respond to crime, prevent crime, and engage in social maintenance tasks such as traffic control. Although not a formal role, responding to and preventing crime has become the de facto purpose of American law enforcement. Local communities and states have empowered agencies to keep records to assist them in anticrime efforts, but many federal, state, and local laws, as well as civil rights groups' efforts, have imposed limits on the types of information the police may gather and retain. Any move to include the police in an intelligence-gathering system alters the expectations local communities have about law enforcement. Communities may decide to empower their police agencies to collect intelligence, but this means changing the focus of police work (see Manning, 1976).

Terrorism, both domestic and international, poses a variety of problems; Richard Best (2001) summarizes well the dilemma over the role for criminal justice. On the one hand, state and local law enforcement agencies are in a unique position to collect and analyze information from their communities. Corrections officials can perform the same role by both incarcerating terrorists and gaining information through jail-house intelligence. Law enforcement and correctional agencies can become the eyes and ears of domestic intelligence. On the other hand, when the criminal justice system has participated in national defense in the past, abuses have occurred. The primary question is whether criminal justice has a role in homeland security. Secondary questions are: Do criminal justice agencies want to assume this role? and Does the public they serve want them to assume it? There are no easy answers to these questions.

National Security and Crime

Among the controversies surrounding counterterrorism law is the role of the criminal justice system, especially law enforcement. The debate comes to a head when the role of intelligence is discussed. There are two general schools of thought about the role of the police in intelligence gathering. One position can be summarized as "eyes and ears." Advocates of this position believe that state and local law enforcement should be used as extensions of, or the eyes and ears of, America's intelligence agencies. They believe the police should collect information and forward it to the appropriate intelligence unit. Extreme proponents of this position would use special police units to collect information beyond potential evidence to be used in criminal investigations. The purpose of such units would be to monitor the activities of political groups that might engage in violence.

Another way of thinking can be called traditional crime response and prevention. Supporters of this perspective fear that police intelligence-gathering activities will interfere with the traditional police missions of fighting crime and providing a social service. They believe that other agencies should gather intelligence. Some other people have a parallel view, fearing expanded police powers.

After September 11, the difference between these two positions became more than an academic debate. Local, state, and federal police agencies began to share information at an unprecedented level. State and local agencies expanded training activities in terrorism, and Attorney General Ashcroft ordered the FBI to create more Joint Terrorism Task Forces (JTTFs). The attorney general also used his prosecutors, the U.S. attorneys who represent the government in the federal court system, to create Anti-Terrorism Task Forces (ATTFs) in all the nation's U.S. attorneys' offices. The name was changed to Anti-Terrorist Assistance Coordinators (ATACs) in 2003. All these federal efforts were based on the assumption that local, state, and federal agencies would work together. The attorney general also called for a seamless interface between law enforcement and defense intelligence. The intelligence role in law enforcement is what frightens civil libertarians.

Intelligence, Networks, and Roles

All levels of law enforcement form nodes in a network opposed to terrorism. Although police agencies have a multitude of other functions, their primary roles in preventing terrorism involve information gathering and sharing, protecting citizens and property, and investigating criminal conspiracies (J. White, 2007). Collecting, analyzing, and storing criminal intelligence requires a criminal predicate. Under the Fourth Amendment, law enforcement personnel cannot collect intelligence without the standard of reasonable suspicion. As stated in federal guidelines (28 CFR Part 23), the police must have a suspicion that a crime is taking place or is about to take place before information can be gathered, analyzed, and stored. Information involved in national security may not meet this test. Law enforcement is not to assume the national security mission. In other words, police officers should continue their assigned role in law enforcement and legally share information (J. White, 2004b, pp. 73–74; Carter, 2009, pp. 5–18). (See the feature later in this chapter titled "Expanding the Concept: The War on Drugs as an Intelligence Model.")

Networks encourage the flow of information. Carter (2009, pp. 192–193) argues that when information is not shared, it loses its value. It is not enough to maintain community partnerships; agencies need to act in cooperation. Total criminal intelligence (TCI) involves sharing; indeed, TCI does not work unless agencies share criminal intelligence. Sharing information neither poses a threat to civil liberties nor reduces the effectiveness of partnerships. Shared information enhances crime prevention and decreases fear inside a community. It allows the intelligence function to operate effectively when it is accomplished within legal guidelines.

Danger to civil liberties appears when agencies inside a network either act illegally or forget their role. The growth of terrorism has thrown law enforcement into an arena traditionally reserved for national security, but police officers are neither intelligence agents nor soldiers. Confronting a terror network requires resources for a long-term struggle and a solidified national will. It does not and should not require extraconstitutional law enforcement actions. Stated more succinctly, the ideological Salafi jihadist network does not threaten American civil liberties, but an improper police response to it may (see Jenkins, 2006, pp. 169–177). Law enforcement's role in national defense is to continue efforts at community partnerships.

In testimony before the House Subcommittee on Homeland Security (C-Span, 2007), Brian Jenkins, Frank Cilluffo, and Salam al Marayati offered an interesting assessment of the role of community partnerships in preventing terrorism. Rather than militarizing the problem, they presented terrorism, especially the jihadist movement, as a social idea. It appeals to young people, especially confused and potentially violent young men. There are times when force must be used, but Jenkins, Cilluffo, and al Marayati equated terrorism to other social problems such as child abuse, illegal drug use, gangs, drunk driving, and family fights. Law enforcement agencies became involved in education, intervention, information gathering, and enforcement in each of these areas. As Jenkins said, they play their role without violating civil rights.

EXPANDING THE CONCEPT

The War on Drugs as an Intelligence Model

The war on drugs has produced a national system of police gathering and disseminating intelligence. Combined federal, state, and local law enforcement agencies operate in conjunction with each other to gather intelligence and conduct operations. Intelligence operations have an impact on civil liberties.

Proponents hail the intelligence system created for drug enforcement as a model of sharing resources and intelligence. They point to cooperation among agencies and investigative information-sharing systems as the answer to the intelligence problem. At the national level, drug intelligence reports are synthesized and disseminated to state and local agencies. On the surface, these multijurisdictional efforts seem to be an effective tool to counter drug traffickers and they do not threaten civil liberties.

Opponents have a different view. Many police administrators believe that the systems are not effective, and they refuse to participate in them. Other people outside law enforcement look at the intelligence network and claim that it is both a failure and an assault on the Fourth Amendment. Proponents of this position state that the war on drugs is ineffective, and civil liberties are the real losers in the process. Critics believe that trying to collect drug intelligence merely leads to labeling certain people or groups without making a dent in drug traffic, and it has militarized policing.

Terrorism represents a tactical change in conflict. Police work has not changed, nor has the police function. Deeper community relationships will enhance law enforcement's role in national security by preventing crime, reducing fear, solving problems, and increasing the flow of information. Police operating deeply in the community in the service role help provide for the common defense. All intelligence gathered by law enforcement agencies, with the exception of the National Security Division of the FBI, must have a criminal predicate. Drug intelligence centers may provide a model for counterterrorism, but critics maintain that the war metaphor leads to militarization.

Emerging Critiques in the Academic Community

Quite a few criminologists, behavioral scientists, and civil libertarians have begun to question the new emphasis on intelligence operations and the role of law enforcement in homeland security. Once again, this illustrates differences between the practice of law enforcement and the academic analysis of the field, and it is indicative of the split between practical and applied criminology. Practitioners tend to develop and/or analyze the processes of homeland security networks, intelligence systems, and partnerships (J. White, 2004a; Carter, 2008 and 2009; Johnson, 2007; Carter and Carter, 2009a and b; Straw, 2009). Although some practitioners are critical of the process (Taylor and Russell, 2012), there is a growing body of behavior literature questioning new intelligence structures. These studies go beyond the operational work of practitioners, and such views are important in the democratic control of intelligence.

Anthony Newkirk (2010) examines a controversial case involving the Maryland State Police to argue that the network of homeland security intelligence operations amounts to an assault on civil liberties. Troopers at a Maryland fusion center gathered data on a wide array of groups from 2005 to 2006. They were able to use a private software system to analyze data from the field. In addition, the system allowed the troopers to conduct data mining operations on their targets. The groups under examination included community activists, peace advocates, environmentalists, death penalty opponents, and advocates for immigrants. These efforts resulted in a tremendous amount of data being placed in numerous files. Newkirk argues that these files were not appropriate because there was no criminal predicate for gathering, analyzing, storing, and sharing the information. One antiwar group had data about political activities stored under the heading "Terrorism: Anti-War Protest." Another entry for an environmental group was stored under "Terrorism: Environmental Extremism." The activities of peaceful political groups, however, are neither terrorism nor subject to government control.

Newkirk sees a number of problems with such intelligence. First, the surveillance itself is scandalous. It is not lawful to spy on American citizens engaged in political activity. Second, the fusion of information leads to a threat to civil liberties. Various levels of law enforcement shared this information with intelligence units and private corporations. This was conducted with murky lines of authority and a lack of public accountability. Finally, the government has no right to maintain security files on innocent people. The history of homeland security since 9/11, Newkirk argues, is a story of violations of liberty. The exacerbated information-sharing environment of the homeland security system, as evidenced in Maryland, is but one example of a system of abuse.

Torin Monahan (2009, 2010; Monahan and Palmer, 2009) of Vanderbilt University argues in a similar vein. Looking at operations during the Obama administration, Monahan uses case data to demonstrate that the homeland security system is too invasive. Rather than protecting civil rights, it threatens them. The primary vehicle behind the threat is the fusion center concept. Stated simply, Monahan claims that law enforcement officials break laws in fusion center operations. His studies suggest that officials illegally infiltrate political groups and collect data. Since many investigations are based on nationality or ethnicity, the resulting data helps to inject racism into the intelligence system. Worst of all, the network of fusion centers has no public accountability.

The intelligence system is justified under the concept of "predictive policing," that is, the analysis of data to prevent crimes before they occur. The world of fusion centers

field contacts: People encountered during normal patrol or investigative operations. Law enforcement officers frequently gather information from such people. The Nationwide SAR Initiative standardizes such information.

is akin to the movie *Minority Report*, a futuristic story of a police unit that arrests and detains potential criminals prior to criminal activity. The only protection from such abuses, according to Monahan, is to introduce democratic accountability.

Suspicious Activity Reporting (SAR), a Department of Justice program designed to systematically analyze information gleaned from law enforcement **field contacts**, is another issue bothering some social scientists. Discussed more fully in the next chapter, the Nationwide SAR Initiative standardizes the manner in which law enforcement information is gathered and stored. Civil rights advocates believe that information should not be gathered and stored based on suspicion alone. In fact, under federal law, such information must be destroyed unless the government can prove that it is directly related a criminal activity. Under terrorism rules, however, information can be stored under the auspices of national security. Kenneth Farrall (2011), of New York University, says this is an affront to personal privacy.

Despite such emerging criticism, there are operators within the homeland security system who are keenly aware of civil rights, privacy issues, and civil liberties. Writing for *Security Management*, Joseph Straw (2009) admits that the tremendous amount of information gathered by the national network of fusion centers could expose innocent citizens to unfair scrutiny. This is why policy guidelines are crucial. They must reflect the law and be rigorously enforced. Ron Brooks (2011), the director of a fusion center in northern California, agrees. Policy guidelines must be enforced and coordinated on a national basis. If power is abused, the fusion center concept, along with security, will be threatened. David and Jeremy Carter (2009) argue that enforceable standards can be used to protect civil liberties.

There is no easy answer to this problem. Technology allows small groups of people to inflict tremendous numbers of casualties, but it can also be used to collect and analyze the information necessary to prevent such destruction. The balance between security and liberty is precarious and will remain so.

Self-Check

> Why must civil libertarians police actions?

> How might community partnerships impact civil liberties?

> What concerns do some academics analysts have about criminal intelligence systems?

Emphasizing the Points

Security systems limit freedom, and they must be regulated. Homeland security involves a constant balancing of safety needs and civil liberties. This is the reason terrorism law and intelligence-gathering legislation have been so controversial. Law enforcement, intelligence, and security interests argue for safety measures while civil libertarians emphasize personal freedom and privacy. Although the USA PATRIOT Act passed by an overwhelming congressional majority after 9/11, it raised concerns among civil libertarians. Debates continued when it was renewed in 2005, 2006, and 2011. Controversial practices expired in 2015 only to be replaced with newly legislated practices. The USA FREEDOM Act renewed most of the powers of the PATRIOT Act, with greater FISA oversight. The Constitution limits government power and will ultimately be involved in terrorism, law enforcement, and intelligence-gathering legislation. Executive power, including law enforcement, will remain limited in our American constitutional democracy.

SUMMARY OF CHAPTER OBJECTIVES

- Increased intelligence activities, homeland security measures, and using governmental power in preventing terrorism must be balanced with the protection of liberty. Civil liberties are diminished when security measures are adopted.
- Civil liberties and human rights are closely related, but they have different meanings. Civil liberty refers to protection of individuals from governmental power. The basic freedoms and protections that should be granted to all people are known as human rights.
- The USA PATRIOT Act, first enacted in 2001, enhanced the gathering and sharing of intelligence. It was renewed in 2005, 2006, and 2011. Controversial provisions dealing with roving wiretaps, lone wolf surveillance, and mega-data dragnets expired in 2015.
- The USA FREEDOM Act was passed shortly after the PATRIOT Act's controversial provisions expired. It restored many law enforcement powers but placed them under greater FISA scrutiny. It also forbade future dragnet mega-data searches.
- The Constitution protects civil liberties and regulates the legal system. Governmental powers are separated so that no one branch gains excessive power. All legislation and executive actions related to terrorism are limited under the Constitution.
- The Bill of Rights directly applies to law enforcement actions. The First Amendment protects assembly and free speech. The Fourth Amendment applies to unreasonable search and seizure. The Fifth Amendment protects suspects from making statements against themselves. The Sixth Amendment guarantees the right to trial and protects defendants from double jeopardy.
- An increase in executive branch powers makes criminal justice more effective, but it threatens civil liberties.
- Recent court decisions have emphasized the importance of (1) balanced power among the branches of government and (2) maintenance of civil rights. Despite the recent increase of executive power, the courts still have the right to review national security laws.
- The Fourteenth Amendment impacts terrorism law. It requires law enforcement and homeland security forces to follow the due process of law before depriving any person of his or her liberty.
- Recent criminal justice scholarship has been taking a more critical view of enhanced governmental powers. It has been focused on the intelligence system and the role of fusion centers. Generally, many researchers feel that law enforcement agencies are collecting too much information beyond criminal intelligence.

LOOKING INTO THE FUTURE

Although it is both frightening and depressing, technological terrorism and massive destruction from a terrorist attack in the United States are possible. American law enforcement agencies, especially JTTFs, have become very good at preventing terrorist attacks, and the intelligence community has honed its skills at gathering and interpreting information. The problem is that security efforts must be successful every time they are employed, if they are to be successful at all. Terrorists only need to get lucky one time.

When the 9/11 terrorists struck, people in the United States literally panicked. National Guardsman with automatic weapons walked through airports, and military forces patrolled the streets of Washington, D.C. The Department of Justice sent thousands of agents to interview tens of thousands of Middle Eastern males simply because they were from the Middle East. Some citizens committed hate crimes against Muslim Americans, and many Muslims were harassed. Civil liberties suffered after 9/11, even before debates surfaced about the PATRIOT Act.

While 9/11 was horrific, imagine a scenario multiplied a hundred times over by some type of technological weapon. The government might well declare marshal law for an extended period of time. It might mandate actions outside the law against certain religious or ethnic groups. It would be comforting to think that this would not happen in America, but unfortunately, the government has authorized such actions in the past. If the country were to enter a nationwide panic, it could happen again. If the United States experiences a massive attack, it will test the constitutional will of Americans to maintain civil liberties.

Many terrorism analysts believe that technological terrorism is unlikely. Such attacks are complicated and require massive logistical systems. They also require sophisticated skill sets for the production of a WMD. Political terrorists who are attempting to win public support have very little incentive to cause massive casualties. Doing so violates the principles of selective terrorism. Eschatological terrorists in search of an apocalypse do not suffer from such limitations.

Civil liberties are difficult to protect, and they are fragile when emotions run high. If America suffers a massive terrorism attack, its moral resolve to maintain a government based on law and individual freedom will be tested.

KEY TERMS

USA PATRIOT Act, p. 354
Military tribunals, p. 354
Civil liberties, p. 356
Bill of Rights, p. 356
Human rights, p. 357

FISA court, p. 358
National Security Letter, p. 358
Roving wiretaps, p. 359
USA FREEDOM Act of 2015, p. 361

Separation of powers, p. 362
First Amendment, p. 363
Fourth Amendment, p. 363
Fifth Amendment, p. 363

Sixth Amendment, p. 363
Reasonableness, p. 364
Fourteenth Amendment, p. 364
Field contacts, p. 372

CHAPTER 16

Law Enforcement, Homeland Security, and the Future

DHS Headquarters, Washington, DC

I n 2014 and 2015, media reports of terrorist attacks in the United States emphasized the danger of lone wolf threats from individuals inspired by groups like ISIS. Other domestic extremist threats were usually not called terrorism. While the George W. Bush administration had used the phrase "war on terror" and spoke of domestic and international terrorists, officials in the Obama administration dropped any references to war as it related to terrorism. Federal officials were also ordered to refer to domestic terrorists as violent criminal extremists (VCE), probably to give the impression that the federal government would not brand political extremists as terrorists. Violent criminal extremism was more politically correct concept than domestic terrorism. Ironically, many terrorism analysts simply ignored the phraseology of both presidential administrations.

LEARNING OBJECTIVES

After reading this chapter, you should be able to:

▶ Describe the relationship between homeland security and community policing.

▶ Define the importance of community partnerships.

▶ Discuss the dangers of militarizing police work.

▶ Outline the methods law enforcement agencies use to obtain military equipment.

▶ List problems caused when tactical units are routinely used for drug enforcement efforts.

▶ Describe the importance of information sharing in the future.

▶ Outline methods for overcoming barriers to information sharing.

▶ Summarize potential problems caused by public–private partnerships.

▶ Describe probable directions in future terrorist attacks.

Threats from domestic and international terrorism increased during the first years of the twenty-first century, and they continued to morph into new forms. Al Qaeda's presence and influence waned as ISIS gained strength. American law enforcement had to stay prepared for organized or lone wolf international attacks and the possibility of an attack equal to or greater than 9/11. Domestically, terrorism saw an upsurge of violent sovereign citizen and racist movements. Law enforcement agencies also had to prepare for Americans inspired by foreign terrorist groups. Recent attacks in Europe also indicated the possibility of violence from citizens returning from foreign conflicts and individuals or small groups sent to engage in terrorism.

The future will probably bring innovative threats and technological attacks from domestic and international terrorists. Major groups will be forced to change continually; for if they remain static, they become vulnerable. The importance of cyber- and technological security will increase. Terrorism will probably become the dominant mode of conflict in the twenty-first century, which implies that all levels of American law enforcement should prepare for it just as they do for other emergencies.

Homeland Security and Community Policing

The U.S. Department of Justice describes community policing as "…a philosophy that promotes organizational strategies, which support the systematic use of partnerships and problem solving techniques, to proactively address the immediate conditions that give rise to public safety issues, such as crime, social disorder, and fear of crime" (DOJ, 2008). Championed by the late Robert Trojanowicz and Bonnie Bucqueroux (2009) of Michigan State University's School of Criminal Justice, community policing is based on extensive familiarization between officers and the public in a given area, the creation of partnerships with local businesses and residents, proactive problem solving, and citizen involvement in crime prevention.

There is a debate about the relationship between community policing and homeland security, and its outcome will determine the future path of American law enforcement (see Thatcher, 2005; Chapel and Gibson, 2009; Oliver, 2009; Jones and Suspinski, 2010; Melekian, 2011). Founders and advocates of community policing argue it is a panacea for a plethora of social problems. It works against crime, solves problems before they occur, and brings law enforcement officers into closer relationships with the people they serve. Since supporters believe community policing works in so many areas, they assume it is a perfect method for approaching homeland security. In theory, citizens become the eyes and ears of the police, who in turn forward information to start the intelligence cycle. Practitioners almost universally believe it to be a tool that should be applied to homeland security, and many analysts and academics support them (see Doherty and Hibbard, 2006).

A number of critiques, primarily from criminologists and other scholars, are more skeptical about the current and future impact of community policing. The research has produced mixed results. Some researchers believe community policing will change, and others even say it will disappear. Their argument generally suggests that American law enforcement has been based on a legal model. The purpose of law enforcement has traditionally been to respond to crime, arrest offenders, and suppress criminal activity. Community policing did not become popular until the 1990s, but after the 9/11 attacks, homeland security doctrine redirected law enforcement to intelligence gathering and the traditional enforcement model of policing. Departments that emphasize homeland security functions, many researchers believe, will separate officers from citizens and in the process weaken homeland security (see Lee, 2010).

This ongoing debate will affect future developments in policing. This is primarily due to the lack of evaluative research on the effectiveness of community policing. Government agencies and law enforcement officials endorse community policing as the only model to achieve homeland security, but they offer very little evidence to support this position (see IACP, 2014b; COPS, 2015). The President's Task Force on Policing in the 21st Century says agencies have not properly evaluated their strategies for handling terrorism (Ramsey and Robinson, 2015, p. 33). Blake Randol (2012) notes that most discussions of the relationship between community policing and homeland security are full of opinion but supported by little empirical evidence. Examining the effectiveness of community policing when applied to homeland security operations will take time, and future research is necessary.

Support for Homeland Security Through Community Policing

Practitioners champion community policing as the way to prevent terrorism and increase homeland security. The Department of Justice's Community Oriented Policing Services (COPS, 2015) has multiple websites devoted to helping state, local, and tribal law enforcement agencies incorporate community policing principles in their homeland security operations. The International Association of Chiefs of Police (IACP, 2014b) flatly states that community policing leads to homeland security. When community members feel comfortable with the police, they will report information, according to the IACP. This association also suggests that law enforcement agencies should send officers to neighborhood events in uniform. It encourages departments to increase communication, establish transparency, and create agency presence on social media. These are the first steps in good community policing and homeland security.

The IACP (2014a) goes on to say that community policing will help prevent homegrown terrorism and radicalization. Family, friends, teachers, and neighbors are generally aware of disruptive behavior in their neighborhoods. They are in a good position to witness radicalization, and social media frequently connects young people in neighborhoods. If officers are deeply connected to their communities, they increase their chances of gathering valuable information. The IACP goes on to say that community policing allows officers to gather information that may reverse or stop the process of radicalization before an act of violence occurs. In addition, community policing provides two-way communication, allowing officers to intervene with potential terrorist recruits and to teach the public about the warning signs of radicalization. The IACP equates community policing with homeland security and effective antiterrorism practices. It should be noted that these arguments are presented with no justification or supporting data. The IACP simply believes that community policing works to stop terrorism.

Blake Randol (2012) examined data from the Bureau of Justice Statistics to determine the impact of community policing on homeland security. Studies are difficult, he writes, because the federal government has provided little leadership in defining homeland security roles for state and local police agencies. Still, he reached some interesting empirical conclusions. Different population concentrations and types of policing (e.g., rural vs. urban) has little impact on how a jurisdiction is prepared to deal with homeland security. The size of jurisdictions, however, affects an agency's ability to prepare for terrorism, and large jurisdictions are positively correlated to homeland security preparedness. In addition, agencies with large budgets and multiple specialized units are better prepared for terrorism than departments lacking these resources.

Randol says his surprise came when he looked at the impact of homeland security on community policing. At the beginning of the research project, he believed he would find that community policing has less influence as agencies place a greater emphasis on homeland security tactics. Instead, he found quite the opposite. Community policing positively correlates with preparation for terrorism. Blake concludes that community policing and homeland security may be complementary, and the concepts are certainly not diametrically opposed. He also believes that community policing is not fading in the face of homeland security.

Jason Lee (2010) went through a similar experience. Lee writes that at the beginning of his empirical research project, he expected to find a negative correlation in the relationship between homeland security and community policing. He based this on an assumed paradox. The literature suggests that law enforcement agencies focused on intelligence gathering and threat prevention would be less concerned with community satisfaction. To his surprise the analysis revealed that as community policing increases, the amount of homeland security planning rises. He tentatively concludes that homeland security blends with community policing, but he cautions that evidence is sparse. More research is needed, Lee says.

Bernard Melekian (2011) also found a positive correlation between community policing and homeland security, and he believes the relationship is growing. Community policing, he says, promotes homeland security through improved training, provision of better equipment, and the availability of more resources. Practitioners support this position. Two former Massachusetts law enforcement executives say that homeland security begins with community policing. Police officers are not merely "first responders," they are "first preventers" (Doherty and Hibbard 2006). Community policing provides the tools for prevention.

Shifting Police Roles

Although it seems that community policing will not diminish in the future, a number of scholars still question the impact of homeland security efforts. Writing in *ACJS Today* one year after 9/11, Melchor de Guzman (2002) says some of the strategies necessary for effective community policing cannot be implemented when law enforcement is tasked with homeland security. Community policing is based on reasonably rationalized behavioral outcomes, and terrorists are not rational. De Guzman says this lack of reasonableness means agencies cannot stop terrorism by winning over local communities. Furthermore, if police are close to the community, they will reveal counterterrorist strategies to potential adversaries. Law enforcement officers must infiltrate communities, detect potential acts of violence, and foil attacks to prevent terrorism. If de Guzman is correct, the future of community policing is bleak.

In a more recent empirical study, MoonSun Kim and de Guzman (2012) found evidence of a fundamental shift in law enforcement practices, and their findings suggest that de Guzman's earlier argument is correct. Police departments deemphasized their relationship with communities after accepting homeland security tasks. This trend holds true in every geographical region of the country, they say. This does not mean state and local agencies will abandon community policing, but it does suggest that attitudes toward communities may change.

Willard Oliver (2006) believes the American police have entered a new era of law enforcement. Police agencies have gone through three transitions since their inception in nineteenth-century America (see Figure 16.1). The political era came first, and it was typified by law enforcement providing a vast array of social services. The next two periods, the reform era and the community police era, were dominated by

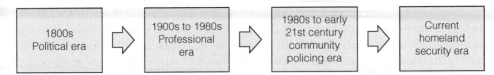

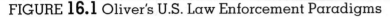

FIGURE 16.1 Oliver's U.S. Law Enforcement Paradigms

legal professionalism and public support, respectively. The police have now entered a fourth paradigm, the homeland security era, and it will change state and local policing. Agencies will be tasked with protecting the public from international and domestic threats. If Oliver is correct, the entire structure of American policing will change.

Oliver believes the homeland security mindset is the result of factors over and above law enforcement's perceptions of and reactions to 9/11. For example, the federal government took an active role in preparing officers for homeland security. These actions ranged from delivering antiterrorist training to supplying departments with technology and military equipment. The American public had a greater awareness of terrorism, which increased their desire for enhanced security. The Department of Justice actively encouraged state and local agencies to accept the homeland security mission, and U.S. attorneys around the country encouraged the police to be "eyes and ears" for the FBI. The Department of Justice asked citizens to join law enforcement by promoting the **Communities Against Terrorism** (CAT) program. Oliver says multiple nationwide political and social forces created the new homeland security era.

Oliver says the new era will usher in several changes in law enforcement. As community policing fades, intelligence gathering and risk analysis will grow. Intelligence will become concentrated in units designed to analyze information. Police agencies will experience a greater degree of centralization that will include centralized decision making. New tactics and technology will accompany these changes. Law enforcement officers will not isolate themselves from the people they serve; rather, relationships will become more formal and professional. Agencies will also remain concerned with crime control and satisfying the public, but the primary effort will be focused on counterterrorism.

Some scholars believe that homeland security has influenced community policing, but not to the extent the aforementioned researchers believe. Allison Chappell and Sarah Gibson (2009) conducted a survey of attitudes among chiefs of police in Virginia. They were seeking information about the chiefs' commitment to community policing in the wake of demands for homeland security. The results were mixed. Chappell and Gibson say the chiefs with bachelor degrees believed their agencies remained loyal to community policing models. So did chiefs from small departments serving fewer than 5,000 people. The more an agency's commitment to community policing prior to demands for homeland security, the less likely it was to abandon community models. Some chiefs did believe that interest in community policing was fading, but the majority of these executives believed deeply in the concept.

Many scholars agree that the role of law enforcement officers is changing, but they maintain that community policing can coexist with homeland security. Chapin Jones and Stanley Supinski (2010) say that some agencies have deemphasized or even abandoned their community policing programs. This trend may not continue because community policing can enhance homeland security, and it is especially effective when dealing with immigrant communities. Robert Friedman and William Cannon (2007) argue that community policing is fading, but it can coexist with and enhance homeland security. The two tasks are not mutually exclusive.

Communities Against Terrorism: (CAT) A program funded by the Bureau of Justice Assistance to help law enforcement agencies provide local businesses with guidelines for detecting suspicious activities. Agencies receive flyers summarizing possible indicators of terrorism for specific industries. Employees are encouraged to report activities to agencies in their area, and the police report this information to an intelligence center or federal counterterrorism contact.

Douglas Page (2011) takes the argument further. Using a case study of Dearborn, Michigan, after 9/11, Page looked at the way the Dearborn police responded to the Arab population in the city. (Dearborn has one of the largest Middle Eastern communities in the country.) After 9/11, the Dearborn Police Department immediately placed officers on 12-hour shifts and stationed them around mosques and schools with large Arab student bodies. They utilized their close relations with community members to assure them the purpose was to protect Muslims from vigilante attacks. They expressed irritation with national figures who claimed Arabs in Dearborn celebrated the attacks. Such accusations were blatantly false, one police official angrily said. The Dearborn police did not abandon their connections with the citizens; on the contrary, they tried to maintain them. Page says the emphasis on homeland security has replaced community policing in some departments, but community policing can be used to increase the flow of information and build strong relationships with the public.

Community Partnerships and the Future

As the community policing movement reached its zenith in popularity in the later part of the twentieth century, Gary Cordner (1995) discussed the importance of community relations. He says that community policing can work only when agencies actively seek input and participation from citizens. The police should avoid claiming they alone have the authority and ability to handle crime, delinquency, drugs, and violence. They need the help of local businesses, community groups, schools, churches, and individuals. In areas where social connections are weak, Cordner says it is even necessary for the police to create organizations within the community to provide assistance. Law enforcement works more effectively when police form partnerships with the communities they serve.

Heather Davis and Martha Plotkin (2005), writing for the Police Executive Research Forum (PERF), recommend community partnerships with organizations and citizens as a means of preventing terrorism. Such partnerships promote problem solving, they say, and since they have a successful track record in crime prevention and addressing other social problems, they will increase homeland security. These researchers urge police agencies to form partnerships with volunteers and cite neighborhood watch as an example. Agencies should seek assistance from experienced people in the community such as retired law enforcement and military personnel and take advantage of their experience. Partnerships are not, of course, the exclusive domain of state and local law enforcement departments; they should extend to the federal government as well. DHS, for example should expand its Citizens Corps and an Emergency Response Team to increase citizen involvement.

The Department of Justice says that community partnerships serve to create more socially and culturally sensitive policies (McCampbell, 2010). Future success depends on the willingness of agencies to give partners increased roles in problem solving. The police tend to approach social problems with standard procedures, but partnerships bring a variety of formal and informal mechanisms that can lead to innovation. If this position is correct, community policing and community partnerships promise success for future homeland security operations in law enforcement.

The Style of Future Policing

It is highly probable that community policing and homeland security will unite in future policing efforts, although more research is needed to either refute or support this argument. Terrorism is primarily a criminal justice problem, and law enforcement agencies need information to counter it. The scholars who suggest that community policing will not work are partially correct. Transparent actions reveal tactics to potential terrorists. However, not all law enforcement units are engaged in community policing. The JTTFs, for example, do not practice community policing tactics. As de Guzman (2002) says, the homeland security mission compels police to infiltrate terrorist organizations so that they can detect and prevent acts of terrorism. Security activities create an environment that can cause the police can be suspicious of just about everybody, and they hide their tactics and operations from public view. The JTTFs operate outside of public view, and the same holds true for drug units and most other undercover operations. These types of units receive intelligence from community police officers operating in cooperation with the people they serve. An agency's primary mission can remain focused on community policing while undercover operations remain secretive (White, 2013). State and local enforcement agencies in cooperation with the federal government will probably continue to increase partnerships through community policing, not only to increase homeland security but also to handle a host of other issues.

✓ **Self-Check**

> How do practitioners view community policing and homeland security?
> What evidence supports these views?
> How might community policing assist with homeland security?

Militarization and Police Work

Part of the federal government's response to 9/11 was to make military equipment available to state and local police agencies and give them funds to purchase it. Federal officials also encouraged agencies to use military equipment to enforce drug laws. Some scholars and civil libertarians believe this increased the military mindset that has been developing in American police work. Indeed, some police agencies have developed units that appear more suited for military functions than for police work. This has spawned a debate. Some administrators have embraced military posturing and utilize military armored cars, uniforms, protective gear, and weapons for many routine operations. Critics from within and outside of law enforcement have questioned this practice. The debate between the two views will become more intense as the role of police in homeland security is institutionalized over time.

The Problem of Militarization

Before discussing the issue, it is necessary to define **militarization**. Military forces are necessary for national defense, and they are organized along principles of rigid role structures, hierarchies, and discipline. A military posture prescribes unquestioning obedience to orders and aggressive action in the face of an enemy. In Clausewitz's sense, military forces are either at war or at peace, and when they are engaged in war, their efforts are targeted toward an enemy. Any bureaucracy can be militarized when it adopts military postures and attitudes, and the police are no exception. If the United States is engaged in a war against terrorism, some policymakers may want the police to look more and more like a military force. In this context, militarization refers to a process in which individual police units or entire agencies begin to approach specific problems with military values and attitudes. They adopt paramilitary dress, behave with military discipline, and, most importantly, prepare to make war with an enemy.

militarization: Responding to social problems with military solutions. In law enforcement, militarization is usually characterized by martial law.

Critics maintain that militarization has been transforming American police. According to Radley Balko (2013, pp. 47–52) the process began as police handled violent demonstrations in the 1960s. Police forces found that the use of military formations and tactics provided a convenient means of controlling crowds. The process was exacerbated as agencies began to develop tactical units. Members of SWAT teams began to look more like soldiers than police officers and many carried military weapons.

Most departments have rejected the idea that their agencies have been militarized. Testifying before the U.S. Senate in 2014, the executive director of the National Tactical Officers Association stressed the need to respond to critical incidents properly (U.S. Senate, 2014). Law enforcement officers had bomb teams and tactical units for emergencies, he said, and riotous crowds necessitate organized responses. The police may have military equipment, but they are not at war with the people they serve. The superintendent of the Massachusetts agreed, writing that high powered rifles and military vehicles should only be deployed in life threatening, emergency situations (Alben, 2014).

Terrorism may bring a change in attitudes. For example, because many forms of terrorism require resources beyond the capacity of local police agencies, law enforcement has been forced to turn to the military for assistance. State and local law enforcement agencies have few international resources compared with the defense and intelligence communities. Finally, terrorism demands a team approach. Law enforcement officers exercise considerable individual discretion when on calls or initiating activities, and they generally work alone or in small groups of two or three. Terrorism, like special events, changes the equation, bringing hundreds of officers together in a single function. The temptation may be to militarize the police response to terrorism.

Two trends may be seen in this area. The first comes from violent demonstrations. The Metro-Dade Police Department in Florida developed an effective method, called the field-force technique, for responding to urban riots after a particularly bad riot in 1980. By 1995, hundreds of U.S. police agencies were using the technique, and it now seems firmly established. The technique calls for responding to a growing disorderly crowd, a situation that can become a precursor to a riot, with a massive show of organized police force. Officers assemble in an area away from the violent gathering. They isolate the area, providing a route for the crowd to disperse. Then they overwhelm it with military riot tactics. A field-force exercise looks as though a small army has moved into an area using nonlethal violence (see Christopher, 1999, pp. 398–407; Kraska and Kappeler, 1999, pp. 435–449).

A second source of militarization comes from police tactical units. These special operations units are called out to deal with barricaded suspects, hostage situations, and some forms of terrorism. They are also frequently used on high-risk drug raids. Tactical units use military weapons, small-unit tactics, and recognized military small-unit command structures (see Cappel, 1979; Jacobs, 1983; Mattoon, 1987). In the past few years, many of the units have abandoned the blue or brown tactical uniforms of police agencies for military camouflage, making it virtually impossible to distinguish them from military combat units.

Peter Kraska (1996) takes exception to these trends in militarization. He argues that police in America have gradually assumed a more military posture after violent standoffs with domestic extremists, and he fears that terrorism will lead to a further excuse to militarize. This will adversely affect democracy, Kraska argues, because it will lead police to picture their jurisdictions as war zones and their mission as military victory. If the problem of terrorism is militarized, other social problems will see the same fate. Kraska's point is well taken. As Michael Howard (2002) states, calling our struggle with terrorism a war creates a variety of conceptual problems. In addition,

Americans have become used to military metaphors for other social problems such as "wars" on drugs or poverty.

Most terrorism analysts believe that counterterrorism efforts are best left to the police whenever possible (see Wardlaw, 1982, pp. 87–102). The difficulty is that the growing potential for single-event devastation sometimes takes the problem beyond local police control. In addition, military forces are often targeted, and they must develop forces to protect themselves (U.S. Department of Defense, 2001; Perl, 2001). Some of the same principles guiding military force protection will eventually spill over into American policing. In the future, state and local police may face subtle social pressure to militarize the terrorist problem and respond to it with paramilitary force.

Obtaining Military Equipment

Tactical units began appearing in U.S. law enforcement agencies in the 1960s and 1970s. By the 1980s, they were prevalent in most large and many medium-sized agencies. They were designed to deal with barricade situations hostage-takers, and other tactical situations. In the 1990s, more and more agencies began using tactical units for drug raids, executing search warrants, and "high-risk" arrest situations. After 9/11, many tactical units took on the appearance of military and commando units, and they were frequently deployed in normal law enforcement operations (see Balko, 2013). Yet, military equipment is expensive, and police budgets are limited. Some people began to wonder how law enforcement agencies were getting armored cars and other military gear. Nobody seemed to know, including the president of the United States.

After the response to demonstrations and violence in Ferguson, Missouri, in 2014, President Barrack Obama created a task force to examine the processes by which the federal government provided military equipment to state and local police. The task force was called the **Law Enforcement Equipment Acquisition Working Group** (LEEWG). Composed of representatives from a variety of federal agencies, the LEEWG found there were several ways to obtain military equipment; there were no common procedures for getting it. The Department of Defense (DOD) with its own procedures provided surplus equipment, including mine-resistant ambush-protected (MRAP) armored combat vehicles freshly returned from battle zones. It also supplied sniper rifles, other weapons, and a host of other combat and noncombat equipment. The General Services Administration (GSA) used another set of procedures. The GSA provided military items through a surplus sharing program. Using another set of criteria DOJ and DHS granted money to buy equipment, and the Treasury Department and DOJ provided money through asset forfeiture funds in drug cases using different processes (LEEWG, 2015). President Obama wanted to systematize and regulate the process, and some officials wanted to stop the distribution of military equipment all together.

The task force gathered nationwide input from associations of law enforcement officers, state and local governments, civil rights groups, and civil liberties organizations. Task force members came from several federal agencies, and members tended to reflect the views of their particular interest group. Generally, police associations wanted to be held accountable for the use of military equipment and recommended punishing departments that did not follow federal guidelines. Spokespersons from state and local governments supported them. Civil liberties and civil rights organizations wanted distribution to cease or to be heavily regulated. Spirited debates within the task force reflected these positions (White, 2015).

The task force made several recommendations to the president. Items such as grenade launchers, heavy weapons, weaponized aircraft, tracked vehicles, and bayonets

Law Enforcement Equipment Acquisition Working Group: (LEEWG) A task force created by a presidential directive in January 2015. The president charged the LEEWG with gathering information on the types of federally supplied military equipment police agencies had acquired and the procedures for obtaining these items. The task force also was to make recommendations for future policies. The LEEWG was co-chaired by the attorney general, secretary of defense, and secretary of homeland security. It resulted in a presidential ban on distributing some types of equipment.

would be banned. Equipment such as desks, office equipment, and computers could be acquired from the federal government without concern, but MRAPs and other equipment made specifically for combat operations would be controlled. The federal government would continue to distribute these items as long as law enforcement agencies justified their need for them and assumed responsibility for using the equipment properly (LEEWG, 2015).

You might wonder why a police agency would need a piece of equipment like an MRAP, a fighting vehicle designed for combat in Iraq and Afghanistan. There may be valid reasons. Although military equipment is distributed to a variety of police units, it is frequently concentrated in tactical units designed for heavily armed confrontations. When suspects are armed, barricaded, or holding hostages, tactical units need firepower and specialized equipment. When police officers or citizens are wounded in a free-fire zone, MRAPs can be used for rescue. MRAPs can also be used to deploy a tactical team or other officers against active shooters. MRAPs are extremely helpful in flood rescue operations. It makes sense to employ military equipment in certain life-threatening situations, but such use needs to be controlled, and agencies must use the equipment properly. State and local agencies will no longer have such easy access to potentially lethal equipment.

Militarization and the "War on Drugs"

Tactical units are designed for emergencies involving combat-style operations, but they are increasingly being used for other situations. In September 2014, a tactical unit in Georgia entered a house to serve a drug warrant. According to the *Washington Post*, the house belonged to David Hooks, who owned a construction company and had a defense contract and a security clearance (Balko, 2014). Hooks's attorney stated that he was asleep around 2:30 a.m., and his wife was in an upstairs craft room. She heard a car enter their driveway at a high rate of speed and saw several people in camouflage and with hoods over their faces. They were running to the back of the house. She called her husband, and he grabbed a shotgun and ran for the back of the house. The back door burst open, and heavily armed men charged into the house. Hooks was shot multiple times and killed. Police searched the house for hours and found no drugs, according to the article.

According to the American Civil Liberties Union (ACLU, 2014), tactical units are routinely utilized for drug raids and search warrants. From 2011 to 2012, tactical units were used for 79 percent of search warrants and 62 percent of drug searches across the nation. The ACLU claims that American law enforcement has militarized the war on drugs. It states that minority communities suffer the majority of militarized actions. Militarized police embrace a warrior mentality and feel they are at war with the communities they serve. Tactical units symbolize militarization.

The purpose of this book is not to evaluate drug policy or methods of executing search warrants. However, these situations present several challenges and frequently put officers' lives in danger. Whether you agree with the ACLU's position or not, a substantial part of the population believes tactical units contribute to the militarization of policing. This is unfortunate because these units are necessary to handle threats and deal with many aspects of homeland security. These perceptions matter. If portions of a community, especially immigrants and minorities, believe the police are acting like a military force and they are the enemy, no amount of community policing can reverse the perception (see DeMichele and Kraska, 2001).

Max Lomax (2014), executive director of the National Tactical Officers Association (NTOA), says there is a problem when specialized units are used improperly. Such situations can cause needless tragedies and negatively impact police–citizen relations. Tactical units are of great value. They save lives, resolve life-threatening situations, and accomplish missions that are often beyond the capabilities of regular patrol and investigative units. The NTOA has established stringent standards for selection, training, and deployment of such units. The problem, Lomax says, is that the standards are voluntary. Any agency can create a tactical unit. Some are highly trained and disciplined; others are not. Lomax could add that some tactical units are clearly identified as civil police officers, and some look like soldiers in a combat zone. Regardless, Lomax concludes that American law enforcement officers, especially tactical officers, cannot view their communities as war zones.

Drug enforcement is dangerous. The future will bring new evaluations of drug policies and law enforcement procedures. It may also be necessary for state boards of police training and standards to develop mandatory guidelines for minimum training standards for tactical units and specialized training for their commanders. NTOA standards would provide an excellent point to begin the process. Americans will also need to rethink phrases such as "war on drugs" and the impact they have on the men and women who enforce antidrug laws. The future should also bring an evaluation of the routine use of tactical units for drug enforcement. If units are overutilized during drug raids and other search warrants activities, perceptions of police militarization will increase.

> **✓ Self-Check**
>
> > What are the types of problems caused by militarizing law enforcement?
> > How do law enforcement agencies obtain military equipment?
> > Will police agencies increase the use of tactical units in drug enforcement? Why?

Future Information Sharing

If homeland security is to function, myriad law enforcement agencies must share information. It must be shared among all levels of government. Fusion centers were supposed to do this, but according to a RAND (Jenkins, Liepman, and Willis, 2014) evaluation, they have been less than effective. Quite a bit of information flows from the DHS, and some of it is helpful. Yet, there are barriers among federal agencies and between federal and local law enforcement agencies. As new terrorist threats appear, the future of information sharing may be in doubt.

Multilevel Communication and Sharing

The people who most frequently encounter terrorism are local law enforcement personnel. First, this means that future antiterrorism activities must operate beyond the federal level and involve state, local, and tribal police agencies. Second, agencies need to develop methods to encourage communication. Although procedures and personal rivalries frequently inhibit communication, organizational leaders need to develop formal and informal connections among agencies and encourage their personnel to use those networks. Third, it is necessary to share information. Policies will not work unless information flows through the system (Wise and Nader, 2008).

These issues may seem overwhelming at first, but obstacles can be circumvented if multiple agencies establish and utilize a network of formal and informal relationships. For example, a study of 500 law enforcement agencies in Illinois revealed that both police executives and local government officials believed that the probability of a terrorist attack was low. They also realized that if an attack were to happen, it would have massive consequences. Therefore, they expanded outreach to other law enforcement agencies and developed methods for sharing criminal intelligence (Giblin, Schafer, and Burruss, 2009). This information, in turn, can be passed on to various federal agencies and incorporated in national policy. Agencies in Illinois developed a formal system of information sharing that resulted in formal and informal communications.

Overcoming Barriers to Sharing

Despite the need to share information, as discussed in Chapter 15, law enforcement agencies are often reluctant to do so. This results from issues other than maintaining bureaucratic power. Information security is important to officer safety and police operations. Misused information can compromise investigations or intelligence operations, and it might put officers' lives in danger. Therefore, agencies usually seek to control intelligence or information about ongoing suspicious activity, even when barriers to information sharing have been minimized. This inhibits efforts to stop criminal activity, including operations aimed at preventing and interdicting terrorism.

Nationwide SAR Initiative: (NSI) A federal program designed to develop common antiterrorism intelligence-reporting procedures among state, local, and tribal law enforcement agencies. SAR is an acronym for suspicious activity report.

A new initiative is being tested, and it will probably dominate law enforcement's role in national security activities in the coming years. The **Nationwide SAR Initiative** (NSI) is designed to overcome both the danger of sharing information, as well as the reluctance many feel to share information about activities that might indicate a terrorist attack is in the making. The initiative is based on two key factors. First, **field contacts** are reported with standardized information gathered from a variety of law enforcement departments. Second, each agency retains control of the information. Department administrators approve all the data that will be released, and departments retain control of information that might jeopardize operations or personnel safety (U.S. Department of Justice, 2010).

field contacts: People who provide information that law enforcement personnel record during patrol operations or investigations. Police officers come into contact with many people during the course of routine patrol or investigations. They frequently encounter suspicious people or circumstances without enough evidence to make an arrest.

The system works as follows. When an officer encounters activity that might indicate potential terrorism, he or she gathers as much information as possible and forwards it in accordance with individual department procedures. The information is reviewed by an intelligence analyst and then goes to a supervisor. If the information appears valid, selected portions may be released on a secure computer server outside the agency's own system. Two more reviews take place before the information can be accessed. First, the local JTTF reviews the data to determine if it threatens any ongoing secret investigation. This is followed by a review from **e-Guardian**. If both of these reviews are positive, the information can be reviewed by other agencies. Any investigator or analyst accessing the information is able to look only at material approved and released by the originating agency.

e-Guardian: An FBI system used to share information about possible terrorist threats.

The NSI began with 12 agencies in an experimental effort to see if the concept would work. All 12 sites were evaluated in 2010. According to the review, executives in the selected agencies took "ownership" of the project, and their actions became a critical factor in the experiment's success. When chiefs, sheriffs, and their top executives actively supported SAR procedures, line officers reported more information.

Officials from the Department of Justice feared that the increased gathering and sharing of information would threaten personal privacy. They believed that the NSI would be dismantled if this happened. As a result, the DOJ convened a board of civil rights organizations to review the procedures, including the American Civil Liberties Union. No organization was asked to approve the NSI, but the government changed procedures for administering the project based on input from these outside reviews (U.S. Department of Justice, 2010).

DOJ officials also decided that no agency should participate in the SAR process unless it had a publicly approved policy for collecting and sharing criminal intelligence that matched the standards set in the **National Criminal Intelligence Sharing Plan** (NCISP) (IIR, 2010b). If an agency had a public policy matching these standards, it was allowed to submit the policy for further review by the Office of the Director of National Intelligence. If approved in this review, the agency was allowed to join the NSI and participate in SAR (U.S. Department of Justice, 2010).

The evaluation in 2010 demonstrated that SAR was effective, but it also revealed a few areas that needed to be addressed. First, criminal analysts need to be trained. As information flow increases, analysts need to know how to look at standardized SAR-generated data. Second, patrol officers and investigators receive SAR training, but an expansion of the system will require training supervisors. New SAR efforts should also include **field training officers** (FTO). Finally, SAR works because it collects specific types of information about criminal activities associated with preparation for terrorist attacks. As terrorist tactics change, SAR indicators must reflect those changes. Future information needs to reflect the actual activities of terrorists. All of these issues can be treated with training and supervision. Based on the initial evaluation, the NSI selected 25 new agencies for expanding SAR (U.S. Department of Justice, 2010).

Procedures such as those related to e-Guardian and the NSI effectively gather and distribute information, but the human factor remains. Individual competition, agency rivalries, and duplication of effort continue to hamper the effective flow of information (*Washington Post*, 2010). Future efforts to improve cooperation among agencies will need to account for the diverse nature of American law enforcement, which is a strength and weakness at the same time. On the one hand, individual rights are protected when the system of law enforcement is ineffective. The many state, local, tribal, and federal law enforcement agencies produce inefficiency. The benefit of this structure is that America does not have a single powerful police agency strong enough to threaten individual freedom. The drawback is that such a system ensures that inefficiencies will continue. The future challenge will be to utilize associations and concepts like SAR and fusion centers to ensure the flow of criminal intelligence.

The Private Industry Problem

Another critical policy link in terrorism prevention comes from the private sector. Effective preventive policies can be enhanced by private–public partnerships. This comes with two problems. First, private businesses operate outside the government, and they are not subject to the same constitutional rules and regulations. They might use information obtained through open government security networks to gain some type of business advantage or to stop a competitor. Second, and somewhat related, private businesses may use their relations with governments to win government contracts.

Tom Barry (2010) believes that one of the emerging critical issues in antiterrorism policy is private businesses developing homeland security industries. He draws a parallel with national defense industries, saying that the term *military-industrial complex* is no longer applicable to the relationship between big defense contractors and the government. These businesses, he argues, have gone far beyond supplying weapons or goods; they provide command and control systems and perform military services. In other words, they are replacing defense activities traditionally performed by the government. Barry cites the increasing number of operations that corporations perform in the DOD and in the intelligence community.

National Criminal Intelligence Sharing Plan: (NCISP) A 2005 set of recommendations designed to overcome barriers to sharing criminal intelligence. The plan contains recommended actions, oversight of operations, and standards for protecting privacy and individual rights.

field training officers: (FTO) Experienced senior patrol officers who ride with police academy graduates. They are responsible for on-the-job training. They mentor and evaluate new recruits.

military-industrial complex: A term coined by President Dwight D. Eisenhower (1890–1969) to describe the relationship between American military forces and private industry.

ANOTHER PERSPECTIVE

DHS Security Mission and Goals

Mission 1: Preventing Terrorism and Enhancing Security

- Goal 1.1: Prevent Terrorist Attacks
- Goal 1.2: Prevent the Unauthorized Acquisition or Use of Chemical, Biological, Radiological, and Nuclear Materials and Capabilities
- Goal 1.3: Manage Risks to Critical Infrastructure, Key Leadership, and Events

Mission 2: Securing and Managing Our Borders

- Goal 2.1: Effectively Control U.S. Air, Land, and Sea Borders
- Goal 2.2: Safeguard Lawful Trade and Travel
- Goal 2.3: Disrupt and Dismantle Transnational Criminal Organizations

Mission 3: Enforcing and Administering Our Immigration Laws

- Goal 3.1: Strengthen and Effectively Administer the Immigration System
- Goal 3.2: Prevent Unlawful Immigration

Mission 4: Safeguarding and Securing Cyberspace

- Goal 4.1: Create a Safe, Secure, and Resilient Cyber Environment
- Goal 4.2: Promote Cyber Security Knowledge and Innovation

Mission 5: Ensuring Resilience to Disasters

- Goal 5.1: Mitigate Hazards
- Goal 5.2: Enhance Preparedness
- Goal 5.3: Ensure Effective Emergency Response
- Goal 5.4: Rapidly Recover

Source: Department of Homeland Security, 2010.

Barry fears that the future will bring a further expansion as defense contractors move into homeland security. As evidence, he says that industrial contracting amounted to 45 percent of DOD's budget in 1960, but that it consumed about 70 percent in 2010. Defense contractors' relationship with the whole government is greater because defense contractors and their subsidiaries have expanded business by providing essential services to other governmental agencies. Several units of government now outsource much of their work to private contractors. Barry says that this has created a "government-industrial complex," and this complex expanding into homeland security operations. *Fortune* magazine reported that DOD was the biggest customer for private contractors, and they donated more than $128 million in lobbying and campaign contributions in 2014 (Dillow, 2015).

Since 9/11, Barry argues, the expanding private incursion into the public sphere has been encouraged by the wars in Iraq and Afghanistan, the focus on homeland security, and the technical requirements of governmental communication systems. He believes that this has resulted in a government–industrial partnership whose boundaries are difficult to determine. More important, blurring lines between entities providing services makes it difficult to determine if national interests are being served.

After September 11, the nation's 10 largest defense contractors immediately created homeland security departments in their companies, and they quickly became the largest contractors under the DHS. They offered a number of security services, including some related to information and communication technology. This cemented their position in homeland security because defense contractors possess skills most governmental agencies do not have. This means that private corporations control vast amounts of intelligence data. The situation is magnified by what Barry calls revolving door security. When government officials who work for agencies tasked with ensuring homeland security leave government service, they are frequently hired by private organizations in the same field. Other government officials form their own consulting corporations and perform essentially the same tasks that they performed in government. Barry believes that future security will be privatized by corporations unrestrained by constitutional limitations on government power.

Dawn Rothe and Jeffery Ian Ross (2010) share Barry's fears. Analyzing the role of private military contractors from a criminological perspective, they present evidence to show that private companies often circumvent constitutional constraints on government power. This happens in a number of ways. Private companies act within their own operational systems and decide what they will and will not report to various stakeholders. Rothe and Ross argue that private military contractors frequently act outside of the rules of warfare. At times, the government has even intervened to protect civilian contractors who have broken local laws, giving them the same protection afforded to the U.S. military forces. Logistical contractors have been given even more freedom because the DOD has reduced the number of people who work to regulate support and supply efforts. Private corporations are doing the work of the government.

These arguments point to a dangerous trend in the future of homeland security. As discussed in several previous chapters, information is power. If Barry is correct, private contractors control both quite a bit of the intelligence flowing through the homeland security system and the manner in which it flows. They also control information about their own activities, and corporations tend to behave in their own self-interest, as Rothe and Ross demonstrated with military contracting. Corporations do not freely share their shortcomings with the government agencies that hire them. If these trends continue, a large portion of private industry will control vast portions of antiterrorist policy. This can be stopped if government agencies hold corporations strictly accountable and if the government is able to take on the tasks of these private entities.

The United States experienced a major recession beginning in 2007, the worst in 75 years, in part because several large banks were on the verge of collapsing. The federal government lent billions of dollars to the banking industry, stating that it would devastate the economy if they were to fail. A similar crisis could develop if private corporations become responsible for homeland security.

Private and public partnerships have produced some positive benefits. These have developed from relations developed between government agencies and businesses as they cooperate to ensure physical security. Rather than purchasing systems or services, this approach involves sharing security information to benefit the entire community. This involves such activities as protecting the infrastructure, analyzing threats, sharing security information, and reducing community vulnerability. When cooperative relationships focus exclusively on community security, the risks posed by government–private industrial relationships are reduced.

✓ Self-Check

> Why is it necessary to create better communication among agencies?

> How might barriers to information sharing be overcome?

> What types of problems do public–private security partnerships cause?

Future Terrorist Tactics

The basic tactics of terrorism remain relatively constant, but terrorists continually develop innovative ways to use them. Such innovation implies that tactics will continue to evolve. Recent innovative methods suggest future tactical trends.

Terrorists may begin attacking multiple targets simultaneously, as the Lashkar-e-Taiba (LeT) did in the 2008 **Mumbai attack**, and they will continue to use secondary attacks after security forces respond to an initial attack. Criminal and terror networks will intersect, even though they will probably not form a common front. Ultimately, terrorists want to destabilize society, but criminals need government stability to operate. Cyberterrorism has yet to reach its full potential, and the United States remains vulnerable to attack. The future path of radicalization will change, but its direction is open to question. Finally, terrorist operations may bifurcate, or break into two branches. Small attacks will continue as they do today, while sophisticated larger strikes will evolve from large groups with logistical support.

Mumbai attack: The LeT launched an attack against multiple targets in Mumbai, India, in November 2008. Terrorists killed dozens of people and took several hostages. The attacks paralyzed the city for several days.

Swarming and Multiple Attacks

On November 26, 2008, several gunmen from the LeT slipped off a hijacked fishing boat in the harbor of Mumbai, India. After slitting the boat captain's throat, they broke into separate teams and slipped into various sections of the city. These destinations had been reconnoitered, photographed, and studied by each group. Their actions were hardly random. Around 9:30 p.m., the small group assigned to the main railway station calmly took assault rifles from their duffle bags and began to shoot into the crowded station. Within minutes, another group shot their way into a hospital while a third group stormed a café. The chaos was just beginning.

The terrorists moved from target to target, even attacking a police station as they drove by. Explosions rumbled through the air as the LeT bombs were detonated. After attacking two hotels, some of the members began to take hostages. Mumbai was in chaos, and the police were outgunned and confused. Their response was ineffective. As security forces sought to regain control, they attempted to respond to each emergency and assess the situation. When the attack ended a few days later, 174 people were dead, and hundreds more were wounded. Small groups of trained terrorists had attacked unarmed civilian targets in a military fashion. It was a new application of an old tactic (BBC, 2008). Europe avoided a similar series of attacks in September 2010 due to proactive police and intelligence work (*Der Spiegel*, 2010).

The LeT learned from its success in Mumbai. Four months later, as a convoy carrying the Sri Lankan cricket team moved through Lahore, Pakistan, the LeT struck again. Nine LeT terrorists appeared from the crowded streets. They attacked the convoy with assault rifles, explosives, and rocket-propelled grenades. Several people were killed, including seven police officers. As the attack ended, the terrorists melted back into the crowd (Page, 2009).

Like the attacks in Mumbai, the violence in Lahore was a copy of an old terrorist tactic. For example, during the Black and Tan War, the IRA attacked a British police station in much the same manner. The LeT attacks represented tactical innovation. Ambushes and assassinations were transformed into small-unit assaults. Bombings were covered by automatic rifle fire and grenades. The **swarming attacks** in Mumbai and Lahore have implications for the future. For example, the Taliban copies the LeT's swarm tactics in Afghanistan (al Jazeera, 2015).

Raymond W. Kelly, former commissioner of the New York City Police Department (NYPD), testified in a congressional hearing about the nature of the two styles

swarming attacks: Attacks launched on multiple targets in the same time frame or attacks involving several attackers suddenly coming to a single location and rapidly dispersing.

of swarming attacks and the future of terrorism. Multiple attacks will be part of the coming wave of terrorism, he said. The **NYPD Intelligence** unit conducted a detailed tactical analysis of the attacks in Mumbai and Lahore and found similarities. Both involved small-unit assaults in densely populated areas. They were preceded by extensive preparation and surveillance, and the actual attacks were coordinated by communication via cell phones and small battery-operated radios. After the initial assaults, teams kept breaking down into smaller units, and local police were outgunned at the time of the initial attacks. All of these factors led the NYPD to conclude that terrorist tactics of sophisticated groups like the LeT will shift from an emphasis on suicide bombings to a focus on military-style assaults by small heavily armed teams (Kelly, 2010).

The FBI generally agreed with the NYPD conclusions (McJunkin, 2010). The FBI analysis of the same two attacks noted that the level of sophistication between the two differed. Mumbai was extremely complicated and required coordination among multiple units. The Lahore attack was simple, involving an initial assault and a retreat. Despite the differences, the FBI agreed with the NYPD due to the similarity in the outcomes of both terrorist strikes. Terrorists do not need sophisticated weapons or WMD to create massive chaos. Small cadres of conventionally armed terrorists can wreak havoc in an urban environment through multiple random murders.

The FBI concluded that the lessons learned from Mumbai and Lahore point to three future responses. First, it is necessary to prepare for strikes by small groups operating without a central command. Lahore demonstrated that a single unit can launch an effective attack, and an individual motivated by radical ideology can do the same. Mumbai showed that larger groups can launch more complex operations. Security forces must prepare for both types of attacks. Second, deep relationships with local communities will be imperative. Local citizens are the best source of information about potential terrorist violence. They are in the best position to note activities that fall outside normal behavior. Third, since ideology and organizations transcend national boundaries, the FBI concluded that law enforcement agencies need to develop international partnerships and sources of information.

Arjen Boin (2009) places such attacks within the larger context of a future global crisis. He says that the structure of international systems and infrastructures will impact the nature, frequency, and consequences of terrorism and other disasters. He examines the impact of Mumbai on an international level but compares such terrorist attacks to natural disasters and other forms of violence. Technology as well as economic and social networks will transform local disasters into transnational crises that will disrupt international systems. In the past, crises had a beginning and an end, and their effects were generally localized. As interdependent global relations grow, future crises will develop lives of their own as they spread new forms of systemic chaos. Boin says that decision makers need to gather information from any emerging crisis and assess its multiple impacts. Future managerial systems must respond to the impact on overlapping infrastructures and international networks. In addition to developing new approaches to crises, officials will need to improve their ability to communicate among multiple organizations and to develop the skills necessary to gather and analyze complex information under pressure.

Another future mode of attack will involve employing multiple explosive devices (see Sweeny, 2005; Ewald, 2006; Bruechner, 2009). If the devices are numerous or large, setting off simultaneous explosions can have a dramatic impact. Secondary devices, which are explosives timed to go off after security forces have responded to an initial attack, have long been used by lone bombers and terrorist groups. Their popularity increased in Iraq and Afghanistan, and they will probably be used in the future.

NYPD Intelligence: A new intelligence operation the New York City Police Department created after the 9/11 attacks to assess domestic and international threats to the city. Its first administrator was a former executive from the CIA. The NYPD sends officers overseas to gather information and assess terrorist threats. Mayor William de Blasio vowed to curtail the unit after his 2013 election, but he maintained many of its functions.

Variations on this theme involve covering an explosive with small arms fire or using explosives in conjunction with a small-unit attack. Explosives can be used to create a specific style of swarming attack, and they can be used to support such attacks. Bombs were present at the beginning of modern terrorism, and they will continue to be an important weapon in the arsenal of terrorism.

Stephen Graham (2009) says that the military view of conflict has moved from state-to-state confrontations with a beginning and an end to an ideology that accepts perpetual warfare in a variety of civilian environments. Shifting terrorist tactics, such as swarming attacks, threaten to turn urban centers into battlefields. This shift, Graham warns, can lead to increased militarization and efforts to control information. Local issues will become global issues, and the distinction between police, military, and intelligence operations will blur. Military models will define criminal justice systems, and command and control structures will be created along military lines. As terrorist tactics shift, state responses will increasingly accept urban environments as war zones.

Blending Criminal and Terrorist Networks

Michael Stohl (2008) says conventional wisdom suggests that terrorist and criminal organizations are merging into common networks. He says that it is important to keep the distinction between criminal and terrorist behavior in mind if law enforcement tactics are to be effective. The differences are often overlooked because terrorists and criminals use similar tactics. Terrorists use violence as a tactical objective to achieve a particular goal, and they seek to destabilize authority. Criminals operate in a different manner. They benefit when recognized political authority is stable. Criminal networks require infrastructure and services—the types of functions governments supply—and they exploit stable systems to bribe or corrupt public officials. The tactical objectives of terrorist and criminal networks differ, and law enforcement agencies need to understand these differences.

Stohl says that there are other differences and similarities between terrorists and organized criminals. Terrorists seek media coverage to enhance their aura, and they want their dramatic criminal activities publicized. Criminals avoid the media, seeking to operate under the public radar. Both criminals and terrorists are frequently charged under the same criminal statutes, but this is often because governments seek to discredit the political claims of terrorists. Criminal groups employ terrorist tactics, and terrorists commit crimes. Terrorists may associate with criminal groups to add to their reputation for ruthlessness. Criminals and terrorists may form alliances, use the same underground networks, share operational motivations, and sometimes even combine operations. It seems that similarities outweigh the differences, and many analysts point to this as evidence of growing collusion.

Stohl says the opposite is true. Overlapping aspects of behavior and shared networks do not signify a growing union between terrorists and criminals. No one disputes, he writes, that criminals and terrorists frequently move in the same circles. The important issue, however, is the relationship between networks. Stohl questions whether networks actually share information or permanently join operations. He also questions whether terrorist networks and criminal organizations can ultimately share long-term alliances and goals.

Networks are dynamic, Stohl argues, and this dynamic structure also impacts relationships. The current thought is that they operate according to a set of rules, but Stohl says that they should be understood as ever-changing structures that flow with social fluctuations. The network metaphor is useful to describe a changing range of linkages among multiple groups. It does not signify a unified hierarchy or a permanent alliance among networked groups.

Different organizational goals, Stohl says, result in separate organizations within networks. Organizations intersect in short-term relations at the nodes where criminal and terrorist needs intersect. For example, terrorists need weapons, and organized criminals may provide them for a profit. Even though the terrorists and criminals are working toward different goals, their interests intersect at the point where weapons are exchanged. Stohl says that the exchange represents the node where law enforcement should direct its attention. Police actions should be focused on denying network connections to terrorist groups and utilizing community policing techniques to isolate terrorists from the public. Law enforcement's eventual goal is not to categorize terrorists as criminals but to create justice systems that can end violence and reintroduce these individuals to their communities. Stohl suggests that the nodes where criminal organizations and terrorist groups intersect also provide opportunities to capture terrorists.

One of the most important intersections between criminals and terrorists occurs in the field of finance. Patrick Hardouin (2009) says that financial institutions will become more critical in the future because they are inevitably used by criminals and terrorists. He also argues that public–private partnerships in this area do not pose risks of unfair competition or private control of governmental functions because each financial institution provides the government with the same type of information. When the banking industry helps law enforcement prevent illegal activities or investigate crimes, they simply serve as a tool for investigations.

John Cassara (2007; Cassara and Jorisch, 2010) agrees with Hardouin, but he suggests that future financial investigations will become more difficult. Terrorists are learning new methods of avoiding financial detection, and lone wolf terrorist activities require little financing. Cassara believes that law enforcement officials need to develop better forensic accounting skills to counter future financial crimes. The nexus between criminal and terrorist networks will continue to intersect in financial nodes, and Cassara believes that a new generation of law enforcement officials must learn new methods to detect illegal transfers of money, goods, and services.

Mette Eilstrup-Sangiovanni and Calvert Jones (2008) do not dispute the fact that criminal and terrorist networks intersect and that future financing is important. They do suggest, however, that the future power of networks may diminish. The reason is that networks are not as tactically efficient as many analysts believe them to be. The prevailing mood of pessimism about future operations, they argue, is premature. Many terrorism analysts believe that the hidden nature of terror networks automatically gives groups the ability to adapt to future changes. Eilstrup-Sangiovanni and Jones argue that this may not be true. Historical and contemporary research suggests that underground movements are vulnerable. Further, organized crime and terrorist networks are not as adaptable as many analysts believe. They offer a detailed examination of al Qaeda to illustrate the point. As its network expands and intersects with other networks, its ability to act as a single entity is diminished. In other words, the networked command structure is less efficient than a single command system. If this line of logic is correct, the future of networks and the meshing of criminals and terrorists may produce more weaknesses than strengths.

Other Tactical Trends

Other tactical trends appear to be in the offing. Former counterterrorism czar Richard Clarke teamed with Robert Knake of the Council on Foreign Relations (Clarke and Knake, 2010) to focus on the need to secure America's cybernetwork. Although their primary focus is on military defense, their warning extends to terrorism. They see cybersystems as an infrastructure in need of protection. Pointing to the 2008 war between Georgia and Russia, they note that Russia jammed Georgia's Internet connections at the start of the war. Nations seeking to attack the United States could achieve a strategic advantage if they were able to disrupt communications, financial systems, and the information technology (IT) infrastructure. For example, China has created a cyber warfare center in the People's Liberation Army, and it hacked into millions of U.S. government personnel record in 2015, according to *Forbes* magazine (Coyer, 2015). *Security* magazine editor Mark McCourt (2010) supports this conclusion, saying that governmental safeguards protect government domains, not the country's infrastructure. The .com, .org, and .edu environments are a matter for the private sector, and they do not enjoy the same protection as .gov systems. The private cybernetwork will be subject to hacking and attacks designed to disrupt systems as well as terrorist groups seeking to use the Internet to raise funds.

Bureau of Justice Assistance: (BJA) A division of the U.S. Department of Justice that assists state, local, and tribal law enforcement agencies.

In late 2010, the **Bureau of Justice Assistance** (BJA) asked three dozen of the nation's leading law enforcement experts in terrorism to attend an informational meeting. Invited analysts were asked to identify emerging trends in their areas of expertise. A number of them noted the bifurcated nature of terrorist attacks. Complex attacks require a lengthy planning period and sophisticated logistical support, but future trends are moving toward smaller individualized attacks. Smaller attacks are more difficult to detect, require shorter planning periods, and appear to be the dominant future trend.

BJA's examination of terrorist attacks revealed other emerging tactical trends. Violent radicals are attempting to infiltrate military and law enforcement ranks, which is primarily a domestic threat. Most of the analysts stated that investigations were pointing toward future individual radicalization, another process that will lead to smaller attacks. Explosives experts pointed to bomb data, demonstrating that the nineteenth century anarchists "philosophy of the bomb" will continue to remain a viable terrorist weapon. The most likely future trend is the use of remote detonation devices. Financial experts pointed to increasing fraud to fund operations, and experts on the domestic right wing noted that many **sovereign citizen** fraud schemes were used for economic gain instead of to fund operations. Several of the participants feared swarming attacks. Finally, experts presented data suggesting that law enforcement officers will be increasingly targeted by violent domestic extremists.

sovereign citizen: A citizen who believes that the original citizens of the United States were free from all governmental control. Sovereign citizens think that they are duped by the government in "schemes" like Social Security, driver's licenses, and car registrations. That is, once people participate in such conspiracies, they lose their natural freedom and become citizens of the United States. Sovereign citizens believe that they can renounce those need to adhere to such regulations and free themselves from American law. This should be noted: Though they free themselves from taxes and fees, they rarely reject government benefits.

One of the greatest fears remains the use of chemical, biological, and radiological weapons. Opinions about the future are varied. Many analysts think that such attacks are inevitable, and others think that they will not happen. The future of WMD security is another issue. Reducing the threat of theft and increasing the security of chemical, biological, and radiological agents are imperative future actions (Bunn, 2009). International law intended to prevent the spread of nuclear weapons already exists. These laws need to be updated, and provisions against trafficking should be added (Joyner and Parkhouse, 2009). James Van De Velde (2010) says diversion is the best way to keep terrorists from using megaweapons. He argues that methods should be employed to steer potential recruits into activities other than terrorism and other forms of crime.

A final development is the issue of active shooters in the United States. Unfortunately, these incidents are increasing, and they will probably continue. Although they usually do not involve political terrorism, some of them could be classified as domestic terrorism, and others must be handled like a terrorist incident. Law enforcement officers are forced to respond to incidents quickly, usually without the assistance

Major Findings from the FBI's Active Shooter Incidents Study

The just-released "A Study of Active Shooter Incidents in the United States Between 2000 and 2013" contains a full list of the 160 incidents used in the study, including those that occurred at Virginia Tech, Sandy Hook Elementary School, the U.S. Holocaust Memorial Museum, Fort Hood, the Aurora (Colorado) Cinemark Century 16 movie theater, the Sikh temple in Wisconsin, and the Washington Navy Yard. Here are some of the study's findings:

> Active shooter incidents are becoming more frequent—the first seven years of the study had an average of 6.4 incidents annually, while the last seven years had an average of 16.4 incidents annually.

> These incidents resulted in a total of 1,043 casualties (486 killed, 557 wounded, excluding the shooters).

> All but six of the 160 incidents involved male shooters (and only two involved more than one shooter).

> More than half of the incidents—90 shootings—ended on the shooter's initiative (i.e., suicide, fleeing), while 21 incidents ended after unarmed citizens successfully restrained the shooter.

> In 21 of the 45 incidents where law enforcement had to engage the shooter to end the threat, nine officers were killed and 28 were wounded.

> The largest percentage of incidents—45.6 percent—took place in a commercial environment (73 incidents); 24.3 percent took place in an educational environment (39 incidents). The remaining incidents occurred in open spaces, military and other government properties, residential properties, houses of worship, or health care facilities.

Source: FBI, 2014

FIGURE **16.2** FBI Analysis of Active Shooters

of tactical units. The FBI (2014) says 160 active shooting incidents took place in the United States between 2000 and 2013. The were an average of 11.4 attacks per year; 486 people were killed and 557 wounded (see Figure 16.2).

Active shooters present an important problem. The debate about the availability of guns in the United States is vitriolic and polarized. Guns are readily available, background checks are ineffective in many cases, and there are millions of guns in circulation. Virtually any person may gain access to a gun, including mentally unstable people and criminals. The United States has the highest rate of gun deaths in the industrialized world. Even stringent control would have little impact on the number of existing firearms. All of these factors indicate that active shooters will continue to attack and that lone wolf domestic and international terrorists will continue to engage in active shooter attacks. Terrorism involving active shooters has taken place around the world.

✓ Self-Check

> How might swarming and simultaneous attacks impact future terrorism?

> Where do organized crime and terror networks intersect?

> What other tactical trends seem to be emerging?

Emphasizing the Points

Although opinions are divided, many scholars and most law enforcement executives believe that community policing strategies will result in better homeland security by increasing the flow of information. Militarization in law enforcement, however, counteracts effective community policing. American law enforcement agencies must reduce perceptions of militarization. They must also begin to gather and systematically share information. Although it is difficult to create public–private partnerships in some instances, both the federal and local governments should seek to do so. Future terrorist attacks suggest that operations will become more complicated. Future cooperation among state and local law enforcement agencies and among differing levels of government is essential for homeland security.

SUMMARY OF CHAPTER OBJECTIVES

- Although some scholars believe that community policing will fade because of an increased law enforcement emphasis on homeland security duties, many researchers believe the two concepts will complement one another. Most practitioners continue to embrace community policing even as they increase homeland security efforts.
- Community partnerships are the essence of community policing. Partnerships between police agencies and community organizations bring the public closer to law enforcement. They provide for innovative problem solving, for two-way communication, and for increasing the flow of information.
- American law enforcement is a civilian occupation. There is a danger when police work is militarized. It separates the police from the public and destroys opportunities for community policing. Much of the future of community policing and homeland security will be influenced by perceptions of law enforcement militarization.
- Law enforcement agencies acquire military equipment in a number of ways. They obtain it by purchasing equipment with federal funds through grants and receiving direct donations from DOD and GSA surpluses. According to a presidential executive order, agencies need to justify their need for many combat items and use them properly.
- Studies indicate that tactical units are frequently used in drug enforcement efforts. The causes officers to take on the appearance of military units, and critics say this creates a warrior mentality among officers. To avoid problems, the NTOA suggests stringent selection criteria, training, and guidelines for deployment.
- Information sharing is necessary for effective homeland security. It starts and completes the intelligence cycle. Future successes in homeland security depend on better information sharing.
- Several federal initiatives have been designed to increase information sharing. The NSI is an attempt to systematically gather and share information among multiple law enforcement agencies. The NCISP is designed to standardize intelligence analysis and sharing.
- Private–public partnerships are complicated because the Constitution limits the power of government, but the same rules do not apply to private industry. Companies may use information for economic advantage. They might also become

so deeply embedded in defense that they would replace military forces in some aspects of national security.

- Swarming attacks will become popular with large terrorist groups. Criminal and terrorist networks will join together when they have common objectives, and cybersystems remain vulnerable to terrorist attacks. Active shooter incidents are increasing and will probably continue to do so.

LOOKING INTO THE FUTURE: A STRATEGIC VIEW

While assessing the strategic future of terrorism is difficult, there is a body of applied and scholarly literature that attempts to do so. The National Intelligence University and the U.S. Army War College teamed together to create Proteus USA, an international think tank designed to consider future strategic problems. Futurists Martin Cetron and Owen Davies (2008) produced one of the project's first papers on the future of terrorism. They identified 55 changes they expect to see in the future based on current trends.

Cetron and Davies suggest that terrorism will grow in the future. They believe that jihadist veterans will return to their native lands and train future jihadists. This will cause terrorism to spread. They suggest that the United States, France, and the United Kingdom are at the greatest risk, and they predict another attack on the scale of 9/11. Emerging technology will impact the effectiveness of security, and it will multiply the force of terrorist groups. New technology will also allow terrorists to strike economic and logistical targets.

They suggest that the three most important courses of future action indicated by current behavior are (1) growing terrorist ranks, (2) probable access to WMD, and (3) spin-off jihadist movements obtaining legitimate political power. These probabilities, they argue, should guide the Western response to terrorism. The 10 most important factors contributing to terrorism are:

- Western economic growth will spawn resentment and radicalization in populations who believe they are victimized by the West. Muslim countries present the greatest risk.
- Militant Islam will gain power and spread.
- Barring nuclear war or some type of global plague, the world's population will reach 9.2 billion by 2050. The United States will continue to prosper, while poverty will increase in poor nations, increasing resentment against the United States. America will remain an attractive terrorist target.
- Recent technological changes are just the beginning of a revolution that will grow exponentially in the coming decades.
- Americans will lose almost all privacy.
- The global economy will continue to grow, and multinational corporations will expand. Economic crime and terrorism will continue to expand with the economy.
- Cities will continue to grow, creating large pockets where religious radicalization will foster and terrorism will grow.
- Internet growth will slow, but it will remain the most important method for planning and administering terrorist operations. Almost all the world's population will have access to the Internet within 20 years. It will serve as a vehicle for recruiting terrorists and may be used to commit financial crimes that will help support operations.

- Communication technology will continue to expand and impact terrorism in a manner similar to Internet growth.
- The United States is losing its technical and scientific leadership to other countries. This has caused an increase in the number of technicians and scientists in lands hostile to the United States. Some scientists will be able to supply terrorists with lethal technologies.

KEY TERMS

Communities Against Terrorism, p. 379
Militarization, p. 381
Law Enforcement Equipment Acquisition Working Group, p. 383

Nationwide SAR Initiative, p. 386
Field contacts, p. 386
e-Guardian, p. 386
National Criminal Intelligence Sharing Program, p. 387

Field training officers, p. 387
Military-industrial complex, p. 387
Mumbai attack, p. 390
Swarming attacks, p. 390

NYPD Intelligence, p. 391
Bureau of Justice Assistance, p. 394
Sovereign citizen, p. 394

GLOSSARY

1978 Civil Service Reform Act A federal law designed to prevent political interference with the decisions and actions of governmental organizations.

1985 hijacking of a TWA flight The hijacking of TWA Flight 847 by a group believed to have links to Hezbollah while it was en route from Athens to Rome. The plane went to Beirut and then to Algeria, where terrorists tortured and murdered U.S. Navy diver Robert Dean Stethem, a passenger on the flight. The plane returned to Beirut, and passengers were dispersed throughout the city. Terrorists began releasing hostages as the incident continued. After Israel agreed to release 700 Shi'ite prisoners, the terrorists released the remaining hostages and escaped.

1993 World Trade Center bombing A carbomb attack by a cell led by Ramzi Youseff. The cell had links to the Egyptian Islamic Group.

9/11 Commission The bipartisan National Commission on Terrorist Attacks upon the United States, created after September 11, 2001, to investigate the attacks.

9/11 Commission Implementation Act of 2007 A federal law requiring selected recommendations of the 9/11 Commission to be implemented. One of its provisions helped create regional fusion centers.

Abbas Musawi (1952–1992) A leader of Hezbollah who was killed with his family in an Israeli attack in 1992.

Abdel Aziz Rantisi (1947–2004) One of the founders of Hamas along with Ahmed Yassin. He took over Hamas after Israeli gunships assassinated Yassin. He, in turn, was assassinated by the Israelis a month after taking charge.

Abdullah Azzam (1941–1989) The Palestinian leader of Hizb ul Tahrir and the spiritual mentor of Osama bin Laden.

Abdullah Ocalan (b. 1948) The leader of the Kurdish Worker's Party PKK. Ocalan was captured in 1999 and sentenced to death, but his sentence was commuted. He ordered the end of a suicide bombing campaign while in Turkish custody and called for peace between Turkey and the Kurds in 2006.

Abimael Guzmán (b. 1934) A philosophy professor who led the Shining Path from 1980 until his arrest in 1992. Guzmán is serving a life sentence in Peru.

Abu Bakr (circa 573–634) Also known as Saddiq, the first caliph selected by the Islamic community (*umma*) after Mohammed's death in 632. Sunnis believe Abu Bakr is the rightful heir to Mohammed's leadership, and they regard him as the first of the *Rishidun*, or Rightly Guided caliphs. He led military expeditions that expanded Muslim influence to the north of Mecca.

Abu Bakr al Baghdadi (b. circa 1971) An Iraqi Sunni who joined the resistance against the U.S. invasion of Iraq in 2003. He may have been a violent radical before the invasion. Regardless, after being held in prison by U.S. forces, he became a hardened radical. He emerged as a leader of AQI, but unlike Zarqawi, he was articulate and charismatic. He assumed control of the ISI in 2010, entered the Syrian civil war, and changed ISI to ISIS. Abu Mohammed al Adnani declared him caliph of the Islamic State in June 2014.

Abu Basir al Tartusi (b. 1953) A Syrian jihadist scholar who fled Syria and began preaching and writing from East London in the 1980s. He has denounced many acts of terrorism but supports Jihadi Salafist ideology. Tartusi has been spotted with an armed group in Syria and supports Europeans who fight the Syrian government.

Abu Muhammed al Jawlani (b. ?) Leader of Jabhat al Nusra. Little is known about Jawlani's background. He is Syrian and left his homeland to fight against U.S. forces in Iraq. He was captured by these forces. After being released from prison, he met Baghdadi, joined ISI, and rose through the ranks. Baghdadi sent him to Syria in 2011, where he formed al Nusra. When Baghdadi tried to absorb al Nusra in 2014, Jawlani broke with ISIS and swore allegiance to Zawahiri.

Abu Mohammed al Maqdisi (b. 1959) A Palestinian scholar now living in Jordan. Maqdisi is one of the most influential Jihadi Salafist scholars in the world today.

Jailed and investigated many times, Maqdisi has influenced many jihadists.

Abu Musab al Zarqawi (1966–2006) A Jordanian criminal who converted to Jihadi Salafism after an extended trip to Afghanistan in 1989 and serving a sentence in a Jordanian prison from 1993 to 1999. He ended up back in Afghanistan and moved to Iraq after the U.S. invasion in 2003. He founded al Qaeda in Iraq, a group that became known for extreme violence. He was killed in an American bombing attack in 2006.

Abu Omar al Baghdadi (?–2010) The first leader of the Islamic State of Iraq who took command after Abu Musab al Zarqawi was killed in 2006. Little is known about his background, and U.S. military forces once believed he was a factious character. He was killed in an American strike in 2010.

Academic consensus definition A complex definition by Alex Schmid. It combines common elements of the definitions used by leading scholars in the field of terrorism.

Actionable intelligence Information that law enforcement agencies, military units, or other security forces can use to prevent an attack or operation.

Adam Gadahn (b. 1958) The American spokesperson for al Qaeda. His *nom de guerre* is Azzam the American.

African Cell A French military unit stationed in Africa and France. It retains between 10,000 and 15,000 troops in various African countries and answers directly to the president of France.

African Union (AU) An organization of 54 African states to promote peace, security, and economic development. Combined AU military forces are sometimes deployed in troubled areas of Africa and employed as peacekeepers.

Ahmed Yassin (1937–2004) One of the founders and leaders of Hamas. Yassin originally started the Palestinian Wing of the Muslim Brotherhood but merged it into Hamas during the first Intifada. He was killed in an Israeli-targeted assassination.

AIDS pandemic Occurred when great numbers of people contracted and were living with and dying form HIV/AIDS. In 2005, Africa had 25.8 million HIV-positive adults and children. Africa has 11.5 percent of the world's population but 64 percent of its AIDS cases. From 1982 to 2005, AIDS claimed 27.5 million African lives.

Al Aqsa Intifada An uprising sparked by Ariel Sharon's visit to the Temple Mount with a group of armed escorts in September 2000. The area is considered sacred to Jews, Christians, and Muslims. Muslims were incensed by the militant aspect of Sharon's visit.

Alberto Fujimori (b. 1938) President of Peru from 1990 to 2000. He fled to Japan in 2000 but was extradited to Peru in 2007. He was convicted of human rights violations and sentenced to prison.

Ali ibn Talib (circa 599–661) Also known as Ali ibn Abi Talib, the son of Mohammed's uncle Abu Talib and married to Mohammed's oldest daughter Fatima. Ali was Mohammed's male heir because he had no surviving sons. The followers of Ali are known as Shi'ites. Most Shi'ites believe that Mohammed gave a sermon while perched on a saddle, naming Ali the heir to Islam. Differing types of Shi'ites accept authority from diverse lines of Ali's heirs. Sunni Muslims believe Ali is the fourth and last Rightly Guided caliph. Both Sunnis and Shi'ites believe Ali tried to return Islam to the purity of Mohammed's leadership in Medina.

Alienation Happens when an individual or group becomes lost in the dominant social world. A person or group of people is alienated when separated from the dominant values of society at large.

Al Jazeera An international Arabic television network.

Al Manar Hezbollah's television network.

Al Shabaab (also known as the Harakat Shabaab al-Mujahedeen, the Youth, Mujahedeen Youth Movement, and Mujahedeen Al Shabaab Movement) Formed as a militant wing of a federation of Islamic courts in Somalia in 2006. Its senior leadership is affiliated with al Qaeda.

Altruistic suicide Occurs when individuals are willing to sacrifice their lives to benefit their primary reference group such as a family, military unit, ethnic group, or country. It may involve going on suicide missions in combat, self-sacrifice without killing others, or self-sacrifice and killing others.

Alvaro Uribe (b. 1952) President of Colombia from 2002 to 2010. He was known for his tough stance against FARC and other revolutionary movements.

American embassy takeover During the Iranian hostage crisis, revolutionary students stormed the U.S. embassy in Tehran with the support of the Iranian government. They held 54 American hostages from November 1979 to January 1981.

Anarchists Those in the nineteenth century who advocated the creation of cooperative societies without centralized governments. There were many forms of anarchy. In the popular understanding of the late nineteenth and early twentieth centuries, anarchists were seen as violent socialist revolutionaries. Today, antiglobalists calling themselves anarchists have little resemblance to their earlier counterparts.

Anders Breivik (b. 1979) A violent right-wing extremist who went on a one-day killing spree in Norway in July 2011. He detonated a bomb in Oslo and went on a shooting spree at a Labor Party youth camp for political reasons.

Anglo-Irish Peace Accord An agreement signed in 1985 that was the beginning of a long-term attempt to stop terrorist violence in Northern Ireland by devising a system of political autonomy and by protecting the rights of all citizens. Extremist Republicans rejected the accord because it did not unite Northern Ireland and the south. Unionists rejected it because it compromised with moderate Republicans.

Anglo-Israelism The belief that the lost tribes of Israel settled in Western Europe. God's ancient promises to the Hebrews became promises to the United Kingdom, according to this belief. Anglo-Israelism predated Christian Identity and is the basis for most Christian Identity beliefs.

Anwar al Awlaki (1971–2011) An American-born Muslim cleric who worked to build U.S.-Muslim relations after 9/11. He became increasingly militant and called for attacks on America. He was arrested in Yemen in 2006 and released in 2007. In 2009, he swore allegiance to AQAP.

Arab nationalism The idea that the Arabs could create a European-style nation based on a common language and culture. The idea faded after the 1967 Six-Day War.

Argentina in 1992 and 1994 In these years there were two bombings in Buenos Aires. Terrorists struck the Israeli embassy in 1992, killing 29 people, and the Jewish Community Center in 1994, killing 85 people. Imad Mugniya is suspected to have been behind the attacks.

Aryan Nations An American antigovernment, anti-Semitic, white supremacist group founded by Richard Butler. Until it was closed by a suit from the Southern Poverty Law Center, the group sponsored the Christian Identity Church called the Church of Jesus Christ, Christian.

Asif Ali Zardari (b. 1955) The husband of Benazir Bhutto, Zardari inherited control of the Pakistan People's Party after Bhutto's assassination in December 2007. He was elected president in 2008.

Ayub Khan (1907–1974) The second president of Pakistan, from 1958 to 1974. Khan seized control of the government in 1958 and then staged elections. He was the first of Pakistan's many military leaders.

Baathist A member of the pan-national Arab Baath Party. Baathists were secular socialists seeking to unite Arabs in a single socialist state.

Bacrims Emerging Colombian drug gangs. A number of violent gangs started to appear after the paramilitary groups were demobilized in 2005. Their ranks include former paramilitary and drug cartel members.

Bacterial weapons Enhanced forms of bacteria that may be countered by antibiotics.

Badr The site of a battle between the Muslims of Medina and the merchants of Mecca in 624. Mohammed was unsure whether he should resist the attacking Meccans but decided God would allow Muslims to defend their community. After victory, Mohammed said that Badr was the Lesser Jihad. Greater Jihad, he said, was seeking internal spiritual purity.

Balfour Declaration A policy statement by the British government in November 1917 that promised a homeland for Jews in the geographical area of biblical Israel. Sir Arthur Balfour was the British foreign secretary.

Balochistan The largest of four states in Pakistan. It is dominated by the Baloch tribe. Many Balochs are fighting a guerrilla war against Pakistan's army in a dispute over profits from natural resources. The central government is creating a deepwater port and international trade center in Gwadar, Pakistan's principal seaport, and displacing many Balochs.

Belfast Agreement Also known as the Good Friday Agreement, an agreement signed in April 1998 that revamped criminal justice services, established shared government in Northern Ireland, called for the early release of prisoners involved in paramilitary organizations, and created the Commission on Human Rights and Equity. Its provisions led to the decommissioning of paramilitary organizations.

Ben Klassen (1918–1993) The founder of the Creativity Movement.

Beslan school Was attacked by Chechen terrorists on the first day of school in September 2004 in North Ossetia. The scene was chaotic, and Russian forces were never able to establish a security perimeter. Although details remain unclear, the incident resulted in the murder of nearly 400 people, including more than 100 children.

Big Man An anthropological term to describe an important person in a tribe or clan. *Big Man* is sometimes used by political scientists to describe a dictator in a totalitarian government.

Bill of Rights The first 10 amendments to the U.S. Constitution.

Black June The rebel organization created by Abu Nidal in 1976. He changed the name to the Fatah Revolutionary Council after a rapprochement with Syria in 1981. Most analysts refer to this group simply as the Abu Nidal Organization.

Black Market Peso Exchange A method for converting illegal profits in U.S. currency to Colombian pesos in an effort to hide the illegal funds. Terrorists have frequently used the system, although they launder less money than organized crime or drug networks.

Black widows Chechen female suicide bombers. In the Chechen language, they are known as Islamic martyrs.

Blind terrorism Tactic used by the FLN. It included indiscriminant attacks against French outposts, which involved bombing, sabotage, and random assassination.

Bourgeois The middle class. *Bourgeoisie* (plural) in Marxist terminology refers to tradespeople, merchants, artisans, and other non-peasants excluded from the upper classes in medieval Europe. Marx called the European democracies after the French Revolution bourgeois governments, and he advocated a democracy dominated by workers.

Brady bill A law that limits gun ownership, named for President Ronald Reagan's press secretary after he was disabled by a gunshot in a 1981 assassination attempt on Reagan.

Branch Davidians Followers of Vernon Wayne Howell, also known as David Koresh. They lived in a compound outside Waco, Texas.

Brüder Schweigen German for "silent brothers," the name used by two violent right-wing extremist groups, Brüder Schweigen and Brüder Schweigen Strike Force II. The late Robert Miles, leader of the Mountain Church of Jesus in Michigan, penned an article about the struggle for white supremacy, "When All of the Brothers Struggle."

Bureaucracy Governmental, private-sector, and nonprofit organizations. It assumes that people organize in a hierarchy to create an organization that will solve problems.

Bureau of Justice Assistance (BJA) A division of the U.S. Department of Justice that assists state, local, and tribal law enforcement agencies.

Camp David Peace Accord A peace treaty between Egypt and Israel brokered by the United States in 1979.

Capone discovery A term used by James Adams to explain the Irish Republican Army's entry into organized crime.

Carlos Marighella (1911–1969) A Brazilian Communist legislator and revolutionary theorist. Marighella popularized urban terrorism as a method for ending repression and eliminating U.S. domination of Latin America. He was killed in a police ambush in São Paulo in 1969.

Cell The basic unit of a traditional terrorist organization. Groups of cells form columns. Members in different cells seldom know one another. In more recent terrorist structures, *cell* describes a tactical group dispatched by the network for selected operations.

Cesare Beccaria (1738–1794) One of the founders of the discipline of criminology. His work *Of Crimes and Punishments* (1764) is the classic Enlightenment study of the discipline.

Chain organizations Temporary associations of diverse groups. Groups in a chain come together for a particular operation and disband after it is over.

Charles Taylor (b. 1948) A warlord in the First War of the Liberian civil war and president of Liberia from 1997 to 2003.

Christian Identity An American extremist religion proclaiming white supremacy. Adherents believe that white Protestants of Western European origin are the true descendants of the ancient Israelites. Believers contend that Jews were spawned by Satan and that nonwhites evolved from animals. According to this belief, white men and women are the only people created in the image of God.

Civil defense Citizens engaged in homeland security.

Civil liberties Individual rights granted to citizens under the U.S. Constitution.

COINTELPRO An infamous FBI counterintelligence program started in 1956. Agents involved in COINTELPRO violated constitutional limitations on domestic intelligence gathering, and the program came under congressional criticism in the early 1970s. The FBI's abuse of power eventually resulted in restrictions on the FBI.

Colombo The traditional capital of Sri Lanka and the country's largest city, with a population of 5,648,000. The Sri Lankan government moved the capital to Sri Jayawardenapura Kotte, five miles away, in 1982. Colombo remains the economic center of Sri Lanka.

Combined Joint Task Force, Horn of Africa (CJTF-HOA) An American-led counterterrorist unit combining military, intelligence, and law enforcement assets of several nations in the Horn.

Committee of Public Safety Assembled by Maximilien Robespierre (1758–1794) to conduct war against invading monarchal powers, it evolved into the executive body of France. The Committee of Public Safety initiated the Reign of Terror.

Communists Socialists who believed in a strong centralized economy controlled by a strong central government. Their ideas were summarized in *The Communist Manifesto*, written by Karl Marx and Friedrich Engels in 1848.

Communities Against Terrorism (CAT) A law enforcement initiative that provides businesses with information about terrorist activities particular to each business or industry. Liaisons from local agencies contact businesses, provide information about the types of preincident activities employees might see in that type of business, and leave contact information.

Copycats People who imitate other criminals after viewing, hearing, or reading a story about a crime. A copycat copies the targets and methods of another criminal.

Creativity The deistic religion of the Creativity movement. It claims that white people must struggle to defeat Jews and nonwhite races.

Criminal intelligence Information gathered on the reasonable suspicion that a criminal activity is occurring or about to occur. It is collected by law enforcement agencies in the course of their preventive and investigative functions. It is shared on information networks such as the Regional Information Sharing System (RISS). Unlike national defense intelligence, criminal intelligence applies only under criminal law. Agencies must suspect some violation of criminal law before they can collect intelligence.

Critical media consciousness The public's understanding of the media and the way stories are presented. A critically conscious audience would not simply accept a story presented in a news frame. It would look for the motives for telling the story, how the story affects social constructs and actions, and hidden details that could cause the story to be told in another way.

Cuban guerrilla war A three-step process as described by Che Guevara: (1) Revolutionaries join the indigenous population to form guerrilla *foco*, as Guevara called them; (2) small forces form columns and control rural areas; and (3) columns unite for a conventional offensive to overthrow government.

Cultural Revolution A violent movement in China from 1966 to 1976. Its main purpose was to rid China of its middle class and growing capitalist interests. The Cultural Revolution ended upon the death of Mao Zedong.

Cyberterrorism Occurs when computers are used to attack other networks or to conduct physical attacks on computer-controlled targets. The most frightening scenario involves an attack designed to create catastrophic failure in the economy or infrastructure.

David Galula (1919–1967) French captain who fought in Algeria from 1956 to 1958. He returned to Paris to analyze the Algerian campaign and produced a critique of the strategy that was followed in the war. His work inspired the development of counterinsurgency doctrine in the U.S. military.

Defense in depth Using social networks in national defense. It is based on Arthur Cebrowski's idea of operating at all levels of society.

Department of Homeland Security (DHS) A federal agency created in 2003 by Congress from the Office of Homeland Security after the attacks of September 11, 2001.

Desert Shield The name of the defensive phase of the international coalition, created by President George H. W. Bush after Iraq invaded Kuwait on August, 2, 1990. Its aim was to stop further Iraqi attacks and to liberate Kuwait. It lasted until coalition forces could begin an offensive against Iraq in January 1991.

Desert Storm The military code name for the January–February offensive in the 1991 Gulf War.

Domestic issues A term used by Gonzalez-Perez to refer to groups within a country fighting to change the social or political structure of that nation.

Dzhokhar Tsarnaev (b. 1993) and **Tamerlan Tsarnaev** (1986–2013) Two brothers who were members of an immigrant family in Boston. Dzhokhar was a naturalized American citizen. They believed the West was at war with their religion and decided to strike back by bombing the 2013 Boston Marathon. Law enforcement officers subsequently killed Tamerlan. Dzhokhar was wounded, taken into custody, convicted of murder, and sentenced to death.

E-Guardian An FBI system to share information about possible terrorist threats.

Embedded reporters Reporters who are placed inside military units during a combat operation.

Emergency response plans Preparations by any agency to deal with natural, accidental, or humanmade disasters. They involve controlling the incident through an organized response-and-command system and assigning various organizations to supervise the restoration of social order.

Endemic terrorism Terrorism that exists inside a political entity. For example, European colonialists created the nation of Rwanda by combining the lands of two tribes that literally hate each other. The two tribes fought to eliminate each other. This is endemic to political violence in Rwanda. The term was coined by J. Bowyer Bell.

Enemy combatants A legal term used to describe nonstate paramilitary captives from Afghanistan. The Bush administration later applied the term to all jihadist terrorists. The Obama administration maintained detention centers after ordering the closing of Guantánamo shortly after President Obama took office in January 2009.

Enhanced interrogation A process of using physical duress while questioning suspects. Supporters argue that such actions are necessary to gain information about future terrorism. Opponents argue that such actions constitute torture, thus violating human rights.

Enlightenment An eighteenth-century intellectual movement that followed the Scientific Revolution. Also called the Age of Reason, the Enlightenment was characterized by rational thought and the belief that all activities could be explained.

Eric Rudolph (b. 1966) A right-wing extremist known for bombing the Atlanta Olympics, a gay nightclub, and an abortion clinic. Rudolph hid from authorities and became a survivalist hero. He was arrested in 2003 and received five life sentences in 2005.

Ernesto "Che" Guevara (1928–1967) Fidel Castro's assistant and guerrilla warfare theorist. Guevara advocated guerrilla revolutions throughout Latin America after success in the Cuban Revolution. He was killed in Bolivia in 1967 while trying to form a guerrilla army.

Eschatology (pronounced es-ka-TAW-low-gee) A Greek word used to indicate the theological end of time. In Judaism and Christianity, it refers to God bringing creation to an end. In some Shi'ite Islamic sects and among Christians who interpret biblical eschatological literature literally, believers contend that Jesus will return to lead a final battle against evil. Other major religions also have end-time theology.

Estates General An assembly in prerevolutionary France consisting of all but the lowest class. The Estates General had not been called since 1614, but Louis XVI assembled them in 1789 in response to demands from the Assembly of Notables, who had been called to address the financial problems of France. Radical elements in the Estates General revolted, and the disruption led the French Revolution.

Expropriation A term used by Carlos Marighella to refer to armed robbery.

Failed state An area outside a government's control. Failed states operate under differing warlords, criminal groups, or competing governments.

Far enemy A jihadist term referring to non-Islamic powers or countries outside the realm of Islam.

Fedayeen Warriors who sacrifice themselves. The term was used differently in Arab history; the modern term is used to describe the secular warriors of Fatah.

Federal Law Enforcement Training Center (FLETC) A law enforcement training academy for federal agencies. Operating in Glencoe, Georgia, FLETC trains agents and police officers for agencies that do not operate their own academy.

Field contacts Information recorded from contacts during patrol operations or investigations. Police officers come into contact with many people during the course of routine patrol or investigations. They frequently encounter suspicious people or circumstances without enough evidence to make an arrest. Field contacts refer to recorded information about such encounters.

Field training officers Experienced senior patrol officers who ride with police academy graduates. They are responsible for on-the-job training. They mentor and evaluate new recruits.

Fifth Amendment Ensures protection against arbitrary arrest, being tried more than once for the same crime, and self-incrimination. It also guarantees due process.

Financial Action Task Force on Money Laundering (FATF) A resolution passed by the United Nations in 1990 and strengthened from 2001 to 2006. It urged member states to adopt measures to hamper money laundering and terrorist financing. It contained 40 recommendations. Nine special recommendations were added to focus specifically on terrorist financing.

First Amendment Guarantees the rights to speech, assembly, religion, press, and petitioning the government.

FISA courts Review federal requests for electronic evidence gathering and search warrants without public review.

Force multiplier A method of increasing striking power without increasing the number of combat troops in a military unit. Terrorists have four force multipliers: (1) technology to enhance weapons or attacks on technological facilities, (2) transnational support,

(3) media coverage, and (4) religious fanaticism.

Force protection Refers to security operations by military forces engaged in securing bases, ports, other areas of operations, and personnel. Military personnel frequently cooperate with local law enforcement and other civil forces when engaged in force protection.

Forensic accounting An investigative tool used to track money used in illegal activities. It can be used in any crime involving the exchange, storage, or conversion of fiscal resources.

Fourteenth Amendment Guarantees that a person cannot be deprived of freedom or property by the government unless the government follows all the procedures demanded for legal prosecution.

Fourteen Words Racist words coined by David Lane, a member of The Order: "We must secure the existence of our people and a future for white children."

Fourth Amendment Particularly applicable to law enforcement and homeland security, it limits government search and seizure, including the elements of arrest.

Francisco Franco (1892–1975) Leader of the nationalist forces during the Spanish Civil War and the fascist dictator of Spain from 1939 to 1975.

Freedom of Information (FOI) Act A law ensuring access to governmental records.

Free State The name given to the newly formed Republic of Ireland after Irish independence.

Free-wheeling fundamentalists White supremacists or Christian patriots who either selectively use Bible passages or create their own religion to further the patriot agenda.

Fusion centers Operations set up to fuse information from multiple sources, analyze the data, turn it into usable intelligence, and distribute intelligence to agencies needing the information.

Globalization A common global economic network that would ideally unite the world through production and international trade. Proponents believe it will create wealth. Critics believe it creates corporate wealth and increases distance between the rich and poor.

Goal displacement Occurs when process is favored over accomplishments. Process should be reasonable and efficient. Too much focus on the process, however, interferes with completion of job tasks.

Golden Temple The most sacred shrine of Sikhism. Its official name is the Temple of God.

Government Management Reform Act of 1994 A federal law designed to prevent political interference in the management of federal governmental organizations and to increase the efficiency of management.

Group think Refers to a bureaucratic process in which members of a group work together to solve a problem; however, innovation and deviant ideas are discouraged as the group tries to seek consensus about a conclusion. Powerful members of the group may quash alternative voices. Intelligence groups tend to resist making any risky conclusion lest they jeopardize their individual careers. Peer pressure creates an atmosphere in which every individual comes to the same conclusion.

Gulf States Small Arab kingdoms bordering the Persian Gulf. They include Bahrain, Qatar, the United Arab Emirates, and Oman.

Habib Akdas (birth date unknown) Also known as Abu Anas al Turki,

the founder of al Qaeda in Turkey. Akdas left Turkey to fight in Iraq after the American invasion. He was killed in a U.S. air strike in 2004.

Hapsburgs The ruling family of Austria (1282–1918), the Austro-Hungarian Empire (1437–1918), and the Holy Roman Empire (1282–1806). Another branch of the family ruled in Spain (1516–1700). Reference here is to the Austrian royal family.

Haqqani network A family in the tribal area of Pakistan that has relations with several militant groups and the ISI. The Haqqani family is involved in organized crime, legitimate businesses, the ISI, and terrorist groups. It is the major power broker in the tribal region.

Hassan al Banna (1906–1949) The founder of the Muslim Brotherhood. He was murdered by agents of the Egyptian government.

Hassan al Turabi (b. 1932) A Sudanese intellectual and Islamic scholar. He served in the Sudanese government during the time Osama bin Laden was in exile in Sudan.

Hassan Nasrallah (b. 1960) The secretary general of Hezbollah. He took over the leadership of Hezbollah after Abbas Musawi's death in 1992. Nasrallah is a lively speaker and charismatic leader.

Hawala system A system of exchanging money based on trust relationships between money dealers. A chit, or promissory note, is exchanged between two Hawaladars, and it is as valuable as cash or other traded commodities because the trust between the two parties guarantees its value.

High-Intensity Drug Trafficking Area (HIDTA) Specialized RICs in regions experiencing a high level of drug trafficking and drug-related crimes. They evolved from RICs and were the direct predecessor to fusion centers. Some HIDTAs simply expanded to become full fusion centers.

Highly enriched uranium (HEU) A process that increases the proportion of a radioactive isotope in uranium (U-235), making it suitable for industrial use. It can also be used to make nuclear weapons. Nuclear weapons are made from either HEU or plutonium.

Hohenzollerns The ruling family of Brandenburg and Prussia that ruled a united Germany from 1871 to 1914.

Homeland Security Act of 2002 A federal law created in 2002 and amended in following years. It established the Department of Homeland Security and reorganized the presidential cabinet. DHS's primary antiterrorism mission is to prevent attacks and respond to them when they occur.

Human rights The basic entitlements and protections that should be given to every person.

Hussein ibn Ali (626–680) Mohammed's grandson and Ali's second son. He was martyred at Karbala in 680. The majority of Shi'ites believe that Hussein is the Third Imam, after Imam Ali and Imam Hasan, Ali's oldest son.

Ibn al Khattab (1969– 2002) Also known as Emir Khattab or the Black Wahhabi, a Saudi international jihadist who went to fight in Chechnya. He tried to move the Chechen revolt from a nationalistic platform to a philosophy of religious militancy. He was killed the Russian secret service in 2002.

Ibrahim al Asiri (b. 1982) Son of a Saudi Arabian career military officer and AQAP's master bomb maker. He is known for perfecting chemical bombs and was behind

several regional and international attempted murders.

Imad Mugniyah (1962–2008) The leader of the international branch of Hezbollah. He has been implicated in many attacks, including the 1983 U.S. marine and French paratrooper bombings. He is also believed to have been behind bombings of the U.S. embassy in Beirut and two bombings of Israeli targets in Argentina. He was assassinated in Damascus in February 2008.

Independent Monitoring Commission (IMC) A commission created in 2004 to investigate paramilitary actions and alleged governmental abuses during the Irish peace process.

Infotainment telesector A sarcastic term to describe cable news networks. It refers to news organizations that produce stories to entertain their audiences under the guise of presenting objective information.

Integration Occurs when illegally gained money is presented into the formal economic system as if it were the result of a legal activity.

Intelligence-led policing A managerial model that focuses on the collection and analysis of information. After analysis, law enforcement resources are deployed to prevent and disrupt crime and to target specific crimes and offenders. Intelligence-led policing is an alternative to using criminal intelligence to support investigations and other forms of reactive policing.

Intelligence product The output of information analysis. Information is analyzed and turned into intelligence. This product is distributed to users.

International focus Gonzalez-Perez uses the term *international focus* to refer to terrorist groups operating in multiple countries.

Inter-Service Intelligence (ISI) The Pakistani domestic and foreign intelligence service, created by the British in 1948. Supporters claim that it centralizes Pakistan's intelligence. Critics maintain that it operates like an independent state and supports terrorist groups.

Intifada The first spontaneous uprising against Israel, lasting from 1987 to 1993. It began with youths throwing rocks and creating civil disorder. Some of the violence became more organized. Many people sided with religious organizations, abandoning the secular PLO during the Intifada.

Iranian Revolution The 1979 religious revolution that toppled Mohammed Pahlavi, the shah of Iran, and transformed Iran into an Islamic republic ruled by Shi'ite religious scholars.

Iran–Iraq War A war fought after Iraq invaded Iran over a border dispute in 1980. Many experts predicted an Iraqi victory, but the Iranians stopped the Iraqi army. The war produced an eight-year stalemate and more than a million casualties. The countries signed an armistice in 1988.

Islamic Courts Union (ICU) A confederation of tribes and clans seeking to end violence and bring Islamic law to Somalia. It is opposed by several neighboring countries and internal warlords. Some people feel that it is a jihadist organization, but others see it as a grouping of clans with several different interpretations of Islamic law.

Izz el Din al Qassam Brigades The military wing of Hamas, named after the Arab revolutionary leader Sheik Izz el Din al Qassam (1882–1935), who led a revolt against British rule.

James W. von Brunn (1920–2010) An American white supremacist and anti-Semite. He entered the Holocaust Museum on June 10, 2009, and began shooting. He killed a security officer before he was wounded and subdued. He died in federal custody while awaiting trial.

Jammu and Kashmir A mountainous region in northern India claimed by both India and Pakistan. It has been the site of heavy fighting during three wars between India and Pakistan in 1947–1948, 1971, and 1999. Kashmir is artificially divided by a line of control (LOC), with Pakistani forces to the north and Indian forces to the south. India and Pakistan made strides toward peace after 2003, but many observers believe that the ISI supports jihadist operations in the area.

Janet Napolitano (b. 1957) The third secretary of homeland security. President Obama appointed her while she was serving her second term of governor in Arizona.

John Walker Lindh (b. 1981) An American captured while fighting for the Taliban in 2001 and sentenced to 20 years in prison.

Joseph Stalin (1878–1953) The dictator who succeeded Vladimir Lenin. Stalin solidified Communist control of Russia through a secret police organization. He purged the government of suspected opponents in the 1930s, killing thousands of people.

Juan Manuel Santos Became president of Colombia in August 2010. He narrowly won a second term in 2014, edging out a conservative candidate who opposed talks with the FARC.

Khalid Meshal (b. 1956) One of the "outside" leaders of Hamas, in Damascus, Syria, Meshal became the political leader of Hamas in 2004. After the 2006 election, he continued to lead from exile.

King Gyanendra (b. 1947) King of Nepal from 2001 to 2008. After the attack and murder of several members of the royal family, Gyanendra became king of Nepal in 2001. He took complete power in 2005 to fight the Maoist rebellion. In the spring of 2006, he was forced to return power to parliament, and he was removed from power in 2008.

King Hussein (1935–1999) King of Jordan. King Hussein drove the PLO from Jordan in September 1970. After his death, his son Abdullah assumed the throne.

Knight Riders The first terrorists of the Ku Klux Klan. Donning hoods and riding at night, they sought to keep newly freed slaves from participating in government and society.

Know-Nothings Different groups of American nationalists in the early nineteenth century who championed native-born whites over immigrants.

Layering Concealing the source of illegal income in confusing, sometimes multiple financial actions.

Law Enforcement Equipment Acquisition Working Group (LEEWG) A task force created by a presidential directive in January 2015. The president charged the LEEWG with gathering information on the types of federally supplied military equipment police agencies had acquired and the procedures for obtaining these items. The task force also was to make recommendations for future policies. The LEEWG was co-chaired by the attorney general, secretary of defense, and secretary of homeland security. It resulted in a presidential ban on distributing some types of equipment.

Leila Khalid (b. 1944) Was a member of the Popular Front for the Liberation of Palestine. In 1969, she was part of a team that hijacked

four aircraft that were destroyed after the passengers and crews disembarked. Arrested in 1970 after another attempted hijacking, she was later released as part of a prisoner exchange.

Leon Trotsky (1879–1940) A Russian revolutionary who led foreign affairs in Stalin's government and later became the commander of the Red Army. He espoused terrorism as a means for spreading White revolution. He was thrown out of the Communist Party for opposing Stalin and was assassinated by Communist agents in Mexico City in 1940.

Liberian civil war Two episodes of conflict involving rebel armies and militias as well as neighboring countries. The First War (1989–1996) ended when a rebel army brought Charles Taylor to Monrovia, the capital. The Second War (1999–2003) toppled Charles Taylor from power. Both wars were characterized by village massacres and conscription of child soldiers.

Liberians United for Reconciliation and Democracy (LURD) A revolutionary movement founded in 1999 in western Africa. LURD was instrumental in driving Charles Taylor from power in 2003.

Longitudinal studies In the social sciences, studies that involve examinations of the same subjects over long periods of time.

Lord's Resistance Army Ugandan guerrilla force opposing the government since 1987. The LRA has conscripted thousands of children, forcing them into its ranks or mutilating and killing them. Dropping all pretense of political activity, it roams through Uganda, southern Sudan, the Democratic Republic of the Congo, and the Central Africa Republic. Its primary tactics are mass murder, mass rape, theft, and enslavement of children. Uganda has referred the LRA to the International Criminal Court.

Made-for-TV dramas Refers to news stories that will keep viewers' attention. H. H. A. Cooper was among the first analysts to recognize the drama that terrorism presented for television.

Madrassas Islamic religious schools.

Mahmud Abbas (b. 1935) The president of the Palestinian Authority since 2005, a founding member of Fatah, and an executive in the PLO.

Majilis council The Islamic name given to a religious council that advises a government or a leader. Some Islamic countries refer to their legislative body as a majilis.

Mandate of Palestine The British Mandate of Palestine was in effect from 1920 to 1948. Created by the League of Nations, the mandate gave the United Kingdom the right to extend its influence in an area roughly equivalent to modern Jordan, Israel, and the Palestinian Authority.

Margherita Cagol (1945–1975) Also known as Mara Cagol. The wife of Renato Curcio and a member of the Red Brigades. She was killed in a shoot-out with Italian police a few weeks after freeing her husband from prison.

Mark Sykes (1879–1919) A British diplomat who signed a secret agreement with Francois Georges-Picot in May 1916. The Sykes–Picot Agreement divided the Middle East into spheres of French, British, and Russian influence.

Marwan Barghouti (b. 1969) A leader of Fatah and alleged leader of the al Aqsa Martyrs Brigades. A Brigades statement in 2002 claimed that Barghouti was their leader. He rose to prominence during the al Aqsa Intifada, but he is currently being held in an Israeli prison.

Max Weber (1864–1920) One of the major figures of modern sociological methods, he studied the organization of human endeavors. Weber believed that social organizations could be organized for rational purposes designed to accomplish objectives.

Meaning The subjective interpretation people give to events or physical objects. Meanings are developed by individuals and groups, and different meanings can be attributed to the same event or physical object because the definitions are always influenced by interpretation. Social scientists in this tradition believe that meanings cause actions.

Meaning framework The definitional boundaries for a particular social meaning. Individuals and groups create boundaries around their experiences and perceptions, and they define issues within them. Meaning frameworks are the social boundaries surrounding those definitions. Juergensmeyer sees the clash between modern values and traditional culture as one of the reasons for terrorism. Religious terrorists look at the modern world and reject it. This world is evil in the meaning framework of religious terrorists, and they refuse to accept the boundaries of the secular modern world.

Militarization Responding to social problems with military solutions. In law enforcement, militarization is usually characterized by martial law.

Military-industrial complex A term coined by President Dwight D. Eisenhower (1890–1969) to describe the relationship between American military forces and private industry.

Military tribunals Venue for military courts to try combatants outside the civilian court system. Trials take place in front of a board of military officers operating under military law.

Militia movement A political movement started in the early 1980s, possibly spawned from survivalism. Militias maintain that the Second Amendment gives them the right to arm themselves and form paramilitary organizations apart from governmental control and military authority.

Mission creep Occurs when too many secondary tasks are added to an organizational unit. Too many jobs divert a unit from its primary mission.

Mogadishu The capital of Somalia. U.S. troops moved into Mogadishu during Operation Restore Hope from December 9, 1992, until May 4, 1993, when the United Nations took over operations. American forces were involved in a major battle in October 1993 involving a downed U.S. army helicopter.

Mohammed Ali Jinnah (1876–1948) The leader of the Muslim League and the founder of modern Pakistan. He served as governor general until his death in 1948.

Mohammed Fneish (age unknown) A Hezbollah politician and minister of energy in the Lebanese prime minister's cabinet.

Mohammed ibn Abdul Wahhab (1703–1792) Also known as Abdul Wahhab; a religious reformer who wanted to purge Islam of anything beyond the traditions accepted by Mohammed and the four Rightly Guided caliphs. He conducted campaigns against Sufis, Shi'ites, and Muslims who made pilgrimages or who invoked the names of saints.

Mohammed Reza Pahlavi (1919–1980) Shah of Iran from 1941 to 1979. The shah led a rigorous program of modernization that turned Iran into a regional power. He left the throne and accepted exile as a result of the 1979 Iranian Revolution.

Mokhtar Belmokhtar (b. 1972) An Algerian jihadist and organized crime figure. Belmokhtar fought in the Soviet–Afghan War and the Algerian civil war. He joined the Salafi Call for Preaching and Combat and later AQIM. He later broke with AQIM. He is also known for criminal activity.

Moorish Nation An African American group that does not recognize the validity of the U.S. government.

Moscow theatre (Theatrical Center, Dubrovka, Moscow, 2002) The site of a Chechen attack where approximately 40 terrorists took 850 hostages. Russian forces stormed the theater on the third day of the siege, killing 39 terrorists and at least 129 hostages.

Mossad The Israeli intelligence agency, formed in 1951. It is responsible for gathering foreign intelligence.

Mullah Omar (b. 1959) The leader of the Taliban. After the collapse of the Taliban government in 2001, Omar went into hiding.

Mumbai attack The LeT launched several attacks in Mumbai, India, in November 2008. Terrorists killed dozens of people and took several hostages. The attacks paralyzed the city for several days.

Muqtada al Sadr (b. 1974) An Iraqi ayatollah. Al Sadr leads the Shi'ite militia known as the Mahdi Army.

Musa Abu Marzuq (b. 1951) The "outside" leader of Hamas. He is thought to be in Damascus, Syria. He is believed to have controlled the Holy Land Foundation.

Muslim Brotherhood An organization founded by Hassan al Banna, designed to recapture the spirit and religious purity of the period of Mohammed and the four Rightly Guided caliphs. The Brotherhood seeks to create a single Muslim nation through education and religious reform. A militant wing founded by Sayyid Qutb sought the same objective through violence. Hamas, a group that defines itself as the Palestinian branch of the Muslim Brotherhood, has rejected the multinational approach in favor of creating a Muslim Palestine.

Najibullah Zazi (b. 1985) A 1999 immigrant to the United States. Zazi was born in Afghanistan and raised in Pakistan. He was arrested in 2009 for planning suicide attacks in New York City and pleaded guilty to charges of terrorism in 2010.

Narcoterrorism A controversial term that links drugs to terrorism in one of two ways: Either drug profits are used to finance terrorism or drug gangs use terrorism to control production and distribution networks.

Nasir al Wuhayshi (d. 2015) The spiritual leader of AQAP and a former aide to Osama bin Laden. Wuhayshi escaped from a Yemeni prison in 2006 to form AQY. In 2009, he joined his group with dissidents in Saudi Arabia to form AQAP.

Nathan Bedford Forrest (1821–1877) A famed and gifted Confederate cavalry commander who founded the Ku Klux Klan in Pulaski, Tennessee. Forrest tried to disband the KKK when he saw the violent path that it was taking.

National Alliance The white supremacist organization founded by the late William Pierce and headquartered in Hillsboro, West Virginia.

National Convention Elected in 1792, it broke from the Estates General and called for a constitutional assembly in France. The White Convention served as the major legislative body of France until it was replaced by the Directory in 1795.

National Counterterrorism Center (NCTC) An organization designed to filter information from the intelligence process, synthesize counterterrorist information, and share it with appropriate organizations.

National Criminal Intelligence Sharing Plan A 2005 set of recommendations designed to overcome barriers to sharing criminal intelligence. The plan contains recommended actions, oversight of operations, and standards for protecting privacy and individual rights. It suggests minimum standards for establishing and managing intelligence operations within police agencies.

National Intelligence University An in-service initiative standardizing training for the entire intelligence community.

National Liberation Movement The Tupamaros' official name.

National security intelligence A system of agencies and networks that gather information about threats to the country. Any threat or potential threat is examined under the auspices of national defense intelligence. Unlike criminal intelligence, people and agencies gathering defense information do not need to suspect any criminal activity. The FBI is empowered to gather defense intelligence.

National Security Letter A mandatory request from the FBI for public and private records. The recipient is not allowed to discuss the contents of an NSL outside FBI interviews.

Nationwide SAR Initiative (NSI) A federal program designed to develop common antiterrorism intelligence reporting procedures among state, local, and tribal law enforcement agencies. SAR is an acronym for suspicious activity report.

Near enemy A jihadist term referring to forms of Muslim governments and Islamic law (*sharia*) that do not embrace the narrow-minded philosophy of Sayyid Qutb.

Netwar One network fighting another network.

Networks Organizations of groups, supplies, weapons, and any structure that supports an operation. Much like a traffic system or the World Wide Web, networks do not have central leadership, and they operate under a variety of rules.

New economy of terrorism A term used by Loretta Napoleoni to describe the evolution of terrorist financing from the beginning strategies of the Cold War to the present. Economic support and antiterrorist policies interact to form the new economy.

New media Any virtual network that allows communication. It includes blogs, multiple Internet postings, and any social network.

News frames Visual, audible, or written packages used to present the news. Communication scholars do not agree on a single definition, but news frames generally refer to the presentation of the news story. They contain a method for beginning and ending the story, and they convey the importance of characters and actions as the story is told.

News media As used in this text, refers to television, radio, and print journalism. It also refers to newer sources on the Internet, including news reporting services, the blogosphere, website pages, and propaganda broadcasts.

New World Order A phrase used by President George H. W. Bush to describe the world after the fall of the Soviet Union. Conspiracy theorists use the phrase to describe what they believe to be Jewish attempts to gain control of the international monetary system and, subsequently, to take over the U.S. government.

Nidal Malik Hasan (b. 1970) A former American soldier of Palestinian descent. Hasan was an army psychiatrist who apparently became self-radicalized and embraced militant Islam. He went on a shooting spree at Fort Hood, Texas, on November 5, 2009, killing 13 people and wounding almost three dozen others. He was wounded, arrested, charged with several counts of murder, and sentenced to death.

Nodes In counterterrorist or netwar discussions, the points in a system where critical components are stored or transferred. The importance of a node is determined by its relationship to the network.

No-go areas Geographical areas that the duly empowered government cannot control (this is an informal term). Security forces cannot routinely patrol these places.

Nordic Christianity A religion that incorporates the ancient Norse gods in a hierarchy under the Christian triune deity. It is similar to Odinism, but it does not completely abandon Christianity.

North-West Frontier Province (NWFP) One of four Pakistani states, inhabited primarily by ethnic Pashtuns. Several areas of the NWFP are controlled by tribes, and jihadists operate in the area. Peshawar, NWFP's capital, served as a base for organizing several mujahedeen groups in the Soviet–Afghan War.

Nuclear black market The system where nuclear material and weapons are allegedly exchanged. When the Soviet Union collapsed, it was difficult to account for all the nuclear weapons that were in the control of military officials and the newly independent states. People feared that these weapons would be sold to terrorists. Similar fears exist for Pakistan's nuclear bombs and nuclear development programs in North Korea and Iran.

NYPD Intelligence After the 9/11 attacks, the New York City Police Department created a new intelligence operation to assess domestic and international threats to the city. Its first administrator was a former executive from the CIA. The NYPD sends officers overseas to gather information and assess terrorist threats.

Omar Hammami (b. 1984) An American leader of Al Shabab; uses the name Abu Mansoor al-Amriki.

Ottoman Empire A Turkish empire that lasted for 600 years, until 1924. The empire spanned southeastern Europe, North Africa, and southwest Asia. It reached its zenith in the fourteenth and fifteenth centuries.

Panga A heavy-bladed machete used in agricultural work. It was the weapon favored by people who took the Mau Mau oath.

Paper terrorism Uses false documents to clog legal, financial, or bureaucratic processes.

Partner capacity As used by Robert Gates, Secretary of Defense 2006–2011, the ability of U.S. military forces to form alliances with security forces and civilian governments inside states threatened with destabilization.

Peace dividend A term used during President William Clinton's administration (1992–2000) to describe reducing defense spending at the end of the Cold War.

People power revolution A mass Philippine protest movement that toppled Ferdinand Marcos in 1986. Marcos ruled as dictator after being elected as president in 1965 and declaring martial law in 1972. When Gloria Macapagal-Arroyo assumed the presidency in January 2001, a position that she held until 2010, her government proclaimed a second people power revolution.

Pervez Musharraf (b. 1943) The president of Pakistan (2001–2008). A career army officer, Musharraf took power in a 1999 military coup and declared himself president in 2001. After 9/11, he sought closer relations with the United States while trying to mollify sources of domestic religious strife.

Philosophy of the bomb A phrase used by anarchists around 1848. It means that social order can be changed only through violent upheaval. Bombs were the first technological force multiplier.

Placement Refers to placing illegal monetary profits in the legitimate financial system.

Plan Colombia A joint effort by the United States and Colombia to reduce violence and illegal drugs. It began in 1999.

Police Service of Northern Ireland (PSNI) The police force created in November 2001 to replace the Royal Ulster Constabulary.

Postmodern A term that describes the belief that modernism has ended; that is, some events are inexplicable, and some organizations and actions are naturally and socially chaotic and defy explanation. A postmodern news frame leaves the consumer thinking there are many possible conclusions.

Preincident indicators The criminal and social actions of individuals and groups before a terrorist attack.

Process orientation Occurs when one pays more attention to the manner of achieving organizational goals than actually achieving them. Process is important when it focuses on ethical and legal requirements. Process orientation goes beyond legal and moral norms, and it becomes dysfunctional when an organization's goal is conceived as maintaining procedures.

Profiling A practical criminological process designed to identify the behavioral attributes of certain types of criminals.

Proteus USA A project designed to identify future threats to national security by assembling panels of experts in various fields that might impact national defense. It was developed by the U.S. Army War College and the National Intelligence University.

Protocols of Zion A forged document written in czarist Russia explaining an alleged Jewish plot to control the world. It was popularized in the United States by Henry Ford. It is frequently cited by the patriot and white supremacy movements. Jihadists also use it as evidence against Jews.

Provisionals The nickname for members of the Provisional Irish Republican Army. They are also known as Provos. The name applies to several different Republican paramilitary terrorist groups.

Pyramid An illustration of the way terrorists organize themselves into hierarchies. It is an analogy showing a large base of support culminating in a small group of terrorists at the top.

Qasim al Raymi (b. 1978) Became the leader of AQAP in June 2015. He escaped from a Yemeni prison 2006 and formed AQY in 2007 with fellow escapee Nasir al Wuhayshi. They merged AQY with

Saudi dissidents in 2009 to form AQAP.

Quadrennial Homeland Security Review (QHSR) Result of a requirement that the secretary of the DHS conduct a review of the department's operations every four years. According to the first report, the Homeland Security Act of 2002, as amended, requires the secretary to "delineate and update, as appropriate, the national homeland security strategy," and to "outline and prioritize the full range of the critical homeland security mission areas of the Nation" (DHS, 2010).

Racial terrorism A dominant group using violence to intimidate a racial minority. Tactics include lynching, murder, beatings, and other forms of violence against a minority group. For example, the Ku Klux Klan historically has practiced racial terrorism.

Radiation sickness Caused by exposure to high doses of radiation over a short period of time. It is characterized by nausea, diarrhea, headaches, and fever. High doses of radiation produce dizziness, weakness, and internal bleeding. It is possible to treat patients who have been exposed to doses of radiation, but higher doses are usually fatal. Other than the two nuclear bombs used in World War II, most radiation sickness has been caused by industrial accidents.

Radical democrats Those who tried to bring democracy to all classes. They sought a more equitable distribution of wealth throughout all economic classes, believing that concentrated wealth and class inequities prevented societies from becoming truly democratic.

Radicalization As used in this textbook, radicalization refers to the psychological process of adopting extremist positions.

Rajiv Gandhi (1944–1991) Prime minister of India from 1984 until 1989; in 1991 he was assassinated by an LTTE suicide bomber.

Ranasinghe Premadasa (1924–1993) President of Sri Lanka from 1989 until 1993, when he was killed by an LTTE suicide bomber.

Raúl Sendic (1926–1989) A Uruguayan revolutionary leader. Sendic founded the National Liberation Movement (MLN), popularly known as the Tupamaros. Following governmental repression in 1973, he fled the country. Sendic died in Paris in 1989.

Raymond W. Kelly (b. 1941) Became commissioner of the New York City Police Department in 2002. A veteran New York City police officer, Kelley previously served as the commissioner from 1992 to 1994. A retired colonel in the U.S. Marine Corps Reserve, Kelly served the NYPD for more than three decades.

Reasonableness Assessment of the actions an average person would take when confronted with certain circumstances. This is a Fourth Amendment doctrine.

Red Army Faction A West German Marxist group modeled as Marighella-style urban guerrillas. They were the most violent and active revolutionary group during the heyday of left-wing European terrorism. After German reunification, the records of the former East German secret police led to the demise of the RAF. It was also known as the Baader-Meinhof Gang when it first formed.

Red Brigades An Italian Marxist terrorist group that had its most effective operations from 1975 to 1990. It amended the centralized Tupamaro model by creating semi-autonomous cells.

Red Corridor The area of Naxalite violence in India. The corridor runs from Nepal through southern India, and from India's east coast to the central regions.

Red Mosque *Lal masjid*, located in Islamabad, with a madrassa and a school for women. It taught militant theology. The government ordered the mosque closed in 2007. This resulted in a shootout and a standoff. Government forces stormed the mosque in July 2007, killing more than 100 students. One of the leaders, Abdul Rashid Ghazi, was killed. His brother Maulana Abdul Aziz, the mosque's other leader, was captured while trying to escape in women's clothing.

Regional Crime Gun Centers (RCGC) ATF intelligence centers similar to RICs but focused on the illegal use of firearms.

Regional Informational Sharing System (RISS) A law enforcement network that allows law enforcement agencies to share information about criminal investigations.

Regional Intelligence Centers (RICs) Originally established to gather drug trafficking intelligence, RICs helped provide the basis for fusion centers.

Reign of Terror The name given to the repressive period in France from 1794 to 1795. The revolutionary government accused thousands of French nobles and clergy of plotting to restore the monarchy. Executions began in Paris and spread throughout the countryside. Large mobs attacked and terrorized nobles in rural areas. Summary executions (executions on the spot without a trial) were quite common.

Renato Curcio (b. 1941) The founder and leader of the Red Brigades in Italy.

Reporting frame The simplest form of a news frame. It is a quick, fact-driven report that summarizes the latest information about a story. It does not need to contain a beginning or an end, and it assumes that the consumer understands the context of the facts.

Revolutionary Guards The militarized quasi police force of the revolutionary government during the Iranian Revolution.

Reza Shah Pahlavi (1878–1944) Shah of Iran from 1925 to 1941. He was forced from power by a British and Soviet invasion.

Richard Butler (1917–2004) A self-made millionaire and white supremacist. Butler founded the Aryan Nations in Hayden Lake, Idaho.

Robert Matthews (1953–1984) The leader of The Order. Killed in a shootout with the FBI.

Routes to terrorism As used by John Horgan, refers to the psychological and social factors that motivate people to join and remain in terrorist groups.

Roving wiretaps A method of quickly intercepting disposable phone or Internet traffic. A roving wiretap allows law enforcement officers to monitor new connections without returning to court for another search warrant.

Royal Irish Constabulary (RIC) The police force established by the United Kingdom in Ireland. It was modeled after the London Metropolitan Police, but it represented British interests. After the Free State was formed, the RIC became the Royal Ulster Constabulary (RUC). In turn, the RUC gave way to the Police Service of Northern Ireland (PSNI) as part of Irish and British attempts to bring peace to Northern Ireland after 1995.

Ruby Ridge The location of a 1992 standoff between survivalists and U.S. federal law enforcement officers in Idaho during which a

U.S. marshal and survivalist Randy Weaver's wife and son were killed.

Ruhollah Khomeini (1900–1989) The Shi'ite grand ayatollah who was the leading figure in the 1979 Iranian Revolution. Khomeini toppled the shah's government and consolidated power by destroying or silencing his enemies, including other Shi'ite Islamic scholars. Iran was transformed into a theocracy under his influence.

Sabri al Banna (1937–2002) The real name of Abu Nidal. Al Banna was a founding member of Fatah but split with Arafat in 1974. He founded militias in southern Lebanon, and he attacked Western and Israeli targets in Europe during the 1980s. In the 1990s, he became a mercenary. He was murdered in Iraq, probably by the Iraqi government.

Salafi movement Used by orthodox Muslims to follow the Prophet and the elders of the faith. Militants narrow the use of the term and use it to justify violence. The Salafi movement refers to those people who impose Islam with force and violence.

SAVAK Mohammed Pahlavi's secret police, established after the 1953 downfall of the democratic government.

Sayyid Imam al Sharif (b. 1951) Also known as Dr. Fadl, one of Egypt's leading militants in the 1970s. While jailed, he embraced Islam and renounced the violence of al Qaeda–style militancy. He is viewed as a traitor by violent jihadists. He has provided much of the information we know about religious militancy, and he continues to publish works denouncing it. Still maintaining anti-Western and antigovernment views, he sees jihad as a necessary part of Islam. Al Qaeda's version, he claims, violates the morality of Islamic law.

Sayyid Qutb (1906–1966) An Egyptian educator who called for the overthrow of governments and the imposition of purified Islamic law, based on the principles of previous puritanical reformers. Qutb formed a militant wing of the Muslim Brotherhood.

Selective terrorism A term used by Michael Collins during the Irish War of Independence (1919–1921). Collins did not launch indiscriminate terror attacks. Rather, he selectively targeted the British military, the police force it sponsored, and the people who supported the United Kingdom.

Separation of powers The distribution of power among the executive, legislative, and judicial branches of government. When powers are separated, there is a balance among the powers. No one branch can control the government.

Shaba farm region A small farming region in southwest Lebanon annexed by Israel in 1981. When Israel withdrew from southern Lebanon in 2000, it remained in the Shaba farm region, creating a dispute with Lebanon, Hezbollah, and Syria.

Shamil Basayev (1965–2006) A jihadist leader in Chechnya, Basayev engineered several operations that resulted in mass civilian casualties.

Sheik Mohammed Hassan Fadlallah (1935–2010) A grand ayatollah and leader of Shi'ites in Lebanon. The spiritual leader of Hezbollah. He was the target of a 1985 U.S.-sponsored assassination plot that killed 75 people.

Sheik Omar Abdel Rahman (b. 1938) A Sunni Islamic scholar linked to the Egyptian Islamic Group. He came to the United States in 1990, even though his name was on a State Department watch list. He was arrested and convicted of conspiracy after the 1993 World Trade Center bombing. He is

currently serving a life sentence in the American federal prison system.

Shell state Created by a political situation in which a government nominally controls its own state but in which large regions are either anarchic or under the control of others. In a shell state, a government is unable to enforce law or provide for other forms of social order.

Sinn Fein The political party of Irish Republicans. Critics claim it represents terrorists. Republicans say it represents their political interests. Despite the debate, Sinn Fein historically has had close connections with extremism and violence.

Six-Day War A war between Israel and its Arab neighbors fought in June 1967. Israel launched the preemptive war in the face of an Arab military buildup, and it overwhelmed all opposition. At the end of the war, Israel occupied the Sinai Peninsula, the Golan Heights, and the West Bank of the Jordan River. It also occupied the city Jerusalem, or al Quds to Muslims.

Six tactics of terrorism As defined by Brian Jenkins: (1) bombing, (2) hijacking, (3) arson, (4) assault, (5) kidnapping, and (6) hostage taking.

Sixth Amendment Guarantees the right to an attorney and a speedy public trial by jury in the jurisdiction where an alleged crime occurred. The amendment also requires that a suspect be informed of any changes against him or her.

Skinheads Young people or groups who embrace racial hatred and white supremacy.

Smart Policing Initiative (SPI) A federal program designed to focus law enforcement resources on a particular type of crime or community problem. Programs are evaluated by external research institutions and modified based on the results of the evaluation.

Social construct The way people view reality. Groups construct a framework around a concept, defining various aspects of their lives through the meanings they attribute to the construct.

Social context The historical, political, and criminological circumstances at a given point in time. The social context affects the way terrorism is defined.

Social geometry As used by Donald Black, the social space occupied by a structure and the direction in which it moves.

Socialists Radical nineteenth century democrats who sought wealth equality in capitalist societies. Some socialists sought governmental guarantees of living standards. Others believed that the state should control industry and divide profits among all members of society. Others believed that people would form cooperative relationships on their own with no need of a government.

Social process As used in this textbook discussion, the way individuals and groups structure themselves, interpret reality, and take action based on those interpretations.

South Lebanon Army A Christian militia closely allied with and supported by Israel. It adopted the name South Lebanon Army in 1980 and operated with Israeli support from 1982 to 2000.

Sovereign citizen A citizen who believes that the original citizens of the United States were free from all governmental control. Sovereign citizens think that they were duped by the government in "schemes" like Social Security, driver's licenses, and car registrations. That is, once people participate in those conspiracies, they lose their natural freedom and become citizens of the United States. Sovereign citizens believe that they can renounce those regulations and free themselves from American law. This should be noted: Though they free themselves from taxes and fees, they rarely reject government benefits.

Spain in 1807 The Peninsular War (1808–1814) began when Spanish and French forces divided Portugal in 1807. Napoleon, whose army entered Spain in 1807, attempted to use his forces to capture the Spanish throne in 1808. British forces under Sir Arthur Wellesley, later Duke of Wellington, joined Spanish forces loyal to the king of Spain and Spanish partisans to fight the French.

Spanish Civil War (1936–1939) A war that pitted pro-Communist Republicans against pro-fascist Nationalists. The war ended with a Nationalist victory and a fascist dictatorship under Franco.

Steganography Occurs when a hidden encoded message is embedded on an Internet site.

Structural framework The idea that social constructs are based on systems that provide order. The systems are social structures that accomplish functions necessary to survive. Human activity occurs to accomplish the functions required to maintain the social structure of the system.

Structure The manner in which a group is organized and its purpose. Social scientists from this tradition feel that a group's structure and purpose cause it to act. They also believe that groups are created for specific functions.

Suppression of the Financing of Terrorism A 1999 UN resolution designed to thwart terrorist financing. It was strengthened after 9/11 by provisions that criminalize terrorist financing, empower states to seize terrorist assets, and require financial institutions to support suspicious activities.

Supreme Council of the IRB The command center of several Republican terrorist organizations, including the Irish Republican Army, the Official Irish Republican Army, and the Provisional Irish Republican Army. The name was transposed from the Irish Republican Brotherhood.

Survivalist A person who adopts a form of right-wing extremism advocating militant rejection of society. The members advocate a withdrawal from society in preparation for a coming internal war. Secluded in armed compounds, they hope to survive the coming collapse of society.

Swarming attacks Attacks launched on multiple targets in the same time frame. Also when several attackers are suddenly brought to a single location from which they rapidly disperse.

Sweet crude A type of oil with less than 0.5 percent sulfur content. Nigeria sits on a large sweet crude field, giving the country potential wealth. The people who live above the oil, however, are poverty stricken, and oil production has harmed the environment.

Symbolic targets Terrorist targets that may have limited military or security value but represent the power of the state under attack. Terrorists seek symbolic targets to strike fear into society and to give a sense of power to the terrorist group. The power of the symbol also multiplies the effect of the attack.

Syrian civil war A war that began in March 2011 in an attempt to overthrow President Bashar Assad. It is characterized by multiple groups fighting multiple enemies and has resulted in the deaths of thousands of people caught in the fighting. Opponents are divided along sectarian, ethnic, and political lines. It has attracted fighters from many countries, including nations in Europe, North America, and Asia.

Taliban The Islamicist group that governed Afghanistan from 1996 to 2001.

Tamils An ethnic minority in southern India and Sri Lanka. The Tamils in Sri Lanka are primarily Hindu, and the Sinhalese majority are mostly Buddhist. However, ethnicity—not religion—defines most of the conflict between the two groups.

Taqi al Din ibn Taymiyyah (circa 1269–1328) Also known as ibn Taymiyya; a Muslim religious reformer in the time of the Crusades and a massive Mongol invasion.

Targeting Violent Crime Initiative (TVCI) A Department of Justice grant program administered through the Bureau of Justice Assistance. Its purpose is to fund multijurisdictional state, local, and tribal law enforcement teams that prevent selected violent crimes through intelligence-led policing.

Task orientation As used in this text, refers to the ability to stay focused on the primary mission of an organization.

Terrorism Screening Center (TSC) A multiagency operation in West Virginia that evaluates information gathered from a variety of governmental sources.

The Order A violent right-wing racist group of the 1980s that killed Jewish radio talk show host Alan Berg and committed other crimes. William Pierce's *The Turner Diaries* inspired the group's formation.

Theory of action A social science theory that assumes human beings take action based on the subjective meanings they attribute to social settings.

Theory of suicide terrorism A theory developed by Robert Pape that states that a group of people

occupied by a democratic power is likely to engage in suicide attacks when there are differences between the religions of the group and the democratic power and when the occupied religious community supports altruistic suicide.

Thermobaric bomb A two-stage bomb. The first stage spreads either a fuel cloud or finely ground powder through the air. The explosive material mixes with the oxygen present in the atmosphere. The second stage detonates the explosive material, which explodes in all directions in a series of shock waves. The cloud can penetrate a number of barriers. A person breathing the material explodes from the inside out when the material is ignited.

Third Position A movement started after the Branch Davidian standoff at Waco. It attempts to unite left-wing, right-wing, and single-issue extremists in a single movement.

Threat analysis The process of examining a community to determine the areas that might be subject to attack and the criticality of those areas to the functions of the community.

Tony Blair (b. 1953) The Labour Party prime minister of the United Kingdom from 1994 to 2007.

Total criminal intelligence Refers to gathering information about all potential crimes, the activities of known and suspected criminals, crime patterns, and potential social problems. Information is analyzed and used to prevent crime. Total criminal intelligence is redundant; that is, several types of crime can be prevented by acting on a single source of information. There are several variations on the theme, including problem-oriented policing, intelligence-led policing, and the smart policing initiative.

Transitional Federal Government (TFG) A group established to

govern Somalia in 2004 until a permanent government could be established. It was backed by the United Nations, with American support, and the African Union.

Tribal areas Refers to Federally Administered Tribal Areas (FATA) in Pakistan along the Afghan border. Seven different Pashtu tribes have control of the region by agreement with the central government.

Triborder region The area where Brazil, Paraguay, and Argentina join. The major city is Cuidad del Este.

Tupac Amaru (d. 1572) An Inca chieftain who led a revolt against Spain in the sixteenth century. His story has inspired many liberation and democratic movements in South America.

Uighar nationalists China's ethnic Turkmen. Some Uighar nationalists organized to revive an eighteenth-century Islamic state in China's Xinjiang province. Using Kyrgyzstan and Kazakhstan as a base, they operate in China.

Ulricke Meinhof (1934–1976) Co-created the Red Army Faction with Andreas Baader in 1970. She was the co-leader of the group. Arrested in 1972, she committed suicide in prison.

Ulster Volunteer Force One of a number of militant Unionist organizations. Such groups wage terrorist campaigns against Catholics and militant Republican organizations.

Umar (circa 580–644) Also known as Umar ibn al Khattab, the second Rightly Guided caliph, according to Sunnis. Under his leadership, the Arab empire expanded into Persia, the southern part of the Byzantine empire, and Egypt. His army conquered Jerusalem in 637.

Umar Farouk Abdulmutallab (b. 1986) According to a federal indictment, smuggled a chemical bomb and chemical igniter in a syringe onto a Northwest flight from Amsterdam to Detroit on December 25, 2009. He was born into a family that practiced Islam. He became radicalized while attending school in the United Kingdom. He was allegedly trained by terrorists in Yemen, who supplied the explosive compound.

Umayyads The first Arab and Muslim dynasty. It ruled from Damascus from 661 to 750. The Umayyads were Uthman's family.

Umbrella Refers to a group that shelters, supports, and inspires smaller terrorist groups. The RAND Corporation refers to this as a hub.

USA FREEDOM Act of 2015 Replaced many of the powers of the PATRIOT Act with greater scrutiny from the FISA court. It also bars the collection of mega-data from dragnet sweeps but allows the collection of specific data based on reasonable suspicion.

USA Patriot Act A law passed in October 2001 that expanded law enforcement's power to investigate and deter terrorism. Opponents claim that it adversely affected civil liberties; proponents claim that it introduced reasonable measures to protect the country against terrorists. The act was amended and renewed in 2006, and the ability to collect and analyze domestic intelligence remained part of the law. Provisions for allowing roving wiretaps, increased power to seize evidence, and increasing wiretaps were approved in 2011.

USS *Cole* A U.S. Navy destroyer attacked by two suicide bombers in the port of Aden, Yemen, on October 12, 2000. Seventeen American sailors were killed in the attack.

Uthman (circa 580–656) Also known as Uthman ibn Affan. The third Rightly Guided caliph, according to Sunnis. He conquered most of the remaining parts of North Africa, Iran, Cyprus, and the Caucasia region. He was assassinated by his own soldiers for alleged nepotism.

Velupillai Pirapaharan (1954–2009) Founder and leader of the LTTE. Pirapaharan's terrorists conducted more successful suicide bombings than any other terrorist group in the world.

Vernon Wayne Howell (or David Koresh, 1959–1993) The charismatic leader of the Branch Davidian cult.

Violent radicalization Refers to the process of adopting extremist positions and engaging in violence based on a new set of beliefs.

Viral weapons Enhanced forms of viruses. The virus is "hardened" so that it can live for long periods and is enhanced for deadlier effects.

Virtual organizations Associations that develop through communication, financial, and ideological links. Like a network, a virtual organization has no central leadership.

Vladimir Lenin (1870–1924) The Russian revolutionary who led a second revolution in October 1917, bringing the Communists to power. Lenin led the Communists in a civil war and set up a dictatorship to enforce Communist rule in Russia.

Vladimir Putin (b. 1952) a former KGB officer and second president of the Russian Federation from 1999 to 2008. He served as Russia's prime minister after his second presidential term and return to the presidency in 2012.

Waco siege The 1993 standoff between members of the Branch Davidian cult and federal law enforcement officers. The standoff ended when FBI agents tried to bring the siege to an end, but Branch Davidian leaders set fire to their compound, killing 82 of the followers.

War of the Spanish Succession (1702–1714) The first global war exported from Europe, pitting the French and Austrians against each other for familial control of the Spanish throne. Although it involved myriad political factors, it set the stage for the evolution of modern Spain. There are several dates given for the end of the war due to the many peace treaties that ended military operations in Europe and around the world.

Waziristan Literally, the land of the Waziris, a tribal region between the North-West Frontier Province and Balochistan. Waziri tribes clashed with the Pakistani army from 2004 to 2006, and they support several jihadist operations in Afghanistan and Pakistan. Al Qaeda and Taliban forces operate in Waziristan.

Weather Underground A left-wing domestic terrorist group operating from 1969 to 1975.

Whiskey Rebellion The uprising that took place in 1791 when a group of Pennsylvania farmers refused to pay a federal tax on corn used to make alcohol. The rebellion ended when President George Washington sent troops to stop the rebellion.

White supremacy A political philosophy claiming that white people are superior to all other ethnic groups.

William Potter Gale (1917–1988) An American military leader who coordinated guerrilla activities in the Philippines during World War II. Gale became a radio preacher and leader of the Christian Identity movement after returning home.

Workers Councils (or Soviets) The lowest-level legislative body in the Soviet Union following the 1917

October revolution. *Soviet* is the Russian word for "council."

Working group A term used in the federal government for a group of subject matter experts who gather to suggest solutions to common problems.

World Islamic Front Against Jews and Crusaders An organization created in 1998 by Osama bin Laden and Ayman al Zawahiri. It represents a variety of jihadist groups that have issued a united front against Jews and the West. It is commonly called al Qaeda.

Yasser Arafat (1929–2004) The name assumed by Mohammed al Husseini. Born in Cairo, he was a founding member of Fatah and the PLO. He merged the PLO and Fatah in 1964 and ran a terrorist campaign against Israel. After renouncing terrorism and recognizing Israel's right to exist, Arafat was president of the Palestinian National Authority from 1993 to 2004.

Yom Kippur War A war between Israel and its Arab neighbors fought in October 1973. Also known as the Ramadan War, hostilities began with a surprise attack on Israel. After initial setbacks, Israel counterattacked and regained its positions.

Yusufiya Followers of the Nigerian Mohammed Yusuf. He ordered them to violently reject all ideas not contained in a strict, intolerant interpretation of Islam.

9/11 Commission Report. *See* National Commission on Terrorist Attacks Upon the United States.

Abbey, E. (1975). *The Monkey Wrench Gang*. Salt Lake City: Roaming the West.

ABC News. (2014). "ISIS Makes Up to $3 Million a Day Selling Oil, Analyst Says." Online: http://abcnews.go.com/International/isis-makes-million-day-selling-oil-analysts/story?id=24814359.

Abinales, P. N. (2008). "The Philippines: Weak State, Resilient President." *Southeast Asia Affairs*: 291–312.

Abinales, P. N., and D. J. Amoroso. (2006). "The Withering of Philippine Democracy." *Current History* (September): 190–195.

Abramson, L., and M. Godoy. (2006). "The Patriot Act: Key Controversies." National Public Radio. Online: http://www.npr.org/news/ specials/patriotact/patriotact provisions.html.

Abuza, Z. (2003). *Militant Islam in Southeast Asia: Crucible of Terror*. Boulder, CO: Lynne Rienner.

Abuza, Z. (2006). "A Breakdown of Southern Thailand's Insurgent Groups." Jamestown Foundation. *Terrorism Monitor* 4(17). Online: http://www.jamestown.org/single/?no_cache=1&tx_ttnews[tt_news]=893.

ACLU (see American Civil Liberties Union)

Adams, D. (2003). "Narcoterrorism Needs Attention." *St. Petersburg Times*, March 10. Online: http:// www.sptimes.com/2003/03/10/Columns/_Narcoterrorism_need.shtml.

Adams, J. (1986). *The Financing of Terror*. New York: Simon & Schuster.

AFP. (2010). "Ex-Guard Says Bin Laden Wants to Use Nukes." Online: http://www.news.copm.au/breaking-news/ex-guard-says-bin-ladin-wants-to-use-nukes/story-e6frfku0.

Afsar, S., C. Samples, and T. Wood. (2008). "The Taliban: An Organizational Analysis." *Military Review* 88(3): 58–73.

Agence France Presse. (2004). "Basque ETA Separatists Call for Unconditional Dialogue." Online: http://www.elkarri.org/en/pdf/Agence_France_Pres_28_10_04.PDF.

Al Arabya News. (2014). "Islamic Jihad Fighters Parade After Gaza War." Online: http://english.alarabiya.net/en/News/middle-east/2014/08/29/Islamic-jihad-fighters-parade-after-Gaza-war.html.

Al Jazeera. (2015). "Dozens Killed in Multiple Attacks Across Kabul." al Jazeera, August 8. Online: http://www.aljazeera.com/news/2015/08/police-academy-kabul-hit-suicide-bomb-150807164338154.html. Accessed: September 2015.

Alban, T. (2014). "The 'Militarization' of Police: Another Perspective." Massachusetts State Police. Online: http://mspcolonel.com/2014/10/25/militarization-police-another-perspective/. Accessed: September 2015.

Alcohol, Tobacco, and Firearms. (2015). "Home Page." ATF. Online: https://www.atf.gov/about. Accessed: September 2015.

Algazy, J. (2004). "Amnesty: IDF Killed 100 Children Last Year." Online: http://www.fromoccupiedpalestine.org/.

Ali, F. (2007). "Dressed in Black: A Look at Pakistan's Radical Women." *Global Terrorism Analysis*. Jamestown Foundation. Online: http://www.jamestown .org/programs/gta/single/?tx_ttnews[tt_news]=4114&tx_ttnews[backPid]=182&no_cache=1.

Ali, T. (2008). *The Duel: Pakistan on the Flight Path of American Power*. New York: Scribner.

Alonso, R. (2001). "The Modernization in Irish Republican Thinking Toward the Utility of Violence." *Studies in Conflict and Terrorism* 24(2): 131–144.

Althaus, S. L. (2002). "American News Consumption During Times of National Crisis." *Political Science and Politics* (September): 517– 521. Online: http://www.apsanet.org/imgtest/AmericanNewsConsumption-Althaus.pdf.

Amble, J. C. (2012). "Combating Terrorism in the New Media Environment." *Studies in Conflict and in Terrorism* 35: 339–353.

American Civil Liberties Union. (2015a). "End Mass Surveillance Under the Patriot Act." Online: https://www.aclu.org/feature/end-mass-surveillance-under-patriot-act.

American Civil Liberties Union. (2015b). "National Security Letters." Online: https://www.aclu.org/national-security-letters.

AMISOM. (2015). ANISOM background. http://amisom-au.org/amisom-background/.

Amon, M. (2004). "Can Israel Survive the West Bank Settlements?" *Terrorism and Political Violence* 16(Spring): 48–65.

Anderson, B. C. (2005). *South Park Conservatives: The Revolt Against Liberal Media Bias.* Washington, DC: Regnery.

Anderson, D. (2005). *Histories of the Hanged: The Dirty War in Kenya and the End of Empire.* New York: W. W. Norton and Company.

Anti-Defamation League (ADL). (2010). "The Lawless Ones." Online: http://www.adl.org/learn/sovereign_movement/sovereign_citizens_movement_report.pdf.

Arbatov, A., A. Pikaev, and V. Dvorkin. (2008). "Nuclear Terrorism: Political, Legal, Strategic, and Technological Aspects." *Russian Politics and Law* 46(1): 50–78.

Armstrong, K. (2000a). *Islam: A Short History.* New York: Modern Library.

Armstrong, K. (2000b). *The Battle for God.* New York: Random House.

Army of God. (n.d.). "The Army of God Manual." Online: http://www.armyofgod.com/AOGhistory.html.

Asia Pacific Economic Cooperation (APEC). (2013). "APEC Strengthens Its Efforts Against Terrorist Financing." Online: http://www.apec.org/Press/News-Releases/2013/1115_financing.aspx.

Asprey, R. B. (2002). *War in the Shadows: The Guerrilla in History.* Lincoln, NE: iUniverse.

Associated Press. (2006). "Provisions in the USA Patriot Act." *San Francisco Chronicle.* May 7. Online: http://sfgate.com/cgi-bin/article.cgi?f=/n/a/2006/03/07/national/w134940S84.DTL.

Associated Press. (2007). "Thousands Protest in Turkey Against an Islamic-Based Government." *International Herald Tribune.* May 20. Online: http://www.iht.com/articles/2007/05/20/africa/ankara.php.

Associated Press. (2015). "Anti-Mining Protestors Square Off with Troops in South Peru." *New York Times.* May 27. Online: http://www.nytimes.com/aponline/2015/05/27/world/americas/ap-lt-peru-mining-protest.html?_r=0.

Azam, J. P. (2005). "Suicide Bombing as an Inter-Generational Investment." *Political Choice* 122: 177–198.

Azani, E. (2009). *Hezbollah: The Story of the Party of God.* New York: Palgrave MacMillan.

Badey, T. J. (2003). "Defining International Terrorism: A Pragmatic Approach." In T. J. Badey (ed.), *Annual Editions: Violence and Terrorism, 2003/2004.* New York: McGraw-Hill.

Baginski, M. (2004). "Statement of Maureen A. Baginski before the House of Representatives Select Committee on Homeland Security." August 22. Online: http://www .gov/congress/congress 04baginsky081704.htm.

Bakier, A. H. (2006). "Lesson from Al Qaeda's Attack on the Khobar Compound." *Terrorism Monitor.* Online: http://jamestown.org/terrorism/news/article.php?issue_id=3830.

Bakunin, M. (orig. 1866; 1987). "Revolution, Terrorism, Banditry." Reprint 1987 in Walter Laqueur and Yonah Alexanderm (eds.), *The Terrorism Reader.* New York: Meridian, 65–68.

Balko, R. (2013). *The Rise of the Warrior Cop: The Militarization of America's Police Forces.* New York: Public Affairs.

Balko, R. (2014). "Meet 59-Year-Old David Hooks, the Latest Drug Raid Fatality." *Washington Post.* October 6. Online: https://www.washingtonpost.com/news/the-watch/wp/2014/10/06/meet-59-year-old-david-hooks-the-latest-drug-raid-fatality/.

Ballard, J. D. (2003). *Nuclear Waste Transportation.* Reno: State of Nevada. Online: http://www.state.nv.us/nucwaste/news2003/pdf/nas_ballard.pdf.

Banerjee, S. (2009). "Reflections of a One-Time Maoist Activist." *Dialectical Anthropology* 33: (3/4) 253–269.

Barber, B. R. (1996). *Jihad vs. McWorld: How Globalism and Tribalism Are Reshaping the World.* New York: Ballantine Books.

Bar-Joseph, U., and R. McDermott. (2008). "Change the Analyst and Not the System: A Different Approach to Intelligence Reform." *Foreign Policy Analysis* 4(2): 127–148.

Barnett, T.P.M. (2004). *The Pentagon's New Map: War and Peace in the Twenty-First Century.* New York: G.P. Putnam's Sons.

Baron, D. P. (2004). "Persistent Media Bias." Online: http://

www.wallis.rochester.edu/conference11/mediabias.pdf.

Barry, T. (2010). "Synergy in Security: The Rise of the National Security Complex." *Dollars and Sense* 287 (March–April): 11–16.

Basile, M. (2004). "Going to the Source: Why Al Qaeda's Financial Network Is Likely to Withstand the Current War on Terrorist Financing." *Studies in Conflict and Terrorism* 27(3): 169–185.

BBC News. (2000). "Turkish Hezbollah: 'No State Links.' " January 23. Online: http://news.bbc.co.uk/1/hi/world/europe/615785.stm.

BBC News. (2003). "Profile: Al Aqsa Martyrs' Brigades." *BBC New World Edition.* July 1. Online: http://news.bbc.co.uk/2/hi/middle_east/1760492.stm.

BBC News. (2005). "Arrest After Stabbing Victim Dies." January 30. Online: http://news.bbc.co.uk/1/hi/northern_ireland/4221599.stm.

BBC News. (2006). "Turkey Seizes 'Al Qaeda Members.' " December 9. Online: http://news.bbc.co.uk/2/hi/europe/6164789.stm.

BBC News. (2012). "US Removes Iran Group MEK from Terror List." September 29. Online: http://www.bbc.com/news/world-us-canada-19767043.

BBC News. (2013a). "Iranian Dissidents 'Killed in Missile Attack.' " December 27. Online: http://www.bbc.com/news/world-middle-east-25523482.

BBC News. (2013b). "Profiles: Colombia's Armed Groups." August 29. Online: http://www.bbc.com/news/world-latin-america-11400950.

BBC News. (2015). "Kenya Attack: 147 Dead in Garissa University Assault." Online:

http://www.bbc.com/news/world-africa-32169080.

BBC. (1998). "World: Europe. Spain's State-Sponsored Death Squads." *BBC News.* July 29. Online: http://news.bbc.co.uk/2/hi/europe/141720.stm.

BBC. (2014). "Profile: Al Qaeda 'Bomb Maker' Ibrahim al-Asiri." BBC News, July 4. Online: http://www.bbc.com/news/world-middle-east-11662143. Accessed: June 2015.

Beck, J. M., and J. D. Markusse. (2008). "Basque Violence: A Reappraisal of Culturalist Explanations." *European Journal of Sociology* 49(1): 91–118.

Bell, D. A. (2007). *The First Total War: Napoleon's Europe and the Birth of War as We Know It.* New York: Houghton Mifflin.

Bell, J. B. (1975). *Transnational Terror.* Washington, DC: American Enterprise Institute.

Bell, J. B. (1976). "Strategy, Tactics, and Terror: An Irish Perspective." In Y. Alexander (ed.), *International Terrorism.* New York: Praeger.

Bell, J. B. (1997). *The Secret Army: The IRA,* 3rd ed. New Brunswick, NJ: Transaction.

Bell, J. B. (1998). "Ireland: The Long End Game." *Studies in Conflict and Terrorism* 21: 5–28.

Bell, J. B., and T. R. Gurr. (1979). "Terrorism and Revolution in America." In H. D. Graham and T. R. Gurr (eds.), *Violence in America.* Newbury Park, CA: Sage.

Benjamin, D., and S. Simon. (2002). *The Age of Sacred Terror.* New York: Random House.

Bergen, P. (2015). "The American Who Inspires Terror from Paris to the U.S." CNN, January 12. Online: http://www.cnn.com/2015/01/11/opinion/

bergen-american-terrorism-leader-paris-attack/. Accessed: June 2015.

Berlet, C., and M. N. Lyons. (2000). *Right-Wing Populism in America: Too Close for Comfort.* New York: Guilford.

Berman, E. (2009). *Radical, Religious, and Violent: The New Economics of Terrorism.* Boston: MIT Press.

Berthelsen, J. (1996). "Room with No View." *Far Eastern Economic Review.* May 9, p. 159.

Best, R. A., Jr. (2001). *Intelligence and Law Enforcement: Countering Transnational Threats to the U.S.* Congressional Reference Service. CRS Report for Congress, December 3. Online: http://www.fas.org/irp/crs/RL30252.pdf.

Best, Jr., R.A. (2014). "Leadership of the U.S. Intelligence Community: From DCI to DNI. *International Journal of Intelligence and Counterintelligence* 27(2): 253–333.

Biersteker, T. J., and S. E. Eckert. (2007). *Countering the Financing of Terrorism.* New York: Routledge.

Bisharat, G. E., T. Crawley, S. Elturk, C. James, R. Mishaan, A. Radhakrishnan, and A. Sanders. (2009). "Israel's Invasion of Gaza in International Law." *Denver Journal of Law and International Policy* 38(1): 41–114.

Bite Back. (2015). "News from the Frontlines." Online: http://www.directaction.info.

BJA/SLATT. (2010). "State and Local Anti-Terrorism Training Program." Online: https://www.slatt.org/ default.aspx.

Black, D. (2004). "The Geometry of Terrorism." *Sociological Theory* 22(1): 14–25.

Bodrero, D. D. (2002). "Law Enforcement's New Challenge to Investigate, Interdict, and Prevent Terrorism." *Police Chief* (February): 41–48.

Boin, A. (2009). "The New World of Crises and Crisis Management: Implications for Policymaking and Research." *Review of Policy Research* 26(4): 367–377.

Boot, M. (2013). *Invisible Armies: An Epic History of Guerrilla Warfare from Ancient Times to the Present*. New York: W. W. Norton and Company.

Booth, W., and A. Gearan. (2014). "Palestinians for a New Unity Government That Includes Hamas." *Washington Post*. June 2. Online: http://www. washingtonpost.com/world/ middle_east/palestinians- form-new-unity-government- including-hamas/2014/06/02/ c681d5c6-ea46-11e3-9f5c- 9075d5508f0a_story.html.

Borum, R. (2004). *Psychology of Terrorism*. Tampa: University of South Florida.

Bouchat, C. J. (2013). *The Causes for Instability in Nigeria and Implications for the United States*. U.S. Army War College, Strategic Studies Institute. Online: http://www. strategicstudiesinstitute. army.mil/pubs/display. cfm?pubID=1163.Ac.

Bowers, S. R., and K. R. Keys. (1998). "Technology and Terrorism: The New Threat for the Millennium." *Conflict Studies* (May). Paper presented by Research Institute for the Study of Conflict and Terrorism.

Bozek, J. (2009). *Sayyid Qutb: Analysis of Jihadist Philosophy*. Saarbrücken, Germany: VDM Verlag.

Bozell, L. B. (2005). *Weapons of Mass Distortion: The Coming Meltdown of the Liberal Media*. New York: Three Rivers Press.

Brackett, D. W. (1996). *Holy Terror: Armageddon in Tokyo*. New York: Weatherhill.

Bradley, E. (2004). *60 Minutes*. CBS.

Bradshaw, B. (1978). "Sword, Word, and Strategy in the Reformation in Ireland." *Historical Journal* 21(3): 475–502.

Branche, R. (2008). "The French State Faced with the Algerian Nationalists (1954–1962): A War Against Terrorism?" In S. Cohen (ed.), *Democracies at War with Terrorism*. New York: Palgrave Macmillan.

Brantly, A. (2014). "Financing Terror Bit by Bit." *CTC Sentinel* 7. Online: https:// www.ctc.usma.edu/posts/ financing-terror-bit-by-bit.

Brar, S. S. (2003). "The Sikhism Homepage." Online: http://www. sikhs.org/.

Bravin, J. (2007). "Terror War Legal Edifice Teeters." *Wall Street Journal*. June 13, p. A4.

Breuil, B., and R. Rozema. (2009). "Fatal Imaginations: Death Squads in Davao City and Medellin Compared." *Crime, Law, and Social Change* 52: 405– 424. Online: http://link.springer. com/article/10.1007%2Fs10611- 009-9191-3#page-1.

Brigitte N., Y. Bloch-Elkon, and R. Shapiro (2008). "Prevention of Terrorism in Post-9/11 America: News Coverage, Public Perceptions, and the Politics of Homeland Security." *Terrorism and Political Violence* 20(1): 1–25.

Brisard, J.C. (2005). *Zarqawi: The New Face of al-Qaeda*. New York: Other.

Brookbank, J. (2006). "Understanding the Terrorism Threats Posed to Medical Technology." *Biomedical Instrumentation & Technology* 40(2): 94–95.

Brooks, R. E. (2011). "Improving Criminal Intelligence Sharing: How the Criminal Intelligence Coordinating Council Supports Law Enforcement and Homeland Security." *Police Chief* 78(February): 34–38.

Brown, I. (2009). "Terrorism and the Proportionality of Internet Surveillance." *European Journal of Criminology* 6(2): 119–134.

Bruce, S. (2001). "Terrorism and Politics: The Case of Northern Ireland's Loyalist Paramilitaries." *Studies in Conflict and Terrorism* 13(2): 27–48.

Bruechner, S. A. (2009). "Swarming Geographic Event Profiling, Link Analysis, and Prediction." Vector Research Center. Online: http:// www. newvectors.net/staff/brueckners/ publications/2009/ gp34SASO_ cameraReady.pdf.

Bryden, M. (2014). "The Reinvention of Al Shabaab." CSIS. Online: http://csis.org/files/ publication/140221_Bryden_ ReinventionOfAlShabaab_Web. pdf.

Bunker, R. J. (1998). "Information Operations and the Conduct of Land Warfare." *Military Review*. September–November, pp. 4–17. Online: http://www.iwar.org.uk/ war/resources/milrev/ bunker/ pdf.

Bunn, M. (2009). "Reducing the Greatest Risks of Nuclear Theft and Terrorism." *Daedulus* 138(4): 112–124.

Bunzel, C. (2015). *From Paper State to Caliphate: The Ideology of the Islamic State*. Center for Middle East Policy at Brookings: Washington, DC. Online: http://www.brookings.edu/~/media/research/files/papers/2015/03/ideology-of-islamic-state-bunzel/the-ideology-of-the-islamic-state.pdf. Accessed: May 2015.

Bureau of Justice Assistance. (2005). *National Criminal Intelligence Sharing Plan.* Online: http://www.it.ojp.gov/documents/National_Criminal_Intelligence_Sharing_ Plan.pdf.

Burleigh, M. (2009). *Blood and Rage: A Cultural History of Terrorism.* New York: Harper.

Burns, J. (2010). "Cameron Says 1972 Killings in N. Ireland Were Unjustified." *New York Times.* June 10. Online: http://www.nytimes.com/2010/06/16/world/europe/16nireland.html.

Burton, A. (1976). *Urban Terrorism.* New York: Free Press.

Bustamante, M., and S. Chaskel. (2008). "Colombia's Precarious Progress." *Current History.* February, pp. 77–84.

Byford, G. (2002). "The Wrong War." *Foreign Affairs* 81(July/August): 34–43.

Byman, D. (1998). "The Logic of Ethnic Terrorism." *Studies in Conflict and Terrorism* 21: 149–169.

Byman, D.L. (2015). "After Death of a Senior Leader in Yemen, al Qaida Faces New Challenges and Opportunities." Brookings Institution, June 18. Online: http://www.brookings.edu/blogs/markaz/posts/2015/06/18-can-aqap-survive-death-of-wuhayshi. Accessed: June 2025.

Cafarella, J. (2014). "Jabhat al-Nusra in Syria: An Islamic Emirate for al-Qaeda." Institute for the Study of War. December. Online: http://www.

understandingwar.org/sites/default/files/JN%20Final.pdf. Accessed: June 2014.

Cahill, T. (2003). *How the Irish Saved Civilization: The Untold Story of Ireland's Heroic Role from the Fall of Rome to the Rise of Medieval Europe.* New York: Bantam/Doubleday.

Calabresi, M., and R. Ratnesar. (2002). "Can We Stop the Next Attack?" *Time.* March 11, pp. 24–37.

Cappel, R. P. (1979). *S.W.A.T. Team Manual.* Boulder, CO: Paladin.

Carafano, J.J., C. Stimpson, S.P. Bucci, J. Malcom, and P. Rosenzweig. (2015). "Section 215 of the PATRIOT Act and Metadata Collection: Responsible Options for the Way Forward." Heritage Foundation, May 21. Online: http://www.heritage.org/research/reports/2015/05/section-215-of-the-patriot-act-and-metadata-collection-responsible-options-for-the-way-forward. Accessed: August 2015.

Carmichael, P., and C. Knox. (2004). "Devolution, Governance, and the Peace Process." *Studies in Conflict and Terrorism* 16(Autumn): 593–621.

Carter, D. L. (2008). *The Intelligence Fusion Process.* East Lansing: Michigan State University.

Carter, D. L. (2009). *Law Enforcement Intelligence: A Guide for State, Local and Tribal Agencies,* 2nd ed. U.S. Department of Justice. Online: https://intellprogram.msu.edu/CARTER_ Intelligence_Guide_2d.pdf. Accessed: September 2015.

Carter, D. L., and J. G. Carter. (2009a). "The Intelligence Fusion Process for State, Local, and Tribal Law Enforcement."

Criminal Justice and Behavior 36(12): 1323–1339.

Carter, D. L., and J. G. Carter. (2009b). "Intelligence-Led Policing: Conceptual and Functional Considerations for Public Policy." *Criminal Justice Policy Review* 20(3): 310–325.

Cassara, J. A. (2006). *Hide and Seek: Intelligence, Law Enforcement, and the Stalled War on Terrorist Finance.* Dulles, VA: Potomac Books.

Cassara, J. A., and A. Jorisch. (2010). *On the Trail of Terror Finance: What Law Enforcement and Intelligence Officials Need to Know.* Washington, DC: Red Cell IG.

Casteel, S.W. (2003). "Narco-Terrorism: International Drug Trafficking and Terrorism. A Dangerous Mix." Testimony, Committee on the Judiciary, U.S. Senate. May 20. Online: http://www.judiciary.senate.gov/testimony.cfm?id=764&wit_id=2111.

CBS, "60 Minutes." (2015). "The Attack on Sony." CBS News, September 6. Online: http://www.cbs.com/shows/60_minutes/video/. Accessed: September 2015.

Center for Consumer Freedom. (2004). "Non-Violent Protests with Guns?" September 4. Online: http://www.consumerfreedom.com/news_detail.cfm/headline/1561.

Center for International Security and Cooperation. (2012a). "National Liberation Army: Colombia." Stanford University. Online: http://web.stanford.edu/group/mappingmilitants/cgi-bin/groups/view/87.

Center for International Security and Cooperation." (2012b). "Revolutionary Armed Forces of Colombia: Peoples' Army."

Stanford University. Online: http://web.stanford.edu/group/mappingmilitants/cgi-bin/groups/view/89.

Cetron, M. J., and O. Davies. (2008). "55 Trends Now Shaping the Future of Terrorism." Proteus USA. Online: http://www.au.af.mil/au/awc/awcgate/army/ proteus-55-terror.pdf.

Chalk, P. (2012). "Profiles of Mexico's Seven Major Drug Trafficking Organizations." *CTC Sentinel* 5(1): 5–8.

Chamberlain, G., and M. Tran. (2009). "Sri Lankan Troops Mop Up Tigers as Leader Said to Have Died in Bunker." *Guardian* (Manchester, UK). May 17. Online: http://www.guardian.co.uk/world/2009/may/17/tamil-surrender-sri-lanka/print.

Chermak, S. L., and J. A. Greunewald. (2006). "The Media's Coverage of Domestic Terrorism." *Justice Quarterly* 23(4): 428–461.

Chermak, S. M., J. D. Freilich, and Z. Shemtob. (2009). "Law Enforcement Training and the Domestic Far Right." *Criminal Justice and Behavior* (36): 1305–1322. Online: http://cjb.sagepub.com/content/36/12/1305.

Chermak, S., and A. Weiss. (2006). "Community Policing in the News Media." *Police Quarterly* 9(2): 135–160.

Chikhi, L. (2014). "Splinter Group Breaks Away from al Qaeda in North Africa." Reuters, September 14. Online: http://in.reuters.com/article/2014/09/14/algeria-security-idINL6N0RF0F020140914. Accessed: June 2015.

Chomsky, N. (2002). "Who Are the Global Terrorists?" Online: http://www.chomsky.info/articles/ 200205–02.htm.

Chothia, F. (2014). "Ahmed Abdi Godane: Somalia's Killed Al Shabab Leader." BBC News. September. Online: http://www.bbc.com/news/world-africa-29034409.

Chothia, F. (2015). "Who Are Nigeria's Boko Haram Islamists?" BBC News. Online: http://www.bbc.com/news/world-africa-13809501. May 4.

Chouvy, P. A. (2004). "Narco-Terrorism in Afghanistan." *Terrorism Monitor: In-Depth Analysis of the War on Terror* 2(29) Online: http://www.jamestown.org/single/?no_cache=1&tx_ttnews%5Btt_news%5D=26379

Christia, F., and M. Semple. (2009). "Flipping the Taliban: How to Win in Afghanistan." *Foreign Affairs* 88(4): 34–45.

Chung, C.-P. (2002). "China's 'War on Terror.'" *Foreign Affairs* 81(4): 8–12.

Cilliers, J. (2003). "Terrorism and Africa." *African Security Review* 12(4): 91–103.Online: http://www.iss.org.za/pubs/ASR/12No4/Cilliers .pdf.

CISC. (*See* Center for International Security and Cooperation)

Clark, J. K. (1988). "Guevara." *Global Security*. Online: http://www.globalsecurity.org/military/library/report/1988/CJK.htm.

Clark, K. (1998). *Petersburg: Crucible of Cultural Revolution*. Cambridge, MA: Harvard University Press.

Clark, R. (1979). *The Basques*. Reno: University of Nevada Press.

Clarke, R. (2010). *Lashkar-i-Taiba: The Fallacy of Subservient Proxies and the Future of Islamist Terrorism in India*. Ft. Leavenworth, KS: U.S. Army War College. Online: http://www.strategicstudiesinstitute.army.mil/pubs/display.cfm?pubID=973.

Clarke, R. A. (2007). "A Back Door for Terrorists." *New York Times*. June 1, Opinion, Editorial.

Clarke, R. A., and R. K. Knake. (2010). *Cyber War: The Next Threat to National Security and What to Do About It*. New York: Ecco/Harper Collins.

Clayton, M. (2005). "Is Black-Market Baby Formula Financing Terror?" *Christian Science Monitor*. June 29. Online: http://www .csmonitor.com/2005/0629/p01s01-usju.html.

Clopper, J.D., and E. Daughtry. (2015). "Re: *New York Times Company v. U.S. Department of Justice*, 14 Civ. 3776 (AT)." January 9. U.S. Department of Justice. Online: https://assets.documentcloud.org/documents/1393145/savage-nyt-foia-doj-ig-report-fbi-702.pdf. Accessed: September 201

Clutterbuck, L. (2004). "The Progenitors of Terrorism: Russian Revolutionaries or Extreme Irish Republicans?" *Terrorism and Political Violence* 16(Spring): 154–181.

CNN. (2006). "House Approves Patriot Act." Online: http://www.cnn.com/2006/POLITICS/03/07/patriot.act/.

CNN. (2014). "Eric Rudolph Fast Facts." September 9. Online: http://www.cnn.com/2012/12/06/us/eric-robert-rudolph---fast-facts/.

Cochrane, P. (2004). "Is Al-Hurra Doomed?" Worldpress.org. Online: http://www.worldpress.org/Mideast/1872.cfm.

Colb, S. F. (2001). "The New Face of Racial Profiling: How Terrorism Affects the Debate." *FindLaw's Legal Commentary*. October 10. Online: http://writ.

news.findlaw.com/200111010. html.

Cole, D., and J. X. Dempsey. (2002). *Terrorism and the Constitution: Sacrificing Civil Liberties in the Name of National Security.* New York: Free Press.

Cole, G. F., and C. E. Smith. (2004). *The American System of Justice.* Belmont, CA: Wadsworth.

Collin, B. (2004). "The Future of Cyber Terrorism: Where the Physical and Virtual Worlds Converge." Online: http://afgen. com/terrorism1.html.

Commission of Inquiry. (2007). "Terrorism, Intelligence, and Law Enforcement: Canada's Response to Sikh Terrorism." Commission of Inquiry into the Investigation of the Bombing of Air India Flight 182. Online: http://www. major-comm.ca/documents/ dossier2_ENG.pdf.

Commission on Accreditation for Law Enforcement Agencies. (1990). *Accreditation Program Overview.* Fairfax, VA: Author.

Commission on the Prevention of Weapons of Mass Destruction Proliferation and Terrorism. (2010). "Report Card: Government Failing to Protect America from Grave Threats of WMD Proliferation and Terrorism." Online: http://www. preventwmd.org/1_26_101/.

Community Oriented Policing Services. (2015). "Homeland Security Through Community Policing." Online: http:// www.cops.usdoj.gov/Default. asp?Item=2487.

Cooley, J. (2002). *Unholy Wars: Afghanistan, America, and International Terrorism.* London: Pluto Press.

Coolidge, S., and J. Prendergast. (2003). "Police Shut Down Crime Ring." *Cincinnati Enquirer.* October 3. Online:

http://www.enquirer.com/ editions/2003/10/03/loc_ crimering03.html.

Cooper, H. (2015). "ISIS Is Cited for Hacking of Central Command's Twitter and YouTube Accounts." *New York Times.* January 12. Online: http://www.nytimes. com/2015/01/13/us/isis-is- cited-in-hacking-of-central- commands-twitter-feed. html?_r=0. Accessed: August 2015.

Cooper, H. H. A. (1977a). "Terrorism and the Media." In Y. Alexander and S. Finger (eds.), *Terrorism: Interdisciplinary Perspectives.* New York: John Jay.

Cooper, H. H. A. (1977b). "What Is a Terrorist? A Psychological Perspective." *Legal Medical Quarterly* 1: 8–18.

Cooper, H. H. A. (1978). "Terrorism: The Problem of the Problem of Definition." *Chitty's Law Journal* 26: 105–108.

Cooper, H. H. A. (2001). "Terrorism: The Problem of Definition Revisited." *American Behavioral Scientist* 44(February): 881–893.

Cooper, H. H. A. et al. (1976). *Task Force Report on Disorders and Terrorism.* Washington, DC: National Advisory Committee on Criminal Justice Standards and Goals.

COPS. (*See* Community Oriented Policing Services)

Cordesman, A. H. (2006). "Preliminary 'Lessons' of the Israeli-Hezbollah War." Center for Strategic and International Studies. Online: http://csis.org/ files/media/csis/pubs/060817_ isr_hez_lessons.pdf.

Cordesman, A. H. (2009). "CSIS: 'The Gaza War.' A Strategic Analysis." Council on Foreign Relations. Online: http://www.

cfr.org/publication/ 18527/csis. html.

Cordner, G. W. (1995). "Community Policing: Elements and Effects." *Police Forum* 7(5): 1–7. Online: http://policeandcommunity. org/pdfs/Archives/2010/ Archives-Alternatives/1995_ CommuntyPolicElemEffects_ Cordner.pdfol.

Coronel, S. S. (2007). "The Philippines: Democracy and its Discontents." *Asian Survey* 47(1): 175–182.

Costigan, G. (1980). *A History of Modern Ireland.* Indianapolis, IN: Bobbs-Merrill.

Cottle, S. (2006). "Mediatizing the Global War on Terror." In A. P. Kavoori and T. Fraley (eds.), *Media, Terrorism, and Theory: A Reader.* Lanham, MD: Rowman & Littlefield.

Council on Foreign Relations. (2002). "Basque Fatherland and Liberty (ETA)." Online: http:// cfrterrorism .org/groups/eta. html.

Council on Foreign Relations. (2004). "Al-Asqa Martyrs Brigades." Online: http://www. cfr.org/publication/ 9127/ alaqsa_martyrs_brigade.html.

Council on Foreign Relations. (2008). "Backgrounder: Colombia's Right-Wing Paramilitaries and Splinter Groups." Online: http://www.cfr.org/colombia/ colombias-right-wing- paramilitaries-splinter-groups/ p15239.

Council on Foreign Relations. (2009a). "Hamas: Backgrounder." Online: http:// www.cfr.org/publication/8968/ hamas.html.

Council on Foreign Relations. (2009b). "Backgrounder: Liberation Tigers of Tamil Eelam (aka Tamil Tigers) Sri Lankan Separatists."

Online: http://www.cfr.org/separatist-terrorism/liberation-tigers-tamil-eelam-aka-tamil-tigers-sri-lanka-separatists/p9242.

Council on Foreign Relations. (2015). "The USA FREEDOM Act of 2015." Online: http://www.cfr.org/intelligence/usa-freedom-act-2015/p36594.

Cowen, T. (2006). "Terrorism as Theater: Analysis and Policy Implications." *Public Choice* 128(1): 233–244.

Coyer, P. (2015). "U.S. Government's Data Breach Exemplifies China's Cyber Insecurities." *Forbes,* July 19. Online: http://www.forbes.com/sites/paulcoyer/2015/07/19/the-opm-data-breach-and-sino-american-competition/. Accessed: September 2015.

Coyle, D. J. (1983). *Minorities in Revolt: Political Violence in Ireland, Italy, and Cyprus.* East Brunswick, NJ: Associated University Presses.

Cram, I. (2006). "Regulating the Media: Some Neglected Freedom of Expression Issues in the United Kingdom's Counter-Terrorism Strategy." *Terrorism and Political Violence* 18(2): 335–355.

Creed, R. D., Jr. (2002). "Eighteen Years in Lebanon and Two Intifadas: The Israeli Defense Force and the U.S. Army Operational Environment." Fort Leavenworth, KS: U.S. Army Command and General Staff College.

Creveld, M. V. (2008). "Bottling the Nuclear Demon." *Nature* 452 (April): 694–695.

Creveld, M. van. (1991). *The Transformation of War.* Cambridge, MA: Harvard University Press.

Criss, N. B. (1995). "The Nature of PKK Terrorism in Turkey." *Studies in Conflict and Terrorism* 18: 17–38.

Critical Incident Analysis Group. (2001). *Threats to Symbols of American Democracy.* Charlottesville: University of Virginia.

Cronin, A. K. (2003). "Al Qaeda After the Iraq Conflict." Congressional Reference Service. *CRS Report for Congress.* Order Code RS21529. May 23. Online: http://www.fas.org/irp/crs/RS21529.pdf.

Cronin, S. (1984). *Irish Nationalism: A History of Its Roots and Ideology.* Dublin: University Press of Ireland.

C-Span. (2007). "Testimony: Brian Jenkins, Frank Cilluffo, and Salam al Marayati." House Subcommittee on Homeland Security, June 14.

Cumming, A., and T. Masse. (2004). "FBI Intelligence Reform Since September 11, 2001: Issues for Congress." Congressional Reference Service. Online: http://www.fas.org/irp/crs/RL32336.html.

Curtis, E. (orig. 1936; 2000). *A History of Ireland from the Earliest Times to 1922.* London: Routledge.

Daily News and Analysis. (2010). "Government to Install Radiation Monitoring Portals at Ports." *Daily News and Analysis, India.* April 25. Online: http://www.dnaindia.com/india/report_govt-to-install-radiation-monitoring-portals-at-ports_1375392.

Dalgaard-Nielsen, A. (2010). "Violent Radicalization in Europe: What We Know and Don't Know." *Studies in Conflict and Terrorism* 33(2): 797–814.

Daly, J. C. K. (2006a). "Saudi Oil Facilities: Al Qaeda's Next Target?" *Terrorism Monitor.* Online: http://jamestown.org/terrorism/news/article.php?articleid=2369910.

Daly, J. C. K. (2006b). "The Baloch Insurgency and Its Threat to Pakistan's Energy Sector." *Terrorism Focus.* Online: http://jamestown.org/terrorism/news/article.php?issue_id=3660.

Daniels, D. A. (2003). "Breaking Barriers: Sharing Information in a Changing World." Law Enforcement Information Sharing Symposium, Office of Justice Programs, U.S. Department of Justice, Arlington, VA. Online: http://www.ojp.usdoj.gov/aag/speeches/deainfosharing.htm.

Danin, R. M. (2013). "Middle East Matters This Week: Iranian Negotiations, Syrian Deterioration, and Palestinian Violence." Council on Foreign Relations. Online: http://blogs.cfr.org/danin/2013/02/28/middle-east-matters-this-week-iranian-negotiations-syrian-deterioration-and-palestinian-violence/.

Danitz, T., and W. P. Strobel. (1999). "The Internet's Impact on Activism: The Case of Burma." *Studies in Conflict and Terrorism* 22: 257–269.

Dawisha, A. (2003). *Arab Nationalism in the Twentieth Century: From Triumph to Despair.* Princeton, NJ: Princeton University Press.

DAWN. (2015). "U.S. Urges Pakistan, Afghanistan to Jointly Combat Terrorism." *DAWN.* Online: http://www.dawn.com/news/1201326. Accessed: August 2015.

de Guzman, M.C. (2002). "The Changing Roles and Strategies of the Police in Time of Terror." *ACJS Today* 22(3): 8–13.

de Silva, M. (1996). "Sunshine Over Jaffna." *Far Eastern Economic Review.* May 5, p. 159.

Debray, J. R. (1967). *Revolution in the Revolution?* Westport, CT: Greenwood.

del Carmen, R. (1991). *Civil Liberties in American Policing: A Text for Law Enforcement Personnel.* Englewood Cliffs, NJ: Prentice Hall.

Della Porta, D. (1995). "Left-Wing Terrorism in Italy." In M. Crenshaw (ed.), *Terrorism in Context.* State College: Pennsylvania State University.

DeMichele, M. T., and P. B. Kraska. (2001). "Community Policing in Battle Garb: A Paradox or Coherent Strategy." In P. B. Kraska (ed.), *Militarizing the American Criminal Justice System: The Changing Roles of Armed Forces and the Police.* Boston: Northeastern University Press, pp. 82–101.

Denson, B., and J. Long. (1999). "Ecoterrorism Sweeps the American West." *Oregonian.* September 26; "Ideologues Drive the Violence." September 27; "Terrorist Acts Provoke Change in Research, Business, Society." September 28; "Can Sabotage Have a Place in a Democratic Community?" September 29. Online: http://www.oregonlive. com/cgi-bin/printer/printer.cgi.

Department of Homeland Security. (2015a). "Homeland Security Information Network (HSIN)." DHS. Online: http://www. dhs.gov/homeland-security-information-network-hsin. Accessed: September 2015.

Der Spiegel. (2010). "Western Officials Concerned About Attack in Europe." *Spiegel Online.* September 29. Online: http://www. spiegel.de/ international/ world/0,1518,720206,00.html

Deutsche Welle. (2015). "Colombian Army and FARC Guerrillas Begin Clearing Landmines." May 30. Online: http://www.dw.de/ colombian-army-and-farc-guerrillas-begin-clearing-landmines/a-18486957.

Deylami, S.S. (2013). "Saving the Enemy: Female Suicide Bombers and the Making of American Empire." *International Feminist Journal of Politics* 115(2): 177–194.

DHS. *See* U.S. Department of Homeland Security.

Dickey, C. (2010). "A Thousand Points of Hate." *Newsweek.* January 11, pp. 34–36.

Dienst, J., K. Nious, and A. Givens. (2015). "Rookie NYPD Police Officer Critically Hurt in Queens Hatchet Attack: I Thought I Was Going to Die." NBC New York. May 7. Online: http://www.nbcnewyork. com/news/local/Hatchet-Attack-Lone-Wolf-Terrorist-Officer-Healey-Queens-Zale-Thompson-Police-NYPD-Shooting-Attack-302630961. html.

Dillon, S. (2001). "A Forum Recalls Unheeded Warning." *New York Times.* October 4, p. A16.

Dillow, C. (2015). "Defense Contractors Outgun Other Industries in Corporate PAC Donations." *Fortune*, July 15. Online: http://fortune. com/2015/07/15/defense-contractors-pac/. Accessed: September 2015.

Discovery Times Channel. (2005). *Media Jihad.* YouTube. Online: https://www.youtube.com/ watch?v=_YQsjKT2z74.

Dixon, P. (2004). "Peace Within the Realms of the Possible? David Trimble, Unionist Ideology, and Theatrical Politics." *Terrorism and Political Violence* 16(Autumn): 462–482.

Dobbins, J. (2005). "Iraq: Winning the Unwinnable War." *Foreign Affairs* 84(January/February): 16–25.

Dobson, C., and R. Payne. (1982). *The Terrorists.* New York: Facts on File.

Doherty, S., and B. G. Hibbard. (2006). "Special Focus: Community Policing and Homeland Security." *Police Chief* 73(2). Online: http:// www.policechiefmagazine. org/magazine/index. cfm?fuseaction=display_ arch&article_id=812&issue_ id=22006.

Donner, H. (2009). "Radical Masculinity: Morality, Sociality, and Relationships Through Recollections of Naxalite Activists." *Dialectical Anthropology* 33: 327–343.

Dostov, V., and P. Shust. (2014). "Customer Loyalty Programs: Money Laundering and Terrorism Risks." *Journal of Money Laundering Control* 17(4): 385–394.

Downs, A. C. (1967). *Inside Bureaucracy.* Boston: Little, Brown.

Doyle, C. (2002). "The USA PATRIOT Act: A Sketch." Congressional Reference Service. *CRS Report for Congress.* Online: http://www.fas.org/irp/ crs/RS21203.pdf.

Drakos, K., and A. M. Kutan. (2003). "Regional Effects of Terrorism on Tourism in Three Mediterranean Countries." *Journal of Conflict Resolution* 45(5): 621–641.

Dreyfuss, R. (2002). "The Cops Are Watching You." March 23. Online: http://www.ccmep. org/ hotnews2/cops_are_ watching052302.htm.

Duekmedjian, J. E. (2006). "From Community to Intelligence: Executive Realignment of the RCMP Mission." *Canadian Journal of Criminology and Criminal Justice* 48(4): 523–542.

Dunn, S., and V. Morgan. (1995). "Protestant Alienation in Northern Ireland." *Studies in Conflict and Terrorism* 18: 175–185.

Durham, F. D. (1998). "News Frames as Social Narratives: TWA Flight 800." *Journal of Communication* 48(4): 100–117.

Durrieu, R. (2013). *Rethinking Money Laundering and Financing of Terrorism in International Law: Towards a New Global Order*. Brill: Online Books and Journals. Online: http://booksandjournals. brillonline.com/content/books/9789004207158.

Dymond, J. (2004). "U.S. and Turkey to Hit PKK." BBC News. October2. Online: http://news. bbc.uk/2/hi/europe/3158686.stm.

Dyson, W. (2011). "Connecting the Dots." Tallahassee, FL: IIR. (Not publically available.)

Dyson, W. E. (2008). *Investigating Terrorism: An Investigator's Handbook*, 3rd ed. Cincinnati, OH: Anderson.

Economist. (2003). "Al Qaeda Operations Are Rather Cheap." October 4, p. 45.

Economist. (2008). "Turkey Invades Northern Iraq." February 28. Online: www. economist.com/displaystory. cfm?story_id=10766808.

Economist. (2009). "Dying Spasms." Online: http://www. economist.com/node/14191335.

Economist. (2010). "Europe: Gone Fishing. Spain and ETA." Online: http://www.economist. com/node/15622351.

ED Armstrong, K. (2000b). *The Battle for God*. New York: The Modern Library.

ED Chalk, P. (2010). "Lashkar-e-Taiba's Growing International Focus and its Links with al-Qaeda." *Global Terrorism Analysis*. The Jamestown Foundation. Online: http://www.jamestown.org/programs/gta/single/?tx_ttnews[tt_news]=36683&tx_ttnews[backPid]=26&cHash=fc945260f6: Accessed: February: 2012.

ED Esposito, J. L., and J. O., Voll. (2001) *Islam and Democracy*. New York: Oxford University Press.

ED Haneef, J. O., (2002). *The Wahhabi Myth: Dispelling Prevalent Fallacies and the Fictitious Link with bin Laden*. Birmingham, UK: Salafi Publications.

ED Knights, M. (2014). "ISIL's Military Power in Iraq." *CTC Sentinel*, August 27. Online: https://www.ctc.usma.edu/posts/isils-political-military-power-in-iraq. Accessed: June 2015.

Egerton, F. (2011). "Alienation and its Discontents." *European Journal of International Relations* 17: 453–474. Online: http://ejt.sagepub.com/content/17/3/453.

Ehrenfeld, R. (2003). *Funding Evil: How Terrorism Is Financed and How to Stop It*. Chicago: Bonus Books.

Eilstrup-Sangiovanni, M., and C. Jones. (2008). "Assessing the Dangers of Illicit Networks: Why Al-Qaida May Be Less Threatening Than Many Think." *International Security* 33(2): 7–44.

Elbe, P. (2000). "The Orange Order in the Wake of Drumcree: Parity of Esteem, Protest, and Propaganda in Northern Ireland, 1995–98." *Archive: A Journal of Undergraduate History*. Online: http://www.sit.wisc.edu/~uwho/Archive/Archive%204%20orange%20order.pdf.

Electronic Frontier Foundation. (2011). "Patterns of Misconduct: FBI Intelligence Violations from 2001-2008." EFF. Online: https://www.eff.org/wp/patterns-misconduct-fbi-intelligence-violations. Accessed: September 2015.

Elkins, E. (2003). "Detention, Rehabilitation, and the Destruction of Kikuyu Society." In J. Lonsdale and E. S. Odhiambo (eds.), *Mau Mau and Nationhood: Arms, Authority, and Narration*. Athens: Ohio University Press.

Ellingsen, S. A. (2008). "Safeguards Against Nuclear Terrorism: HEU v. Plutonium." *Defense and Security Analysis* 24(2): 129–146.

Elliot, A. (2010). "The Jihadist Next Door." *New York Times Magazine*. January 31, pp. 26–35, 42–47.

Emerson, S. A. (2002). *American Jihad: The Terrorist Living Among Us*. New York: Free Press.

Emery, T. (2009). "It's Official: The FBI and ATF Don't Get Along." *Time*, October 29. Online: http://content.time.com/time/nation/article/0,8599,1932091,00.html. Accessed: September 2015.

Enteshami, A. (1995). *After Khomeini: The Iranian Second Republic*. London: Routledge.

Epstein, B. (2001). "Anarchism and the Anti-Globalism Movement." *Monthly Review* 53(4): 1–14.

Epstein, D. (2014). "East of Mumbai: Naxalism and the Future of India." *Harvard International Review* 36(1, Summer). Online: http://hir.harvard.edu/archives/7270.

Esposito, J. (1999). *The Islamic Threat: Myth or Reality*. New York: Oxford University Press.

Esposito, J. L. (2002). *Unholy War: Terror in the Name of Islam.* New York: Oxford University Press.

Ewald, S. (2006). "Twisted Rail WMD: An ARES Response." *QST* 90(5): 78–82.

Fairfield, R. P. (1959). "Cyprus: Revolution and Resolution." *Middle East Journal* 13(3): 235–248.

Farah, C. (2000). *Islam.* Hauppage, NY: Baron's.

Farrall, K. (2011). "Suspicious Activity Reporting: U.S. Domestic Intelligence in the Postprivacy Age?" *Research in Social Problems and Public Policy* 19: 247–276.

FBI. (2004). "Counterterrorism Website." October 12. Online: http://www.fbi.gov/terrorinfo/terrorism.htm.

FBI. (2014). "FBI Releases Study of Active Shooter Incidents." Online: https://www.fbi.gov/news/stories/2014/september/fbi-releases-study-on-active-shooter-incidents.

FBI. (2015). "Protecting America from Terrorist Attack: Our Joint Terrorism Task Forces." FBI. Online: https://www.fbi.gov/about-us/investigate/terrorism/terrorism_jttfs. Accessed: September 2015.

FBI. (n.d.) "Counterterrorism." Online: http://www.fbi.gov/terrorinfo/counterterrorism/waronterrorhome.htm. Accessed: October 2014.

FBI. (n.d.). "Counterterrorism." Online: http://www.fbi.gov/terrorinfo/counterrorism/waronterrorhome.htm.

Federation of American Scientists. (2010). "Types of Chemical Weapons." Online: http://www.fas.org/programs/bio/chemweapons/cwagents.html.

Ferrero, M. (2002). "Radicalization as a Reaction to Failure: An Economic Model of Islamic Extremism." DIW workshop on The Economic Consequences of Global Terrorism. Berlin. June.

Fields, G. (2002). "U.S. Probe of Intelligence Lapses to Go beyond CIA and FBI." *Wall Street Journal.* May 3, p. A4.

Financial Action Task Force (FATF). (2014). "United States." Online: http://www.fatf-gafi.org/countries/u-z/unitedstates/.

Financial Action Task Force (FATF). (2015). "FATF." Online: http://www.fatf-gafi.org.

Fingar, T. (2011). *Reducing Uncertainty: Intelligence Analysis and National Security.* Stanford, CA: Stanford University Press.

Fingar, T.A. (2011). *Reducing Uncertainty: Intelligence Analysis and National Security.* Stanford, CA: Stanford University Press.

Finley, M. I. (1983). *The Politics of the Ancient World.* Cambridge: Cambridge University Press.

Firestone, R. (1999). *Jihad: The Origins of Holy War in Islam.* New York: Oxford University Press.

Fisher, M. (2007). "Abbas Calls Emergency as Hamas Routs Fatah." *Gazette* (Montreal). June 15.

Fitzpatrick, S. (2001). *The Russian Revolution.* New York: Oxford University Press.

Fletcher, H. (2008). "Mujahadeen-e-Khalq (MEK) (aka People's Mujahedin of Iran or PMOI)." Council on Foreign Relations. Online: http://www.cfr.org/publication/9158/mujahadeenekhalq_mek_aka_peoples_mujahedin_of_iran_or_pmoi.html.

Flynn, S. (2002). "America the Vulnerable." *Foreign Affairs* 81: 60–74.

Flynn, S. (2004a). *America the Vulnerable.* New York: Harper Collins.

Flynn, S. (2004b). "The Neglected Home Front." *Foreign Affairs* 83 (September/October): 20–33.

Flynn, S. E. "Homeland Insecurity." Council on Foreign Relations. Online: http://www.cfr.org/world/homeland-insecurity/p19238. Accessed: September 2015.

Foreign Policy Association. (2004). "Great Decisions Guides: Terrorism.The Basque ETA." Online: http://www.fpa.org/newsletter_info2478/newsletter_info_sub_list.htm?section=The%BasqueETA.

Foster, R. F. (2001). *The Oxford History of Ireland.* New York: Oxford University Press.

Fox News. (2014). "Extremely Dangerous Survivalist Named Suspect in Pennsylvania State Trooper Ambush." September 16. Online: http://www.foxnews.com/us/2014/09/16/authorities-release-profile-gunman-who-ambushed-pennsylvania-state-troopers/.

Fraley, F., and E. L. Roushanzamir. (2006). "Critical Media Theory, Democratic Communication, and Global Conflict." In A. P. Kavoori and T. Fraley (eds.), *Media, Terrorism, and Theory: A Reader.* Lanham, MD: Rowman & Littlefield.

Francis, D. (2015). "Controversial MEK Leader Asked to Talk to Islamic State, Instead Talks to Iran." *Foreign Policy.* April 29. Online: http://foreignpolicy.com/2015/04/29/controversial-mek-leader-asked-to-talk-islamic-state-instead-talks-iran/.

Fraser, B. (2007). "No Longer Silent: Women and Children Who Survived Peru's Civil War Find Hope, Strength Together."

National Catholic Reporter. March 16.

Freeh, L. J. (2005). *My FBI: Bringing Down the Mafia, Investigating Bill Clinton, and Fighting the War on Terror.* New York: St. Martin's.

Freeman, M. (ed.). (2012). *Financing Terrorism: Case Studies.* Burlington, CT: Ashgate.

Friedman, T. L. (2000). *From Beirut to Jerusalem.* New York: Harper Collins.

Frielich, J. D., S. M. Chermak, and D. Caspi. (2009) "Critical Events in the Trajectories of Domestic Extremist White Supremacist Groups: A Case Study Analysis of Four Violent Organizations." *Criminology and Public Policy* 8(3): 497–530.

Fromkin, D. (2001). *A Peace to End All Peace: The Fall of the Ottoman Empire and the Creation of the Modern Middle East.* New York: Owl Books, Henry Holt.

Frontline. (2002). "Interview: Jihad Ja'Aire, Al Asqa Martyrs Brigade Leader." PBS. Online: http://www.fromoccupiedpalestine.org/node.php?id=745.

Fung, B., and A. Peterson. (2015). "The Centcom Hack that Wasn't." *Washington Post.* January 12. Online: http://www.washingtonpost.com/blogs/the-switch/wp/2015/01/12/the-centcom-hack-that-wasnt/.

Gaines, L. K., and G. W. Cordner. (1999). *Policing Perspectives: An Anthology.* Los Angeles: Roxbury.

Galula, D. (orig. 1963; reprint 2006 with forward by B. Hoffman). *Pacification in Algeria, 1956–1958.* Santa Monica, CA: RAND.

Gambetta, D. (2005). *Making Sense of Suicide Missions.* Oxford: Oxford University Press.

Gange, D. (2015). "Peru's Shining Path Allied with Columbian Drug Traffickers." In SightCrime. Online: http://www.insightcrime.org/news-briefs/peru-shining-path-guerrillas-allied-with-colombian-drug-traffickers.

Ganguly, S. (2009). "India in 2008: Domestic Turmoil and External Hopes." *Asian Survey* 49(1): 39–52.

Ganor, B. (2011). "An Intifada in Europe? A Comparative Analysis of Radicalization Processes Among Palestinians in the West Bank and Gaza Versus Muslim Immigrants in Europe." *Studies in Conflict and Terrorism* 34: 587–599.

Garrison, A. H. (2004). "Defining Terrorism: Philosophy of the Bomb, Propaganda by Deed, and Change Through Fear and Violence." *Criminal Justice Studies* 17(3): 259–279.

Gartenstein-Ross, D. (2009). "The Strategic Challenge of Somalia's Al Shabab: Dimensions of Jihad." *Middle East Quarterly* 16(4): 25–36.

Gartenstein-Ross, D., and L. Grossman. (2009). *Homegrown Terrorists in the U.S. and U.K.: An Empirical Analysis of the Radicalization Process.* Washington, DC: Foundation for the Defense of Democracies.

Gato, P., and R. Windrem. (2007). "Hezbollah Builds a Western Base." NBC News, MSNBC. Online: http://www.msnbc.msn.com/id/17874369.

Gause, F. G., III. (2005). "Can Democracy Stop Terrorism?" *Foreign Affairs* 84(5): 62–76.

General Electric. (2012). "Top Ten Vulnerabilities for Control Systems." GE. Online: https://www.gemeasurement.com/sites/gemc.dev/files/top_10_cyber_vulnerabilities_english.pdf. Accessed: September 2015.

Gentry, J. A. (2008). "Intelligence Failure Reframed." *Political Science Quarterly* 123(2): 247–262.

Gerges, F. A. (2006). *Journey of the Jihadist: Inside Muslim Militancy.* Orlando, FL: Harcourt.

Giblin, M. J., G. W. Burruss, and J. A. Shafer. (2014). "A Stone's Throw from the Metropolis: Re-Examining Small Agency Homeland Security Practices." *Justice Quarterly* 31(2): 368–393.

Giblin, M. J., J. A. Schafer, and G. W. Burruss. (2009). "Homeland Security in the Heartland: Risk, Preparedness, and Organizational Capacity." *Criminal Justice Policy Review* 20(3): 274–289. Online: http://cjp.sagepub.com/content/20/3/274.

Gil-Alana, L. A., and Carlos P. Barros. (2010). "A Note on the Effectiveness of National Anti-Terrorist Policies: Evidence from ETA." *Conflict Management and Peace Science* 27(1): 28–46. Online: http://cmp.sagepub.com/cgi/content/abstract/27/1/28.

Gilboa, E. (2005). "Global Television News and Foreign Policy: Debating the CNN Effect." *International Studies Perspectives* 6(3): 325–341.

Gindersah, I. (2014). "Indonesia's Struggle Against Terrorism." Council of Foreign Relations, Council of Councils. Online: http://www.cfr.org/councilofcouncils/global_memos/p32772. Accessed: August 2015.

Giraldo, J. K., and H. A. Trinkunas (eds.). (2007). *Terrorism*

Funding and State Responses: A Comparative Perspective. Stanford, CA: Stanford University Press.

Giroux, H. A. (2002). "Democracy and the Politics of Terrorism: Community, Fear, and the Suppression of Dissent." *Cultural Studies Critical Methodologies* 2(3): 334–342.

Glasser, S. B., and S. Coll. (2005). "The Web as a Weapon." *Washington Post.* August 1. Online: http://www.washingtonpost.com/wpdyn/content/article/2005/08/08/AR2005080801018.html.

Global Jihad. (2007). "Habib Akdas." Online: http://www.globaljihad.net/?p=3002

Global Security.org. (n.d.). "Sikhs in Punjab." Online: http://www.globalsecurity.org/military/world/war/punjab.htm.

Global Witness. (2003). *For a Few Dollars More: How Al Qaeda Moved into the Diamond Trade.* London: Global Witness.

Goldberg, B. (2003). *Bias: A CBS Insider Exposes How the Media Distort the News.* New York: Perennial Editions (HarperCollins).

Gonzalez-Perez, M. (2008). *Women and Terrorism: Female Activity in Domestic and International Terror Groups.* New York: Routledge.

Goodman, A. (2003). "Basque Question: Spain's Pressing Problem." CNN. Online: http://www.cnn.com/SPECIALS/201/basque/stories/overview.html.

Goodwin, C. (2010). "The Blonde's Bombshell: Nuclear Armageddon Is Closer Than We Think, Warns a Terrifying New Documentary by Lucy Walker." *Sunday Times* (London). May 16. Online: http://entertainment.timesonline.co.uk/tol/arts_and_entertainment/film/article7125512.ece.

Goodwin, D. K. (2005). *Team of Rivals: The Political Genius of Abraham Lincoln.* New York: Simon & Schuster.

Gordon, M. R., and B. E. Trainor. (2006). *Cobra II: The Inside Story of the Invasion and Occupation of Iraq.* New York: Pantheon.

Gordon, N. (1999). "Terrorism in the Arab-Israeli Conflict." South Bend, IN: University of Notre Dame, Joan B. Kroc Institute for International Peace Studies, Occasional Paper.

Gorritti, G. (2006). "The Fog of Forgetting: Thirteen Years and Two Trials After First Sentencing, the Leader of Peru's Shining Path Is Back in Court." *Index on Censorship* 3: 6–15.

Graber, D. (2003). "Styles of Image Management During Crises: Justifying Press Censorship." *Discourse and Society* 14(5): 539–557. Online: http://das.sagepub.com.ezproxy.gvsu.edu:2048/cgi/content/abstract/14/5/539.

Graham, S.(2009). "The Urban Battlespace." *Theory, Culture & Society* 26(7–8): 278–288.

Grare, F. (2013). "Balochistan: The State Versus the Nation." Carnegie Endowment for International Peace. Online: http://carnegieendowment.org/files/balochistan.pdf.

Greer, S. (1995). "De-Centralised Policing in Spain: The Case of the Autonomous Basque Police." *Policing and Society* 5(1): 15–36.

Grob-Fitzgibbon, B. (2004). "From the Dagger to the Bomb: Karl Heinzen and the Evolution of Political Terror." *Terrorism and Political Violence* 16(Spring): 97–115.

Groseclose, T., and J. Milyo. (2005). "A Measure of Media Bias." *Quarterly Journal of Economics* 4(November): 1191–1239. Online: http://www.polisci.ucla.edu/faculty/groseclose/Media-Bias.8.htm.

Grossman, M. (1999). "Cyberterrorism." Computer Law Tip of the Week. Online: http://www.mgrossmanlaw.com/articles/1999/cyberterrorism.htm.

Guha, R. (2007). "A War in the Heart of India." *Nation.* July 16, pp. 28–31.

Gunaratna, R. (1998). "International and Regional Implications of the Sri Lankan Tamil Insurgency." Institute for Counter-Terrorism. Online: http://www.ict.org.il/.

Gunaratna, R. (2000). "Suicide Terrorism: A Global Threat." *Jane's Intelligence Review.* Online: http://www.janes.com/security/international_security/news/usscole/jir001020_1_n.s.html.

Gunaratna, R. (2002). *Inside Al Qaeda: Global Network of Terror.* New York: Columbia University Press.

Gunaratna, R., and M. B. Ali. (2009). "De-Radicalization Initiatives in Egypt: A Preliminary Insight." *Studies in Conflict and Terrorism* 32: 277–291.

Gunter, B. (2008). "Media Violence: Is There a Case for Causality?" *American Behavioral Scientist* 51: 1061–1122. Online: http://abs.sagepub.com/cgi/content/abstract/51/8/1061.

Gurr, T. R. (1988). "Political Terrorism in the United States: Historical Antecedents and Contemporary Trends." In M. Stohl (ed.), *The Politics of Terrorism.* New York: Dekker.

Haddad, S. (2006). "The Origins of Popular Support for Lebanon's Hezbollah." *Studies in Conflict and Terrorism* 29: 21–34.

Hagby, M., A. Goldberg, S. Becker, D. Schwartz, and Y. Bar-Dayan. (2009). "Health Implications of Radiological Terrorism: Perspectives from Israel." *Journal of Emergencies, Trauma, and Shock* 2(2): 117–123.

Halm, H. (1999). *Shi'a Islam: From Religion to Revolution*. Princeton, NJ: Marcus Wiener.

Hamas. (1988). "Hamas Character." Translated and copied by Mid-EastWeb. Online: http://www.mideastweb.org/hamas.htm.

Hambling, D. (2004). "Experts Fear Terrorists Are Seeking Fuel-Air Bombs." *New Scientist*. Online: http://www.newscientist.com/news/news.jsp?id=ns99994785.

Hamilton, C. (2007). *Women and the ETA: The Gender Politics of Radical Basque Nationalism*. Manchester: Manchester University Press.

Hamilton, I. (1971). "From Liberalism to Extremism." *Conflict Studies* 17: 5–17.

Hamm, M. S. (2007). *Terrorist Recruitment in American Correctional Institutions: An Exploratory Study of Non-Traditional Faith Groups*. National Institute of Justice. Online: www.ncjrs.gov/pdffiles1/nij/grants/220957.pdf.

Hamm, M. S. (2009). "Prison Islam in the Age of Sacred Terror." *British Journal of Criminology* 49: 667–685. Online: http://bjc.oxfordjournals.org/cgi/content/abstract/49/5/667.

Hammond, B. (2013). "Sensenbrenner Tells European Parliament Panel that NSA Ignored USA PATRIOT Act's Civil Liberties Terms." *Cybersecurity Policy Report*. November 18, p. 1.

Hammond, T.A. (2010). "Intelligence Organizations and the Organization of Intelligence." *International Journal of Intelligence and Counterintelligence* 23(4): 680–724.

Hanzich, J. (2003). "Dying for Independence." *Harvard International Review* 25(2): 32–36.

Harel, A., and A. Issacharoff. (2008). *34 Days: Israel, Hezbollah, and the War in Lebanon*. New York: Palgrave MacMillan.

Harik, J. P. (2004). *Hezbollah: The Changing Face of Terrorism*. London: I. B. Taurus.

Harris, E. (1995). *Guarding the Secrets: Palestinian Terrorism and a Father's Murder of His Too-American Daughter*. New York: Scribner.

Harris, W. (1998). *Burglary for the Patrol Officer*. Longview, TX: Rough Edge Publications.

Hauser, C., and A. O'Connor. (2007). "Arrested in Plot to Attack Fort Dix." *New York Times*. May 8. Online: http://www.nytimes.com/2007/05/08/us/08cnd-dix.html?ex=1336276800&en=85a2795016f8037f&ei=5088&partner=rssnyt&emc=rss.

Haynes, M. R., and M. J. Giblin. (2014). "Homeland Security Risk and Preparedness in Police Agencies: The Insignificance of Actual Risk Factors." *Police Quarterly* 17(1): 30–53.

Healy, S., and M. Bradbury. (2010). "Endless War: A Brief History of the Somali Conflict. Conciliation Resources." Online: http://www.c-r.org/accord-article/endless-war-brief-history-somali-conflict.

Heilman, J. P. (2010). "Family Ties: The Political Genealogy of Shining Path's Comrade Norah." *Bulletin of Latin American Research* 29(2): 155–169.

Helms, R., S. E. Constanza, and N. Johnson. (2012). "Crouching Tiger or Phantom Dragon: Examining the Discourse on Global Cyber-Terror." *Security Journal* 25(1): 57–75.

Henderson, D. (2006). "Former Detectives Arrested in McCord Probe." *Independent*. August 9. Online: http://news.independent.co.uk/uk/ulster/article1217930.ece.

Hereen, M. W., and S. A. Brown. (2002). *Christ in Celtic Christianity: Britain and Ireland from the Fifth to the Tenth Century*. Rochester, NY: Boydell Press.

Herman, E. S. (1983). *The Real Terror Network*. Boston: South End Press.

Herman, E. S. (1999). *The Myth of the Liberal Media: An Edward Herman Reader*. New York: Peter Lang.

Herman, S. (2001). "The USA PATRIOT Act and the U.S. Department of Justice: Losing Our Balances." *Jurist*. December 3. Online: http://jurist.law.pitt.edu/forum/forumnew40.htm.

Hewitt, C. (2003). *Understanding Terrorism in America: From the Klan to Al Qaeda*. New York: Routledge.

Hewitt, C. *Understanding Terrorism in American: From the Klan to al Qaeda*. New York: Routledge.

Hill, S., and R. Beger. (2009). "A Paramilitary Policing Juggernaut." *Social Justice* 36(1). Online: http://www.socialjusticejournal.org/archive/115_36_1/115_03_Hill-Beger.pdf.

Hinnen, T. M. (2004). "The Cyber-Front in the War on Terrorism: Curbing Terrorist Use of the Internet." *Columbia Science and Technology Law Review*. Online: www.stlr.org/html/volume5/hinnen.pdf.

Hinton, H. L. (1999). *Combating Terrorism: Observations on*

Biological Terrorism and Public Health Initiatives. Washington, DC: General Accounting Office.

Hiro, D. (1987). *Iran Under the Ayatollahs.* London: Routledge & Kegan Paul.

Hirsch-Hoefler, S., and C. Mudde. (2014). " 'Ecoterrorism:' Threat or Political Ploy?" *Studies in Conflict and Terrorism* 37(7): 586–603.

History Channel. (2000). "100 Years of Terror." Four-part series. New York: A&E Television Networks.

Hitt, G., and D. S. Cloud. (2002). "Bush's Homeland Security Overhaul Faces Obstacles." *Wall Street Journal.* June 10, p. A4.

Hobijn, B. (2002). "How Much Will Homeland Security Cost?" Federal Reserve Bank of New York. Online: http://www.security management.com/library/Bart_Homeland0203.pdf.

Hocking, J. (2004). *Terror Laws: ASIO, Counter-Terrorism, and the Threat to Democracy.* Sydney: University of South Wales Press.

Hoffman, B. (1995). "Holy Terror: The Implications of Terrorism Motivated by a Religious Imperative." *Studies in Conflict and Terrorism* 18: 271–284.

Hoffman, B. (1998). *Old Madness, New Methods.* Santa Monica, CA: RAND. Online: http://www.rand.org/publications/randreview/issues/rr.winter98.9/methods.html.

Hoffman, B. (2009). "Radicalization and Subversion: Al Qaeda and the 7 July 2005 Bombings and the 2006 Airline Bombing Plot." *Studies in Conflict and Terrorism* 32: 1100–1116.

Holden, R., and J. White. (2010). "Elements of Radicalization." Bureau of Justice Assistance. Online: https://www.slatt.org.

Holland, J. J. (2005). "House Approves Extension of PATRIOT Act." Associated Press. December 14. Online: http://news.yahoo.com/s/ap/20051214/ap_on_go_co/patriot_act.

Holman, M., J. L. Merolla, and E. J. Zechmeister. (2011). "Sex, Stereotypes, and Security: A Study of the Effects of Terrorist Threat on Assessment of Female Leadership." *Journal of Women, Politics and Public Policy* 32: 173–192.

Horchem, H. J. (1986). "Terrorism in West Germany." *Conflict Studies* 186.

Horgan, J. (2005). *The Psychology of Terrorism.* New York: Routledge.

Horgan, J. (2009). *Walking Away from Terrorism.* New York: Routledge.

Horgan, J., and K. Braddock. (2010). "Rehabilitating the Terrorists? Challenges in Assessing the Effectiveness of De-Radicalization Programs." *Terrorism and Political Violence* 22: 267–291.

Hourani, A. (1997). *A History of the Arab Peoples.* Cambridge, MA: Belknap.

Hourdin, P. (2009). "Banks, Governance, and Public-Private Partnership in Preventing and Confronting Organized Crime, Corruption, and Terrorism Financing." *Journal of Financial Crime* 16(3): 199–209.

Hourdin, P. (2009). "Banks, Governance, and Public-Private Partnership in Preventing and Confronting Organized Crime, Corruption, and Terrorism Financing." *Journal of Financial Crime* 16(3): 199–209.

Howard, M. (2002). "What's in a Name? How to Fight Terrorism." *Foreign Affairs* 81(January/February): 43–59.

Howard, R. D. (2004). "Understanding Al Qaeda's Application of the New Terrorism." In R. Howard and R. Sawyer (eds.), *Terrorism and Counterterrorism: Understanding the New Security Environment.* New York: McGraw-Hill.

Hudson, A. (2006). "Antiterror Grant to Probe Bingo Halls Criticized." *Washington Times.* April 12. Online: http://washingtontimes.com/national/20060411-115930-6028r.htm.

Hudzik, J., and G. Cordner. (1983). *Planning in Criminal Justice Organizations and Systems.* New York: Macmillan.

Hughes, J., and C. Donnelly. (2004). "Attitudes to Community Relations in Northern Ireland: Signs of Optimism in the Post Cease Fire Period?" *Terrorism and Political Violence* 16: 567–592.

Humud, C., A. Arief, L.P. Blanchard, J.M. Sharp, and K. Katzman. (2014). "Al Qaeda-Affi;iated Groups: Middle East and Africa." Congressional Research Service, October 10. Online: http://fas.org/sgp/crs/mideast/R43756.pdf. Accessed: June 2015.

Hutchcroft, P. D. (2008). "The Arroyo Imbroglio in the Philippines." *Journal of Democracy* 19(1): 141–155.

IACP. (*See* International Association of Chiefs of Police)

IIR. (2010). "National Criminal Intelligence Sharing Plan." Institute for Intergovernmental Research. Online: http://www.iir.com/global/ncisp.htm.

Imperial Knights of the Ku Klux Klan of America. Online: http://www.k-k-k.com/items.html.

In SightCrime. (n.d., circa 2011) "ELN Profile." Online: http://

www.insightcrime.org/colombia-organized-crime-news/eln-profile.

In SightCrime. (2015). "Shining Path." Online: http://www.insightcrime.org/peru-organized-crime-news/shining-path-profile.

Inserra, D. (2015). "69th Islamist Terrorist Plot: Ongoing Spike in Terrorism Should Force Congress to Finally Confront the Terrorist Threat." Heritage Foundation. Online: http://www.heritage.org/research/reports/2015/06/69th-islamist-terrorist-plot-ongoing-spike-in-terrorism-should-force-congress-to-finally-confront-the-terrorist-threat. Accessed: September 2015.

Institute for Counter-Terrorism. (2001). *Countering Suicide Terrorism*. Herzliya, Israel: Author.

Institute for Counter-Terrorism. (2004). "The Moral Infrastructure of Chief Perpetrators of Suicide Terrorism." Online: http://www.ict.org.il/Article/903/The%20Moral%20Infrastructure%20of%20Chief%20Perpetrators%20of%20Suicidal%20Terrorism.

International Association of Chiefs of Police. (2001). *Terrorism Response*. Alexandria, VA: Author.

International Association of Chiefs of Police. (2014a). *Homegrown Violent Extremism*. Awareness Brief. Washington, DC: Office of Community Oriented Policing Services. Online: http://ric-zai-inc.com/Publications/cops-w0738-pub.pdf.

International Association of Chiefs of Police. (2014b). *Twitter and Violent Extremism*. Awareness Brief. Washington, DC: Office of Community Oriented Policing Services. Online: http://ric-zai-inc.com/Publications/cops-w0741-pub.pdf.

International Crisis Group. (2004). "Indonesia Backgrounder: Jihad in Central Sulawesi." February 3. Online: http://www.crisisgroup.org/library/documents/asia/indonesia/074_jihad_in_central_sulawesi_mod.pdf.

Irwin, A. S. M., J. Slay, K-K. R. Choo, and L. Liu. (2012). "An Analysis of Money Laundering and Terrorism Financing Typologies." *Journal of Money Laundering Control* 15(1): 85–11

International Crisis Group. (2005). "Recycling Militants in Indonesia: Dural Islam and the Australian Embassy Bombing." February 22. Online: http://www.crisisgroup.org/library/documents/asia/indonesia/074_jihad_in_central_sulawesi_mod.pdf.

International Crisis Group. (2006a). "Pakistan: The Worsening Conflict in Balochistan." Online: http://www.crisisgroup.org/home/index.cfm?id=4373&l=1.

International Crisis Group. (2006b). "Sri Lanka: The Failure of the Peace Process." November 28. Online: http://www.crisisgroup.org/library/documents/asia/south_asia/sri_lanka/124_sri_lanka_the_failure_of_the_peace_process.pdf.

International Crisis Group. (2009). "Women and Radicalization in Kyrgyzstan." September 3. Online: http://www.crisisgroup.org/~/media/Files/asia/central-asia/kyrgyzstan/176_women_and_radicalisation_in_kyrgyzstan.ashx.

International Crisis Group. (2013). "Sri Lanka's Potemkin Peace: Democracy Under Fire." Online: http://www.crisisgroup.org/~/media/Files/asia/south-asia/sri-lanka/253-sri-lankas-potemkin-peace-democracy-under-fire.

International Crisis Group. (2015). "Sri Lanka Between Elections." Online: http://www.crisisgroup.org/~/media/Files/asia/south-asia/sri-lanka/272-sri-lanka-between-elections.

Isikoff, M., and M. Hosenball. (2004). "Paying for Terror." *Newsweek*. Web Exclusive, March 12. Online: http://www.msnbc.msn.com/id/4963025/.

Isseroff, A. (2004). "A History of the Hamas Movement." MidEastWeb. Online: http://www.mideastweb.org/hamashistory.htm.

Jacobs, J. (1983). *S.W.A.T. Tactics*. Boulder, CO: Paladin.

Jacobson, M., and M. A. Levit. (2009). "Interrupting the Money Flow." *Security Management* 53(6): 38–39.

Jamal, A. (2010). "The Asian Tigers: The New Face of the Punjabi Taliban." *Terrorism Monitor* 8(20). Online: http://www.jamestown.org/programs/gta/single/?tx_ttnews[tt_news]=36398&tx_ttnews[backPid]=457&no_cache=1.

Jamestown Foundation. (2010). "Will India Deploy Its Army Against Maoist Terrorists?" *Terrorism Monitor*. June 17. Online: http://www.jamestown.org/programs/gta/single/?tx_ttnews[tt_news]=36502&tx_ttnews[backPid]=457&no_cache=1.

Jamestown Foundation. (2012). "Shining Path Faces Leadership Vacuum in Upper Huallaga Valley." *Militant Leadership Monitor*. March 12. Online: http://mlm.jamestown.org/single/?tx_ttnews%5Btt_news%5D=39201&tx_ttnews%

5BbackPid%5D=539&cHash=
a6028a22ae8ad466650d6ad5a
2c5cdf0.

Jamwal, N. S. (2002). "Hawala:
The Invisible Financing System
of Terrorism." *Strategic Analysis*
26(2): 181–198.

Jarboe, J. (2002). "FBI Testifies
to House Ecoterror Hearing."
Testimony Before the U.S.
House of Representatives,
House Resource Committee,
Subcommittee on Forests
and Forest Health. February
12. Online: http://www.
furcommission.com/news/
newsF04f.htm.

Jeffers, A., and D. Milton. (2014).
"Three Hurdles to Peace:
Negotiating with the FARC
in Colombia." *CTC Sentinel*
7(6, June): 13–17. Online:
https://www.ctc.usma.edu/v2/
wp-content/uploads/2014/06/
CTCSentinel-Vol7Iss6.pdf.

Jenkins, B. (1987). "Will Terrorists
Go Nuclear?" In W. Laqueur
and Y. Alexander (eds.), *The
Terrorism Reader.* New York:
Meridian.

Jenkins, B. M. (1984). "The Who,
What, When, Where, How,
and Why of Terrorism." Paper
presented at the Detroit Police
Department Conference on
Urban Terrorism: Planning or
Chaos? Detroit, November.

Jenkins, B. M. (2004a). "The Operational Code of the Jihadists."
Briefing prepared for the Army
Science Board, RAND, April 1
(unpublished).

Jenkins, B. M. (2004b). "Where
I Draw the Line." *Christian
Science Monitor.* Online: http://
www.csmonitor.com/specials/
terrorism/lite/expert.html.

Jenkins, B. M. (2009). "Outside
Expert's View." In D.
Gartenstein-Ross and L.
Grossman (eds.), *Homegrown
Terrorists in the U.S. and

U.K.: An Empirical Analysis
of the Radicalization Process.*
Washington, DC: Foundation
for the Defense of Democracies.

Jenkins, B. M. (2010). "Would-Be
Warriors: Incidents of Jihadist
Terrorist Radicalization in the
United States Since September
11, 2001." RAND Corporation.
Online: http://www.rand.org/
pubs/occasional_ papers/2010/
RAND_OP292.pdf.

Jenkins, B. M., A. Liepman,
and H. H. Willis. (2014).
*Evolving Terrorist Threats and
the Continuing Challenges
of Domestic Intelligence
Collection and Information
Sharing.* RAND Corporation.
Online: http://www.rand.org/
content/dam/rand/pubs/conf_
proceedings/CF300/CF317/
RAND_CF317.pdf.

Jenkins, B.M. (2006).
*Unconquerable Nation:
Knowing Our Enemy,
Strengthening Ourselves.* Santa
Monica, CA: RAND.

Jenkins, P. (2009). "Terror Begins at
Home." *American Conservative*
8(6): 16–17.

Jensen, R. B. (2004). "Daggers,
Rifles, and Dynamite: Anarchist
Terrorism in Nineteenth
Century Europe." *Terrorism and
Political Violence* 16(Spring):
116–153.

John, W. (2005). "The Roots of
Extremism in Bangladesh."
Jamestown Foundation.
Terrorism Monitor 3(1,
January 13). Online:
http://www.jamestown.
org/publications_details.
php?volume_id=411&issue_
id=3196&article_id=2369092.

Johnson, B.R. (2011). "Fusion Centers: Strengthening the Nation's
Homeland Security Enterprise,"
The Police Chief 78 (February):
pp. 62–68. Online: http://www.
policechiefmagazine.org/magazine/

index.cfm?fuseaction=display_
arch&article_id=2315&issue_
id=22011#top. Accessed:
September 2015.

Jones, C and S. Supinski. (2010).
"Policing and Community
Relations in the Homeland
Security Era." *Journal Of
Homeland Security &
Emergency Management*
January7(1): 1–14.

Jones, S. G. (2014). "The Extremist
Threat to the U.S. Homeland:
Testimony presented to the
House Homeland Security
Committee, January 15, 2014."
RAND. Online: http://www.
rand.org/content/dam/rand/
pubs/testimonies/CT400/CT403/
RAND_CT403.pdf.

Jones, S. G., and M. C. Libicki.
(2008). *How Terrorist Groups
End: Lessons for Countering
Al Qa'ida.* Santa Monica, CA:
RAND Corporation. Online:
http://www.rand.org/pubs/
monographs/MG741-1/.

Jones, S.G. (2014). *A Persistent
Threat: The Evolution of
al Qa'ida and Other Salafi
Jihadists.* Santa Monica, CA:
RAND.

Jonsson, M. (2010). "Counter
Terrorist Financing." *CTC
Sentinel* 3. Online: https://
www.ctc.usma.edu/posts/
countering-terrorist-financing-
successes-and-setbacks-in-the-
years-since-911.

Jordan, L. J. (2005). "Homeland
Security Information Network
Criticized." *Washington Post.*
May 10. Online: http://www.
washingtonpost.com/wp-dyn/
content/article/2005/05/09/
AR2005050901076.html.

Joscelyn, T. (2015). "AQAP
Confirms Death of Senior
Leader." Long War Journal,
June 16. Online: http://
www.longwarjournal.
org/archives/2015/06/

aqap-confirms-death-of-senior-leader.php. Accessed: June 2015.

Joshi, M. (1996). "On the Razor's Edge: The Liberation Tigers of Tamil Eelam." *Studies in Conflict and Terrorism* 19: 19–42.

Josson, P. (2006). "New Profile of the Home-Grown Terrorist Emerges." *Christian Science Monitor*. June 26.

Joyner, C. C., and A. I. Parkhouse. (2009). "Nuclear Terrorism in a Globalizing World: Assessing the Threat and Emerging Management Regime." *Stanford Journal of International Law* 45(2): 203–242.

Juergensmeyer, M. (1988). "The Logic of Religious Violence." In D. C. Rapoport (ed.), *Inside Terrorist Organizations*. New York: Columbia University Press.

Juergensmeyer, M. (2003). *Terror in the Mind of God: The Global Rise of Religious Violence*. Berkley: University of California Press.

Juergensmeyer, M. (2003). *Terror in the Mind of God: The Rise of Religious Violence*. Berkley, CA: University of California Press.

Kahn, A. (2013). "The Magazine That Inspired the Boston Bombers." *PBS Frontline*. Online: http://www.pbs.org/wgbh/pages/frontline/iraq-war-on-terror/topsecretamerica/the-magazine-that-inspired-the-boston-bombers/.

Kamminga, J. (2013). "Peace with the FARC: Integrating Drug-Fueled Guerrillas into Alternative Development Programs." *CTC Sentinel* 6(6): 26–29. Online: https://www.ctc.usma.edu/posts/peace-with-the-farc-integrating-drug-fueled-guerrillas-into-alternative-development-programs.

Kanable, R. (2011). "Fusion Centers Grow Up." *Law Enforcement Technology*. September, pp. 8–16.

Kaplan, D. E. (2003). "The Saudi Connection: How Billions in Oil Money Spawned a Global Terror Network." *U.S. News & World Report*. December 15. Online: http://www.usnews/issue/031215/usnews/15terror.htm.

Kaplan, D. E. (2005). "Paying for Terror." *U.S. News & World Report*. December 5. Online: http://www.usnews.com/usnews/news/articles/051205/5terror.htm.

Kaplan, E. H., A. Mintz, S. Mishal, and C. Samban. (2005). "What Happened to Suicide Bombings in Israel? Insights from a Terror Stock Model." *Studies in Conflict and Terrorism* 28: 225–235.

Karam, P. A. (2005). "Radiological Terrorism." *Human and Ecological Risk Assessment* 11: 501–523.

Karim, K. H. (2001). *Islamic Peril: Media and Global Violence*. Ottawa: Black Rose Books.

Karman, E. (2000). "Hamas' Terrorism Strategy: Operational Limitations and Political Constraints." *Middle East Review of International Affairs* 4(1, March). Online: http://meria.idc.ac.il/journal/2000/issue1/jv4n1a7.html.

Katersky, A. (2010). "Faisal Shahzad Pleads Guilty in Times Square Car Bomb Plot, Warns of More Attacks." ABC News. June 21. Online: http://abcnews.go.com/Blotter/faisal-shahzad-pleads-guilty-times-square-car-bomb/story?id=10970094.

Katz, L. R. (2001). "Anti-Terrorism Laws: Too Much of a Good Thing." *Jurist*. November 24. Online: http://jurist.law.pitt.edu/forum/forumnew39.htm.

Kayyali, N. (2015). "Section 215 of the PATRIOT Act Expires in June. Is Congress Ready?" Electronic Frontier Foundation. Online: https://www.eff.org/deeplinks/2015/01/section-215-patriot-act-expires-june-congress-ready.

Kayyem, J., and A. M. Howitt (eds.). (2002). *Beyond the Beltway: Focusing on Hometown Security*. Cambridge, MA: Harvard University.

Keathley, J. (2002). "Conducting Undercover Terrorism Investigations." Tallahassee, FL: IRR (unpublished).

Keats, A. (2002). "In the Spotlight: Al Jihad (Egyptian Islamic Jihad)." Center for Defense Information. Online: http://www.cdi.org/terrorism/aljihad.cfm.

Keefer, W. J. (2006). "The PATRIOT Act Reauthorized." *Jurist*. Online: http://jurist.law.pitt.edu/forumy/2006/03/patriot-act-reauthorized.php.

Keinon, H. (2004). "Israel Preparing for Wave of Terror." *Jerusalem Post*. May 21.

Kelly, R. W. (2010). "Statement of Raymond W. Kelly, Commissioner, New York City Police Department." The Mumbai Attacks: A Wakeup Call for America's Private Sector. Hearing before the Subcommittee on Transportation Security and Infrastructure Protection of the Committee on Homeland Security, U.S. House of Representatives. Online: http://www.gpoaccess.gov/congress/index.html.

Kepel, G. (2002). *Jihad: The Trail of Political Islam*. Cambridge, MA: Belknap.

Kepel, G. (2004). *The War for Muslim Minds: Islam and the West*. Cambridge, MA: Belknap.

Kershaw, S. (2010). "The Terrorist Mind: An Update." *New York Times*. January 10, Week in Review.

Ketcham, C. C., and H. J. McGeorge. (1986). "Terrorist Violence: Its Mechanics and Countermeasures." In N. C. Livingstone and T. E. Arnold (eds.), *Fighting Back*. Lexington, MA: Heath.

Khashan, H. (2003). "Collective Palestinian Frustration and Suicide Bombings." *Third World Quarterly* 24(6): 1049–1067.

Khatami, S. (1997). "Between Class and Nation: Ideology and Radical Basque Ethnonationalism." *Studies in Conflict and Terrorism* 20: 395–417.

King, A. (2009). "Islam, Women, and Violence." *Feminist Theology* 17: 292–328. Online: http://fth.sagepub.com/cgi/content/abstract/17/3/292.

King, M., and D. M. Taylor. (2011). "The Radicalization of Homegrown Jihadists: A Review of Theoretical Models and Social Psychological Evidence." *Studies in Conflict and Terrorism* 23: 602–622.

Kirchner, L. (2015). "Whatever Happened to 'Eco-terrorism?'" *Pacific Standard*. Online: http://www.psmag.com/nature-and-technology/whatever-happened-to-eco-terrorism. Accessed: September 2015.

Klausen, J. (2015). "Tweeting the Jihad: Social Media Networks of Western Foreign Fighters in Syria and Iraq." *Studies in Conflict and in Terrorism* 38: 1–22.

Klite, P. (2000). "Media Can Be Antibiotic for Violence." *Quill* 88(3): 32–34.

Kohlman, E. F. (2004). *Jihad in Europe: The Afghan-Bosnian Network*. New York: Berg.

Kohlmann, E. (2005). "Spreading Terrorist Dogma." MSNBC. Online: http://www.msnbc.msn.com/id/13848605.

Konotorovich, E. V. (2002). "Make Them Talk." *Wall Street Journal*. June 18, p. A12.

Korn, D. A. (1995). "Interview with Abdullah Ocalan." Online: http://kurdstruggle.org/index.shtml.

Kraska, P. B. (1996). "Enjoying Militarism: Political/Personal Dilemmas in Studying U.S. Police Paramilitary Units." *Justice Quarterly* 13: 405–429.

Kraska, P. B. (2014). "Police Use of Military Equipment." C-SPAN. Online: http://www.c-span.org/video/?321337-1/hearing-militarization-police-forces.

Krasna, J. S. (1997). "Narcotics and the National Security Producer States." *Texas Law Review*. Online: http://www.lib.unb.ca/Texts/JCS/s96/articles/krasna.html.

Kunnath, G. J. (2006). "Becoming a Naxalite in Rural Bihar: Class Struggle and Its Contradictions." *Journal of Peasant Studies* 33(1): 89–123.

Kurtzleben, D. (2015). "Americans Say They Want the Patriot (sic) Act Renewed…but Do They Really?" NPR, June 1. Online: http://www.npr.org/sections/itsallpolitics/2015/06/01/411234429/americans-say-they-want-the-patriot-act-renewed-but-do-they-really. Accessed: August 2015.

Kurz, A. (1994). "Palestinian Terrorism: The Violent Aspect of a Political Struggle." In Y. Alexander (ed.), *Middle Eastern Terrorism: Current Threats and Future Prospects*. New York: Hall.

Kurzman, C. (2001). "Critics Within: Islamic Scholars' Protest Against the Islamic State of Iran." *International Journal of Politics, Culture and Society* 15(2): 341–359.

Kurzman, C. (2004). *The Unthinkable Revolution in Iran*. Cambridge, MA: Harvard University Press.

Kushner, H. W., and B. Jacobson. (1998). "Financing Terrorist Activities Through Coupon Fraud and Counterfeiting." *Counterterrorism and Security International* 5(Summer): 10–12.

Kuusisto, A.-K. (2001). "Territoriality, Symbolism, and the Challenge." *Peace Review* 13(1): 59–66.

Labeviere, R. (2000). *Dollars for Terror: The United States and Islam*. New York: Algora.

Lake, E. (2004). "Hamas Agents May Be Lurking in U.S.: Fears Rantisi's Vow to Attack May Awaken Operatives Here." *New York Sun*. April 29.

Lamloum, O. (2009). "Hezbollah's Media: Political History in Outline." *Global Media and Communication* 5(3): 353–357.

Laqueur, W. (1987). *The Age of Terrorism*. Boston: Little, Brown.

Laqueur, W. (1999). *The New Terrorism: Fanaticism and the Arms of Mass Destruction*. New York: Oxford University Press.

Lau, S. (2003). "An Analysis of Terrorist Groups' Potential Use of Electronic Steganography." SANS Institute. Online: http://www.sans.org/reading_room/whitepapers/steganography554.php.

Law Enforcement Equipment Working Group. (2015). "Recommendations Pursuant to Executive Order 13688 Federal Support for Law Enforcement Equipment Acquisition." White House, Executive Office of the President. Online: https://www.

whitehouse.gov/sites/default/files/docs/le_equipment_wg_final_report_final.pdf.

Lee, A. M. (1983). *Terrorism in Northern Ireland*. New York: General Hall.

Lee, G. D. (2005). *Conspiracy Investigations: Terrorism, Drugs and Gangs*. Upper Saddle River, NJ: Prentice Hall.

LEEWG. (*See* Law Enforcement Equipment Working Group)

Lemieux, A. F., J. M. Brachman, J. Levitt, and J. Wood. (2014). "*Inspire* Magazine: A Critical Analysis of Its Significance and Potential Impact Through the Lens of Information, Motivation, and Behavioral Skills Model." *Studies in Conflict and in Terrorism* 26: 354–371.

Lesser, I. O. (1999). "Changing Terrorism in a Changing World." In I. O. Lesser, B. Hoffman, J. Arquilla, D. Ronfeldt, M. Zanni, and B. M. Jenkins, *Countering the New Terrorism*. Santa Monica, CA: RAND.

Levi, M. (2007). *On Nuclear Terrorism*. Cambridge, MA: Harvard University Press.

Levin, D. (2003). "Structure of News Coverage of a Peace Process." *Press/Politics* 8(4): 27–53.

Levit, L. (2006). *Hamas: Politics, Charity, and Terrorism in the Service of Jihad*. New Haven, CT: Yale University Press.

Levitt, L. (2002). "A Fed-Friendly NYPD? Not Yet." *Newsday*. January 28. Online: http://nypdconfidential.com/columns/2002/020128.html.

Levitt, M., and M. Jacobson. (2008). "The Money Trail." Washington Institute. Online: https://www.washingtoninstitute.org/uploads/Documents/pubs/PolicyFocus89.pdf.

Lewis, B. (1966). *The Arabs in History*. London: Hutchinson University Press.

Lewis, B. (1995). *Cultures in Conflict: Christians, Muslims, and Jews in the Age of Discovery*. New York: Oxford University Press.

Lewis, B. (1998). "License to Kill: Usama bin Ladin's Declaration of Jihad." *Foreign Affairs*. 77(4): 14–19.

Lewis, B. (2003). *The Crisis in Islam: Holy War and Unholy Terror*. New York: Random House.

Lewis, B. (2004). *From Babel to Dragomans: Interpreting the Middle East*. New York: Oxford University Press.

Liff, S., and A. S. Laegren. (2003). "Cybercafes: Debating the Meeting and Significance of Internet Access in a Café Environment." *New Media & Society* 5(3): 307–312.

Lindeman, M. (2010). "Laboratory of Asymmetry: The 2006 Lebanon War and the Evolution of Iranian Ground Tactics." *Military Review* 90(3): 105–116.

Linstone, H. (2003). "The 21st Century: Everyman as Faust. Technology, Terrorism, and the Multiple Perspective Approach." *Technological Forecasting and Social Change* 70(3): 283–296.

Linstroth, J. P. (2002). "History, Tradition, and Memory and the Basques." *History and Anthropology* 13(3): 159–189.

Liptak, A. (2002). "Changing the Standard." *New York Times*. May 31. Online: http://nytimes.com/2002/05/31/national/31ASSE.html.

Liptak, A. (2010). "Court Affirms Ban on Aiding Groups Tied to Terror." *New York Times*. June 21. Online: http://www.nytimes.com/2010/06/22/us/politics/22scotus.html?sq=pkk&st=cse&adxnnl=1&scp=5&adxnnlx=1277326830-HE9VnglcrJmh/Z3oVX1iNQ.

Livingstone, N. C., and T. E. Arnold (eds.). (1986). *Fighting Back*. Lexington, MA: Heath.

Llora, F., J. M. Mata, and C. L. Irvin. (1993). "ETA: From Secret Army to Social Movement. The Post-Franco Schism of the Basque Nationalist Movement." *Terrorism and Political Violence* 5: 106–134.

Logan, S. (2013). "The Sinaloa Federation's International Presence." *CTC Sentinel* 6(4): 6–10. Online: https://www.ctc.usma.edu/posts/the-sinaloa-federations-international-presence.

Lomax, M. (2014). "Written Testimony of Mr. Mark Lomax; Executive Director of the National Tactical Officers Association before the Senate Committee on Homeland Security and Governmental Affairs for the hearing on 'Oversight of Federal Programs for Equipping State and Local Law Enforcement Agencies.' " U.S. Senate. September 9. Online: http://leaksource.info/2014/09/10/senate-hearing-on-militarization-of-us-police-homeland-security-govt-affairs-cmte/.

Lonsdale, J. (2003). "The War Within Mau Mau's Fight for Land and Freedom." In Lonsdale and E. S. Odhiambo (eds.), *Mau Mau and Nationhood: Arms, Authority, and Narration*. Athens: Ohio University Press.

Lufti, A. (2004). "Uyghur Separatism and China's Crisis of Creditability in the War on Terror." Jamestown Foundation. *China Brief* 4(3, February 4). Online: http://www.jamestown.

org/single/?no_cache=1&tx_ttnews[tt_news]=3624.

Lynn, W. J., III (2010). "Defending a New Domain: The Pentagon's Cyberstrategy." *Foreign Affairs*. September/October. Online: https://www.foreignaffairs.com/articles/united-states/2010-09-01/defending-new-domain.

Lyons, T. (2015). "Ethiopia and the Search for Regional Peace in the Horn of Africa." CSIS. Online: http://csis.org/story/ethiopia-and-search-regional-peace-horn-africa.

MacDonald, A. [William Pierce]. (1985). *The Turner Diaries*. Arlington, VA: National Vanguard.

MacDonald, A. [William Pierce]. (1989). *Hunter: A Novel*. Hillsboro, WV: National Alliance.

MacDonald, R. (1972). "Electoral Politics and Uruguayan Political Decay." *International Economic Affairs* 26: 24–45.

Mackay, C. S. (2004). *Ancient Rome: A Military and Political History*. New York: Cambridge University Press.

Mackey, R. (2010). "Another Middle-Class Terror Suspect." *New York Times*. May 4. Online: http://thelede.blogs.nytimes.com/2010/05/05/another-middle-class-terror-suspect/?scp=1&sq=mackey%20&st=cse.

Macleod, S. (2008). "Who Killed Imad Mugniyeh?" *Time*. February 13. Online: http://mideast.blogs.time.com/2008/02/13/who_killed_imad_mughniyeh/.

Maier, T. (2003). "Counterfeit Goods Pose Real Threat." *Insight on the News*. November 10, p. 21.

Main, R. (2015). "Law Enforcement, Peter King at Odds About Which Groups Pose the Greatest Threat." *Long Island Press*. June 26. Online: http://www.longislandpress.com/2015/06/26/law-enforcement-peter-king-at-odds-about-which-extremist-groups-pose-greatest-threats/

Makarenko, T. (2002). "Terrorism and Transnational Organized Crime: The Emerging News." In P. Smith (ed.), *Transnational Violence and Seams of Lawlessness in the Asia-Pacific: Linkages to Global Terrorism*. Honolulu: Asia Pacific Centre for Security Studies.

Maleeha, A. (2012). *Gender-Based Explosions: The Nexus Between Muslim Masculinities, Jihadist Islamism and Terrorism*. New York: United Nations Press.

Manning, P. K. (1976). *Police Work: The Social Organization of Policing*. Cambridge, MA: MIT Press.

March, A. (2005) "Guerrilla War, a Method." Che Guevara Studies Center and Ocean Press. Online: http://www.marxists.org/archive/guevara/1963/misc/guerrilla-war-method.htm.

Marighella, C. (1969). *The Minimanual of the Urban Guerrilla*. U.S. Army Military Intelligence School (unpublished). Online: http://www.marxists.org/archive/marighellacarlos/1969/06/minimanual-urban-guerrilla/.

Marighella, C. (1971). *For the Liberation of Brazil*. J. Butt and R. Sheed (trans.). Harmondsworth, UK: Pelican.

Markon, J. (2011). "Post 9/11 Security Focus Has Created Sometimes Tense Rivalry between FBI, NYPD." *Washington Post,* November 25. Online: http://www.washingtonpost.com/politics/post-911-security-focus-has-created-sometimes-tense-rivalry-between-fbi-nypd/2011/11/22/gIQAZoH7vN_story.html. Accessed: September 2015.

Marquise, R. A. (2006). *Scotbom: Evidence and the Lockerbie Investigation*. New York: Algora.

Marshal, M. A. (2009). "Domestic Terrorism: Veterans Are the Focus of Reports on Extremism." *Officer* 85(6): 16–17.

Marshall, A. (2008). "Lost Girls of the Jungle." *Marie Claire* 15(2): 108–112.

Martin, M. (2007). "Jailhouse Conversion Takes 'Extreme' Turn." National Public Radio, Interview with Mark Hamm. August 8. Online: http://www.npr.org/templates/story/story.php?storyId=12587106.

Mason, C. (2004). "Who's Afraid of Virginia Dare? Confronting Anti-Abortion Terrorism after 9-11." *Journal of Constitutional Law*. April, pp. 796–817. Online: http://64.233.179.104/scholar?hl=en&lr=&q=cache:wXS6hyrjQHUJ:www.law.upenn.edu/conlaw/issues/vol6/num4/mason.pdf+%22eric+rudolph%22+abortion.

Massie, R. K. (1991). *Dreadnought: Britain, Germany and the Coming of the Great War*. New York: Random House.

Masters, J. (2014). "Mujahadeen-e-Khalk (MeK)." CFR Backgrounder. Online: http://csis.org/files/publication/140304_Meacham_Colombia_Web.pdf.

Matthews, M. M. (2008). *We Were Caught Unprepared: The 2006 Hezbollah-Israeli War*. Fort Leavenworth, KS: U.S. Army Combined Arms Center, Combat Studies Institute Press. Online: http://www.cgsc.edu/carl/download/csipubs/matthewsOP26.pdf.

Mattoon, S. (1987). *S.W.A.T. Training and Deployment.* Boulder, CO: Paladin.

Matusitz, J. (2010). "Cyberterrorism: Postmodern State of Chaos." *Journal of Digital Forensics* 3(2–4): 115–123.

May, P., J. Sapotichne, and S. Workman. (2009). "Widespread Policy Disruption: Terrorism, Public Risks, and Homeland Security." *The Policy Studies Journal* 27(2): 171–194.

Mazzei, J. (2009). *Death Squads or Self-Defense Forces? How Paramilitary Groups Emerge and Challenge Democracy in Latin America.* Chapel Hill: University of North Carolina Press.

McCampbell, M. S. (2010). *The Collaboration Toolkit for Community Organizations: Effective Strategies to Partner with Law Enforcement.* COPS, U.S. DOJ. Online: http://ojp. gov/fbnp/pdfs/Collaboration_ Toolkit.pdf.

McCampbell, M.S. (2010). "The Collaboration Toolkit for Community Organizations: Effective Strategies to Partner with Law Enforcement." COPS Office. Online: http://ojp. gov/fbnp/pdfs/Collaboration_ Toolkit.pdf. Accessed: September 2015.

McCants, W. (2006). (see Abu Bakr Naji, "The Management of Savagery.")

McCants, W. (2014). "State of Confusion: ISIS' Strategy and How to Counter It." *Foreign Affairs.* Online: https://www. foreignaffairs.com/articles/ iraq/2014-09-10/state- confusion. Accessed: June 2015.

McCants, W. (n.d., ca. 2014). "The Sectarian Apocalypse Online." University of California, Berkeley. Online: https://vimeo. com/110515042. Accessed: May 2015.

McCourt, M. (2010). "Is Cyber Your Biggest Threat?" *Security* 47(8): 12.

McGinn, D. (2006). "IRA Has Changed Drastically." *Independent.* October 4. Online: http://news.independent.co.uk/ uk/ulster/article1794267.ece.

McGreal, C. (2006). "Fatah Struggles with Tainted Image." *Guardian.* January 24. Online: http://www.guardian.co.uk/ world/2006/jan/24/israel.

McGregor, A. (2015). "After Garissa: Kenya Revisers Its Security Strategy to Counter Al Shabaab's Shifting Tactics." *Terrorism Monitor,* Jamestown Foundation. Online: http:// www.jamestown.org/programs/ tm/single/?tx_ttnews%5Btt_ news%5D=43807&tx_ttnews% 5BbackPid%5D=26&cHash=a0 472536606dc527783d7487e4ce 18bb#.VVT-PGCp3dk.

McJunkin, J. W. (2010). "Statement of James W. McJunkin, Deputy Assistant Director, Counterterrorism Division, Federal Bureau of Investigation." The Mumbai Attacks: A Wakeup Call for America's Private Sector, Hearing before the Subcommittee on Transportation Security and Infrastructure Protection of the Committee on Homeland Security, U.S. House of Representatives. Online: http://www.gpoaccess.gov/ congress/index.html.

Meacham, K., D. Farah, and R.D. Lamb. (2014). *Colombia: Peace and Security in the Post-Conflict Era.* Center for Strategic and International Studies. Online: http://csis.org/files/ publication/140304_Meacham_ Colombia_Web.pdf.

Melekian, B. K. (2011). "Back to the Future: Why Community Policing Is More Relevant Than Ever." *Sheriff* 63(4): 52–53.

Miller, A. (1982). *Terrorism, the Media, and the Law.* New York: Transnational.

Miller, J., S. Engelberg, and W. Broad. (2001). *Germs: Biological Weapons and America's Secret War.* New York: Simon & Schuster.

Millman, G. J. (2014). "Does Anti-Money Laundering Work? Rick McDonell of FATF Answers His Critics." *Wall Street Journal.* April 8. Online: http://blogs.wsj.com/ riskandcompliance/2014/04/08/ does-anti-money-laundering- work-rick-mcdonell-of-fatf- answers-critics/.

Miniter, R. (2005). *Disinformation: 22 Media Myths that Undermine the War on Terror.* Washington, DC: Regnery.

Mintz, J. (2005). "Security Spending Initiates Disputes." *Washington Post.* March 13. Online: http:// www.washingtonpost.com/ wp-dyn/articles/A47964- 2005Apr12.html.

Mironova, V., L. Mrie, and S. Whit. (2014). "The Motivations of Syrian Islamist Fighters." *CTC Sentinel* 7(10). Online: https://www.ctc.usma.edu/v2/ wp-content/uploads/2014/10/ CTCSentinel-Vol7Iss10.pdf. Accessed: October 2014.

Mitchell, A., and C. Hulse. (2002). "Accountability Concern Is Raised over Security Department." *New York Times.* June 27. Online: http://www. nytimes.com/2002/06/27/ national/27RIDG.html.

Moghadam, A. (2008). "The Salafi-Jihad as a Religious Ideology." *CTC Sentinel* (February 15). Online: https://www.ctc.usma. edu/posts/the-salafi-jihad-as- a-religious-ideology. Accessed: June 2015.

Momen, M. (1985). *An Introduction to Shi'a Islam.*

New Haven, CT: Yale University Press.

Monaghan, R. (2004). "An Imperfect Peace: Paramilitary Punishments in Northern Ireland." *Terrorism and Political Violence* 16: 439–461.

Monahan, T. (2009). "The Murky World of 'Fusion Centers.' " *Criminal Justice Matters* 75(1): 20–21.

Monahan, T. (2010). "The Future of Security? Surveillance Operations at Homeland Security Fusion Centers." *Social Justice* 37(2/3): 84–98.

Monahan, T., and N. A. Palmer. (2009). "The Emerging Politics of DHS Fusion Centers." *Security Dialogue* 40(6): 617–636.

Montlake, S. (2007). "The Philippines Fights Leftists, Fair or Foul." *Far Eastern Economic Review* 170(3): 2–5.

Montpetit, J. (2008). "Tricky to Track Terrorist Cash." *Toronto Star*. April 28, p. A13.

Moore, R. F. (2006). "Deep Inside City Jails, Top Cops Keep a Watchful Eye Out for Terror." *New York Daily News*. August 13. Online: http://www.nydailynews.com/front/story/443116p-373179c.html.

Morlin, B. (@015). "'Shot Caller' in California White Supremacist Gang Pleads Guilty." Southern Poverty Law Center. Online: https://www.splcenter.org/hatewatch/2015/01/30/shot-caller-california-white-supremacist-gang-pleads-guilty. Accessed: September 2015.

Moss, R. (1972). *Urban Guerrillas*. London: Temple Smith.

Moxon-Browne, E. (1987). "Spain and the ETA." *Conflict Studies* 201.

MSNBC. (2007). "DOJ Statement on JFK Airport Plot Arrests." MSNBC. June 2. Online: http://www.msnbc.msn.com/id/19002569/.

Mullendore, K., and J. R. White. (1996). "Legislating Terrorism: Justice Issues and the Public Forum." Paper presented at the Academy of Criminal Justice Sciences Annual Meeting. Las Vegas, NV, March.

Munck, R. (1992). "The Making of the Troubles in Northern Ireland." *Journal of Contemporary History* 27(2): 211–229.

Munson, Z. (2008). "Terrorism." *Context* 7(4): 78–79.

Muro, D. (2009). "The Politics of War Memory in Radical Basque Nationalism." *Ethnic and Racial Studies* 32(4): 659–678.

Murphy, P. (2015). "Ecuador Says Hosted Peace Talks with Colombia Gov't, ELN Rebels." Reuters. May 13. Online: http://www.reuters.com/article/2015/05/13/us-ecuador-colombia-eln-idUSKBN0NY2RE20150513.

Myers, G. (2012). "Investing in the Market of Violence: Toward a Micro-Theory of Terrorist Financing." *Studies in Conflict and Terrorism* 35: 693–711.

Nacos, B. L. (2005). "The Portrayal of Female Terrorists in the Media: Similar Framing Patterns in the News Coverage of Women in Politics and in Terrorism." *Studies in Conflict and Terrorism* 28: 435–451.

Naji, A.B. (2006). "The Management of Savagery: The Most Critical Stage through which the Umma Will Pass." Translated by William McCants. Olin Institute for Strategic Studies, Harvard University. Online: https://azelin.files.wordpress.com/2010/08/abu-bakr-naji-the-management-of-savagery-the-most-critical-stage-through-which-the-umma-will-pass.pdf. Accessed: June 2015.

Nance, M. W. (2003). *The Terrorist Recognition Handbook*. Guilford, CT: Lyons Press.

Napoleoni, L. (2003). *Modern Jihad: Tracing the Dollars Behind the Terror Networks*. London: Pluto.

Nasr, K. B. (1997). *Arab and Israeli Terrorism*. Jefferson, NC: McFarland.

National Commission on Terrorist Attacks upon the United States. (2004). *The 9/11 Commission Report: Final Report of the National Commission on Terrorist Attacks upon the United States*. New York: Norton. Online: http://www.9-11commission.gov/report/911Report.pdf.

National Conference of State Legislatures. (2003). "Cyberterrorism." Online : http://www.ncsl.org/programs/lis/ CIP/cyberterrorism.htm.

National Counterterrorism Center. (2015). "Al Qa'ida in the Lands of the Islamic Maghreb (AQIM)." NCTC. Online: http://www.nctc.gov/site/groups/aqim.html. Accessed: June 2015.

National Counterterrorism Center. (2015a). "Al Aqsa Martyrs Brigade." Online: http://www.nctc.gov/site/groups/al_aqsa.html.

National Counterterrorism Center. (2015b). "Revolutionary Armed Forces of Colombia (FARC)." Online: http://www.nctc.gov/site/groups/farc.html.

National Public Radio. (2009). "Gutanamo Detainee Decision Soon." NPR, October 15. Online: http://www.npr.org/templates/story/story.php?storyId=113840271. Accessed: September 2015.

National Public Radio. (2009). "Holder: Guantánamo Detainee

Decision Soon." October 15. Online: http://www.npr. org/templates/story/story. php?storyId=113840271.

National Public Radio. (2015). "Right-Wing Extremists More Dangerous than Islamic Extremists in U.S." Online: http://www.npr. org/2015/06/24/417192057/ right-wing-extremists-more-dangerous-than-islamic-terrorists-in-u-s.

National Strategy for Combating Terrorism. (2006). "National Strategy for Combatting Terrorism." Online: http://fas.org/ irp/threat/nsct2006.pdf. Accessed: October 2006.

Navarro, J. (2005). *Hunting Terrorists: A Look at the Psychopathology of Terror*. Springfield, IL: Charles C. Thomas.

Navarro, J., and M. Karlins. (2008). *What Every BODY Is Saying: An ex-FBI Agent's Guide to Speed Reading People*. New York: Harper.

Navarro, P. (2010). "A Maoist Counterpoint: Peruvian Maoism beyond Sendero Luminoso." *Latin American Perspectives* 37(1): 153–171. Online: http:// lap.sagepub.com/cgi/content/ abstract/37/1/153.

Navias, M. S. (2002). "Financial Warfare as a Response to International Terrorism." *Political Quarterly* 73(August): 57–79.

NBC News. (2015a). "Cyber Attack on Power Grid Could Cost $1 Trillion: Report." Online: http://www.nbcnews.com/tech/ security/cyber-attack-power-grid-could-cost-1-trillion-report-n388581.

NBC News. (2015b). "Freed Nigerian Women Tell of Boko Haram Horror." May 2. Online: http://www. nbcnews.com/storyline/

missing-nigeria-schoolgirls/ freed-nigerian-women-tell-boko-haram-horror-n352866.

NCTC. (see National Counterterrorism Center).

Nechaev, S. (1987). "Catechism of the Revolutionist." In W. Laqueur and Y. Alexander (eds.), *The Terrorism Reader*. New York: Meridian.

Nelson, R., and R. Wise. (2013). "Homeland Security at a Crossroads: Evolving DHS to Meet Next Generation of Threats." Center for Strategic and International Studies. Online: http://csis.org/ publication/homeland-security-crossroads-evolving-dhs-meet-next-generation-threats.

Ness, C. D. (2005). "In the Name of the Cause: Women's Work in Religious and Secular Terrorism." *Studies in Conflict and Terrorism* 28: 353–373.

Neuberger, L.C., and T. Valentini. (1996). *Women and Terrorism*. New York: St. Martin's.

Neuman, P. R. (2007). "Negotiating with Terrorists." *Foreign Affairs* 86(3): 128–138.

New American. (2009). "New Push to Criminalize Dissent." *New American* 25(14, July 6): 6.

New York Times. (2009). "Shining Path." March 18. Online: http://topics.nytimes.com/ topics/reference/timestopics/ organizations/s/shining_path/ index .html.

New York Times. (2010). "Umar Farouk Abdulmutallab." February 10. Online: http:// topics.nytimes.com/top/ reference/timestopics/ people/a/umar_farouk_ abdulmutallab/index.html?scp= 1-spot&sq=umar%20 farouk%20 abdulmutallab&st=cse.

New York Times. (2012). "Times Topics: USA PATRIOT Act."

May 15. Online: http://topics. nytimes.com/top/reference/ timestopics/subjects/u/usa_ patriot_act/index.html.

Newkirk, A. B. (2010). "The Rise of the Fusion-Intelligence Complex: A Critique of Political Surveillance after 9/11." *Surveillance and Society* 8(1): 43–60.

Nice, D. C. (1988). "Abortion Clinic Bombings as Political Violence." *American Journal of Political Science* 32: 178–195.

Nilson, C., and T. Burke. (2002). "Environmental Extremists and the Eco-Terrorism Movement." *ACJS Today* 24: 1–6.

Nima, R. (1983). *The Wrath of Allah: Islamic Revolution and Reaction in Iran*. London: Pluto.

Non-State Armed Groups. (2008). "Palestinian Islamic Jihad or Islamic Jihad Movement in Palestine." Harvard University Graduate Institute, Geneva. Online: http://www.armed-groups.org/6/section.aspx/ ViewGroup?id=69.

Nordland, R., S. Yousafzi, and B. Dehghanpisheh. (2002). "How Al Qaeda Slipped Away." *Newsweek*. August 19, pp. 34–41.

Northern Ireland Office. (2007). "The Agreement." Online: http://nio.gov.uk/the-agreement.

Norton, A. R. (2009). *Hezbollah: A Short History*. Princeton, NJ: Princeton University Press.

NPR. (*See* National Public Radio)

Nuclear Threat Initiative. (2009). "Civilian Uses of HEU." Online: http://www.nti.org/db/heu/civilian. html.

O Corrain, D. (2000). "Prehistoric and Early Christian Ireland." In R. F. Foster (ed.), *The Oxford Illustrated History of Ireland*. New York: Oxford University Press.

O'Connor, T. (2004). "Civil Liberties and Domestic Terrorism." North Carolina Wesleyan College. Online: http://faculty.ncwc.edu/toconner/429/429lect19.htm. Accessed: Summer 2006.

O'Connor, T. (2004). "Civil Liberties and Domestic Terrorism." North Carolina Wes-leyan College. Online: http://faculty.ncwc.edu/toconner/429/429lect19.htm. Accessed: October 2006.

O'Neill, K. M., J. M. Calia, C. Chess, and L. Clarke. (2007). "Miscommunication During the Anthrax Attacks: How Events Reveal Organizational Failures." *Research in Human Ecology* 14(2). Online: http://www.human ecologyreview.org/pastissues/her142/oneilletal.pdf.

Oetken, J. (2009). "Counterinsurgency Against the Naxalites in India." In S. Ganguly and D. P. Fidler (eds.), *India and Counterinsurgency: Lessons Learned*. New York: Routledge.

Office of Homeland Security. (2002). *National Strategy for Homeland Security*. Washington, DC: Author.

Office of National Drug Control Policy. (2015). "High Intensity Drug Trafficking Areas (HIDTA) Program." The White House. Online: https://www.whitehouse.gov/ondcp/high-intensity-drug-trafficking-areas-program. Accessed: September 2015.

Office of the Director of National Intelligence. (2015). "Leading Intelligence Integration." ODNI. Online: http://www.dni.gov/index.php. Accessed: September 2015.

Okeowo, A. (2015). "The People vs. Boko Haram." *New York Times Sunday Edition Magazine*.

January 28. Online: http://www.nytimes.com/2015/01/28/magazine/the-people-vs-boko-haram.html?_r=0.

Oliver, H. J. (2002). *The Wahhabi Myth: Dispelling Prevalent Fallacies and the Fictitious Link with Bin Laden*. Birmingham, UK: Salafi Publications.

Oliver, M. (2004). "Israel Targeting Entire Hamas Leadership." *Guardian*. May 23. Online: http://www.guardian.co.uk/israel/Story/0,2763,1175986,00.html.

Oliver, W. M. (2006). "The Fourth Era of Policing: Homeland Security." *International Review of Law, Computers & Technology* 20(1/2): 49–62.

Oliver, W. M. (2009). "Policing for Homeland Security." *International Review of Law, Computers, and Technology* 20(3): 49–62.

Oliverio, A., and P. Lauderdale. (2005). "Terrorism as Deviance or Social Control." *International Journal of Comparative Sociology* 46(1/2): 156–169.

Onoucha, F. C. (2012). "The Audacity of Boko Haram: Background, Analysis, and Emerging Trend." *Security Journal* 25(2): 134–151.

Organization for the Prohibition of Chemical Weapons. (2000). "Nerve Agents: Lethal Organo-Phosphorus Compounds Inhibiting Cholinesterase." Online: http://www.opcw.nl/chemhaz/nerve.htm.

Osborn, R. (2007). "On the Path of Perpetual Revolution: From Marx's Millenarianism to Sendero Luminoso." *Totalitarian Movements and Political Religions* 8(1): 115–135.

Osterholm, M. T., and J. Schwartz. (2000). *Living Terrors*. New York: Delta.

Othman, R., and R. Ameer. (2014). "Institutionalization of Risk Management Framework in Islamic NGOs for Suppressing Terrorism Financing: Exploratory Research." *Journal of Money Laundering and Control* 17(1): 96–109.

Owen, M., and K. Maurer. (2012). *No Easy Day: The Firsthand Account of the Mission That Killed Osama Bin Laden*. New York: Penguin Group (USA), Ltd.

Page, D. (2011). "Community Policing or Homeland Security: A 'Sophie's Choice' for Police?" *Law Enforcement Technology*, 38(9): 18–22.

Page, J. (2009). "Sport in Line of Fire as Terrorists Target Sri Lankan Cricket Team." *Sunday Times*. March 4. Online: http://www.timesonline.co.uk/tol/news/world/asia/article5841980.ece.

Pan, E. (2005). "Turkey's EU Bid." Council on Foreign Relations. September 30. Online: http://www.cfr.org/publication/8939/turkeys_eu_bid.html.

Pantucci, R. (2010). "Europol Report Suggests Separatism Rather Than Islamism Constitutes Biggest Terrorist Threat to Europe." *Terrorism Monitor* 8(22, June 4). Online: http://www.jamestown.org/articles-by-author/?no_cache=1&tx_cablanttnewsstaffrelation_pi1%5Bauthor%5D=473.

Pape, R. A. (2003). "The Strategic Logic of Suicide Bombing." *American Political Science Review* 97(3): 1–19. Online: http://www.danieldrezner.com/research/guest/Pape1.pdf.

Pape, R. A. (2005). *Dying to Win: The Strategic Logic of Suicide Terrorism*. New York: Random House.

Parachini, J. (2003). "Putting WMD Terrorism into Perspective." *Washington Quarterly* 26(4): 37–50. Online: http://www.twq.com/03 autumn/docs/03autumn_parachini .pdf.

Parker, L. (2002). "A Frenzied Race for Answers, Antibiotics." *USA Today.* January 23.

Paul, J., and M. Spirit. (2008). "War and Politics." *Britain's Small Wars.* Online: http://www.britains-small-wars.com/cyprus/war.html.

Payne, S. (1971). "Catalan and Basque Nationalism." *Journal of Contemporary History* 6(1): 15–33.

Paz, R. (2004). "Hamas' Solidarity with Muqtada al-Sadr: Does the Movement Fall under the Control of Hizbollah and Iran?" Herzliya, Israel: PRISM Series of Special Dispatches on Global Jihad, No. 4/2.

Pecquet, J. (2015a). "Congressional Invite to MEK Sparks Furious Backlash." *Al Monitor.* April 28. Online: http://www.al-monitor.com/pulse/originals/2015/04/congress-mek-testimony-backlash-maryam-rajavi.html#. Accessed: September 2015.

Pecquet, J. (2015b). "MeK Uses Congressional Spotlight to Push Regime Change in Iran." *U.S. News and World Report.* April 30. Online: http://www.usnews.com/news/articles/2015/04/30/mek-uses-congressional-spotlight-to-push-regime-change-in-iran.

Percox, D. A. (2003). "Mau Mau and the Arming of the State." In J. Lonsdale and E. S. Odhiambo (eds.), *Mau Mau and Nationhood: Arms, Authority, and Narration.* Athens: Ohio University Press.

Perl, R. F. (1998). *Terrorism: U.S. Response to Bombings in Kenya and Tanzania: A New Policy Direction?* Congressional Reference Service, *CRS Report for Congress.* Online: http://nsarchive.gwu.edu/NSAEBB/NSAEBB55/crs19980901.pdf

Perl, R. F. (2001). *National Commission on Terrorism: Background and Issues for Congress.* February 6. Online: http://nsarchive.gwu.edu/NSAEBB/NSAEBB55/crs20010206.pdf

Perlinger, A. (2006). *Middle Eastern Terrorism.* New York: Chelsea House.

Perry, M. (2010). *Talking to Terrorists: Why America Must Engage with Its Enemies.* New York: Basic Books.

Peters, R. (1996). *Jihad in Classical and Modern Islam.* Princeton, NJ: Marcus Wiener.

Petrou, M. (2009). "Hosted by Terrorists?" *Maclean's* 122(10/11, March 23): 24–26.

Pew Foundation. (2005). "Islamic Fundamentalism: Common Concern for Muslim and Western Public." Online: http://www.pewglobal.org/2005/07/14/islamic-extremism-common-concern-for-muslim-and-western-publics/.

Philp, C., and M. Evans. (2009). "Fear and Mistrust on Both Sides: Analysis." *Times* (London). October 20.

Pillar, P. R. (2004). "Counterterrorism after al Qaeda." *Washington Quarterly* 27(3): 101–113.

Pitcavage, M. (1999a). "Anti-Government Extremism: Origins, Ideology, and Tactics." Tallahassee, FL: Institute for Intergovernmental Research.

Pitcavage, M. (1999b). "Current Activities and Trends." Tallahassee, FL: Institute for Intergovernmental Research.

Pitcavage, M. (1999c). "Old Wine, New Bottles: Paper Terrorism, Paper Scams, and Paper Redemption." *Militia Watch Dog.* November 8. Online: http://archive.adl.org/mwd/redemption.html.

Pizam, A., and A. Fleischer. (2002). "Severity Versus Frequency of Acts of Terrorism: Which Has a Larger Impact on Tourism Demand?" *Journal of Travel Research* 40(3): 337–339.

Plachta, M. (2014). "Europol Releases Its Report on Terrorism." *International Enforcement Law Reporter* 30(9, September): 337–340.

Pluchinsky, D. (1982). "Political Terrorism in Western Europe: Some Themes and Variations." In Y. A. and K. A. Myers (eds.), *Terrorism in Europe.* New York: St. Martin's.

Pochon, C. "Applying the Holder Standard to Speech That Provides Material Support to Terrorism in the *United States v. Mehanna, No. 09-10017-GAO* (D. Mass. 2012)." *Harvard Journal of Law and Public Policy* 36(1): 375–389.

Polk, W. R. (2013). "Understanding Syria: From Pre-Civil War to Post-Assad." *Atlantic.* Online: http://www.theatlantic.com/international/archive/2013/12/understanding-syria-from-pre-civil-war-to-post-assad/281989/.

Poloni-Staudinger, L., and C. Orbtals. (2014). "Abbottabad: Agency and Hegemonic Masculinity in the Age of Global Terror." *Gender Issues* 31(1): 34–57.

Poole, R. (2006). "New Study Calls for Rethinking TSA's Role." *Aviation Security Newsletter* 17(January). Online site no longer active.

Porath, N. (2010). "Civic Activism Continued Through Other Means: Terror-Violence in the

South of Thailand." *Terrorism and Political Violence* 22(4): 581–596.

Porteous, T. (2006). "The Al Qaeda Myth." Online: http://www.truth-out.org/archive/component/k2/item/62043-tom-porteous--the-al-qaeda-myth.

Posner, R. A. (2004). "The 9/11 Report: A Dissent." *New York Times*. August 29. Online: http://www.nytimes.com/2004/08/29/books/review/29POSNERL.html?ex=1094787860&ei=1&en=b755-f3ccc383aefd.

Post, J. M. (2007). *The Mind of the Terrorist: The Psychology of Terrorism from the IRA to Al-Qaeda*. New York: Palgrave Macmillan.

Pratt, N. (2012). "The Gender Logistics of Resistance to the 'War on Terror': Constructing Sex-Gender Difference Through the Erasure of Patriarchy in the Middle East." *Third World Quarterly* 33(10): 1821–1836.

Priest, D., and W. M. Arkin. (2010). "Top Secret America." *Washington Post*. July 19. Online: http://projects.washingtonpost.com/top-secret-america/articles/a-hidden-world-growing-beyond-control/.

Pruitt, D. G. (2007). "Readiness Theory and the Northern Ireland Conflict." *American Behavioral Scientist* 50(11): 1520–1541.

Rabasa, A., P. Chalk, K. Cragin, S. A. Daly, H. S. Gregg, T. W. Karasik, K. A. O'Brien, and W. Rosenau. (2006). *Beyond Al Qaeda: Part II. The Outer Rings of the Terrorist Universe*. Santa Monica, CA: RAND.

Radelet, L., and D. Carter. (2000). *Police and the Community*, 7th ed. New York: Macmillan.

Raman, B. (2003). "Istanbul: The Enemy Within." *Asia Times*.

Online: http://www.atimes.com/atimes/Middle_East/EK22Ak01.html.

Ramsey, C and L. Robinson. (2015). "Final Report of the President's Task Force on 21st Century Policing." COPS Office. Online: http://www.cops.usdoj.gov/pdf/taskforce/TaskForce_FinalReport.pdf. Accessed: September 2015.

Randal, J. (2004). *Osama: The Making of a Terrorist*. New York: Andrew A. Knopf.

Randol, B. M. (2012). "The Organizational Correlates of Terrorism Response Preparedness in Local Police Departments." *Criminal Justice Policy Review* 23(3): 304–326.

Ranstorp, M. (1994). "Hizbollah's Command Leadership: Its Structure, Decision-Making Relationship with Iranian Clergy and Institutions." *Terrorism and Political Violence* 6(3, Autumn). Online: http://www.st-andrews.ac.uk/academic/intrel/research/cstpv/pages/terrorism.html.

Ranstorp, M. (1996). *Hizb'Allah in Lebanon: The Politics of the Western Hostage Crisis*. New York: St. Martin's.

Rashbaum, W. (2010). "Qaeda Leader Indicted in New York Subway Plot." *New York Times*. July 7. Online: http://www.nytimes.com/2010/07/08/nyregion/08terror.html?_r=1&ref=najibullah_zazi.

Rashdan, M.A. (2012). "An Analytical Study of the Financial Intelligence Units' Enforcement Mechanisms." *Journal of Money Laundering Control* 15(4): 483–495.

Rasler, K. (1996). "Concessions, Repression, and Political Protest in the Iranian Revolution." *American Sociological Review* 61(February): 132–152.

Rath, S.K. (2015). *Fragile Frontiers: The Secret History of the Mumbai Terrorist Attacks*. London: Routledge.

Raufer, X. (1993). "The Red Brigades: Farewell to Arms." *Studies in Conflict and Terrorism* 16: 313–325.

Raymond, C. Z. (2006). "The Threat of Maritime Terrorism in the Malacca Straits." *Terrorism Monitor* 4(3, February 9). Online: http://jamestown.org/terrorism/news/article.php?issue_id=3614.

Read, C. (1996). *From Tsar to Soviets: The Russian People and Their Revolution, 1917–21*. New York: Oxford University Press.

Regan, T. (2004). "New Skirmishes in the Patriot Act Battle." *Christian Science Monitor*. July 14. Online: http://www.csmonitor.com/2004/0714/dailyUpdate.html.

Renard, T. (2009). "Europol Report Describes Afghanistan-Pakistan Connection to Trends in European Terrorism." *Terrorism Monitor* 7(12, May 8). Online: http://www.jamestown.org/articles-by-author/?no_cache=1&tx_cablanttnewsstaffrelation_pi1%5Bauthor %5D=539.

Renwick, R., and S. Hanson. (2014). "FARC, ELN: Colombia's Left-Wing Guerrillas." CFR Backgrounder. Online: http://www.cfr.org/colombia/farc-eln-colombias-left-wing-guerrillas/p9272.

Reuters. (1996). "Israel Arch Foe Hizbollah Tough Nut to Crack." April12. Online: http://www.nando.net/newsroom/nt/412/r/whoiz.html.

Ricks, T. E. (2006). *Fiasco: The American Military Adventure in Iraq*. New York: Penguin.

Ridley, N., and D. C. Alexander. (2012). "Combatting Terrorist Financing in the First Decade of the Twenty-First Century." *Journal of Money Laundering Control* 15(1): 38–57.

Riedel, B. (2008). "Pakistan: The Critical Battlefield." *Current History* 107(712): 355–361.

Riessenfeld, L. (2015). "Sophisticated Argentina Kidnapping Gang Allegedly Include Fmr (*sic*) Shining Path Guerrillas." In SightCrime. May 8. Online: http://www.insightcrime.org/news-briefs/sophisticated-argentina-kidnapping-gang-shining-path-guerrillas.

Riley, K. J., and B. Hoffman. (1995). *Domestic Terrorism*. Santa Monica, CA: RAND. Online: http://www.rand.org/publications/MR/MR505/MR505.pdf.

Rinehart, C. S. (2009). "Volatile Breeding Grounds: The Radicalization of the Egyptian Muslim Brotherhood." *Studies in Conflict and Terrorism* 32: 953–988.

Riordan, R. J., and A. B. Zegart. (2002). "City Hall Goes to War." *New York Times*. July 5. Online: http://www.nytimes.com/2002/0.7/05/opinion/05RIOR.html.

Risen, J., and J. L. Thomas. (1998). "Pro-Life Turns Deadly: The Impact of Violence on America's Anti-Abortion Movement." January 26. Online: http://www.rick-ross.com/reference/a-abortion/a-abortion2.html.

Robb, A. (2010). "Not a Lone Wolf." *Ms. Magazine* 20(2): 26–32.

Roberts, A. (2002). "The Changing Faces of Terrorism." BBC News. August 27. Online: http://www.bbc.co.uk/history/war/sept_11/changing_faces_01.shtml.

Robinson, S. E., and N. Mallik. (2015). "Varieties of Homeland Security: An Assessment of US State-level Definitions." *Journal Of Homeland Security & Emergency Management*, 12(1): 67–80.

Rogers, M. (2012, February). Private conversation with Congressman Michael Rogers (R-MI), Chair of the United States House Permanent Select Committee on Intelligence.

Roggio, B. (2013). "U.S. Adds Belmokhtar's Brigade to Terrorist Lists." Long War Journal, December 18. Online: http://www.longwarjournal.org/archives/2013/12/us_adds_belmokhtars.php. Accessed: June 2015.

Rohlinger, D. A. (2002). "Framing the Abortion Debate: Organizational Resources, Media Strategies, and Movement-Countermovement Dynamics." *Sociological Quarterly* 43(4): 479–507.

Rollins, J. (2010). "Al Qaeda and Affiliates: Historical Perspective, Global Presence, and Implications for U.S. Policy." Congressional Research Service. Online: http://fpc.state.gov/documents/organization/137015.pdf.

Ross, J. I. (2007). "Deconstructing the Terrorism News Media Relationship." *Crime, Media, Culture* 3(2): 215–225. Online: http://cmc.sagepub.com/cgi/content/refs/3/2/215.

Rothe, D. L., and J. I. Ross. (2010). "Private Military Contractors, and the Terrain of Unaccountability." *Justice Quarterly* 27(4): 593–617.

Rothem, D. (2002). "In the Spotlight: Al-Asqa Martyrs Brigades." Center for Defense Information. Online: http://www.cdi.org/terrorism/asqa.cfm.

Roul, A. (2010). "Little-Known Ghazi Brigade Now a Major Player in the Punjabi Jihad?" *Terrorism Monitor* 8(28). Online: http://www.jamestown.org/programs/gta/single/?tx_ttnews[tt_news]=36621&tx_ttnews[backPid]=457&no_cache=1.

Ruane, M. E. (2009). "The Life of James W. von Brunn." WashingtonPost.com. July 6. Online: http://www.cbsnews.com/stories/2009/07/06/politics/washingtonpost/main5136822.shtml.

Rubenstein, R. E. (1987). *Alchemists of Revolution*. New York: Basic Books.

Rubin, B. (2003). "Lessons from Iran." *Washington Quarterly* 26(3): 105–115.

Ruthven, M. (2000). *Islam in the World*. New York: Oxford University Press.

Ryan, J. (2007). "The Four P-Words of Militant Islamist Radicalization and Recruitment: Persecution, Precedent, Piety, and Perseverance." *Studies in Conflict and Terrorism* 30: 985–1011.

Saab, B. Y., and A. W. Taylor. (2009). "Criminality and Armed Groups: A Comparative Study of FARC and Paramilitary Groups in Colombia." *Studies in Conflict and Terrorism* 32: 455–475.

Saeed, A., and H. Saeed. (2004). *Freedom of Religion, Apostasy, and Islam*. Aldershot, UK: Ashgate.

Sageman, M. (2004). *Understanding Terror Networks*. Philadelphia: University of Pennsylvania.

Sallot, J. (2006). "Auto Thefts Help Finance Terrorism, Day Says." *Globe and Mail* (Canada). June 9, p. A15.

Samuels, D. (2012). "The New Mastermind of Jihad." *Wall*

Street Journal (April 6). Online: http://www.wsj.com/articles/SB1 0001424052702303299604577 3237350859163544 Accessed: June 2015.

Saupp, K. (2010). "Fusion Liaison Officer Programs: Effective Sharing of Information to Prevent Crime and Terrorism." *Police Chief* 77(2, February). Online: http://policechiefmagazine. org/magazine/index. cfm?fuseaction=print_ display&article_ id=2013&issue_id=22010.

Savage, C. (2015). "Justice Department Declassifies Inspector General 2012 Report on FBI Activities under FISA Amendments of 2008." *New York Times,* January 11. Online: http://www.nytimes. com/interactive/2015/01/12/ us/12-doj-ig-fbi-702-foia.html. Accessed: September 2015.

Savage, C. (2015). "Surveillance Court Rules the N.S.A. Can Continue Bulk Data Collection." *New York Times.* June 30. Online: http://www.nytimes. com/2015/07/01/us/politics/fisa-surveillance-court-rules-nsa-can-resume-bulk-data-collection. html?_r=0.

Scarman, L. (1972). *Violence and Civil Disturbance in Northern Ireland in 1969.* London: Her Majesty's Stationary Office.

Schabner, D. (2004). "ELF Making Good on Threat." ABCNews. com. January 30. Online: http:// abc-news.go.com/sections/us/ DailyNews/elf010130.html.

Schachter, J., Y. Guzansky, and Y. Schweitzer. (2010). "Nuclear Terrorism: Threat to the Public or to Credibility." Tel Aviv: Institute for National Security Studies. April 29. Online: http:// canadafreepress.com/index.php/ article/22594.

Scheuer, M. (2006). *Through Our Enemies' Eyes: Osama Bin Laden, Radical Islam, and the Future of America.* Washington, DC: Potomac Books.

Schmid, A. P. (1992). "The Response Problem as a Definition Problem." *Terrorism and Political Violence* 4(4, Winter): 7–25.

Schmid, A. P., and A. J. Jongman. (2005). *Political Terrorism: A New Guide to Actors, Authors, Concepts, Data Bases, Theories, and Literature.* Somerset, NJ: Transaction Books.

Schmid, A., and J. deGraaf. (1982). *Violence as Communication.* Newbury Park, CA: Sage.

Schmitt, E. (2002). "Administration Split on Local Role in Terror Fight." *New York Times.* April 29. Online: http://www. nytimes.com/2002/04/29/ politics/29IMMI.html.

Schneider, F. (2002). "Money for Terrorism: The Hidden Financial Flows of Islamic Terrorist Organisations. Some Preliminary Results from an Economic Perspective." Paper prepared for the workshop on The Economic Consequences of Global Terrorism, organized by DIW. Berlin, June 14–15.

Schoof, M., and G. Fields. (2002). "Anthrax Attack Summary." *Wall Street Journal.* March 25.

Schramm, M., and M. Taube. (2002). "The Institution Foundations of Al Qaida's Global Financial System." Related papers not presented at The Economic Consequences of Global Terrorism. Berlin, June 14–15.

Schweitzer, Y. (2000). "Suicide Terrorism: Development and Characteristics." Institute for Counter-Terrorism. Online: http://www.ict.org.il/_home. htm.

Scott-Joynt, J. (2003). "Charities in Terror Fund Spotlight." BBC News. October 15. Online: http://news.bbc.co.uk/2/hi/ business/3186840.

Seale, P. (1992). *Abu Nidal: A Gun for Hire.* New York: Random House.

Seelye, K. Q. (2002). "War on Terror Makes for Odd Twists in Justice System." *New York Times.* June 23. Online: http:// www.nytimes.com/2002/06/29/ national/23SUSP.html.

Seixas, X.-M. N. (2005). "Nation in Arms Against the Invader: On Nationalist Discourses During the Spanish Civil War." In C. Ealham and M. Richards (eds.), *The Splintering of Spain: Cultural History and the Spanish Civil War, 1936– 1939.* Cambridge: Cambridge University Press.

Serafino, N. M. (2002). "Combating Terrorism: Are There Lessons to Be Learned from Foreign Experiences?" Congressional Reference Service. Online: http://fpc.state.gov/ documents/organization/7957. pdf.

Service, R. (1995). *Lenin: A Political Life,* Vol. 3: *The Iron Ring.* Bloomington: Indiana University Press.

Service, R. (2005). *A History of Modern Russia: From Nicholas II to Vladimir Putin.* Cambridge, MA: Harvard University Press.

Shafer, J. R. (2010). *Psychological Narrative Analysis: A Professional Method to Detect Deception in Written and Oral Communications.* Springfield, IL: Charles C. Thomas.

Shafer, J. R., and J. Navarro. (2004). *Advanced Interviewing Techniques: Proven Strategies for Law Enforcement, Military, and Security Personnel.*

Springfield, IL: Charles C. Thomas.

Shahar, Y. (2002). "The Al-Asqa Martyrs Brigades: A Political Tool with an Edge." Institute for Counter-Terrorism. Online: http://www.ict.org.il/articles/articledef.cfm?articleid=430.

Shaikh, F. (2008). "Pakistan's Perilous Voyage." *Current History* 107(712): 362–368.

Sharma, D. (2006). "Historical Traces of Hundi, Sociocultural Understanding, and Criminal Abuses of Hawala." *International Criminal Justice Review* 16(12): 99–121. Online: http://icj.sagepub.com/cgi/reprint/16/2/99.pdf.

Shay, S. (2002). *The Endless Jihad: The Mujahidin, the Taliban, and Bin Laden.* Herzliya, Israel: Institute for Counter-Terrorism.

Shepard, W. S. (2002). "The ETA: Spain Fights Europe's Last Active Terrorist Group." *Mediterranean Quarterly.* Winter, pp. 55–68.

Sherewell, P., and A. Spillius. (2009). "Fort Hood Shooting: Texas Army Killer Linked to September 11 Terrorists." *Daily Telegraph.* November 7. Online: http://www.telegraph.co.uk/news/worldnews/northamerica/usa/6521758/Fort-Hood.

Shoshoni, A., and M. Sloan. (2008). "The Drama of Media Coverage of Terrorism: Emotional and Attitudinal Impact on the Audience." *Studies in Conflict and Terrorism* 31: 627–640.

Simms, K. (2000). "The Norman Invasion and Gaelic Recovery." In R. F. Foster (ed.), *The Oxford Illustrated History of Ireland.* New York: Oxford University Press.

Simpson, C., and S. Gorman. (2009). "Suspected Fort Hood Shooter Believed to Be Self-Radicalized." *Wall Street Journal.* November 18.

Singh, P. (2000). *The Sikhs.* New York: Alfred Knopf.

Sinha Roy, M. (2009). "Magic Moments of Struggle: Women's Memory of the Naxalbari Movement in West Bengal, India (1967–1975)." *Indian Journal of Gender Studies* 16(2): 205–232.

SITE. (2011). "Abu Musab al Suri Theory of Jihad." Online: http://news.siteintelgroup.com/blog/index.php/about-us/21-jihad/21-suri-a-mili. Accessed: June 2015.

Sjoberg, L. (2009). "Feminist Interrogations of Terrorism/Terrorism Studies." *International Relations* 23(1): 69–74. Online: http://ire.sagepub.com.

Skeen, L. (2014). "A Shining Path Resurgence?" North American Conference on Latin America. Online: https://nacla.org/news/shining-path-resurgence.

Slisli, F. (2000). "The Western Media and the Algerian Crisis." *Race and Class* 41(3): 43–57.

Smith, B. L. (1994). *Terrorism in America: Pipe Bombs and Pipe Dreams.* Albany: State University of New York Press.

Smith, B. L., and K. R. Damphousse. (2002). *American Terrorism Study: Patterns of Behavior, Investigation, and Prosecution of American Terrorists, Final Report.* U.S. Department of Justice. Online: http://www.ncjrs.gov/pdffiles1/nij/grants/193420.pdf.

Smith, B. L., and P. Roberts. (2005). "Pre-Incident Indicators of Terrorist Activities: The Identification of Behavioral, Geographic, and Temporal Patterns of Preparatory Conduct." National Institute of Justice. Online: http://www.ojp.usdoj.gov/nij/maps/savannah2005/papers/Smith.ppt#397.

Sofer, K., and J. Addison. (2012). "The Unaddressed Threat

of Female Suicide Bombers: Women Terrorists Are an Increasing Problem." Center for American Progress. Online: http://www.americanprogress.org/issues/2012/01/female_suicide_bombers.html.

Sonmez, S. F., and Graefe, A. R. (1998). "Influence of Terrorism Risk on Foreign Tourism Decisions." *Annals of Tourism Research* 25(1): 112–144.

Southern Poverty Law Center (SPLC). (2015a). "Hate and Extremism." Online: http://www.splcenter.org/what-we-do/hate-and-extremism.

Southern Poverty Law Center (SPLC). (2015b). "Ku Klux Klan." Online: http://www.splcenter.org/get-informed/intelligence-files/ideology/ku-klux-klan.

Southern Poverty Law Center. (2015). "Sovereign Citizen Movement." SPLC. Online: https://www.splcenter.org/fighting-hate/extremist-files/ideology/sovereign-citizens-movement. Accessed: September 2015.

Spencer, A. T., and S. M. Croucher. (2008). "Basque Nationalism and the Spiral of Silence: An Analysis of Public Perceptions of ETA in Spain and France." *International Communication Gazette* 70(2): 137–153. Online: http://gaz.sage-pub.com/cgi/content/abstract/70/2/137.

Stanton, B. (1991). *Klanwatch: Bringing the Ku Klux Klan.* New York: Grove Weidenfeld.

Sterling, C. (1986). *The Terror Network.* New York: Dell.

Stern, J. (2003a). "When Bombers Are Women." *Washington Post.* December 18. Reprint, Harvard University, John F. Kennedy School of Government. Online: http:// www.ksg.harvard.edu/news/opeds/2003/stern_women_bombers_wp1121803.htm.

Stern, J. (2003b). *Terror in the Name of God: Why Religious Militants Kill*. New York: Harper Collins.

Stern, J., and J. M. Berger. (2015). *ISIS: The State of Terror*. New York: HarperCollins.

Stohl, M. (2008). "Networks, Terrorists and Criminals: The Implications for Community Policing." *Criminal Law and Social Change* 50(1/2): 59–72.

Storey, I. (2007). "Malaysia's Role in Thailand's Southern Insurgency." Jamestown Foundation. *Terrorism Monitor* 5(5, May15). Online: http://www.jamestown. org/terrorism/news/article. php?articleid=2370279.

Stout, D. (2009). "Museum Gunman a Longtime Foe of Government." *New York Times*. June 10. Online: http://www. nytimes.com/2009/06/11/ us/11shoot.html.

Stratfor. (2015). "In Kenya, Al Shabaab Kill en Masse Again." Stratfor. Online: https://www. stratfor.com/analysis/kenya-al-shabaab-kills-en-masse-again.

Straw, J. (2009). "Connecting the Dots, Protecting Rights." *Security Management* 53(8): 22–24.

Suri, A.M. (2005). "A Call to Global Islamic Resistance." SITE (translation). Online: http://news.siteintelgroup.com/ blog/index.php/about-us/21-jihad/21-suri-a-mili. Accessed: June 2015.

Sutter, D. (2001). "Can the Media Be So Liberal? The Economics of Media Bias." *Cato Journal* 20(3): 431–451. Online: http:// cato.org/pubs/journal/cj20n3/ cj20n3-7.pdf.

Swanson, C. R., L. Territo, and R. W. Taylor. (2001). *Police Administration: Structures, Processes, and Behavior*, 5th ed.

Upper Saddle River, NJ: Prentice Hall.

Sweeny, E. M. (2005). "The Patrol Officer: America's Intelligence on the Ground." *FBI Law Enforcement Bulletin* 74(9): 14–22.

Taber, R. (2002). *The War of the Flea: The Classic Study of Guerilla Warfare*. Dulles, VA: Potomac Books.

Taheri, A. (1987). *Holy Terror*. Bethesda, MD: Adler & Allen.

Talkleft. (2003). "Victory Act: Redefining Drug Crimes as Terrorism." August 20. Online: http://www.w3c.org/TR1999/ REC-html1401-19991224/ loose.dtd.

Tamas, G. M. (2001). "The Decay of Terrorism." *East European Constitutional Review* 10(4). Online: http://www.law.nyu.edu/ vol10num4/features/tamas.html.

Taylor, A. (2014). " 'Dead' Boko Haram Leader Tells Nigeria: 'I'm Still Alive.' " *Washington Post*. Online: http://www. washingtonpost.com/blogs/ worldviews/wp/2014/10/02/ dead-boko-haram-leader-tells-nigeria-im-still-alive/.

Taylor, D. G. (2011). "Revise the PATRIOT Act to Increase Government Oversight of Surveillance." Politifact.com. Online: http://www.politifact. com/truth-o-meter/promises/ obameter/promise/179/revise-the-patriot-act-to-increase-oversight-on-go/.

Taylor, L. (2006). *Shining Path: Guerrilla War in Peru's Northern Highlands, 1980–1997*. Liverpool, UK: Liverpool University Press.

Taylor, R. W. (1987). "Terrorism and Intelligence." *Defense Analysis* 3: 165–175.

Taylor, R. W., and A. L. Russell. (2012). "The Failure of 'Fusion' Centers and the National

Criminal Intelligence Sharing Plan." *Police Practice and Research* 12(2): 184–200.

Tenet, G. (2007). *At the Center of the Storm: My Years at the CIA*. New York: Harper Collins.

Thachik, K., M. E. Bowman, and C. Richardson. (2008). "Homegrown Terrorism: The Threat Within." National Defense University. Online: http://www.dtic.mil/cgi-bin/ GetTRDoc?AD=ADA482139

Thaoor, I. (2014). "Indonesia Quashed al Qaeda. Now it Faces New Islamic State Threat." *Washington Post*, September 25. Online: https://www. washingtonpost.com/news/ worldviews/wp/2014/09/25/ indonesia-quashed-al-qaeda-now-it-faces-new-islamic-state-threat/. Accessed: August 2015.

Tharu, S. (2007). "Insurgency and the State in India: The Naxalite and Khalistan." *South Asian Survey* 14(1): 83–100.

Thatcher, D. (2005). "The Local Role in Homeland Security." *Law and Society* 39(2): 635–676.

Theidon, K. (2006). "The Mask and the Mirror: Facing up to the Past in Post War Peru." *Anthropologica* 48(1): 87–100.

Thony, J. T., and C. A. Png. (2007). "FATF Special Recommendations and UN Resolutions on the Financing of Terrorism." *Journal of Financial Crime* 14(2): 150–169.

Throup, D. W. (1988). *Economic and Social Origins of Mau Mau, 1945–1953*. London: James Currey.

Tilly, C. (2004). "Terror, Terrorism, and Terrorists." *Sociological Theory* 22(1): 5–13.

Times of India. (2003). "Dawood, Osama Share Smuggling Routes." November 19. http:// timesofindia.indiatimes.

com/cms.dll/html/uncomp/articleshow?msid=291478.

Tofangsaz, H. (2015). "Rethinking Terrorist Financing: Where Does this all Lead?" *Journal of Money Laundering Control* 18(1): 112–130.

Tosini, D. (2009). "A Sociological Understanding of Suicide Attacks." *Theory, Culture, Society* 26(4): 67–96. Online: http://tcs.sagepub.com/cgi/content/abstract/26/4/67.

Trautsoult, J., and J. Johnson. (2012). "International Anti-Money Laundering Regulation of Alternative Remittance Systems: Why the Current Approach Does Not Work in Developing Countries." *Journal of Money Laundering Control* 15(4): 407–420.

Trojanowicz, R. C., B. Busqueroux, V. E. Kappeler, and L. K. Ganines. (1998). *Community, NJ Policing: A Contemporary Perspective*. Cincinnati, OH: Anderson.

Trojanowicz, R., and B. Bucqueroux. (2009). *Community Policing: A Contemporary Perspective*. Newark, NJ: Matthew Bender and Company, Inc.

Trundle, R. C., Jr. (1996). "Has Global Ethnic Conflict Superseded Cold War Ideology?" *Studies in Conflict and Terrorism* 19: 93–107.

Tucker, N. B. (2008). "The Culture Revolution in Intelligence: Interim Report." *Washington Quarterly* 31(2): 47–61.

Tupman, W. A. (2009). "Ten Myths About Terrorist Financing." *Journal of Money Laundering Control* 12(2): 189–205.

U.S. Congress, Office of Technology Assessment. (1995). *Environmental Monitoring for Nuclear Safeguards*. Washington, DC: Government Printing Office.

U.S. Department of Defense. (2001). "DOD USS *Cole* Commission Report." January 9. Online: http://www.defenselink.mil/pubs/cole20010109.html.

U.S. Department of Defense. (2005). *Homeland Security*. U.S. Joint Chiefs of Staff. Online: http://www.dtic.mil/doctrine/jel/new_-pubs/jp3_26.pdf.

U.S. Department of Defense. (2015). "Frequently Asked Questions. Under Secretary of Defense for Policy. Online: http://policy.defense.gov/OUSDP Offices/ASDforHomeland DefenseGlobalSecurity/HomelandDefenseIntegration DSCA/faqs.aspx#Section5. Accessed: September 2015.

U.S. Department of Homeland Security. (2004). *Securing Our Homeland*. Online: http://www.dhs.gov/inter-web/assetlibrary/DHS_StratPlan_ FINAL_spread.pdf.

U.S. Department of Homeland Security. (2009). "National Infrastructure Protection Plan." DHS. Online: http://www.dhs.gov/xlibrary/assets/NIPP_Plan.pdf. Accessed: September 2015.

U.S. Department of Homeland Security. (2010). "Executive Summary: Quadrennial Homeland Security Review Report." Online: http://www.dhs.gov/xlibrary/assets/qhsr_executive_summary.pdf.

U.S. Department of Homeland Security. (2014). "Fusion Center Success Stories." Online: http://www.dhs.gov/fusion-center-success-stories.

U.S. Department of Homeland Security. (2015). "DHS Announces Grant Guidance for Fiscal Year (FY) 2015 Preparedness Grants." DHS, April. Online: http://www.dhs.gov/news/2015/04/02/dhs-announces-grant-guidance-fiscal-year-fy-2015-preparedness-grants. Accessed: September 2015.

U.S. Department of Homeland Security. (2015b). "State and Major Urban Areas Fusion Centers." DHS. Online: http://www.dhs.gov/state-and-major-urban-area-fusion-centers. Accessed: September 2015.

U.S. Department of Justice. (2003). "Members of the Palestinian Islamic Jihad Arrested, Charged with Racketeering and Conspiracy to Provide Support for Terrorists." Press Release. February 20. Online: http://www.usdoj.gov/opa/pr/2003/February/03_crm_099.htm.

U.S. Department of Justice. (2006). "Combat Terrorism." Online: http://www.usdoj.gov/whatwedo/whatwedo_ct.html.

U.S. Department of Justice. (2007). "United States Attorneys." Online: http://www.usdoj.gov/usao/index.html.

U.S. Department of Justice. (2008). "Community Policing Dispatch." Online: http://cops.usdoj.gov/html/dispatch/january_2008/nugget.html.

U.S. Department of Justice. (2010). "The Nationwide SAR Initiative." Online: http://nsi.ncirc.gov/.

U.S. Department of Justice. (2013). "Uniting and Strengthening America by Providing Appropriate Tools to Gather and Obstruct Terrorism (USA PATRIOT) Act." Online: https://it.ojp.gov/PrivacyLiberty/authorities/statutes/1281.

U.S. Department of Justice. (2015). "Offices of the United States Attorneys." DOJ. Online: http://www.justice.gov/usao/mission. Accessed: September 2015.

U.S. Department of Justice, Office of Justice Programs. (2006). *Fusion Center Guidelines*.

Online: http://it.ojp.gov/documents/fusion_center_guidelines_law_enforcement.pdf.

U.S. Department of State. (2004b). *Patterns of Global Terrorism, 2003*. Online: http://www.state.gov/s/ct/rls/pgtrpt/2003/.

U.S. Department of State. (2015). "Foreign Terrorist Organizations." Online: http://www.state.gov/j/ct/rls/other/des/123085.htm.

U.S. Department of the Treasury. (2003). "Informal Value Transfer Systems." Online: http://www.fincen.gov/advis33.pdf.

U.S. Department of the Treasury. (2015). "National Money Laundering Risk Assessment, 2015. Online: http://www.treasury.gov/resource-center/terrorist-illicit-finance/Documents/National%20Money%20Laundering%20Risk%20Assessment%20–%2006-12-2015.pdf

U.S. Immigration and Customs Enforcement. (2005). "Two Dearborn Residents Plead Guilty to Document and Visa Fraud." Online: http://www.ice.gov/pi/news/newsreleases/articles/050714detroit.htm.

U.S. Marshals Service. (2005). *Monitor*. Online: http://www.usdoj.gov/marshals/monitor/autumn05.pdf.

U.S. Navy. (2008). "Palestinian Islamic Jihad (PIJ)." Naval Post Graduate School. Online: http://www.nps.edu/Library/Research/SubjectGuides/SpecialTopics/TerroristProfile/Current/PalestineIslamicJihad.html.

U.S. Office of the Director of National Intelligence. (2007). "An Overview of the United States Intelligence Community." http://www.dni.gov/who_what/061222_DNIHand-book_Final.pdf.

U.S. Senate, Committee on Homeland Security and Governmental Affairs. (2014). "Oversight of Federal Programs for Equipping State and Local Law Enforcement (Testimony Mark Lomax)." Online: http://www.hsgac.senate.gov/hearings/oversight-of-federal-programs-for-equipping-state-and-local-law-enforcement. Accessed: January 2015.

Ulph, S. (2006a). "Internet Mujahadeen Intensify Research on U.S. Economic Targets." *Terrorism Focus* 3(2). Online: http://www.jamestown.org/terrorism/news/article.php?issue_id=3588.

Ulph, S. (2006b). "Internet Mujahideen Refine Electronic Warfare Tactics." *Terrorism Focus* 3(5). Online: http://www.jamestown.org/terrorism/news/article.php?issue_id=3611.

Unger, C. (2007). "From the Wonderful Folks Who Brought You Iraq." *Vanity Fair*. March. Online: http://www.vanityfair.com/politics/features/2007/03/whitehouse200703.

United Nations. (1948). "Universal Declaration of Human Rights." Online: http://www.un.org/Overview/rights.html.

United States of America v. Mohamad Youseff Hammoud, et al. (March 2002). U.S. District Court, Western District of North Carolina, Charlotte Division. Docket No. 3:00CR147-MU.

United States of America v. Mousa Mohammed Abu Marzook, et al. (2003). U.S. District Court, Northern District of Illinois, Eastern Division. Docket No. 03 CR 978.

University of Singapore. (2007). "Contemporary Post-Colonial and Post-Imperial Literature in English: Frantz Fanon." Online: http://www.scholars.nus.edu.sg/post/poldiscourse/fanon/fanonov.html.

Uris, L. (1977). *Trinity*. New York: Bantam Books.

Valburn, M. (2002). "Air Marshal Program Drains Other Agencies." *Wall Street Journal*. February 4, p. A18.

Van De Velde, J. R. (2010). "The Impossible Challenge of Deterring 'Nuclear Terrorism' by Al Qaeda." *Studies in Conflict and Terrorism* 33(8): 682–699.

Van Dongen, T. (2012). "The Naxalite Insurgency in India: No End in Sight." Aspen Institute Italia. Online: http://www.aspeninstitute.it/aspenia-online/article/naxalite-insurgency-india-no-end-sight.

Vergani, M. (2014). "Neo-Jihadist Prosumers and Al Qaeda Songle Narrative: The Case Study of Giuliano Delnevo." *Studies in Conflict and in Terrorism* 37: 604–617.

Verhoeven, C. (2009). *The Odd Man Karakozov: Imperial Russia, Modernity, and the Birth of Terrorism*. Ithaca, NY: Cornell University Press.

Vest, G. (2007). "Ohio Local Law Enforcement Information Sharing Network: Policy Issues in Data Exchange." *Police Chief* 72(6). Online: http://policechief-magazine.org/magazine/index.cfm?fuseaction=display_arch&article_id=612&issue_id=62005.

Vidino, L. (2009). "Homegrown Jihadist Terrorism in the United States: A New and Occasional Phenomenon?" *Studies in Conflict and Terrorism* 32(1): 1–17.

Vidino, L. (2011). "The Buccinasco Pentiti: A Unique Case Study of Radicalization." *Terrorism and Political Violence* 23: 398–418.

Voelkel, C. (2015). "Colombia: The ELN's Long and Slow

March to Peace." International Crisis Group. Online: http://blog.crisisgroup.org/latin-america/2015/01/19/colombia-the-elns-long-and-slow-march-to-peace/.

von Hippel, K. (2002). "The Roots of Terrorism: Probing the Myths." *Political Quarterly*. Online: www.blackwell-synergy.com/doi/pdf/10.1111/1467-923X.73.s1.4.

von Knop, K. (2007). "The Female Jihad: Al Qaeda's Women." *Studies in Conflict and Terrorism* 30: 397–414.

Wade, S. J., and D. Reiter. (2007). "Does Democracy Matter? Regime Type and Suicide Terrorism." *Journal of Conflict Resolution* 51(2): 329–348.

Walby, K., and R. K. Lippert. (2015). "The Difference Homeland Security Makes: Comparing Municipal Corporate Security in Canada and the United States." *Security Dialogue* 46(3): 238–255.

Walker, S. (1985). *Sense and Nonsense about Crime: A Policy Guide*. Pacific Grove, CA: Brooks/Cole.

Walker, S. (1992). *The Police in America*. New York: McGraw-Hill.

Wall Street Journal Research Staff. (2005). "A Chronology of Violence." *Wall Street Journal*. November 11, p. A16.

Wallach, J., and J. Wallach. (1992). *Arafat in the Eyes of the Beholder*. Rocklin, CA: Prima.

Walter, J. P. (2002). "National Drug Control Strategy: Combating Narcoterrorism." May 2. Online: http://fpc.state.gov/9908.htm.

Wardlaw, G. (1982). *Political Terrorism: Theory, Tactics, and Counter-Measures*. London: Cambridge University Press.

Warwick, D. P. (1975). *A Theory of Public Bureaucracy: Politics, Personality, and Organization in the State Department*. Cambridge, MA: Harvard University Press.

Washington Post. (2010). "Experts Discuss the Government's Growing Intelligence Network: Is It Too Big?" July 25. Online: http://www.washington-post.com/wp-dyn/content/article/2010/07/24/AR2010072400164.html.

Watson, D. L. (2002). *The Terrorist Threat Confronting the United States*. Washington, DC: Federal Bureau of Investigation. Online: www.fbi.gov.

Weaver, M.A. (2015). "Why Do the Go?" *New York Times Magazine*, April 19: 42–47 and 58–60.

Wedgwood, R. (2002). "The Enemy Within." *Wall Street Journal*. June 14, p. A12.

Wege, C. A. (1994). "Hizbollah Organization." *Studies in Conflict and Terrorism* 17(2): 151–164.

Weimann, G. (2008). "The Psychology of Mass-Mediated Terrorism." *American Behavioral Scientist* 52: 69–86. Online: http://abs.sagepub.com/cgi/content/abstract/52/1/69.

Weimann, G., and K. von Knop. (2008). "Applying the Notion of Noise to Countering Online Terrorism." *Studies in Conflict and Terrorism* 31(10): 883–902.

West, D. M. (2012). *A Vision for Homeland Security in the Year 2025*. Brookings Institution. Online: http://www.insidepolitics.org/brookingsreports/homeland_security.pdf.

Westcott, K. (2000). "Who Are Hamas?" BBC News Online. October 19. Online: http://news.bbc.co.uk/1/hi/world/middle_east/978626.stm.

Westphal, K. (2003). "Steganography Revealed." Online: http://www.securityfocus.com/infocus/1684.

Whine, M. (1999). "Cyberspace: A New Medium for Communication, Command, and Control by Extremists." Institute for Counter-Terrorism. Online: http://www.ict.org.il/ articles/articledet.cfm?articleid=76.

White, J. R. (1986). *Holy War: Terrorism as a Theological Construct*. Gaithersburg, MD: International Association of Chiefs of Police.

White, J. R. (1997). "Militia Madness: Extremist Interpretations of Christian Doctrine." *Perspectives: A Journal of Reformed Thought* 12: 8–12.

White, J. R. (2000). *The Religious Roots of Criminal Behavior*. Tallahassee, FL: Institute for Intergovernmental Research.

White, J. R. (2001). "Political Eschatology: A Theology of Antigovernment Extremism." *American Behavioral Scientist* 44: 937–956.

White, J. R. (2002). *Political Violence*. Tallahassee, FL: Institute for Intergovernmental Research.

White, J. R. (2004). *International Terrorism in Transition*. Tallahassee, FL: Institute of Intergovernmental Research.

White, J. R. (2007). "Networks and Netwars." Destin, FL: First National Fusion Center Conference. February (unpublished).

White, J. R. (2010). "Paths to Radicalization." Tallahassee, FL: Institute for Intergovernmental Research (unpublished).

White, J. R. (2013). "The Nature of Modern Terrorism." *Huffington*

Post. April 21. Online: http://www.huffingtonpost.com/jonathan-r-white/confusion-about-boston_b_3128995.html.

White, J. R. (2015). Unpublished personal notes taken during meetings and subcommittee meetings of the Law Enforcement Equipment Working Group. Washington, DC, January through May.

White, R. W. (1989). "From Peaceful Protest to Guerrilla War: Micromobilization of the Provisional Irish Republican Army." *American Journal of Sociology* 94(6): 1277–1302.

White, R. W. (1993). *Provisional Irish Republicans: An Oral and Interpretative History.* Westport, CT: Greenwood Press.

Wickham-Crowley, T. P. (1992). *Guerrillas and Revolution in Latin America: A Comparative Study of Insurgents and Regimes Since 1956.* Princeton, NJ: Princeton University Press.

Wieviorka, M. (1993). *The Making of Terrorism.* Chicago: University of Chicago Press.

Wikas, S. (2002). "The Hamas Ceasefire: Historical Background, Future Foretold?" Peacewatch. Online: http://www.washingtoninstitute.org/watch/Peacewatch/peacewatch2002/357.htm.

Wilber, D. Q. (2010). "Von Brunn, White Supremacist Holocaust Museum Shooter Dies." *Washington Post.* January 7. Online: http://www.washingtonpost.com/wpdyn/content/article/2010/01/06/AR2010010604095.html?sid=ST2010010604659.

Wilkinson, P. (1997). "The Media and Terrorism: A Reassessment." *Terrorism and Political Violence* 9(Summer): 51–64.

Wilkinson, P. (2006). *Terrorism Versus Democracy.* New York: Routledge.

Williams, B. G., and F. Altindag. (2004). "El Kaide Turka: Tracing an Al-Qaeda Splinter Cell." Jamestown Foundation. *Terrorism Monitor* 2(22, November 18). Online: http://www.jamestown.org/print_friendly.php?volume_id=400&issue_id=3148&article_id=2368888.

Williams, P. (2007). "Warning Indicators and Terrorist Finances." In J. K. Giraldo and H. A. Trinkunas (eds.), *Terrorism Funding and State Responses: A Comparative Perspective.* Stanford, CA: Stanford University Press.

Willis, C. (2005). *The I Hate Ann Coulter, Bill O'Reilly, Rush Limbaugh, Michael Savage, Sean Hannity Reader.* New York: Thunder's Mouth Press.

Wilner, A. S., and C.-J. Dubouloz. (2011). "Transformative Radicalization: Applying Learning Theory to Islamist Radicalization." *Studies in Conflict and Terrorism* 34: 418–438.

Winchester, S. (1974). *Northern Ireland in Crisis.* New York: Holmes and Meier.

Wingate, J. E. (2006). "Steganography: Threat or Hype?" *Homeland Security Report* 167. Online: http://www.terrorisminfo.mipt.org/pdf/hsr167.pdf.

Wise, C. R., and R. Nadar. (2002). "Organizing the Federal System for Homeland Security: Problems, Issues, and Dilemmas." *Public Administration Review* 62(s1): 44–57.

Wise, C. R., and R. Nader. (2008). "Developing and Homeland Security System: An Urgent and Complex Task in Intergovernmental Relations." In T. J. Conlon and P. L. Posner (eds.), *Intergovernmental Management for the Twenty-First Century.* Washington, DC: Brookings Institution Press.

Wise, D. (2002). "Spy Game: Changing the Rules so the Good Guys Win." *New York Times.* June 2. Online: http://www.nytimes.com/2002/06/02/weekinreview/02WISEhtml.

Wise, R. (2011). "Al Shabaab." CSIS. Online: http://csis.org/files/publication/110715_Wise_AlShabaab_AQAM%20Futures%20Case%20Study_WEB.pdf

Wolf, J. B. (1981). *Fear of Fear.* New York: Plenum.

Wolfsfeld, G. (2001). "The News Media and the Second Intifada: Some Initial Lessons." *Press/Politics* 6(4): 113–118.

Woodcock, G. (2004). *Anarchism: A History of Libertarian Ideas and Movements.* Peterborough, ON: Broadview Press, Broadview Encore Editions.

Woodworth, P. (2001). *Dirty Wars, Clean Hands: ETA, the GAL, and Spanish Democracy.* Cork, Ireland: Cork University Press.

Wright, J., and K. Bryett. (2000). *Policing and Conflict in Northern Ireland.* New York: Palgrave Macmillan.

Wright, L. (2002). "The Man Behind Bin Laden: How an Egyptian Doctor Became a Master of Terror." *New Yorker.* September 16. Online: http://www.newyorker.com/archive/2002/09/16/020916fa_fact2?currentPage=all.

Wright, L. (2006). *The Looming Tower: Al Qaeda and the Road to 9-11.* New York: Knopf.

Wright, M. (2008). "Technology and Terrorism." *Forensic Examiner* 17(4): 13–21.

Wright, R. (2000). *The Last Great Revolution: Turmoil and Transformation in Iran.* New York: Knopf.

Wyss, J. (2015). "Colombia's ELN Guerrillas Inch Toward Peace Talks." *Miami Herald.* January 7. Online: http://www.miamiherald.com/news/nation-world/world/americas/colombia/article5576874.html.

Young, J. A. T., and J. Collier. (2002). "Attacking Anthrax." *Scientific American* (March): 48–59.

Zackie, M.W. (2013). "An Analysis of Abu Musab al Suri's 'Call to Global Islamic Resistance.'" *Journal of Security Studies* 6(1): 1–18. Online: http://scholarcommons.usf.edu/cgi/viewcontent.cgi?article=1230&context=jss. Accessed: June 2015.

Zassoursky, Y. N. (2002). "Media and Communications as the Vehicle of the Open Society." *International Journal for Communication Studies* 64(5): 425–432.

Zenko, M. (2006). "Intelligence Estimates of Nuclear Terrorism." *Annals of the American Academy of Political and Social Science* 607: 87–102. Online: http://ann.sagepub.com/cgi/content/abstract/607/1/87.

Zenn, J. (2012). "Northern Nigeria's Boko Haram Al Qaeda's Africa Strategy." Jamestown Foundation. November 26. Online: http://www.jamestown.org/single/?tx_ttnews%5Btt_news%5D=40153&no_cache=1#.VdoiUHip3dk.

Zenn, J. (2013). "How to End Boko Haram's Terror: James Zenn, The Jamestown Foundation." YouTube. Online: https://www.youtube.com/watch?v=5VkVYyHmV4o.

Zenn, J. (2014a). "Boko Haram and the Many Faces of Abubakar Shekau." *Africa Arguments.* Online: http://africanarguments.org/2014/09/30/boko-haram-and-the-many-faces-of-abubakar-shekau-by-jacob-zenn/.

Zenn, J. (2014b). "Exposing and Defeating Boko Haram: Why the West Must Unite to Help Nigeria Defeat Terrorism." Bow Group. Online: http://www.bowgroup.org/sites/bowgroup.uat.pleasetest.co.uk/files/Jacob%20Zenn%20Bow%20Group%20Report%20for%2022.7.14.pdf.

Zenn, J. (2014c). "Leadership Analysis of Boko Haram and Ansaru in Nigeria." *CTC Sentinel,* Combating Terrorism Center at West Point. Online: www.ctc.usma.edu/posts/leadership-analysis-of-boko-haram-and-ansaru-in-nigeria.

Zill, O., and L. Berman. (2014). "The Black Peso Money Laundering System." PBS. Online: http://www.pbs.org/wgbh/pages/frontline/shows/drugs/special/blackpeso.html.

Zissis, C. (2006). "The Sri Lankan Conflict." Council on Foreign Relations. September 11. Online: http://www.cfr.org/publication/11407/sri_lankan_conflict.html?breadcrumb=%2Fregion%2F289%2Fsri_lanka.

Zissis, C. (2007). "Terror Groups in India." Council on Foreign Relations. March 5. Online: http://www.cfr.org/publication/12773/terror_groups_in_india.html#4.

Zulaika, J. (2003). "Anthropologists, Artists, Terrorists: The Basque Holiday from History." *Journal of Spanish Cultural Studies* 4(2): 139–150.

INDEX